A
LITERARY
HISTORY
OF
FRANCE

A LITERARY HISTORY OF FRANCE

General Editor: P. E. CHARVET
Fellow of Corpus Christi College, Cambridge

THE MIDDLE AGES , v. 1
by JOHN FOX
Professor of French at the University of Exeter

RENAISSANCE FRANCE , v. 2
by I. D. McFARLANE
Professor of French Literature at the University of Oxford

THE SEVENTEENTH CENTURY 1600–1715 , v. 3
by P. J. YARROW
Professor of French at the University of Newcastle upon Tyne

THE EIGHTEENTH CENTURY 1715–1789 , v. 4
by ROBERT NIKLAUS
Professor of French at the University of Exeter

THE NINETEENTH CENTURY 1789–1870 , v. 5
by P. E. CHARVET

THE NINETEENTH AND TWENTIETH CENTURIES 1870–1940 , v. 6
by P. E. CHARVET

A LITERARY HISTORY OF FRANCE

THE MIDDLE AGES

A LITERARY HISTORY OF FRANCE

The Middle Ages

JOHN FOX

Professor of French, University of Exeter

LONDON · ERNEST BENN LIMITED

NEW YORK · BARNES & NOBLE BOOKS

First published 1974 by Ernest Benn Limited
Sovereign Way, Tonbridge, Kent &
25 New Street Square, Fleet Street, London EC4A 3JA
and Barnes & Noble Books, 10 East 53rd Street, New York 10022
(a division of Harper & Row Publishers Inc.)

Distributed in Canada by
The General Publishing Company Limited Toronto

© John Fox 1974

Printed in Great Britain

ISBN 0–510–32201–8

ISBN 06–492218–9 (USA)

FOREWORD BY THE GENERAL EDITOR

IN HIS QUEST for the past, the historian proper deals with a variety of evidence, documentary and other, which is of value to him only for the light it sheds on events and on the men who played a part in them. The historian of literature has before him documents in manuscript or print that exist in their own right, books and ever more books, as the centuries unfold. Within the space allotted to him, his first task must be to give the maximum amount of relevant information about them, but if he is to avoid producing a mere compilation of unrelated and therefore meaningless facts, he is bound to organise his matter into some sort of pattern.

Time itself does this for him to some extent by keeping alive the memory of those writers and books that retain their relevance, and, often enough, setting one school of writers against another, as successive generations seek to establish their own originality by revolt against their immediate predecessors.

At whatever point in time the historian of literature may stand, he is bound to adopt as a basis of his work the patterns time gives him, although he knows well enough that, just as the tide and the waves may alter the patterns they themselves are for ever imprinting on the sands of the sea shore, time, bringing with it changing tastes and values, will alter these patterns, at least in detail or emphasis.

Within these broad natural patterns come problems of arrangement. Here inevitably a degree of arbitrariness creeps in. Some writers are dubbed precursors, as though they themselves had consciously played the role of prophet in a wilderness, others are marked down as 'epigoni' – poor fellows! Had they but known! – others again are lumped together because they are seen to have in common the characteristics of an age, though they may have had no relations with each other; chronology must often be sacrificed to the need of tidiness. Thus does the historian of literature try to create from the vigorous and confused growth he is faced with, at least on the surface, an ordered garden, where the reader may wander and get an impression to store away in his memory, of neatness and controlled change, an impression helpful, indeed indispensable, as a preliminary to the study of the subject, but not to be confused with the reality.

Nor is this all. Should the historian of literature, need he, smother his personal responses? And if he should (which we doubt and indeed have not tried to do), is this really possible? Within the kindly Doctor Jekyll, recording in detached tones his literary history, seeking to give an objective picture of an age, explaining, elucidating, lurks Mr Hyde, the critic, ready to leap out at the reader on the slightest provocation and wreak his mischief. As in all of us, the levels of his personality that may respond to stimuli are numerous: intellectual, emotional, moral, spiritual; more numerous still the sources of interest whence the stimuli may come: historical and social, psychological, linguistic and stylistic, aesthetic. Literature is a vast catchment area all these streams flow into; a book, a great book is like a burning glass that concentrates the rays of human experience into one bright point; it burns itself into our memories and may even sear the soul.

If he be wise, Mr Hyde the critic will use as his criterium of judgement only the degree to which he feels his own experience has been enriched, his own perceptiveness extended. Thus will he avoid being too rigid or narrow in his attitudes and avoid the temptation of for ever seeking some underlying principle that controls the whole mechanism. Since the corpus of a writer's work is the expression of his experience, since the writer belongs to a given age, a given people, the works may easily become the pretext for an exercise in individual or national psychology. Conversely, the idea of race, the age, the accumulated legacy of history – its momentum, in a word – may be invoked as cause and explanation of the works. Or again, since the works have their place in one or more given art-forms, they may be seen as no more than moments in the evolution of these.

Such ideas and unifying theories have their value no doubt; the people, the society, the age, the art-forms all bear on the question, but who is to assess their impact? They leave the mystery of individual genius and of artistic creation intact; to emphasise them at the expense of the latter is really using the history of literature for other ends. Admittedly books do not spring from nothing, but whether we consider them historically or critically, in the last resort they stand, as we observed at the outset of this foreword, in their own right, and their value depends upon their impact on the individual; every book has three aspects: what the author meant to express, what the book contains, and the image the reader carries away with him; this latter changes with every reader of the book and depends as much upon himself as upon the book and the author.

From its early beginnings in the ninth century down to the present day, French literature can claim a continued existence of 1100 years. What country, besides our own, can boast such literary wealth, such resource, such powers of renewal? The authors of this history, the first of its kind in English, have been only too well aware of the difficulties attendant upon so vast an enterprise. Their hope is that it may give to all readers of French literature a coherent background against which particular periods or writers may be studied and enjoyed in greater depth.

P.E.C.

PREFACE

OF the many debts incurred in the writing of this volume, the greatest by far is owed to Professor Armel Diverres who, despite a busy life as Head of the French Department in the University of Aberdeen, devoted much time to the reading of the first draft, and made numerous valuable suggestions from which this book has benefited greatly. I should also like to express my gratitude to P. E. Charvet, general editor of the series, for having placed so generously at my disposal his wisdom and experience, and to my colleagues and friends of many years' standing, Professor Robert Niklaus and Professor Philip Yarrow, for their constant encouragement. Last of all, but first in my thoughts, is my wife, who has at times succeeded in breathing some French clarity into my own English mists.

Despite generous help and advice from several quarters, no book of these or much larger dimensions could possibly hope to reflect adequately the tremendous scope and variety of medieval French literature on the one hand, or the scholarship which many modern critics devote to it on the other. It is a chastening thought that every year over three hundred studies of different kinds are published, all devoted to medieval French literature.[1] The reader can expect to find in these pages no more than an introduction to certain vital aspects of the subject. More important, in the footnotes and bibliography, he will find indications for further reading and study in this subject which year by year attracts keener interest as the early centuries of European vernacular literature are at last given their due.

J.F.

Exeter
March 1973

NOTE

1. Over four hundred in fact in 1970, see R. Rancœur, *Bibliographie de la littérature française du Moyen Age à nos jours*, Paris, 1963–, published annually.

CONTENTS

LIST OF ABBREVIATIONS

ALMA   R. S. Loomis, ed., *Arthurian Literature in the Middle Ages, A Collaborative History,* Oxford, 1959
BHS   *Bulletin of Hispanic Studies*
CCMe   *Cahiers de Civilisation Médiévale*
CFMA   Classiques français du moyen âge
DLF   *Dictionnaire des Lettres Françaises: Le Moyen Age,* Paris, 1964
EETS   Early English Text Society
FMLS   *Forum for Modern Language Studies*
FS   *French Studies*
MA   *Le Moyen Age*
MAe   *Medium Aevum*
MHRA   *Annual Bulletin of the Modern Humanities Research Association*
MLN   *Modern Language Notes*
Mor.   J. Morawski, *Proverbes français antérieurs au XVe siècle,* Paris, CFMA, 1925
MP   *Modern Philology*
N   *Neophilologus*
OED   *Oxford English Dictionary*
PQ   *Philological Quarterly*
R   *Romania*
RF   *Romanische Forschungen*
RHLF   *Revue d'Histoire Littéraire de la France*
RPh   *Romance Philology*
RR   *Romanic Review*
SATF   Société des anciens textes français
SN   *Studia Neophilologica*
Sp   *Speculum*

TLF   Textes Littéraires Français
VR   Vox Romanica
ZRP   Zeitschrift für Romanische Philologie

INTRODUCTION

A COMPREHENSIVE survey of some six hundred and fifty years of French literature – from the middle of the ninth century to the end of the fifteenth – in a volume of this size is impossible, the more so as the last four of those centuries saw a prolific outpouring of literary works of all kinds. Moreover, since we are here concerned with the first period of French literature, some space, however small, must be allotted to the factors leading up to its beginnings. It must also be realised that, despite the keen interest which many scholars have shown during the past century or so in the early literature of France, some important texts are still inadequately known at the present day. Even some widely held views of better-known works must be regarded as tentative and as certain to be modified in the future. It is paradoxical but true that the literature of the past is changing constantly. In the face of these difficulties, the scope of the present volume has been restricted to the study of a number of *focal points* whose importance in the history of medieval French literature is beyond question. This concentration on particular aspects of the subject will begin in the remaining paragraphs of this introduction, it will continue in the historical survey of the period and throughout each chapter in the limited range of texts chosen for analysis and commentary. It is often claimed that medieval authors wrote according to certain deeply entrenched formulas and that, in consequence, a few well-chosen works can represent the literary output of the age. The present author regards this as a misleading hypothesis, however convenient. No claim is made here that this is a fully characteristic selection, but only that an attempt is made in these pages to give an insight, however brief, into certain vital aspects of the literature of these centuries.

A first point for consideration involves the term 'Middle Ages', which came into use in the seventeenth century to designate what was considered to have been the barbaric interval of a thousand years between the collapse of the Roman Empire and the rebirth of learning in Italy. The arbitrariness and sheer inappropriateness of the term are its sole features on which all scholars would agree nowadays. Its most frequent use at the present time[1] is with reference to the four centuries following A.D. 1000. From the particular point of view of French literature this calls for some modification, since the very few texts extant from the ninth and tenth centuries are not markedly different in kind from those of the eleventh century.[2] At the other extreme, it would be necessary to prolong the period to about 1500, even though the beginnings of the Renaissance in France are uncertain, and the object of much research which has been continued very actively over the last few decades.[3] Whatever the imperfections of the expression 'Middle Ages', and they are many, and those of the corresponding adjective 'medieval' which does not seem to have been used before the nineteenth century, these terms are used in the present work in a fairly loose manner to designate the pre-Renaissance period in France from the ninth century onwards, and the literature it produced.

How did the language we call French come into being, and why did the first French texts appear when they did, in the course of the ninth century? Even the most perfunctory answer to these questions has to move far back in time to the Roman occupation of Gaul, which took place in the south between 125 and 121 B.C., and was completed in the north by Julius Caesar between 58 and 50 B.C. The native population was predominantly Celtic, but so thorough was the Roman conquest that the natives were induced to abandon their own language in favour of Latin, a simpler, more practical form of the language than the Classical Latin used by the outstanding writers and orators of Rome. Although schools were set up in many towns to which the sons of those who could pay fees were sent, the majority of people remained illiterate. Their language gradually evolved away from its Latin origins, acquiring characteristics of its own, as did the Latin spoken in other areas of the Roman Empire. As long as the centralising power of Rome remained strong, it exercised control over regional peculiarities of language. Western Europe was more closely united than it has ever been since, with a single spoken idiom, usually referred to as Vulgar Latin, whose dialectal variations were not sufficiently marked to prevent its being understood from the western boundaries of the Empire (modern Portugal) right through to its easternmost extremities (modern Romania).

Of greater importance in the later centuries of the Empire was the gradual spread of Christianity, which was facilitated by the baptism of the Emperor Constantine in A.D. 312 and his recognition of Christianity as a 'religio licita'. The long era of persecutions and martyrdom of Christians was almost over, the triumph of this dynamic religion was now assured, and its system of administration and regional representation was rapidly elaborated during the fourth century. Even so, it had to overcome rival religions and it was not until about A.D. 500 that a substantial part of the population of western Europe was Christian. The Church's role as the sole bastion of culture once Roman power had waned was to be immense.[4]

Among the many reasons for the fall of the Roman Empire, a particularly significant one was the Romans' continual failure to subdue the many Germanic tribes along their eastern frontiers. Men of Germanic origin were absorbed into the armies of the later Empire, and allowed to settle within its frontiers, but these measures were not enough to prevent the invasions from sweeping across western Europe in the fifth and sixth centuries. In the north of Gaul large numbers of Frankish tribes became established, but un-like the Romans 500 years earlier, they gradually adopted the language of the native inhabitants, even though they modified vocabulary and speech habits. Their influence on the history of western Europe was second only to that of Rome. In the anarchical conditions created, conflict between rival tribes was inevitable. Late in the fifth century the Salian Franks, originally inhabiting the extreme north-east of Gaul, extended their domain under the leadership of Clovis (c. 466–511), most outstanding of the Merovin-gian kings,[5] who in 486 defeated Syagrius, the last Roman governor of Gaul, and won a series of victories over other Germanic tribes, in particular the Alamanni, the Visigoths, and the Burgundians. He married Clotilda, a Burgundian princess, and under her in-fluence was converted to Christianity. It was during his reign that the Salic Law was issued.[6] On his death his kingdom was almost the size of modern France, but it was divided between his four sons. The continual warfare that followed led to fresh territorial divisions and a rapid weakening of the kingdom. In the eighth century, as the Merovingian dynasty declined, effective power passed more and more into the hands of the Carolingian family,[7] who owned large estates and served the king as mayors of the palace. Not until 751 was the *de facto* situation recognised, when Pepin the Short was elected king in place of the last Merovingian, Childeric III. The 'regnum Francorum' was destined to achieve unity and to expand further under Pepin's descendant Charlemagne, king of the Franks from 768 to 814 and Western emperor from 800 to 814.

At the Church Council of Tours, held at Charlemagne's instiga-tion in 813, the clergy were required to use the 'rusticam romanam linguam' (i.e., the spoken language) in their sermons, thereby ack-nowledging the futility of attempting to preach to the people in Latin which they could not understand. Disintegration of the Roman Empire had destroyed the relative unity of Vulgar Latin, and the spoken idioms of the different regions had moved along rapidly diverging paths; it has become traditional to refer to the language of Gaul from the end of the fifth century to the middle of the ninth century as Gallo-Romance.[8] Towards the end of the ninth century the first lives of saints to have survived in the vernacular were recorded. They were not original compositions, but were translations or adaptations of earlier Latin works. Latin did not yield quickly, and for centuries was to remain firmly entrenched as the written language *par excellence*, but this did not prevent the vernacular from making rapid progress in recorded form, particularly from the later eleventh century onwards. The earliest text extant in the vernacular, as we shall see in the following chapter, is not a hagiographical work, but a military treaty of considerable importance nowadays not only for the light it sheds on the events of the age, but even more for the information it provides on the early history of the French language.

NOTES

1. According to *OED*.

2. The expression The Dark Ages is occasionally used for some or all of the centuries between the collapse of the Roman Empire and the year A.D. 1000 or thereabouts, but becomes less justifiable as more is discovered about the period in question. A recent book devoted to a study of the artistic brilliance of these early centuries is paradoxically entitled *The Dark Ages* (ed. D. T. Rice, London, 1965) on the grounds that this label is 'generally familiar'.

3. See in particular F. Simone, *The French Renaissance, Medieval Tradition and Italian Influence in Shaping the Renaissance in France*. Translated from the Italian by H. Gaston Hall, London, 1969. Charles VIII's Italian expedition of 1495, for long spoken of as heralding the dawn of the Renaissance in France, is viewed more cautiously by Simone as no more than a momentary confrontation, allowing Italy to intensify her participation in an already existing cultural activity in France (p. 41). See also *L'Originalité du XVe siècle*, being the proceedings of the 22nd Congress of the Association Internationale des Études Françaises, published in the *Cahiers* of the Association, May 1971.

4. See below, pp. 6–10.

5. So called from Merovech, grandfather of Clovis.

6. This was a penal code in Latin, but with many Frankish terms, giving a long list of fines for various offences. It also contains the stipulation that daughters cannot inherit land, later taken to mean that the crown should never pass to a woman.

7. So called because in the eighth and ninth centuries, eight of its members bore the name Charles.

8. cf. Italo-Romance, Ibero-Romance, Daco-Romance for other regions of the former Empire.

Chapter 1

THE HISTORICAL BACKGROUND

I. THE EARLIEST SURVIVING DOCUMENT IN FRENCH

TRADITIONALLY regarded as the first text extant in French, the *Serments de Strasbourg* is a historical document relating to the year 842, twenty-eight years after the death of Charlemagne. It concerns a defensive alliance between two of Charlemagne's grandsons, Louis the German, leader of the Germanic-speaking Franks, and Charles the Bald, leader of the Romance-speaking Franks, against their older brother Lothair. Each swore, in the language of the other, to support his brother to the best of his ability.[1] In the following year the three brothers reached a settlement in the Treaty of Verdun. Charles was allotted the region known as *Francia occidentalis* (latina, gallicana, romana), roughly from beyond the Pyrenees including Pamplona in the west and Barcelona in the east, to the vicinity of the Rhône, the Saône, and the Marne; Lothair the central territories, *Francia media*, between the Meuse and the Rhine, which came to be known as Lotharingia, whence the name Lorraine, a region destined throughout its history to be a bone of contention between the powerful countries which grew up on its western and eastern frontiers; while Louis the German was allotted the eastern section of Francia – *Francia orientalis* – also known as Austria or Austrasia; to this day Franconia designates the region of the right bank of the Lower Rhine. Each of the brothers had the right to style himself 'rex Francorum', and the term *Francia* alone could still embrace the whole of the former empire of the Franks, with the exception of Italy.[2] The subsequent meaning of the term varied according to historical developments. Not until the later fifteenth century did it designate almost all the territory which it covers today.

The artificiality of referring to the 'French language' as early as the ninth century is easily demonstrated by a quick glance at the opening sentences of the *Serments de Strasbourg*:

Pro Deo amur et pro christian poblo et nostro commun salvament, d'ist di in avant, in quant Deus savir et podir me dunat, si salvarai eo cist meon fradre Karlo et in ajudha et in cadhuna cosa, si cum om per dreit son fradra salvar dift . . .[3]

5

Quite clearly this is not 'French' as we know it, but equally clearly this is a language which has evolved far beyond its Latin origins. Certain linguistic features such as the slurring of endings, whose presence was so vital to Latin – *amur, christian, commun, salvament*, etc. – tip the scales more in favour of French than Latin, and from this point of view it is worth noting that this ninth-century document is further removed from Latin than are certain twentieth-century Romance languages such as Italian and Spanish. Even so, there was no 'French language' at this time, but only a number of dialects.[4] Francien, the dialect of the Ile-de-France, was eventually to prevail over its main rivals the Norman and Picard dialects, largely for political reasons, being that used by the royal Court and the capital. Already in the twelfth century certain writers refer to its prestige over other dialects,[5] but these continued in literary usage into the fourteenth century and beyond, and are still alive in the spoken medium. Modern French is essentially the descendant of Francien, particularly as spoken in Paris, though it was to absorb a large number of terms from other districts, and countries, in the course of time.

II. ASPECTS OF MEDIEVAL SOCIETY

Certain features of medieval life and literature characterised already the reign of Charles the Bald, their origins sometimes stretching much further back in time. They can best be expressed as a series of *relationships*, to which brief consideration will be given in the following pages. Most far-reaching in its effects was the relationship between Church and state. After 753 all royal Carolingian documents bore the words 'King of the Franks *by the grace of God*', so making the king the anointed of the Lord as David and Saul had been. In the year 800 the Imperial crown was placed on Charlemagne's head by Pope Leo III in the basilica of St Peter in Rome. Subsequently, the custom of anointing the king at his coronation became firmly established. From the time of Philip Augustus onwards at the end of the twelfth century, the consecration usually took place in Rheims cathedral, since according to tradition the Merovingian King Clovis had been baptised there by St Remigius at the end of the fifth century A.D. The idea that the monarch was God's elect, that there was such a thing as the Divine Right of Kings, was of considerable help in the gradual extension of his sovereignty and in making the crown hereditary and not elective as it had been until the late tenth century. At times there were bitter quarrels between king and Church,[6] but on the whole throughout the Middle Ages each benefited from the support of the other. It is

arguable that Joan of Arc's greatest service to Charles VII lay not
in her actual victories over the English but in her insistence that he
be anointed king in Rheims cathedral, an act which served to rally
around this erstwhile feeble monarch the support of his fellow
countrymen.

The relationship between the individual and his faith, and that
between the two rival religions of the age, Christian and Moslem,
were also important in what is so often referred to nowadays as the
Age of Faith. The earliest literary texts in the French language
concern stories of Christian martyrs who suffered torture and death
rather than relinquish their faith. That so many heroes of so long
ago – the first French hagiographical work extant is set in the
early fourth century A.D.[7] – bore such witness to their faith was a
great encouragement to the Christians of later centuries, whose
steadfastness was put to the test when the Arabs invaded Spain in
A.D. 711. So firmly did they establish themselves there that it took
some five centuries for the *Reconquista* to reassert Christian rule.
In 732 Charlemagne's grandfather, Charles Martel, inflicted a
decisive defeat on the Arabs near Poitiers, and when Pepin III captured Narbonne, their last stronghold in France, in 751, the Arabs'
power in western Europe was effectively limited to southern Spain.
By the eleventh century the religious fervour which followed the
passing of the millennium brought numbers of Christian soldiers to
Spain to fight the Moslems there, along with pilgrims on their way
to worship at the shrine of St James of Compostela in Galicia.
Towards the end of the century, the extreme difficulty of access to
Jerusalem led to Pope Urban II's preaching the first crusade in
1095 in order to free the Holy Land. This new zeal led to a 'rewriting' of earlier history so that Charlemagne became the prototype of the crusading knight, a more implacable foe of the Arabs
than he had in fact been,[8] and the lives of the saints were now
paralleled by a more militant form of Christian literature, the
chansons de geste.[9] There were in all eight principal crusades, from
1095 to 1270, in most of which men from the north of France played
a dominant role. The influence of the crusades was immense, not
least in bringing Christians into contact with a civilisation in numbers of respects more refined than their own. The increase in trade
with the Orient that resulted, from the twelfth century onwards,
transformed the economic life of France, and led to a taste for
luxuries – jewellery, fine silks and cloths in particular – which we
shall find reflected in the courtly literature of that century and
later.[10]

The influence of Christianity is revealed in other ways. Not long
after the appearance of the first hagiographic works in French, the
abbey of Cluny was founded by Duke Guillaume I d'Aquitaine in

910. The first abbots were men of strong character and religious conviction who did much to further the Christian cause, recognising no authority apart from the Holy See. A veritable Cluniac empire was built up, eventually possessing in Provence alone forty-four monasteries and eighty-one priories and extending its influence over much of Europe. Cluny brought a new discipline and sterner spirit to the monasteries which had begun to spring up as early as the sixth century, based on the rule of St Benedict, drawn up originally for his own abbey, that of Monte Cassino. At the very end of the eleventh century yet another order, ascetic and well disciplined, came into being: the white monks, or Cistercians, named from Cîteaux in Burgundy where they originated. The most formidable of their order, an uncompromising religious reformer, was St Bernard, born in 1090, probably at Fontaines-les-Dijon. His forceful preaching at Vézelay and elsewhere did much to launch the second crusade (1147). He was active in many spheres: he condemned Abelard's new dialectic applying Aristotelian logic to theology; he opposed the Cluniacs on occasions; and even deposed princes and replaced bishops. He was canonised in 1174, twenty-one years after his death.

Not until the thirteenth century did the mendicant, or wandering, friars appear. The Franciscan order was founded in 1209 by St Francis of Assisi, the gentle mystic who, like the legendary St Alexis,[11] renounced earthly goods and relationships in order to live in poverty and humility; five years later the Dominican order was founded by a Spanish nobleman, St Dominic, with the original aim of combating heresies and preaching to the pagans. Already in the thirteenth century the Dominicans were bitterly attacked in French literature[12] for not observing the poverty and humility to which they too had dedicated themselves, following the rule of St Augustine.

The most visible and impressive testimonies to medieval religious faith are of course the many churches and cathedrals of western Europe, few earlier than the eleventh century because wood was for long used extensively in their construction. From that century onwards many were built of stone in the Romanesque style, whose spread through Burgundy and France owed much to the monks of Cluny, in particular to one of their abbots, William of Volpiano, a native of Lombardy whence the style, preserving something of Roman traditions of vaulting, originated; this abbot of the early eleventh century employed masons from Lombardy. A few of the many notable examples of Romanesque style still to be seen in France are the southern transept of the third abbey church at Cluny (1088–1130) – contemporary with the nave of Durham cathedral – Autun cathedral, the basilica of the Magdalen at Vézelay, the priory of La-Charité-sur-Loire dating from the first half of the twelfth century, and, from the second half of the same century, the cathedrals of Arles and Avignon. At this time the pointed arches of the Gothic style became popular, inspired, it is believed, by the abbey of Saint-Denis near Paris, begun in 1140, followed by Notre-Dame of Paris (1163), and the cathedrals of Bourges and Laon, begun a few years later. Only desultory information has survived concerning the master-craftsmen and sculptors who built and decorated the churches and cathedrals. Beneath the tympanum of the western doorway of Autun cathedral is carved *Gislebertus hoc fecit*. It is likely that this outstanding sculptor was trained in the workshop responsible for Cluny abbey. His influence has been discerned in other Burgundian churches, and even at Chartres. He was, however, only one of many, most of whom remain anonymous. Different regions evolved styles of their own, their individualities developing within a common framework. The only architect's sketchbook to have survived from before the fifteenth century is that of Villard de Honnecourt, dating from about 1235 and revealing much about the working practices of French architects in the early Gothic period.[13]

Closely allied to the religious faith of the Carolingian epoch, destined to come to fruition in later centuries, as were so many aspects of that crucially important age, was the revival of learning undertaken on Charlemagne's initiative. His reforming zeal was put into effect by the eminent scholar of the day, Alcuin, who, after fifty years in his native York, of whose cathedral school he had become the head, was invited by the emperor to take charge of the palace school at Aachen (Aix-la-Chapelle). He ended his days as abbot of St Martin's abbey in Tours, encouraging monks to work on Carolingian minuscule, the marvellously clear script which is the ancestor of modern Roman type.

One other manifestation of the individual's relationship to his faith must be explored, and here too ultimate causes must be sought in the Carolingian epoch and even earlier. The region of Languedoc had been more thoroughly romanised but less thoroughly Christianised than the north. Other faiths became established there as a result, notably that of the Cathars, in all respects more ascetic than medieval Christianity. Their name derives from a Greek word meaning 'pure', and they have been referred to as the puritans of the Middle Ages. Influenced probably by the Bogomils who flourished in the Balkans from the tenth century onwards, they followed Manichean dualism, believing in the co-existence of two ultimate and utterly opposed principles, a good deity who created spirit and light, an evil force who created matter and darkness. Everything to do with the material world was under the

control of the latter, so that all enjoyment of life on earth was condemned. Bearing children was evil in that it imprisoned their souls
within bodies, whereas suicide was not, in that it liberated the
spirit. They denied the meaning of Christ's crucifixion, and rejected
the authority of Church and state. They were repeatedly condemned
by the Church not merely for their doctrinal heresy, but because
they were considered a threat to family, state, and all society. The
Catharist faith was eventually destroyed in the ruthless Albigensian
crusades (1209–29) – so called because Albi was one of their principal centres, along with Toulouse and Carcassonne – led by the
fanatical Simon de Montfort. The Inquisition, founded by Pope
Lucius III in 1183, could override all tribunals in the bid to wipe
out heresy. Whatever the achievement from the Christian point of
view, the effect on the civilisation of the south of France, in some
ways more refined than that of the north, was disastrous.

Another type of relationship which was to have enormous influence on medieval life and literature was that between the rulers
of different regions. We have seen that the three grandsons of
Charlemagne reached an agreement among themselves. In an age
when territorial divisions were exceedingly complex, such agree-
ments were very necessary. They were often made among relatives,
moreover, since from the tenth century onwards at least, the
younger sons of royal families were given domains which became
hereditary, reverting to the crown when there were no descendants.
Since each had his own forces, disagreements frequently resulted
in conflict and civil war, which continued intermittently into the
first half of the fifteenth century. The two dynastic quarrels most
fraught with consequence for the history of medieval France were
first William, duke of Normandy's successful claim to the throne
of England in 1066, and secondly Edward III of England's un-
successful claim to the throne of France in 1328, which was responsible for the Hundred Years War, fought entirely on the
continent.

Relationships between rulers and their subjects were governed by
feudalism, only the main elements of which can be mentioned here.
The system of vassalage and benefice, whereby an individual cere-
moniously swore allegiance to a lord and promised to undertake
military service on his behalf, sometimes legal and administrative
duties also, dates from the early Carolingian era. In return the
vassal could hope for a benefice, consisting as a rule of a grant of
land, although vassals without a benefice remained numerous. In
principle, even the smallest grant of land was enough to provide at
least for the vassal and his family, and to enable him to afford a
warhorse and such accoutrements as the stirrup, which appeared in
the West in the eighth century and revolutionised the use of

cavalry.[14] Vassalage to the king became a particularly privileged
and wealthy status, and each royal vassal granted land in his turn
to a number of sub-vassals. Vassalage was a personal relationship
which lapsed on the death either of the vassal or of the lord, but a
vassal would normally expect a lord's successor to re-grant him his
benefice, and would endeavour to make it hereditary; evidence of
this dates from the eighth century and becomes more abundant in
the ninth. From the end of the ninth century instances are recorded
of vassals holding benefices from more than one lord, a growingly
intricate state of affairs. At this period a new term, synonymous
with benefice, came into use; this was 'feodum' (also 'feudum' or
'fevum') which gave 'fief' in English and French (also 'fee' in the
former), and benefice gradually became limited to an ecclesiastical
sense. Feudal institutions in France were to last as long as the
ancien régime, but the growth of towns and the rise of the bourgeoisie meant that by the end of the thirteenth century the feudal
system no longer governed every aspect of society.

Already in the ninth century society was divided broadly into
three categories: the fighting-men, the clergy, the peasants, relationships between them being clearly established. The fighting-men,
consisting of the lord of a territory and his vassals, easily became
dominant, not merely because the power was in their hands, but
also because their strongholds offered protection from invading
forces, particularly important at this time when the Northmen were
constantly marauding and pillaging, before settling in what was to
become Normandy. Courage in battle, loyalty to his leader, were
originally the sole requisites of the knight, but with the intervention
of the Church further moral duties were added, which are frequently mentioned in the early *chansons de geste*:[15] defence of
Christianity, protection of the weak, safeguarding of the rights of
widows and orphans. So was born the concept of chivalry, and by
the twelfth century knighthood had become a jealously guarded
caste system, reserved for the sons of knights. Heraldry, whatever
its ultimate origins may have been, rapidly acquired great elabora-
tion in the twelfth century, each knight bearing the family coat-
of-arms on his shield. A special kind of symbolism was involved,
and an esoteric vocabulary, much of it French. Each knight also
had his armorial banner, and his armour, principally the coat of
mail in the eleventh and twelfth centuries (as shown in the Bayeux
Tapestry), developing towards the use of plate armour from the
late thirteenth century onwards. The knight's life was governed by
a highly formalised ritual, not merely as his lord's vassal. After he
had served his apprenticeship, the young knight, called the
'bachelier', received the *accolade* from his father or another knight,
consisting of a touch on the shoulder with the flat of a sword,

followed by the *adoubement* in which he was invested with his
armour. This was an initiation not merely into a certain class but
into a very particular way of life given up largely to the pursuit of
warfare, whether on the field of battle or in the lists. Even in tournaments knights were frequently wounded or killed. The squires,
originally no more than the knights' shield-bearers, acquired aristocratic status themselves, though at a lower level.

The clergy enjoyed great prestige, more in the north of France
than in the south, and privileges such as the right to be tried in
ecclesiastical courts, usually more lenient than their civil counterparts. The Church possessed no army of its own, but it had a
formidable and much-feared weapon in its powers of excommunica-
tion, and from the eleventh century the interdict, preventing all
religious ceremonies throughout the territories of any noble who had
incurred the Church's wrath. Celibacy was required of the clergy,
but not always faithfully observed. Church Councils in the tenth
and eleventh centuries regularly protested against the marriages of
clerics which were declared invalid at the First and Second Lateran
Councils of 1123 and 1139. Such marriages, or concubinage,[16] were
not altogether eliminated as a result, but only became common
again during the moral laxity of the Hundred Years War.

Very little information has survived on the peasants and working
classes, although, as we shall see, the occasional literary text gives
a vivid description of the sordidness of their existence.[17] The
counterparts of the slaves of Roman times were still known as serfs
(Latin *servos*) and could neither leave a domain nor take a wife
from outside it without the landowner's permission, whereas the
freemen were not subject to such restrictions, and the *corvées* (forced
labour) and taxes (often paid in kind) fell more lightly on them than
on the serfs. The latter were quite often granted their freedom in
return for a payment, sometimes made collectively to the lord,
resulting in an *abornement* (or *abonnement*), a limitation of his
former power over them.

The rise of the bourgeoisie dates from after the Carolingian
era, beginning in the late eleventh century as a result of increasing
trade. The principal trade-routes of western Europe passed through
France. A particularly important one followed the valleys of the
Rhône and Saône, then, crossing the hills, followed the Seine to
Champagne. Trade-fairs were held from the twelfth century onwards at Beaucaire in the south and at Troyes in Champagne,
whereas the flourishing 'foire du lendit', held annually at Saint-
Denis, is rather older, going back to the preceding century. Goods
such as cloths, silks, leather, fur, horses, and cattle were sold in
the main trade-fairs, which brought together merchants from as
far afield as Flanders, Germany, Italy, and Spain. Towns became

increasingly prosperous and were granted charters setting out their privileges, limiting those of the nobility, and defining each citizen's rights and duties. At about the same time the different crafts were formed into guilds ('métiers'), each determined to safeguard its particular interests. By the late thirteenth century several hundred guilds existed in Paris alone. The members of a guild formed a *confrérie* which celebrated the feast of the guild's patron saint, sometimes having poetry or a play written specially for the occasion.

From the time of Charles the Bald onwards, society moved slowly and unevenly towards more settled conditions. After the millennium, internal warfare diminished, partly as a consequence of the crusades. Life for all but the humblest peasants and workers gradually became more refined and sophisticated. Not until this stage had been reached in what was essentially a man's world does much consideration appear to have been given, whether in life or literature, to his relationships with the fair sex, which henceforth were to remain one of the basic preoccupations of French and indeed of European literature generally, down to the present day. Renewed interest in classical literature, the works of Ovid in particular, influenced this development, as also did the spread of what has come to be known as *amour courtois* from Limousin where it flourished as early as the eleventh century. In court circles, at least from the twelfth century onwards, manners and etiquette required that women be treated with respect, and the resultant gallantry, with all that it implies, was to leave a profound impression on French civilisation.[18]

III. THE DYNASTIES OF MEDIEVAL FRANCE

Seven centuries (ninth–fifteenth) and the reigns of over twenty sovereigns are involved in this brief background survey. Only the reigns and achievements of some of the more outstanding monarchs can be mentioned here. Between 888 and 987 the region formerly allotted to Charles the Bald had four rulers of the Carolingian dynasty and three descended from Robert the Strong, count of Anjou and Blois, most gifted of Charles's *missi dominici* (envoys, representatives), who died fighting the Normans in 866. In 987 Hugues Capet of the Robertian line mounted the throne and began the rule of the Capetian kings which was to remain unbroken throughout fifteen reigns up to 1328. An important consequence of this regularity of succession was that the system came to matter more than the individual monarch, a state of affairs reflected, not uncritically, in certain *chansons de geste*.[19] Some of the finest kings France has ever known belonged to this dynasty, outstanding among

them being Louis VI (1108–37), who succeeded in reducing the
many internal dissensions of the kingdom, leading his armies in
vigorous campaigns against rebellious barons; Philip Augustus
(1180–1223), whose dynamism on the field of battle and in political
intrigue destroyed the powerful Angevin empire through the occupation of Normandy, Anjou, Touraine, and Poitou, the English
claim to those territories being abandoned eventually by Henry III
in the Treaty of Paris (1259); Louis VIII (1223–26), who as a result
of the Albigensian crusades took definitive possession of Languedoc
in 1226; Louis IX (1226–70), renowned not only for his piety and
crusading zeal, for which he was canonised in 1297, but also for his
internal reforms; Philip IV (1285–1314), called the Fair (le Bel),
who extended the royal domains northwards to include Lille, Douai,
and Béthune, and in the centre to include Champagne (through
marriage), while in the south suzerainty was established over the
Lyonnais, Barrois, and Vivarois.

Charles IV, the last Capetian king, died without male issue in
1328. An assembly of vassals, prelates, and nobles elected as their
new monarch Philip, son of Philip the Fair's brother Charles de
Valois, rejecting the claims of Edward III of England, son of
Philip the Fair's daughter. Philip VI reigned from 1328 to 1350.
He added the Dauphiné to the royal domains, the title Dauphin
being adopted for the king's eldest son. The major event of his
reign was the outbreak of the Hundred Years War in 1337 when
Edward III decided to press his claim to the French throne. Charles
V (1364–80), most adroit of the early Valois monarchs, surrounded
himself with wise counsellors and placed at the head of his army
the experienced soldier of Breton origin Bertrand Du Guesclin, whose
tactical skill reduced the English possessions in France to the ports
of Calais, Cherbourg, Brest, and Bordeaux. Charles VI's reign
(1380–1422) was as disastrous as that of his father had been triumphant. Only twelve years of age on his father's death, he became
subject to fits of madness in 1392 when only twenty-four, thus
giving the powerful dukes – those of Anjou, Bourbon, Burgundy,
Brittany, and Orleans in particular – the occasion to war among
themselves and to increase taxes, thereby causing riots in Paris (the
rioters were called 'maillotins' since they were armed with 'maillets',
mallets), Rouen, Amiens, and other cities. The military wisdom of
Du Guesclin was sorely missed. Henry V's victory at Agincourt in
1415 led to his being acknowledged heir to the French throne, and
to his son Henry VI's coronation in Paris as king of the French in
1431. Charles VII (1422–61) was an ineffective king until Joan of
Arc's inspired leadership enabled him to crush, not merely the
English, but also the rebellious barons. At the end of his reign only
Burgundy, Flanders, and Brittany remained outside his jurisdiction.

Louis XI (1461–83), a most astute and ruthless politician, annexed to the royal domain the immensely wealthy duchy of Burgundy in 1482. His successor Charles VIII (1483–98), a considerably weaker figure, added Brittany to the kingdom through his marriage to Anne de Bretagne.

IV. EDUCATION AND GOVERNMENT

Two developments taking place over several reigns and concerned with vital aspects of medieval life remain to be mentioned: the educational system and the machinery of government. Already at the time of the Roman Empire, numbers of schools were set up in the north of Gaul as well as in the south, and the whole country was a relatively cultured area of the Empire.[20] These schools undoubtedly suffered greatly at the time of the Germanic invasions in the fifth and sixth centuries A.D., and the Church was left with the monopoly of education. Church schools were originally intended to train priests or monks, but education was not of a narrowly theological kind and was particularly thorough in its study of language, exclusively Latin for many centuries. The seven liberal arts taught in the Roman schools had developed a clear pattern by the eleventh century: the *trivium*, consisting of grammar, rhetoric (a study of the effective use of language, a discipline of classical origins with which the subject known nowadays as stylistics has some affinities), and dialectic (limited originally to the few works of Plato and Aristotle available in Latin translation); and the *quadrivium*, consisting of music (mainly church singing), arithmetic, geometry, and astronomy (the last-named confined originally to the calculation of the date of Easter).[21]

In the course of the twelfth century, thirst for knowledge increased rapidly, resulting in the formation towards the end of the century of the University of Paris, though no precise date for its founding can be quoted. It was a process of gradual change and development rather than a sudden dramatic step forward. In the mid-twelfth century Abelard had taught in the open air on the Mont Sainte-Geneviève for want of suitable accommodation. Activities of this kind, along with the growth of the Cathedral School of Paris, led to the formation of a *studium generale* (meaning a place of study for students from all parts. *Studia generalia* appeared about the same time also in Bologna and Salerno), later the *Universitas magistrorum et scholarium*. Already in the thirteenth century four faculties had developed – Theology, Canon Law, Medicine, and the Liberal Arts – and students were attracted from all over Europe. They were divided up according to 'nations' in a manner showing how different such concepts were in those days: the French nation included Italian and Spanish students; the Norman nation students of the north and west of France; the English nation students from Germany as well as England; the Picard nation those from Picardy and the Low Countries. The university, which awarded the *licentia docendi* (the modern 'licence'), was based on the collegiate system. In 1257, Robert de Sorbon, almoner of St Louis, founded the college whose name was later to serve for the whole university: the Sorbonne. Other universities were founded at Toulouse and Montpellier in the thirteenth century and at Orleans in the fourteenth. Montpellier became famous for its study of medicine, Toulouse for the study of law, Paris for theology and philosophy, attracting the finest minds of the age – Roger Bacon, Duns Scotus, Albertus Magnus, Thomas Aquinas among them. Philosophical disputations often hinged on extremely subtle points, and however archaic scholasticism may sometimes appear, Thomism, arising from Thomas Aquinas's rational investigations of the divine truth contained in the Scriptures, still arouses much interest at the present day. In studying the vernacular literature of medieval France, it must always be borne in mind that we are automatically excluding thereby the finest minds of the age, which in speech and writing invariably expressed themselves in Latin. Only towards the end of the Middle Ages did the occasional distinguished theologian, such as Jean Gerson, sometimes write in French, and even so Latin remained paramount.

The system of education was geared principally to the production of clergy and teachers, but some were able to find posts in the law courts and in administration, which from the time of Philip Augustus had been growing more elaborate. In his reign the offices of government outgrew the mainly domestic functions which they had for long had and whose origins were reflected still in titles such as *connétable* (from *comes stabuli*, originally the officer in charge of the royal stables) and *seneschal* (originally a Germanic term meaning 'senior servant', used to designate the officer in charge of the royal table). Following a model already established in Normandy, Philip Augustus created the office of *baillis* (bailiffs), called *seneschaux* in the south. Their duties included the administration of justice in the assize courts, the calling-up of vassals for military service, and the collecting of taxes. Louis IX appointed *enquêteurs* (inspectors), whose duty it was to investigate complaints against the *baillis*. Towards the end of Louis IX's reign, a change in the organisation of the *curia regis* – the King's Council – brought into being the *Parlement* of Paris, consisting originally of prelates, nobles, officials, and lawyers,[22] and the *Chambre des Comptes* for financial matters. Each evolved an infrastructure of its own in the course of time. Numbers of writers of the later Middle Ages belonged to the administrative and legal *milieux* of the capital, occupying positions as bailiffs, court officials, or as secretaries to the king, the pope in Avignon, or one of the dukes. Despite the increasing variety of openings, not all the pupils of the schools, and later the graduates of the universities, were able to find posts, but this was by no means a new problem. Already in the eleventh century, earlier possibly, numbers wandered from region to region – the *clerici vagantes* as they were called, or *Goliardi* (named apparently after a certain Golias, the otherwise unknown founder of their 'order') – making a living as best they could, sometimes becoming minstrels and jong-leurs, popular entertainers who would recite or sing the lives of the saints, the *chansons de geste*, or early romances to gatherings in castles or public squares at a time when the majority of people, including even the nobles, were illiterate and manuscripts rare and precious. Some may well have chosen this life rather than have had it thrust upon them, for, apart from material hardship, it seems to have been a carefree existence beyond the authority of the Church, of which they were notably disrespectful. They wrote verses in Latin for the delectation of others of the *Ordo Vagorum*, a lively poetry in praise of wine, women, and the gay life, imbued with a simple 'carpite florem' philosophy.

The biggest failure of the French Middle Ages, among whose effects it is no exaggeration to number the Revolution of 1789, was that no adequate system of representation was developed. The States-General, bringing together representatives of the three estates (the Church, the nobility, and all others, referred to, in an expression found for the first time in 1484, as the *tiers état*), met in desultory fashion during the fourteenth and fifteenth centuries, usually when the monarch required help of some kind. The first meeting appears to have been held after the French defeat by the English at Crécy in 1347 (the assembly of 1302 called by Philip the Fair, and those of 1314–46, seem to have been gatherings of notables without the representative value of the States-General). As the king became stronger, meetings became rarer, and the powerful centralised monarchy that emerged at the end of the Middle Ages already bore the seeds of its own destruction and that of the régime on which it depended.

V. DISCOVERIES AND INVENTIONS

Finally, certain discoveries of great consequence deserve mention: from the twelfth century, possibly earlier, the compass in the form of a magnetised needle set on a piece of wood floating in water, which greatly facilitated navigation;[23] the discovery of gunpowder which began to change the nature of warfare in the fifteenth century, although the bow remained for long the most formidable weapon of the foot-soldiers; the discovery of printing in Germany, leading to the setting-up of the first French press in the University of Paris in 1470. Reading and study were now open to a far wider public than hitherto, and intellectual life was revolutionised as a result. From the special point of view of medieval literature this change was not all benefit, since some of the prose romances printed in large numbers were late and degenerate forms of earlier literature. Many of the finest medieval works, in their original and best forms, lay forgotten in their manuscripts for centuries. Only a few scholars referred back to medieval manuscripts in the course of the sixteenth, seventeenth, and eighteenth centuries, and though some produced distinguished work, it was not really until the nineteenth century that the vast treasure house of medieval French literature began to be explored.

NOTES

1. The text of the document is preserved in the chronicles of the brothers' cousin Nithard, the sole surviving copy of which dates from about 1000, over a century and a half after the swearing of the oaths, so that the reliability of the text is open to question.

2. That a restriction of meaning indicative of future usage was already taking place is revealed in the linguistically important *Glossary of Reichenau*, an eighth-century work defining terms in the fourth-century Vulgate which were becoming obsolete. *Gallia* is explained as *Frantia* (confusion of -ti- and -ci- before a vowel was common in spelling; cf. *naciones*) without the addition of a qualifying adjective such as *occidentalis*. That the two names were wholly synonymous at this period is most unlikely.

3. 'For the love of God and the Christian people and our common salvation, from this day onwards, to the extent that God has granted me knowledge and power, I shall save this my brother Charles both in aid and in everything, just as one must by right save one's brother . . .'

4. An essential difference between dialects of the north and those of the south of France, the former represented nowadays by French, the latter by Provençal (or 'occitan'), is in their treatment of Latin vowel *a*. In the former, when stressed and final of its syllable, it gave *e*: *mare>mer*, *firmare>fermer*, whereas in the latter, as in other Romance languages, it remained unchanged: *mar*, *fermar*, etc. They came to be designated by their particles of affirmation, the language of the north being the *langue d'oïl*, that of the south *langue d'oc* (hence the name of the region).

5. See below, p. 6.
6. See below, pp. 42–50.
7. See below, p. 20.
8. See below, p. 76.
9. See below, chapter 3. The *chansons de geste* were not concerned exclusively with the wars against the Arabs, though this is the subject of many of them.
10. See below, chapter 5.
11. See below, pp. 21–34.
12. See below, p. 221.
13. Some of his sketches are reproduced by G. Henderson, *Gothic*, Harmondsworth, 1967, 1972.

14. The effect of the stirrup was to put the whole force of the charging horse into a spearthrust instead merely of that of the rider's arm. The stirrup has even been called the most significant invention in warfare prior to gunpowder. The use of the saddle and horseshoes began at about the same period.

15. See below, pp. 78–9.

16. Medieval *fabliaux* refer to 'la feme au prestre', see below, p. 229. The problem of 'married' clergy comes up in the works of writers of the second half of the thirteenth century such as Adam de la Halle and Rutebeuf.

17. See below, pp. 262–3.

18. See below, pp. 119–20.

19. See below, p. 85.

20. Certain linguistic features are usually ascribed to the influence of the schools, such as the retention of a two-case system in the vernacular at a time when other regions had abandoned the case system altogether except for personal pronouns. See below, p. 362.

21. The division of the seven arts into the *trivium* and *quadrivium* is said to date from the time of Boethius in the sixth century A.D., though the effective organisation of the system owed much to Alcuin of York. See H. Rashdall, *The Universities of Europe in the Middle Ages*, new ed. Oxford, 1936, I, 34, note 2.

22. The *Parlement* of Paris was more a high court of justice than a parliament in the English sense of the term. It was unrepresentative, and eventually became a body of hereditary lawyers.

23. It is referred to in this form in the *Bible* of Guiot de Provins, see below, pp. 266–7.

Chapter 2

VARIATIONS ON HAGIOGRAPHIC THEMES

I. THE EARLIEST SURVIVING LITERARY TEXTS

THE oldest hagiographic text extant in French is the *Cantilène de Sainte Eulalie*, dating from about 880.[1] In its short span of twenty-nine lines, this Passion story depicts the unyielding faith of an early fourth-century Spanish martyr, the persecution she suffered, and her decapitation at the command of 'li rex pagiens' (the Emperor Maximian). Based on a Latin *Sequentia*, this little poem provides no more than a threadbare account, interesting, however, for its early date of composition and its aptness as a starting-point for the lives of the saints in the vernacular, indeed for French literature as a whole. Like the other extant works of the ninth and tenth centuries, very few in number, the *Cantilène de Sainte Eulalie* is studied today mainly as a linguistic document.

The *Vie de Saint Léger* was written in the following century, so that it too must be numbered among the earliest extant French works.[2] It gives a much fuller biography, containing 240 octosyllabic lines divided into 40 stanzas of 6 lines each. Here too literary merit is slim. It is an abrupt, disjointed, clumsily written account of St Léger's career, his appointment as abbot of the monastery of St Maxentius in Poitiers, later as bishop of Autun. We are told briefly of his quarrel with Ebroin, mayor of the palace in Neustria (the text merely refers to him as 'un compte', line 55), leading to Léger's downfall, his imprisonment, torture, and martyrdom, which took place in A.D. 678.

The *Chanson de Sainte Foy* was composed in the second half of the eleventh century.[3] From the south of France, one of the earliest Provençal works to have survived, this poem begins with an incredible gasconade in its claim to be 'sweeter than honey or spiced wine' and to make 'a beautiful dance'. That this grim story of the torture and decapitation of an eleven-year-old girl should be considered such pleasant entertainment is surprising, even though stories of martyrdom were intended to bring inspiration and joy to medieval Christianity rather than sorrow and mourning. It has been suggested that this allusion to song and dance was borrowed from some secular work, now lost, and had nothing to do with the original song of Sainte Foy. Only the lilting verse measure, and the simple melody to which it was set, may be said to go some little way towards justifying the unknown author's boast:

Canczon audi q'es bella 'n tresca,	I heard a song which is beautiful as a dance,
Que fo de razo Espanesca;	
Non fo de paraulla Grezesca	Which was of Spanish subject matter.
Ne de lengua Serrazinesca	It was not in Greek words
Dolz' e suaus es plus que bresca	Nor in the Saracen tongue.
E plus qe nulz pimentz q'om mesca . . .	It was sweet and soothing more than a honeycomb
(lines 14–19)	And more than any spiced wine that one may mix . . .

In the following pages, three important hagiographic texts from the eleventh and twelfth centuries – the *Vie de Saint Alexis*, the *Vie de Saint Brendan*, and the *Vie de Saint Thomas* – will be analysed in some detail. Attention will also be paid to their style and versification, since their characteristics are shared, with some modification, by many contemporary and later works, including the *chansons de geste* and the romances.

II. THE 'VIE DE SAINT ALEXIS'

Possibly the most famous of the lives of the saints to have been recorded in the vernacular languages of western Europe is that of St Alexis.[4] Although it came to be set down in at least eleven languages, the French version can claim to be the earliest and best of all those written in a modern European tongue. Much information has been brought to light concerning the formation and growth of this legend, its success and propagation. It is as well, however, to begin with a brief account of the work as it appears in the most complete and reliable of the seven extant manuscripts of the first French version, one copied out in the early twelfth century, some time before 1123.[5]

Euphemianus, a rich Roman noble of early Christian times, is sorrowful because his wife is unable to bear him a child. Together they pray that God might grant them a child to His liking. The wife bears a son whom they christen Alexis. Brought up and educated with care, he eventually enters the emperor's service. Euphemianus does not wish to die before his son marries, and accordingly arranges a suitable match for him. Alexis, however, desires to devote his whole life to God. On his wedding night he abandons his wife and sets sail for Laodicea. He departs thence for Edessa, having heard of a miraculous icon of the Virgin Mary in that city. Settling there, he gives away all his possessions and lives on alms, retaining just enough for his own needs, distributing the remainder among the poor. In Rome meanwhile, his parents and wife grieve over his disappearance, and servants are dispatched to look for him. They find him eventually in Edessa and give him alms, but fail to recognise him in his beggar's guise. This failure brings only joy to Alexis, and he praises God. In Rome his parents and wife mourn for him as though he is dead. For seventeen years Alexis remains in Edessa, until one day the miraculous icon proclaims: 'Seek the man of God'. It becomes clear that this is Alexis, and people begin to revere him. Not wishing this, he flees back to Laodicea and from there to Rome. He seeks shelter in his father's house as a beggar beneath the staircase and there, still unrecognised and scorned even by the servants, he lives for a further seventeen years, keeping, as before, just enough food for his own needs, giving the remainder to other beggars. Shortly before his death he calls for ink, parchment, and pen and writes down the story of his life. Three times a voice summons the faithful to church, and there they are ordered to seek the man of God who is in Rome. The pope, the emperors,[6] and all the people of Rome pray to God for guidance, and the voice then proclaims: 'Seek him in the house of Euphemianus. There shall you find him'. Only after his death is he discovered, with the parchment on which he has written his life-story clutched in his hands. When this becomes known the grief of his parents and wife redoubles. The body of Alexis, meantime, works great miracles and many sick people are cured. The people of Rome flock to the funeral in great numbers. Because of Alexis the souls of his parents and wife are saved, and they are united with him in Paradise.

The story ends with the *Pater noster* ...

The prologue to this tale of asceticism and self-sacrifice describes it, rather surprisingly, as an 'amiable song', though this choice of adjective is no more surprising than that of a modern editor who finds it 'thrilling'.[7] So complete a renunciation of normal human relationships on the part of Alexis can hardly be termed 'amiable',[8] and so complete an absence of action does not make for a 'thrilling' story. What, then, are the salient characteristics of this work, and wherein lies its claim to be the first masterpiece of French literature? Remarkable is the creation of atmosphere, an atmosphere similar in important respects to that achieved in the icons of the early Eastern Church, particularly those emanating from Byzantium in the eleventh and twelfth centuries. A contemplation of such works can contribute to an understanding of the *Vie de Saint Alexis*. These portrayals of the Virgin and Child, of the Apostles or the Saints, reveal the same austerity and simplicity as our text, the same severe symbolism, the same aloofness, the same mysticism suggestive of the spiritual life even though human affections still have a part to play. Just as the parents and wife of Alexis represent the warmth and depth of personal emotions, so, in the pose of the Mother and Child in an icon such as the famous Our Lady of Vladimir, the tenderness of the relationship is portrayed even though the individual figures themselves are clearly not wholly of this world. It is in such a blending, and contrasting, of divine love and earthly love, in this transcendence of earthly ties even while their importance is acknowledged, that the *Vie de Saint Alexis* deserves its reputation.

The story even has the same static effect as the paintings, for the attitude of Alexis remains quite constant, as also does that of his parents and wife, whose grief is not effaced by the passing years. The likeness is not mere coincidence, for as we shall see later, the legend reached the Western world from the East, by way of Constantinople.

The importance of this text which stands at the very threshold of French literature is such that a closer examination is called for. In its details, as in its creation of atmosphere, it reveals several significant features. From the opening lines the reader cannot but be struck by the regularity of the verse structure, an analysis of which will not be out of place here, since this same measure was to enjoy a tremendous vogue among vernacular works of the twelfth century, the *chansons de geste* in particular. It at once becomes clear that this is not a primitive literature at a rudimentary stage in its development, still seeking an adequate mode of expression. The framework is firm, based on conventions as well established as those of later periods, for which this medieval verse sets the pattern in its reliance on the number of syllables in a line, rather than feet as in Classical Latin verse. The basic pattern of every line is decasyllabic, with a caesura after the fourth syllable. Variety could be achieved by accepting at the end of either or both hemistiches an unstressed e: Bons fut li secles (line 1), Velz est e fraisles (line 9), etc. The formula may be represented thus: $4 (+e) - 6 (+e)$, allowing a total of four possible variations for these lines:[9]

Bons fut li secles al tens ancïenur,
Quer feit i ert e justise ed amur;
S'i ert creance, dunt or n'i at nul
    prut.
Tut est müez, perdut ad sa colur:
Ja mais n'ert tel cum fut as
    anceisurs.

Al tens Noë ed al tens Abraham
Ed al David, qui Deus par amat
    tant,
Bons fut li secles; ja mais n'ert si
    vailant.
Velz est e fraisles, tut s'en vat
    declinant:
Si'st ampairét, tut bien vait
    remanant.   (lines 1–10)

Good was the world in the time of the ancients, for there was faith, justice, and love. There was also trust, from which there is no profit now. The world is quite changed, and has lost its colour. Nevermore will it be as in the time of our ancestors.

In the time of Noah, in the time of Abraham and that of David, whom God loved so much, good was the world. Nevermore will it be of such worth. It is old and feeble, quite degenerate. It has grown worse, all good deeds remain undone.

Only 40 out of the total of 625 lines have one syllable too few or too many, but these may be the fault of the scribe rather than the poet. The fourth and tenth syllables (eleventh where the first hemistich ends in *e*) bore a stress, but there was no regular placing of

stress accents elsewhere in the line. The lines are divided into groups
of five, as the passage quoted above reveals. Each stanza has the
same assonance, according to which the final stressed vowel is
identical, but not necessarily the consonants which follow it (*prut*:
colur: *anceisurs*, etc.). When the final consonants eventually became
identical in later texts, assonance had given place to rhyme. The
last four lines quoted above (ending in *tant*: vail*ant*: declin*ant*:
reman*ant*) show that the *Vie de Saint Alexis* was already at times
close to achieving this.

Aesthetically this verse was admirably suited to the function it
was required to fill. It was essentially intended for singing or de-
claiming in the presence of an audience rather than for reading in
private by the individual. Its qualities are accordingly of an *oral*
nature. In the asymmetrical 4 – 6 structure, the voice rose on the
accent of the caesura and fell on that of the assonance or rhyme,[10]
thus imparting a circumflex pattern to the line of verse. Assonance
contributed adequately to the acoustic effects of the whole without
the greater artistic potentialities of rhyme (which were achieved
at the expense of an inevitably narrower range of suitable words)
and without that additional appeal to the eye, a characteristic of
rhyme which would have served no purpose here.

How had this verse pattern, differing in important respects from
that of Classical Latin, come into being? This simple question is by
no means easy to answer – indeed all questions relating to the origins
of medieval literature are difficult, and usually controversial. It is
clear, however, that changes were inevitable once Classical Latin
distinctions between long and short vowels and syllables began to
disappear, as they did from the third century A.D. onwards. Hence
the very foundations of classical verse, the iambics ($\cup$ –), trochees
(– $\cup$), spondees (– –), anapests ($\cup\cup$ –), and dactyls (– $\cup\cup$), were
threatened, although they did not disappear overnight, the change
from one system to the other being evolutionary rather than revolutionary. Classical Latin offered considerable variation in metre;
thus the iambic metron $\cup$ – $\cup$ – could be varied by making the first
syllable (the anceps) long: – – $\cup$ –, and the pattern could be further
modified by substituting two short syllables for one long one
$\underset{\cup\cup}{\cup}$ $\underset{\cup\cup}{}$ $\cup$ –. Similar licence existed for trochaic feet, and in the
dactylic hexameter any one of the first four feet could be replaced
by a spondee: – $\cup\cup$ > – –. Within a constant number of feet
the number of syllables was obviously free to vary considerably. In
the medieval Latin hymns of the fourth–sixth centuries, this wide
choice was abandoned, in particular the option of substituting two
short syllables for one long one, so that while Classical Latin metre
was still respected, a new state of affairs arose in that the number
of syllables now remained constant, a feature which was gradually

to become predominant until eventually the concept of the metric foot disappeared, not surviving beyond medieval Latin into the vernacular. The caesura was retained as a break towards the middle of lines of ten syllables or more, though only the earliest of octosyllabic lines were so divided. So it was that the new system evolved from and within the Classical Latin system and did not begin as something completely foreign to it. The matching of sounds at the ends of lines, though not a feature of classical verse, bears some resemblance to the rhetorical device known as *similiter cadens*,[11] and gradually became a feature of Latin hymns in answer to the need for a new prosody. The structure of works such as the *Vie de Saint Alexis*, no less than their contents, owed much to early Christianity.

It is not only the verse form of the *Vie de Saint Alexis* that is adequately characterised by its opening lines. Light is thrown too on the poet's vocabulary and hence on the intellectual level of his work. The first stanza contains no fewer than five abstract nouns – *foi, justice, amour, croyance, prut* – and a metaphorical use of *colur* in the sense of 'lustre', 'brightness', a usage evidently borrowed from Latin, where it was found only in rhetorical language. Throughout the work a certain level of sophistication is maintained, and many are the details revealing a considerable degree of literary skill. The characters of what could so easily have been a dull and insipid tale are brought to life by the frequent use of direct speech, e.g., the parents' prayer to God:

E! reis celeste par ton cumandement Amfant nus done ki seit a tun talent!	Oh heavenly king, through your command, grant us a child according to your wishes!

(24–5)

or the quaint manner in which Euphemianus urges his reluctant son to sleep with his newly wedded wife:

. . . 'Filz, quar t'en vas colcer Avoc ta spuse, al cumand Deu del ciel'.	'Son, pray go to bed with your wife, at the command of God in heaven'.

(52–3)

It will be noted that the father cleverly found the argument most likely to convince his single-minded son – 'al cumand Deu del ciel' – but it had no effect, as is shown by Alexis's extraordinary admonitions before his departure:

'Oz mei, pulcele! Celui tien ad espus Ki nus raenst de sun sanc precïus. An icest secle nen at parfit' amor; La vithe est fraisle, n'i ad durable honur; Cesta lethece revert a grant tristur'.	'Listen to me, girl. Keep for husband the one who redeemed us with his precious blood. In this life there is no perfect love. Life is frail, there is no lasting honour. This happiness turns to great sadness'.

(66–70)

On seeing his wife in the marital bed Alexis exclaimed:

'E! Deus! dist il, cum fort pecét   'Oh God! what great sin afflicts me!'
  m'apresset!'
(59)

so that sexual relations even in marriage are rejected by him as sinful, a condemnation which has made at least one modern scholar wonder whether there is not here a reflection of the Catharist heresy.[12] The most effective use of direct speech occurs in the depiction of the parents' and wife's grief over Alexis's disappearance, as in this example of apostrophe, in which Alexis's mother addresses the room in which her son had grown up:

'Cambra', dist ela, 'ja mais n'estras   'Room', she said, 'never again will
  parede,   you be adorned, nor shall joy be
Ne ja ledece n'ert an tei demenede'.   shown in you'.
(141–2)

Apostrophe is extensively used when all three express their sorrow by addressing Alexis directly in his absence, each according to his or her character and interests. The wife thinks of his handsome appearance:

'O bele buce, bel vis, bele   'Oh handsome mouth, handsome
  faiture . . .'   face, handsome appearance . . .'
(481)

The mother thinks of her only child whom she has lost, the father of the disastrous effect of Alexis's disappearance on his mother:

'Filz Alexis, de ta dolenta medra!   'Son Alexis, such affliction for your
Tantes dolurs ad pur tei   grieving mother. She has endured so
  anduredes . . .'   much sadness because of you'.
(396–7)

and bitterly regrets that there will be nobody to succeed him after his death:

'O filz, qui erent mes granz ereditez,   'Oh son, to whom will my great in-
Mes larges terres dunt jo aveie asez,   heritances belong, my great domains
Mes granz palais de Rome la citét?'   of which I possessed an abundance,
(401–3)   my great palaces in the city of
                                Rome?'

Particularly interesting in the structure of many lines is the search for balance and symmetry. For example, Alexis's encounter with his father's servants, who gave him alms, is summarised thus:

Il fut lur sire, or est lur almosners.   He was their lord, now he is their
(124)   servant.

The stripping of Alexis's room by his grieving mother:

Sa grant honur a grant dol ad   Its great honour to great grief has
  turnede.   turned.
(145)

The parallel grief of mother and wife is summed up by the former:

'Tu tun seinur, jol ferai pur mun   'You will do it for your husband, I
   filz'.   for my son'.
                   (155)

The pope summarises reactions to the discovery of Alexis's body, which brought health to the sick:

'Chi chi se doilet, a nostr'os est il   'Whoever may grieve here, for our
   goie'.   purpose it is a matter for joy'.
                   (503)

The effect of the miraculous cures is likewise compressed into one line:

Alquant i cantent, li pluisur jetent   Some sing there, many shed tears,
   lermes,
                   (584)

and, in an equally lapidary fashion:

Ki vint plurant, cantant l'en fait   Whoever came weeping, singing he
   raler.   made them depart.
                   (560)

Interest in symmetry is shown in other ways, although it is true that not all of these are of the French author's invention. Three times in Edessa the statue of the Virgin was heard to proclaim 'Seek the man of God', the third time telling where he was to be found. Years later, in Rome

Vint une voiz treis feiz en la citét   There came a voice three times in
          (292)   the city

and again, on the third occasion, the exact whereabouts of the man of God were revealed. But above all – any analysis of the *Vie de Saint Alexis* cannot but return to this point, for it is here that the French version achieves its finest effects – the poet's artistry was directed towards the depiction of the grief of Alexis's relatives over his disappearance.[13] This is the author's way of toning down the harshness of the legend, counterbalancing Alexis's seeming indifference to his relatives. In fact 155 of the 625 lines are devoted to this feature. Alexis, like the eponymous hero of the *Chanson de Roland*, is already dead when little more than half the story has been told, and most of the remainder is taken up with reactions to his death. Stanza 22 makes father, mother, and wife speak in turn:

Ço dist li pedres: 'Cher filz, cum   The father said: 'Dear son how I
   t'ai perdut!'   have lost you!' The mother replies:
Respont la medre: 'Lasse! qu'est   'Alas, what has become of him?'
   devenut?'   The wife said: 'Sin has taken him
Ço dist la spuse: 'Pechét le m'at   from me . . .'
   tolut . . .'
          (106–8)

Later in the story, after the discovery of Alexis's body, each speaks at greater length, in the same order as in the stanza just quoted. It is as though they represent the three panels of a medieval triptych on the subject of grief. Repetition and accumulation are effectively used throughout these passages, as in this description of the mother's reaction to the finding of Alexis's body:

Chi dunt li vit sun grant dol demener,	Whoever saw her lamenting so grievously, beating her breast and throwing herself on the ground, tearing her hair and scratching her face, pulling her dead child close to her, would have been very hard-hearted had he not felt constrained to weep.
Sum piz debatre e sun cors dejeter,	
Ses crins derumpre et sen vis maiseler,	
Sun mort amfant detraire ed acoler,	
Mult fust il dur ki n'estoüst plurer	
(426–30)	

The verse measure allowed some liberty in the distribution of the sense pauses. The second hemistich usually continues or qualifies the first:

Eufemien/si out a nom li pedre . . . (16)	Eufemien, such was the father's name . . .
Fud baptizét/si out num Alexis . . . (31)	He was baptised and was called Alexis . . .

The sense pause at the caesura varies considerably in strength. It may be quite distinct:

Tuz l'escarnissent/sil tenent pur bricun;	All of them scorn him, and consider him an idiot. They pour water over him and wet his wretched bed.
L'egua li getent/si moilent sun liçon.	
(266–7)	

but more frequently it is weak, imposing no real break in the continuity of the line:

Sainz Alexis/est el ciel senz dutance,	St Alexis is in heaven without a doubt, along with God and His band of angels.
Ensembl' ot Deu/e la compaignie as angeles.	
(606–7)	

A complete change of subject in the second hemistich is very rare indeed:

Vait s'en li pople./Le perë e la medra	The people depart. The father and mother and girl never separated.
E la pulcela/unches ne desevrerent.	
(601–2)	

Sense divisions correspond more to the ends of lines, but even so overflow is sometimes encountered, as in the lines just quoted.[14] Throughout, the language remains terse and concentrated despite the static, repetitive nature of the story. Only very occasionally has the need to write a line of ten syllables, the last tonic vowel of which respects the assonance, produced some padding:

Dunc an eisit danz Alexis *a certes* . . .	Then Alexis went out in truth . . .

(83)[15]

Finally, a not inconsiderable characteristic of the story lies in its author's reticence. Alexis's action in abandoning his wife on their wedding night must have seemed as unprincipled and as extraordinary in the eleventh century as it does now. Why did he not disappear *before* the marriage could take place? Similarly his absolute indifference to the suffering he caused his relatives, which he witnessed daily and at close quarters when he lived beneath his father's staircase, seems incomprehensible and indeed un-Christian, but the poet simply tells his tale. He does not attempt to explain, to excuse, to condone. Here is the story of a very special being: the man of God – *l'ume Deu, le Deu serf* – here is what happened. The author avoids becoming entangled in comments and justifications. Only at the end does he point to the story's ultimate significance, without excessive moralising and always without specific comment on Alexis's behaviour:

Ki ad pechét bien s'en pot recorder,	Whoever has sinned can bear this
Par penitence s'en pot tres bien salver.	well in mind, through penitence he can well save himself. This life is
Briés est cist secles, plus durable atendeiz.	short, prepare for a more lasting one. Let us pray to God, the Holy
Ço preiums Deu, la sainte trinitét,	Trinity, that along with God we may
Qu' o Deu ansemble poissum el ciel regner.	reign in heaven.

(546–50)

Later versions of the story became longer and more tedious when their authors could not refrain from adding their own commentaries on Alexis's behaviour. When moral and social considerations were brought in of such matters as the attitude towards marriage, then, as we shall see, the revisions became very confused.

Such, in brief, are the contents and characteristics of this first French text of real literary merit. It was not a story which had its origins in France. Indeed, when the first French version appeared, the legend already had a centuries-old history behind it, for it was in existence long before the language of northern Gaul had developed far enough to be called French. The earliest version of all has been preserved in three Syrian manuscripts copied out in the sixth century A.D. Alexis is not named here, but is referred to simply as the Man of God. Composed between 450 and 475,[16] this marks the beginning of the legend which, in a modified and expanded form, was to spread throughout the Christian world. It tells

how the Man of God, born to a life of luxury though his preference
was for one of poverty and humbleness, departed from his parents'
house in Rome[17] on the day fixed for his wedding, without even
setting eyes on the fiancée whom his parents had chosen for him. He
settled in Edessa, where he fasted all day, and in the evening begged
for alms at the entrance to the church. At night while the other
beggars slept, he would pray with his arms outstretched in the form
of a cross, touching the walls of the church. He died in Edessa and
was buried in the common grave there. This account, simple and
straightforward, gives the impression of being largely factual,
and its modern editor believes that this was indeed the case.[18] The
sole miracle concerned the disappearance of his body when it was
decided that it should be exhumed and given a more appropriate
burial.

Five later Syrian manuscripts, the earliest from the ninth century,
the latest from the thirteenth, give this same account in a lengthened
form. An episode has been added which is possibly an adaptation of
the final scenes in the life of another holy man, John the Calybite
(Hut-dweller), whose story was well known in Constantinople.[19]
According to this, the Man of God, whose body was not found in
Edessa, did not in fact die there, but left that city when he began to
acquire a reputation for holiness. He returned to his parents' house,
and lived the remainder of his days in the vestibule there (in a hut
nearby in the original story of John the Calybite), unrecognised,
scorned by his father's servants. This expansion of the original story
of the Man of God is believed to have originated in Constantinople,
whence it returned to Syria, so testifying in its travels to the close-
ness of the relationship between Byzantium and Syria.[20]

In subsequent Greek versions the story was further modified and
the name Alexis was added. The story did not become known in
Western Christendom before the end of the tenth century. It
appears to have reached Rome for the first time when the archbishop of Damascus, Sergius, took refuge there in 977 and founded
a Graeco-Roman community centred on the church of St Boniface.[21]
Not for nothing does this church figure prominently in the Latin[22]
and vernacular versions of western Europe, where it is referred to as
the resting-place of Alexis's body:

Sainz Boneface, que l'um martir
    apelet,
Aveit an Rome un' eglise mult bele.
Iloec an portent danz Alexis a
    certes,
Ed attement le posent a la terre.
Feliz le liu u sun saint cors
    herberget!

St Boniface, who is called martyr,
had a very fine church in Rome.
There they carry Lord Alexis in
truth, and lay him to rest in the
ground as is befitting. Blessed the
place where his holy body lies!

(566–70)

Where, when, and in what circumstances the first French version
of the story was composed, is not clear. The suggestion that it was
owed to a certain Tedbalt de Vernon, canon of Rouen, writing towards the middle of the eleventh century, is based on nothing more
than the assertion by one of Tedbalt's contemporaries that he translated several lives of saints 'from their latinity, not without
eloquence, and made pleasant songs of them with a tinkling
rhythm'.[23] Renewed attention has recently been paid to the fact
that the earliest and best French version was copied out in England
and forms part of the manuscript known as the St Albans Psalter.[24]
This work was removed from St Albans to the abbey of Lamb-
springen in Germany by Benedictine monks of the seventeenth century and is now at Hildesheim in Hanover. It may have been
intended originally for presentation to Christina of Markyate
(1096?–1155?), anchoress and afterwards prioress of the nunnery
at Markyate near St Albans.[25] Forced by her parents into marriage
despite her vow of virginity at the relics of St Albans, Christina
abandoned her husband soon after her marriage in order to devote
herself to the religious life. Her marriage was eventually dissolved
by the archbishop of York. The inclusion of the story of St Alexis
in the psalter may therefore have been no mere chance, but a discreet allusion to Christina's own life, and indeed a justification of it.
The story of her life was eventually recorded in Latin in its turn,
as a work of edification for the nuns whose priory she had founded.[26]

In view of the wide dissemination of the Alexis legend and the
popularity it enjoyed, it is strange that only three places in western
Europe north of the Alps had churches dedicated to St Alexis:
Paderborn in Germany, Bec in Normandy, and a chapel of the
abbey church of St Albans.[27] Between Bec and St Albans there was
an interesting connection which may well have had a bearing on
the St Alexis legend, as has recently been shown:

... since the first Norman abbot of St Albans, Paul, Lanfranc's nephew,
came from Bec to England the possibility has to be borne in mind that the
cult of the exotic Graeco-Roman saint was introduced into England via
Normandy. The two great late eleventh century abbots of Bec, Lanfranc
and Anselm, were of Italian extraction which in its turn would help to
explain the spreading of the Alexis cult from Italy to Normandy and would
make the genealogical line complete.[28]

The author of this hypothesis goes on to suggest that, provided
there are no linguistic objections to dating the French original as
late as 1120[29] – the approximate date of the St Albans Psalter –
'there would be a strong case for regarding St Albans, towards
which we have a unique combination of circumstances converging
at this time, as the birthplace of the Alexis poem in French'.[30] The
abbot of St Albans in the 1120s was a Frenchman, Geoffrey of

Maine, who is known to have been interested in the case of Christina.[31]

The seeker of the sources of medieval works is constantly endeavouring to complete a jigsaw puzzle in which half the pieces or more have been lost. Clearly there remains a strong possibility that there was an earlier French version, composed probably at Bec in Normandy, that it was eventually taken to St Albans in England, and that the extant version is accordingly a copy (or a copy of a copy . . .) of this lost original. Further research may throw more light on this enigma. Meantime the *Vie de Saint Alexis* must be considered an anonymous work, the exact date of composition of which is unknown, but the copy preserved in the St Albans Psalter may be assigned to 1115–19.

The later history of the legend in its French form can be traced more easily. Revised versions appeared in the twelfth, thirteenth, and fourteenth centuries, the importance of which depends on the light they throw on some of the less praiseworthy aspects of later medieval literature. The later twelfth-century version is over twice the length of the Anglo-Norman prototype, a rather ominous change in itself. The author's aim was evidently to put flesh on the bare bones of the original. Not for nothing has the title been changed to *Le Roman de Saint Alexis*.[32] Attempts made to introduce picturesque effects and vivid details have resulted in a loss of concentration of aesthetic purpose and have introduced a note utterly foreign to the ascetic spirit of the legend. Thus, in the wedding-chamber, Alexis looks at the wife he is about to abandon:

Assés i ardent candoiles et lanternes,	Many were the candles and lanterns
Mout la vit gente et couvoiteuse et bele.	burning there, and he saw that she was comely, desirous, and beautiful.
(lines 125–6)	

However, the sole effect is to inspire him to deliver an extremely long sermon, over ten times the length of that in the Anglo-Norman text. He then cuts his wedding-ring in half, keeps one half, and gives the other to his wife. He tells her that if he does not bring his half back in a year's time, she is free to marry again. A romantic, tearful leavetaking, heavily overladen with sentiment, follows:

Estes les vous belement departis,	Behold the beauty of their separa-
Plorent des oels, ne se porent tenir,	tion. They weep, they could not
Et la pucele gentement li a dit:	refrain, and the maiden spoke nobly
'Or t'en vas, sire, Dieus te laist revenir,	to him: 'Now you are leaving, my lord, may God grant that you re-
Quant autrement ne te puis retenir.	turn, since I cannot otherwise keep
Dolante en ert cele qui te nori,	you. She who brought you up will
Si ert li peres qui toi engenui,	be grief-stricken, and the father who
Et jou meisme qui t'avoie a mari...'	engendered you, and I myself who
(285–92)	had you for husband...'

Alexis is full of remorse because of the suffering he has caused his relatives (whereas the Man of God in the earlier versions was not beset by these human sentiments) and feels as a result that there can be no salvation for him:

Qui çou a fait, comment porra garir?

He who did this, how can he be saved?

(565)

The statue, however, thinks differently, for having called out 'Seek the man of God', it adds five lines of suitable explanation. The most extraordinary addition occurs after Alexis's death. The letter in which he had given an account of his sufferings flies aloft and swoops down to lodge in his wife's bosom, an event which the story-teller is not slow to explain at length:

'Oiés, signour, con grande loiauté
Tout home doivent a lor moiller
   porter
Car tel moustrance fist le jour
   Damedés,
Que a sa mere ne vaut la carte aler
Ne a son pere qui l'avoit engenré
Mais a l'epouse ki bien avoit gardé
Le compaignie de son ami
   carnel...'

'Hear, my lords, what great loyalty all men must show to their wives, for such a proof did the Lord God give that day, that the letter did not want to go to his mother, nor to his father who had engendered him, but to the wife who had loyally kept the company of her husband...'

(1106–12)

The half ring of course turns up in this letter. It too leaps up into the air, and then joins with the other half ring in the possession of Alexis's wife, so that the joints cannot be seen. These additions to the story are highly significant. They show how perplexed the author of the revised version must have been over the attitude towards marriage revealed by the legend. He has invented this ingenious but highly contrived way of correcting possible misconceptions concerning the attitude of the Church to marriage. Unfortunately, in trying to forestall one misinterpretation, he has introduced a far more serious one which makes nonsense of the spirit of the legend, utterly foreign to sugary sentiment and romance. Unwittingly he has produced a complete negation of the original version, a veritable anti-Alexis. His successors, however, were evidently grateful to him for this interpolation which they all adopted, with varying degrees of astonishment expressed by the assembly and by Alexis's wife in particular as she plucks the letter from her bosom:

'Sire', dist ele, 'jou sui moult esgarée...'

'My lord', said she, 'I am most perplexed...'

(1124)

Utterly gone from these later French versions is the noble and ascetic atmosphere of the first one, touching in its very simplicity, effective because of the innate good taste and judgement it reveals. The more Alexis is humanised, the more is he de-sanctified. The Man of God becomes a man of the world.[33] No medieval version, however, can rival Desfontaines's seventeenth-century tragedy on St Alexis for sheer absurdity. There the essential details of the legend had to be contained within a period of 24 hours. Alexis flees from his wife, is shipwrecked, returns to his father's house, unrecognised since the fatigue he has suffered has changed his appearance, also 'à cause du poil qui luy estoit venu depuis son départ', falls ill with chagrin on seeing the suffering his departure has caused, and dies – all within the space of one day! The letter he addressed to his wife ends grimly with these words:

'Le Ciel aura mon âme, et dans la sépulture Tu pourras posséder mon corps'.

'Heaven will have my soul, and in the tomb you can possess my body'.

To return to the earliest vernacular version of the legend as preserved in the St Albans Psalter is clearly a necessary, and rewarding, task. It can justifiably claim to be the best of all, for here the spirit of the story, and the expression of it, are in close harmony. In its depiction of the reaction of Alexis's relatives it has a greater human interest than its Syrian, Greek, and Latin antecedents, with none of the absurdities and irrelevant preoccupations of later French versions. A sober work, an ascetic one severely limited in range, but a true masterpiece none the less.

III. THE 'VIE DE SAINT BRENDAN'

In one of the principal extant manuscripts of early hagiographical works in French, the story of the life of St Alexis is followed immediately by that of St Brendan. *Incipit Vita Sancti Brendani* is the new heading.[34] A later manuscript also associates these two works[35] even though they were of radically different origin and atmosphere. It is tempting to assert that, strictly speaking, the story of St Brendan should not be classed as a life of a saint, since a mere seven years of Brendan's life are dealt with, and there is no martyrdom. However, such a claim would clearly impose restrictions on this literature of a type which did not exist in medieval times, as the above-mentioned title and juxtapositions indicate. The story is in effect a Christian version of the 'quest' type of literature, encountered in classical times in such diverse works as the *Odyssey*, or the story of Jason and the Argonauts, or that of the *Aeneid*, and found also in the East in the fabulous story of Sinbad the Sailor. The central theme is Brendan's voyage in search of heaven and hell, a voyage which takes him and his followers through a series of incredible adventures. In the following summary the less important of the many episodes are omitted.

St Brendan, of royal Irish lineage, abandons his inheritance in order to become a monk. In time he is chosen for abbot, although, being of a modest nature, he has not sought this position for himself. Because of his great virtue many join the order. Before his death Brendan longs to see Paradise and Hell, and begs God to grant him this wish. After seeking advice of the wise hermit Barintus, who in the course of his travels has visited an island near Paradise, he chooses fourteen of his monks and acquaints them with his project. They agree to accompany him and to obey him in all things. They journey to the coast and come to a rocky promontory known since as Brandan Head ('le Salt Brandan', line 164). There Brendan has a boat built of pine, with ox-hide stretched over the outside, smeared with grease so that it can sail swiftly through the waves.[36] They take forty days' supply of food on board. At the last minute they are joined by three felonious monks, all of whom are to perish in the course of the voyage, as Brendan predicts. They set off, the East wind carrying them in a westerly direction. They take to the oars when the wind slackens, steering no particular course, but putting their trust in God. They row on for a month, and just as food and strength are giving out, land comes into sight and a wind springs up. For three days they skirt towering cliffs in search of a mooring place. On landing they come across a splendid palace, with food and drink in abundance, but no occupants are to be found. Having rested and attended to their needs, they proceed on their way. After several months of hardship, they come to an island where they discover sheep as big as stags. They take one of them and prepare to eat it, since Easter Day is not far off. A messenger from God brings them bread and tells them to land on another island nearby. After holding a service in the boat, they cook their meal on the second island. As they do so, it begins to quake and move. The monks scramble into the boat and the island recedes at great speed, until all they can see of it is the fire they lit there. Brendan tells his astonished monks that what they have taken for an island is in fact the back of a giant fish. Pursuing their course, they come to the mouth of a river. They pull the boat upstream with ropes from the shore until they reach a tree as white as marble whose leaves are spotted white and red. Its top is higher than the clouds and it is covered with beautiful white birds. One of them flies down and tells Brendan that they are in fact fallen angels, followers of Satan, deprived of the glory of God's presence. The place is called the Paradise of Birds. Brendan also learns that not for another six years will he and his followers set eyes on Paradise, and that each year they will celebrate Easter on the back of the giant fish. This latter prophecy, surprisingly enough, provokes no particular reaction among the sailor monks. After a rest they re-embark with several months' supply of food and drink. A long voyage eventually brings them to land once more. The cliffs are high and forbidding, and they sail around them for forty days before finding a harbour. Eventually a monk meets them and takes them to a nearby abbey where they are shown the relics and treasures. They learn that this is the abbey founded by St Ailbe who died some eighty years earlier. The monks sail on and are becalmed at a time when food is running low. Driven to land by a storm, they drink of an intoxicating spring which makes them sleep for three days. On their way once more, they come to the big fish, on whose back they celebrate Easter and then proceed to the land of the huge white tree and white birds, where they are made welcome. Sailing on, they are threatened in turn by a giant sea-serpent and a griffin, vividly portrayed. The intervention of other monsters saves them at the last minute, and the monks understand that such ordeals serve to test the strength of their faith. When it comes to the feast of St Peter, Brendan joyfully sings hymns at the top of his voice, much to the alarm of his monks, who, seeing a shoal of giant fish, fear that Brendan's singing will annoy them. The contrary happens, for the fish come to the surface, escort the ship, and enjoy the hymns. Next the monks come to an enormous pillar of jacinth surmounted by a tent of gold cloth containing an altar of emerald and a sacrarium of sardonyx. They stay there for three days and sing mass before pursuing their course. As they go on their way the sky grows dark, and Brendan reminds the monks of the purpose of their quest: they will now be afforded a glimpse of hell, but, safe in God's keeping, they must remain firm as ever in their faith. Burning rocks and towering flames surround them, and white-hot blades of metal shoot through the air, hurled by the giant smithy of hell. Sailing unscathed through the boiling sea, they come to a smoke-capped mountain. On a rock nearby they find a naked man who has been singled out for special torment. They learn that he is Judas, whose damnation is owed, not to his treachery, but to his dying as a suicide without confession. His sufferings, described at length, move Brendan to pity. As always at Eastertime, they return to the giant fish, but now the seventh and final year of their quest has arrived. Setting a course eastwards, they enter a thick mist in which a narrow channel the width of a street remains clear for them. This leads to an enormous wall, whiter than any snow, resplendent with gems of all kinds, with, behind, a mountain of pure gold. The Garden of Paradise is full of sweetly perfumed flowers and many different fruits. The young man who acts as their guide tells them that they have seen only a tiny corner of Paradise, and that they would only know it fully when they returned in spirit. With the purpose of their mission achieved, they set sail for home and in three months are back in Ireland. People flock from far and wide to hear Brendan tell of his adventures. On his death he enters the Kingdom of Heaven, as do many others through St Brendan's good graces.

This Anglo-Norman version of the story is a free rendering of an earlier Latin prose work which had been written about 950 in Ireland. The author, or translator, of the vernacular text names himself, somewhat enigmatically, as 'Li apostoiles danz Benedeiz', which seems to mean no more than 'the monk Benedeiz'.[37] Nothing is known about him, though it has been suggested that he was the same person as Benedict of Gloucester, author of a Latin life of St Dubricius.[38] The *Vie de Saint Brendan* was dedicated to Maud (of Scotland), first wife of Henry I, but later versions, including the best of the extant manuscripts,[39] substituted for her name that of Henry's second wife, Adeliza (of Louvain), whom he married in 1121. Whether Benedict himself was responsible for this substitution is not known. His original version must have dated from about 1106.[40]

Although the *Vie de Saint Brendan* is found juxtaposed to the *Vie de Saint Alexis* in at least two extant manuscripts, it would clearly be difficult to find two texts contrasting more sharply. Let those who would accuse medieval hagiography of dullness and monotony, or of conforming rigorously to set patterns, or of lack

of inventiveness, pay heed! In the *Vie de Saint Alexis* also, long
sea voyages take place, but they are dismissed in a mere fourteen
lines and provide no more than a rapid transition from one scene
to the next, whereas in the *Vie de Saint Brendan* – the *Voyage of
St Brendan* (*Navigatio sancti Brendani*) is the more appropriate title
of the early Latin prose versions – the sea voyages constitute almost
the entire story, no more than forty of the eighteen hundred lines
being concerned with Brendan's life on land. The sober asceticism
of the one has given way to the colourful fantasy of the other, and
the irony is that all the magic of the East is found in the tale centred
in Ireland, whereas the tale which was of wholly Eastern origin is
a simple monochrome quite lacking in oriental splendour. All that
the two have in common is the unshakeable faith of the central
figure, and a lack of interest in sexual relationships, though what is
a deliberate renunciation in Alexis is a mere absence, or irrelevance,
in *Brendan*. In the latter, as in the former, we can single out creation
of atmosphere as being the most striking feature rather than such
aspects as development of plot, subtlety of intrigue, character portrayal, etc. It should be added, however, that whereas Alexis is
clearly defined by his actions, even when these appear to be of a
negative kind, Brendan is not. He emerges, to be sure, as a man of
great piety, gentle and merciful, but he does little except assure his
monks that all will work out well as long as they do not lose faith.
His companions remain shadowy and unsubstantial figures, not
described, not even named. Detailed descriptions are admittedly
given of some of the characters they encounter on their voyage, but
only when they are sufficiently fantastic – the smithy of hell, for
example – and even so they are descriptions of appearance only, so
that their effect is to add to the general atmosphere of the story,
vivid and romantic in the extreme. Throughout its numerous Latin
and vernacular forms (like the *Vie de Saint Alexis*, this story was
translated into numbers of European vernaculars, French being the
earliest) despite the strong tradition of inherited literary and folklore
themes, despite the author's evident lack of precise knowledge of
seamanship,[41] this is a yarn that has retained something of the tang
of the sea: the sailing ship making landfall, finding only tall, forbidding cliffs, edging patiently around the coast until a safe anchor-
age is found; a ship becalmed in a still, smooth sea 'as thick as a
marsh' (line 793), or tossed by giant waves, or creeping through a
thick mist in which strange shapes loom up. There is all the superstition of ancient seafaring peoples in this phantasmagoria of fire-
breathing sea-serpents and griffins, fish the size of whole islands,
birds that speak with human voices, smoke-capped mountains, dark
caves whose gloomy depths lead down to hell, and at journey's end,
beyond these Stygian horrors, far in the hidden distance, the tall

white walls of the Promised Land. It is a gripping and romantic rime of an ancient mariner-monk, a rime whose fantasies reflect the magic and terror that the unexplored expanses of the earth's surface held in that age when the mysteries of space extended out horizontally, rather than vertically as they do today.

The appearance of so intriguing and inventive a tale at the very dawn of French literature raises a number of questions, foremost among them inevitably: who was St Brendan, and how did the legend come into being? An historical personage, Brendan is believed to have been born in Kerry, in the region of present-day Tralee, about 484 and to have died about 577. He belonged to the main branch of the Ciarraige who had settled in south-western Ireland. Brendan was the founder of several abbeys, the most famous that of Cluain Fearta (Clonfert in English), in the county of Galway in Connaught, between 558 and 564, probably also the church and monastery of Ard Fearta. It is likely that he undertook at least one sea-voyage, travelling no further, possibly, than Rockall off the western Irish coast, or some of the islands off the western coast of Scotland. Another hagiographical work refers to Brendan's visit to St Columba in Iona. How did the historical Brendan become the Brendan of legend? On this subject there is bound to be much surmise, and only the general pattern of the story's formation is fairly clear. Legends tend to accrue around the names of certain prominent figures, and Brendan was a sufficiently important person in that active period when Irish missionaries were setting forth to Britain and the continent for various stories to gather around his name. These tales accrued from a variety of sources, as happened in a more limited way with Alexis. The first additions may have come from native Irish sources, from the *immrama*, tales of the marvellous adventures of travellers at sea that would arise naturally among a seafaring island people. One of the four extant *immrama*, *The Voyage of Maeldúin*, resembles the *Vie de Saint Brendan* in several specific features: (1) against their will the travellers were joined by three felons (Maeldúin's foster brothers) who were later killed in the course of the adventures; (2) they landed on an island of tall trees covered with talking birds; (3) they encountered a deserted palace where they found an abundance of food and drink; (4) they found some springs running with intoxicating drink; (5) they came to an enormous silver pillar in the sea. Dating from the early twelfth century, this story was contemporary with the Anglo-Norman *Vie de Saint Brendan*, later therefore than the Latin prose version of the latter. It is possible that this Irish *imram* has borrowed from the Brendan legend rather than vice versa.[42]

However, it contains many extraordinary features not found in *Brendan*, such as the shaggy horse which whirls its skin round and round its body like a millstone, and the likelihood is that it shared a common source with the Brendan story (perhaps classical in the case of the silver column and that of the talking birds) without deriving directly from it. These resemblances are interesting because they show that the Brendan legend had affinities with a type of literature well established in Ireland though not wholly native to that country. In addition, however, the story of Brendan had absorbed material from quite a different source, no trace of which is to be found in the *immrama*. It has been conjectured that shortly before or after 900 an Irish monk on pilgrimage to Syria heard the story of Sinbad the Sailor in some form, and on his return adapted it to the Brendan legend. The main similarities are: (1) the Whale-Back Island on which Sinbad landed bears a close resemblance to Brendan's adventure on the back of the giant fish, even in details such as the lighting of the fire; (2) the Roc recalls the Griffin encountered by Brendan; (3) the seven years of travel by Brendan call to mind the seven adventures of Sinbad; (4) in both tales there is an island abounding in giant sheep; (5) both tales contain volcanic islands communicating with the lower world. The resulting synthesis provides a fascinating illustration of the formation of a medieval legend. Only the occasional discrepancy betrays the disparate origin of the material. For example, when first Brendan and his monks encounter the giant fish, its behaviour is hostile, exactly as in the first voyage of Sinbad, but it unexplainedly becomes very friendly in their subsequent encounters (line 1624: '. . . li peisuns est lur servanz') (the fish is their servant), possibly, in the poet's mind, because of the importance of the fish in Christian symbolism. One wonders too why Brendan has to wander about for seven years, coming back to the same places at the same time of year, before finally he is allowed his glimpse of Paradise. A Christian explanation, added later, is that this was a punishment of Brendan for having disbelieved an account of marvellous adventures which had come into his hands. He was condemned to wander during a sacred cycle of years until he had seen all the marvels he had refused to believe in.[43] The final result is this extraordinary Christian Odyssey, rooted in Irish history and legend, yet permeated with oriental influence.

Before we leave our study of the *Vie de Saint Brendan*, some attention must be paid to the form in which it was written, not only for its own intrinsic merits, but also because, like the very different structure of the *Vie de Saint Alexis*, it uses a type of verse that was to become extremely popular in the twelfth and thirteenth centuries. Its octosyllabic rhyming couplets possess two characteristics which betray its insular origin, and its relatively early date. Whereas in most continental octosyllabic verse, a final weak *e* was a supernumerary not counting in the measure, as in the introduction to Chrétien de Troyes's *Lancelot*:

Puisque ma dame de champ⁸aigne	Since my lady of Champagne wants
Vialt que romans a faire	me to undertake a romance . . .
anpr⁸aigne . . .	

Puisque ma dame de champaigne
Vialt que romans a faire
   anpraigne . . .

Since my lady of Champagne wants me to undertake a romance . . .

in the *Vie de Saint Brendan* a final *e* counted as any other vowel:

Donna Aaliz la reïne

Par qui valdrat lei divine . . .

Lady Adeliza, the queen, through whom the divine law will prevail . . .

This treatment of feminine rhyme in exactly the same way as the masculine has meant that the former, very much in the minority in continental works because of the special treatment it received, here constitutes a much larger proportion of the total.[44] A second feature of the octosyllabic line in the *Vie de Saint Brendan* is that it contained a caesura after the fourth foot, whereas in the twelfth-century continental works, the caesura was abandoned in all lines of less than ten syllables. In practice its retention meant little more than the avoidance of having the fourth syllable of the line fall in the interior of a word, except when an unstressed *e* followed that syllable. Thus we find, not

Cum furent endormit trestuit
              (309)

When all were asleep

but

Cum endormit furent trestuit

but on the other hand

De naissance fud des Ireis
             (20)

He was of Irish descent

could have been written

Fud de naissance des Ireis

These relatively minor differences – greater freedom in one respect, greater restraint in another – do not prevent this verse from sharing with the continental octosyllabic certain basic characteristics: a lively, springy, quick-moving pace admirably suited to the telling of an adventure story. The narrative proceeds swiftly from episode to episode: 'On they sailed until they came to . . .' is the basic formula followed with but minor variations. It is not all action and movement, however. Vivid thumbnail sketches of scenery and characters are included. Indeed, this verse measure was alien only to the expression of solemn or tragic or epic material, for which the more ponderous decasyllabic was better fitted.

As examples of the Anglo-Norman poet's skill in breathing life into a scene of pure fantasy, the following examples are noteworthy:

The fight of the sea-serpents

Justedes sunt les dous bestes;
Drechent forment halt les testes;
Des narines li fous lur salt,
Desque as nües qui volet halt;
Colps se dunent de lur noës,
Tels cum escuz, e des podes.
A denz mordanz se nafrerent,
Qui cum espez trenchant erent;
Salt en li sanz as aigres mors
Que funt li dent en cez granz cors;
Les plaies sunt mult parfundes,
Dun senglantes sunt les undes.

(937–48)

The two beasts have joined in combat. They rear their heads high, fire spurts from their nostrils and flies to the clouds. They exchange blows with their fins, as though they were shields, and with their paws. They wound each other with their sharp teeth which cut like spears. The blood flows out from the terrible bites which the teeth make in those mighty bodies. The wounds are very deep and make the waves bloody.

The giant smithy of hell

Jetant flammes de sa gorge,
A granz salz curt en sa forge.
Revint mult tost od sa lamme
Tute ruge cume flamme;
Es tenailes dun la teneit
Fais a dis bofs bien i aveit.
Halcet la sus vers la nue,
E dreit vers eals puis la rue;
Esturbeiluns plus tost ne vait,
Quant sus en l'air li venz le trait,
Ne li quarels d'arbaleste,
Ne de funde la galeste.

(1145–56)

Spurting flames from his throat, he bounds into his forge. He came back very quickly with his blade as red as flame. In the tongs with which he held it there was a load for a good ten oxen. He raises it aloft and then hurls it straight at them. No whirlwind travels faster, when the wind drives it through the air, no quarrel from a crossbow, no stone hurled from a sling.

Many of the similes employed in these passages, as in the entire text, are obvious enough, but their effect is not entirely spoiled as a result. Some, however, are unusual and quite arresting, such as the description of the white-hot blades of metal, glowing still, even when they have fallen into the depths of the sea 'like heather in a clearing' (1162), or the description of the magic birds' flight, making a noise 'like the chiming of a bell' (512).

To encounter such a picturesque, dramatic, and inventive tale so near the threshold of French literature is inevitably a great surprise. The element of edification is central and yet incidental; the monks' survival in the face of so many perils is owed to their faith in God, which remains absolute because of the courage and piety of their leader. Far more space is devoted, however, to a description of the wonders and perils through which they sail than to an evocation of their faith, so that the element of entertainment is paramount throughout. This story which provides a link between past and present in its debt to the classical pagan world as well as to medieval Christendom, a link also between contemporary civilisations in its drawing on Islamic sources as well as Christian ones,[45] testifies ultimately to the perennially popular, universal appeal of a tale of mystery and imagination which lifts people out of the humdrum of their daily lives, unfolding before their eyes the romantic and colourful spectacle of an otherworld where dreams and reality converge.

IV. THE 'VIE DE SAINT THOMAS'

The final text that we have chosen for this trilogy is the oldest and most important of the several extant medieval French versions of the life of Thomas Becket. Almost ten times the length of the *Vie de Saint Alexis*, over three times that of the *Vie de Saint Brendan*, and composed in alexandrine verse to boot, the *Vie de Saint Thomas* by Guernes de Pont-Sainte-Maxence, a wandering cleric, provides a useful corrective to the impression that hagiography was necessarily an accruement of legendary material.[46] In this historical work the author took great pains to give a wholly factual and truthful account, as he points out no less than four times in his conclusion:

Ci n'a mis un sul mot se la verité nun.
(line 6159)

He has not written a single word here if not the truth.

N'i ad mis un sul mot qui ne seit veritez.
(6163)

He has not written a single word that is not the truth.

Mainte feiz en ostai ço que jo ainz escris,
Pur oster la mençonge.
(6169–70)

Many times I removed what I had at first written, to remove lies.

. . . ço sacent tuit cil qui ceste vie orrunt
Que pure verité par tut oïr purrunt.
(6171–2)

Let all who hear this life know that they can hear throughout the absolute truth.

Begun within two years of Thomas's martyrdom in 1170 (6166–7), the work took almost four years to complete (144) and brought the author from France to Canterbury (146–50, 6168) so that he could learn the truth from Thomas's servants and friends. His principal sources, however, were the Latin *Vitae* by two eyewitnesses of the murder, Edward Grim, a monk who was himself severely wounded in the fray, and William of Canterbury.[47] This endeavour to give an authentic version of Thomas's life in a vernacular text is significant, since it accords to the French language the dignity usually accorded in those times to Latin. Not only was the martyrdom of Thomas Becket of the highest importance in itself, but also it involved one of the most serious political issues which arose in medieval Europe, namely, the relationship between ecclesiastical and secular authorities.[48] This is dealt with at length and with many pertinent comments. The vernacular was not to be used simply for legends and edifying or entertaining tales for the common people. Like Latin, it could deal with the vital issues of the times, a fact acknowledged by one Latin version of Thomas's life which has this French poem as its main source. Light is also thrown on the attitude towards the use of the vernacular by the author's curious comment in his conclusion:

Mis languages est bons, car en France fui nez.	My language is good, for I was born in France.

(6165)

In view of the limited meaning of 'France' in the twelfth century the implication may well be that the dialect of the Ile-de-France already enjoyed greater prestige than did that of other regions.[49]

Guernes's story was not intended to be read in private, any more than were those of his contemporaries writing in the vernacular. It was, he tells us, the text of a sermon which he preached himself on numerous occasions at St Thomas's tomb in Canterbury:

Guernes li Clers del Punt fine ici sun sermun	Guernes the cleric of Pont-Sainte-Maxence finishes here his sermon concerning the martyrdom of St Thomas and his passion. And many times he read it at the nobleman's tomb.
Del martir saint Thomas e de sa passiun.	
E mainte feiz le list a la tumbe al barun.	

(6156–8)

However, he goes on to claim, rather proudly even if a little inconsistently:

Ainc mais si bons romanz ne fu faiz ne trovez.	Never was such a good romance written or composed.

(6161)

Whoever listened attentively to the entire sermon, and whoever today reads carefully every one of the six thousand lines, has been through a fruitful, even though somewhat harrowing, experience.[50] Clearly a man of the highest moral purpose, possessing a considerable command of language, Guernes de Pont-Sainte-Maxence was without doubt a truly formidable sermoniser. He was endowed with an active, didactic mind, always ready to find symbolical meaning even in apparently minor details of Thomas's life. 'Ici a signifiance grant . . .' (183), or a similar expression, introduces many a lengthy digression in which the author's views on numerous topics are unfolded – on human nature, on free will, on the death penalty, on the duties of clerics and kings, on the relationship between Church and state. He drew on a tremendous store of apophthegms and an intimate knowledge of the Old Testament. The verve and conviction with which his opinions are expressed prevent his sermon from losing impetus. Even when verbose, he managed to remain caustic, vigorous, and outspoken, helped in this by the strength of his own prejudices and by that very increase in the Church's prestige and authority which had been a direct outcome of Thomas's martyrdom. Guernes's ideas on the world at large can have contained nothing new, but the forthrightness of expression, the firmness and clarity of style, and the skill with which one phrase is balanced with another, give them considerable impact:

De mult divers curages e de diverse vie	People on this earth have very different outlooks and ways of life,
Sunt en cest siecle gent, n'est nul hom kil desdie.	nobody can deny that. Many are poor, some are rich. Some love wis-
Plusurs unt povreté, li alquant manantie;	dom, many love folly. Some love God, Satan controls many.
Alquant aiment le sen e plusur la folie;	
Li alquant aiment Deu, Sathan les plusurs guie.	

(16–20)

The author begins this biography with an account of the several dreams of Thomas's mother when Thomas was still in the womb, and of their meaning. Thomas's childhood is passed over rapidly, though one anecdote describes at some length how he was miraculously saved from drowning. His rise to the chancellorship is also dealt with in a few lines, and we learn little about his years in that office, more than 90 per cent of the work being devoted to his career as archbishop. We are told, however, that in his early career Thomas was haughty and overbearing, and brief references are made to his 'evil ways' (552), although

Chastes ert de sun cors e en espirit sains.	He was chaste in his person and healthy in his mind.

(298)

No attempt is made to depict Thomas's relatively carefree life at this time. It was left to the imagination of a much later, and far more literary-minded, author, to conjure up

> Fluting in the meadows, viols in the hall,
> Laughter and apple-blossoms floating on the water,
> Singing at nightfall, whispering in chambers . . .[51]

VARIATIONS ON HAGIOGRAPHIC THEMES 45

Thomas's intimate relationship with the king during his years as chancellor receives no more than a dry mention in a single line:

Nul hume a cel contemple n'a li
reis plus amé.

(380)

No man at that time did the king love more.

Characteristically, Guernes dwells at far greater length on Thomas's later atonement for his dissolute life as chancellor. Several references are made to his habit when archbishop of wearing a hair-shirt swarming with lice. This, comments Guernes, was the first martyrdom of Thomas, and the more terrible, for what took place in the cathedral was quickly over, and led to eternal bliss:

Car mult plus grief martyre suffri,
tant cum fu vis,
Que ne fist el mustier, la u il fu
ocis:
Car erramment transi e en joie fu
mis;
Mais cele grant vermine dunt il
esteit purpris,
Le quivra plusurs anz, e les nuiz e
les dis.

(5811–15)[52]

For he suffered a far greater martyrdom during his lifetime than when he was killed in the church, for he died immediately and found bliss, but that abundant vermin with which he was infested covered him day and night for many years.

Not content with this, Thomas had himself scourged frequently by the clergy. On the very day of his martyrdom he had been whipped three times. He even tore at his flesh with his own hands to express his scorn of it:

Il meïmes perneit sun cors a
depescier,
A l'une de ses mains sa char a
detrengier.

(3963–4)

He himself began to tear at his body and to rip his flesh with one of his hands.

The central issue in Guernes's poem, as indeed in Thomas's career as archbishop, concerned the king's attempt to impose on the Church acceptance of the 'customs of the realm'. Above all, the king was anxious that the clergy should be subjected to the laws of the land, and Guernes states the king's views fairly enough:

Par tut le munde est leis, tut par
dreit establie,
E en cristïenté e nis en paenie,
Qui pris est a embler u a tel felunie
La justise en seit faite e pleniere e
furnie;
Pur pere ne pur frere n'est a
esparnier mie.

Everywhere it is the law, established by justice, in the Christian and even in the pagan world, that whoever is caught stealing or in some such felony, must be punished fully and completely. He is not to be spared for father or brother.

Pur ço voleit li reis, e il e si barun,
Que se nuls ordenez fust pris a
mesprisun,
Cumme de larrecin u murdre u
traïsun,
Dunc fust desordenez par itele
raisun
E puis livré a mort e a desfactiun.

(1111–20)

On this account the king, along with his barons, desired that if any ordained priest was caught committing a crime like robbery or murder or treason, he should be defrocked on that account and then delivered up to death and destruction.

Thomas was willing to make some concessions: that a cleric should be deprived of holy orders for a criminal offence, but that no further proceedings should be taken against him unless there was a second offence (1146–55). Guernes does not hesitate to condemn the archbishop for this concession, maintaining that it is not in man's power to undo what God has ordained:

E ki puet dessacrer ço que Deus
ad sacré?

(1264)

And who can rob of holy estate whatever God has made holy?

Thomas, however, remained firm on the basic principle that a man should not be punished twice for the same offence (1146–7). The loss of holy orders was already a terrible punishment in itself:

D'un sul mesfait ne deit nuls huem
dous feiz perir.
Quant li clers pert sun ordre nel
puet hum plus hunir.

(1171–2)

No man must perish twice for a single offence. When a man of the Church loses his holy orders, he can suffer no greater shame.

The bishops sided with the king, and Thomas was quite alone (1184–5). Guernes unerringly concentrates attention on important issues of this kind. The topical value of his work was great as a result, and it remains throughout a polemic against secular usurpation of ecclesiastical authority. Guernes does not hesitate to address the king directly, giving him stern advice founded on the idealistic view of monarchy, widely accepted in his day:

'Reis, se tu es enuinz, curune d'or
portant,
Ne deiz estre en orgueil, mais en
bien reluisant;
A tun pueple deiz estre e chiefs
e lur chalant.
Ne la portes adés, n'avoec ne fus
naissant.
La glorie d'icest mund n'est
lungement durant'.

(1241–5)

'King, if you are anointed and wear the golden crown, you must not be arrogant, but must shine forth in virtue. You must be the head of your people and their protector. You will not always wear it, you were not born with it. The glory of this world does not last for long'.

At the same time, he wags his finger in an equally severe manner at the churchmen, reminding them of their role in society, and of

their duties (1246–50). His attitude towards the bishops who sup-
ported the king and not the archbishop is also made clear in no
uncertain terms:

'Ahi, las e chaitif! Dites mei que
  cremez?
Cremez vus que vus toille li reis
  voz poestez?
Par ma fei, nel fera, se tenir les
  osez.
Vus n'estes pas evesque, le sul nun
  en portez.
Ço que a vus apent un sul puint ne
  guardez'.

'Ah you miserable wretches! Tell me
what you fear? Do you fear that the
king may strip you of your powers?
By my faith he will not do so if you
dare to hold on to them. You are not
bishops, you only bear the name.
You neglect your duty entirely'.

(1191–5)

A long, hard-hitting diatribe follows. No attempt is discernible to
make 'literature' out of the story. Thus when the king and his
barons meet Thomas and his supporters, Guernes does not conjure
up the scene by describing the robes they wear or their physical
appearance. He simply gives a list of the names of those present and
refers to the main topics discussed. Also little attempt is made to
heighten the drama of the story by showing Thomas's internal
conflict of loyalties, or that of the king. Thomas does show something of his mental anguish on one occasion:

'. . . jo ne quier al rei ne mal ne
  deshonur.
N'a humme en tut le siecle qui plus
  desirt s'onur;
E mult sui jo dolenz que jo ai sa
  haür.
E se s'espee trenche, la meie ad
  grant reidur;
E obeïr m'estuet al suverain
  seignur'.

'I seek no ill and no dishonour for
the king. No man in all the world
desires his honour more. And I am
very grieved that I have his hatred.
And if his sword cuts, mine has
great strength, and yet I am compelled to obey my sovereign lord'.

(1601–5)

The king's early affection for Thomas is briefly alluded to, as we
have seen, but apart from these chance references, the king is mostly
in a perpetual rage, for ever exclaiming 'God's eyes!' when he hears
of Thomas's measures intended to uphold the Church's authority.
Guernes shows how attempts at reconciliation failed because of the
king's mistrust and fickle temper,[53] though criticism of Thomas was
widespread, and he became more and more isolated as a result:

Tuz perdi les Franceis saint Thomas
  a cel jur;
Par France l'apeleient felun e
  traïtur . . .

On that day St Thomas lost the
support of Frenchmen. Throughout
France they called him a felon and
a traitor . . .

(4166–7)

Thomas emerges as a lonely man, struggling courageously to uphold the rights of the Church in the face of fierce opposition and

despite lack of support from the bishops, and gradually becoming aware of the eventual inevitability of his martyrdom.

The final impression is of a text that achieves its results through the vigour of its language. Many a scene springs to life even though, as we have seen, there is remarkably little description. One remembers the barons mocking Thomas 'a hu e a desrei' (1918) (with hue and cry) after one of his altercations with the king:

'Li traïtres s'en vait: veez lei, veez lei!'

(1919)

'The traitor is leaving. Look at him, look at him!'

One remembers too how King Henry's messengers addressed the pope in very indifferent Latin, an occasion which seems to have appealed to the wry humour of Guernes the pedagogue:

Devant la pape esturent li messagier real.
Alquant diseient bien, pluisur diseient mal,
Li alquant en latin, tel buen, tel anomal,
Tel qui fist personel del verbe impersonal,
Singuler e plurel aveit tut parigal.

(2256-60)

The royal messengers stood in the pope's presence. Some spoke well, many spoke badly, some in Latin, good or bad, some made impersonal verbs personal, singulars and plurals were all confused.

Many other scenes deserve a passing mention: King Louis's remarks on France as a refuge for the persecuted:

'Pur ço est France franche . . .
Que cil ki mestier unt i viengent
a refui . . .'

(2207-8)

'France is a free country . . . in order that those in need may seek shelter there'.

the prophetic remarks of the bishops, that excessive provocation of the English king would result in his abjuring the papacy (3266-70); Guernes's comment on the king's wrath:

Curuz de rei n'est pas gius de petit enfant;

(1636)

A king's wrath is no child's play;

the bishop of London's angry retort when Thomas insisted on presenting himself to the king wearing his full regalia:

'Fous', fait il, 'tuzdis fustes, e estes e serrez,
Quant vus, l'espee traite, desur le rei venez'.

(1671-2)

'Madman', he said, 'you always were, are, and will be, when you dare come to the king with drawn sword'.

Above all one remembers the unequivocal, uncompromising view of the relationship between Church and king:

Li prelat sunt serf Deu, li reis les
  deit cherir;
E il sunt chiés des reis, li reis lur
  deit flechir.
Deus est chiés des prelaz, pur sa
  lei maintenir
Devreient il estendre les cols, prez
  de murir:
Deus suffri mort en cruiz pur s'iglise
  franchir.

(2806–10)

Prelates are God's serfs, the king
must cherish them, and they are the
heads of kings, the king must bend
his knee to them. God is the head of
the prelates, to maintain His law
they ought to risk their necks, ready
to die. Christ suffered death on the
cross to free His Church.

and Thomas's summing-up of his relationship with his king:

'Mes reis estes, pur ço vus dei aveir
  mult chier;
Mes fiz estes en Deu, si vus dei
  chastïer'.

(3069–70)

'You are my king, on this account
I must hold you dear. You are my
son in God and I must chastise you'.

No change in technique is made for the actual scenes of the
martyrdom. It is largely a factual account, giving the names of the
assassins, what was said in the quarrel between them and the
archbishop, who it was who struck the first blow, the effects of that
blow, etc. The pathos of the scene is lessened somewhat by Guernes's
rather portentous moralising. Thus, when Thomas stands with his
back against one of the cathedral pillars, Guernes digresses as
follows:

Car sainz Thomas s'esteit apuiez al
  piler
Qui suffri mort en cruiz pur s'iglise
  estorer;
Ne l'en poeit nuls huem esluignier
  ne oster.
Mais ore en coveneit un sul a mort
  livrer,
Al piler del mustier, pur le pueple
  salver.

(5551–5)

For St Thomas had leaned against
the pillar which suffered death on
the cross to establish His Church. No
man could remove him from it. But
now a single man had to die at the
pillar of the church to save the
people.

Once more the dramatic, literary potentialities of the story are not
deliberately exploited by the author, even though the terse sobriety
and directness characterising the greater part of his narrative is
effective.

The structure of the *Vie de Saint Thomas* resembles that of the
Vie de Saint Alexis in that it is based on stanzas of five lines each,
although a simple mono-rhyme has here replaced the earlier assonance, and the lines contain twelve, not ten, syllables, as the passages
quoted above reveal. Guernes, evidently proud of his work, drew
attention to its verse forms in his conclusion:

Li vers est d'une rime en cinc
clauses cuplez.

(6164)

The verse is based on one rhyme for
every five lines.

This was not, of course, the first work to appear in alexandrines.
The first text in this measure to have achieved renown is the mid-
twelfth-century *Roman d'Alexandre* by Lambert li Tors.[54] Most of
Guernes's lines are carefully constructed with a caesura clearly perceptible after the sixth syllable:

Mis languages est bons, car en
France fui nez.

(6165)

My language is good, for I was
born in France.

but this is by no means always the case:

'Tu iés Pieres, e sur ceste piere
ferai M'iglise . . .'

(3117–18)

'You are Peter, and on this rock I
shall build my church . . .'

These lines also show the author's readiness to use overflow. The
advantage of the medieval alexandrine was that it allowed, even
more than the decasyllabic, a full development of a serious subject.
Le Roman d'Alexandre exploited its characteristics in a different
way, showing its value for scenes of vivid descriptions and violent
actions,[55] but the full aesthetic potentialities of the line were not to
be revealed for another five hundred years.

Ascetic legend – Christianised pagan myth – contemporary history. These three texts chosen as principal examples to illustrate the
early hagiographical literature of France differ widely. It may even
be felt that not one of them is wholly representative of its genre.
But what was that genre? If we speak of a 'typical' life of a saint,
we are presumably implying that these works followed a pattern
and reveal a certain uniformity when this is manifestly not the case.
It is of course true that all were concerned with a study of the life,
or part of the life, of a monolithic character, the steadfastness of
whose faith provides the basic subject and the central issue. This
fundamental requirement engendered monotony only in the works
of devout but unimaginative writers. Talented authors found ample
scope within the genre for variety and invention, and in fact in the
course of numbers of these works, many aspects of medieval life are
touched upon.

No attempt has been made in this chapter to provide a comprehensive survey of medieval French hagiography despite the fact that
this is a comparatively neglected aspect of medieval French literature. Since such a survey would have to cover some two hundred
works, many of considerable length, this task would clearly be quite
beyond the scope of this entire volume. However, in order to

broaden the picture a little, and to enable the reader to view the examples chosen for detailed analysis in relation to other lives of saints, these concluding paragraphs are devoted to a rapid survey of some of the many other hagiographic works of the French Middle Ages.

v. THE 'VIE DE SAINT NICOLAS', THE 'VIE DE SAINTE MARGUERITE', AND THE 'VIE DE SAINT GILLES'

Among those of the twelfth century should be mentioned two by Wace, a native of Jersey better known as a chronicler: a *Vie de Saint Nicolas*, that most popular of saints whose miraculous powers we shall find described in Jean Bodel's splendid play *Le Jeu de Saint Nicolas*, which was composed in the early years of the thirteenth century, and a *Vie de Sainte Marguerite*,[56] a simple account of this early Christian martyr, probably of the fourth century, the firmness of whose faith despite all kinds of torture by her Roman captors won many converts to Christianity, five thousand of whom (so the text relates) were executed in a single day on the orders of the Roman prefect Olybrius, who had hoped to destroy Marguerite's adherence to Christianity and marry her. Following Latin accounts, Wace relates that the pagan executioner, awestruck by hearing Marguerite converse with a voice from on high, was reluctant to kill her, and that she herself peremptorily ordered him to cut her head off. Failure to do this would deprive him of his chance of entering Paradise with her:

'Frere, dist ele, des or fier'.
'Dame, dist il, ne t'ous tocher.
Dame, coment ferir te dei,
Quant l'angele Deus parole o tei?
Mais prie por mei ton seignor
Que j'aie pardon por t'amor'.
'Se tu, dist elle, ne m'ocis,
N'iras o moi en Paradis,
Mais fai ce que t'est comandé,
O mei iras el regne Dé'.
(lines 693–702)

'Brother', she said, 'strike your blow at once'. 'Lady', he said, 'I dare not touch you. Lady how can I strike you when the angel of the Lord speaks to you? But pray for me to your lord that I may be pardoned for love of you'. 'If you do not kill me', she said, 'you shall not go with me to Paradise, but do what is commanded of you and you shall go with me to God's kingdom'.

Martyrdom was a privilege, not an infliction.

One of the most readable and entertaining of all twelfth-century French texts is Guillaume de Berneville's *Vie de Saint Gilles*, written in the 1170s about the same time as Guernes de Pont-Sainte-Maxence's *Vie de Saint Thomas*.[57] The story of St Giles became extremely well known in medieval times, and his name is commemorated to this day in numerous place-names and churches in

England and on the continent. St Giles was of Greek origin, and
early acquired a reputation as a healer of the sick. Like Alexis he
sought only obscurity, and accordingly set sail for foreign shores.
In his description of this voyage, which took St Giles to Marseilles,
the author reveals a knowledge of sea and ships far more precise
than anything in the *Vie de Saint Brendan*. He can paint a vivid
picture of a storm-tossed boat, evoking very successfully its violent
up-and-down motion:

Esclaire e tone e plot e vente.	There is lightning and thunder, rain
Tant de la mer tant del grant vent	and wind. What with the sea and
Pur poi ke cele nef ne fent;	the mighty wind that ship nearly
L'unde la porte contre munt,	splits asunder. One wave carries it
L'autre la treit vers le parfunt,	aloft, the next drags it down into the
L'une la peint, l'autre la bute,	depths, one strikes it, the next
Pur poi k'ele ne desront tute.	pushes it, and it nearly bursts open.

(lines 786–92)

His vocabulary abounds in technical terms which he seems to
accumulate for the very pleasure of using them. His notions of the
wild life of the south of France – the region between the Rhône
and Montpellier where St Giles lived the life of a hermit – were
somewhat fantastic, in common with those of his contemporaries
describing any region of western Europe. Lions and elephants
roamed there according to him, and – a delightful juxtaposition
here – 'Vipers, tigers, and tortoises' (1236). Such beliefs did not
prevent him from being extremely knowledgeable on the subject of
hunting, and here too he made full use of the precise terminology.[58]
He paints a vivid picture of his hero's life, whether in the desert with
only his faithful white hart for company, or in the Courts of nobles
and kings, including Charlemagne (an anachronism here, since St
Giles lived in the seventh century), or as head of the abbey which he
founded. In his closing lines the author gives his name, Guillaume
de Berneville, and refers to himself as a canon. The modern editor
has surmised that he was of Norman origin but lived and wrote in
England. He may have taken his name from Barnwell priory in
Cambridge where there were two canons of this name towards the
end of the century.[59] This hypothesis would not be weakened in any
way by a line such as:

Il les welcume en sa language.	He welcomes them in his language.

(2467)

This canon with an observant eye and a keen interest in the world
around him has avoided the claustrophobic atmosphere characteristic of so many hagiographic works, and has related his story very
successfully and convincingly to the practicalities of daily life.

VI. THE 'VIE DE SAINTE MARIE L'EGYPTIENNE' AND THE 'VIE DE SAINTE ELYSABEL'

The thirteenth-century author Rutebeuf is remembered above all for his play, the *Miracle de Théophile*, and for his lyric poems and polemical writings.[60] He also wrote, or rather adapted from the Latin, two lives of saints, the *Vie de Sainte Marie l'Egyptienne* and the *Vie de Sainte Elysabel*.[61] The former reached the West from Greek sources, as did the *Vie de Saint Alexis* and the *Vie de Saint Gilles*. It tells the story of a fourth-century saint, very famous in medieval times, who led the life of a prostitute, but repented and spent many years as a hermit in the desert where she was found by the monk Zozimas shortly before her death. The story of her life illustrated Christ's words 'I am not come to call the righteous, but sinners to repentance' (Matthew 9:13). Rutebeuf has written a plain, sober account which dismisses the saint's early years very quickly and dwells mainly on the austerity of her life in the desert, where she deliberately destroyed the physical attractiveness which she had exploited in her early years:

A paine deïst ce fust ele
Qui l'eüst veü damoisele,
Quar ne paroit en li nul signe.
Char ot noire com pié de cigne;
Sa poitrine devint mossue,
Tant fu de pluie debatue.
Les braz, les lons dois et les mains
Avoit plus noirs, et c'ert du mains,
Que n'estoit pois ne arremenz.
(lines 449–57)

Whoever had seen her as a girl could scarcely have said that it was her, for there was no means of recognising her. Her flesh was as black as a swan's foot; her breast became mossy because of all the rain that had fallen on it. Her arms, long fingers, and hands were blacker, and this is an understatement, than pitch or ink.

His *Vie de Sainte Elysabel* was a more topical work since it was written some thirty years only after the death of the saint, Elizabeth of Hungary, which took place in 1231. She was an extremely pious woman, of royal lineage, who did not actually renounce her wealth and position in the way Alexis, Brendan, and others had done, but devoted herself to the service of the sick and needy, founding hospitals, washing and tending the sick herself, paying the debts of the poor:

Ou que ce fust, ou loing ou pres,
Aloit les malades veoir
Et delez lor lit asseoir.
Ja si ne fust la mesons orde,
Tant ot en li misericorde
Que ne redoutoit nule ordure,
Quar d'aus aidier avoit grant cure.
(lines 804–10)

Wherever it was, near or far, she would go to visit the sick and sit at their bedside. However dirty the house, she had so much pity that she had no fear of the filth, for she had a great desire to help them.

For St Mary of Egypt Rutebeuf had some sympathy because, like him, she had known misery and destitution.[62] However, he was more drawn towards Elizabeth because she reflected something of the ideal person of noble birth praised so constantly by this penniless mercenary poet and others like him, that is the nobleman or woman who, mindful at all times of the importance of charity, put inherited wealth to practical use, distributing gifts of money and fine clothes among the poor. Once her early years were behind her, Mary of Egypt became a remote, mysterious, ethereal figure, hovering a forearm's length above the ground as she said her prayers, whereas Elizabeth, with her feet planted firmly on the ground, remained closer to the realities of existence in that age when pestilence was rife and it was not necessary to look far afield in order to find those in desperate need of help.

Rutebeuf's account of Elizabeth's ascetic existence devoted to the service of others becomes very repetitive, and the author apologises somewhat ruefully on more than one occasion:

... Je dout qu'il ne vous anuit.   ... I am afraid it may bore you.
(2078)

The difficulty he clearly experienced in sustaining his own, and his readers', interest, reflects a basic difficulty of the entire genre: the difficulty, that is, of writing about virtue. Throughout the ages, writers have found vice to be a far more fascinating subject, whereas virtue and purity have a oneness, a uniformity that defies prolonged description. The author of *Saint Alexis* avoided the difficulty by describing at length the grief of Alexis's relatives over his disappearance. The author of *Saint Brendan* simply got on with describing the marvels encountered by the seafaring monks and took his hero's virtue for granted. The *Vie de Saint Thomas* provided an excellent moral story on the superiority of ecclesiastical authority over the secular powers, and the author could insist on the spiritual virtue of his hero even while acknowledging his foibles. The *Vie de Saint Gilles* scores as a literary work, in particular, when the author's eye strays away from the strait and narrow path trod by his hero, and takes a sharp look at the world around him. The tendency in all these works was to concentrate attention either on the forces against which the saint had to struggle or on attendant circumstances, as in the case of Alexis and that of St Giles. Conversely, none illustrates more effectively the monotony that threatens the portrayal of absolute virtue and goodness than Rutebeuf's *Vie de Sainte Elysabel*. Given this potential drawback of hagiography as a literary medium – a somewhat false and narrow view since it neglects their mainly religious and didactic function – it is surprising that these texts provide as much variety and interest as they do. The problem that faced the early vernacular writers was a very real one. These can never have been easy works to write, and the wonder is that their medieval authors, these pioneers of the vernacular, have surmounted the difficulty as well as they have done.

NOTES

1. For the text, with commentary and translation, see A. Ewert, *The French Language*, 2nd ed., London, 1943 (latest reprint 1964), 353–4.

2. ed. J. Linskill, Paris, 1937.

3. ed. E. Hoepffner and P. Alfaric, Paris, 2 vols., 1926.

4. C. Storey ed., *La Vie de St Alexis, Texte du Ms de Hildesheim*, Geneva–Paris, 1968. All references to the text in the following pages will be based on this edition.

5. O. Pächt, C. R. Dodwell, F. Wormald, *The St Albans Psalter*, London, Warburg Institute, 1960, 278–80.

6. Pope Innocent I (401–17). Arcadius (377–408) and Honorius (384–423) were the sons of the Emperor Theodosius, on whose death in 395 the former became emperor in Constantinople, the latter in Rome. Henceforth there were (*de facto* if not *de iure*) two empires instead of one as hitherto.

7. V. L. Dedeck-Héry, *The Life of St Alexis*, New York, 1931, 1.

8. This adjective has been taken to refer specifically to the rhythm and structure of the 'song', but only in support of a very tentative hypothesis.

9. i.e., 4 – 6; 4 – 6e; 4e – 6; 4e – 6e. The 4e pattern of the first hemistich was a useful device on occasions, although it inevitably imposed a certain word-order. In the first line 'Li secles fut bons . . .' would have given a hemistich of five syllables, as also would 'Fraisles est e velz . . .' in line 9. So, in the *Chanson de Roland*, numerous similar hemistiches – 'Bels fut li vespres . . .' (line 157), 'Cler le visage . . .' (line 3116), but on the other hand 'Les oz sont beles . . .' (line 3346) – were the result of necessity, not of a stylistic choice. Where there was a choice, e.g., 'Grans est la noise . . .' or 'La noise est granz . . .', 'Clers est li jurz' or 'Li jurz est clers . . .', the order with adjective at the beginning was preferred whenever the context called for emphasis. Line 77 of the *Vie de Saint Alexis* reads: 'La nef est preste ou il deveit entrer . . .'. The adjective calls for no particular stress here, hence there was no need to write 'Preste est la nef . . .'. Similarly, a narrative passage describing the parents' reaction to Alexis's disappearance contains the line: 'Ço fut granz dols quet il unt demenét' (line 104), whereas in a later passage of direct speech, Euphemianus, giving keen expression to his grief, exclaims: 'Granz est li dols ki sor mai est vertiz' (line 463). Another factor may have intervened to prevent the poet from writing 'Ço est granz dols . . .', viz., a dislike of hiatus – cf. 'Ço'st sa merci . . .' (line 363), 'Ço'st ses mesters . . .' (line 367), but such hiatuses were not proscribed altogether in medieval French. It has been pointed out that in the *chansons de geste* the order with adjective first is particularly common at the beginning of the *laisses* (although eleven of the seventeen examples cited admit of no choice!) and was probably felt to have an intonatory value (J. Rychner, *L'Art épique de Jongleurs*, Geneva, 1957, 72).

10. G. Lote, *Histoire du vers français*, I, Paris, 1949, 277.

11. See the *Rhetorica ad Herennium*, a rhetorical manual widely used in the Middle Ages, when this anonymous work was attributed to Cicero. It has been edited by H. Caplan for the Loeb Classical Library, London, 1964; chapter II, 298–301.

12. H. Sckommodau, 'Zum Altfranzösischen Alexiuslied', *ZRP*, LXX, 1954, 161–203. However, nothing in the legend encourages extrapolation from Alexis's own very special case.

13. K. D. Uitti, 'Recent Alexis Studies from Germany', *RPh*, XXIV, 1970, 128–37, esp. 133–4. This same author has provided a valuable survey of Alexis scholarship, and a close analysis of the legend's sources, in 'The Old French *Vie de Saint Alexis,* Paradigm, Legend, Meaning', *RPh*, XX, 1966–67, 262–95.

14. cf. 6–7, 72–3, 88–9, 133–4, 533–4, etc.

15. cf. 147, 568.

16. A. Amiaud, *La Légende syriaque de Saint Alexis*, Paris, 1889, XLVII.

17. 'Rome' here is usually taken to mean the new Rome, i.e., Constantinople, cf. Storey, ed. cit., 19.

18. Amiaud, op. cit., xxix.

19. ibid., LXIX–LXXII.

20. ibid., XLI–XLII, L, LIV. See also G. Paris, *R*, VIII, 1879, 163–4. Amiaud believes that the first passage of the legend from Syria to Byzantium took place orally (LII).

21. Now the church of San Bonifazio e Alessio on the Aventine. Ten years after Sergius's arrival in Rome the first references to St Alexis were recorded there.

22. On immediate Latin sources, see Uitti, 'Recent Alexis Studies', 128–133.

23. G. Paris and L. Pannier, *La Vie de Saint Alexis*, Paris, 1872, 43–5.

24. First discussed by A. Goldschmidt, *Der Albanipsalter in Hildesheim*, Berlin, 1895, and now taken up and developed in Pächt, Dodwell, Wormald, op. cit.

25. Objections to this hypothesis have been made by Professor Dominica Legge in her review of C. Storey's latest edition of *La Vie de Saint Alexis*, *MAe*, XXXIX, 1970, 188.

26. C. H. Talbot, *The Life of Christina of Markyate*, Oxford, 1959.

27. The cult of the saint in St Albans was of short duration, confined in the main to the twelfth century, see Pächt, op. cit., 135, note 2.

28. ibid. As Dr Pächt points out, there is no means of ascertaining when the St Alexis cult became established at Bec, i.e., whether it really antedated that of St Albans. Moreover, the antecedents of the St Albans *Alexis* were clearly Italian (ibid., 142), but there is no indication that these Italian sources were ever available in France. Dominica Legge reports that it was perhaps brought to Bec by Lanfranc when he returned from Rome in 1050 (op. cit., 187).

29. No such objections have been raised. Professor Legge has produced evidence to show that the poem cannot have been copied after 1123, and may well date from 1115–19. 'It must therefore be recognised that this is the earliest surviving copy, French or Anglo-Norman, of an eleventh-century text, and that the text itself is the only survivor from the eleventh century' (ibid., 188).

30. Pächt, op. cit., 143.

31. ibid.; Talbot, op. cit., 9.

32. For the text of this and later medieval French versions, see Paris and Pannier, op. cit.

33. A fourteenth-century version, described as 'unappealing and pedantic', has survived in the recueil *Tombel de Chartrose*, for which see Uitti, 'Recent Alexis Studies', 134–7.

34. This is a manuscript belonging to the Bibliothèque Nationale in Paris (Nouvelle acquisition française 4503), a description of which is given in E. G. R. Waters ed., *The Anglo-Norman Voyage of St Brendan*, Oxford, 1928, xi–xii.

35. ibid., cxvi.

36. cf. the Irish 'curragh', and Welsh 'coracle'.

37. Waters, op. cit., xxvii, and E. Walberg, 'Sur le nom de l'auteur du Voyage de St Brendan', in *SN*, XII, 1939, 46–55.

38. Waters, op. cit., xxviii. On the possibility that he was a contemporary at Bec of the author of *St Alexis*, see Legge, op. cit., 188.

39. This manuscript belongs to the British Museum (Cotton Vesp. B X(1). Waters, op. cit., ix–xi).

40. R. L. G. Ritchie, 'The Date of the Voyage of St Brendan', *MAe*, XIX, 1950, 64–6.

41. Contrast what is said later about the *Vie de Saint Gilles*. See below, p. 52.

42. Indeed, reference is made to Brendan in one of the episodes.

43. C. R. Beazley, *The Dawn of Modern Geography*, New York, 1949 (reprint of work first published in 1897), I, 230–9, esp. 236.

44. 33 per cent as against 20 per cent average in continental works. See Lote, op. cit., II, Paris, 1951, 113.

45. Unless the two go back to a remote common source in a store of old Indo-European folk-tales, kept alive over the centuries by word of mouth.

46. The best edition is that by E. Walberg, *La Vie de Saint Thomas le Martyr*, Lund, 1922. The work has also been edited by the same scholar in CFMA series, 1936.

47. ibid., Introduction, chapter II.

48. See above, pp. 6–7.

49. On the difficulty of determining the meaning of 'France' at this period see F. L. Ganshof, 'A propos de ducs et de duchés au haut moyen âge', *Journal des Savants*, 1972, 13–24, 14. It is worth noting, however, that the author's birthplace, Pont-Sainte-Maxence, is indeed situated in the Ile-de-France, and that is the likely meaning of the term here.

50. Since the story of Becket's life and martyrdom is well known, and since Guernes's claim to have produced an accurate account is on the whole well founded (Walberg, *La Vie de Saint Thomas*, ch. v of 1922 Introduction) even though his attitude was far from unbiased, a full summary of his work will not be included here.

51. T. S. Eliot, *Murder in the Cathedral*.

52. cf. 3936–70.

53. In actual fact Thomas was at least partly to blame, but Guernes does not acknowledge this; Walberg, *La Vie de Saint Thomas*, note to lines 4146–60.

54. The *chanson de geste* entitled *Le Pèlerinage de Charlemagne* (ed. P. Aebischer, Paris–Geneva, 1965) appears to be the earliest extant text in alexandrine verse.

55. See below, p. 139.

56. Wace's *Vie de Saint Nicolas* was edited by E. Ronsjö, Lund, 1942, his *Vie de Sainte Marguerite* by E. A. Francis, Paris, CFMA, 1932. Mention should also be made of a third religious work by Wace, the *Concepcion Nostre Dame*, ed. W. R. Ashford, Chicago, 1933.

57. G. Paris and A. Bos eds., *La Vie de Saint Gilles par Guillaume de Berneville, Poème du XIIᵉ siècle*, Paris, SATF, 1881.

58. See esp. 1587–8, 1625–30.

59. D. Legge, *Anglo-Norman Literature and its Background*, Oxford, 1963, 254.

60. See below, pp. 189–95, 249–50.

61. E. Faral and J. Bastin eds., *Œuvres Complètes de Rutebeuf*, 2 vols., Paris, 1959–60, II, 9–166.

62. cf. his attitude to Théophile in *Le Miracle de Théophile*. See below, pp. 249–50.

Chapter 3

VARIATIONS ON EPIC THEMES

I. THE CHANSONS DE GESTE

MANY narrative poems extant from the period beginning with the late eleventh or early twelfth century and continuing into the fourteenth century are known by the generic term *chansons de geste*, meaning 'songs of heroic exploits' (*geste*<Latin *gesta*). For some medieval writers the term was sufficiently broad to include even the lives of the saints, with their tales of heroic resistance to the enemies of the Church,[1] but for most the reference was to exploits in battle. Some were concerned with feudal conflict, some with religious warfare between Christendom and Islam, some with both. Rather fewer than a hundred *chansons de geste* have survived, varying in length from 2,000 lines or so to over 10,000. The most outstanding are those dealing with the wars against the Saracens, and are set in Spain or in the south of France (occasionally in the north) rather than in the Holy Land. Dating as they do from the crusading era, at their best from the late eleventh to the late twelfth century, they substitute an active, dynamic hero for one who was passive, though no less courageous. Warrior replaced saint, and the cross assumed the shape of the sword.[2]

The relationship of the *chansons de geste* to the wars against the Arabs in the south of France and in Spain, and to the incessant feudal strife of the centuries preceding and following the millennium, raises the vexed question of the origins of the genre. This subject has been the centre of a long, closely and often bitterly argued controversy among specialists over the past hundred years or so. Though it may seem to the general reader to be an essentially academic, even arid, debate, it is none the less a vitally important matter and one that holds tremendous fascination for all who become involved in it, to such an extent that most of the voluminous work on the *chansons de geste* to have appeared in modern times is devoted to this problem. The fact that the *chansons de geste* are set in a later period than numbers of the lives of the saints does not of course mean that they were necessarily composed later. It is universally accepted that the earliest surviving texts of the *chansons*,

58

which date from the early twelfth century, are not necessarily the earliest to have existed. Much has been lost, not only because of the burning of libraries and destruction of manuscripts, but also because of the importance in early times of oral tradition. But did the first tales of heroic exploits originate, in some simple, primitive form that was perhaps never set down in writing, among the first Christian soldiers to oppose the Arab invaders, or even earlier, or did they only come into being centuries later, at a time when the Church was broadening the struggle, sending its armies not merely into Spain but as far as the Holy Land, in that period of tremendous religious fervour and fanaticism which characterised western Europe and France in particular, in the years following the millennium? Between the period of composition of the earliest extant *chansons de geste* and the epoch in which their action is set, usually that of Charlemagne or of his son Louis, there is a gap of some 300 years. What songs, if any, existed during those three centuries? If any did exist, what was their form and subject-matter? Were the few historical facts, which the *chansons* intermingle with much legendary material, culled from the Latin chronicles by writers of the crusading era, anxious, no doubt, to assure the crusaders that they were fighting for the cause defended so valiantly by their ancestors, or was their presence owed to an unbroken oral tradition which originated shortly after the actual events? Such, in the broadest outlines, is the nature of the problem, a problem to which we shall return, albeit briefly, in the course of the chapter.

Most extant *chansons de geste* have survived in groups known as cycles, or 'gestes'. The success of a song about one particular hero resulted in numbers of others being written about him. A song dealing with his death could be followed by a later one describing his early life, so that his literary existence could begin with the end of his life and end with the beginning. In the same way, his ancestors could come into being after him, and those *chansons* celebrating the earliest heroes of a particular clan are often relatively late compositions, dating from the thirteenth or fourteenth century. In the course of the thirteenth century attempts were made to tidy up the very confused state of affairs that had gradually come into being. The result was the compilation of the cyclic manuscripts of which a number have survived. The three cycles that came to be recognised are alluded to briefly in an early thirteenth-century poem:

N'ot que iii gestes en France la garnie:	There were only three families of warriors[3] in France, that land rich in heroes: that of the king of France was the finest as regards splendour and chivalry. The next (very right that I should say it) is that of the hoary bearded Doon of Mayence
Dou *Roi de France* est la plus seignorie	
E de richesse et de chevalerie.	
Et l'autre après (bien est drois que jo die)	

Est de *Doon* a la barbe florie
Cel de Maiance qui tant ot baronie.
En son lignage ot gent fiere et
hardie
De tote France eüssent seignorie . . .
Se il ne fussent plain de tel
felonie . . .
La tierce geste ke moult fist a
proisier
Fu de *Garin de Montglane* le fier.
De son lignage puis je bien
temoignier
Que il n'i ot ne coart ne lainnier
Ne traïtor ne felon losengier.[4]

who had such courage. In his lineage were men proud and bold who would have had dominion over all France had they not been full of such felony . . . The third family deserved great praise, that of the proud Garin de Montglane. In his lineage, I can well testify, there was no coward or faint heart, no traitor, no deceitful flatterer.

The *Cycle du Roi* groups those concerned with Charlemagne's wars, the best known of which is the *Chanson de Roland*. The *Cycle de Doon de Mayence* is named after the supposed ancestor of this line of rebel barons, though in fact the historical personages on whom they were based — wherever these existed and can be identified — lived at different periods and rebelled against different kings: Girart de Roussillon, in the *chanson de geste* named after him, rebelled against Charles Martel — against Charles the Bald (le Chauve) in historical fact;[5] the renegade Isembart, in *Gormont et Isembart*, rebelled against King Louis I, Charlemagne's son (against King Louis III in historical fact); Ogier the Dane (le Danois), in the *chanson* of that name, rebelled against Charlemagne, which is in accordance with historical fact.[6] The third cycle is known as the *Cycle de Garin de Monglane* or the *Cycle de Guillaume d'Orange* according to whether one chooses to name it by the traditional ancestor of this line of heroes or by his great-grandson who was the most distinguished and celebrated of them all. The *Cycle de Guillaume d'Orange* has considerably more cohesion than the others, the links between several of its poems being very close indeed. The analyses that follow deal with three works from this cycle: the *Couronnement de Louis*, the *Charroi de Nîmes*, and the *Prise d'Orange*. From the cycle of rebel barons *Gormont et Isembart* has been chosen, and from the *Cycle du Roi*, that with which we begin, the poem generally acknowledged as the masterpiece of the entire genre, the *Chanson de Roland*.[7]

II. THE 'CHANSON DE ROLAND'

Not only is the *Chanson de Roland* the most famous of the extant *chansons de geste*, one of the several medieval French works whose fame has reached far beyond the sphere of the specialist, it is also the earliest. Seven manuscripts of the text, copied out between the twelfth and fifteenth centuries, have survived. The earliest, dating from the second quarter of the twelfth century, is owed to an Anglo-Norman scribe. It can be seen in the Bodleian Library at Oxford or in a photostatic copy published by the *Société des Anciens Textes Français*. The version of the *Chanson de Roland* of which this appears to be a faithful copy is believed to have been written towards the end of the eleventh century. The following analysis is based on the text of the Bodleian manuscript.

In the course of the seven years he has spent in Spain, Charlemagne has subdued all opposition save only that of the Saracen king, Marsile of Saragossa. Feeling himself hard pressed, Marsile assembles his 'dukes and counts' and asks them for advice. Only one, Blancandrins de Castel del Valfunde, speaks up. He urges Marsile to swear to follow Charlemagne back to Aix and there to become a Christian. This oath, which he would later disregard, would induce Charlemagne's army to leave Spain. Charlemagne receives the Saracen deputation, led by Blancandrins, in a vast orchard where he is relaxing with Roland and Oliver and with leaders of his army. The young knights are fencing together while the older ones play chess. Marsile's message is debated at length by the barons. Roland is the first to speak; he reminds Charles of the treachery shown earlier by the Arabs and urges him to pursue the war against them to the end. He is immediately opposed by his stepfather Ganelon who finds the Saracen offer a reasonable one. Others agree, and the surrender is accepted. The next problem is the choice of a messenger to send to Marsile. When Roland volunteers, he is at once opposed by Oliver on the grounds that Roland's impetuous temperament is quite unsuitable for such negotiations. Oliver himself offers to go, but Charlemagne refuses, adding that he will not risk any of the twelve peers on this mission. When an impasse is reached, Roland suggests that Ganelon should be chosen – the first and only time that a name is put forward of a person who has not actually volunteered. Ganelon reacts angrily, but cannot withdraw his name without appearing a coward. He swears that, if he returns alive from the mission, he will obtain his revenge, and becomes all the more incensed when Roland tauntingly offers to go in his place. Ganelon drops the glove, symbol of office, an evil omen which causes dismay among the French. As Ganelon rides off with Blancandrins, he cannot conceal his hatred of Roland, presenting him as the real obstacle to peace. Before they reach Saragossa they agree that Roland shall be killed. Ganelon warns Marsile not to attempt to fight the main French army, but to attack only the rearguard which will be commanded by Roland and Oliver. The death of Roland will deprive Charlemagne of his desire to wage war.

Back once more in the French camp, Ganelon reports to Charlemagne that all is well and that they are free to return to France. While the French pitch camp for the night, the Arabs are taking up their positions for the ambush. Charlemagne is warned in dreams of impending disaster. The next day he asks his barons to decide who will take charge of the rearguard. Ganelon at once proposes Roland's name, and Roland (in the position in which he had put Ganelon earlier) is obliged to accept. The emperor offers Roland half his army, an offer haughtily rejected by Roland, who, aided by his eleven peers, chooses the 20,000 men of the rearguard. The army begins its homeward march through the narrow defiles of the Pyrenees, until finally only the rearguard is left in Spain. Charlemagne recalls his foreboding dreams and is filled with anguish. Meantime the Saracens make ready for battle, and one by one the leaders of Marsile's army come forward, begging for the privilege of dealing the first blow against Roland. From a nearby hilltop Oliver sees them approaching. He warns the French of the impending battle, and three times urges Roland to recall the main army while there is still time. Roland refuses, his main reason being that his reputation is at stake. He sweeps aside Oliver's reproaches and reminds him of their duties towards their suzerain lord. The archbishop Turpin addresses the men and absolves them of their sins. Roland strikes the first blow, killing Marsile's nephew, the first of the Saracens who had boasted that he would overcome Roland, while Oliver emulates him by killing the second Saracen who had boasted likewise. At first all goes well for the French, but the superior numbers of the enemy gradually begin to tell. In France, from the Mont-Saint-Michel to Saintes, and from Besançon to Wissant, a fiercesome storm hangs over the land, and there is darkness at noon.

When only sixty Frenchmen remain alive, Roland decides that he will blow the oliphant to recall Charles and the main army. Oliver opposes this suggestion, saying that it is now too late and that Roland will bring disgrace to all his family. He condemns Roland for his recklessness in not having summoned reinforcements earlier. However, when Turpin supports Roland, the decision is taken. In sounding the oliphant with tremendous force Roland bursts a blood vessel in his temples. It is from this that he is eventually to die. Charlemagne hears the oliphant and at once decides to return despite Ganelon's protests. Ganelon's treachery is now clearly revealed. He is put in chains and handed over to the army cooks until the trial. Meanwhile the few remaining companions fight on. After the death of Oliver, only Turpin and Roland are still alive, both wounded, the latter only from his efforts to recall Charlemagne. Roland wanders over the battlefield and assembles the bodies of the twelve peers so that they can receive the archbishop's blessing. Turpin staggers towards a nearby stream to fetch some water for Roland, but collapses when he has covered a few yards. Roland takes the oliphant and his sword and makes towards a high hill. When a Saracen feigning death tries to seize Roland's sword, Roland summons his last remaining strength and strikes him dead with the oliphant. He tries in vain to shatter his sword on the rocks, and feeling death near, places them on the ground beneath him, his face turned towards the pagan army. As Roland calls aloud his *mea culpa,* angels from heaven descend towards him and bear his soul aloft.

Charlemagne and the main army return to the scene of the massacre and mourn the loss of their friends and relatives. The decision is quickly taken to pursue the enemy, leaving only a small force to watch over the bodies of Roland and his men. To help Charlemagne, God holds the sun still in the sky as he rides towards Saragossa. Many Arabs are cut down by the sword while others, trying to escape, are drowned in the deep waters of the swiftly flowing Ebro. Charlemagne kneels on the ground to give thanks to God. When he rises to his feet, the sun has set.

In the first year of the seven that Charlemagne had spent in Spain, Marsile had sent a letter to the emir Baligant in Babylon imploring him to send help. From forty kingdoms the emir assembled an army which eventually set sail in a vast fleet, the lanterns of which lit up the sea at night. They sail up the Ebro and reach Saragossa the day after the wounded Marsile took refuge there. Marsile presents the keys of the city to the emir and urges him to join battle with the French army which has pitched camp seven leagues away. At daybreak, as Charlemagne is returning to Roncevaux, news of the emir's arrival reaches him. His army is rapidly organised in ten divisions: the first two of Frenchmen (i.e., of the Ile-de-France), the third Bavarians, the fourth Germans, the fifth Normans, the sixth Bretons, the seventh Poitevins and Auvergnats, the eighth Flemish and Frisians, the ninth men of Lorraine and

Burgundy, the tenth the barons of France, the élite of the entire army. The Saracen drums and trumpets sound as the massive Arab army draws up in thirty divisions, and battle is joined. The climax is reached in the encounter between Charlemagne and Baligant, in which the emperor, with the exhortations of the angel Gabriel ringing in his ears, is the victor. On the death of their leader the Arabs take to flight and the battle of the two main armies is over. The French occupy Saragossa, where many 'pagans' are converted to the Christian faith. When they return to France, Roland's oliphant is left on the altar of Saint-Seurin in Bordeaux and at Saint-Romain in Blaye the bodies of Roland, Oliver, and Turpin are deposited. At Aix Charlemagne is met by Roland's fiancée Alde, who, hearing of Roland's death, falls dead at the emperor's feet.

When Charlemagne has assembled his barons, the trial of Ganelon begins, and is finally decided by a single combat between Pinabel, a relative of Ganelon, and Thierry, brother of one of the twelve peers who died at Roncevaux. The victory of Thierry results in the putting to death of Ganelon and all his relatives. Marsile's wife is converted to Christianity and baptised in the name of Juliane. Charlemagne learns from the angel Gabriel that his struggles are by no means over and that Christians besieged by the pagan armies are crying out for his help:

'Deus, dist li reis, si penuse est ma vie!' (line 4000)	'God, said the king, so painful is my life!'

With this glance ahead to a difficult and uncertain future, the *Chanson de Roland* ends:

Ci falt la geste que Turoldus declinet. (4002)	Here ends the story which Turoldus narrates[?][8]

The word 'epic' is so overworked in the English language today, both as adjective and noun, that it is as well to recall its full and original meaning before seeking to apply it to the *Chanson de Roland*. An epic has been defined as 'a long narrative poem recounting heroic deeds set against a background of war and the supernatural, having a serious theme developed in a coherent and unified manner, written in a dignified style, and marked by certain formal characteristics' (Webster). There is nothing in this general definition to prevent its being taken as a precise description of the *Chanson de Roland*. The only feature that readers unfamiliar with early epic poetry may wish to call into doubt is the style of the work. Can one speak of the dignified style of a poem so much of which deals crudely with butchery and massacre and which describes, with no discretion, no reticence, the effect of blows given and received? Such features are to be found in the epics of most early civilisations, and rarely are they dwelt on for their own sake. They are there in this instance because this is a poem about a battle and its aftermath. They form an integral part of the whole and merely take up their appropriate space in the narrative. It could well be argued that their very forthrightness has a dignity of its own. Undoubtedly revolting is the execution of Ganelon, whose limbs were strapped to four horses which were made to gallop across a field. Here too, however, there is no morbid insistence, for the scene is quickly dismissed in nine lines, and the poet rounds it off, apologising almost for its ferocity, in a short, sharp conclusion:

Hon ki traïst altre, nen est dreiz
　　qu'il s'en vant!
　　　　　　(3974)

It is not right that a man who betrays another should boast about it!

About the work as a whole, and about Charlemagne, Roland, and their followers, there hangs a princely distinction, a nobleness, and high moral purpose which no utterance betrays, even when they give vent to their hatred of the enemy or their contempt of the traitor Ganelon. Dominant throughout is a tremendous admiration and respect for these courageous warriors ready to endure every kind of physical torment, to drive themselves to the limits of their capacities, to die with their bodies hacked to pieces, for the sake of a religious and patriotic ideal. Not for them a life of pleasurable dalliance in court circles. Life according to this view, no less ascetic than that of the early hagiography, must be spent in a perpetual struggle against the enemies of one's faith. When, at the end of the poem, Charlemagne looks ahead to the future, he sees only more conflict, more hardship. Despite the dismay this prospect causes him, we are left in no doubt that he will face it with steadfastness.

Strangely enough, the poet's admiration is not withheld by any means from the Arabs. No Christian of that age could possibly have admitted that they too were courageous defenders of a magnificent faith, but at least they are presented as worthy opponents, and often the poet remarks of one of them: what a man of great worth he would have been, if only he had been a Christian:

Fust chrestïens, asez oüst barnét.
　　　　　　(899)

Had he been a Christian, he would have had all the qualities of a baron.

The *Chanson de Roland* is, therefore, a Christian epic imbued with the fervour of the crusading era. But is it not something quite different besides, is it not a story of the clash of two forceful personalities, the account of a quarrel between two men and of the consequences of that quarrel? Apart from its epic and Christian characteristics, the poem is indeed a human drama concerned very much with individuals and their temperaments. Roland's insolent implication that Ganelon could be spared to go on the dangerous mission to the Arabs, after Charles had made it clear that he would not allow any of his best barons to be sent, made Ganelon swear to obtain his revenge on Roland, a revenge which culminated in the annihilation of the rearguard at Roncevaux. Every aspect of the action at this level is psychologically convincing: Ganelon is proud, haughty, and quarrelsome, as also is Roland, and hence, with the former a partisan of peace moves and the latter anxious to pursue the war to its end, the inevitability of their conflict, exacerbated by the traditional rivalry between stepfather and stepson.[9] Ganelon's plans were very neatly laid and could hardly fail. When he discussed the details with the Arabs, it had not yet been decided that Roland with the eleven other peers should lead the rearguard, but Ganelon knew that he had only to propose this for it to be accepted. Since he had yielded to Roland's suggestion that he should carry the message to the Arabs, Roland could hardly refuse to accept Ganelon's suggestion that he should take charge of the rearguard – a sort of tit-for-tat on Ganelon's part – and, Roland's character being what it was, Ganelon knew that Roland would not recall the main army before battle had been joined. Roland's impetuosity was bound to make him eager for the fray without a care for the tremendous odds against which the rearguard had to fight. When Roland boasted that Charlemagne would not lose even a packhorse to the enemy without its being bitterly contested over the sword, Ganelon replied in quietly ironical terms: 'You speak the truth, I'm well aware of that' (760). According to a definition of tragedy that has become well known, it is like a trap, a well-set, carefully prepared trap that is bound to go off; it is simply a matter of waiting.[10] This is hardly a simile in this instance, it is the literal truth, and nowhere does the poet seek to conceal the inevitability of disaster. Before it had even begun, the assembly of barons at which the Arabs' peace offer was accepted was referred to as the council that led to disaster (179). As the Arabs were preparing their ambush, the poet exclaims

Deus! quel dulur que li Franceis nel sevent	God! how tragic that the French are unaware of it.

(716)

The storm that raged over France while the battle at Roncevaux was in progress and even before Roland had decided to recall Charlemagne was

li granz dulors por la mort de Rollant	the great mourning for the death of Roland.

(1437)

Later, as Charlemagne turned back his army, the poet several times declared that it was too late to save Roland and his men. Charlemagne, moreover, clearly foresaw the impending disaster, but was powerless to prevent it. The *Chanson de Roland* is a tragedy, then, because of the inevitability of disaster and the total absence of what Anouilh so vividly terms 'le sale espoir', whose presence turns tragedy to melodrama.

The poem can also be deemed a tragedy from a rather different point of view. Roland, true to Aristotle's description of the tragic hero, reveals a *hamartia* (a fatal flaw, defect), that is responsible for the massacre of the rearguard and Roland's own death. This fatal flaw is his extreme arrogance and impetuosity (*desmesure* was the contemporary term), traits which quickly became apparent in the first main scene even before his clash with Ganelon. These self-same traits were responsible for his quarrel with his stepfather and for his rashness in not recalling Charlemagne while there was still time. Towards the end of the engagement, when only a handful of the rearguard remained alive, Oliver reproached Roland bitterly:

. . . vasselage par sens nen est folie,	Courage combined with sense is no
Mielz valt mesure que ne fait estultie.	folly. Moderation is better than recklessness. Frenchmen have died be-
Franceis sunt morz par vostre legerie . . .	cause of your heedless behaviour . . .

(1724–6)

This condemnation is all the fiercer in that it reflects proverbs well known and often repeated in that age which set great store by moral apophthegms of this kind. *Mesure*, in particular, was a quality much praised in proverbs and didactic writings alike.

Roland, the great hero, had thus brought on himself the angry and heartfelt reproof of his close friend and wise counsellor, and yet his courage and intransigence in the face of the foe, his simple enduring confidence in the rightness of the Christian cause, his sheer prowess as a warrior, were qualities which attracted the greatest admiration, not least from Oliver, who had long been aware of his companion's defects.

Why, eventually, did Roland recall Charlemagne despite Oliver's taunt, flinging Roland's earlier remarks back in his face:

'. . . vergoigne sereit grant	'. . . it would be great shame, and
E reprover a trestuz vos parenz'?	reproach for all your relatives'.

(1705–6)

Was it an act of repentance, was Roland confessing the folly of his decision, had his overweening pride at last taken a fall? Only at this point did Ganelon's plan break down, for he had not believed that Roland would ever deign to summon reinforcements, an admission of failure wholly out of character. Here as always the poet is sufficiently canny not to have interpolated explanations and comments of his own, and we have only Roland's actions, and sparse words, to guide us. Nowhere does he openly confess his error in not following Oliver's advice, but, as he laments the death of so many of his men, he seems to accept responsibility:

'Barons franceis, pur mei vos vei
  murir
Jo ne vos pois tenser ne guarantir'.
              (1863-4)

'French barons, for me I see you
dying, I cannot save or protect you'.

Unfortunately these important lines contain an ambiguity, for 'pur mei' can mean either 'for my sake', or 'because of me'. Even the former meaning contains a measure of self-accusation, and the remark made by Roland to Oliver that follows these lines carries at least an implication of failure:

'Oliver frere, vos ne dei jo faillir'   'Oliver brother, you I must not fail'
              (1866)

not, as it could have been, 'jo ne vos dei faillir'. The full implication of the actual wording appears to be: 'I have failed all those who lie here dead, but you, my best friend, you I must not fail'. None the less Roland died, a proud figure to the very end, for he turned his face to the enemy as proof that he had died, as he had boasted he would, 'cunquerrantment' (2867) – as a conqueror. When he confessed his sins, he made no direct reference to his lack of foresight which had resulted in the death of so many of Charlemagne's men. If we judge him by his actions, however (and in a *chanson de geste* actions inevitably speak louder than words), it can well be maintained that Roland had at last repented and had placed the Christian cause as a whole before his own personal glory. Even if the sounding of the oliphant did entail admission of defeat, even were it to bring shame on Roland and his relatives as Oliver said it would, still it had to be sounded because, as Turpin pointed out, the massacre of the rearguard should not go unavenged.

Different interpretations of Roland's death have been put forward. It has been claimed, for example, that it can be explained in purely heroic terms, without any reference to Christianity.[11] Possibly so, but this is manifestly not the view expressed in the text as we have it, for Roland, as he lay dying, confessed his sins, and angels carried the soul of this warrior saint aloft to Paradise. It has also been suggested that Roland in effect acknowledged his failure as Charlemagne's most trusted captain, and relinquished his command – again a highly idiosyncratic reading which demands much torturing of the text before it can find even the remotest justification.[12] To explain the strange cause of Roland's death it has been argued that 'Roland must die at his own hand (although not a suicide) as punishment for a sin which, although forgiven, has not yet been expiated'.[13] Nowhere does the text itself offer, or even hint at, such an explanation, and nowhere does it speak of Roland's impetuosity in engaging action without first summoning Charles, as a *sin*. What the text does is to present Roland as a superhuman, utterly invincible warrior, and this seems an adequate explanation for the manner of his death: no man alive was capable of killing him. The question has even been asked why Roland had to die at all, for was he not after all the victor in the field?[14] The reasons are obvious enough. It is not simply that the Roland of history did indeed die at Roncevaux, but above all, surely, the death of Roland was an artistic necessity without which much of the pathos and grandeur of the poem would have been lacking. The whole ethos of the work could not allow Roland to live on when all his friends and the men who had depended on his leadership lay dead. The heroes of later *chansons de geste* who did survive such encounters are *ipso facto* less impressive figures.[15] Yet another much-debated question is why the poem did not end with the death of Roland. Aesthetically, would this not have been more satisfying? For the modern reader no doubt so, but within the historical context of the crusading era the Baligant episode appears justified and represents, as has been pointed out, the final unfolding of the work as it passed from drama to epic, from epic to myth.[16] The Baligant episode most certainly does not represent 'the triumph of Christendom over Islam, and, by extension, the coming of the Kingdom of God'[17] for, as we have seen above, at the very end of the poem, the weary Charlemagne learns that his triumph over the 'pagans' is only momentary, and it is made very clear to him that the Kingdom of God is not yet at hand. Perhaps the author had an eye to history as he wrote these concluding lines, for he well knew that Charlemagne's reign had not resulted in the triumph of Christendom over Islam, and that in his own day even, this triumph was still no more than a remote possibility that could not be achieved without a long and bitter struggle.

The broadest issues which the poem raises are concerned, not with the death of Roland, nor with the clash between Roland and Ganelon, but with the contrast between the two companions Roland and Oliver. The poem provided people with interesting points of debate, for surely men discussed the great heroes of their literature then as they have done throughout the ages. Indeed they were even closer to them inasmuch as literature lived more through oral tradition, and these poems were not read in private but recited – performed might be a more apt word – in front of whole groups of people.[18] Discussion might well have been concerned with heroism: was the ideal hero the Roland type who fought quite recklessly in defence of his cause, without pausing to weigh up the possible consequences of his course of action, or was the ideal hero the equally courageous, but more cautious, more thoughtful Oliver? This is, as it were, a personification, almost an allegory, of a favourite medieval *topos*: *fortitudo* versus *sapientia*. The poet, as usual, refrained from comment, beyond pointing out the difference in their temperaments and emphasising that Oliver's courage was not inferior to that of Roland, a fact illustrated not only by his deeds of prowess, but also by the specific comment

| Rollant est proz e Oliver est sage | Roland is bold and Oliver is wise, |
| Ambedui unt meveillus vasselage | both have amazing courage. |

(1093–4)

The question can easily be carried further, for it concerns the nature of true courage. Must it be quite uncompromising and intransigent, as illustrated by Roland, or can it be tempered with reason and moderation, can it in fact admit of compromise, as illustrated by Oliver? The poet clearly expected his audience to admire Roland, whose courage was that of a superhuman, courage of a purity and intensity unattainable by ordinary men, but to approve rather of Oliver and his saner, more practical approach, one that others could safely imitate. It was easier to be an Oliver than a Roland, for the one was the courage of a good, brave, and experienced soldier, the other that of a fanatic. Oliver's attitude could well have been preferred to that of Roland, and it is interesting to note that several instances have been recorded of fathers in the late eleventh century christening one son Oliver, another Roland, always in that order. Not before the 1120s did it become the custom to call the first boy Roland, the second Oliver. Why this difference? Various explanations have been put forward, but it could well be that in the eleventh century the cooler, more rational temperament of Oliver was thought preferable to that of Roland, and only later, in the years of tremendous fervour that followed the first crusade, was Roland given precedence.[19]

In the final analysis, the contrast between the two companions is a matter of idealism on the one hand, and realism on the other, a true reflection of the spiritual and mental conflict of that turbulent age. The crusades of St Louis, like those of his predecessors (even those in whom materialistic motives were strong), were to represent the triumph of idealism of an extreme kind over realism and any suggestion of compromise. There was to be, so to speak, no premature blowing of the oliphant, and the heroic defeat of Roncevaux was to find its counterpart in many an ill-fated crusade to the Holy Land. In a way too, long after the crusading ardour was spent, this same uncompromising spirit so characteristic of the French nation was responsible for many a defeat in the battles that were to be fought on French soil in the later Middle Ages. At Crécy, Poitiers, Agincourt, and many other battlefields, honour and glory, the fear of appearing cowardly, eagerness to plunge into the fray, took precedence over the hard practicalities of military tactics, and the more unassuming, pragmatic approach of the enemy prevailed . . . until, that is, the advent of Joan of Arc, and how could she have succeeded without the intense idealism and fervour with which she inspired the men she led? At the end of the Middle Ages, was it not the Roland spirit that eventually triumphed and brought the French nation into being? Even in the late twentieth century, such concepts as 'l'honneur', 'la grandeur', 'la gloire' are still part of the French psyche and can still be a dynamic and ennobling force, chauvinistic though they may appear to other eyes.

To assess the qualities of this great, shaggy, uneven masterpiece is a wellnigh impossible task. Any contact we have with the text is bound to be of a kind utterly different from that intended by the author, or authors. Like other *chansons de geste*, the *Chanson de Roland* was meant to be chanted, or possibly sung to a simple, repetitive melody, by a jongleur before a gathering in castle hall, public square, or marketplace. Its peculiar characteristics are owed to this oral presentation: the varying length of the sections, known as *laisses*, changing according to the episode being dealt with; the use, not of rhyme, but of assonance, so much less demanding on a man reciting long passages from memory, since, as we have seen, assonance is far more tolerant of slight variations and the choice of words is far greater; the use of stereotyped expressions to describe particular characters or places whenever they are mentioned, a useful mnemonic device and a ready means for the jongleur's audience of identifying and remembering the principal characters; the habit of naming in the first line of the *laisse* the person who is to be its principal subject, again a formula which could only be of immense help to the jongleur reciting from memory this work of over 4,000 lines. Also, oral presentation was responsible for a particular use of repetition, in passages known as the *laisses similaires*, which would quickly have become monotonous and pointless in a prose narrative intended for reading in private by the individual. Three times Oliver urged Roland to recall Charlemagne before battle had been joined, and each time Roland refused on the grounds that he would lose his reputation were he to do this. The change of assonance from *laisse* to *laisse* produced a slightly different wording on each occasion:

Cumpaign Rollant, kar sunez vostre corn!	Companion Roland, pray sound your horn!
(1051)	
Cumpainz Rollant, l'olifan car sunez!	Companion Roland, pray sound the oliphant!
(1059)	
Cumpainz Rollant, sunez vostre olifan . . .	Companion Roland, sound your oliphant!
(1070)	

When Roland finally sounded the oliphant, three successive *laisses* recounted the episode in similar terms. (In the same way, Marsile's questioning of Ganelon was repeated with only slight variation of wording. Roland's attempt to destroy his sword Durendal receives similar treatment, as also does the splendid scene of Roland's death and the ascent of his soul into heaven.) The poet, or his predecessor or predecessors, had discovered this extremely effective technique of slowing down the action at a crucial point in the narrative, so building up an atmosphere of tension and expectancy in the audience, and causing the most dramatic moments of the story to stand out in strongly marked relief. Even in a private reading of the work today, when so many of its distinguishing features are inevitably lost, this skilful manipulation of essentially oral techniques such as those revealed in the *laisses similaires* can hardly pass unnoticed and unfelt.

A substantial proportion of the text is taken up with direct speech, approximately 1,700 lines,[20] well over a third of the total. The nature of the direct speech is such that the jongleur must have been required to change the tone frequently, so much so that he clearly needed the vocal control and artistry of an actor, all the more so if the text was sung to some simple melody. Thus, when Roland's name is put forward by Ganelon for command of the rearguard, Roland replies twice, on the first occasion officially, in the hearing of all:

'Sire parastre, mult vos dei aveir cher.
La rereguarde avez sur mei jugiét . . .'

'Sir stepfather, I owe you great esteem. You have assigned the rearguard to me . . .'

(754–5)

The second occasion that follows immediately is an angry aside to Ganelon which calls for a very different tone:

'Ahi, culvert, malvais hom de put aire!'

'Ah wretch, evil man of vile birth!'

(763)

Later, when Oliver reproaches Roland with his failure to sound the oliphant in time, we find a very strange juxtaposition:

'Cil ki la sunt ne funt mie a blasmer.
Kar chevalchez a quanque vos püez!
Seignors baruns, el camp vos retenez!'

'The men over there deserve no blame. Pray ride on for all you are worth! Lord barons, stand firm in the field!'

(1174–6)

The first line is addressed still to Roland, the following lines to the rearguard as a whole, without any warning passage to mark the transition, such as 'Next, he turned to the men and said . . .'.[21] To recite these lines at one level of voice, without a short break after the first line quoted and a change in tone for those following, would

risk making nonsense of the entire passage. Also, to read them to
oneself, without pausing to note the unannounced switch, is to miss
an important detail, a clever touch of realism. Later, when Oliver
reproaches Roland with his failure to sound the oliphant, he ends
his tirade with the lines

'Se vos cornez, n'ert mie hardement.
Ja avez vos ambsdous les braz
  sanglanz'.

'If you sound your horn, it will be
no act of courage. I see both your
arms are bloody'.

(1710–11)

Clearly the last line does not follow on logically from the preceding
one, for it is an expression of concern and sympathy demanding
quite a different intonation. It was this abrupt change of tone that
had to take the place of an explanatory comment such as 'He then
noticed that Roland appeared to be wounded, and exclaimed . . .'.
Numerous other examples could be quoted showing how the jongleur's delivery had to adapt itself constantly to the nature of the
text, such as the many lines, the second half only of which consists
of direct speech:

Dist a Rollant: 'Tut fol, pur quei
  t'esrages?'

He said to Roland: 'You utter madman, why are you in a rage?'

(286)

In order to spring into life, the text clearly depended to a considerable degree on the skill of the jongleur.

The dramatic features of the work, and its essentially oral nature,
inevitably benefited from the rich sonority of the language in its
early stages. As a language to be *heard* rather than read in silence,
the early vernacular was undoubtedly superb. Although the exact
nature of many of the sounds is not known, it is certain that words
were more fully pronounced then than now, with very little of the
slurring of endings and final consonants so characteristic of modern
French. A more complete, more deliberate enunciation than nowadays meant that this full-throated, virile language harmonised
wonderfully with the spirit of the *chansons de geste*, forming a
coherent whole that could be only imperfectly re-created in any
modern idiom. In order to appreciate this, the opening lines of the
chanson should be read aloud, with a vigorous rolling of the rs and
a full pronunciation of all word-endings according to their spellings:

Carles li reis, nostre emperere
  magnes,
Set anz tuz pleins ad estét en
  Espaigne,
Tresqu'en la mer cunquist la tere
  altaigne.
N'i ad castel ki devant lui remaigne,
Mur ne citét n'i est remés a
  fraindre,

Charles the king, our mighty emperor, seven full years has been in
Spain, right down to the sea he has
conquered the high [?proud?] land.
No castle holds out against him, no
wall or city remains to be shattered,
apart from Saragossa, which is on a
mountain. King Marsile holds it
who loves not God, he serves

Fors Sarraguce, ki est en une
  muntaigne;
Li reis Marsilie la tient ki Deu
  nen aimet,
Mahumet sert et Apollin recleimet;
Ne. s poet guarder que mals ne l'i
  ateignet.

(1–9)

Mahomet and invokes Apollin. He is
powerless to prevent evil coming
upon him.

In the general organisation of the work, particularly striking is the coherent, tightly knit structure in which everything is closely related to the central tragedy, always pointing inwards to the core in a wording that is terse, sober, but vivid by reason of its very economy. Thus the Pyrenees become a physical manifestation of the atmosphere of tension and anxiety:

Halt sunt li pui, e li val tenebrus
Les roches bises, les destreiz
  merveillus...

(814–15)

High are the mountains and the valleys deep in shadow, the rocks dark, the passes awe-inspiring...

Later this description reappears with slight variation, like some ominous refrain sounding a death knell as the main French forces turn back too late to help the ill-fated rearguard:

Halt sunt li pui e tenebrus e grant
Li val parfunt e les ewes curant...

(1830–1)

High are the hills, deep in shadow and mighty, the valleys deep and the waters swift...

The darkness that hangs over France as the battle rages has the same effect:

Cuntre midi tenebres i ad granz,
N'i ad clartét, si li ciels nen i fent;
Hume nel veit ki mult ne s'espaent.

(1431–3)

Towards noon there was great darkness, no light save when the sky split open. No man seeing this could fail to be terrified.

There is an incantatory effect about many such atmosphere-creating lines, or in those describing Charlemagne's portentous dreams where the expression *Carles se dort* is used as is the opening line of a rondeau, twice repeated in the course of the poem:

Tresvait le jur, la noit est aserie,
Carles se dort, li empereres riches;
Sunjat qu'il eret as greignurs porz
  de Sizer,
Entre ses poinz teneit sa hanste
  fraisnine;
Guenes li quens l'ad sur lui saisie,
Par tel aïr l'at crullee e brandie
Qu'envers le cel en volent les
  escicles.
Carles se dort, qu'il ne s'esveillet
  mie.

The day passes, the night has grown dark, Charles is asleep, the mighty emperor. He dreamt he was in the great [lit. 'greater'] Col de Cize, in his fists he held his spear-shaft of ash. Ganelon the count seized it from him, with such anger he shook and brandished it that splinters from it flew to the sky. Charles is asleep and does not wake up.

Aprés iceste altre avisiun sunjat:
Qu'il ert en France a sa capele ad Ais,
El destre braz li morst uns vers si mals.
Devers Ardene vit venir uns leuparz,
Sun cors demenie mult fierement asalt.
D'enz de la sale uns veltres avalat
Que vint a Carles les galops e les salz,
La destre oreille al premer ver trenchat,
Ireement se cumbat al lepart.
Dient Franceis que grant bataille i ad,
Il ne sevent li quels d'els la veintrat.
Carles se dort, mie ne s'esveillat.

(717–36)

After this one he dreamed another dream: that he was in France at his chapel in Aix, a very fierce boar bit him in his right arm. From the Ardennes he saw a leopard coming which attacked his very person extremely fiercely. From out of the hall a hound came leaping and bounding to Charles, it bit off the boar's right ear, and angrily fights the leopard. The French say that there is a great battle. They know not which of them will win. Charles is asleep and did not wake up.

Colour is by no means lacking from the descriptions, but is usually concerned with the soldiers and their armour or their horses, natural enough in a work over a quarter of which is given up to detailed accounts of battle scenes and their effects. No description is more vivid (or more frequently quoted) than that of Turpin's horse, in which is reflected something of the fighting man's tremendous affection for his 'destrier':

Li destrers est e curanz e aates,
Piez ad copiez e les gambes ad plates,
Curte la quisse e la crupe bien large,
Lungs les costez e l'eschine ad ben halte,
Blanche la cue e la crignete jalne,
Petites les oreilles, la teste tute falve;
Beste nen est nule ki encontre lui alge

(1490–6)

The steed is swift and speedy, its hooves hollow, its legs slender, its haunches short, its crupper very wide, its flanks long, its back very high, its tail white and its mane yellow, its ears small and its head quite tawny. No beast can compete with it.

Passages of this nature give the work an intense visual effect. A skilful jongleur can have had no difficulty in bringing the many scenes to life before the eyes of his audience. In those times a mere recital of the poem must have had a more telling effect than a Technicolor film can have in our own day, for the scenic effects of a film constantly limit and control the imagination, whereas the text opens it out and gives it the fullest possible scope, the eternal advantage of the written or spoken word over all other art-forms, save possibly music.

III. THE ORIGINS OF THE 'CHANSON DE ROLAND'

No single problem concerning their field of interest has pre-occupied students of medieval French literature more than that of the origins of the *Chanson de Roland*.[22] Like the medieval pilgrims who travelled the various routes that crossed western Europe and converged eventually on the shrine of Saint James of Compostela in Galicia, these scholarly pilgrims embark at least once in their lives on this long and perilous quest, the very converse of that earlier one however, for here the point of departure is always the same, but no single destination awaits them at journey's end. They are likely to end their progress somewhere in one of two regions, finding themselves at worship among the 'traditionalists' (or 'neotradition-alists') on the one hand, or the 'individualists' on the other. These terms will be explained briefly in the following pages, although it is not our purpose here to set out on this quest and to explore after so many others its many byways and blind alleys. However, we are in duty bound, as tourists rather than pilgrims, to pay it a respectful salute in passing.

The annihilation of Charles's rearguard as he returned from Spain to France was no mere poetic fiction. The Royal Annals contemporary with Charles's Spanish campaign make no mention of the defeat. It was recorded for the first time in a revision of the annals some twenty years later. A more detailed account appears in the *Vita Karoli* of Eginhard, composed about 830. Dealing with the year 778, the relevant passage runs as follows:

Whilst waging uninterrupted war against the Saxons, Charles stationed garrisons at appropriate places along the frontier and attacked Spain with all the forces he could muster. He crossed the Pyrenees and received the submission of all the strongholds on his route. He brought his army safely back, except that, crossing the Pyrenees, he suffered from the perfidy of the Basques. His army was moving in an extended line in accordance with the narrowness of the road. The Basques had prepared an ambush on the hill-tops. The place, thickly wooded, was well chosen. They descended on the baggage trains and the troops of the rearguard who were protecting the main body of the army. They drove them into a valley, engaged battle, and annihilated our men. Having pillaged the baggage, they scattered very quickly in all directions, favoured by the oncoming night. They were helped by the lightness of their armour and the lie of the land. The Franks, on the other hand, were hindered by their cumbersome weapons and low position. In this battle were killed the seneschal Eggihard, Anselme count of the palace, and Roland duke of the March of Brittany amongst many others. This aggression could not be avenged on the spot because the enemy dispersed and nobody knew in what direction to look for them.

A slightly later text says of those who died in the ambush: 'Since their names are well known I shall not repeat them here'. Various

other historical records mention the defeat, though nowhere is
Roncevaux referred to by name. The eighth-century historio-
graphers appear to have been somewhat embarrassed by this
episode, at first passing it over in silence, later alluding to it briefly.
It may have been a defeat of greater dimensions than they cared
to confess. The historical basis of the *Chanson de Roland* is
undeniable, therefore, but it has clearly been 'arranged' from a
Christian point of view. Charles's rearguard was ambushed in actual
fact by the Christian Basques, although it is possible that they were
in league with Arab factions as Charles himself had been when he
undertook the invasion of Spain. Roland did indeed die in the battle
along with the other men of the rearguard, but he is not presented
in the annals as having been more important than the others named
there, neither of whom is as much as mentioned in the *Chanson*.
There is no reference in the annals to Ganelon and his treachery,
no reference to Roland's close companion Oliver. On the other
hand, the archbishop Turpin who played such a prominent role in
the poem was indeed an historical figure, but he died ten years
after the battle in which, according to the poem, he met a heroic
death.

Between the actual historical events of the late eighth century
and the earliest surviving version, of the *Chanson de Roland*, dating
from the early twelfth century, what was the relationship? Are the
so-called 'traditionalists' or 'neotraditionalists' right when they
maintain that there must have been an unbroken oral tradition
connecting the two, beginning not long after the event? Are the
'individualists' right in believing that the *Chanson* was essentially
the work of individual poets of the eleventh century? Can both
areas of belief contain a measure of truth?

The first iconographical references to the *Chanson de Roland*
are to be found in the scenes carved over the main porch of the
cathedral of Angoulême. They date from some time between 1120
and 1130. The scholars responsible for this important discovery
believe that, for Roland to be represented in this way, equal in
importance to the most famous figures of the Bible, a tradition of
several centuries was indispensable.[23] This belief, it must be said,
is gratuitous, for the decades which ended the eleventh century and
began the twelfth saw the religious fervour which for so long had
been gaining momentum reach its height in the first crusades to the
Holy Land, and the importance attached to the Christian warrior
in those years increased not unnaturally with great rapidity.

Onomastic evidence of an interesting kind was brought to light
when it was shown that in the eleventh century it became fashionable for fathers to christen one of their sons Roland, another Oliver.
At first the earliest instances were thought to go back as far as 1030,

but it has recently been demonstrated that this was not so. The earliest in fact date from the 1060s and 1070s.[24]

Available textual evidence predating the earliest and best versions of *Roland* consists of various fragments of Latin texts – some discovered quite recently – but it cannot be said with certainty that they take us back earlier than the 1060s or 1070s. The latest discovery, known as the *Nota Emilianense*, is generally accepted as fairly firm proof of the existence of a *Song of Roland* in the 1070s, possibly a little earlier, a simpler and no doubt considerably shorter tale than the earliest extant version, Digby 23.[25] This short fragment is included here so that the version of the disaster which it gives may be contrasted with that quoted above from the contemporary annals. The transformation it has undergone is of the greatest interest:

> In the year 778 King Charles came to Saragossa. At that time he had twelve nephews, and each was accompanied by 3,000 armed knights; among them may be mentioned Roland, Bertrand, Ogier Shortsword, Guillaume Curvednose, Olivier, and the bishop Turpin. Each of them served the king for one month a year along with his body of knights. The king stopped at Saragossa with his army. After the lapse of a certain time the king was advised by his men to accept the numerous presents offered him so that his army would not perish from hunger and could return home. This was done. The king decided that to protect the men of his army, Roland the courageous warrior should have charge of the rearguard. When the army passed through the Col de Cize, Roland perished, killed by the Saracens.[26]

The evidence brought to light so far cannot be said to establish the existence of a *Song of Roland* earlier than the 1060s.[27] The neo-traditionalists will remain quite dissatisfied with statements of this kind. They point to the futility of relying on written evidence for something whose primary existence was essentially oral and therefore unrecorded. Their belief in a long unbroken chain of oral legend has therefore to be taken on trust. It is in the end a faith, an inner conviction: 'clearly, it must have been so'. The non-specialist who is not personally involved in such scholarly furores can rest content with the knowledge that the extant poem was certainly preceded by earlier, shorter versions from the 1060s or 1070s, so that there may well be some truth in the several assertions that have survived to the effect that, as they went into battle, the Normans at Hastings were accompanied by a jongleur who sang about the heroic Roland. Indeed, it has been plausibly suggested that the *Chanson de Roland* was essentially a Norman composition.[28] New evidence, new interpretations of old evidence, will certainly throw further light on this fascinating problem of the ancestry of the most famous of medieval French texts, though whether the whole truth will ever be known remains extremely doubtful. The aura of mystery surrounding this great work may well have been present already in the eleventh century, for even then the full history of its genesis is unlikely to have been known to the jongleur's audience.

IV. THE 'COURONNEMENT DE LOUIS'

Composed about half a century after the *Chanson de Roland*, some time between 1131 and 1150, the *Couronnement de Louis*[29] is concerned with the end of Charlemagne's reign and the beginning of that of his son Louis. It was not intended specifically as a continuation of the *Chanson de Roland* in the way that the thirteenth-century *Chanson d'Aspremont* was, for in the latter the French army, returning from the Spanish campaign, decided on Charlemagne's initiative to begin fresh campaigns immediately against the Saracens in the south of France, particularly at Narbonne.

The *Couronnement de Louis* tells how the aged Charlemagne is no longer able to bear arms, and decides that his son Louis should be crowned in his place. The barons rejoice on learning that they are not to have a foreign king. In their presence the emperor addresses his son, advising him on his moral duties: he is to commit no lechery, no treason, and is not to disinherit orphans and widows. He is to lead the Christian armies across the Gironde, attack the pagans, and conquer their lands. The crown is placed on the altar, but when Charlemagne finishes speaking, Louis, still only a boy of fifteen, does not step forward. The barons weep and Charlemagne bursts out with bitter reproaches, accusing his son of cowardice. One of the barons, Arneïs d'Orléans, offers to lead the armies for a period of three years. Arneïs is about to be crowned king when Guillaume, returning from the hunt, learns of these events. Guillaume enters the church and goes up to Arneïs. He draws his sword, but, mindful of where he is and of Christianity's condemnation of murder, he thrusts it back into its scabbard and instead deals Arneïs a mighty blow with his fist on the back of the neck, casting him down dead at his feet. Guillaume exclaims that he only intended to punish Arneïs, but since he has betrayed his rightful lord he deserves to die. Guillaume now seizes the crown and places it on Louis's head, to the great satisfaction of Charlemagne who reiterates his earlier advice to his son. Guillaume obtains from Charlemagne permission to depart on a pilgrimage to Rome, and he sets off with a retinue of sixty knights.

In Rome the pope learns that the Saracens have attacked Capua and taken many prisoners who will soon be put to the sword unless help is forthcoming. He asks advice from Guillaume, whose first instinct is to send to the king of France for reinforcements, since his own force is insignificant. The pope promises Guillaume all manner of indulgences in return for his help. Encouraged by this concession, Guillaume calls his men to arms, along with the 3,000 men of the pope's army. The pope meantime parleys with the pagans in an attempt to avert bloodshed. The Saracen emir, addressing the pope as 'sire with the broad hat', suggests that each side should select a champion, and that the combat between them should decide the issue. The pope accepts, but is dismayed when he sees the enemy's choice: the giant Corsolt, a shaggy, massive figure, so tall that merely from shoulder to waist he measures a full six foot. Guillaume is the inevitable choice for the Christian champion. At the sight of Corsolt, Guillaume dismounts, turns to the East, and prays to God, the giant standing meekly by until Guillaume has finished. Then the two exchange insults, and the combat begins. Corsolt, confident of victory, deals Guillaume the first blow. Guillaume charges at full tilt, his lance passing right through the giant's body. The giant fights back fiercely despite the severity of his wound. He strikes Guillaume a mighty blow which severs the nose-piece of his helmet and cuts off the end of his nose, a blow later to earn Guillaume a new nickname: Guillaume al Cort Nés. This same blow cuts Guillaume's horse in two. Once dismounted, Guillaume cannot reach Corsolt to inflict any further wounds. Thinking him beaten, Corsolt leans over, intending to pick him up and lay him across his saddle. Seeing his chance Guillaume aims a mighty blow at Corsolt's head, splits it open, and casts him dead over the neck of his steed, rejoicing at being avenged for the loss of his nose: his nose may be shorter, but his reputation is now longer. The Saracen army is demoralised by the death of their champion. Their king Galafre, taken prisoner and converted to the Christian faith, arranges the release of those Christians captured at Capua and makes preparations for Guillaume to marry his beautiful daughter when messengers from France bring the news that Charlemagne is dead and that traitors are threatening to depose Louis. Guillaume has no option but to return to France.

On his way Guillaume joins forces with two of his nephews leading a body of knights to the help of Louis who is held prisoner in Tours. On hearing that the baron Richart de Rouen is planning to crown his son Acelin king, Guillaume vows that he will plant the crown on his head in such a way that his brains will fall at his feet. With the help of a gatekeeper loyal to Louis, Guillaume enters the city with his men and posts detachments at each of the city gates. He finds Louis hiding in the church, and quickly drives out those members of the clergy disloyal to him. Then Guillaume takes away the traitors' harness while they sleep. In the ensuing confusion the traitors try to flee the city, but find Guillaume's men waiting for them at the gates. Guillaume himself kills Acelin, using a wooden stake for the purpose, not deigning to sully his weapons with traitors' blood, but spares the life of Acelin's father, Richart de Rouen.

For the next three years Guillaume wears his helmet daily, fighting the king's cause, taking land for him in Poitou, conquering King Amarmonde near Bordeaux, Dagobert of Carthage near Pierrelate, and waging campaigns in Andorra and at Saint-Gilles in the Gard. On hearing that Guillaume is now marching north to the Mont Saint-Michel and intends to pass through his territory, Richart de Rouen plots his murder. In the ensuing encounter Guillaume unsaddles Richart, who falls in such a way that the spike of his helmet is stuck in the ground and his spurs point to the sky. Richart is taken prisoner, handed over to the king, and dies later in prison.

Just as Guillaume is thinking of laying down his arms, messengers arrive from Rome announcing the deaths of Galafre and the pope and begging for help since Rome has been attacked by Gui d'Alemagne. Within a fortnight Guillaume musters 50,000 men ready for the march on Rome. He attacks under cover of a thick mist and kills many of Gui's men. Then Gui suggests that the issue be decided by a single combat. Guillaume is the obvious choice for France once more, and after a bitter struggle, described blow by blow, he is again the victor. But his longing for peace and rest is shattered by new revolts against Louis that keep him busy for a further year, until at last Louis's power is firmly established.

A basic theme unites the four principal episodes of this work: the duty of a Christian knight, a twofold duty towards the king on the one hand, towards the Church on the other. In the first episode Guillaume prevented an upstart from deposing the king; in the second he prevented the Saracens from overrunning Rome and killing the pope; in the third he saved Louis from an insurrection by one of his barons; in the fourth he prevented Gui d'Alemagne from destroying Rome and occupying the whole region. This simple alternating pattern lacks subtlety and invention, but results in a fast-moving tale of adventure offering excitement and entertainment while at the same time showing a didactic motivation of a type quite clear to the people of twelfth-century France. The whole work revolves around a remarkable discrepancy, for it begins with a vigorously-worded but conventional portrait of the ideal king:

Reis qui de France porte corone
   d'or
Prodom deit estre et vaillanz de
   son cors;
Et s'il est om qui li face nul tort,
Ne deit guarir ne a plain ne a bos
De ci qu'il l'ait o recreant o mort:
S'ensi nel fait, donc pert France
   son los;
Ce dit l'estoire coronez est a tort

(lines 20–6)

The king who wears the golden crown of France must be noble and valiant in his person. If any man does him wrong, he must not go free whether in the plains or woods, until the king has made him submit or has killed him. If this he does not do, then France loses her reputation. So says the story, he is wrongfully crowned.

Louis, however, turns out to be a weak, vacillating monarch who cannot be excused solely on the grounds of youth, and even the loyal Guillaume eventually loses patience with him and addresses him as

'. . . povre reis, lasches et asso-
   tez . . .'

'. . . wretched king, cowardly and besotted . . .'

(2249)

Was the implication therefore that Louis was wrongfully crowned? Evidently so according to the preamble, but not so in actual practice, for Louis was Charles's legitimate heir and the barons who attempted to depose him are roundly condemned as traitors. In remaining loyal to Louis despite his complete lack of kingly qualities, Guillaume was doing his duty and is very clearly the dominant hero of the work. Implicit in the poem, therefore, is the idea that the system was greater than the individual. Even when the king was no Charlemagne, even when he was a puny, unimpressive figure, he still had the right to his subjects' loyalty and obedience. The loyalty was to the position, not to the man, and this is clearly propaganda in favour of the hereditary monarchy. The idea that the strongest or most venturesome figure should assume the leadership is condemned, the implicit reason being that this would result in civil war and anarchy. Hence, when Charlemagne announced that his son would succeed him, the barons were greatly relieved:

'Pere de gloire, tu seies mercïez
Qu'estranges reis n'est sor nos
    devalez'.

'Father of glory, may you be thanked
that a foreign king has not descended on us'.

(59–60)

The *Couronnement de Louis* is accordingly an adventure story
with political and religious implications. It is on a lower plane than
the *Chanson de Roland*, never reaching to the heights of tragedy,
never seeking to do so. The hero who survived has now succeeded
to the hero who gave his life, and death now seems to be reserved
for traitors and pagans. It is very much of a fighting man's poem,
all the admiration being reserved for the loyal-hearted man of
action, while the clergy are treated with some disdain. When
Charlemagne accused his son of cowardice, he added scornfully
that he would make a churchwarden of him: his hair would be
shorn and he could devote himself to bell-ringing. Even the pope
cuts a sorry figure, being quick to lose heart, declaring that not even
Roland and all the twelve peers could overcome the mighty Corsolt,
a remark which Guillaume seems to have found almost sacrilegious.
The clergy are spoken of as owing allegiance to the king and are
given short shrift by Guillaume when suspected of treachery:

Li cuens Guillelmes de neient ne
    se targe,
Tresqu'al chancel en est venuz en
    haste,
Ou a trové et evesques et abes;
Por le pechié ne les volt tochier
    d'armes,
Mais as batons les desrompent et
    batent,
Fors del mostier les traïnent et
    chacent,
Ses comanderent a quatre vinz
    deables.
Qui traïson vuelt faire a seignorage
Il est bien dreiz que il i ait
    damage!

Count Guillaume does not delay at
all, he came swiftly to the chancel
where he found both bishops and
abbots. Because of the sin involved
he does not wish to touch them with
his weapons, but they [Guillaume
and his companions] set about them
and beat them with sticks, and drag
them and chase them out of the
church and consigned them to eighty
devils. Whoever betrays his lord, it
is very right that he should suffer
for it!

(1768–76)

An element that constantly appears in the *Couronnement* and
which is extremely rare in the *Chanson de Roland* is the earthy
humour, frequently concerning the hero: Guillaume's resolve to
strike the traitor Anseïs d'Orléans with his fists rather than with his
sword in order not to kill him, though he does in fact break his neck
at the first blow; his sarcastic retort when the pope bestows all
manner of indulgences upon him:

Onc mais nuls clers nen ot le cuer
    si large

Never before did any cleric have so
generous a heart;

(399)

his satisfaction on killing the giant Corsolt because in so doing he avenged the loss of the end of his nose:

'Deus', dist Guillelmes, 'com j'ai   'God', said Guillaume, 'how I have
    mon nés vengié!'   avenged my nose!';
                        (1122)

his neat upturning of Richart de Rouen who landed head-first on the ground, followed by his bundling of the captive Richart on to his horse 'come cofre en somier' (2186) (like a chest on a pack-horse). Noteworthy also is Bertran's greeting of his somewhat battered uncle after one of his numerous exploits:

... 'De vostre brant vei sanglent   'I see all the steel of your sword is
    tot l'acier,   bloody, and your shield is not al-
Et vostre escuz n'est mie toz entiers: together whole. You have been up
Alcun malice avez vos comencié'.   to some mischief'.
                    (2191-3)

Guillaume was a sort of folk hero, a common man's ideal of a baron and Christian knight, lacking refinement of manner and thought, not much of a lady's man,[30] a hale and hearty, back-slapping, swash-buckling adventurer, physically powerful, a wonderful fighter, stead-fastly loyal to his rightful king, and a devout Christian withal. His character colours and controls the entire narrative, which takes on the dimensions, and the limitations, of its hero. The coronation of Louis is the starting-point of the story, and in several ways the most dramatic and original of the four episodes, but the main action is taken up almost wholly with the testing of Guillaume, who emerges triumphant from the various ordeals imposed upon him by his conception of duty.

After Guillaume the most impressive figure is undoubtedly that of Corsolt, whose presence introduces a supernatural element into the story. This Goliath possesses the awe-inspiring physical traits of the giants of popular myth and folklore, a figure which crops up again in the romances and is presaged already in some of the fantastic pagan heroes against whom Roland and his peers fought at Roncevaux.[31] Corsolt looked upon himself as God's personal enemy. God had killed his father with a thunderbolt, now Corsolt was avenging his father's death:

'Quant je la sus ne puis Deu   'Since I cannot wage war on God
    guerreier,   up there, I do not want to leave
Nul de ses omes ne vueil ça jus   any of His men down here, and I
    laissier,   and God have nothing to discuss.
Et je et Deus n'avons mais que   Mine is the earth, His shall be the
    plaidier: heavens'.
Meie est la terre et suens sera li
    ciels'.
                (534-7)

Little wonder that the pope, to whom this astonishing diatribe was addressed, felt dismayed. The ultimate effect of Corsolt's might was simply to enhance Guillaume's glory. The more redoubtable his enemies, the greater was his achievement in overcoming them, and the remarkable thing is that in the process Guillaume did not himself become a mythical figure, but remains solidly human and 'real'.

The question has inevitably been asked: is the *Couronnement de Louis* in any way a comment on the history of France at the time the poem was composed, in the second third of the twelfth century? Was it intended as a warning to Frenchmen of those times to be mindful of their real duties and to avoid the perils of civil war? Was it written in an age when the French monarch was indeed a weak, vacillating figure?[32] The opening scene has been taken as a veiled reference to the crowning of the eleven-year-old Louis VII by his father Louis VI in 1131. Louis VI actually reigned for another six years, dying in 1137. (In the poem Charlemagne dies five years after crowning his son.) The very fact that Louis VI deemed it necessary to ensure the succession in this way shows that the turbulence of the powerful feudal barons, as depicted in the *Couronnement de Louis*, was no mere figment of the poet's imagination, but a very real and a very disturbing part of the history of twelfth-century France:

> ...Louis VI found that the task to which he had resolved to devote himself, of bringing peace into the royal domain, was an arduous undertaking, and one that required persistent effort on his part. Even in 1108, immediately on his accession to the throne, he was involved in war with Hugh of Crécy, who, not content with ravaging the country, had crowned his offences by capturing Eudes, Count of Corbeil, and imprisoning him in the dungeons of La Ferté-Alais. To set him free it was necessary to besiege that fortress, which only surrendered to the king after a long struggle, full of vicissitudes. A few months later, in the spring of 1109, Louis VI was again in the field. This time he was besieging Mantes, which he recovered after a strenuous fight from his half-brother Philip, the son of Bertrada of Montfort.[33]

It is clear that the general atmosphere created by the text reflects closely that of twelfth-century France, but it would be unwise to seek precise and detailed parallels between the text and the century in which it was composed. Louis VI was certainly no Charlemagne, but he was a fine king and an active leader of his armies; his son Louis VII, on the other hand, though considerably less astute and energetic than his father, and less skilful in controlling the ever-rebellious barons, was not the entirely negative figure that his literary namesake was. (Neither was the historical Louis, son of Charlemagne, for that matter.) The weakness of Louis in the *Couronnement* was necessary in order to show up to good effect the energy and heroism of Guillaume. This does not imply that the text lacked a historical basis, for it has been shown that the author knew

and followed a ninth-century chronicle, the *Vita Hludovici* of
Thegan, on the life of Charlemagne's son Louis le Débonnaire, in
which Charlemagne crowned his son king and showered advice on
him as the *Couronnement* relates.[34] This episode is described as
follows in the *Cambridge Medieval History*:

> In September of the year 813 an Assembly was held at Aachen and
> Charles with his nobles resolved to raise Louis, his only surviving son, to the
> position of Emperor, while a grandson Bernard, the son of his dead son
> Pepin, was to be appointed under-king of Italy. In his robes as Emperor,
> Charles advanced to the altar, knelt in prayer, addressed warning words to
> his son, caused him to promise fulfilment of all commands, and finally bade
> Louis take a second crown that was lying upon the altar and place it
> himself upon his head.[35]

It is quite clear that the *Couronnement de Louis* made no attempt
at a faithful account of this episode of ninth-century history any
more than it attempted a direct reference to twelfth-century history.
The differences between the actual coronation of Charlemagne's son
and the opening scene of the *Couronnement* have been made very
clear by Joseph Bédier:

> Il est bien vrai que Charlemagne, à Aix, en l'an 813, a solennellement
> associé à l'empire son fils Louis.
> Mais ce n'était pas, comme dans le roman, le jour de la consécration de
> la chapelle. – Mais le pape n'était pas présent. – Mais Louis n'était pas un
> enfant de quinze ans: il avait trente-cinq ans. – Mais il n'a pas hésité à
> prendre la couronne: il l'a prise aussitôt et résolûment. – Mais personne n'a
> troublé la fête: le couronnement a eu lieu au milieu de la jubilation univer-
> selle. – Mais personne à la cour de Charlemagne ne s'appelait Arneïs
> d'Orléans. – Mais aucun Guillaume, que l'on sache, n'a assisté à la céré-
> monie. – Mais Charlemagne n'a pas survécu cinq ans à l'événement: il est
> mort quatre mois après.[36]

The tale has a general basis in ninth-century history, skilfully
adapted to reflect aspects of twelfth-century history, with additions
and modifications necessary for the telling of an exciting story
centring around the exploits of the indefatigable hero Guillaume al
Cort Nés.

Was Guillaume himself a historical figure? As Bédier points out in
the passage just quoted, there is no record of any Guillaume having
been present at the coronation of Louis I. However, the Guillaume
who is the hero of this and several other *chansons de geste* does seem
to have had an actual prototype in Count Guillaume de Toulouse,
cousin of Charlemagne, who became the principal counsellor of the
emperor's son Louis long before his coronation, when Louis in fact
was still only twelve years old. Guillaume's principal duty was to
combat Arab invasions from across the Pyrenees and though he was
not always victorious, he did eventually triumph in the year 803
when his forces captured Barcelona. As with the person of Roland

then, there was in the name, character, and role of Guillaume undoubtedly a historical foundation, but the structure erected on all
such foundations in the *chansons de geste* owed much to poetic
invention and imagination, coloured strongly by the political and
religious climate of the crusading era, in particular the twelfth
century.[37] Exactly how, and exactly when, the transformation from
history to legend took place is scarcely less controversial a matter
than it is in the case of the *Chanson de Roland*. It is not our purpose to summarise the various hypotheses advanced in recent years,
but it should be recalled that the *Nota Emilianense*, quoted earlier
in connection with the *Chanson de Roland*,[38] makes mention of a
certain Guillaume 'Curvednose' (Ghigelme alcorbitanas) as one of
Charlemagne's nephews. This Guillaume is not likely to have been
other than the hero of the *Couronnement de Louis*, Guillaume al
Cort Nés, probably originally *al corb nés*, as he is indeed called in
the *chanson* that bears his name.[39] We have seen that his historical
prototype was indeed a relative of Charlemagne, but a cousin, not
nephew. The only safe conclusion that can be drawn from the *Nota
Emilianense* and other Latin fragments such as the *Fragment de la
Haye*[40] is that there was already a legendary Guillaume, as there
was also a legendary Roland, before the *chansons de geste* that we
have inherited, but nothing that has so far come to light authorises
one to trace the origins of such legends further back with absolute
certainty than the second half of the eleventh century.

V. THE 'CHARROI DE NÎMES'

In the manuscripts that have preserved the text of the *Couronnement de Louis*, Guillaume's adventures continue in *Le Charroi de
Nîmes*,[41] which tells the following tale.

On returning to Paris from a hunt, Guillaume is met by his nephew
Bertran with the news that the king has distributed fiefs among his barons,
but has overlooked Guillaume. Without further ado Guillaume goes immediately to the palace and seeks the king. He reminds Louis of his long
and faithful service and is told in reply that when one of the barons dies,
he will be granted his lands and his wife too if he is so inclined. That he
has to wait for a dead man's shoes fills Guillaume with rage, and he reproaches the king bitterly with his failure to give him his due reward. In a
fierce diatribe, Guillaume recounts his many exploits on Louis's behalf,
so summarising much of the action of the *Couronnement*. Louis in despair
offers various territories to Guillaume, who turns them down on the grounds
that the rightful heirs to these lands would have to be dispossessed. Louis
then offers him a quarter of his own kingdom, an offer which Guillaume
also rejects since the other barons would accuse him of being a usurper. A
solution to the resulting impasse is found by Bertran, who suggests that
Guillaume could ask for the lands in the south of France and in Spain still

in the hands of the Saracens. Louis is reluctant, and would willingly part
with the crown in favour of Guillaume, but is finally persuaded to accept
Bertran's proposition, and an army of 30,000 men is assembled. Guillaume,
on hearing just before his departure that Aymon, a baron, is accusing him of
exposing the kingdom to attacks and leaving it helpless, hastily returns to
the palace, dispatches the baron in his favourite pugilistic manner,[42] and
throws the body out of the window. He then sets off. Their journey south
is carefully described, coresponding in fact to pilgrim routes from the
north of France to Saint-Gilles. They travel to Brioude, and then on through
Berry and Auvergne leaving Clermont-Ferrand on their right, down along
the 'voie de Regordane',[43] turning off to Le Puy in order to pray at the
church of Notre Dame and to leave offerings there. They then don their
armour, expecting to meet the Saracens as they journey further in the direction of Nîmes. On their way they meet a peasant on whose cart is a large
barrel of salt. This prompts one of Guillaume's knights to suggest that they
withdraw to Regordane, commandeer a thousand such carts, oxen, and
barrels in which to hide the knights, and capture Nîmes. This is done
and the ox-drivers dress up as merchants. Bertran wears a rough woollen
tunic and large ox-hide shoes with the tops burst open. Guillaume makes
fun of him and laughs at his clumsy efforts to get his cart moving. Guillaume
fares little better, riding a feeble mare, wearing a long woollen garment
that hangs down to his knees and a woollen bonnet on his head. The
whole convoy successfully enters the city of Nîmes and Guillaume opens
negotiations with the Arab leaders. The Saracens make fun of the disguised Guillaume and pull his beard, whereupon Guillaume loses his
temper and deals their leader a mighty blow with his fist 'que gros ot et
quarré' (line 1375), breaking his neck, as he had done earlier with the
traitors Arneïs and Aymon. He then sounds his horn and the knights sally
forth from their barrels. The battle is fierce but quickly over, and Guillaume
is master of the city of Nîmes.

An important feature of medieval literature well illustrated by the
Charroi de Nîmes is the ability to mix the serious with the humorous
without loss of effectiveness. Once more the character of Guillaume
epitomises the whole work. In several different ways he is a comical
figure despite himself, or so he can hardly fail to appear in modern
eyes: in running to see the king he bursts the leather straps of his
gaiters; he shatters his bow as he leans on it in the king's presence
(sure signs of Guillaume's agitation, and clumsy strength); he
solemnly greets Bertran's suggestion that he should carve his fief
out of Arab-held territories with the unconvincing remark that he
had had the same idea himself. This uninhibited figure without
a care for his personal dignity is something of an anti-Roland when
he dons a peasant's woollen bonnet and mounts 'une jument molt
foible' (a very feeble mare), with ancient stirrups and spurs. But
he has his pathetic moments too. Having rejected Louis's offer of
half his kingdom for fear of being thought a usurper, he reflects as
they encamp after the first day's march southwards that he has
perhaps been wrong and that it would now be said of him that he
was quite mad to go off and endeavour to conquer territories where
he had no rightful inheritance. Bertran puts a peremptory stop to

such thoughts in a manner not uncharacteristic of the entire work by suggesting that it is high time they had their supper. Guillaume's depression soon passes. He is at his most impressive and grandiose, and the text in consequence at its most nearly epic, in his fierce diatribe against the king:

'Quant el mostier Marie Magdalaine
Et Herneïs por son riche lignage
Vot la corone par devers li atrere,
Quant ge le vi, de bel ne m'en fu gaire;
Ge li doné une colee large,
Que tot envers l'abati sor le marbre:
Haïz en fui de son riche lignage,
Passai avant si con la cort fu large,
Que bien le virent et li un et li autre,
Et l'apostoile et tuit li patriarche;
Pris la corone, sor le chief l'enportastes.
De cest servise ne vos remenbre gueres,
Quant vos sanz moi departistes voz terres'.

(169–81)

'When in the church of Mary Magdalene I saw Herneïs trying to get the crown for himself because of his powerful lineage, this scarcely pleased me. I gave him a mighty blow which spreadeagled him on the marble. In so doing I earned the hatred of his powerful lineage. I came to the front across the width of the Court in full view of everybody including the pope and all the patriarchs. I took the crown, you wore it on your head. To this service you pay little heed, when without me you shared out your lands'.

In such lines there is a clear, noble ring, a note of indignation and just outrage that can only have met with a sympathetic response from a twelfth-century audience accustomed to the idea that the feudal system imposed certain duties and loyalties on the suzerains as well as on the vassals. That Guillaume's claims were legitimate, that he deserved his reward, must have seemed perfectly obvious, and must have met with even more sympathy when he refused any offer which would deprive others of their rightful inheritance. This was no trivial issue, and it is no mere chance that it takes up some 600 lines of the total of 1,486, whereas the scenes of actual fighting in the streets of Nîmes take up a mere sixty. Its very seriousness gives an almost lyrical note to Guillaume's reproaches:

'Looÿs, sire', Guillelme a respondu,
'Tant t'ai servi que le poil ai chanu,
N'i ai conquis vaillissant un festu,
Ne en ta cort en fusse mielz vestu;
Encor ne sai quel part torne mon huis.
Looÿs, sire, qu'est vo sens devenuz?
L'en soloit dire que g'estoie voz druz.
Et chevauchoie les bons chevaus crenuz,
Et vos servoie par chans et par paluz.

'Louis, sire', Guillaume replied, 'I have served you so long that my hair is white, and I have got not a farthing out of it, nor was I better clad in your Court as a result. I still do not know in what direction to turn. Louis, sire, are you out of your mind? It used to be said that I was your favourite and I used to ride fine horses with flowing manes, and serve you over fields and marshland. May God curse anyone who ever profited from this or who got a

Maldahé ait qui onques mielz en
  fu,
Ne qui un clo en ot en son escu
Se d'autrui lance ne fu par mal
  feru.
Plus de vint mile ai tüé de faus
  Turs;
Mes, par celui qui maint el ciel
  lasus,
Ge tornerai le vermeill de l'escu.
Fere porroiz que n'ere mes vo dru!'
                (256–71)

single nail in his shield because of
it, unless it was pierced by another's
lance. More than 20,000 treacherous
Turks have I killed, but by the God
in heaven above, I shall forsake my
allegiance. You could act in such a
way that I was no longer your
favourite!'

Only in its reflection of vital feudal issues can the text claim to be
in any way historical. Long before Charlemagne's time and that of
his son Louis, in the reign of Charles Martel, Nîmes was in fact
twice occupied by the Saracens, in 719 and 737, but it need hardly
be said that Charles Martel's retaking of the town bore no resemblance to the method adopted by Guillaume.[44] Despite his bitterness,
and the occasional moment of depression, Guillaume remains the
character that he had been in the *Couronnement*: though serious
when the mood demanded, he was normally gay and hearty,
Rabelaisian almost as he laughed out loud at some remark or jest –
's'en a un ris geté' is a favourite expression applied to him – an
inspiring leader of men but without that single, high-minded
purpose characteristic of Roland which would never have allowed
that more noble and tragic hero to resort to subterfuge in order to
vanquish the pagan foe as Guillaume did not hesitate to do.
Guillaume's *amour-propre* was more moral than physical. He had
no objection to dressing up as a peasant, but he would not allow the
king to treat him like one.

Particularly comical is Guillaume's attitude to the fair sex and
its total lack of courtly pretence. One scene describes his alarm
when a lady takes him into an upstairs room and falls at his feet:

Cuidai, beau sire, qu'el queïst
  amistiez
Ou itel chose que fame a home
  quiert.
Se gel seüsse, ne m'en fusse
  aprochiez
Qui me donast mil livres de
  deniers.
Demandai li: 'Dame, fame, que
  quierz?'
– 'Merci, Guillelemes, nobile
  chevalier.
De ceste terre quar vos preigne pitié,
Por amor Deu qui en croiz fu
  drecié'.
                (561–8)

I thought, good sir, that she was
after love or whatever a woman
expects of a man. Had I known that
such was the case, I would not have
gone near her for a thousand pounds.
I asked her: 'Lady, woman, what do
you want?' 'Mercy, Guillaume, noble
knight, please take pity on this land
for love of Christ who was crucified'.

Guillaume is vastly relieved to discover that what is expected of him is not romance and love but merely a military campaign to rid the region of Arab invaders, a request with which he is only too happy to comply, for this at least is a matter in which he feels some competence.

VI. THE 'PRISE D'ORANGE'

Guillaume's campaign of conquest in the south of France takes on a different aspect in *La Prise d'Orange*,[45] which follows *Le Charroi de Nîmes* in the cyclic manuscripts:

It is early summertime, the woods are in flower, the meadows growing green, and even Guillaume's fancies lightly turn to thoughts of love. After all, life in Nîmes is boring, the more so as they have no minstrels to entertain them, no damsels to help while away the time. It would, Guillaume muses, be a good idea to send for a thousand maidens from the north to bring some pleasure into their dull lives. While such delectable, and uncharacteristic, thoughts are going through his mind, a Christian, by name Guillebert, who has just escaped from the Turks in Orange, arrives dishevelled and starving on the scene. After being revived with a copious meal of cranes, wild geese, and peacocks in pepper sauce, he tells Guillaume about the magnificent fortress of Orange and the force of 20,000 pagans holding it under King Arragon, son of Tibaut. Queen Orable, Tibaut's wife, most beautiful lady of the whole Orient, whose skin is as white as blossom, is also there. She lives in a splendid palace, resounding with the song of birds, the calls of falcons and hawks, the neighing of horses, the braying of mules, and the merrymaking of the Saracens. Guillaume decides then and there that he will take 'la dame et la cité'. Now firmly enamoured of the oriental princess, he sets off in disguise with some followers to see Orable in Orange – an apparently onomastically (or mnemonically) inspired beginning to the fantastic tale of adventure that follows. At Orange they are well received when they present themselves as Turks newly arrived from Africa with news of King Arragon's father and pretend they have been held prisoners on the way by the mighty Guillaume in Nîmes. On setting eyes on Orable, Guillaume can only exclaim 'This is Paradise', the nearest he was ever to come (in this work at least) to paying her a compliment, nor is it at all obvious that he is thinking of her, for he could very well have been referring to the splendours of the palace. In the ensuing conversation he takes advantage of his disguise to tell her what a splendid fellow Guillaume is, though the features he picks out for special mention hardly seem calculated to please a lady: large fists, powerful arms, and the strength to cut Saracens in two with his sword! While they are conversing Guillaume is recognised and challenged. After saying a quick prayer, he lays about him with his stick, and his companions do likewise, to such effect that they kill fourteen Turks. Guillaume, Guielin, and Guillebert (the text makes great play with their names) soon have the palace of Gloriete to themselves, and Orable. She gives Guillaume her husband's best armour and equips the other two as best she can. Thus accoutred, they easily repel the Saracens' attacks and all would have been well had it not been for a secret underground passage leading the enemy into the palace. The three Christians are overwhelmed and would have been killed on the spot had it not been for the intervention of Orable. The Christians are thrown into prison. Their

suspicions that Orable has betrayed them are quickly dispelled when the
queen offers to release them and become a Christian provided Guillaume will
marry her. Guillaume is delighted by this proposition (or proposal) and they
are free once more. Through another secret tunnel Guillebert is dispatched
to Nîmes and informs Bertran of their perilous plight. Meantime King
Arragon learns of their escape, and Guillaume and Guielin, along with
Orable, are recaptured and thrown into a dungeon. There Guielin taunts his
uncle with the folly of his amorous exploit: Guillaume Fierebrace (William
Strongarm) would be known henceforth as Guillaume l'Amïable (William
Loverboy). Uncle and nephew are brought before Arragon for their fate to
be decided. They escape once more, fighting with whatever weapons they
can set hands on, to such effect that fourteen Turks lie dead and the Saracens are driven out of the palace. Soon after, Bertran and his men, led by
Guillebert, enter the palace through the secret passageway, and Orange is
in Christian hands.[46] Guillaume, Guillebert, and Guielin thus emerge triumphant from their incredible adventures, and Orable becomes Guillaume's
wife and is baptised Guibourc! Guillaume and Guibourc, Guillebert and
Guielin, along with their army, live for thirty years in Orange, repelling
daily attacks by the Saracens. The reader is left to suppose that, some time
in that period, Tibaut, who had been summoned by Arragon, at last turned
up from Africa with his army, and was defeated by Guillaume.

This swashbuckling, preposterous, cloak-and-dagger melodrama
indisputably brought a new and startling dimension to the Guillaume
cycle only faintly presaged by the *Charroi de Nîmes*. It would be
tempting to dismiss the *Prise d'Orange* as a tardy excrescence, an
interlude in the series of crusading and feudal wars whose aim
was to provide Guillaume with a wife of suitably heroic stature and
at the same time to develop the comic relief already present in the
second half of the *Charroi*, were it not that there are good grounds
for believing that this late twelfth-century *chanson* was a revision of
one now lost which dated from the beginning of the century and
which was possibly earlier than either the *Couronnement* or the
Charroi.[47] Since this earlier version has not survived, the extent
of the revision cannot be measured. Orange may have been captured
in that earlier and scarcely less fictitious account as a result of a
more conventional siege.[48] It is likely also that Orable figured
already in the early version, though how romantic that story was
cannot be said. Not that the extant story is particularly romantic.
Not one direct compliment does Guillaume pay Orable, there are no
sighs, no tender glances, no declarations of eternal love of the type
prescribed by the *fin' amors* doctrine.[49] Not once is Guillaume referred to as a handsome or prepossessing figure, and it is difficult
to understand why Orable should fall in love with him and eventually propose marriage (conveniently forgetting her ageing Saracen
husband), for, as we have seen, it was indeed from her that the proposal came. It is as though the poet had no idea of how to
handle scenes of affection and tenderness, or was singularly uninterested by them, and solved the predicament by sending his

characters hurtling about violently in all directions, the three Christians spending much of their time belabouring Saracens with clubs. Orable's first act, which shows that Guillaume has gained her favours, is to give him her husband's best armour, which Arragon has coveted but has never been allowed to wear. However, she gives it to Guillaume not out of affection, but out of pity because of his desperate plight. Pity evidently yields to admiration as a result of Guillaume's tremendous prowess, and this young Saracen beauty doubtless likes her men to be rough, tough, and bawdy . . . Guillaume must be the clumsiest lover in all French literature, and their courtship, if indeed their series of lightning encounters in and out of secret tunnels, dungeons, and palaces can be so called, is the most hair-raising and hectic of all times. The sole visible effect of love on Guillaume is that, compared with the hero of the *Couronnement* and the *Charroi*, he appears to act in a somewhat dazed and absentminded fashion. Not one of his famous punches does he deliver, and he stands meekly by while his nephew Guielin executes a perfect imitation of the famous right hook, of which Guillaume has so far been the only practitioner.[50] Orable for her part is more of a companion and counsellor, at times a sort of *dea ex machina*, than a true lady of courtly stamp, but the story invites us to be indulgent because of her great beauty.

Judgements of this work have understandably been extremely harsh, and it has to be admitted that at first sight it appears unworthy of those that precede it in the cycle, and certainly unworthy of the *Chanson de Roland*, for it lacks almost totally that strong sense of mission and purpose which, affecting the others in different ways and in varying degrees, lifted them beyond the level of mere adventure stories: the crusading ardour of Roland and Charlemagne, Guillaume's strict devotion to the rightful king and so to the Christian religion, with all that such a twofold devotion involved. Not until the second half of the *Charroi de Nîmes* does the sense of purpose and urgency diminish, but the motivation for that adventure is firmly based: Guillaume was to extend the king's domains, and at the same time obtain for himself a fief which he would hold under Louis's sovereignty. Though the reasons for the taking of Orange were basically the same, they seem less important than Guillaume's desire to set eyes on the beautiful Saracen princess, a desire which determined the peculiar nature of the enterprise and prevented the intervention of the Christian army until the very last moment. However, to condemn the *Prise d'Orange* as unworthy of the genre is shortsighted: clearly this was not the feeling in the late twelfth and thirteenth centuries when the cyclic manuscripts were prepared. Evidently the term *chanson de geste* was sufficiently broad to embrace many different types of activity and

feats of arms. It is, the preamble claims, a 'chançon de bone geste'.
A certain amount of parody and horseplay was not precluded, and
the *Chanson de Roland* was not the sole worthy model. The author
of the *Prise d'Orange* has been reproached with inconsistencies and
'invraisemblance', but a certain lack of attention to details, such
as Guillaume's conversing directly and effortlessly with the Saracens
when in fact he had taken Guillebert with him as interpreter, merely
invites the complicity of the audience and was probably not found
at all shocking by those for whom it was designed.[51] The dominating
features of the poem make of it, in the view of a recent editor, 'un
chef d'œuvre d'humour', and his comparison of the *Prise d'Orange*
with that other delightful parody of not altogether dissimilar themes,
Aucassin et Nicolete, seems particularly apt.[52]

VII. THE 'CHANSON DE GUILLAUME'

Our next analysis looks beyond the cyclic manuscripts to the
poem which bears the name of the eponymous hero: the *Chanson
de Guillaume*.[53] This work, brought to light in 1901, has survived
in one isolated Anglo-Norman manuscript, limited to this one text.
We have chosen this work rather than one of the half-dozen or so
that follow the *Prise d'Orange* in the cyclic manuscripts because,
alone of the hundred or so *chansons de geste* to have survived, it has
been judged by some scholars the equal or near equal of the
Chanson de Roland. This is a matter of opinion, but it is a fair
claim that nowhere in the many thousands of lines singing the
exploits of Guillaume Fierebrace is the epic spirit more poignantly
expressed than in the first two thousand lines of the *Chanson de
Guillaume*. Many problems surround this work, none more thorny
than that of its date of composition. That competent scholars should
differ in their estimates by a century or more is an indication of the
extreme difficulty involved. The extant version is probably late
twelfth century or early thirteenth, judging from linguistic evidence,
but how can the date be determined of the earlier versions which
have not survived? Consensus of opinion, in so far as there is any consensus, places the composition of the original work some time in the
twelfth century, so making it a later work than the *Chanson de
Roland*, and possibly, though by no means certainly, later also than
the poems of the Guillaume cycle analysed above. At least on the
face of it – though nothing in the *chansons de geste* can or should
ever be taken solely at face value – a late dating appears justified,
for in this poem the doughty warrior Guillaume is old and tired:

'Veil sui e feble, ne puis armes   'I am old and feeble, I can no longer
   porter'.   (line 1336)   bear arms'.

a line recalling the Charlemagne of the *Couronnement de Louis*, but this avowal by Guillaume was made in a moment of discouragement that was not to last for long, despite the fact that he was by this time 350 years old, a ripe old age even by epic standards! Moreover, Guillaume is no longer invariably in the foreground, the sole dominating figure that he was in the *Couronnement* and the *Charroi*. Not least among his supporters is his faithful and courageous wife Guibourc, who at one stage raises an army to enable the vanquished Guillaume to return to the fray. Guillaume's role, it will be observed, recalls that of Charlemagne in the *Chanson de Roland*, while that of his nephew Vivien seems to combine the roles of Roland and Oliver.[54]

The first line of the *Chanson de Guillaume* promises a poem of 'great battles and violent conflicts'. A messenger arrives at Bourges and announces to Tedbald, his nephew Esturmi, and Vivien, Guillaume's nephew, that King Deramed has left Cordova, sailed up the Gironde, and is destroying the churches and capturing the knights in the region of Archamp-sur-mer. Tedbald, although returning from vespers, is so drunk that he can hardly stand up. Vivien advises Tedbald to send the news at once to Guillaume, but Esturmi disagrees since Guillaume is sure to be given all the credit for any victory. Three times Vivien urges Tedbald to ask Guillaume for his help, but Tedbald merely calls for wine, drinks a toast to Esturmi, and boasts that they will soon be shattering Arabian armour. The next day Tedbald is alarmed to see the Saracen army approaching, and cannot remember whether he has summoned Guillaume or not. He dons his armour and leads 10,000 men on to the field of battle. On seeing the size of the Saracen fleet Tedbald is terrified and will not engage battle without Guillaume. Vivien points out that to withdraw before battle has even been joined would disgrace Christianity. As the Saracen army disembarks and advances towards the wooded country, the ground trembles beneath their feet and the sunlight flashing on their armour lights up the woods all around. Tedbald and Esturmi tear down their banners, trample them underfoot so that they are not recognised as the leaders, and flee, leaving Vivien in charge of the Christians. The men acknowledge him as their new commander, and Vivien, raising his banner aloft, proclaims Charlemagne's warcry 'Monjoie'. Vivien kills the first Saracen, while the cowards among the Christians follow Tedbald's example and take to flight. As Tedbald passes near some gallows where four robbers are hanging, his horse rears up and one of the corpses brushes against his mouth. So terrified is Tedbald that he empties his bowels. He is pursued by the young Girard, cousin of Vivien, who unhorses Tedbald so that his helmet sinks into the ground. While Girard rides back to join Vivien in the fray, Tedbald remounts and continues his terrified flight through a flock of sheep. He reaches Bourges with the head of a sheep caught fast in his stirrups. The Christians under Vivien fight valiantly, but outnumbered and without Guillaume to help them, they are steadily cut down by the Arabs. Descriptions of the wounded Christians leave nothing to the imagination: bloodstained harness, pools of blood on the saddles between their legs, men holding in their bowels to prevent the horses from trampling them underfoot. Their numbers are gradually reduced. Out of 10,000 only a hundred remain, half of them wounded. Vivien urges them to leave the field of battle, and for a short time remains alone with Girard, but, finding themselves surrounded, the Christians rejoin their leader. Vivien sends Girard, still unwounded, through the enemy lines to summon help from Guillaume. Girard's horse collapses beneath him, and he continues on foot, tormented by thirst in the hot, dry atmosphere. One after the other he abandons his weapons and pieces of armour until only his sword remains, and in that state he finally reaches Guillaume and gives him the news. Meantime Vivien fights on, with twenty men, then ten, until finally he is left alone. The Arabs surround him and harass him like a pack of hounds attacking a wild boar. Vivien is hacked to death and his body hidden so that the Christians will not find it.

In Barcelona Guillaume receives from Girard the news of the Christian massacre. Only three days previously Guillaume had returned from a battle in which he had lost many men. Had it not been for Guibourc's entreaty he would have refused to go to the help of his nephew. Meantime Guibourc serves Girard, who has not eaten for three days, with a gigantic meal at which he drinks a gallon of wine in two gulps – a sure sign, says Guibourc, that he is of Guillaume's lineage. The next day Guillaume and Girard set off for Archamp with an army of 30,000. The battle, not described at all, lasts from Monday until Thursday, and finally only three Christians are left: Guillaume, Girard, and Guibourc's nephew Guischard. At length, finding himself the sole survivor, Guillaume departs:

N'en fuit mie Willame, ainz s'en vait.	Guillaume does not flee, he just goes away.

(1225)

Meanwhile, in Barcelona Guibourc has assembled another Christian army of 30,000 men. She comforts the vanquished Guillaume, and having asked his permission to lie to the men she has gathered, she tells them that her husband has returned victorious, and has killed the Saracen King Deramed, but has been unable to annihilate the enemy. Now it is their duty to accompany Guillaume on this final mission. Gui, a young nephew of Guillaume's not yet fifteen years old, asks permission to go with him. He argues fiercely when Guillaume refuses, forcing his uncle to admit

'Cors as d'enfant e si as raisun de ber'.	'You have the body of a child but the mind of a man'.

(1479)

Despite his diminutive stature

Mielz portad armes que uns hom de trente anz	He carried his arms better than a thirty-year-old man.

(1556)

There is only a foot and a half of him showing above the saddle bow, but Guillaume eventually agrees to let him fight after Gui has demonstrated how well he can handle his horse. The battle rages from Monday to Wednesday (1771, 1919) until finally only Guillaume and his nephew remain. Gui weeps not because of the battle, but because of his extreme hunger. Guillaume sends him to the place where they had surprised the Saracens taking their meal, and continues the fight alone. Gui eats heartily and returns just in time to save Guillaume whose horse has been killed beneath him. So mighty are Gui's blows that the remaining Saracens think that he is Vivien come back to life, and flee:

Ço fu grant miracle que nostre sire fist;	This was a great miracle that Our Lord accomplished. Because of a single man 20,000 took to flight.
Pur un sul home en fuirent vint mil.	

(1858–9)

Gui gives Guillaume his horse and follows on foot. They meet and kill the Saracen King Deramed, and their victory is then complete:

Lores fu mecresdi	Then it was Wednesday. Now Guil-
Ore out vencu sa bataille Willame	laume had won his battle.
(1979–80)	

Although the series of battles which had cost the lives of some 70,000 Frenchmen was over, the sole extant version of the *Chanson de Guillaume* does not end at this point. Like the *Chanson de Roland*, *Raoul de Cambrai*, and others, the *Chanson de Guillaume* appears to reach its climax long before the end, little more than half-way through. However, the remaining episodes are believed by many scholars to be the work of a different author and to have been added to the original *chanson* by a late revisor. They are taken up principally with the exploits of Rainouart, a giant who, with his 'tinel', a club made out of a tree trunk, slaughters Saracens by the hundred and ensures final victory for the Christians. Such a fantastic folklorish figure presented the author with numerous opportunities for developing an element of farce and buffoonery, and he took full advantage of this, as when the giant decides that he would carry seven shields at a time, wear seven hauberks on his back and seven helmets on his head, or when, having shattered his tree trunk, he becomes even more redoubtable using his bare fists, or when, condescending for a time to use a sword, he is delighted to find it so sharp and declares that each knight should carry four of these little things. Although the escapades of Rainouart may have formed a separate work originally – the *Chanson de Rainouart* as some scholars have called them – the very fact that the sole surviving manuscript has attempted to fuse the two *chansons* into one work[55] reveals that medieval propensity for passing from the sublime to the ridiculous in a manner which the modern reader can only find disconcerting. Tragedy, comedy, and farce were not then the separate entities they were to become in later epochs, even though some of the best works were wholly serious and others wholly farcical. There were no fixed rules, doctrines, and precepts of the type later to dominate French literature. We may imagine that a medieval audience listening to a performance of the *Chanson de Guillaume* in the form in which it has come down to us would have reacted with anger and scorn on hearing of Tedbald's cowardice, wept bitterly as Vivien met his heroic end, loved and admired Guillaume, their favourite hero of old, as again and again he returned to the fray, and roared with delight at the fantastic exploits of the giant Rainouart. They were carried through a whole gamut of violent emotions and are not likely to have been unduly worried by the inconsistencies and changes in style which a study of the text reveals. Farce, moreover, is by no means limited to the later episodes, as the details of Tedbald's cowardice reveal, or the amusing episode of Gui, a dwarf figure as redoubtable in his way as was the great Rainouart in his. It would be unwise to hazard a guess at which scenes of so disparate a work lingered on in the medieval mind longer than others, but a modern reader is most likely to remember above all the martyrdom of Vivien, not only because in such scenes the *chansons de geste* appear as a specific genre with no rival elsewhere, but because even within the genre itself there are few scenes to rival this one. Buffoonery of the Rainouart type, on the other hand, was common currency found also in the romances and *fabliaux*.

Apart from its geography – so fantastic that one wonders whether it could ever have been written by a continental Frenchman – the first half of the work is marked by a strong vein of realism. The Christian heroes, Vivien chief among them, die a death without divine intervention, for no angels appear from on high to bear their souls to God, as happened with Roland. It is a death without that stylisation so much in evidence in the *Chanson de Roland* which robs death of its harshness and cruelty. The author knows the appearance of death, and describes it exactly as he has seen it:

Troble out le vis, e pasle la
maissele,
Turnez les oilz qui li sistrent en la
teste;
Tote la langue li pendit sur
senestre,
Sur le mentun li enbrunchat sun
halme.

(lines 1298–1301)[56]

His face was troubled, his cheeks pale, his eyes turned upwards in their sockets. All his tongue hung out on the left, and his helmet slumped over his chin.

It is death without hope, for no trumpets, however far off, have promised Vivien that help is on the way. It is death without supernatural glory and poetic beauty, death as it happened on the battlefield, the crusaders' heroic sacrifice receiving no visible acknowledgement in the heavens above: it all had to come from within, a matter of personal conviction and devotion to beliefs. Realism is shown in other ways too: the Christians are not all perfect and saintly warriors, even though the pagans for their part are uniformly evil. There are cowards, drunkards, and braggarts among the Christian leaders,[57] and even the most courageous cannot fight for hours on end without being tormented by hunger and thirst. Their bodily needs are not held in abeyance as they fight on behalf of their religion, as seems to happen in the first masterpiece of the genre. This is a *Chanson de Roland* brought down to earth: the sun will not stand still in the sky, angels will not be heard shouting exhortations, men scream with pain as they are cut to pieces. There is epic exaggeration in the huge numbers of Saracens killed by the

Christian heroes in their superhuman efforts, but apart from this characteristic of the genre there is no idealisation and remarkably little glorification of the Christian cause. The heroes are not diminished thereby, rather is their stature increased, for they stand on their own and there can be no assurance of ultimate victory.

Realism, and lack of stylisation and symbolism of the kind found in the *Chanson de Roland*, do not mean that the *Chanson de Guillaume* is devoid of poetic qualities. These are perhaps most in evidence in the technique of repetition that the poet uses so frequently and to such dramatic, indeed lyrical, effect. When Girard leaves the battle in order to bring help to Vivien, he abandons one after the other his weapons and pieces of armour until at last only his sword remains:

LX

'Ohi, grosse hanste, cume peises al braz;
Nen aidera a Vivien en l'Archamp
Qui se combat a dolerus ahan'.
Dunc la lance Girard en mi le champ.

'Oh mighty spear, how you weigh on my arm. I cannot help Vivien in the Archamp, fighting in such pain and suffering'. Then Girard throws it into the middle of the field.

LXI

'Ohi, grant targe, cume peises al col;
Nen aidera a Vivié a la mort'.
El champ la getad, si la tolid de sun dos.

'Oh mighty shield, how you weigh on my neck. I cannot help Vivien at his death'. Into the field he threw it, and removed it from his back.

LXII

'Ohi, bone healme, cum m'estunes la teste;
Nen aiderai a Vivien en la presse
Ki se cumbat el Archamp sur l'erbe'.
Il le lançad et jetad cuntre terre.
(716–26)

'Oh good helmet, how you daze my head. I cannot help Vivien in the fray, fighting in the Archamp on the grass'. He hurled it away and cast it to the ground.

Earlier, when Vivien gives Girard his message for Guillaume, the same technique is used, this time in the form of questions:

LIII

'Sez que dirras a Willame le fedeil?
Se lui remenbre del chanp Turlen le rei,
U jo li fis batailles trente treis...'
(655–7)

'Do you know what you will tell Guillaume the faithful? Remind him of the war with Turleen the king, where I fought thirty-three battles for him...'

LIV

'Sez que dirras a Willame le bon franc?
Se lui remenbre de la bataille grant
Desuz Orenge de Tedbalt l'esturman...'
(666–9)

'Do you know what you will tell the good noble Guillaume? Remind him of the great battle beneath Orange of Tedbalt the steersman...'

LV

'Sez que dirras a Guiot mun petit
  frere?
De hui a quinze anz, ne deust
  ceindre espee.
Mais ore la ceindrat pur secure le
  fiz sa mere ...'

'Do you know what you will tell
Guiot my little brother? For the next
fifteen years he should not gird on a
sword. But now he will do so to help
his mother's son ...'

(679–81)

Another striking feature of the *chanson* is the recurrence as a
sort of refrain of a hemistich indicating the day and time of day
when the battle was fought: 'Lunesdi al vespre' (Monday in the
evening) (repeated 15 times), 'Joesdi al vespre' (Thursday in the
evening) (seven times), etc. There is an ominous ring in these expressions, a sort of knell that marks the crucial points of the long-
drawn-out series of battles. The resemblance of such techniques to
those of popular poetry, particularly to those of early ballad forms,
has often been noticed.

> In its metrical form, in its conception and execution, in the dominance
> of the poet by his material, it [the *Chanson de Guillaume*] has the un-
> mistakable stamp of the popular heroic poetry. Its affinities lie with the
> ballad poetry, with the rude and vigorous productions of the wandering
> minstrel. Of especial significance in this connection are the repetitions, 'the
> soul of balladry' according to one of the latest writers on the subject ...[58]

Miss Pope goes on:

> The similarity between the *Willelme* [i.e., the *Chanson de Guillaume*] and
> the ballad extends to ... the short two-, three- or four-lined strophe and
> the rudimentary refrain. It is equally apparent ... in all the other marked
> features of the poem, as for instance, the terseness, baldness, even triviality
> of the diction, the use of short question and answer, the slightness of the
> characterisation and absence of all detailed description of the enemy, all
> well known characteristics of the 'ballad' poem – and all we may add
> absent from the *Roland*.[59]

For Miss Pope these traits were proof of the earliness of the *Chanson
de Guillaume*, but it would be as well at this juncture to heed
Professor McMillan's warning: '... qui dit poésie populaire ne dit
pas nécessairement poésie ancienne'.[60] Although popular refrain
songs, possibly associated with dancing, may well have existed in
France in a wide variety of forms already in the early Middle
Ages, very little is known about them. Their descendants are
the relatively sophisticated fixed forms – the *ballades*, *rondeaux*,
and *virelais* – of which the earliest extant date from the thirteenth century. Indeed the word *ballade* (from Late Latin
ballare, to dance, cf. French *bal*, *ballet* and English *ball*), of
Provençal origin, is not attested in northern France before
the mid-thirteenth century, and though the popular ballad was to
have a long and immense vogue in England, it is difficult to produce

irrefutable proof that it flourished there before 1300.[61] Accordingly, the exact relationship of the *Chanson de Guillaume* to medieval balladry remains something of a mystery. Inevitably, various hypotheses have been put forward. The resemblance has been adduced as evidence of theories that existed before the *Chanson de Guillaume* was known, to the effect that the *chansons de geste* originated as series of popular ballads run together. Conversely it has been suggested that the fragmentation of the *chansons de geste*, which indeed are often episodic in nature, led to the formation of the ballads. The only safe conclusion is that in varying degrees both *chansons de geste* and ballads were types of composition relying on an essentially oral art, needing to be read or sung aloud to achieve their full effects, hence the artistic use in both media of repetitions, whether this was the 'incremental repetition' used in the ballads and certain passages of the *Chanson de Guillaume*, or the more sophisticated use of *laisses similaires* to be found in most *chansons de geste* and which are used to the greatest effect in the *Chanson de Roland*.

VIII. 'GORMONT ET ISEMBART'

Affinities with the popular ballad are also found in the surviving fragment of a twelfth-century *chanson de geste* known as *Gormont et Isembart*.[62] The 661 lines which are extant are taken up entirely with the account of a battle which took place near Cayeux-sur-mer in Picardy between the army of King Louis, son of Charlemagne, and a Saracen army led by Gormont and a Christian renegade, Isembart. Gormont wrought great havoc among the Christian ranks, and every time he killed an opponent, his victory was hailed in a refrain with a strongly marked rhythm:

Quant il ot mort le bon vassal	When he had killed the brave young
Ariere enchalce le cheval	nobleman, he drives his horse back.
Puis mist avant sun estandart:	Then he brought forward his stan-
L'em la li baille un tuënart	dard and is given a shield.
(lines 5–8, 37–40 etc . . .)	

So strong was Gormont that his spear sometimes passed right through his opponent and killed the knight behind him as well. After numerous attempts had been made to overcome him, he was finally killed by King Louis himself, though the king suffered so much from his efforts that he died thirty days later. Isembart the renegade, abandoned by the Saracens, pursued by the Christians, fought against his father in the thick of the fray without recognising him. He was finally cut down, and repented just before his death, calling on the Virgin Mary to intercede with Christ on his behalf. This legend, fuller details of which are known from other sources,[63] is based on an historical event, the invasion of the region of Ponthieu and Vimeu in northern France by a Norman army in 881 and the defeat of that army by King Louis III, who reigned from 879 to 882.[64] The Normans have become Saracens in true *chanson de geste* style, their leader is Gormont l'*Arabi*,[65] and their opponent has become Louis son of Charlemagne (lines 276, 289), who, despite the absence of Guillaume and his numerous nephews to whom the fragment makes not the slightest allusion, acquits himself valiantly in the battle. The *laisse similaire* technique is not in evidence in this work, the structure of which is unusual: assonanced octosyllabic verse in *laisses* which vary in length from under ten lines to over fifty. Many lines bear a tonic accent on the fourth syllable,[66] imparting a strongly marked rhythm and swift movement to these lines qualified by Bédier as 'petits vers pressés, robustes, fougueux':[67]

Or fu Hugon al pré a pié,	Now Hugo was dismounted in the meadow, twice wounded by the great spear. Then his charger escaped from him. When Isembart the renegade saw the horse running wild, he promised himself one thing: if he could lay his hands on it, he would let himself be cut to pieces rather than lose it for any man. He went in that direction at a gallop. With the shaft of his spear he wanted to get the horse by the neck. The horse reared its head up high and he could not get hold of it.
Navré dous feiz del grant espié.	
Dunc li eschapa sun destrier.	
Quant Isembart le reneié	
Vit le cheval cure estraer,	
D'une chose s'est afichié:	
S'il poeit as puins baillier,	
Que einz se lerreit detrenchier	
Que mes pur home le perdist.	
Cele part vent tut eslessé;	
Od le restiu de sun espié	
Vot acoler le bon destrier;	
Le cheval porta haut le chef,	
Que il nel pot mie baillier.	

(299–312)

When they tell of the devotion of a heroic knight to the Christian cause, a devotion which often led to his death on the battlefield, the *chansons de geste* are Passion stories whose affinities with the lives of the saints are obvious. When a love element is introduced and such devices as secret disguises and escapes through hidden tunnels, the affinities are rather with the romances which began to appear in the twelfth century. It would be quite wrong to look for a smooth progression from the one to the other. This is impossible to trace in any case, since even the approximate dating of many of these texts is a matter for conjecture, but it was very possible for a *chanson* dealing with martyrdom on the field of battle to appear late in the twelfth century, whereas one of more lighthearted vein could well have appeared earlier. The *Pèlerinage de Charlemagne*, for example, which seems to be something of a parody of the genre, appears to be quite an early work.[68] It tells how Charlemagne and the twelve peers, after bragging about their prowess, are constrained to prove that this is not mere idle boasting. In most *chansons*, the frequent intervention of humour, usually of a coarse and naïve kind, has to be noted. One critic has referred to their 'mélange inattendu du tragique et du comique'.[69] But why 'unexpected'? Unexpected and disconcerting for the modern reader, no doubt, but probably not at all so for the medieval audience. It is true that there is no comic relief in the *Chanson de Roland*, though the scene in which the traitor Ganelon is handed over to the cooks of Charlemagne's household is sometimes looked upon as a farcical interlude. In other *chansons*, particularly those concerned with Guillaume, there is usually some light relief, and for the medieval audience this was probably an advantage of this genre over the more ascetic and edifying hagiographic literature. You could laugh with Guillaume, for he had a robust sense of humour, you could laugh at him when the end of his nose was chopped off or when he decked himself out in peasant garb and rode an ancient mare, but this did not prevent you from admiring his prowess or from weeping for him in moments of danger and disillusionment. These characters were more fully rounded than those depicted in hagiography, superhuman no doubt in their wielding of the sword and in facing the most incredible odds on the battlefield, but downright earthy personalities as well. Not just doughty warriors, but intensely alive figures also; even rebellious barons such as Isembart or Raoul de Cambrai could attract pity and were certainly meant to do so. If we return to the definition of epic poetry quoted earlier: 'a serious theme developed in a coherent and unified manner, and written in a dignified style', we see that, for the majority of the *chansons de geste*, some qualification is needed. The theme was serious, but not necessarily invariably so, the manner was not always coherent and unified, and the style could doff its dignity on occasions. Not, then, a stiff-laced and starchy manifestation of the epic genre, but, after all, neither was the Homeric epic or indeed that of most early civilisations. The mixed genre does not usually go down well with modern readers, but this could be our failing rather than that of the texts themselves.

NOTES

1. 'Hagiographie et poésie épique étaient, dans le monde roman, étroitement entremêlées; dès avant l'époque carolingienne les saints étaient les héros de la Gaule' – C. A. Robson, 'Aux origines de la poésie épique romane', *MA*, LXVII, 1961, 55.

2. The preceding chapter will have made it clear that lives of saints continued to appear throughout the crusading era and were not neglected and abandoned the moment the crusades started. It is certain, however, that the militaristic Christian heroes of the *chanson de geste* seemed more relevant to contemporary conditions, and were more popular, than the early Christian martyrs at the time of the crusades.

3. The meaning of 'gestes' is uncertain. It might stand for 'families' here as it certainly does in other contexts, but it might also be little more than 'stories', 'series of exploits'.

4. Bertran de Bar-sur-Aube, *Girart de Viane*, ed. P. Tarbé, Rheims, 1850, and F. G. Yeandle, New York, 1930, lines 1448 ff. A late and shortened version, based on the Cheltenham ms., has been edited by D. M. Dougherty and E. B. Barnes, under the title *La Geste de Monglane*, Eugene, Oregon, 1966.

5. There was in fact a century between them, Charles Martel (Charlemagne's grandfather) having died in 741, whereas Charles the Bald became king of France in 840.

6. J. Bédier, *Les Légendes Epiques*, Paris, 4 vols., 1908-13, 2nd ed. 1914-1921, II, 302-3.

7. The edition used here is that of F. Whitehead, Oxford, 1947. Those of J. Bédier, Paris, 1921, and G. Moignet, Paris, 1969, include translations into modern French. The most reliable, and recent, English version is that by D. D. R. Owen, *The Song of Roland*, London 1972.

8. The meaning of this line has been much disputed, as also has the identity of Turoldus. Was he a mere jongleur who recited the poem, did he compose an early version, or possibly a later revision? The truth is not known and there are many hypotheses.

9. Ganelon's declaration (3758) that Roland had cheated him of some gold and possessions either points to an earlier quarrel between them, or is an excuse invented by Ganelon to explain his attitude towards his stepson.

10. Anouilh, *Antigone*.

11. G. F. Jones, 'Roland's Lament', *RR*, LIII, no. 1 (1962), 3-15; and J. E. White, 'La Chanson de Roland, Secular or Religious Inspiration?', *R*, LXXXIV, 1963, 398-408.

12. A. Renoir, 'Roland's Lament', *Sp*, XXXV, 1960, 572-83; and White, op. cit., 399-401.

13. ibid., 406-7.

14. ibid., 404-8.

15. See below the analysis of the *Chanson de Guillaume*, pp. 93-5.

16. P. Le Gentil, *La Chanson de Roland*, Paris, 2nd ed., 1967, 105-16. On the question of whether or not the Baligant episode is a later interpolation scholars are still divided. That it is, is argued by D. D. R. Owen, 'Charlemagne's dreams, Baligant and Turoldus', *ZRP*, LXXXVII, 1971, 197-208, and in *The Song of Roland*, 15. For the opposite view see A. Burger, 'Remarques sur la composition de l'épisode de Baligant', *Mélanges . . . Delbouille*, Paris, 1964, II, 59-69.

17. White, op. cit., 407.

18. See above, p. 16 and below, p. 200.

19. As Professor D. McMillan has observed, it is not difficult to invent circumstances which might justify the sequence Oliver-Roland. See his article 'Du Nouveau sur la "Chanson de Roland"?', *MLR*, XLVII, 1952, 339, note 1. See also F. Lecoy's review of R. Menéndez Pidal's *La Chanson de Roland et la tradition épique des Francs*, *R*, LXXXIV, 1963, 117-19.

20. This figure includes half-lines, e.g.

Dist li paiens: 'Mult me   The pagan said: 'I marvel greatly
puis merveiller . . .'   . . .'
(537)

21. A different reading is possible, taking the second line quoted, along with the first, as referring to Roland. The break would then come between the second and third lines of the quotation.

22. For a recent appraisal of the many attempts to solve this problem, which concerns the whole genre, see P. Le Gentil, 'Les Chansons de Geste: Le Problème des Origines', *RHLF*, LXX, 1970, 992-1006.

23. R. Lejeune and J. Stiennon, *La Légende de Roland dans l'art du moyen âge*, Brussels, 2 vols., 1966, I, 402.

24. McMillan, op. cit., 334-9; also Lecoy, op. cit., 88-133.

25. ibid., 132; see also Robson, op. cit., 57-8.

26. Le Gentil, *La Chanson de Roland*, 45-6.

27. Robson, op. cit., esp. 56-8.

28. D. Douglas, 'The "Song of Roland" and the Norman conquest of England', *FS*, XIV, 1960, 99–116.

29. ed. E. Langlois, Paris, CFMA, 1925.

30. He was not averse to marrying a beautiful Saracen princess, conveniently forgetting his wife Orable, as the text points out (1433). Only circumstances prevented this marriage from taking place. Although the exceptional indulgences granted to Guillaume by the pope would have allowed it, Guillaume's loyalty does not seem to have extended to his matrimonial affairs. The concept of *amour courtois* that was soon to reach northern France from the south (and which may have reached it already) demanded absolute loyalty of a lover to a lady who was not his wife, but this loyalty consisted in secrecy and steadfastness, not in bigamous offers of marriage!

31. J. Frappier, *Les Chansons de geste du cycle de Guillaume d'Orange*, I, Paris, 1955; II, Paris, 1965; II, 83.

32. R. Van Waard, 'Le Couronnement de Louis et le principe de l'hérédité de la couronne', *N*, XXX, 1945, 52–8; also U. T. Holmes, *History of Old French Literature*, New York, 1948, 104.

33. L. Halphen, in *Cambridge Medieval History*, V, 1926, 596.

34. D. Scheludko, 'Neues über das Couronnement de Louis' in *Zeitschrift für französische Sprache und Literatur*, LV, 1931, 425–74.

35. G. Seeliger, in *Cambridge Medieval History*, II, 1913, 624–5.

36. *Les Légendes Épiques*, I, 246. Quoted also Frappier, op. cit., II, 77.

37. ibid., I, 65–8.

38. See above, p. 77.

39. See below, p. 92, and Frappier, op. cit., I, 89–94.

40. Le Gentil, *La Chanson de Roland*, chapter iv, 35–64. See also I. Siciliano, *Les Chansons de geste et l'épopée*, Turin, 1968, chapter x.

41. ed. J.-L. Perrier, Paris, CFMA, 1931; 2nd ed. 1968; and more recently D. McMillan, Paris, 1972. Quotations are from the latter.

42. Compare the fate of Arneïs d'Orléans in the *Couronnement de Louis*; see above, p. 78.

43. Frappier, op. cit., II, 190, note 1.

44. ibid., 189.

45. ed. C. Régnier, Paris, 1967 (Bibliothèque Française et Romane, Série B, no. 5).

46. The action appears to be a reversal of that of the *Charroi*, in which the Christians entered Nîmes secretly from the outside. In the *Prise d'Orange*, they made their entry secretly into Orange from *within*.

47. Frappier, op. cit., II, 185–6, 267.

48. Orange was certainly captured by the Arabs, and changed hands several times, in the course of the first half of the eighth century, but Guillaume de Toulouse, historical prototype of our hero, was never involved; ibid., 273, note 3, and 274.

49. See below, p. 120.

50. Guillebert dealt a similar kind of blow to a Saracen who got in his way while he was escaping from Orange, lines 119–23.

51. Régnier, ed. cit., 28–9.

52. ibid., 31.

53. ed. D. McMillan, Paris, SATF, 2 vols. 1949–50.

54. Frappier, op. cit., I, 156–62.

55. Not without serious inconsistencies: Guillaume finds Vivien still alive on the battlefield, whereas he had been killed in the first main encounter, Guibourc is now in Orange and not Barcelona, Gui's weapons are now referred to as being of normal size, Guillaume finds himself face to face with a Saracen king who had been killed in the first encounter. Even within the *Chanson de Guillaume* proper there are inconsistencies, as when Guischard is taken prisoner after he has been killed (line 1722). Frappier, op. cit., I, 142–4.

56. However harshly realistic such descriptions may be, there is no undue insistence on them, any more than there is in the *Roland*. An analysis of the first thousand lines reveals the surprising fact that nearly 50 per cent of them are taken up with dialogue (cf. above, pp. 71–2 on dialogue in the

Chanson de Roland), just over 10 per cent are concerned with fighting, and a little over one per cent only with description of wounds, though it is sometimes difficult to distinguish between these last two categories.

57. In the *Chanson de Roland* even Ganelon was no coward.

58. M. K. Pope, 'Four Chansons de Geste: A Study in Old French Epic Versification', *MLR*, VIII, 1913, 365. The quotation 'the soul of balladry' is taken from F. B. Gummere, *The Popular Ballad*, 1st ed. 1907; reprinted New York, London, 1959, 324.

59. op. cit., 366. This last remark is qualified as follows in a note: 'the baldness of diction alone excepted'.

60. *Chanson de Guillaume*, II, 127.

61. M. J. C. Hodgart, *The Ballads*, London, 1950, 32.

62. ed. A. Bayot, Paris, CFMA, 3rd ed., 1931.

63. Bédier, *Les Légendes Epiques*, IV, 27–38.

64. Bayot, ed. cit., xiii.

65. On whether or not Gormont was a historical personage see Bédier, *Les Légendes Epiques*, IV, 59–81.

66. Bayot, ed. cit., vii; cf. the *Vie de St Brendan*, for which see above, pp. 34–42.

67. *Les Légendes Epiques*, IV, 30.

68. Aebischer, ed. cit., gives it the title *Le Voyage de Charlemagne à Jérusalem et à Constantinople*.

69. J. Bédier and P. Hazard, *Littérature française*, I, Paris, 1923 (revised eds. 1948, 1955), 19.

Chapter 4

TWELFTH-CENTURY LYRIC POETRY

I. THE TROUBADOURS

T HE earliest extant texts in the vernacular to have been composed in France in which love is the dominant theme are the
lyric poems of the troubadours. They are written in the language known as Provençal, although it was in fact spoken in a region
much wider than Provence. Indeed, the earliest troubadours came
from the regions of Limousin and Poitou, between the Loire and the
Garonne, rather than Provence. The first of those surviving date
from the late eleventh century, and were imitated in the north of
France in the last third of the twelfth century. Latin poems of an
affective kind take us much further back in time, to Claudian in the
fourth century and Venantius Fortunatus in the sixth, but here it is
either a matter of epithalamia praising the bride in an important
wedding, or, where the poet's own feelings are involved, of expressions
of tenderness which, as in monastic exchanges of letters and verses,
lean heavily on Ciceronian concepts of *amicitia*, and, inevitably, on
Christian *caritas*.[1] By the twelfth century the feelings portrayed
in Latin verse were of a more passionate kind, but by that time it is
possible that influences had flowed the other way, and that the
Latin verse bore the imprint of the vernacular lyrics.[2] The Provençal
poems appear to have been preceded in the vernacular by the
Mozarabic verse of Spain, which in its earliest surviving forms dates
from the first decades of the eleventh century. Possible Arabic influence on the Romance love lyrics has for long been a hotly
debated subject. Recent research has produced evidence suggesting
that the Arabic *muhwashshahas* were, at least in part, of Romance
origin.[3] Cultural links between the Arabs of Spain and the Courts
of the south of France may have been closer than is generally
realised, but of this there is no concrete proof. Although the Provençal lyric has some affinities with medieval Latin and Mozarabic
verse, and may have been influenced by them in certain respects,
it is a direct continuation of neither. On the other hand, a classical
poet whose influence was immense was Ovid, and indeed the twelfth
century has been referred to as the 'aetas ovidiana'.[4] Since Ovid's
ironical recommendations tended to be taken seriously by medieval
poets, it has been suggested that the whole tone of their poetry can

be explained by the formula 'Ovid misunderstood',[5] though it is readily admitted that it was a consistent and indeed deliberate mis-understanding[6] reflecting the outlook of eleventh- and twelfth-century society. The medieval lover's professedly submissive attitude towards the lady, lacking the hypocrisy and calculated self-interest of his Ovidian counterpart, has given rise to the notion that the Middle Ages discovered the passion and sorrow of love, a view recently challenged by P. Dronke:

> I am convinced that this received opinion, this belief in a wholly new conception of love, is false. I am convinced that the question, why did this new feeling arise at such a place, at such a time, in such a society, is a misleading one. For I should like to suggest that the feelings and conceptions of *amour courtois* are universally possible, possible in any time or place and on any level of society. They occur in popular as well as in learned or aristocratic love-poetry ... I should like to introduce the term 'the courtly experience' to designate something which cuts across the notions of popular and courtly poetry. The courtly experience is the sensibility that gives birth to poetry that is *courtois*, to poetry of *amour courtois*.[7]

At least within the relatively narrow sphere of the vernacular literature of medieval France, the 'courtly experience' was clearly a novelty. That its first manifestation should have been in the south of France is not surprising in view of the history of that region. Although the Visigoths were established there for some centuries, although the Vandals passed through on their way to Spain, although there were later incursions by the Arabs until their decisive defeat by Charles Martel, this comparatively refined and cultured region of the former Empire, in which the Romans had established many schools, remained almost undisturbed, free to develop along its own lines:

> Bordeaux, Toulouse, Arles, Lyons and other towns were flourishing and brilliant centres of civilisation at a time when Northern France was struggling with foreign invaders. It was in Southern Gaul, again, that Christianity first obtained a footing; here the barbarian invasions of the fifth and sixth centuries proved less destructive to civilisation than in Northern France, and the Visigoths seem to have been more amenable to the influences of culture than the Northern Franks ... The climate, again, of Southern France is milder and warmer than that of the North, and these influences produced a difference which may almost be termed racial.[8]

This freedom, which certainly helped the troubadour literature to evolve, contributed also to its eventual demise in the thirteenth century, for the Catharist heresy had been allowed to take root in the region,[9] leading to the terrible Albigensian crusades (1209–29).[10]

What were the characteristics of the troubadours' love-poems? So much has been written about the so-called *amour courtois*[11] doctrine, so many generalisations according to the beliefs and temperament of the particular scholar and the intellectual and moral climate in which he was writing – it has been variously termed platonic, mystical, sensual, erotic – that the individuality of the troubadours has been largely lost sight of. Space will allow us no more than a brief look at the work of a few of the 460 troubadours whose works are extant (many are known by a single poem or fragment), but this should enable us to form some idea, however approximate, of their poetry.

II. GUILLAUME IX: FIRST KNOWN TROUBADOUR

Guillaume IX, seventh count of Poitiers, ninth duke of Aquitaine, first known troubadour, was born in 1071 and died in 1127. The vast estates which he inherited from his father before the age of fifteen were larger than those of the king of France. A dissolute figure, 'vehemens amator feminarum' as the chronicles call him, 'totius pudicitiae ac sanctitatis inimicus',[12] an ineffective soldier who led a crusading army of 60,000 into ambush and near annihilation in one of the earliest major setbacks suffered by the Christian armies in Palestine, Guillaume is clearly not a very promising figure with whom to begin the story of 'courtly love'. Nevertheless, he has been considered not just as the first troubadour whose works have survived, but as the first in historical fact.[13] This is unlikely for a number of reasons which will shortly become apparent. Of the eleven poems attributed to Guillaume, five are of a coarse, barrack-room type wholly in keeping with the debauched character depicted in the chronicles. One, which reflects well enough the tone of the other four, tells how the poet met two married women, and pretended to be dumb. All he could manage to articulate was 'Babariol, Babariol, Babarian'. They took him to a house where they were alone, put his dumbness to the test by running the claws of a large ginger cat down his naked back, and finding that he remained silent, indulged their sexual appetites with him for a whole week, at the end of which he was utterly exhausted, having worn out his 'block and tackle'. Clearly this is the sexually obsessed bawdiness of an essentially male milieu without the slightest pretension to refinement or courtly behaviour.[14] The remaining poems are of an altogether more refined nature, even though allusions to sexual pleasure are by no means absent:

Enquer me lais Dieus viure tan   May God let me live long enough
C'aja mas manz soz so mantel!   to have my hands beneath her cloak!

exclaims Guillaume in one of his milder anticipations of the ultimate success of his wooing of the fair lady. It has been plausibly argued that, while the obscene ditties are undoubtedly the work of Guillaume, the courtly songs are not, and that they were in fact the work of a contemporary of Guillaume's, Eble II de Ventadour, and became attached in the manuscripts to those of Guillaume because of his greater fame and power.[15] Medieval studies are replete with arguments of this nature which are plausible without being wholly convincing, and the very incompleteness of the evidence means that the final proof must always be lacking. Another attempt to introduce some order into this seemingly confused and contradictory state of affairs sees the rude songs as the work of Guillaume in his early years, and the refined ones as the work of his maturity.[16] However, it is not inconceivable that the two veins, concerning very different types of women – the whores who made advances to the men, the courtly ladies who had to be wooed with some delicacy – were composed by one and the same author at about the same time, designed on the one hand for military, on the other for courtly, circles. The modern mind is constantly intrigued by the violent extremes of the medieval mentality, and strives to rationalise them, forgetting that our own age can juxtapose extremes of bawdiness and delicacy without undue embarrassment.

The following poem is characteristic of Guillaume's courtly vein:

I

Ab la dolchor del temps novel
Foillo li bosc, e li aucel
Chanton chascus en lor lati
Segon lo vers del novel chan;
Adonc esta ben c'om s'aisi
D'acho don hom a plus talan.

In the sweetness of springtime the woods break into leaf and the birds sing, each in its own tongue, according to the new season's melody. Then it is good to take pleasure in that for which one has the greatest desire.

II

De lai don plus m'es bon e bel
Non vei mesager ni sagel,
Per que mos cors non dorm ni ri,
Ni no m'aus traire adenan,
Tro que sacha ben de la fi,
S'el' es aissi com eu deman.

From the source of all that is good and beautiful in my eyes, I see no messenger arriving and no letter. As a result I cannot sleep or rejoice and dare take no further steps until I know for sure that our pledge remains as I ask.

III

La nostr' amor vai enaissi
Com la branca de l'albespi
Qu'esta sobre l'arbre tremblan,
La nuoit, a la ploja ez al gel,
Tro l'endeman, que. l sols s'espan
Per las fueillas verz e. l ramel.

Our love is like the hawthorn branch, trembling on the tree at night in the rain and frost, until the next day when the sun spreads its rays through the green leaves on the boughs.

IV

Enquer me membra d'un mati
Que nos fezem de guerra fi,
E que. m donet un don tan gran,
Sa drudari' e son anel:
Enquer me lais Dieus viure tan
C'aja mas manz soz so mantel!

I still remember one morning when we put an end to our quarrel and she gave me a great gift, her love and her ring. May God let me live long enough to have my hands beneath her cloak!

v

Qu'eu non ai soing d'estraing lati	For I do not worry lest the gossip of
Que. m parta de mon Bon Vezi,	others part me from my 'Good
Qu'eu sai de paraulas com van	Neighbour',[17] for I know how words
Ab un breu sermon que s'espel,	are spread around in small talk, for
Que tal se van d'amor gaban,	some go boasting about love, but we
Nos n'avem la pessa e. l coutel.[18]	have all that we need [lit.: 'we have
	the piece (of bread) and the knife'].

One is immediately struck by the rigorously controlled form and structure. Not a syllable is out of place. Each stanza contains six octosyllabic lines. Not only is the same rhyme scheme retained throughout: *a a b c b c*, but the same sounds are used: *-el, -el, -i, -an, -i, -an* in the first two stanzas, the order changing in the last three: *-i, -i, -an, -el, -an, -el*. This scrupulous attention to the detail of composition is characteristic, not merely of Guillaume's courtly songs (his bawdy compositions tend to be less elaborate, three of them being based on a simple monorhyme), but of the whole subsequent troubadour tradition, and many stanzaic patterns were evolved,[19] along with the music which always accompanied these poems (songs is a more apt term) and which was often composed by the troubadours themselves. It is now established that both the complex verse structure and the music of the troubadours' love-poetry were heavily indebted to Latin liturgical hymns, in particular to the *versus* of the very important abbey of Saint-Martial at Limoges:[20]

Ces chansons [i.e., those of Guillaume IX] s'appelleront un *vers*, traduction exacte de *Versus*, dont il y a lieu de noter l'emploi au singulier de part et d'autre; le nom même de *trobador* est, d'après les hypothèses actuellement admises, un dérivé direct de *tropator*, faiseur de trope – de même que *trobar*, trouver, dérive de *tropare*. De nombreux troubadours ont eu une éducation monastique – tel Gausbert de Puycibot, élevé à Saint-Léonard de Limoges ... ou Peire Guilhem, représenté en costume de moine; à tout le moins, leurs relations avec les monastères sont évidentes, et du reste inhérentes à la civilisation de l'époque: Guillaume IX jure par Saint Martial, et on relève dans les chroniques de notre monastère, en 1215, un cierge *pro Bertrando de Born* qui pourrait bien être consécutif à la mort de ce troubadour et permettre ainsi de la dater ... Entre la versification latine des *versus* et la versification des trouveurs les correspondances sont considérables. La répartition régulière des accents de mots ou de phrase, à peu près constante chez les trouveurs à quelques licences près, est aussi chez eux une marque distinctive: on ne la trouve pas dans les autres secteurs de la poésie provençale ou française, même lorsqu'elle est chantée. Or elle semble empruntée à la versification latine d'église dont nos *Versus* sont parmi les premiers monuments. Enfin l'étude des mètres ... donne également des résultats impressionnants: presque tous les rythmes relevés dans les chansons des plus anciens troubadours ont leur équivalent dans les *Versus* ... il en est de même pour le groupement des vers en strophes, la répartition des rimes, les procédés de refrain, les assonances léonines, etc.[21]

The transposition from one genre to another seems to have been fully accomplished by Guillaume's day, and the elaborate form and

refined tone of this and others of Guillaume's courtly songs make it
very hard to accept that he was indeed the first troubadour. The
setting of the song in the springtime, the parallel drawn between
the breaking of the woods into fresh green and the awakening of the
poet's feelings, is in any case a *topos* found also in Latin verse.
Whatever its precedents, and whatever Guillaume's true feelings
or motives, the song quoted above has considerable charm and
delicacy. The lover anxiously awaits some sign from his lady that
his feelings are requited, and the fragility of their love is beautifully
reflected in the protracted simile of the third stanza. That
Guillaume does not intend their relationship to remain a platonic
one is clearly revealed in the suggestive ending of the fourth stanza.
The veiled reference to the lady as 'Bon Vezi' (Good Neighbour) is
paralleled in many a later poem. This discretion is sometimes taken
as a sign that the relationship was an adulterous one, but that this
was inevitably so with all troubadouresque love-poetry has been
vigorously denied in recent years.[22]

The most enigmatic of Guillaume's poems introduces a very
different note:

I

Farai un vers de dreyt nien:
Non er de mi ni d'autra gen,
Non er d'amor ni de joven,
    Ni de ren au,
Qu'enans fo trobatz en durmen
    Sobre chevau.

I shall write a poem about absolutely
nothing. It will not be about me
or anybody else, it will not be about
love or youth or anything, but it
was composed while I was asleep on
horseback.

II

No sai en qual hora. m fuy natz:
No suy alegres ni iratz,
No suy estrayns ni sui privatz,
    Ni no. n puesc au,
Qu'enaissi fuy de nueitz fadatz,
    Sobr' un pueg au.

I know not when I was born, I am
not happy or sad, stranger or friend,
and I cannot do anything about it,
for thus was I fated at night, on a
high hill.

III

No sai quora. m suy endurmitz
Ni quora. m velh, s'om no m'o ditz.
Per pauc no m'es lo cor partitz
    D'un dol corau:
E no m'o pretz una soritz,
    Per sanh Marsau!

I know not when I am asleep or
awake unless I am told. My heart
is nearly bursting with a deep sorrow,
but I care not a fig about it, by St
Martial!

IV

Malautz sui e tremi murir,
E ren no. n sai mas quan n'aug dir;
Metge querrai al mieu albir,
    E no sai cau;
Bos metges er si. m pot guerir.
    Mas non, si amau.

I am ill and fear I shall die, and
know nothing about it save what I
hear said. I shall seek a doctor of
my choice, I know not who. He will
be a good doctor if he can cure me,
but not if I get worse.

V

Amigu' ai ieu, no sai qui s'es,	I have a lady-love, I know not who

Amigu' ai ieu, no sai qui s'es,
Qu'anc non la vi, si m'ajut fes;
Ni. m fes que. m plassa ni que. m
    pes,
Ni no m'en cau,
Qu'anc non ac Norman ni Frances
Dins mon ostau.

I have a lady-love, I know not who
she is, for never have I seen her, so
help me my faith. She has never
done anything to please or grieve
me, and I care not, for never have
I had a Norman or a Frenchman in
my abode.

VI

Anc non la vi e am la fort,
Anc no n'aic dreyt ni no. m fes tort;
Quan non la vey, be m'en deport,
No. m pretz un jau,
Qu'ie. n sai gensor²³ et bellazor,
    E que mais vau.

I have never seen her yet love her
dearly, she has never done me right
or wrong. When I do not see her, I
get along very nicely and care not
in the least, for I know one more
noble and fair and of better worth.

VII

Fag ai lo vers, no say de cuy;
E trametrai lo a selhuy
Que lo. m trametra per autruy
    Lay vers Anjau,
Que. m tramezes del sieu estuy
    La contraclau.   (Poem IV)

I have written the song, I know not
about whom, and I shall send it to
the one who will send it through another over towards Anjou, so that he
can send me the key to it from his
own wallet.

This poem is referred to by its editor as a 'devinalh', a riddle, and
clearly there is something of the 'Guess what I am' atmosphere
about it. However, it has been given two interpretations, utterly
opposed, a consideration of which throws light on the poetry of
Guillaume IX and on the difficulties of interpreting it. According
to one view, this is a vital poem reflecting a fundamental change in
Guillaume's outlook: '... des plaisanteries grossières il a passé d'un
bond à la vraie poésie, expression de ses sentiments les plus per-
sonnels'.²⁴ The poem therefore provides in this view a link between
Guillaume's obscene ditties and love-songs. It shows the emergence
of a new 'état d'âme'²⁵ as Guillaume is beset by a mysterious influence which he himself is unable to define or understand.
Guillaume, it is suggested, was profoundly influenced by Robert
d'Arbrissel, the stern and ascetic founder of the abbey of Fontevrault,
to which his first wife, from whom he was divorced in 1091, retired, to
be followed by his second wife, and also his daughter. According
to this hypothesis Guillaume gradually replaced the religious mysticism of the epoch by a more secular mysticism which finds its first
adumbrations in this poem. Out of this ill-defined feeling, a new
doctrine was to emerge in which 'courtoisie' was put to the service
of love, and the lady was to be exalted. Drawing heavily on the
spirit and outlook of his age, Guillaume, 'le porte-parole général des
aspirations de toute une société féodale',²⁶ united and crystallised
them in this new poetry and so became in effect the first troubadour.
It is no mere coincidence, claims Bezzola, that of the 460 troubadours'

names known to us, not one appears to be earlier than that of
Guillaume.[27] This romantic, far-reaching interpretation reads a
great deal into Guillaume's poems without, however, examining
them closely in the details. The first stanza, for example, calls for a
simple, but important, observation. Guillaume declares that his
poem will not be about himself or anybody else, it will not be about
love and youth – a declaration, surely, that this is to be a poem out
of the ordinary, avoiding conventional subjects. This much of the
poem makes sense and is well borne out by what follows. The implication therefore is that love was already an established theme.
However, much stronger arguments reinforce this belief, for it has
been claimed that this poem, far from being the mystical creation
that Bezzola saw in it, was a deliberate burlesque of the poetic
convention of *amour courtois* which must have been in full flower
for his joke to have had a point.[28]

After a close analysis of this and other poems by Guillaume

The conclusion . . . is that he is neither the founder nor even an exponent
of *amour courtois*, that he was conscious of it around him, exasperated,
beguiled and amused by it, and that at times he used it as a point of
departure for saying something which is entirely his own.[29]

Guillaume was doubtless too autocratic a figure to feel or even to
feign the subservience to the lady that was to characterise the verse
of most troubadours, although he does observe, somewhat stiffly
perhaps, that

Obediensa deu portar	Whoever wishes to love must show
A motas gens qui vol amar,	obedience to many people, and it
E coven li que sapcha far	behoves him to behave pleasantly
Faigz avinens,	and to take care at Court not to
E que. s gart en cort de parlar	speak in villainous fashion.
Vilanamens.[30]	

Of these two radically opposed interpretations, that of Bezzola,
that of Dronke, the latter seems the more convincing when one
remembers the high degree of sophistication and polish in the
structure of the poems, the very complexity of which presupposes
a period of evolution, not all of which can be assigned to the hymno-
logy of Saint-Martial de Limoges.

III. CERCAMON

Cercamon, one of the few troubadours of the first half of the
twelfth century whose works have survived, wrote a poem lamenting
the death in 1137 of Guillaume X, son of the first known troubadour.
Seven songs by this Gascon poet have survived, five of which concern love.[31] He portrays the torments of an unrequited love:

Las! qu'ieu d'Amor non ai conquis
Mas cant lo trebalh e l'afan,
Ni res tant greu no. s covertis
Com fai so qu'ieu vau deziran;
Ni tal enveja no. m fai res
Cum fai so qu'ieu non posc aver.
(ɪ, lines 7–12)

Alas! all that I have gained of love
is the pain and suffering it brings,
and nothing is as hard to obtain as
what I desire. Nothing gives me as
much longing as what I cannot have.

and, like Guillaume, he does not disguise the sensual nature of his feelings:

Dieu prejarai qu'ancar l'ades
O que la vej' anar jazer
(ɪ, 23–4)

I pray to God that I may yet touch
her or see her going to bed

though there is a conscious effort to achieve a tone of refinement and distinction. He is clearly proud to proclaim in the concluding lines of one song that it was written

Ses mot vila, fals, apostitz,
E es totz enaissi bastitz
C'ap motz politz lo vau uzan . . .
(ɪɪɪ, 32–4)

Without any villainous, false, hypocritical word and in its composition
I have used polite terms throughout.

Indeed, so careful is the tone of this song, so cautious and timid when compared with the more forthright note of Guillaume's poems, that its modern editor could not decide whether it was addressed to the poet's lady or the Virgin Mary, and accordingly gave it as title 'Chanson pieuse (?)'. It is in fact clearly concerned with his lady, since mention is made of her fickle nature, and he relates in a theme which was to recur constantly in the lines of later troubadours the joy, the exaltation, that his love brought him. Physical descriptions of the lady are of a general kind:

Aqesta don m'auzetz chantar
Es plus bella q'ieu no sai dir;
Fresc' a color e bel esgar
Et es blancha ses brunezir;
Oc, e non es vernisada,
Ni om de leis non pot mal dir,
Tant es fin' et esmerada.
(ɪɪ, 15–21)

She of whom you hear me sing is
more lovely than I can tell. She has
a fresh complexion and lovely eyes
and her skin is white and un-
blemished. Yes, and she wears no
make-up, nor can anything adverse
be said about her, so pure and
refined is she.

This is characteristic of most troubadour verse, as is the preoccupa-tion with the poet's own feelings, varying constantly according to the lady's moods and attitude towards him: sad and downcast when she appears to neglect him, but even so not giving way to despair:

Cercamons ditz: greu er cortes
Hom qui d'amor se desesper.
(ɪ, 57–8)

Cercamon declares: with difficulty
will he be courtly, the man who
despairs of love.

At other times the poet is filled with exaltation, sometimes at the mere thought of the lady's beauty, sometimes when she gives him

some encouragement, often switching abruptly from one emotion
to another:

Amors es douza a l'intrar	Love is sweet at the beginning and
Et amara al departir,	bitter at the end, for one day it
Q'en un jorn vos fara plorar,	makes you weep, the next it makes
Et autre jogar e burdir . . .	you rejoice and be merry . . .
(ii, 36–9)	

However much he constantly fed his hope with the desire that he
would one day lie naked with his love in bed, it is a poetry almost
wholly taken up with the feelings that love awakens in a man's
heart (hence the inclusion of physical desire) and is not a celebration
of eroticism as such. Cercamon's verse is less striking, less filled with
the dominant personality of its author, than that of Guillaume,
but it is not lacking in skill and grace, and a high ideal is revealed.
Deceit and insincerity were the lover's greatest possible crimes:

Fals amador, al meu semblan,	False lovers, in my view the loss will
Vostr'er lo danz e no. n pueis mai;	be yours, and I cannot help it. You
De gran folor es acordan	are all acting in the same mad way
Can l'us l'autre gali'e trai . . .	when you trick and betray one an-
(iv, 22–5)	other.

IV. JAUFRÉ RUDEL

Jaufré Rudel, like Guillaume, was a troubadour of noble origin;
his thirteenth-century biography refers to him as the prince of
Blaya.[32] Several allusions in his poems to a distant love, along with
the fact that he took part in the second crusade,[33] gave rise to the
legend, recorded in his biography and retold by several modern
authors (Rostand, Carducci, Uhland, Heine), that he fell in love
with the countess of Tripoli whom he had never seen, but whose
praises he had heard sung by pilgrims returning from Antioch. He
took the Cross and set off on the voyage, but fell ill, and eventually
died in the countess's arms. This highly romantic concoction is at
least faithful to the atmosphere of Jaufré Rudel's poems, of which
only six have survived. The most famous is the following, of whose
seven stanzas the first three are quoted here:

Lanquan li jorn son lonc en may	When days are long in May, sweet
M'es belhs dous chans d'auzelhs de	in my ears is the song of birds far
lonh,	away. And when I have gone on my
E quan mi suy partitz de lay	way, I recall a love far away. I go
Remembra. m d'un' amor de lonh:	sad and downcast so that the bird-
Vau de talan embroncx e clis	song and the hawthorn blossom
Si que chans ni flors d'albespis	please me no more than winter's
No. m platz plus que l'yverns gelatz.	frost.

Be tenc lo Senhor per veray
Per qu'ieu veirai l'amor de lonh;
Mas per un ben que m'en eschay
N'ai dos mals, quar tan m'es de
lonh.
Ai! car me fos lai pelegris,
Si que mos fustz e mos tapis
Fos pels sieus belhs huelhs remiratz!

Be. m parra joys quan li querray,
Per amor Dieu, l'alberc de lonh:
E, s'a lieys platz, alberguarai
Pres de lieys, si be. m suy de lonh:
Adoncs parra. l parlamens fis
Quan drutz lonhdas ert tan vezis
Qu'ab bels digz jauzira solatz.

(v, lines 1–21)[34]

Well do I hold the Lord for true, through whom I shall see that love far away. But for one piece of good fortune I have two misfortunes, for she is so far away. Ah, would that I were a pilgrim there, so that my staff and cloak could be mirrored by her lovely eyes!

Very apparent will my joy be when, through love of God, I seek that shelter far away. And if it pleases her, I shall take my shelter near her, however far away I am now. Then there will be true love-talk, when this distant lover will be so close that he can enjoy the solace of her lovely discourse.

A remarkable feature is the repetition of 'de lonh' at the end of every second and fourth line, the sole variation being that 'lonh' only is repeated in the fourth lines of the fourth and fifth stanzas. This stylistic feature contributes strongly to the atmosphere of desire and longing for the seemingly unattainable that characterises this beautiful poem. The problem of the significance of this distant love (echoed in four of the other five extant poems by Jaufré Rudel) has received several very different solutions in recent years. In the view of one scholar, the poet is singing of his love for the Holy Land, but this is improbable to say the least, since he desires to meet his love in a room or garden![35] This same discreet but undeniable physical allusion[36] makes other proposed identifications equally unlikely: Aliénor d'Aquitaine, Helen of Troy, the Virgin Mary.[37] Certainly the reference was to a lady, but whether real or legendary, or a figment of the poet's imagination, is not known. Psychological interpretations have been proposed which are sometimes far-reaching:

L'*amor de lonh* ne vient-il pas chez Jaufré Rudel de cette 'mélancolie de l'imperfection', qui sent que 'quelque chose' manque toujours au bonheur absolu, et de cette auto-limitation volontaire, qui a besoin du lointain? Le lointain est un élément nécessaire de tout amour, aussi nécessaire que le contact – ces troubadours ont en somme senti la *selige Sehnsucht* de Goethe, aspirant au milieu du plaisir du lit conjugal vers une *andere Begattung*. C'est le lointain qui donne à la tenue morale un rayonnement métaphysique et un sens à l'amour, comme la mort le donne à la vie.[38]

Jaufré Rudel maintains a fascinating dichotomy, not merely the joy of love contrasted with the sadness of separation, nor the happiness that wounds, nor an ethereal longing that does not exclude a sensual desire, but a quest, earnestly pursued, occupying the poet's whole mind and heart; yet it is a quest for the unattainable. This is a particularly romantic, subjective version of the 'quest' theme, a theme which took many very varied forms in the Middle Ages both in historical fact – were not pilgrimages and crusades a form of quest?[39] – and in fiction.

V. BERNARD DE VENTADOUR

Non es meravelha s'eu chan
melhs de nul autre chantador . . .
(1, lines 1–2)[40]

It is no marvel if I sing better than
any other singer . . .

so boasted Bernard de Ventadour who did not number modesty among his many virtues. His claim did not go unchallenged in his day, since it was not Bernard, but Giraut de Borneilh, who was hailed as the 'Maestre dels Trobadors'.[41] His modern editor calls Bernard 'le troubadour le plus lyrique du XIIᵉ siècle, et l'un des plus grands poètes de l'amour de tous les temps'.[42] Of humble origin according to his thirteenth-century biography,[43] no certain information is possessed about him: '. . . nous devons humblement confesser notre totale ignorance quant à la vie de Bernard de Ventadour, ses origines, son destin et sa fin'.[44] In the forty-four songs attributed to him, there is a much greater unity than in the eleven attributed to Guillaume IX or even in the seven attributed to Cercamon. Love is his constant theme, and he treats it with that apparent effortlessness and that versatility which characterise the master of any genre. His starting-point may be the same as that of others, but his development is bolder, more unexpected:

Lancan folhon bosc e jarric,
e. lh flors pareis e. lh verdura,
pels vergers e pels pratz,
e. lh auzel, c'an estat enic,
son gai desotz los folhatz,
autresi. m chant e m'esbaudei
e reflorisc e reverdei
e folh segon ma natura.
(6, 1–8)

When woods and groves break into
leaf and flowers and verdure appear
in orchards and meadows, and birds
which have been sad are gay under
the foliage, I too sing and rejoice
and break into flower and leaf
according to my nature.

Love in his view is no mere dalliance or narcissistic preoccupation, for only love can give a man his true quality, an idea soon to be put to the test in the romances of northern France:

Nuls om ses amor re non vau.
(11, 29)

No man is worth anything without love.

He himself cannot live without it:

Qu'eu no posc viure ses amar
que d'amor sui engenoïtz
(42, 15–16)

I cannot live without loving, for I
was engendered through love.

Does this last line mean that he regarded himself as a scion of Love, or that he was engendered in the act of love? A physical reference of this kind would not be out of place in his poetry, for the sensual basis of the lover's longings is clearly indicated, although quotations out of context make it appear more dominant than it is:

Amors, e que. m farai?	Love, what am I to do? Shall I ever
Si garrai ja ab te?	be cured by you? I think I shall die
Ara cuit qu'e. n morrai	from the longing that comes to me,
del dezirer que. m ve,	if the lovely lady does not welcome
si. lh bela lai on jai	me near her in the place where she
no m'aizis pres de se,	lies, so that I can touch her and
qu'eu la manei e bai	kiss her and hold close to me her
et estrenha vas me	white body, plump and smooth.
so cors blanc, gras e le.	

(18, 28–36)

It is above all a matter of longing rather than of actually consummated love, for in one poem, having spoken of the whiteness of the lady's body, he adds

eu non o dic mas per cuda,	I only suppose it to be so,

(16, 38)

and goes on in true poetic hyperbole to say that, compared to her, snow is brown. If at times there is a certain 'préciosité' about this verse, it nevertheless conveys that impression of involving the whole mind and personality of the poet, which is to be found in all truly great lyric poetry:

Chantars no pot gaire valer,	A song can scarcely have any worth
si d'ins dal cor no mou lo chans;	unless it comes from within the
ni chans no pot dal cor mover,	heart, and it cannot come from the
si no i es fin'amors coraus.	heart if pure love is not implanted

(2, 1–4) there.

Best known of all his verse is the beautiful and moving skylark song, the first three of whose seven stanzas are quoted here:

Can vei la lauzeta mover	When I see the skylark beating its
de joi sas alas contra. l rai,	wings for joy in the rays of the sun,
que s'oblid' e. s laissa chazer	when unmindful of itself it swoops
per la doussor c'al cor li vai,	down because of the sweetness in its
ai! tan grans enveya m'en ve	heart, oh! such great envy comes to
de cui qu'eu veya jauzion.	me of whomsoever I see rejoicing. I
meravilhas ai, car desse	marvel that my heart does not at
lo cor de dezirer no. m fon.	once melt with longing.
Ai, las! tan cuidava saber	Alas! I thought I knew so much
d'amor, e tan petit en sai,	about love, and know so little, for I
car eu d'amar no. m posc tener	cannot refrain from loving the one
celeis don ja pro non aurai.	who will do me no good. She has
Tout m'a mo cor, et tout m'a me,	robbed me of my heart and my very
e se mezeis e tot lo mon;	being, herself and the whole world.
e can se. m tolc, no. m laisset re	In so doing she left me nothing but
mas dezirer e cor volon.	desire and a yearning heart.

Anc non agui de me poder
ni no fui meus de l'or en sai
que. m laisset en sos olhs vezer
en un miralh que mout me plai.
Miralhs, pus me mirei en te,
m'an mort li sospir de preon,
c'aissi. m perdet com perdet se
lo bels Narcisus en la fon.

(31, 1–24)

Never did I have any power over
myself, never was I mine from the
time when she let me look into her
eyes, into a mirror which pleased me
greatly. Mirror, since I mirrored
myself in you, sighs from the depths
have killed me, for I have been my
own undoing like the handsome Narcissus at the spring.

VI. OTHER TROUBADOURS: THEIR VERSE, DOCTRINE, AND MUSIC

Many fine and varied qualities of the numerous troubadours
whose works have survived can find no mention in these pages. The
passions they celebrated were by no means always of an amorous
kind. The spirited Bertran de Born, who wrote in the second half
of the twelfth century,[45] rejoiced in springtime not at the burgeon-
ing of his love but at the sight of armies of knights assembled for
battle:

Be. m platz lo gais temps de pascor,
que fai fuolhas e flors venir;
e platz mi, quan auch la baudor
dels auzels, que fan retentir
lor chan per lo boschatge;
e platz mi, quan vei sobre. ls pratz
tendas e pavilhos fermatz;
  et ai gran alegratge,
quan vei per champanha rengatz
chavaliers e chavals armatz.

(41, lines 1–10)

Gay springtime, bringing leaves and
flowers in its wake, pleases me well.
It pleases me to hear the gay bird-
song echoing in the woods. It pleases
me to see tents and pavilions set up
on the meadows, and I feel great
exultation when I see armed
knights and horses drawn up in
ranks in the countryside.

Raimbaut de Vaqueiras, writing in the late twelfth and early
thirteenth centuries, also 'found true fulfilment in the heroic and
chivalric life of the world . . . rather than in contemplation or
amorous dalliance'.[46] Raimbaut d'Orange, first of the truly
Provençal troubadours, writing in the second half of the twelfth
century, satirised the courtly love theme, and was not above advising
the wooer of an obdurate lady to seek her favours by punching her
on the nose![47] Elsewhere, forsaking the comic vein, he successfully
fused courtly with divine elements.[48] His contemporary Peirol wrote
with dogged persistence on the unrequited-love theme, but met with
such indifference or hostility that his importunate obstinacy may
have caused him to be banished from Court.[49] Even so, that 'joi
vertadier' (true joy) experienced by other troubadour-lovers was
not entirely foreign to him.[50] At the same period, Peire Cardenal
vigorously satirised love by rejecting all the customary avowals:

I don't claim that I am assailed by love or that my heart has been stolen away. I don't claim that I'm dying for the most beautiful woman or that my fair one is keeping me languishing. I don't beg her for her love, I don't adore her, I don't ask for her favours, and I don't desire her . . .[51]

He also wrote much satire of a political and religious nature. Giraut de Borneilh, his contemporary, sang the praises of love with as much versatility as Bernard de Ventadour, but usually in a more *recherché*, deliberately obscure, style, the *trobar ric* or *trobar clus* rather than the less esoteric *trobar plan* or *trobar leu* practised by Bernard, even though it was towards this style that Giraut's later poetry evolved. The virtuosity of a highly developed formalistic art was carried further by the complex Arnaut Daniel who wrote at the same period, practitioner *par excellence* of the *trobar ric*, of art for art's sake, though the intricacies of his verse structures and imagery were not matched by the quality of the feelings depicted. His fame today rests more on the praises showered on him by Dante than on his own verse.[52] Poetic genres as well as personalities and techniques revealed something of the troubadours' versatility: the *tenso* or *joc-partit* was a debate between two poets, often of a rather *précieux* kind, on the subject of love, while the *sirventes* was a satirical or moralising mode.

The *albas* – 'dawn-songs' – in which the lovers part reluctantly at daybreak, when 'night's candles are burnt out', were a very old genre finding a parallel in many literatures. A Latin dawn-song with a Provençal refrain survives in a late tenth-century manuscript.[53] Some fifteen are extant in Provençal, and four in French. The *pastorelas*, of which some thirty have survived in Provençal and as many as two hundred in French, the latter dating mainly from the mid- and late thirteenth century, tell of the meeting of a knight and shepherdess. The knight makes advances and usually finds the girl a good deal more sharp-witted than he had expected. Sometimes he succeeds in carrying her off, sometimes he is rebuffed, with the help, on occasions, of her rustic lover.

In the face of so much diversity, it is clearly difficult to speak in terms of an 'amour courtois' doctrine embracing the works of the troubadours as a whole. As we have seen, the very term *amour courtois* was exceedingly rare in the Middle Ages. The one favoured by the troubadours was *fin' amors* ('true love', 'pure love') and it is not without significance that this concerns a quality of mind rather than a social distinction. The following quotation gathers together numbers of the salient features of *fin' amors*, even though the author has in mind one particular troubadour, an outstanding personality not so far mentioned in these pages, Marcabru, who lived in the first half of the twelfth century and whose tempestuous Gascon temperament led him to condemn in the most forthright terms the excesses of

fol' amor and the adultery it often implied,[54] even while he painted
an idealistic picture of *fin' amors*:[55]

No single concept can be substituted for it without diminishing the
poem – not God, or love of God, or love of neighbour, or faithful sexual
love: it is all these and more. One might indicate it best by saying, *fin'
Amors* is all that is true, truly loved or truly loving, in whatever mode,
earthly or heavenly, it finds expression; all that is genuinely felt, devoid of
treachery or dissembling, calculation or greed or fear.[56]

The best aspects of *fin' amors* were to provide the essence of what
was to become a vital influence on the literature and social behaviour
of western Europe: the introduction of *courtoisie* between the sexes.
The situation which the love-poetry of the troubadours presupposes
is as follows: in the relationship between the sexes, it is the man who
has the initiative; he is the dynamic partner who makes the advances,
but he voluntarily renounces his superiority and leaves the woman
complete freedom of choice. He deliberately humbles himself and
shows absolute deference to the lady's whims and desires. Moreover,
the troubadour promises her complete discretion, referring to her
indirectly by means of a pseudonym, and assuring her that he would
respect her honour and dignity at all times. This setting of the lady
on a pedestal had the interesting effect of reducing, at least in
theory, distinctions of rank among the troubadours. Guillaume IX
and Jaufré Rudel were of noble birth, whereas Bernard de Ventadour and Giraut de Borneilh appear to have been of humble origins.
What determined their success was their skill as poets and musicians,
and their ability to instil into their compositions that essential aura
of authenticity. Since the commoners were able to compete on an
equal footing with the nobles,[57] the implication was that the man
mattered more than his rank, a lesson which moralists were never
tired of repeating in that age of a highly stratified society, and which
is here seen to have had an actual application.

To do full justice to the aesthetic value of the troubadours' work
it would be necessary to study in some detail the musical accompaniment, forming as it did a vital part of the structure. There is
unfortunately no space for such an enterprise here,[58] and in any case
difficulties would arise owing to the relative scantiness and incompleteness of surviving musical material. Melodies of only 10 per cent
of extant Provençal poems have survived (only one fragment for
Guillaume IX, but eighteen melodies for Bernard de Ventadour),
and the inadequacies of the simple square-note notation, to which
no time-values are assigned, make interpretations controversial.
Moreover, the modern ear, unattuned to the rhythmic freedom of
medieval monody, may react in ways quite different from those of
the troubadours and their contemporaries. None the less, a question
that must be asked when the text is the main consideration, as here,

is this: is the music liable to influence significantly, perhaps even to modify, our interpretation of the actual word-matter? Future research may provide the answer. Meantime, it has been suggested that the complex, subtly varied melodic patterns evolved by the troubadours lift their songs above the frequent sensuality of the words and that, through its melodies, this art-form of noble endeavour transcends the emotions expressed by the words which provide no more than a starting-point.[59]

VII. THE TROUVÈRES OF NORTHERN FRANCE

The propagation in the north of France of the troubadours' poetry and their concept of *fin' amors* owed much to the marriage in 1137, at the age of fifteen, of Aliénor d'Aquitaine, granddaughter of Guillaume IX, to Prince Louis, soon to become Louis VII of France. She attracted troubadours to the Court of the French king, among them Bernard de Ventadour. The two daughters of this marriage both became active patronesses of letters: Marie married Henry I of Champagne in 1164; Chrétien de Troyes and Andreas Capellanus were both to become indebted to her, as we shall see eventually; Marie's sister Alix married Henry's brother, Thibaut V of Blois, in the same year, and it was at their Court that Gautier d'Arras composed his *Eracles*. Aliénor's marriage to Louis was dissolved in 1152, and two months later she married the future Henry II of England, by whom she had three daughters and four sons, among them Richard Cœur-de-Lion. The Anglo-Norman poet and chronicler Wace dedicated his *Brut* to her,[60] and Thomas's version of the Tristan legend may have been written for her, as also Benoît de Sainte-Maure's *Roman de Troie*. The influence on the French literature of the times of this formidable queen and her numerous descendants was truly immense. Other factors, too, were of importance: the crusades united northerners and southerners in a common cause, and poets from the north and south are known to have travelled widely: Marcabru visited Blois,[61] while Guiot de Provins lived for a time in Arles:

A Arle oï conteir molt gent	At Arles I heard many relate the
lor vie, en l'englise Saint Trophe	philosophers' lives, in the church of
	Saint Trophime.[62]

Many other contacts have doubtless gone unrecorded, and it is rather surprising that imitation of the troubadours, judging at least from extant texts, does not appear to have begun much before the 1170s. What vernacular poems already existed in the north of France before that time? The difficulty of dating most of the surviving poems, all the greater because of the possibility that some thirteenth-century compositions were deliberately given an archaic flavour,[63] makes a categorical answer impossible. The earliest French song to which a clear date can be given is a crusading poem which alludes in its refrain to Louis VII's participation in the second crusade of 1147.[64] Here are the first and third stanzas:

Chevalier mult estes guariz
Quant Deu a vus fait sa clamur
Des Turs e des Amoraviz
Ki li unt fait tels deshenors,
Cher [=Car] a tort unt cez fieuz
    saisiz.
Bien en devums aveir dolur,
Cher [=Car] la fud Deu primes servi
Et reconnu pur segnnur.
    Ki ore irat od Loovis
    Ja mar d'enfern n'avarat pouur,
    Char s'alme en iert en pareïs
    Od les angles nostre segnor . . .

Knights, your salvation is at hand, when God calls out to you concerning the shame brought on Him by the Turks and Saracens, for they have wrongfully seized His fiefs. We have good cause to grieve, for it was there that God was first served and acknowledged as Our Lord.

Who now goes with Louis need never fear hell, for his soul will be in Paradise with the angels of Our Lord.

Prenez essample a Lodevis
Ki plus ad que vus n'avez
Riches reis e poestiz
Sur tuz altres est curunez
Deguerpit ad e vair e gris
Chastels e viles e citez
Il est tornez a icelui
Ki pur nus fut en croiz penez.
    Ki ore . . .[65]

Model yourself on Louis, a mightier man than you. A rich and powerful king, he is crowned above all others. He has forsaken furs, castles, and towns and cities and has turned to that one who for us was crucified. Who now . . .

Crusading songs of this kind were composed by troubadours and *trouvères* alike in the course of the twelfth and thirteenth centuries, and throw an interesting light on this vital aspect of contemporary history.

For long thought to be the earliest love-poems in northern France were the *chansons de toile* or *chansons d'histoire* which, according to a thirteenth-century poet, Jean Renart, were sung by the women as they worked at their spinning or embroidery. They are not subjective poems, but tell simple tales, as the title *chansons d'histoire* implies, concerning, for example, a girl's love for a knight who is away on a crusade:

Quant vient en mai, que l'on dit as
    lons jors,
que Franc de France repairent de
    roi cort,
Reynaud repaire devant el premier
    front,
si s'en passa lez lo mes Arembor,
ainz n'en deigna le chief drecier a
    mont.
    e Raynaut amis!

When days are long in the month of May, and Frenchmen of France are returning from the king's Court, Reynaud returns at their head and passed by Arembor's house without deigning to look up. Oh Raynaut my love!

Bele Erembors a la fenestre au jor	Fair Erembors in the daylight at the
sor ses genolz tient paile de color;	window holds coloured silk on her
voit Frans de France qui repairent	knees. She sees the Frenchmen of
de cort,	France returning from the king's
e voit Raynaut devant el premier	Court and Raynaut at their head.
front:	Aloud she speaks, and has expressed
en haut parole, si a dit sa raison.	her thoughts. Oh Raynaut my love!
e Raynaut amis![66]	

The use of assonance, the borrowing of terms such as *Franc de France* from epic works, a concept of love showing no trace of Provençal influence are some of the factors suggesting an early date for this and other such songs, some time in the first half of the twelfth century, contemporary with the first troubadours. However, a close analysis of the linguistic and stylistic characteristics of such poems has led one scholar to the conclusion that they are 'du faux ancien', composed in the thirteenth century with a deliberately old-fashioned flavour.[67] Furthermore, the pre-courtly nature of the love they portray is not an indisputable proof of earliness (neither is their sophisticated tone and atmosphere a proof of lateness), for the two concepts, however different, may have co-existed for a time.[68] On the other hand, the discovery, since Faral's article, of eleventh-century love-poems in Mozarabic Spain in which, as in the *chansons de toile*, the lady, not the knight, sings of her love, may be a sign that this was indeed an early genre which in the surviving *chansons* has suffered a late revision.[69] Late versions of what was probably also an early genre are provided by the *rondels* preserved in various thirteenth-century romances, principally Jean Renart's *Roman de la Rose*, also known as the *Roman de Guillaume de Dole*.[70] These were short dance-songs, whose simplest forms contained a refrain of one line only:

La jus, desoz la raime,	Yonder 'neath the branches, – that's
– *einsi doit aler qui aime,* –	the way the lover goes – brightly
clere i sourt la fontaine, y a!	springs the water, oh! that's the way
Einsi doit aler qui bele amie a.[71]	for lover and lass.

The *trouvères* of northern France were not able to renew the troubadouresque tradition, indeed they detracted from it by subduing, almost eliminating, the passion expressed in the words of the southerners' love-songs.[72] It is all in a lower key, less sensual, less hot-blooded, so that the love the *trouvères* professed to feel seems unreal by comparison and within its narrower confines fell more readily into stereotyped patterns. What in the south was a literary theme but something more as well, has now become literary theme only. It is perhaps no mere coincidence that it was further south, in Italy, that the Provençal love-poetry was to find a true renewal, in the *dolce stil nuovo*. Like the vine and the olive, *fin' amors* never seemed to flourish north of the Loire, save possibly in the objective form of the courtly romance, and even in that form it was frequently hedged about with moral considerations. Despite these strictures, the northern love-poetry often has considerable charm and a delicate grace which must be sought principally in the subtle variations on a given theme, always expressed, as in the south, within a carefully controlled structure. The wonder is that, within the limits they set themselves, the *trouvères* still managed to vary their material and to express something of their personality, as the following brief survey will endeavour to show.

VIII. CONON DE BÉTHUNE

There are roughly as many late twelfth-century *trouvères* whose names and works have survived as there are Provençal troubadours of the first half of the century. Earliest of all appears to be Chrétien de Troyes, far better known for his romances than for his two songs.[73] Outstanding among the early *trouvères* was Conon de Béthune, born towards the middle of the twelfth century of noble stock related to the House of Flanders. Henry IV's minister Sully was a descendant of the *trouvère*'s brother. A person of considerable historical importance, the archives and chronicles of the day relate Conon de Béthune's participation in the crusades. He became one of the leaders of the fourth crusade, a mediator whose eloquence was much appreciated, and played an important part in the founding of the Latin empire. He died in the East in 1219 or 1220. In his lyric poems, of which ten have survived, he presents his departure on the crusades in terms of separation from his lady, just as Charles d'Orléans, over 200 years later, was to speak of his long imprisonment in England:

Ahi! Amors, com dure departie
Me convenra faire de la millor
Ki onques fust amee ne servie!
Dieus me ramaint a li par sa douçor
Si voirement con j'en part a dolor!
Las! K'ai je dit? Ja ne m'en part
    je mie!
Se li cors va servir Nostre Signor,
Mes cuers remaint del tot en sa
    baillie.

Oh! Love, how grievous my departure from the best lady who was ever loved and served! May God in His mercy bring me back to her as truly as I part in grief! Alas! what have I said? I never leave her. If my body goes to serve Our Lord, my heart remains entirely in her power.

Por li m'en vois sospirant en Surie,
Car je ne doi faillir mon
    Creator ...[74]

For her I depart sighing to Syria, for I must not fail my Creator ...

As the poem proceeds, love and the lady disappear from view, and this is clearly no forlorn, swooning poet pouring his heart into his verse, but an intent, purposeful crusading knight, courtly lover by proxy only, whose real interests and devotion soon pierce the carapace of literary fashion:

Dieus est assis en son saint iretaige;
Ore i parra con cil le secorront
Cui il jeta de la prison ombraje,
Quant il fu mis ens la crois ke Turc ont.
Honi soient tot chil ki ramanront,
S'il n'ont poverte ou viellece ou malaige!
Et cil ki sain et jone et riche sont
Ne poevent pas demorer sans hontaige[75]

God is in His heavenly abode. Now we shall see what help He will receive from those He released from the dark prison, when He was put on the cross which the Turks now have. A plague on all those who stay behind unless they are poor, old, or ill. The healthy, the young, and the rich cannot stay behind without disgrace.

A somewhat impetuous, part-time wooer of the fair sex, he was quicker than many to direct his attentions elsewhere when they were clearly not wanted:

Dame, lonc tans ai fait vostre servise,
La merci Deu! c'or n'en ai mais talant,
Que m'est ou cuer une autre amor assise
Que me requiert et alume et esprant . . .

Lady, for a long time I have served you, God be praised, I have no desire for it any longer, for another love is planted in my heart, which seeks me out, sets me alight, and consumes me . . .

(ix, st. iii)

One poem of his vividly records how the relationship between lover and lady could so easily turn sour. A harsh note of realism is heard in these crisply worded stanzas which suggest that the courtly manners of the south had not as yet struck deep root in the north:

L'autrier avint en cel autre païs
C'uns chevaliers eut une dame amee.
Tant com la dame fut en son bon pris,
Li a s'amor escondite et veee.
Puis fu un jors k'ele li dist: 'Amis,
Mené vous ai par parole mains dis;
Ore est l'amours coneüe et provee.
Des or mes sui tot a vostre devis'.

Li chevalliers la regarda el vis,
Si la vit mout pale et descoulouree.
'Dame', fait il, 'certes mal sui baillis
Ke n'eüstes piech'a ceste pensee.
Vostres cler vis, ki sambloit flors de lis,
Est si alés, dame, de mal em pis
K'il m'est a vis ke me soiés emblee.
A tart avés, dame, cest consell pris . . .

The other day it happened in another country that a knight had loved a lady. As long as the lady was in her prime she refused to grant him her love. Then came the day when she said to him: 'My friend, I have put you off with words for many a day. Now your love is known and proved. Henceforth I am all yours'.

The knight looked her in the face, and saw she was very pale and discoloured. 'Lady', said he, 'in truth I deeply regret that you did not have such a thought long ago. Your clear complexion, which resembled a lily, has grown so much worse, lady, that you seem to have been stolen away from me. This idea has come to you too late, my lady. . .

(x, st. i, ii)

The poem becomes an exchange of insults in which the last word is left with the knight. Neither he nor the lady is shown in a good light, though Conon's intention seems to have been to attack ladies who keep their suitors dangling too long. Less fully committed to the fashionable literature of the day than other *trouvères*, he was none the less proud of his verse, and when attacked at Court for his northern dialect, in the presence of Marie de Champagne, he protested stoutly:

Encoir ne soit ma parole franchoise
Si la puet on bien entendre en
   franchois.[76]

My words may not be French, but they are perfectly understandable in French.

Poet and man of action, as vigorous and independent in the one sphere as in the other, not without reason has Conon de Béthune been called the most passionate and the most personal of the early lyric poets of northern France.[77]

IX. GUIOT DE PROVINS

The moralising note occasionally felt in Conon de Béthune's verse is far more evident in the verse of Guiot de Provins, author of *La Bible*, a satirical analysis, some 2,700 lines in length, 'du siecle puant et orrible' (of this stinking horrible age).[78] Only five of Guiot's songs, written between 1170 and 1190, have survived, representing probably 'une faible partie de l'œuvre lyrique de notre poète'.[79] They are, in the words of their editor, 'froidement conventionnelles', possessing 'une grâce qui tient plutôt au genre qu'à l'apport personnel du poète'.[80] None the less, a personal note is heard from time to time, as in the following lines, composed possibly when he was away on the third crusade:[81]

Molt avrai lonc tans demoré
Fors de ma douce contree
Et maint grant enui enduré
En terre malëuree.
Por ceu, n'ai je pas oblïé
Lo douz mal que si m'agree
Don ja ne quier avoir santé
Tant ai la dolor amee.

I shall have stayed for a long time away from my sweet homeland and endured many a great encumbrance in an ill-fated land. For all this, I have not forgotten that sweet ache which brought me such delight, of which I never seek to be cured, so dear to me is the pain.

Lonc tens ai en dolor esté
Et mainte larme ploree:
Li plus bels jors qui est d'esté
Me semble nois et jalee
Quant el païs que je plus hé
M'estuet faire demoree:
N'avrai mais joie en mon aé
S'en France ne m'est donee.[82]

I have sorrowed for a long time and wept many a tear. The finest summer day seems like snow and ice to me since I am compelled to stay in the country I hate the most. Never again shall I have joy in my life, unless it is given to me in France.

Towards the end of his life he forsook love's 'douz mal', and became a monk, first at Cîteaux, then at Cluny.

X. GUI, CHATELAIN DE COUCY

Fifteen songs have survived by Gui, chastelain de Coucy, who is
referred to in documents between 1186 and 1201.[83] They possess
considerable charm and liveliness:

Bien cuidai vivre sens amor
Desore en pais tot mon aé
Mais retrait m'a en la folor
Mes cuers dont l'avoie escapé.
Empris ai greignor folie,
Ke li fols emfés ki crie
Por la bele estoile avoir
K'il voit haut et cler seoir.
                    (III, st. i)

I really thought I could live without
love, in peace and quiet my whole
life through, but my heart has
dragged me back into that madness
from which I had rescued it. I am
acting far more foolishly than the
silly child who cries because he
wants the lovely star that he sees
high and bright in the sky.

Fond of springtime openings – six of his fifteen poems have
them – he gave them a freshness not always possessed by this well-
worn *topos*:

Li noviaus tens et mais et violete
Et rosignols me semont de canter,
Et mes fins cuers me fait d'une
        amorete
Si douc present, ke ne l'os refuser.
Or me laist Dius en tel honor
        monter
Ke chele ou j'ai mon cuer et mon
        penser
Tiegne une fois entre mes bras
        nuete,
    Ains ke voise outre mer.
                    (IX, st. i)

Springtime and May and the violet
and the nightingale invite me to
sing, and my true heart makes me a
sweet present of a love which I dare
not refuse. Now may God increase
my honour by allowing me to hold
naked in my arms the one in whom
I have placed all my heart and
thoughts, before I go overseas.

He was also, as these lines reveal, a crusading poet like Conon de
Béthune and Guiot de Provins, a less distinguished crusader than the
former no doubt, but a bolder poet to judge by the last line but one,
which according to one scholar, who has a keen eye for such things,
is the sole eroticism in the poetry of the early *trouvères*.[84]

XI. GACE BRULÉ

Regarded by some scholars as 'le classique de la lyrique courtoise
française',[85] is Gace Brulé, rivalled for the number of extant songs
attributed to him with fair certainty – sixty-nine – only by Thibaut

de Champagne in the following century, to whom sixty-one are attributed.[86] Belonging to the lesser nobility, Gace Brulé was born about 1160–65 in the region of Brie. He frequented the Court of Marie de Champagne and followed a career as a professional song-writer. His work bears the clear imprint of Provençal influence, in vocabulary (*fin amant, fine amor, fin cuer* are favourite expressions of his), in style, versification, and theme. Like Bernard de Venta-dour, he claims that his songs find their source in the true love with which his heart is filled:

Li pluseur ont d'Amours chanté Par esfors et desloiaument; Més de ce me doit savoir gré C'onques ne chantai faintement. Ma bone fois m'en a guardé, Et l'amours, dont j'ai tel plenté Que merveille est se je rienz hé Neïs cele anuieuse gent.	Many have sung about Love out of duty, and insincerely, but I am to be thanked inasmuch as I never sang in hypocritical fashion. My good faith kept me from this, and love, of which I have such an abundance that it is a marvel if I have any hate in me, even for love's detractors.
Certes, j'ai de fin cuer amé Ne ja n'amerai autrement . . . <div align=center>(XI, lines 1–10)</div>	To be sure, I have loved truly and never shall I love any other way . . .

Although here and elsewhere his themes are conventional, he is able on occasions to reach beyond them and to attain a truly lyrical note:

Les oiseillions de mon païs
  Ai oïs en Bretaigne.
A lor chant m'est il bien avis
Q'en la douce Champaigne
  Les oï jadis,
  Se n'i ai mespris.
Il m'ont en si dolz panser mis
K'a chanson faire me sui pris
Tant que je parataigne
Ceu q'Amors m'a lonc tens
  promis . . .
<div align=center>(I, 1–10)</div>
	I have heard in Brittany the birds of my own region. Their song tells me that I heard them long ago in sweet Champagne, unless I am mistaken. They have put such sweet thoughts into my head that I have begun to write a song that I shall continue until I achieve what Love has for long promised me . . .

It is usually the sadness of an unrequited and dominating love that he sings of rather than the joy and exaltation which provide one of the troubadours' favourite themes. He was as dedicated to love as Bernard de Ventadour, but his prevailing melancholy reflects a cooler and less sunny climate:

Bien est voirs qu'amours me desfent Joie et deport et gieu et ris . . . <div align=center>(XV, 33–4)</div>	Very true it is that love forbids me joy, happiness, play and laugh-ter . . .

Similar declarations can be found in the troubadours' poetry, but what for them was a passing cloud is here a sky of almost unbroken greyness.

XII. A THEORETICAL WORK: THE 'DE AMORE' OF ANDREAS CAPELLANUS

This chapter concludes, somewhat artificially, with a brief look at Andreas Capellanus's treatise on love, because it is often mentioned in association with the poetry of the *trouvères*, although in fact it is more closely related to the romances; from this point of view it will provide a suitable link between this chapter and the next. The troubadours appear to have produced no theoretical treatise on love. The early fourteenth-century *Leys d'Amors* was composed in a partially successful bid to keep Provençal alive as a literary language at a time when the troubadours' poetry had passed its peak, and, despite its title, is concerned essentially with grammar and the art of poetry-writing. However, the north filled the gap with the *De Amore* of Andreas Capellanus (André le Chapelain), composed possibly between 1184 and 1186 at the Court of Marie de Champagne. It is not simply a straightforward codex of the *fin' amors* doctrine,[87] and in any case its relative lateness means that it is unlikely to have been a formative influence on the poetry of the early *trouvères*. Besides, as indicated above, the *De Amore* bears closer affinities to the romances than to the love-poetry, and the nature and number of Andreas's *exempla* suggest that his literary interest lay rather in that direction. Whereas the troubadours and *trouvères* were concerned principally with the workings of love on the poet's mind and feelings, the *De Amore* was interested more in the sophistry of arguments and counter-arguments concerning various *social* implications of love rather than in its mental effects. In what circumstances may love properly flourish? What makes a man worthy of being loved? Does a man violate love's precepts if his lady is from a lower class? What sort of behaviour does love demand according to the rank of the man on the one hand, the woman on the other? Can true love exist between married people? These are some of the questions debated in this litigious work, much of which is presented in the form of dialogues, or debates, between a man and a woman chosen from different social classes. The answer to the last question was provided by Marie de Champagne herself: 'We declare and we hold as firmly established that love cannot exert its powers between two people who are married to each other'.[88] This could be a reflection of *fin' amors*, but it is more likely owed to the influence of Ovid (Naso magister erat) who is several times quoted in the course of the work. The *Ars Amatoria* contains exactly the same idea: the lack of all obstacles and restraint in marriage blunts the edge of love.[89] The chaplain's scholastically-oriented casuistry is fully employed in his distinction between 'pure love' which can have an erotic base but stops short of actual intercourse, and 'mixed love' which does involve intercourse. 'Pure love' is preferable,

> for this love goes on increasing without end, and we know that no-one ever regretted practising it, and the more of it one has the more one wants. This love is distinguished by being of such virtue that from it arises all excellence of character, and no injury comes from it, and God sees very little offence in it.[90]

Even clerics are not obliged to refrain from this love, for God made them no differently from others and they are subject to the same temptations as other men.

The two books comprising the *De Amore* are followed by a third, the *De Reprobatione Amoris*, a strange recantation, for the enthusiasm with which love has been discussed and advocated is now followed by a condemnation, given, however, a rational explanation in the opening paragraph: innocence must be based, not on ignorance, but on a full knowledge: 'For God is more pleased with a man who is able to sin and does not, than with a man who has no opportunity to sin'.[91] Understanding of carnal temptation gives a man full choice, and it is in the proper exercise of that choice that the true Christian reveals himself.

The success of the *De Amore* was considerable, as is shown by the twelve manuscripts in which it has survived, two thirteenth-century translations into French, two into Italian, and two into German. It has been hailed as 'one of those capital works which reflect the thought of a great epoch and which explain the secret of a civilisation'.[92] This is fulsome praise, but the interest of the *De Amore* is that it does indeed reveal something of the preoccupations of the aristocratic literary circles of northern France in the late twelfth century and the difficulties which the rapidly developing society of those times was facing, difficulties which found very different expression in the romances of Chrétien de Troyes.

NOTES

1. P. Dronke, *Medieval Latin and the Rise of European Love-Lyric*, 2 vols., Oxford, 1965–66, I, 192–220.
2. ibid., 263.
3. B. Dutton, 'Some new evidence for the Romance origins of the Muhwashshahas', *BHS*, XLII, 1965, 73–8.
4. For ways in which Ovid may be said to adumbrate medieval notions on love, see Dronke, op. cit., I, 163–81.
5. C. S. Lewis, *The Allegory of Love*, London, 1936; latest ed. 1965, 7.
6. H. Davenson, *Les Troubadours*, Paris, 1961, 132; 2nd ed., this time under the author's real name, H.-I. Marrou, Paris, 1971, 135.
7. op. cit., I, 2–3.
8. H. J. Chaytor, *The Troubadours*, Cambridge, 1912, 5.
9. It has been suggested that there was a close relationship between

Provençal love-poetry and the Catharist heresy: '... le lyrisme courtois fut *au moins inspiré* par l'atmosphère religieuse du catharisme'. (D. de Rougemont, *L'Amour et l'occident*, Paris, 1939, 84). This gratuitous view has not found general favour.

10. See above, pp. 10, 14.

11. The expression *amour courtois* was coined by Gaston Paris in the nineteenth century. Troubadour poetry appears to contain only one such instance: *cortez' amors* in Peire d'Alvernhe according to Dronke, op. cit., I, 46.

12. 'A keen lover of women, an enemy of all decency and sanctity'.

13. R. R. Bezzola, *Les Origines et la formation de la littérature courtoise en occident*, 5 vols., Paris, 1944–62, II, 2, 275–316.

14. This same theme was known to Boccaccio.

15. Maria Dumitrescu, 'Eble II de Ventadorn et Guillaume IX d'Aquitaine', *CCMe*, XI, 1968, 379–412. The argumentation is subtle but somewhat forced in the view of F. Lecoy, *R*, XCI, 1970, 428.

16. Bezzola, op. cit., 275–316.

17. The lady was never named, but was referred to in a pseudonym, as here, known as a 'senhal'.

18. A. Jeanroy ed., *Les Chansons de Guillaume IX*, Paris, CFMA, 2nd ed. 1927, Poem x on pp. 24–6.

19. For details of different 'coblas', see Marrou, op. cit., 69.

20. The *versus* in its lyric form has been defined as '... à peu près tous les chants strophiques ne faisant pas partie de l'office, qu'ils soient profanes ou pieux'. See J. Chailley, *L'École musicale de Saint Martial de Limoges jusqu'à la fin du XIe siècle*, Paris, 1960, 152.

21. ibid., 370–1.

22. Dronke, op. cit., I, 46–8; and A. R. Press, 'The Adulterous Nature of Fin' Amors: A Re-examination of the theory', *FMLS*, VI, 1970, 327–41.

23. 'gensor' can also mean 'better-looking'.

24. Bezzola, op. cit., II, 2, 296.

25. ibid., 296.

26. ibid., 311.

27. ibid., 316.

28. P. Dronke, 'Guillaume IX and Courtoisie', *RF*, LXXIII, 1961, 327.

29. ibid., 338.

30. Poem VII, st. vi.

31. ed. A. Jeanroy, Paris, CFMA, 1922.

32. J. Boutière and A.-H. Schutz eds., *Biographies des Troubadours, textes provençaux des XIIIe et XIVe siècles*, Toulouse–Paris, 1950, 202–3. Even though these biographies are often sketchy and unreliable, the fact that they were written at all shows something of the interest in the troubadours in the Middle Ages.

33. The troubadour Marcabru addressed a poem to 'Jaufre Rudel outra mar' (across the sea), see J.-M.-L. Dejeanne ed., *Poésies complètes du troubadour Marcabru*, Toulouse, 1909, Poem xv, line 38.

34. ed. A. Jeanroy, Paris, CFMA, 1924.

35. G. Frank, 'The Distant Love of Jaufré Rudel', *MLN*, LVII, 1942, 528–34.

36. P. Dronke, *The Medieval Lyric*, London, 1968, 120.

37. For these hypotheses, see Marrou, op. cit., 162–3.

38. L. Spitzer, 'L'Amour lointain de Jaufré Rudel', in *Romanische Literaturstudien 1936–1956*, Tübingen, 1959, 363–417.

39. It is not surprising that critics have readily associated Rudel's poem with the crusades; ibid., 416.

40. M. Lazar ed., *Bernard de Ventadour, Chansons d'Amour*, Paris, 1966.

41. E. Hoeppfner, *Les Troubadours dans leur vie et dans leurs œuvres*, Paris, 1955, 77.

42. Lazar, op. cit., 12.

43. ibid., 54.

44. ibid., 13.

45. ed. A. Stimming, *Bertran von Born*, Halle, 2nd ed., 1913; and C. Appel, *Die Lieder Bertrans von Born*, Halle, 1932. The poem is no. 41 in Stimming's edition.
46. J. Linskill ed., *The Poems of the Troubadour Raimbaut de Vaqueiras*, The Hague, 1964, 16.
47. Hoeppfner, op. cit., 74.
48. Dronke, *Medieval Latin and the Rise of European Love Lyric*, I, 107–12.
49. S. C. Aston, *Peirol, Troubadour of Auvergne*, Cambridge, 1953, 10.
50. See poems v, vi, xxiii, xxiv, xxv.
51. R. Lavaud, *Poésies complètes du troubadour Peire Cardenal*, Toulouse, 1957, Poem i, lines 19–24.
52. Hoeppfner, op. cit., 94.
53. Dronke, *The Medieval Lyric*, 170.
54. Maritz qui l'autrui con grata / Ben pot saber que. l sieus / pescha . . .   A husband who tickles another's — should realise that his own may well be up to no good . . .
(xi, lines 49–50)
55. Ja non creirai, qui que m'o jur, / Que vins non iesca de razim / Et hom per Amor nos meillur . . .   I shall never believe – whoever swears it is the truth – that wine does not come from grapes, and that a man is not improved by love . . .
(xiii, lines 25–7)
56. Dronke, *The Medieval Lyric*, 210.
57. Provided they were educated men versed in the ways of courtesy. Merchants whose only interest lay in the accumulation of wealth were excluded.
58. On medieval music and instruments, the following may be consulted: T. Gérold, *La Musique au moyen âge*, Paris, CFMA, 1932; J. Chailley, *Précis de musicologie*, Paris, 1958; G. Reese, *Music in the Middle Ages*, London, 1941 (chapter 7, 'Secular Monody', is particularly informative on the musical settings of the troubadours' verse); H. van der Werf, *The Chansons of the Troubadours and Trouvères. A Study of the Melodies and their Relation to the Poems*, Utrecht, 1972.
59. Marrou, op. cit., 89.
60. See below, pp. 279–80.
61. Dejeanne, ed. cit., Poem xx, stanza vi.
62. J. Orr ed., *Les Œuvres de Guiot de Provins*, Manchester, 1915, *La Bible*, 12, lines 70–1.
63. See below, p. 123.
64. The date of this poem is referred to in N. H. J. van den Boogaard, *Rondeaux et refrains du XIIᵉ siècle au début du XIVᵉ*, Paris, 1969, 10–11.
65. A facsimile of the manuscript may be seen, along with a transcription of the text, in P. Aubry, *Les Plus Anciens Monuments de la musique française*, Paris, 1905, Planche III. See also P. Meyer, *Recueil d'anciens textes*, Paris, 1877, 366.
66. The complete text of this poem, six stanzas altogether, may be seen in A. Pauphilet ed., *Poètes et Romanciers du Moyen Age*, Bibliothèque de la Pléiade, vol. 52, 2nd ed. 1952, 825–6; also in B. Woledge ed., *The Penguin Book of French Verse*, vol. I, Harmondsworth, 1968, 83–4.
67. E. Faral, 'Les Chansons de Toile ou Chansons d'Histoire', R, LXIX, 1947, 433–62.
68. Dronke, *The Medieval Lyric*, 98–9.
69. P. Le Gentil, *La Littérature française du Moyen Age*, Paris, 1963, 69.
70. See van den Boogaard, op. cit.
71. ibid., 27.
72. See the remarks of M. Lazar in *Amour Courtois et fin' amors dans la littérature du XIIᵉ siècle*, Paris, 1964, 266–7.
73. Chrétien's songs have been edited by W. Foerster in *Kristian von Troyes, Wörterbuch zu seinen sämtlichen Werken*, Halle a.S., 1914, Part II, 202–9.

74. A. Wallensköld ed., *Les Chansons de Conon de Béthune*, Paris, CFMA, 1921, Poem ıv, lines 1–10.
75. Lines 17–24 of the same poem.
76. Poem ııı, lines 10–11.
77. DLF, 220.
78. See Orr, ed. cit., *La Bible*, line 1, and below pp. 266–7.
79. ibid., xix.
80. ibid., xii, xix.
81. xiii, 114.
82. First two stanzas of Chanson ııı, ibid., 5.
83. F. Fath, *Die Lieder des Castellans von Coucy*, Heidelberg, 1883.
84. Lazar, *Amour Courtois*, 267.
85. *DLF*, 290.
86. ed. H. P. Dyggve, *Gace Brulé, trouvère champenois*, Helsinki, 1951.
87. Different views have been expressed on this, cf. *MAe*, XXXII, 1963, 56–60, P. Dronke's review of F. Schlösser's work on Andreas Capellanus.
86. ed. H. P. Dyggve, *Gace Brulé, trouvère champenois*, Helsinki, 1951.
York, 1941; reprinted 1959, 1964, 106.
89. Book III, lines 583–8.
90. Parry, op. cit., 122.
91. ibid., 187.
92. R. Bossuat, quoted ibid., 3.

Chapter 5

TWELFTH-CENTURY ROMANCE

I. THE ROMANS D'ANTIQUITÉ

TOWARDS the middle of the twelfth century, when Provençal influence had not yet made an impact on the literature of northern France, several works based on Latin, or Latinised Greek, sources appeared, principally the *Roman de Thèbes*, composed about 1150; *Piramus et Tisbé*, dating from about the same period, or possibly a little later; the *Roman d'Eneas*, composed about 1160; the *Roman de Troie* about 1165; *Narcisus* about 1170.[1] Also, from about the beginning to beyond the end of this century, various versions of the story of Alexander the Great appeared. These are the earliest French works traditionally known as romances,[2] and because of their sources are usually referred to nowadays as the 'romans d'antiquité'. They occupy an important place in the history of medieval French literature and deserve more attention than can be given them in a manual of this type. They represent a confluence of different traditions: that of the *chansons de geste*; that of classical authors, Ovid in particular; and eventually that of the Provençal Courts, perceptible mainly in one of the latest *romans d'antiquité*, the *Roman de Troie*, dedicated by its author Benoît de Sainte-Maure to Aliénor d'Aquitaine. Classical influence reached beyond the stories themselves to matters of style and presentation, works such as the *Rhetorica ad Herennium*, attributed in those times to Cicero, being studied in the church schools. Besides forming the scholars who made their careers in the Church, these schools also produced numbers of clerks in minor orders who appear to have been the authors of the romances, even though most of these were mundane and secular in inspiration. Particularly illuminating is a comparison of these stories with their chief Latin sources, of which they are free adaptations rather than faithful translations. The differences introduced by the medieval poets throw light on their particular interests and those of the *milieux* for which they were writing. The brief portrait given by Statius of Argia and Deiphile, daughters of Adrastus, is expanded enormously in the *Roman de Thèbes*, as the following passages reveal:

... mirabile visu,
Pallados armisonae pharetrataeque ora Dianae
aequa ferunt, terrore minus, nova deinde pudori
visa virum facies: pariter pallorque ruborque
purpureas hausere genas, oculique verentes
ad sanctum rediere patrem.[3]

Mout furent gentes les puceles,	The girls were extremely good-looking, unrivalled in any country. Never did Pallas or Diana surpass their beauty. They are very lovely and pleasant to behold, neither too big nor too small, of the same height and appearance, with nothing displeasing. Their long hair fair and fine hangs down to their feet, their faces are open, their foreheads white, their eyebrows slender and charming; their eyes are bright and loving, no man saw such marvellous ones. Their long slender noses were well set, neither too small nor too big. Their mouths were straight and majestic, their teeth white, small, and even ...
en nul païs n'en ot tant beles;	
onques Palla ne Dyana	
la leur biauté ne sormonta.	
Mout sont gentes et avenanz,	
ne trop petites ne trop granz,	
d'une grandeur et d'un semblant,	
rien n'i avoit mesavenant.	
Cheveux ont blonz, lons et deugiez,	
si lor descendent jusqu'as piez,	
les vis aperz et les fronz blanz,	
grelle sourcils et avenanz;	
les eulz ont vers et amoreux,	
nus hom ne vit si merveillex;	
lons nés traitis et bien seanz,	
ne sont trop petiz ne trop granz.	
Bouches ont droites et roiaux,	
menues denz blanches, ygaux ...[4]	

Iseut in Béroul's *Tristan*, Camille in *Eneas* are described in similar terms. The likelihood is, it has been said, that 'all three authors reproduce a model description picked up in the schools or from the arts of poetry and rhetoric of the times'.[5] Significant is the change from *oculi verentes* (timid eyes) to 'eulz ... amoreux' (loving eyes). The love element is not yet fully developed in this early romance, but it is noteworthy that Ismène's lament over the death of her fiancé Atys fills one line and a half in Statius's *Thebaid*, and sixty in the *Roman de Thèbes*.[6] This is also in marked contrast to the *Chanson de Roland*, where Alde's lament over the death of her fiancé Roland covers a mere two and a half lines.

The story of the tragic love of Pyramus and Thisbe, which occupied only 111 lines of Ovid's *Metamorphoses* (Book IV, 55–166), was expanded in a Norman poem written sometime in the later twelfth century to 921 lines, far more attention being devoted to the lovers' expression of their feelings.[7] Ovid is intent on telling a sad little tale to explain how the mulberry-tree got its dark-coloured berries, which once had been white, but which had been stained by Pyramus's blood when, wrongly believing that Thisbe had been killed by a lion, he stabbed himself to death beneath its branches. The French author, while not discarding this aspect, was more interested in the love story for its own sake. Whereas direct speech takes up only a small part of Ovid's tale and is devoted mainly to soliloquies, the lovers' self-questioning monologues take up over half the French tale (484 out of 921 lines) and are presented with considerable skill. A line of only two syllables sometimes completes the meaning of the preceding line, sometimes introduces a sentence completed in the following lines, and always has the same rhyme as the group of two, three, or four octosyllabic lines following:

'Las, cheitif, tristes et dolent,
Soufferai longues cest tourment?
Tous tens ai duel, joie noient,
Et plus me dueil et plus m'esprent
    Amour.
Amour la nom? Mes est ardour,
Qui einsi vient de jour en jour.
Fletrist ma face et ma coulour,
Com fait gelee tenre flour.
    Hé las!'

'Alas, wretch that I am, sad and downcast, shall I suffer this torment for long? I have constant grief, no joy at all, and the more I grieve the more does love set me alight. I call it love? Rather is it an ardour which comes on like this from day to day. It withers my face and my complexion as the frost withers a tender flower. Alas!'

(150–9)

Only two short monologues do not follow this pattern, consisting of octosyllabics on the same rhyme, whereas the narrative sections are composed of octosyllabic rhyming couplets. The heterometric verse conveys in its broken and uneven gait something of the lovers' emotional stress, cleverly brought out since the dissyllabic line often carries an exclamation, a question, or a word of particular importance. The author's aim was clearly to harmonise content and form. Nurtured in the rhetorical tradition, he brought various stylistic devices into play in order to achieve the maximum effect. However, there is as yet no evidence of Provençal influence. This is simply a tale of the innocent love of two adolescents with none of the sophistication and artifices of the troubadours' doctrine.

Similar techniques are followed in *Narcisus*,[8] where in place of Ovid's 171 lines in the *Metamorphoses* (Book III, 339–510) the French poet has 1,010, consisting entirely of octosyllabic couplets. Much of the text is given up to the skilfully exploited technique of self-questioning and self-analysis, firstly by Danae after she has fallen in love with Narcisus, then by the latter after seeing his reflection in the water. Mythical characters such as the nymph Echo are eliminated, and a purely human situation is created. The very nature of this story, in which the girl falls in love with the boy, who remains stonily indifferent, was bound to isolate it from the courtly tradition, although it is mentioned by certain troubadours.

Eneas modifies its principal source in a rather similar manner. Whereas Vergil never informs us what were the feelings of Lavinia for Aeneas,[9] the medieval French poet tells at inordinate length of the effects of love on each of them. In the following passage, Lavinia has been bitten, not by a mad dog as one could suppose, but by love:

Ele comance a tressüer,
a refroidir et a tranbler,
sovant se pasme et tressalt,
sanglot, fremist, li cuers li falt,
degiete soi, sofle, baaille:
bien l'a Amors mise an sa taille![10]

She begins to perspire, to feel cold,
and to tremble, often she faints and
shudders, she sobs, she shivers, her
heart fails her, she throws herself on
the ground, she pants, she sighs.
Love has really got her in his grip!

Clearly, in all such cases, Vergil has been pushed into the back-ground, and once more it is Ovid who is the guide. Ovid's satirical intent is absent, or at least greatly subdued, but the treatment of love is lively and often amusing, as when Queen Amata, surprised to find that her daughter Lavinia does not love Turnus, asks her the name of her lover, and receives an incoherent sigh-interrupted reply:

... 'Il a non E ...'
puis sospira, se redist: 'ne ...',
d'iluec a piece noma: 'as ...'
(lines 1553–5)

... 'He is called E ...' then she
sighed, and spoke again: 'ne ...'
and after some time she added:
'as ...'

Meantime Aeneas, as torn asunder as his name, fares no better and spends as tormented a night as does Lavinia. Such developments set the pattern for many a later romance:

... désormais, dans tous les romans courtois, il sera de règle que les amants, inspirés par Ovide et par lui [i.e., the unknown author of *Eneas*], décrivent, en de longs monologues intimes, leurs sentiments, débattent des problèmes de casuistique amoureuse, et, travaillés par l'insomnie et la fièvre, discourent sur le Dieu d'Amour, sur la douceur ou sur la cruauté de ses lois, sur les flèches d'or qui font aimer, sur ses flèches de plomb qui font haïr.[11]

It has been claimed that, already in the *Roman de Thèbes* and in *Eneas*, French romance was completely and fully defined.

The 30,000 lines of Benoît de Sainte-Maure's *Roman de Troie*[12] make use of the same basic elements, with, possibly, greater refine-ment and elegance, and certainly greater erudition, revealed in 'une masse de renseignements géographiques, zoologiques, cosmo-logiques, minéralogiques, ethnographiques'.[13] This heterogeneous material may seem out of place in a romance, but it is a bagatelle when set beside Jean de Meun's endless lucubrations in the thirteenth-century *Roman de la Rose*. Benoît knew no Greek, and relied on two early medieval Latin sources by writers who made the preposterous claim – still accepted long after Benoît – that they had witnessed the Trojan wars: Dares's *De excidio Trojae historiae*, described by Benoît's editor as 'horriblement monotone', and Dictys's *Ephemeris*. It is to Benoît's credit that he breathed life into this unpromising material, though his tale does have what the French refer to as 'des longueurs'. A section of 500 lines describes the facial appearance of each of the heroes and heroines of the Trojan wars. Contrived and artificial though this portrait gallery may be, it shows that the writers of romances were becoming more interested in their characters as individuals, for what they were, not simply for what they could do. It is true that already in the *Chanson de Roland* an attempt is made to typify the Saracen and Christian protagonists, but such portraits are less specific than those of the romances. Favourite pastimes are sometimes included, and social accomplishments begin to loom large. Here, for example, is the portrait of Priam:

Mout par fu beaus e lons e granz,
Ço dit l'Escriz, li reis Prianz.
Le nes e la boche e le vis
Ot bien estant e bien asis;
La parole aveit auques basse,
Soëf voiz ot e douce e quasse.
Mout par esteit bons chevaliers,
E matin manjot volentiers.
(lines 5295–302)

King Priam, according to the story, was very handsome and tall. His nose, mouth, and face were of fine appearance and well set. His voice was rather low, soft, gentle, and deep in tone. He was a very fine knight, and ate heartily in the morning.

Battles there still are in abundance – twenty-two, for example, outside the walls of Troy, but the love element too is by no means neglected. In the following passage Achilles has just set eyes on Polyxena:

Sovent mue color sa face:
Sovent l'a pale, et puis vermeille.
A sei meïsme se conseille
Que ço puet estre que il sent,
Qu'ensi freidist e puis resprent . . .
(17606–10)

His face often changes colour, often pale, then crimson. He deliberates with himself as to what it is that makes him feel hot and then cold . . .

A comparison of this passage with that quoted from *Eneas* shows the continuing interest in the psychology of love, and how a particular style and vocabulary were crystallising around it. This description of Achilles's plight is followed by over a hundred lines of direct speech in which he analyses his feelings, made the more complex because his love is for the sister of Hector whom he has killed. This situation was to find a parallel in Chrétien de Troyes's *Yvain*, in which the hero falls in love with the widow of a knight he has killed. Benoît, like his anonymous predecessors, has a keen eye for all that is luxurious and beautiful: rich silken materials made in India 'par nigromance et par merveille' (13343) (by magic and wonder), palace rooms sparkling with the twelve most precious stones that God made (14636 ff.), carved pillars of jasp and onyx, and a splendid array of musical instruments (14781 ff.). The changing tastes of courtly society, increasing knowledge of oriental luxuries brought about by the prospering commerce with the East, the broadening and enriching of the lives of the twelfth-century nobility are faithfully reflected in such details.

The *Roman d'Alexandre* was expanded from an early twelfth-century octosyllabic Franco-Provençal version by Alberic de Pisançon, of which only 105 lines are extant, based on the pseudo-Callisthenes of the second century A.D. Through a decasyllabic version it developed to the late twelfth-century compilation in lines of 12 syllables, whence the name alexandrine verse. In the course of its growth at the hands of various authors, some anonymous, some whose names at least have survived, it acquired from different sources a large number of exotic, fantastic elements, referred to collectively as 'le merveilleux'. Although it probably predated *Eneas* and the *Roman de Troie* in this respect, this was not necessarily the first story to introduce oriental fantasies to the people of northern France – the earliness of the *Vie de Saint Brendan* must not be forgotten – but they are certainly much more elaborate here and in a far richer variety. The medieval romance has here acquired another of its characteristics.

II. THE LEGEND OF TRISTAN AND ISEUT

In the first half of this most dynamic and creative of the medieval centuries, the poets of northern France found a new source in Celtic material. Among the earliest Celtic legends to be exploited is one whose fame, thanks to the interest shown in it by the French poets, has far transcended its own times: the story of Tristan and Iseut. This tragic tale of lovers in the grip of an overwhelming passion which transgressed all social and moral conventions ranks among the world's masterpieces. The lost original was probably owed to a mid-twelfth-century poet of northern France, or possibly an Anglo-Norman poet of the same period. The tale quickly acquired tremendous popularity and was several times retold by various of his contemporaries, but no complete French version has survived from the twelfth century. The largest single fragment extant from that century, 4,485 octosyllabic lines attributed to Béroul, may be the work of two authors, but this, like so many aspects of the legend, is hotly contested,[14] whereas what is indubitably owed to a single author, Thomas, has survived in nine fragments.[15] A further complication is that, whereas Béroul's version is usually considered to be closer in nature than Thomas's to the lost original (commonly referred to, from a passage in Béroul, lines 1789–92, as the *Estoire*), Béroul appears to have composed his version in the last decade of the twelfth century,[16] whereas Thomas's was composed earlier, between 1155 and 1170. It is possible that both were written in England.[17] Thomas in particular seems anxious to please an English audience, and paints a glowing picture of the glories of London:

Lundres est mult riche cité	London is a most splendid city, there

Lundres est mult riche cité
Meliur n'ad en cristienté
Plus vaillante ne melz preisiee,
Melz guarnie de gent aisiee.
Mult aiment largesce e honur,
Cunteinent sei par grant baldur.
(2651–6)

London is a most splendid city, there
is none better in Christianity, none
more worthy or more esteemed or
better supplied with people of ample
means. They have a great love of
generosity and honour, and are very
joyful in their behaviour.

Béroul's version is paralleled by the Middle High German romance by Eilhart von Oberge, composed about the same time or a little earlier,[18] whereas Thomas's more courtly version was the source of Gottfried von Strassburg's *Tristan und Isolt*, written about 1210, which has been hailed as the greatest poem of the Middle Ages after the *Canterbury Tales* and the *Divina Commedia*. The Norwegian prose saga by the Monk Robert, from about 1226, and the Middle English *Sir Tristrem* from the last decade of the thirteenth century, are also indebted to Thomas, and have indeed been used by the modern editor of Thomas's poem to fill the many gaps in what has survived of the French poem. From twelfth-century French literature several episodic pieces concerning Tristan have also survived. Particularly worthy of mention are two with the title *La Folie Tristan*, one a Norman poem of 572 lines, the other an Anglo-Norman poem of 998 lines; also the *Lai du Chievrefeuil*, by the earliest known French poetess, Marie de France, who lived and wrote in England in the latter half of the twelfth century.[19] Other twelfth-century French versions, possibly of the complete legend, are known to have existed: one by a certain La Chievre,[20] the other by Chrétien de Troyes, the most outstanding author of romances of the century. The French prose *Tristan*, composed between 1215 and 1235, whose popularity is attested by the large number of manuscripts and translations and adaptations in English, German, Italian, Russian, and Spanish,[21] is a much-adulterated version of the legend, although the author seems to have known both the Béroul and Thomas versions:

Of the original character of the Tristan poems, of the blendings of magic and tragedy which had made the legend great, few traces remain in the prose romance, and fewer still in its modern adaptations.[22]

As regards its sources, the story is an amalgam which bears the strong imprint of twelfth-century northern France. It is, in the words of Professor Ewert, 'a compound of Celtic, popular and classical lore'.[23] The Celtic origin is reflected in a number of ways, most obviously in the names, particularly that of the hero:

The name is of Celtic origin, being connected with the name (*Drest–Drostan*) borne by Pictish kings in the seventh–ninth centuries, transmitted through Welsh (*Drystan*), Cornish (*Tröstan*) and possibly English (*Trystan*) to the French as *Tristan*[24] and also in resemblances, at times very close, to Irish tales such as that of Diarmaid and Grainne.[25] On the other hand, Graeco-Latin mythology is reflected in elements of the story which seem to have been part already of the *Estoire*: the influence of the Minotaur legend may account for Morholt's exacting of a tribute of young men and women from Cornwall, and that of Theseus for the use of a white or black sail according to whether Iseut is or is not on board the ship bringing Tristan the last hope of a cure for his poisoned wound. Even this theme, however, has latterly been ascribed to a Breton tradition.[26] The Celts may never have possessed the story of the tragic lovers in a fully developed romance. Whether or not the *Estoire* was a fully constituted French romance in all its textual detail must remain an open question.[27]

A comparison of the various extant versions enabled the brilliant medieval scholar Joseph Bédier to reconstruct the essential elements of the *Estoire*, an exercise which, however hypothetical, remains invaluable.[28] The following account is based on that reconstruction, but, intended only as an outline, does not follow all the episodes.[29]

Rivalen, king of Loonois [=Lothian], marries Blanchefleur, sister of King Mark of Cornwall. The queen dies giving birth to a boy. Born in sadness, he is called Tristan.[30] Entrusted to a wise master, Governal, Tristan enters the service of his uncle Mark and eventually attains the age of knighthood. At this time the giant Morholt, whose sister is married to the king of Ireland, lands in Cornwall to demand a tribute of young men and women. Tristan offers to fight him. In the ensuing combat the giant is mortally wounded and Tristan is poisoned by his weapon. Morholt is taken by his companions to Ireland, where he dies. Still suffering from his wound, Tristan casts off alone in an open boat to seek death or a cure. He lands in Ireland where he pretends to be a jongleur, Tantris by name. The king hears him play on his harp and takes him to his palace. Cured by Iseut, daughter of the king of Ireland,[31] Tristan returns to Cornwall. King Mark, greatly attached to him, desires to treat him as his heir, but his barons object and persuade him to marry. Reluctant, Mark declares that he will only marry the woman to whom belongs the golden hair that a swallow has carried through the window. Tristan sets off on a quest to find her and once more lands in Ireland. He kills a dragon that has been terrorising the inhabitants, but is poisoned by its tongue. He is cured as before by Iseut. He tells her that King Mark of Cornwall desires to marry her. The king of Ireland gives his consent, and Tristan and Iseut set sail accompanied by the latter's confidant Brangain, to whom the queen has given a love-potion, to be drunk by Mark and Iseut on their wedding-night. Those who take it will be bound by an indissoluble love.[32] Brangain gives the potion to Tristan and Iseut in error, and they fall in love. The boat lands at Tintagel, and the wedding of Mark and Iseut takes place. Brangain, yielding to the entreaties of the lovers (for whose plight she was responsible) takes her mistress's place in the wedding-bed. Tristan and Iseut keep their love secret for some time but are eventually denounced by the barons, and Tristan is banished from Court. Their secret meeting-place in an orchard is discovered by the king's dwarf. Mark is informed and hides in a tree. The lovers notice his shadow and pretend that they are innocent. Mark, deceived, recalls Tristan to Court.

The dwarf prepares another trap for them, and they are caught and sentenced to death. Tristan escapes and rescues Iseut. They go to live in the forest of Morrois[33] along with Tristan's old master Governal and his faithful dog Husdent. One day the king finds them asleep, separated by Tristan's sword. The king replaces it with his own, and departs. In response to this sign of clemency, Iseut returns to Court and gives Tristan her ring, to be used by any messenger he sends to her. Tristan offers his services to Hoël, duke of Brittany, defeats his enemies, and marries his daughter Iseut aux Blanches Mains, attracted by her name as much as by her beauty.[34] Ever mindful of the first Iseut, he is unable to consummate the marriage. His wife eventually confesses to her brother Kaherdin that she is still a virgin. Tristan takes Kaherdin to Cornwall so that he can see for himself the beauty of the Iseut Tristan can never forget. They are received in secret by Iseut and Brangain. Forced to depart in the morning, Tristan later returns in various disguises: as a leper, as a penitent, as a madman. In this last disguise[35] Tristan, in the presence of Mark and Iseut, intersperses his incoherences with allusions to his life with Iseut, to whom he shows the ring she has given him. The king, not recognising him, finds him amusing and allows him to stay, but Tristan has to depart once more when servants discover the ruse. Back again in Brittany, he is gravely wounded in a combat and only Iseut, who twice before has cured him, can save him. A messenger is sent in secret to her. If she returns in the boat, it will carry a white sail; if not, a black one. Tristan's wife discovers his secret, and jealously announces that the sail is black. Tristan dies of grief. Iseut, arriving shortly afterwards, kisses his body and dies at his side. Mark at last learns the full story of how they had been bound together by the magic potion. They are buried side by side, and two trees grow on their grave and entwine their branches.

The Béroul fragment contains the central section of the story, beginning with the lovers' meeting beneath the tree in whose branches Mark is hiding, and ending with various episodes, not apparently in the *Estoire*, intercalated between the reconciliation of Mark and Iseut after the Morrois interlude and Tristan's entering the service of the duke of Brittany. In some of these, King Arthur and his knights are introduced. In the final extant scenes, Tristan kills two of the malevolent barons who had constantly opposed him. Only one remains alive, whose very name, Ganelon, was enough to earn him the hatred of a medieval audience. The greater extant part of Thomas's poem deals with Tristan's marriage to the second Iseut and with the final episodes of the work. The first of the Thomas fragments, a mere 52 lines, follows Mark's discovery of the lovers asleep in the forest. No direct comparison of the two versions is possible, since the surviving portions do not overlap. It is clear, however, that their ways of telling the story were very different. Béroul, *chanson de geste* style, keeps the narrative moving at a smart pace and adds a minimum of comment. The characters are delineated by their words and deeds more than by description, and they have no time for lengthy introspection. Béroul is wholly involved in the story, and his sympathies are entirely on the side of the lovers, as were doubtless those of the *Estoire*'s author, for the exposure of the lovers was owed to an evil, misshapen dwarf who had powers of necromancy – 'Dehé aient tuit cil devin!' (line 646) (A curse on all these soothsayers!) exclaims Béroul. The three barons who sought Tristan's discomfiture had in fact a very good case, for they knew of his adultery but not of the magic potion; however, they had been jealous of Tristan's success at Mark's Court even before Iseut joined it, and found in his adultery a convenient motive for getting rid of him. Béroul refers to them as the 'felons' (582) and even expresses regret that Tristan did not kill them much earlier than he did (825). He peppers his narrative with exclamations and exhortations, as though he were one of the audience constantly surprised and excited by the action, eager to know what would happen next. When Tristan resolves to speak to the queen at the risk of giving away their love, Béroul interjects: 'Dex! quel pechié! trop ert hardiz!' (700) (Oh God! what folly! he will be too bold!). Again, when Tristan acts strangely in his endeavour to outwit the dwarf, Béroul himself seems astonished: 'Dex! porqoi fist? Or escoutez' (728) (Oh God! why did he do that? Now listen). He is occasionally crude, showing, as Ewert says, a 'predilection for the earthy and the barbarous'.[36] There are touches of a rough and boisterous humour, as when a band of lepers prepares for action like grotesque caricatures of knights, their leader shouting: 'Now to your crutches, men!' (1251). The main impression his narrative leaves is owed to its terse, crisp, unflagging style as he whisks his audience from one episode and one character to another, but despite the emphasis on action, the characters are well drawn. Particularly noteworthy, apart from the lovers themselves, is King Mark, deeply attached to his nephew, pathetically reluctant to think ill of him, constantly swinging between extremes as he is torn this way and that:

Li rois n'a pas coraige entier	The king is not of one mind, at one
Senpres est ci et senpres la.	time he's here, at another there.
(3432–3)	

Thomas was equally interested in human nature, but his approach is altogether different. When Tristan decides to marry Iseut aux Blanches Mains in a desperate bid to forget his love for the queen, Thomas exclaims:

| Cum genz sunt d'estrange nature! | How strange are the ways of men! |
| (286) | |

He goes on in a lengthy digression to condemn man's restless search for novelty, ever dissatisfied with his lot:

Novelerie fait gurpir	Novelty makes men forsake good
Buen poeir pur malveis desir . . .	power for evil desire . . .
(307–8)	

Among the texts dealt with so far in this volume, only one bears comparison with Thomas from this point of view. However incongruous the comparison may seem, that text is the *Vie de Saint Thomas* by Guernes de Pont Sainte-Maxence, for that poet too – writing about the same time as Thomas – was always ready to push his narrative aside for a moment, sometimes a lengthy one, in order to reflect on the vicariousness of men's motives and to moralise on the foibles of humanity. Thomas's digressions seem less justifiable and more contrived because of the very different nature of the story and because he is after all writing about a man whose feelings are governed by a drug which allows him no choice and no respite. The potion's effect in Thomas's version was not of limited duration (2495–8). Thomas's handling of the legend is more fashionable than Béroul's. Thus Tristan analyses his feelings at length and argues with himself in the *ratiocinatio* pattern that we have observed in the 'romans d'antiquité'. Iseut, Tristan tells himself, really should comfort him in his distress:

Ele, de quei? – D'icest ennui.
– U me trovereit? – La u jo sui.
– Si ne set u ne en quel tere.
– Nun? e si me feïst dunc querre!
– A que faire? – Pur ma dolur.
– Ele n'ose pur sun seignur
Tuit en oüst ele voleir.
(139–45)

Why should she? – Because I am troubled. Where would she find me? – Where I am. She knows not where nor in what land. No? she ought to look for me then! What for? – Because of my suffering. She dares not because of her husband, however much she might wish it.

In such details, at least, Thomas is closer to the courtly tradition than is Béroul, but the legend does not become courtly for all that, since '. . . the spirit of *courtoisie* and the spirit of the Tristan story are incompatible'.[37] Thomas himself was at pains to explain that Tristan's attitude towards the second Iseut was not inspired by 'fin' amur' (371–3). The tragedy which affects the lovers and all associated with them is quite different in atmosphere from love celebrated by the troubadours, even though the outward situation had some resemblance: the love was an adulterous one, they were surrounded by 'losengiers' (jealous hypocrites) determined to bring about their downfall. The husband, however, was not among their number, for he is a pathetic figure in love with his wife yet attached to his nephew Tristan. This is no delicate toying with feelings, a wishful thinking, a lover's flirtation with the aspirations of his own heart, but an illicit love lived right through to its final and bitter consequences. It is to Thomas's credit that he relates the final scenes with a minimum of intervention. All, at the end, is 'Mesaise, deshait e dolur' (2043) (Misfortune, unhappiness and grief), and the pathos and poetry of the death scene are not vitiated. The overall impression left by Thomas, particularly when compared with

Béroul, is of his cleverness with words, a cleverness which takes a scholastic turn as he explores, for example, the different implications of *désir* and *vouloir* (641–65), and as he shows his obvious delight in analysing at length the niceties of the situation: Tristan is married to the second Iseut, Mark to the first. Of the four, which was happiest in love, which the most unhappy? Having expounded the situation and asked the question, he leaves others to pronounce judgement:

Le jugement facent amant	Let lovers pass judgement as to
A quel estoit mieuz de l'amor	which was happiest in love, or had
Ou qui en ait greignor dolor.	the greatest grief.

(1089–91)

At times he is like a man triumphantly assembling the pieces of a very intricate jigsaw puzzle. His dexterity with words met its match in the poem, for which he provided the model, by Gottfried von Strassburg, telling this immortal story of

ein senedaere, ein senedaerîn,	a young man, a young woman, in
ein man, ein wîp; ein wîp, ein man,	love, a man, a woman, a woman, a
Tristan, Îsôt, Îsôt, Tristan.	man, Tristan, Iseut, Iseut, Tristan.

(lines 128–30)[38]

The words entwine together like the branches growing over the lovers' grave, as they do also in Marie de France's *Lai du Chievre-feuil*:

Bele amie, si est de nus	Sweet lady-love, so it is with us: no
Ne vus sanz mei, ne mei sanz vus.	you without me, no me without you.

(lines 77–8)[39]

French poets of the twelfth century may not have composed the finest versions of the legend, but without them, it would in all likelihood never have been recorded for posterity.

III. THE ROMANCES OF CHRÉTIEN DE TROYES

Chrétien de Troyes has been dubbed not merely 'le meilleur écrivain français du Moyen Age', but more ambitiously 'le plus grand romancier du Moyen Age'.[40] He wrote in the last third of the twelfth century, between 1170, or a few years earlier, and 1190, but these dates are still open to question.[41] He was a court poet, one of whose romances, *Le Chevalier de la Charrete* (also known, as are his other works, by the name of the hero – in this case Lancelot), was dedicated to Marie de Champagne, and his last, unfinished one, *Le Conte du Graal* (*Perceval*), to Philippe d'Alsace, count of Flanders. His extant works, in addition to the two lyric poems mentioned earlier,[42] are: *Philomena*, an adaptation of a grisly tale told by Ovid in *Metamorphoses* (Book VI, lines 426–674), surviving only in a late thirteenth-century version, the *Ovide moralisé*,[43] *Erec et Enide* (1170?), the earliest surviving Arthurian romance in French; *Cligès* (1176?); *Le Chevalier de la Charrete* (1177–81?); *Le Chevalier au lion (Yvain)* (1177–81?); *Le Conte du Graal* (1179–90?). The authorship of another romance, *Guillaume d'Angleterre*, is much disputed, some scholars attributing it to Chrétien,[44] others doubting that he was the author.[45] It is not an Arthurian legend and differs considerably in subject-matter from the romances known to be by Chrétien.

The principal formative influences on his writings were the following:

(i) Ovid

Among the author's works listed in the opening lines of *Cligès* figure *Les Comandemenz d'Ovide* and *L'Art d'Amours*, neither of which has survived, though *Philomena*, mentioned above, remains as a testimony to Chrétien's 'formation ovidienne', described as follows by Frappier:

> Elle se révèle d'abord dans l'emprunt des sujets qui constituaient la suite des *Ovidiana*, œuvres de jeunesse très probablement. Mais ses effets se prolongent dans *Cligès* et même dans les romans postérieurs, comme le prouvent des comparaisons et des développements métaphoriques. D'une façon plus subtile, Chrétien semble avoir hérité de son modèle latin le tour piquant, l'élégance de la narration, l'art d'une beauté plastique et musicale du vers.[46]

(ii) The 'romans d'antiquité'

The influence of these works on Chrétien was extensive in matters of style, technique, and description far more than in actual themes. What the late twelfth- and thirteenth-century romances inherited generally from the *romans d'antiquité* has been summed up as follows:

> Goût de la description, sens du merveilleux, règles du portrait, peinture des objets d'art, rôle de l'intrigue amoureuse, théorie de l'amour, poncifs et clichés, adresses de style et lieux communs, en tout cela éclate l'imitation des romans antiques.[47]

Certain resemblances may be owed to a common source rather than to direct imitation by Chrétien of the *romans d'antiquité*.[48] The long self-analyses of characters falling in love[49] are not exploited by Chrétien in *Erec*, but feature in most of his later works.

(iii) Geoffrey of Monmouth's 'Historia Regum Britanniae'

This was written in 1136. Wace's adaptation of it in the vernacular, dating from 1155, the *Roman de Brut*, so called from Brutus, mythical founder of the British race,[50] was also an influence. Geoffrey of Monmouth's inextricable blend of fact and fiction, a 'prose-epic', as it has been aptly described,[51] was intended to attract the Norman conqueror's sympathy to the British in preference to the Anglo-Saxons, and also provided propaganda for the incipient imperial ambitions of the House of Normandy in France. Tremendously popular in its day, as the 180 surviving manuscripts testify, it was to exercise a prodigious influence:

... as a source-book for the imaginative writing of others, as an inspiration for poetry, drama and romantic fiction down the centuries, it has had few if any equals in the whole history of European literature.[52]

Although Arthur is only one of 99 kings named by Geoffrey, a fifth of his work deals with Arthur's life and exploits, a tremendous expansion of the meagre references to Arturus in earlier chronicles such as Nennius's *Historia Britonum*. There is as yet no Round Table in Geoffrey, but it appears for the first time in extant literature in Wace's *Brut*,[53] which has survived in 20 manuscripts, and is only one of several adaptations of Geoffrey's chronicle. The influence of these seminal works on Chrétien is less extensive than one might suppose, and is in fact more apparent in later writers. Of forty names of Arthurian knights quoted in *Erec* (lines 1672–706; 1885–1962) only five appear in Wace.[54] It was the general ambiance of his romances, and their style and technique, that were influenced above all:

... peintre excellent dans tous les genres, paysagiste autant que peintre de fresques historiques et de petits tableaux plus intimes, Wace est le maître de Chrétien surtout et avant tout dans l'art de la description.[55]

The real importance of Geoffrey and Wace in their own century lay in their raising of Arthur to the legendary stature of Charlemagne and Alexander, so paving the way for the Arthurian romances. Arthur was in fact more of a legendary figure than either of these two, for it is not even certain that he existed, though many scholars now believe that he did.[56]

(iv) Celtic sources

Wherever oral sources are mentioned, there is inevitably much uncertainty, much hypothesis, and debate. That Chrétien invented all his Arthurian themes and names is out of the question, the more so since some are demonstrably of Celtic origin and bear resemblances to the Welsh *mabinogion*, of which at least one, *Culhwch and Olwen*, is usually considered to have been earlier than Chrétien's romances.[57] Later tales of the *mabinogion* – *The Lady of the Fountain* (basically the same story as *Yvain*), *Peredur* (resembling the *Conte du Graal*), *Geraint son of Erbin* (resembling *Erec et*

Enide) – show French influence, but even so they were not necessarily complete borrowings. Their subject-matter is sufficiently different from that of the continental poets to suggest that the Welsh and French versions derived from common sources, yet another much-debated topic.[58] That earlier written versions existed and have been lost in the course of time is also possible. One may surmise that Celtic bards, perhaps from Ireland, Wales, Scotland, Cornwall, or Brittany,[59] were both numerous and active in the twelfth century, possibly earlier, and that what has survived of their richly imaginative tales is no more than the tip of the iceberg. That the bards travelled widely is suggested by the famous Modena archivolt in north Italy, on which are carved figures from the Arthurian legends with early and primitive forms of their names (e.g., Winlogee for Queen Guenièvre), but, though this may well be an early twelfth-century work, we are not altogether certain. Also of interest is the visit of a Breton *conteur*, Bleheris, or Breri,[60] to Guillaume IX's Court at Poitiers, which may explain the early references to the Tristan legend in the poetry of Bernard de Ventadour.

R. S. Loomis sums up as follows the results of his epoch-making (though sometimes controversial) research on Chrétien's Celtic sources:

Evidently there was a great ferment in the Welsh imaginations during the Dark Ages which blended into one great seething mass the hereditary lore of the Goidelic and Brythonic peoples. And what the *cyvarwyddon* recited in Wales they passed on to the Breton *conteurs* before the year 1000, and doubtless later as well. These tales, gradually adapted to French tastes, given a new localization in Anglo-Norman Britain after the Conquest, receiving new authority from the quasi-historical production of Geoffrey of Monmouth and Wace, were the great sensation of the twelfth century and enjoyed great favour wherever French was understood.[61]

French poets like Wace and Chrétien do not reflect faithfully the other-worldly, mystical qualities of their Celtic sources, either because they failed to comprehend their spirit, or because, sceptical and lucid in their approach to life, as the French mind has been through the ages, it suited them to dissipate somewhat the Celtic mists and to treat the fantasy and magic rather in the spirit of the oriental *merveilleux* of the *Roman d'Alexandre*. In a well-known passage of his *Roman de Rou*, Wace relates how, having heard the Bretons' stories concerning the magic properties of the 'fontaine de Barenton' in the forest of Brocéliande,[62] he went to see for himself:

Vi la forest et vi la terre,	I saw the forest and I saw the land,
Merveilles quis, mais nes trovai,	I sought miracles but I found none,
Fol m'en revinc, fol i alai,	I came away a fool, I went there a
Fol i alai, fol m'en revinc,	fool, I went there a fool, I came
Folie quis, por fol me tinc.[63]	away a fool, I sought foolishness, I
	considered myself a fool.

This quotation is interesting, for if we venture to generalise on its implications, it can be said to reveal something of the contrast between the Breton and Norman mentalities, something too, possibly, of the shortcomings, but also some of the qualities, of the French mind: too matter-of-fact and rational for the spirit of fantasy ever really to take wing, but endowed with a gentle, yet penetrating, scepticism which makes the French unparalleled observers of the human condition. It is in part to this last quality that Chrétien de Troyes owes his reputation.

(v) The Tristan legend

This deserves to be singled out from other Celtic themes as having been of special importance for Chrétien. Poet of the happy ending and sensible compromise, haunted, shocked even, by the tragedy of these ill-fated lovers to which he alludes many times, Chrétien devoted much attention to conjugal love, the very possibility of which seemed to be denied both by the Tristan legend and the love-poetry from the south. We have already had occasion to quote Marie de Champagne's unequivocal statement[64] that love between husband and wife is an impossibility. The contention, in *Erec*, in *Cligès* and *Yvain*, that love and marriage can cohabit has every appearance, in the literature of the day, of considerable originality. This view may have been expounded already in Chrétien's version of the Tristan legend, though this can only be inferred from the title, which alone has survived: *Del roi Marc et d'Yseut la blonde*. One of his two extant lyric poems makes a direct allusion to the legend.[65] The poet claims that his love is superior to Tristan's because it is based on deep tenderness and is in accord with his own will. What is clearly rejected by implication is the blind, all-consuming passion to which everything else must be subjugated. Chrétien's only depiction of such an indomitable love is in *Le Chevalier de la Charrete*, the theme of which was provided for him, as he tells us, by Marie de Champagne. It has recently been argued very plausibly that this work, which he left to another to complete, is in fact an implied criticism of a love which escapes from the control of *raison* and *mesure* and becomes an obsession. Viewed in this light, Lancelot falls in line with Chrétien's other works.[66] Marriage can and should be a love-match: in the twelfth century the effect of three of Chrétien's romances was to show this as convincingly as did numbers of Molière's plays in the seventeenth century, though Chrétien clearly realised that such a marriage, in the aristocratic society of the day, was not without difficulties of its own. If the love is too absorbing, it can have the effect of turning the couple in upon itself, so that social duties are neglected. Neglect of a knight's duties can lead to charges of 'recreantise' (cowardice); the wife may blame herself for this, and the husband may suspect, perhaps wrongly, that his wife doubts him. This is the situation that is created, and explored at some length, in *Erec et Enide*. *Yvain* is a mirror-image of this same situation, for here the crisis is reached when the hero neglects his functions, not as a knight, but as a husband. *Cligès*, on the other hand, has been variously described as an *anti-Tristan* or a *neo-Tristan*. An important theme of this romance is that a woman should belong to one man only and should not be divided between lover and husband as Iseut was. Chrétien seems strangely insensitive to the splendid poetic overtones of the Celtic tragedy, and is determined to look at it from the point of view of the realities and practicalities of daily life. He creates a similar situation to that in *Tristan*, but gives it a totally different, less plausible, but more 'sensible', and ultimately happy, outcome.

An exhaustive analysis of Chrétien's romances, along with an account that would do justice to all the scholarship that has been devoted to them in recent years,[67] is beyond the scope of this volume. The following pages give only brief synopses of the principal works, along with descriptions of certain important features.

Erec et Enide

In his introduction Chrétien claims to have turned an adventure story into 'une molt bele conjointure' – a well-organised narrative. Previous tales concerning Erec, son of King Lac, had been split up into fragments and so ruined, but Chrétien's version will last as long as Christianity.

One Eastertime at Cardigan in Wales, Arthur assembles a mighty Court. He wishes to revive an old custom, the Hunt for the White Stag. The successful knight will be rewarded with a kiss from the fairest maiden. As they ride along following the hunt, Queen Guenièvre and Erec encounter a knight accompanied by a lady and a dwarf. The dwarf insults Guenièvre's maid, and Erec himself. Unarmed, Erec is unable to challenge the knight. He decides to follow them until he can exact revenge. Meantime Arthur himself takes the white stag, but final celebrations are deferred until Erec's return. Erec, following the knight, arrives at a fortified town and is offered shelter by a poor vavasour, from whom he learns that the knight he is following is expected to be the victor next day in a tournament for which the prize is a sparrow-hawk. The vavasour lends his arms to Erec, who declares that he will give the hawk to his host's beautiful daughter Enide, whose charms are described at some length. Erec loses no time in asking for her hand in marriage, which is readily granted when he roundly declares: 'Filz sui d'un riche roi puissant' (line 650) ('I am the son of a rich and powerful king'), and that he will make her queen of ten cities. Next day Erec defeats the offending knight Yder[68] and sends him to join Arthur's Court. Erec takes leave of the vavasour, whose daughter is well received by the king. Arthur bestows on her the kiss that concludes the White Stag episode and what is in effect the prologue to the story: 'Ici fenist li premiers vers' (1796)[69] ('Here ends Part I').

After his wedding Erec is the victor in a mighty tournament at Edinburgh, but after that he is so smitten with love for his wife that he forgets all else.

Enide learns that Erec is being reproached for his inactivity and early one morning speaks her regrets aloud, blaming herself for Erec's neglect of chivalry, ending with the words 'Amis, con mar fus'.[70] On waking up Erec hears this last remark and asks her to explain. Enide tells him: 'recreant vos apelent tuit' (2551) (they are all calling you a coward). Without further ado Erec orders her to put on her best dress and make ready to ride off. He dons his armour, described at length. Enide rides in front and Erec forbids her to speak to him. They soon meet three robber knights intent on mischief. Despite his orders Enide warns Erec of their approach. Erec overcomes all three. Further adventures follow, preceded always by Enide's anxious self-questioning. Fearing to disobey her husband, she fears even more for his safety, and despite his repeated orders to remain silent, warns him of imminent danger. Finally her love has been sufficiently tested, and Erec is reassured:

il aparçoit et conuist bien	he perceives and realises full well
qu'ele l'ainme sor tote rien.	that she loves him above all else.

(3753-4)[71]

Their perils reach a climax after their reconciliation, in the *Joie de la Cort* episode in which Erec has to traverse an invisible wall of air in order to defeat a gigantic knight, Maboagrain. This final achievement brings joy to Arthur's Court and puts a triumphant end to the adventures of Erec and Enide.

Erec et Enide offered court circles of northern France entertainment of the most complete kind set against a novel background dominated by King Arthur, this hero cut to the pattern of twelfth-century knightly ideals, a pattern in which the social graces gave a new dimension to valour and prowess. Henceforth, without courtly manners, these qualities could not exist. Another essential element, suggesting troubadour influence, was love. The very sight of Enide increased Erec's strength (910) and gave him the victory over the powerful Yder, but what is here little more than a passing mention was to become a dominant theme in *Le Chevalier de la Charrete*. Love and adventure, a courtly amusement where a damsel's kiss is the ultimate reward, fierce hand-to-hand encounters in which villainous knights were pierced by lances and hacked by sword-thrusts, vivid descriptions all aglow with life and colour: a bustling, fortified town, huntsmen and hounds, horses, hawks, knights, shields, lances, armour, tapestry, dresses, jewels, a wedding-feast, ivory carvings showing:

comant Eneas vint de Troye,	how Aeneas came from Troy, how
comant a Cartaige a grant joie	Dido welcomed him joyfully in Car-
Dido an son leu le reçut,	thage, how Aeneas deceived her,
comant Eneas la deçut,	how she killed herself because of him,
comant ele por lui s'ocist,	how Aeneas went on to conquer
comant Eneas puis conquist	Laurentum and all Lombardy ...
Laurente et tote Lonbardie ...	

(5291-7)

all are paraded before our eyes as though the author had set out to record something of the social life of the twelfth-century aristocracy. The central thread is the love uniting Erec and Enide, and the testing of that love. No long internal monologues are devoted to their nascent feelings for one another – indeed the beginnings of their love are not even mentioned – but Enide does analyse her conflicting emotions each time she warns her husband of impending danger. Erec was sometimes equally aware of the peril, but remained silent to see how she would react. Here and elsewhere a certain sly humour peeps through. We know that Erec knows of the approach of danger, and we wait with him to observe Enide's behaviour. After considerable heart-searching she produces a quavering:

'Sire'.
– 'Cui?' fet il, 'que volez vos dire?'
– 'Sire, merci! dire vos vuel
que desbunchié sont d ce bruel
cinc chevalier, don je m'esmai'. . .
(2979–83)

'My lord'. 'Who?' says he, 'what do you want to say?' 'Mercy, my lord, I just want to tell you that five knights have ridden out of that wood, and I am worried . . .'

The adventures are not just there for the thrills and spills. They are motivated by the psychological core of the story.

Whatever the sources of the story, in its actions and implications its concern is very much with the real world. It is not set in the mysterious aura of a Celtic Otherworld, for though reality and fantasy mingle, the former predominates. This is revealed in the rationalising of Celtic sources. The White Stag episode, for example, has been deemed to be the dilution of an early Breton tale in which '. . . a fay offers her love on condition that the hero pursue a white stag with the aid of a white hound which she provides . . .',[72] and the strange *Joie de la Cort* episode was originally a Celtic tale of a giant held captive by a fairy.[73]

One further detail deserves attention. Chrétien claims that his story will last as long as Christianity. This pride and confidence in the literary value of his work, and in his erudition, inherited, as he points out in *Cligès*, by Rome from Greece and then by France from Rome, is a mark of humanism, and it is in part at least as a humanist that Chrétien deserves to be remembered. The reading of *Erec et Enide*, as Frappier well remarks, helps us to understand that there really was such a thing as a twelfth-century renaissance. With this romance the vernacular literature of northern France has come of age.

Cligès[74]

Alixandre and Alis are the sons of the emperor of Constantinople. The former, attracted by King Arthur's reputation, joins his Court at Winchester. As he sails with Arthur and his Court for Brittany, Soredamor, Gauvain's sister, falls in love with him, and he with her. They do not dare reveal their feelings, but in long internal monologues dissect their symptoms. The queen assumes from their troubled countenances that both are sea-sick. For long they suffer in silence, and eventually the Court returns to England on receiving news that Angrès of Windsor has seized London. Before the start of battle Alixandre is dubbed knight and receives from the queen the gift of a silken shirt. He distinguishes himself in the ensuing fighting. One evening, when Soredamor and Alixandre are in the queen's tent, she invites Soredamor to tell Alixandre of her contribution to his silken shirt: one of her hairs, brighter than the gold thread, has been woven into it. In this way each at last becomes aware of the other's love. Alixandre's prowess is now boundless: he enters Angrès's palace at Windsor with a handful of men, and takes him prisoner. He returns in triumph and the queen arranges his marriage with Soredamor. A boy is born to them whom they call Cligès.

On the death of the emperor, Alis, the younger brother, mounts the throne, having been wrongly informed of the death of Alixandre in Brittany. It is agreed that Alis shall keep the crown but that Alixandre shall have the effective power. Also Alis is to remain single in order to leave Cligès heir to the throne. Alis eventually breaks this promise, having been persuaded by his barons to marry Fénice, who is in fact in love with his nephew Cligès. Fénice asks her old nurse Thessala to prepare a magic potion so that, married to Alis, she can remain intact for the one she loves. Cligès meantime, having given proof of his courage in battle, departs for Arthur's Court, where he wins new honours. Returning to Greece, he confesses his love to Fénice, who tells him of the magic potion. Another is prepared to enable her to feign death. Her 'body' will be 'resurrected' by Cligès and they will live in secret together. This is achieved despite the strong suspicions of three doctors from Salerno. After some time Alis discovers the truth. Cligès and Fénice escape and return to Arthur's Court. Alis dies of rage and Cligès and Fénice are married in Constantinople, where Cligès is crowned emperor.

This composite story has one foot lightly planted in Arthur's realm and the other firmly set in Greece, where much of the action takes place. In this respect *Cligès* is related to the *romans byzantins* which, like the *Roman d'Alexandre*, were usually based on Latin intermediaries of Greek legends. Another such romance was *Eracles*, by Chrétien's contemporary Gautier d'Arras, completed in 1164. Chrétien gives as his source a book belonging to the cathedral of St Peter in Beauvais, but this has not survived.

The bare bones of the tale, as exposed above, do no justice to Chrétien's telling of it. It is far less stiff and contrived than a brief synopsis suggests. Chrétien's skill as a storyteller and creator of character breathes life and vigour into it, and it is only afterwards, when his spell is broken, that one becomes fully aware of the far-fetched nature of certain aspects, particularly Fénice's manner of escaping from her husband. The story is modelled to some extent on that of *Tristan*,[75] as the bipartite structure reveals. Like the Tristan legend, *Cligès* begins with the life of his parents, here dealt with more fully. Both couples in *Cligès* succeed in overcoming considerable difficulties. In the case of Alixandre and Soredamor they are of an inward, psychological kind; in the case of Cligès and Fénice they are of an outward, social kind. As with *Erec et Enide*, both end with the lovers happily married. The final, almost exultant, outcome is that: 'L'amour est compatible avec le mariage: il s'accroît même d'une tendresse et d'une confiance toujours plus profondes'.[76]

Cligès, like others of Chrétien's romances, lives through its characters rather than through its plot. Thus Soredamor's self-questioning, as she falls in love with Alixandre, is skilfully handled:

'... Fole, qu'ai je a feire,
Se cist vaslez est deboneire,
Et larges, et cortois, et proz?
Tot ce li est enors et proz.
Et de sa biauté moi que chaut?
Sa biauté avoec lui s'an aut.
Si fera ele maugré mien,
Ja ne l'an voel je tolir rien.
Tolir? Non voir! Ce ne vuel mon ...'
(lines 889–97)

'Fool that I am, what does it matter to me if this young man is noble, generous, courtly, and brave? This is all to his honour and good. What care I for his handsomeness? He can take it away with him and will do despite me. I do not wish to rob him of it. Rob? No indeed! I assuredly do not wish for this ...'

Most outstanding, however, is Fénice, who has been called 'un des personnages les plus vivants de la littérature médiévale'.[77] She is quite determined that she is not going to be torn between husband and lover as Iseut had been, and expresses herself unequivocally:

'Mialz voldroie estre desmanbree
Que de nos deus fust remanbree
L'amors d'Ysolt et de Tristan,
Don mainte folie dit an,
Et honte en est a reconter.
Ja ne m'i porroie acorder
A la vie qu'Isolz mena'.
(3105–11)

'I would rather be torn to pieces than have the two of us serve as a reminder of the love of Ysolt and Tristan, concerning whom many foolish things are said, the mere telling of which is a disgrace. I could never bring myself to accept Ysolt's way of life'.

As far as she was concerned 'Qui a le cuer, cil a le cors' (3123) (The one who has the heart has the body). To some extent she was motivated by fear of gossip and the blame attached to an adulterous love, a fear characteristic of the courtly convention:

'Se je vos aim, et vos m'amez,
Ja n'en seroiz Tristanz clamez,
Ne je n'an serai ja Yseuz,
Car puis ne seroit l'amors preuz,
Qu'il i avroit blasme ne vice'.
(5199–203)

'If I love you, and you love me, never will you be called Tristan on that account, nor I Yseut, for then our love would be sullied and blame and vice attached to it'.

Above all, however, she declares roundly that she could never bring herself to accept the life that Iseut had perforce to lead. 'Ceste amors ne fu pas resnable' (3117) (This love was not reasonable) – a most interesting and revealing choice of adjective; and her preoccupation, like that of Chrétien himself in his lyric poems,[78] is ultimately with the way one spends one's life. The inference is that life should not be tragic; it is meant to be enjoyed, but to achieve happiness is not easy. Passion must be brought under control by reason, and commonsense must in the end prevail. When Tristan and Iseut drank their magic potion, they drank their death, as Thomas dramatically observed. Fénice, on the other hand, drank her death-feigning potion in order to escape from an unhappy situation and so to marry the man she loved. The underlying meaning is clearer here than in *Erec*, even though neither work is to be considered simply as a *roman à thèse*, for they are too rich and diverse for that. Cligès is an epithalamium to marriage as a love-match, and the paradox is that, to achieve so natural an end, Chrétien had to resort to so artificial a means. But how else could he steer the Tristan situation, into which he had deliberately placed Fénice, Alis, and Cligès, to a happy outcome for the lovers? Alis is less the victim of gross injustice than may appear, since in marrying Fénice he had broken his promise to remain single, so that his death was ultimately of his own making.

In rewriting the *Tristan* legend – for this is what he has done in *Cligès* – Chrétien doubtless had strong motives, for the tragic legend ran so counter to his concept of love as revealed in his lyric poems and in his other romances.

Yvain[79]

Calogrenant, one of Arthur's knights, tells the assembled Court of a strange adventure which has befallen him. In the forest of Brocéliande he met a monstrous herdsman guarding some wild bulls in a clearing, who, learning that the knight was seeking adventure, told him where he could find a magic spring with a slab of precious stone beside it. By sprinkling water on the slab he would provoke a mighty tempest. This Calogrenant did, only to find himself challenged by a knight, Esclados le Roux, who asked him why he had caused such devastation and then attacked him, knocking him off his horse. Calogrenant had had to flee on foot. Arthur decides to visit the site, but Yvain precedes him and avenges his cousin's discomfiture by mortally wounding Esclados. He pursues him to a castle, but a portcullis crashes down in front of Yvain and another just behind him, cutting his horse in two and slicing off his spurs. He is taken through a secret passageway by a maiden, Lunete, to whom he has recently shown kindness at Court. The dead knight's household are eager to take him prisoner, and so Lunete gives him a ring to make him invisible.[80] As he watches the funeral procession, Yvain falls in love with the beautiful widow Laudine who is full of hatred for her husband's murderer. However, as Lunete later points out to her, a knight has to be found to take Esclados's place as defender of the fountain, and who better than the one who has overcome him? The widow's attitude gradually changes and the wedding is eventually celebrated.

Gauvain urges Yvain to set off with him to participate in tournaments:

'Comant! seroiz vos or de çax', ce disout mes sire Gauvains, 'qui por leur fames valent mains?' (lines 2486–8)

'What then? would you be one of those', Sir Gauvain said, 'who lose their worth because of their wives?'

Yvain, unable to resist such taunts, accepts 'que l'an ne l'apialt recreant' (2563) (in order not to be called coward). Laudine agrees to let him go for a year. If he stays away longer, her love will turn to hatred. Despite Yvain's great reluctance to part he fails to return in the allotted time. The news that Laudine has turned against him drives the repentant Yvain out of his mind and he lives like a wild man in the woods. On regaining his sanity he embarks on a long series of expiatory adventures. He rescues a lion from a dragon's clutches and it becomes his faithful companion, actually helping him in some of his combats. After a long period full of fighting and perilous adventures, Yvain forces the issue with Laudine by provoking a mighty tempest at the fountain. With the intercession once more of the ever resourceful Lunete, Yvain and Laudine are happily reunited.

Yvain has often been spoken of as Chrétien's masterpiece, 'The most accomplished of the romances of the twelfth century'.[81] It closely resembles *Erec* in theme and development: events lead to a marriage; a crisis threatens the marriage, the hero's prowess dominates the crisis and leads to a happy ending.[82] There is no polemic as in *Cligès*, no doctrine as in *Lancelot*. Chrétien is here the complete master of his craft, weaving an intricate pattern of adventures real and fantastic, of characters drawn from life or imagination, of individuals and crowds, princes, noble ladies, poor girls in threadbare garments slaving over the sumptuous gold-embroidered fabrics of the wealthy, a monstrous herdsman, a bright-witted lady-in-waiting. This is his most complete, all-embracing picture of humanity. In this virtuoso performance Chrétien seems to have set himself what appears an impossible task for the simple pleasure of surmounting it: to make a woman lament in sincere tones the death of a noble and valiant husband – 'le meillor des buens' (1209) (the best of the good) – and three days later to make her marry his murderer without this volte-face appearing artificial or unconvincing. It is true that he was helped by the fact that the dead husband's place as defender of the fountain and fief had to be filled in any case, but Chrétien did not rest content with this explanation. The change in Laudine's attitude is explored through the favourite technique of the inner dialogue. She imagines a conversation with Yvain in which she puts him on trial and convinces herself that he was blameless:

'Viax tu donc', fet ele, 'noier
que par toi ne soit morz mes sire?'
– 'Ce', fet il, 'ne puis je desdire,
einz l'otroi bien'. – 'Di donc por coi
feïs le tu? Por mal de moi,
por haïne, ne por despit?'
– 'Ja n'aie je de mort respit
s'onques por mal de vos le fis'.
– 'Donc n'as tu rien vers moi
    mespris
ne vers lui n'eüs tu nul tort,
car s'il poïst, il t'eüst mort . . .'
(1762–72)

'Do you mean to deny', said she, 'that my husband died by your hand?' – 'That I cannot deny', said he, 'but I accept it entirely'. – 'Then tell me why you did it, to do me wrong out of hatred, or spite?' – 'May I never have any respite from death if I did this to wrong you'. – 'And so you have not acted wrongfully towards me, and you did him no wrong, for had he been able to, he would have killed you . . .'

Although Yvain is already in love with her, and intimidated by her to boot, as a true courtly lover should be:

'... peor n'aiez de ma dame qu'el ne vos morde' (1968–9)	'Do not fear my lady. She will not bite you'

says Lunete, there is as yet no question of love on her part. Her instinctive hatred of Yvain has first to be destroyed, but this happens quickly as she reasons the matter out in her mind, and realises that there could be no better defender of the fountain than Yvain. Laudine finally accepts her vassals' entreaties that she should marry him:

Ce qu'ele feïst tote voie, qu'Amors a feire li comande ce don los et consoil demande ... (2140–2)	which she would have done anyway, for Love commands her to do what good counsel and advice demand ...

The approval of her vassals was essential, for on no account did she wish to be known as

... cele qui prist celui qui son seignor ocist (1811–12)	the woman who married her husband's murderer.

There is no long account of love's beginnings, which would surely have seemed out of place. Later, when Yvain appears to have deserted her, Laudine's love, shown by her anxiously counting off the days of his absence (2759), is swiftly transformed to hatred once more, only overcome much later, when Lunete tricks her into forgiving Yvain.

Although Chrétien's plots are at times contrived, his analyses of people's motives and feelings are invariably subtle and convincing. It was perhaps his classical training that made him eager to penetrate the minds of his protagonists in order to explore their reactions, partly to events, mainly to one another. Particularly striking is Yvain's violent emotional reaction to the news that Laudine had turned against him:

Lors se li monte uns torbeillons el chief, si grant que il forsane; si se dessire et se depane et fuit par chans et par arees, et lessa ses genz esgarees qui se mervoillent ou puet estre: querant le vont destre et senestre par les ostex as chevaliers, et par haies et par vergiers ... (2806–14)	Then a storm mounts into his head, so great that he loses his senses. Then he tears at his clothes and runs away over fields and ploughed land, and left his household bewildered, wondering where he can be, seeking him right and left, through the knights' lodgings, through hedges and orchards ...

Above all, one feels, Chrétien was interested in people, and his invention of extraordinary situations helped him to develop his curiosity about human behaviour. 'How strange people are!' – Chrétien would have been ready to echo Thomas's cry as he explored unceasingly the vicissitudes of human nature.

Chrétien's treatment of Laudine may give rise to a suspicion of anti-feminism: 'feme a plus de cent corages' (1440) (woman has more than a hundred minds), said the lovelorn Yvain, more hopefully than accusingly, and with no great originality; but the very thoroughness with which Laudine's changing attitude is analysed averts any charges of fickleness or callousness on her part, and at the end, the deference Yvain pays her shows that her place in marriage and society, like that of Enide, Soredamor, and Fénice, was an honoured and respected one. The wife's rights were different from her husband's, but not inferior to them. There is no misogyny here, and the very character of Laudine's confidant Lunete, alert, charming, and intelligent, is further evidence of this. There is a refreshing lack of prejudice on Chrétien's part, not shared, alas, by many medieval authors.

Chrétien's earlier works suggest that his interests were confined to the upper classes, an idea that is shattered in *Yvain*. It is true that the monstrous herdsman is largely a figure of myth and folklore, but no personage in Chrétien's romances is wholly mythical, and for all his terrifying appearance he speaks to the knights who question him in a meek and friendly fashion. Of far greater interest, however, is Chrétien's vivid description of the ill-clad, ill-fed girls slaving away with threads of gold and silk at the clothes of the rich:

vit puceles jusqu'a trois cenz
qui diverses oevres feisoient:
de fil d'or et de soie ovroient
chascune au mialz qu'ele savoit;
mes tel povreté i avoit
que desliees et desceintes
en i ot de povreté meintes;
et as memeles et as cotes
estoient lor cotes derotes,
et les chemises as dos sales;
les cos gresles et les vis pales
de fain et de meseise avoient.
(5188–99)

he saw as many as three hundred girls working at various tasks. With threads of gold and silk each was working to the best of her ability. But such was their poverty that many were bareheaded and ill attired. Their dresses were gaping open at their breasts and ribs, and their petticoats were dirty on their backs. Their necks were thin, their faces pale because of starvation and hardship.

One of them tells Yvain that, whereas twenty shillings a week were hardly a living wage, not one of them earned more than five (5305–9). This very precision makes one suspect that this was something drawn from real life.[83] It was doubtless easier for Yvain to rescue them in the romance than it was for Chrétien to help them in reality, but it is greatly to Chrétien's credit, as a chronicler of his times, that he observed them with compassion, that he felt very clearly the injustice of their fate and described it so poignantly.

Much has been written on the sources of this work, but they remain obscure in many respects. The 'Chevalier au lion' theme is undoubtedly a reminiscence of the story of Androcles and the lion, well known in the Middle Ages.[84] That Celtic elements may have coloured the lion episodes is not impossible.[85] Particularly intriguing is the adventure at the magic fountain, which, as we have seen above,[86] was known to Wace. It is remarkable that this fountain still exists at the present day: the 'Fontaine de Barenton' in the forest of Paimpont, some 25 miles west of Rennes. A common folklore theme, this too may represent a fusion of Celtic and classical elements. Affinities with the Arician Diana myth have been claimed,[87] but more recently R. S. Loomis has seen numbers of resemblances to the legend of the Irish god Curoi in the saga *Bricriu's Feast* belonging to the Ulster cycle.[88] The synthesis of various elements, among which must be included the *Vie de Saint Brendan*, since after the storm at the fountain a chorus of singing birds settles on the pine overlooking the spring, recalling the Paradise of Birds in that text, may well have been accomplished already in Chrétien's source. It is present, for example, in the Welsh *mabinogi The Lady of the Fountain* which, though later than *Yvain* and possibly influenced by it, very likely shared a common source with it. Medieval romances such as *Yvain* owe much to the encounter of two civilisations: that of ancient Rome and that of the Celtic races, but the stories that emerged were indebted to the skill, the wide reading, and resourcefulness of the twelfth-century poets of northern France, among whom Chrétien de Troyes was outstanding.

Le Chevalier de la Charrete (Lancelot)[89]

As Arthur holds his Court at Camelot, a knight bursts into the assembly. He claims that he holds many of the king's subjects prisoners, but promises to release them if Queen Guenièvre is entrusted to a knight able to defeat him in the nearby forest. Seneschal Keu accepts, but, always something of a pantaloon, is defeated and taken with Guenièvre into captivity. Gauvain sets out to rescue the queen and encounters another knight, as yet unnamed, on the same quest. A dwarf offers to take this unknown knight, whose horse has died under him, into his cart. After hesitating for a moment to accept so shameful a conveyance, his love for the queen gets the better of reason, and he accepts. He is taken to a castle where he survives perilous adventures. The following morning, through his window, he catches sight of the queen riding with a troop of knights. In his anxiety to watch her for as long as possible he almost jumps out of the window. Gauvain and the knight eventually learn that the queen has been taken by Meleagant, son of Bademagus, to the kingdom of Gorre 'don nus estranges ne retorne' (line 641) (whence no stranger returns). A large, swift-flowing river, resembling 'li fluns au deable' (3012; i.e., the Styx), will eventually have to be crossed, either by *Le Pont Evage*, an underwater bridge, or the even more dangerous *Pont de l'Epee*, as narrow and as sharp as a sword-blade. Gauvain chooses the former, the unknown knight the latter. Lost as ever in his lovelorn thoughts of the queen's beauty:

ne set s'il est, ou s'il n'est mie,
ne ne li manbre de son non,
ne set s'il est armez ou non,
ne set ou va, ne set don vient . . .
(716–20)

he does not know if he exists, or does not exist, he does not remember his name, he does not know if he is armed or not, he does not know where he is going, he does not know where he is coming from . . .

the knight is carried along by his horse, which without his guidance comes to a ford and crosses it. A knight defending the ford knocks him into the water, which has the salutary effect of bringing him back to his senses. He is the victor in the ensuing fight. Subsequent adventures demonstrate his utter devotion to the queen. Also he succeeds in raising the lid of a tombstone on which is inscribed: 'He who raises this slab unaided will release the men and women held captive in this land' (1900–3). At last he reaches the swordbridge:

d'une espee forbie et blanche
estoit li ponz sor l'eve froide;
mes l'espee estoit forz et roide,
et avoit deus lances de lonc.
De chascue part ot un grant tronc,
ou l'espee estoit closfichiee.
(3022–7)

the bridge over the cold water was made of a polished, gleaming sword, strong and stiff, of the length of two lances. On each side there stood a tall tree-trunk into which the sword was thrust.

Those looking at it are so awestruck that they think they see two lions or leopards waiting at the other end. With much pain and difficulty the knight struggles across, and when he reaches the far bank, the apparition of the lions fades away. At last he is able to fight the evil Meleagant. The queen watches the fight and it is from her lips that we first learn his name:

Lanceloz del Lac a non
li chevaliers, mien esciant.
(3660–1)

Lancelot del Lac is the knight's name, in my opinion.

When Lancelot sees her he stares ecstatically at her and fights his assailant from behind his back in order to remain facing her. He is the victor and the queen is freed as well as all the other prisoners. She receives Lancelot very coldly, and only later does he learn that this is because of his moment of hesitation before climbing into the infamous cart. The two are reconciled and Lancelot sleeps with the queen. As he departs on a quest to find Gauvain, Lancelot is taken prisoner by the treacherous Meleagant, and it is Gauvain who finally returns the queen in triumph to Arthur's Court. Unknown to Meleagant, Lancelot is released on parole to take part *incognito* in a tournament. The queen suspects it is he, and to find out for sure orders him to fight in cowardly fashion. This he does, his obedience proving to her his identity and continued devotion. When allowed to fight normally, he is once more the victor. After further adventures he fights and kills Meleagant. Lancelot is received in triumph by the king and Court, and the queen awaits a propitious moment for them to renew their love discreetly.

This extraordinary palinode appears to run counter to the three preceding romances, for it tells of the triumph of an adulterous love which reflects the *fin' amors* tradition of the southern Courts. In his prologue, Chrétien is at pains to point out that 'ma dame de Champagne', that is Marie de Champagne, provided both the 'matière', the actual subject-matter, and the 'sen', the basic idea, of the story, and that his sole contribution was in the 'painne et antancïon' (care and attention) which he had devoted to the writing of it. When this is considered along with the fact that Chrétien left the story incomplete, the last thousand lines having been written by Godefroi de Leigni at Chrétien's request (7102–7), the suspicion is inevitably aroused that this romance was not to Chrétien's taste and that his interest, lukewarm to start with, ran cold long before the end. It is important, yet wellnigh impossible, to determine Chrétien's attitude towards the main character, for so much depends on this. Does he admire him as an exponent of the courtly doctrine, does he imply criticism of his extravagant behaviour, does he caricature him as an impossibly idealistic, quixotic figure, or was he at heart indifferent to him? The text provides no clue, and the behaviour of the characters betrays no categorical outlook or dogma as in *Cligès*. It is possible to interpret the work in various ways: it may have been one with which Chrétien was not wholly in sympathy and with which he just did the best he could before passing it on to another. Against this it must be pointed out that Lancelot is perhaps his most remarkable creation as a character (save possibly for Perceval), destined – supreme irony! – unlike the relatively unimpressive Cligès to rival and even surpass Tristan. Whereas so many of his heroes possess highly idealised traits which only in subtly observed details bear the stamp of an individual character, Lancelot is a more obviously individualised portrait. He possesses a peculiar characteristic (which reappears, it is true, in Perceval) in the trance-like state into which he so often falls as his love for the queen fills the whole of his mind and determines all his actions. Moreover, he is a man apart, predestined in his role as liberator of the captives of Gorre, and those who came into contact with him sensed this special quality:

il vialt a si grant chose antendre
qu'ainz chevaliers n'osa enprendre
si perilleuse ne si grief . . .
(1275–7)

He intends to devote his attention to a matter of such importance that never did a knight dare to undertake so perilous or so grievous a one . . .

But is this strange figure not ridiculed when he prepares to jump out of the window rather than lose sight of Guenièvre? Or when he obtains Guenièvre's comb and gently withdraws the hairs sticking to it, kissing them and hugging them to his bosom 'entre sa chemise et sa char' (1469) (between his shirt and his flesh)? Or when he stares joyfully at Guenièvre in the midst of a fight with a dangerous opponent, waggling his sword at him behind his back rather than lose sight of the queen? What would Chrétien's audience, connoisseurs of the tournament, have made of this grotesque behaviour? It must be acknowledged, however, that what may be so clearly a figure of fun in the eyes of a casual modern reader may not have been so in medieval eyes, or they may well have laughed at his foibles while admiring him as the model of the perfect lover, a devoted and steadfast servant of his lady, and a courageous fighter withal. If we knew the exact nature of the 'sens' that Marie de Champagne imposed on Chrétien, these problems would not be so intractable. Many views have been put forward. Mario Roques has suggested that this 'sens' was 'l'amour s'emparant peu à peu du cœur altier d'une dame souveraine, et triomphant de sa naturelle et légitime réserve, devant la grandeur continue de l'adoration et des sacrifices du vassal'.[90] This, however, would make the queen the main figure, though she plays little part in the first half of the story and is not as dominant as might be supposed in the second half. More recently, it has been argued that Marie de Champagne may have asked Chrétien to write a romance showing the pitfalls that could trap a knight and his lady if they failed to cultivate the qualities of *raison* and *mesure*, and this they indeed signally fail to do, at least until the end of the story, when

... reisons anferme et lie son fol cuer, et son fol pansé ... (6846–7)[91]	... reason closes in on his foolish heart and foolish mind, and holds them fast ...

This interpretation implies that it is not so much *fin' amors* that is condemned as the hero and heroine's failure to live up to this doctrine which, however immoral it may have been, at least insisted on absolute tact and discretion. Even if this is admitted, it still remains a moot point whether or not Chrétien approved of this doctrine even when faithfully observed. It can also be argued that he shows the pitfalls into which *fin' amors*, with its cult of extremes of devotion (better suited, he may have felt, to songs than romances), could lead even such exemplary characters as Lancelot and the queen. The suggestion has been made, with particular reference to this romance, that Chrétien's real interest was simply in love, not specifically marital courtly love: 'The essential for him was that Love should be courtly, a source of good for the world; this means it should lead to the preservation of society, helping to defend that society from within by courtliness and from without by prowess'.[92] It is possible to turn the argument in several directions, and the controversial nature of Lancelot is second only to that of Perceval.

The 'matière' provided by Marie de Champagne poses as many problems as the 'sens'. That a legend concerning the abduction of Arthur's wife, Gwenhwyfar (i.e., Guenièvre), by a certain Melwas (i.e., possibly Meleagant) existed before Chrétien's time is shown by the *Vita sancti Gildae* attributed to a Welsh clerk, Caradoc of Llancarvan, and written probably before 1136. She was taken, according to this account, to Glastonbury, called l'Ile de Voirre (the Isle of Glass) in medieval French according to a false etymology,[93] of which Gorre (or Goirre), the forms in Chrétien's *Lancelot*, may be corruptions. There was, however, no Lancelot in this tale, which has clearly undergone much modification and expansion in Chrétien's version. Mario Roques writes on the ever thorny question of sources:

Pour les motifs, si celui de l'enlèvement de la reine Guenièvre peut être de caractère mythologique et a de nombreuses analogies avec des motifs celtiques, il est difficile d'assurer qu'il ne soit pas aussi influencé par des thèmes antiques (Eurydice, Perséphone, Alceste etc.) . . .

Themes of this kind 'échappent à toute précision d'origine'.[94] Once more one has the impression of a confluence of classical themes having been recast in a Celtic mould and then brought back to northern France where, with further additions from classical sources, and much 'painne et antancïon' from the poets of northern France, a new form emerged. It is likely that the contribution of Chrétien de Troyes himself was immense and indeed crucial.

Perceval[95]

A young Welsh lad has been brought up by his mother in a house in a forest in total ignorance of chivalry and all social life, because her two other sons have died in tournaments and her husband, himself wounded, has died of grief as a result. One day he meets five knights riding in the forest and is so dazzled by their armour that he takes them for angels and asks their leader: 'Are you God?' The knights are not too surprised at his ignorance, believing that

Galois sont tot par nature
Plus fol que bestes en pasture
(lines 243–4)

Welsh people by their very nature
are more stupid than the beasts of
the meadows.

Returning home, he tells his mother that he is going to become a knight. Reluctantly, she helps prepare his departure and showers advice on him: he is to honour 'dames et puceles' ('ladies and maidens') and to pray to God in church; but this only provokes the question 'Mere . . . que est eglise?' (573) ('Mother . . . what is a church?'). As he rides off, he glances back and sees that his mother has fallen to the ground in a faint. He continues at a gallop without turning back. That night he sleeps in the forest, and next day comes to a splendid tent which he takes to be a church. He enters, intending to pray, but inside finds a girl in bed, to whom he says:

. . . 'Pucele, je vos salu
Si com ma mere le m'aprist'.
(682–3)

. . . 'Maiden, I greet you, just as
my mother taught me'.

Under the impression that his mother has told him to kiss girls ('if they consent', she had specified), this he proceeds to do against her will, and seizes the ring on her finger – another misunderstanding of his mother's advice. He makes off after helping himself to food in the tent. The girl's lover returns from the woods, accuses her of infidelity, and they ride off, the knight swearing he will have the Welsh lad's head. The lad makes a clownish entry into Arthur's Court, riding into the hall on his horse, but he soon distinguishes himself by killing the Crimson Knight who has insulted Arthur and the queen. At the castle of Gornemant de Goort he learns much about weapons and chivalry, and is told among many other things not to keep on saying 'My mother told me...'. Remembering how he left his mother, he decides to return home. On the way he rescues a damsel, Blanchefleur, from the clutches of a cruel knight, and to her he owes his first experience of love. On leaving her he comes to a river; two men fishing in a boat invite him to stay the night in the nearby castle. At table, the young man sees a strange procession pass through the hall, but, mindful of Gornemant's advice to restrain curiosity, asks no questions. First comes a young man carrying a lance (3191), from the tip of which a drop of blood flows down to his hand; next two young men holding candelabra of pure gold, each with at least ten candles; next a damsel bearing a 'graal' (3220; grail), which gives off a light so bright that the candelabra are as stars to the sun; finally a damsel bearing a silver platter. The procession passes through the hall during each change of course, and each time the young man remains silent. Next morning the castle is empty, and the drawbridge is raised the moment he leaves. In the forest he meets a maiden. When she asks him his name he 'guesses' (3574) that it is Perceval le Gallois, and is right without knowing it (3576). He learns from her that he has spent the night at the castle of the Fisher King who, wounded between the thighs, is unable to ride a horse, and fishes in a boat as a distraction. Had he asked questions about the Grail procession the king would have been cured, but this could not happen because of his sin in abandoning his mother, who has died of grief in his absence. Perceval receives the news calmly, and suggests that the damsel, whose knight has been killed, can follow him, and for both it would be a case of 'Les mors as mors, les vis as vis' (3630) (The dead to the dead, the living to the living). She refuses, and he rides off. He meets the damsel whom he kissed in the tent and brings about a reconciliation between her and her lover. On his way again, he comes across three drops of blood in the snow where a falcon had caught a wild goose. The bright colours remind him of Blanchefleur's complexion, and he becomes lost in contemplation as he stares at the drops.[96] Arthur's Court is nearby. Several of his knights make fun of Perceval, who easily unhorses them and returns to his contemplations. Only Gauvain is able to bring him to his senses, and he is well received by Arthur.

To the Court comes an ugly damsel, who reproaches Perceval bitterly for his silence at the castle of the Fisher King, as a result of which the whole kingdom would suffer. Hearing from her that a maiden is in distress, Gauvain decides to go to her help, but Perceval leaves on a quest to find the Grail, despite the warning that the Fisher King will never hold his kingdom in peace now that the opportunity has been lost. The story then follows Gauvain's adventures for some time before returning to Perceval and his quest. For five years Perceval has not entered a church, but one Good Friday he meets a group of penitents walking barefoot who send him to a hermit in the woods to confess his sins. Once more he learns that his sin in not returning to his mother has caused him to remain silent in the castle of the Fisher King: 'Pechiez la langue te trencha' (6409) (Sin cut your tongue out). The Grail served the Fisher King's father, the hermit's brother, and the Fisher King was Perceval's cousin. The host carried in the Grail had kept the Fisher King's father alive for twelve years: 'Tant sainte chose est li graals'

(6425) (such a holy object is the Grail). Perceval remains for two days with the hermit and at last expresses true repentance. The story returns once more to the mundane adventures of Gauvain, and, left incomplete by Chrétien at his death, leaves Perceval's quest unfinished.

Perceval is the most ambitious, the most fascinating, the most intriguing of Chrétien's romances. The gradual development of the hero from a simple country bumpkin of the rudest kind to a 'verray parfit gentil knight' is very skilfully brought about by Chrétien. Perceval's slow discovery of himself is symbolised in his strange, intuitive guessing of his own name. Whereas Lancelot is first named by the queen, Perceval eventually finds his own name, and there is more than one quest in this story as he sets out in search of his real identity and ultimate destiny. He had much to learn: easiest of all was the handling of a knight's weapons, for despite his total ignorance, to this son of a knight, whose mother too was of noble birth, this matter

...li venoit de nature. Et quant nature li aprent Et li cuers del tot i entent, Ne li puet estre rien grevaine La ou nature et cuers se paine. (1480–4)	...came to him naturally. And when nature teaches him and his mind is entirely absorbed in it, nothing can stand in his way since nature and his mind are striving together.

Courtly manners too had to be acquired, partly by meeting and mixing with others, partly by listening to advice, but he had to learn not to apply advice unthinkingly and in too literal a fashion. More elusive was consideration for others, the lack of which is shown in his incredibly callous treatment of his mother, the consequences of which were grave and irremediable, and in his brutal, though innocent, treatment of the girl in the tent. Only love could bring him understanding of others, and maturity of mind: the difference between the callow lad and the knight lost in contemplation of the blood on the snow is tremendous. Even when enriched by many experiences, he still spent a period of five years without once entering a church. The Christian faith is the last of his acquisitions, the final stage in the long enriching evolution that characterised this knight's Progress. At long last, having been told so often about his sins, he was able to understand them, and confessed in contrite manner to the hermit that he had lived without love of God. When we leave him, he seems to have found divine grace or to be ready to receive it. His own personal quest, at least, is over. How did Chrétien intend the story to finish? No threads are left dangling in his other works, all ends neatly and happily, and we may surmise that, as in certain of the continuations of *Perceval* owed to later poets, Gerbert and Manessier in particular, he would have found the Fisher King's castle once more, posed the necessary questions, and brought health and wellbeing to the king and his stricken kingdom. This, however, remains surmise, and it must be remembered that Perceval set out on the quest despite the warning that it could no longer succeed. The very fact that he sets out at all on so noble, seemingly hopeless, a mission, while Gauvain continues the more banal type of knightly adventure which seems trivial in comparison, does promise a ray of hope, and the underlying optimism that inspires so much of Chrétien's writing may not have left that hope unfulfilled.

The question that hangs over the whole romance is inevitably the significance of the Grail procession. Many answers have been given by later writers of medieval romance, by modern authors, by modern students of Arthurian romance, and still the question remains. 'The Grail legend is a Celtic heritage', says R. S. Loomis,[97] and the same claim is made for the story of the maimed king whose sterility affected the whole of his kingdom. Despite all the thoroughness of Loomis's research, and that of other scholars of like bent, that the elements of the Grail procession were Celtic in origin remains hypothetical, for other possible explanations have been given. Reference has been made to the Christian faith, particularly in the Crucifixion so often represented in medieval art from the tenth century onwards. The first description of these elements in Chrétien's romances is purely extrinsic, for we look at them through Perceval's eyes without any understanding, but the hermit later tells him that the Grail, which carried the host for the Fisher King's father, was 'tant sainte chose'. The Christian exegesis thus finds justification in the text.[98] Even so, interpretation of details at times offers considerable difficulty, and the following explanation cannot be regarded as definitive:[99] the lance is a reference to that of the Roman soldier Longinus with which he pierced the Saviour's side; the fresh drop of blood symbolises the eternal and universal nature of the Redemption; the Grail might represent the vessel used in the Last Supper, or more precisely that in which Christ's blood was received, held in medieval crucifixion scenes by a young woman who depicted Ecclesia, the Church. The silver dish at the end of the procession could represent the paten which receives the host at Holy Communion, bringing pardon and salvation to all believers. It may be that, had Perceval asked the right questions, he could have brought about the Christianisation of the Fisher King's realm and hence its salvation.

Whatever the truth of the matter, the very absence of an explanation by Chrétien himself – the only one that could have been authentic – has contributed to the success of the legend by firing the imagination of many generations, not only in medieval times. It is after all fitting that the work of this splendid pioneering poet, reaching, in his last endeavour, beyond the secular world of chivalry and courtly behaviour he has so far depicted, should end in this way without a true end, alive still for all men of goodwill. In the last resort, each individual reader must embark on his own quest for an explanation, and find the truth which satisfies him the most.[100]

IV. THE LAYS OF MARIE DE FRANCE

A contemporary author who, it is sometimes asserted, was almost Chrétien's equal was Marie de France,[101] for long looked upon as the author of three main works written in the octosyllabic verse which had become so fashionable: a collection of twelve lays, varying in length between 118 and 1,184 lines;[102] a collection of 103 fables, rarely over a hundred lines in length, based, so Marie tells us, on an English version of Aesop's fables owed to King Alfred;[103] and the *Espurgatoire Saint Patrice*, telling how the knight Owein descended into a purgatory first revealed to St Patrice, and how the sight of the tortures of the damned, more grisly than anything seen by St Brendan, had a purifying effect on him.[104] It is usually claimed that this represents the order of composition, so that Marie progressed from entertainment through moralisation to edification.[105] Doubts have always existed as to whether Marie, named most fully in the epilogue to the fables: 'Marie ai nun, si sui de France' (line 4), and as Marie in one of the lays (*Guigemar*, line 3) and in the *Espurgatoire* (line 2297), really was one and the same person. They have recently been revived in a thesis[106] which argues that whereas the *Lais* are usually dated from the third quarter of the twelfth century, between 1160 and 1170,[107] the *Espurgatoire* is based on a Latin work composed probably about 1210, considerably later than previous estimates.[108] Moreover, the collection of *lais* is marked by certain 'divergences difficilement explicables dans l'œuvre d'un seul auteur'.[109] The fables for their part may date from as late as the mid-thirteenth century.[110] These findings, running counter to the consensus of opinion of recent years, are still only tentative, and as so often, the limited amount of available evidence may never allow the whole truth to be known. For our immediate purposes the sole work of importance is the *Lais*, and there seems no reason to reject Professor Ewert's conclusion that their author Marie

... was a native of France, that she lived and wrote in England, that she knew English, as well as Latin, that she was well known to (and possibly on familiar terms with) royalty, that she felt a definite literary vocation, writing for the pleasure and profit of her public, and that she was jealous of her literary reputation.[111]

Attempts to identify her have led to no positive conclusion. The *Lais* are dedicated to a noble king, thought to be Henry II (d. 1189), and the fables to a count William, who may have been Guillaume de Mandeville, earl of Essex.[112]

That the lay was not a distinct literary genre is evident, for, as we have seen,[113] sharply defined categories did not exist as such in medieval times.[114] As we have it in the collection attributed to Marie de France, and in various anonymous works, mostly later, the *lai* was in effect a miniature romance[115] relating a single sentimental adventure, lacking the sustained literary effort, the *conjointure*, needed in a romance of several thousand lines. Most were based on the 'matière de Bretagne', and Marie's importance in recording this subject-matter and bringing it into the orbit of the recorded literature of northern France is considerable. Marie claims in her prologue that her sources were oral, and that to find 'aukune bone estoire' (a good story) she turned to them rather than to Latin works which others had translated into French. The nature of her sources is described as follows by Rychner:

A l'époque de Marie, des jongleurs originaires de Bretagne armoricaine chantaient, en s'accompagnant de la rote ou de la harpe, des chansons qu'ils nommaient des *lais* et que le public appelait lais bretons, à cause surtout de l'origine de ceux qui les chantaient. Nous ne savons pour ainsi dire rien de certain sur ces chansons, dont l'existence cependant, abondamment attestée, ne saurait faire de doute.[116]

Marie tells her stories in a vivid and charming manner, her descriptive technique and style showing the influence of *Eneas* and Wace's *Brut*, but not that of Chrétien de Troyes, suggesting that she was writing shortly before him.[117] However, she does show something of Chrétien's tendency to concentrate on the realistic and psychological aspects of her material more than on its fantastic elements, but in so doing 'ce n'est pas le merveilleux que Marie tue, c'est la vie qu'elle poétise'.[118] To give some idea of the nature and contents of her lays, five of them are analysed briefly in the following pages.

Lanval

King Arthur is holding Court at Carlisle. A handsome young knight, Lanval, is overlooked by the king in his distribution of lands and gifts. Son of a king though he is, he is far from his native land and has exhausted his resources. In the countryside he meets a beautiful fairy who grants him her love on condition that he keeps it secret. If he does this, he will want for nothing. Moreover, he will be able to speak to her whenever he wishes. No others present will see or hear her. The queen notices his isolation at Court and offers him her love. When he refuses, she accuses him of being interested only in young men. He is stung into retorting that he loves a lady so beautiful that her poorest maidservant far surpasses the queen in beauty, in upbringing, and kindness. The queen is offended, Lanval's secret is out, and his contact with the fairy lost. Lanval is put on trial by the king. His barons decide that Lanval shall be condemned unless he can show them the lady of whom he had boasted. This he cannot do, but when the barons are about to pass sentence, the fairy arrives on her horse. Her beauty is such that Lanval is forgiven, and the two ride off to Avalon – 'Ceo nus recuntent li Bretun' (line 642) (So the Bretons relate) – never to be seen again.

Sometimes spoken of as Marie's masterpiece,[119] *Lanval* is the only one of her lays to have an Arthurian setting. Particularly skilful, as Ewert has pointed out,[120] is her adapting of the injunction to secrecy, a commonplace of fairy tales, to contemporary theories of *fin' amors* with their insistence on the importance of discretion.[121]

Chievrefeuil (Honeysuckle)

Tristan has been banished from the Court by King Mark because of his love for Iseut, and has gone 'En Suhtwales, u il fu nez' (line 16) (To South Wales where he was born). Longing to see her again, he goes to Cornwall, learns that the king is going to hold Court at Tintagel, and hides in a wood near the road they will take. He cuts a branch of a hazel-tree, carves his name on it, and leaves it on the road. The queen has earlier been warned by letter to be on the lookout for such a message.[122] The two of them are like the hazel and the honeysuckle, which grow well together but quickly die when separated. The queen finds the hazel branch and stops to rest a while in the woods – so she tells the barons. The lovers spend a short time together and Iseut tells Tristan that Mark has regretted his banishment. Tristan departs once more to Wales until his uncle sends for him. In honour of the occasion, Tristan, 'ki bien saveit harper' (112) (who could play the harp well), composes a new lay:

Gotelef l'apelent Engleis, Chievrefoil le nument Franceis. (115–16)	Goatleaf the English call it, and the French call it chèvrefeuille [honeysuckle].

The shortest of Marie's lays, this is the only one referring to the Tristan legend. Its ultimate source, and relationship to the legend as a whole, have been frequently discussed, but remain uncertain.[123]

Les Deus Amanz

A king in Neustria, now called Normandy, grows very attached to his daughter after the death of his wife and is reluctant for her to marry. He declares that, to be successful, any suitor will have to carry her to the top of a high hill near Pitres. Many try, but even the strongest never reaches more than half-way. His daughter, meanwhile, has fallen in love with a young man at Court, and, to enable him to carry her to the top of the hill, she sends him to an aunt of hers in Salerno who will give him an electuary enabling him to accomplish this feat and so marry her. Meantime she starves herself to make his task easier. Overjoyed and over-confident, the young man scorns to take the electuary. He reaches the top of the hill, but his heart fails and he dies. The girl dies of grief at his side and the two are buried there.

To this day a steep hill near Pitres still bears the name *la Côte des Deux-Amants*, and the legend is still alive in the region. The name is owed to a nearby twelfth-century priory, now in ruins, the *prieuré des Deux-Amants*, so called in fact because it was dedicated to an ascetic couple, Injuriosus and Scholastica of Auvergne. The legend was thus made up later to explain the name.[124]

Equitan[125]

Equitan, lord of the region of Nantes, falls in love with his seneschal's wife. She returns his love, but despairs at the thought that he will one day marry and so leave her. He declares that he will marry her if only her husband were dead, and accordingly she plots his murder. Equitan and her husband will be bled and then each will take a bath. The water in her husband's would be boiling and he will die scalded. Shortly after the baths have been prepared, the seneschal surprises Equitan and his wife together. Equitan – 'pur sa vileinie covrir' (line 294) (to cover his villainy) – leaps into a bath – the wrong one – and dies. Realising the truth, the seneschal plunges his wife into it as well, and she too is killed. So it happens that those who plot evil for others often bring evil on themselves.

Bisclavret

This lay is called Bisclavret in Breton, Garwaf (werewolf) in Norman. A nobleman in Brittany disappears for three days every week. When his wife presses him for an explanation, he tells her that he becomes a werewolf and lives in the woods. If he is unable to change back into his clothes, he will remain a werewolf. The wife is terrified, and yields to the entreaties of a knight who has for long been paying her court. She arranges for him to take her husband's clothes. This is done, and when no more is heard of her husband, she marries the knight. A year later the king catches the werewolf, and, surprised by its intelligence, keeps it with him at Court. It becomes quite tame and harmless, but, when the knight who has married his wife comes to Court one day, the werewolf springs at him, to the surprise of the nobles, who suspect the knight as a result. Later, when the wife too comes to Court, the werewolf bites her nose off. The knight and the lady are questioned, and the truth discovered. The werewolf, given his clothes back, becomes a knight once more. His former wife and her second husband are banished and have several children, who live 'esnasees' (line 314) (without noses).

Eliduc

Eliduc, longest of the lays, tells how the hero, out of favour with his king in Brittany, comes to Totnes in Devon. Though happily married, he falls in love with the daughter of a king who lives near Exeter, and helps her father defeat his enemies. After various adventures, Eliduc's wife, though deeply attached to her husband, enters a nunnery so that he can marry the girl.

The same basic theme, considerably modified and expanded to the dimensions of a romance, is treated by Gautier d'Arras in

Ille et Galeron.[126] The remaining *lais*: *Chaitivel, Guigemar, Le Fresne, Yonec, Milon, Laüstic*[127] are all love-stories, sometimes very slight, characterised by a delicacy of touch and economy of wording which only *Eliduc* does not share. Otherwise the contrasts between them are considerable. Some end happily, some tragically, some are marked by a sordid realism, some are fairy-tale and fantasy. Some see love as a tender and beautiful relationship, others as a criminal passion. Some – *Equitan* for example – have a moral ending like the *fable* and *fabliau*;[128] most have a short conclusion of four lines giving the Breton name of the lay. Above all, they were intended to distract and entertain. They exist for themselves and to a great extent the 'matière' is the 'sens' without the distinction implied by Chrétien in *Lancelot.*[129] Perhaps something of the heterogeneous nature of their oral, or supposedly oral, origins is reflected in their diversity, but all are skilfully told and can deservedly be called poetic creations. Not surprisingly, contemporary testimony bears witness to their popularity:

E dame Marie autresi,
Ki en rime fist e basti
E compassa les vers de lais,
Ke ne sunt pas del tut verais;
E si en est ele mult loee
E la rime par tut amee
Kar mult l'aiment, si l'ant mult
    cher
Cunte, barun e chivaler;
E si enaiment mult l'escrit
E lire le funt, si unt delit,
E si les funt sovent retreire.
Les lais solent as dames pleire,
De joie les oient e de gré
Qu'il sunt sulum lur volenté.[131]

And lady Marie, who composed in rhyme the lines of the lays which are not at all true. She is greatly praised because of them and the rhyme is appreciated everywhere, for counts, barons, and knights are very fond of it[130] and have her work read out and take delight in it, and often have it recited. The lays usually please the ladies, who hear them gladly since they are to their liking.

They have been edited no fewer than nine times in recent years, testifying to the interest which they still arouse even today.

V. OTHER TWELFTH-CENTURY ROMANCES

Various romances of the twelfth century not so far mentioned, or referred to only *en passant*, will now be described very briefly.

If *Guillaume d'Angleterre* is by Chrétien de Troyes,[132] it is different in many respects from his other extant works.

Guillaume, king of England, a pious and gentle character, is ordered by God to abandon his riches and go into exile. His wife follows him, and gives birth to twins. All four are separated, and only after a long series of perilous adventures, in which their trust in God holds firm throughout, are they happily reunited.

A *roman d'aventure*, based, so its author, who names himself as Chrestiiens, claims, on a story from the monastery of St Edmond (in Suffolk), it makes no mention of King Arthur and his knights, and there is no *amour courtois* similar to that in *Cligès*, *Yvain*, and *Lancelot*. The story has affinities with the legend of St Eustace, also that of Apollonius of Tyr.

The legend of *Robert le Diable*[133] tells of this son of a duchess of Normandy who, for long childless, gives birth to him after praying to the devil to grant her a child. He grows through an unruly childhood into an evil, immensely strong tyrant who, after many atrocities, such as the destruction of twenty abbeys in less than a year, repents, is converted to the Christian faith, and becomes a redoubtable enemy of the Saracens.

This *roman d'aventure* appears to date from the end of the twelfth century,[134] but the story was retold in various forms in the later Middle Ages. It was taken by the Normans to Sicily, where four of its episodes are depicted in fourteenth-century paintings on the ceiling of the Chiaramonti Palace in Palermo.[135]

Partonopeu de Blois[136] has affinities with Marie de France's *Lanval* and, like it, derives from Celtic sources.

The hero swears not to look at his fairy mistress Melior, whom he has met only in the dark, until they are married. His mother persuades him to break the oath; his mistress loses her magic powers as a result and turns against him. After he has demonstrated his prowess in numerous tournaments, they are reconciled and all ends well.

This work, written before 1188 and showing the influence of *Eneas* and the *Roman de Thèbes*, was very popular in the Middle Ages and was translated into several languages, including English.

Floire et Blancheflor[137] is a romantic idyll written in the third quarter of the twelfth century, set partly in the fabulous East (one reason for its success throughout medieval Europe) and telling of lovers – Floire, son of a pagan king; Blancheflor, daughter of a Christian noblewoman – for long separated, but at last happily united after many adventures. The theme resembles that of *Aucassin et Nicolete*[138] and the two stories have often been compared.

Renaud de Beaujeu is one of the relatively few authors' names to have survived from this period when the fashion of including the name in a prologue or epilogue was slowly becoming established. His *Guinglain* or *Le Bel Inconnu*,[139] written about 1190, is an Arthurian tale telling how the young hero rescues the daughter of a king of Wales transformed by an evil spell into a dragon, from which he has to receive the 'fier baiser' which puts an end to the spell and also reveals to him his name Guinglain, and that of his father, no other than Gauvain. After further adventures the couple are eventually married. The story shows the influence of Chrétien de Troyes.[140]

Hue de Rotelande (possibly Rhuddlan in Flintshire), writing in the 1180s, is the author of two extant romances, *Ipomedon* and *Protheselaus*.[141] The former tells how Ipomedon, son of the king of Apulia, after a series of adventures in which his prowess is demonstrated, eventually marries the duchess of Calabria. Protheselaus, son of that marriage, after his share of adventures, becomes king of Apulia.

Horn is a romance dating from about 1170 by a certain 'mestre Thomas'.[142]

Horn, son of King Aälof of Suddene [possibly south Devonshire], having been carried off in childhood by the Saracens, eventually becomes their implacable enemy. Having proved himself worthy of Rigmel, daughter of King Hunlaf of Brittany, they are eventually married.

The versification of *Horn* is interesting in that, instead of the octosyllabic rhyming couplets used in the majority of these romances, it is composed of monorhymed *laisses* of alexandrines, of varying length.

Jaufré,[143] written in the late twelfth century,[144] is of interest as one of only two surviving Arthurian romances in Provençal.

Jaufré, the hero, undergoes a series of perilous adventures in pursuit of Taulat, a knight who has insulted Arthur. He is eventually the victor both on the field of combat and in bed, where he wins Brunissen, the lady of his heart, after their love has been analysed, according to the fashion of the later *romans antiques* and Chrétien's *Cligés*, in internal monologues.

A discreet irony in the treatment of the characters already heralds Cervantes.

The legend of the Seven Sages of Rome, destined to become extremely popular throughout western Europe, appears to have reached France, ultimately from oriental sources, in the twelfth century. Jean de Hauteseille's *Historia de Rege et Septem Sapientibus*, also known as the *Dolopathos*, a Latin prose work written between 1184 and 1212,[145] was followed by a version in French verse dating from the later twelfth or early thirteenth century,[146] a thirteenth-century prose version of which at least twenty-four manuscripts are extant,[147] and various continuations and adaptations.[148] In its basic structure the story bears some resemblance to the *Thousand and One Nights*.

A stepmother accuses her stepson of attempting to violate her. The son's father, the king, orders him to be put to death. Seven wise men tell the king a series of stories to convince him of the malice of women – with such success that the son is eventually pardoned and the stepmother executed.

In one of the versions of this well-known legend Shakespeare found the theme of *The Merchant of Venice*.

Romance represents only one aspect of twelfth-century vernacular literature, without doubt the most inventive, the most imaginative, the most popular aspect at the time: that concerned principally with entertainment, though on occasions these stories impart much edification also. For Chrétien at least, they contain a 'sens' as well as 'matière'. If the outlines given above make them sound repetitive, it must be remembered that, like the songs of the troubadours, their appeal, and their originality, lay often in the subtly varied detail, consideration of which would fill a volume this size. What has been written of one particular romance is true of many: '. . . son principal mérite . . . est dans l'habileté du métier, dans la pertinence des touches, la couleur des descriptions, le piquant des observations, la vivacité du mouvement qui attachent le lecteur ayant accepté le genre littéraire offert à son agrément'.[149] The world which they create is remarkable for its peculiar charm and attraction, though it retains a pertinence and relevance to life. So often these early poets of northern France have suffused the world of Celtic myth – or classical myth on occasions – with a solidly-planted psychological realism, and their art was to entwine the real and the fantastic in such a way that each contributed to the effect of the other. Their influence on succeeding centuries was to be immense.

NOTES

1. The chronology of all these works, and their order of appearance, has often been debated, and remains an open question. Future research may throw further light on this problem. M. M. Pelan and N. C. W. Spence eds., *Narcisus (poème du XIIe siècle)*, Paris, 1964, 33–4. R. Jones. *The Theme of Love in the Romans d'antiquité*, London, *MHRA* diss. series no. 5, suggests tentatively the following order of composition: *Thèbes, Piramus et Tisbé, Narcisus, Eneas, Troie, Alexandre*, judging by the growing interest in psychological development and the passage from adaptation to invention (p. 69).
2. The word 'romance' derives from a Latin adverb, *romanice*, meaning 'in Roman fashion'. By the first half of the twelfth century it is found as a substantive 'romanz' in the sense of 'langue vulgaire du Nord de la France', then 'texte français qui est le résultat d'une traduction ou d'un remaniement d'un texte latin'. In the second half of the century it is attested with the meaning 'récit en langue française'. W. von Wartburg, *Französisches Etymologisches Wörterbuch*, Bonn, 1928– (still in process of publication).
3. Statius, *Thebaid*, I, lines 534–9. Text and following translation from the Loeb edition, London–New York, 1928, 380–1: '. . . in countenance, marvellous to tell, like to quiver-bearing Diana and warrior Pallas, yet without their terror. They spy the new faces of the heroes and are shamed; pallor at once and blushes made havoc of their bright cheeks, and their timorous eyes resought their reverend sire'.
4. G. Raynaud de Lage ed., *Le Roman de Thèbes*, Paris, CFMA, 2 vols., 1966–68, I, lines 969–86.
5. A. Ewert ed., *The Romance of Tristran* by Béroul, 2 vols., Oxford, 1939–70, II, 151. It is worth noting that medieval gentlemen preferred blondes, a preference which has left a vestige in the language to this day in the expression 'blue-blooded' and 'to have blue blood in one's veins', for the veins show up more easily in fair-skinned people.

6. *Thebaid*, Book VIII, lines 653–4; *Roman de Thèbes*, 6073–134.

7. C. de Boer ed., *Piramus et Tisbé, poème du XIIe siècle*, Paris, CFMA, 1921.

8. Pelan and Spence, ed. cit.

9. J. Conington, P. *Vergili Maronis Opera*, III, London, 1871, 394, note to line 64.

10. J.-J. Salverda de Grave ed., *Eneas, Roman du XIIe siècle*, Paris, CFMA, 1925, lines 8073–8.

11. Bédier and Hazard, op. cit., I, 24.

12. ed. L. Constans, Paris, SATF, 6 vols., 1904–12.

13. Bédier and Hazard, op. cit., I, 25.

14. Ewert, ed. cit., II, 1–3.

15. J. Bédier ed., *Le Roman de Tristan* by Thomas, Paris, SATF, 2 vols., 1902–05.

16. Ewert, ed. cit., II, 36. Béroul's treatment of the octosyllabic is based on that of Chrétien de Troyes, according to F. Whitehead, 'The Early Tristan Poems', *ALMA*, 140.

17. Ewert, ed. cit., II, 32–3; Bédier, *Le Roman de Tristan*, II, 39.

18. J. Bédier's hypothesis that the versions of Béroul and Eilhart were based on the same source, itself a derivative of the *Estoire*, has been challenged by G. Schoepperle, *Tristan and Isolt, A Study of the Sources of the Romance*, 2nd ed., New York, 2 vols., 1960, I, 83. See also Whitehead, op. cit., 137.

19. Bibliographical details concerning editions of these texts are given by Ewert, ed. cit., II, 46–9.

20. ' . . . Tristant, dont La Chievre fist . . . Et fables et chançons de geste . . .' (. . . Tristan concerning whom La Chievre wrote . . . both fables and chansons de geste). M. Roques ed., *Le Roman de Renart*, Branches II–VI, Paris, CFMA, 1951, lines 3737–9.

21. Ewert, ed. cit., II, 37–8.

22. E. Vinaver, 'The Prose Tristan', *ALMA*, 347.

23. ed. cit., II, 161.

24. ibid., 79–80. Professor Ewert adds that a fancied connection with the adjective *triste*, a variant of which was *tristre*, would account for the two forms Tristan, Tristran.

25. Schoepperle, op. cit., II, 401–8; also H. Newstead, 'The Growth of the Tristan Legend', *ALMA*, 127.

26. ibid., 129; also R. S. Loomis, 'Tristan Scholarship after 1911', in Schoepperle, op. cit., II, 578.

27. Ewert, ed. cit., II, 40.

28. Despite the fact that it has been criticised on several grounds by Schoepperle, op. cit., I, 66–111.

29. For the full reconstruction see Bédier, ed. cit., II, 194–319.

30. A convenient etymological explanation. The true origin of the name was quite different, see above, p. 140.

31. According to Eilhart, Iseut provided the herbs, but did not actually meet Tristan on this occasion. That Eilhart represents the *Estoire* in this respect is argued by Schoepperle, op. cit., I, 84–9.

32. Béroul and Eilhart differ from Thomas in that they give its effects a limited duration: the former three years, the latter four, though Eilhart specifies that it would not become completely ineffective after that period (ibid., 72–84). Whereas Bédier thinks that Thomas represents the original legend in this respect (i.e., the potion having unlimited duration), Schoepperle thinks that Béroul and Eilhart are closer to the original; cf. Whitehead, op. cit., 137, and Vinaver, op. cit., 341, note 1 and, more comprehensively, E. Vinaver, 'The Love Potion in the primitive Tristan Romance', in *Mediaeval Studies in Memory of Gertrude Schoepperle Loomis*, Paris–New York, 1927, 75–86.

33. Perhaps Moray in Scotland; Loomis, in Schoepperle, op. cit., II, 572.

34. On the origins of this theme, see ibid., 580.

35. cf. the two *Folie Tristan* poems mentioned above, p. 140.

36. ed. cit., II, 175.

37. C. B. West, *Courtoisie in Anglo-Norman Literature*, Oxford, 1938, 40.

38. A. Closs ed., *Tristan und Ísolt*, Oxford, 1944.

39. A. Ewert ed., *Marie de France, Lais*, Oxford, 1947.

40. J.-C. Payen, *Le Moyen Age des origines à 1300* (in the series *Littérature française*, general editor C. Pichois), Paris, 1970, 158, 275.

41. J. Frappier, *Chrétien de Troyes*, new ed., Paris, 1968, 5–9.

42. See above, p. 124.

43. The attribution of this work (ed. Ch. de Bœr, Paris, 1909) to Chrétien is sometimes contested, unjustifiably so according to J. Frappier, *Chrétien de Troyes*, 63–4.

44. Payen, op. cit., 158.

45. Frappier, *Chrétien de Troyes*, 81.

46. ibid., 16.

47. E. Faral, *Recherches sur les sources latines des contes et romans courtois du moyen âge*, Paris, new printing 1967, 418.

48. For example, the painting of the seven arts on Amphiaraus's chariot (*Thèbes*, lines 4752–62) and the designs woven into Erec's robe depicting Geometry, Arithmetic, Music, and Astronomy (M. Roques ed., *Erec et Enide*, Paris, CFMA, 1955, lines 6684–728). Chrétien here names his source as Macrobius.

49. See the passage quoted from *Eneas*, p. 137.

50. The most recent, and best, translation of Geoffrey of Monmouth's work is by Professor Lewis Thorpe, and was published in the Penguin Classic series (Harmondsworth, 1966, reprinted 1968). Wace's *Brut* has been edited by I. Arnold, Paris, SATF, 2 vols., 1938–40.

51. Thorpe, ed. cit., 28.

52. ibid.

53. C. Foulon, 'Wace', *ALMA*, 99–100.

54. Frappier, *Chrétien de Troyes*, 39.

55. M. Pelan, *L'Influence du* Brut *de Wace sur les romanciers français de son temps*, Paris, 1931, 69.

56. K. H. Jackson, 'The Arthur of History', *ALMA*, 10.

57. Earlier than 1100 according to I. L. Foster, 'Culhwch and Olwen and Rhonabwy's Dream', *ALMA*, 38. *Mabinogion*, as Foster explains (31), is a modern plural form of the medieval Welsh *mabinogi*, corresponding in meaning to the French *Enfances*, the story of a hero's youth from conception and birth to early manhood. Further evidence of the Celtic ancestry of some of Chrétien's names is provided by R. Bromwich, *Trivedd Ynys Prydein. The Welsh Triads*, Cardiff, 1961. The section headed 'Notes to Personal Names' (263–523) contains many allusions to Chrétien's works, in connection with names such as *Enid*, *Owein* (*Yvain* in French), *Peredur* (to which *Perceval* approximates in French), *Gwalchmei* (Gauvain in French), etc.

58. I. L. Foster, 'Gereint, Olwein and Peredur', *ALMA*, 192.

59. Above all Brittany according to R. S. Loomis, 'The Oral Diffusion of the Arthurian Legend', *ALMA*, 52–63.

60. For information on this 'famous fabulator' see Bromwich, op. cit., cxv. Interesting evidence concerning the existence in Britain of professional interpreters ('latimers'), who may well have formed the vital links between the Celtic populations and the Normans, is provided by C. Bullock-Davies, *Professional Interpreters and the Matter of Britain*, Cardiff, 1961.

61. *Arthurian Tradition and Chrétien de Troyes*, New York, 1949, 467–468.

62. Mentioned also in Chrétiens *Yvain*; see below, p. 155.

63. H. Andresen ed., *Roman de Rou et des Ducs de Normandie* by Maistre Wace, Heilbronn, 1877, lines 6416–20. A new ed. by A. J. Holden is being published by SATF. Vol. I appeared in 1970, vol. II in 1972.

64. According, at least, to Andreas Capellanus; see above, p. 129.

65. Frappier, *Chrétien de Troyes*, 69, and Foerster, op. cit., II, 202–9; also G. Toja, *Lirica cortese d'oïl*, Bologna, 1966, 183–90.

66. A Diverres, 'Some Thoughts on the *Sens* of *Le Chevalier de la Charrette*', *FMLS*, VI, 1970, 24–36.

67. See bibliography in Frappier, *Chrétien de Troyes*, 243–55.

68. cf. the name Isdernus on the Modena archivolt and in Geoffrey of Monmouth's *Historia Regum Britanniae*, for which see above, pp. 146–7.

69. On the full implication of 'vers', cf. Roques, *Erec et Enide*, ix, note 1.

70. Line 2503. Having earlier said the same of herself. The expression, occurring frequently in the *chansons de geste* in laments for dead heroes, is difficult to render. *Mar* derives from *mala hora*, 'in an evil hour', the implication being 'what a waste your life has been', 'your life has been all to no purpose, since this is all it has led to'.

71. cf. lines 4883–7, in which Erec addresses Enide:

'. . . bien vos ai de tot essaiee.   'I have put you fully to the test. No
Or ne soiez plus esmaiee,   longer must you feel dismay, for I
c'or vos aim plus qu'ainz   love you more than ever, and I for
mes ne fis,   my part am sure and certain that you
et je resui certains et fis   love me truly'.
que vos m'amez parfitemant.'

It is thus made quite clear that Erec's intention in setting out on his series of adventures is not merely to put an end to gossip about his supposed cowardice, but also to put their love for each other to the test. For this test to be fully effective, Erec obviously cannot explain it to Enide beforehand, but only later, as here. This has not always been appreciated, as in the following comment: 'There can be no doubt that technically it was a mistake to allow Enide to accompany her husband on his quest' (J. P. Collas, 'The Romantic Hero of the Twelfth Century', in *Medieval Miscellany presented to Eugène Vinaver*, Manchester, 1965, 95). But how else could Enide's love have been put to the test, and how else could she have been made to see with her own eyes the falseness of the 'recreantise' charges?

72. Loomis, *Arthurian Tradition*, 70.

73. Frappier, *Chrétien de Troyes*, 92–3, and for a fuller account Loomis, *Arthurian Tradition*, 168–84.

74. The latest edition is by A. Micha, Paris, CFMA, 1957.

75. The possibility has been envisaged that Thomas wrote his version of *Tristan* after Chrétien's *Cligès*, and borrowed from it, but the borrowing was most likely the other way round, see Whitehead, op. cit., 135–6.

76. Micha, ed. cit., xii.

77. ibid., xiii.

78. See above, p. 124.

79. The latest edition is by Mario Roques in the CFMA series, Paris, 1960.

80. They know he is present, though invisible, because the wounds on the body reopen and bleed afresh – cf. for this superstition, Shakespeare, *Richard III*, Lady Anne's exclamation as Gloucester approaches Henry VI's 'corse':

     O, gentlemen, see, see! dead Henry's wounds
     Open their congealed mouths and bleed afresh.
                     (Act I, Scene ii)

81. Collas, op. cit., 80.

82. That the structure of both is more bipartite than tripartite, since in each the middle section is very short, has been shown by Collas, ibid., 84.

83. Frappier, *Chrétien de Troyes*, 156.

84. Frappier, *Etude sur Yvain ou le Chevalier au Lion de Chrétien de Troyes*, Paris, 1952, new ed. 1968, 108–9.

85. ibid., 110.

86. p. 148.

87. W. A. Nitze, 'The Fountain Defended', *MP*, VII, 1909, 145–64: 'The most notable and most widely known fountain-deity we have is the Arician Diana. With her myth the *Yvain* has more points in common than with any similar story now extant' (162).

88. *Arthurian Tradition*, 278–93.

89. The latest edition is by Mario Roques in the CFMA series, Paris, 1958.

90. *Le Chevalier de la Charrette*, xxv.
91. Diverres, op. cit., 36. Professor Diverres views the romance as an attack on the conception of the *dompna* as a woman insisting on blind obedience for her lover in all circumstances, so forcing him into humiliating situations.
92. F. D. Kelly, *Sens and Conjointure in the Chevalier de la Charrette*, The Hague–Paris, 1966, 84.
93. Loomis, *Arthurian Tradition*, 219.
94. *Le Chevalier de la Charrette*, v–vi.
95. The latest edition is by W. Roach in the *TLF* series, Geneva–Paris, 1959.
96. Is this the first 'réminiscence involontaire' in French literature, of the type that Marcel Proust was to make so famous?
97. *Arthurian Tradition*, 373.
98. It has been suggested, however, that the hermit episode was interpolated by a later author; see A. Brown, 'Did Chrétien identify the Grail with the Mass?', *MLN*, XLI, 1926, 226–33. The debate continues; see D. G. Hoggan, 'Le péché de Perceval', *R*, XCIII, 1972, 50–76 (à suivre).
99. See for fuller details Mario Roques, *Le Graal de Chrétien et la demoiselle au Graal*, Geneva–Lille, 1955, and Martin de Riquer, 'Le Graal', *DLF*.
100. J. Frappier, in his conclusion to a most useful survey of recent Grail scholarship – 'Le Graal et ses feux divergents', *RPh*, XXIV, 1970–71, 373–440 – points out that the books he reviews offer six different interpretations of the Grail, to which, he remarks, should be added a seventh: his own. Each hypothesis is vigorously defended.
101. E. Hoeppfner, *Les Lais de Marie de France*, Paris, 1935, 166.
102. ed. A. Ewert, Oxford, 1944 (several reprints); and J. Rychner, Paris, 1966.
103. In fact not all have their source in the Aesop collection, and the English versions were not by King Alfred, see A. Ewert and R. C. Johnston eds., *Marie de France, Fables*, Oxford, 1942, xi. For a complete edition see K. Warnke ed., *Die Fabeln der Marie de France*, Halle, 1898.
104. T. A. Jenkins ed., *The Espurgatoire saint Patriz of Marie de France*, with a text of the Latin original, Chicago, 1903.
105. Ewert and Johnston, ed. cit., vii.
106. R. Baum, *Recherches sur les œuvres attribuées à Marie de France*, Heidelberg, 1968. For a criticism of this work, see J. Rychner's review in *VR*, XXXI, 177–80.
107. Rychner, *Lais*, xii.
108. Baum, op. cit., 217.
109. ibid., 167.
110. ibid., 217.
111. Quoted from his edition of the *Lais*, vi.
112. Rychner, *Lais*, ix; and S. Painter, 'To whom were dedicated the Fables of Marie de France?', *MLN*, XLVIII, 1933, 367–9.
113. See above, p. 58.
114. The whole concept of the *lai*, with particular reference to medieval uses of the term, is examined by Baum, op. cit. See also, by the same author, 'Les Troubadours et les Lais', *ZRP*, LXXXV, 1969, 1–44, esp. 43.
115. Collas, op. cit., 85.
116. *Lais*, xii.
117. ibid., xi–xii.
118. ibid., xviii.
119. *DLF*, 499 .
120. *Lais*, 173.
121. See above, pp. 119–20.
122. The passage concerned, 56–61, is a difficult one. The interpretation followed here is that of Ewert (*Lais*, 184), whereas for Rychner (*Lais*, 276–9) the whole message was written on the hazel branch.
123. See the notes to Ewert's edition, 183–4.
124. Ewert, *Lais*, 177, and Rychner, *Lais*, 261–2.
125. The attribution of this tale to Marie de France has been doubted by some scholars.

126. ed. F. A. G. Cowper, Paris, SATF, 1956. Collas, op. cit., 89–93.
127. Marie gives the French and English equivalents for this Breton word:

Ceo est russignol en franceis	This is 'rossignol' in French and
E nihtegale [i.e., nightin-	nightingale in English.
gale] en dreit engleis.	
(lines 5–6)	

128. See below, pp. 225–32.
129. See above, pp. 161–2.
130. 'her' possibly, rather than 'it'. Masculine 'cher' offers difficulty with either interpretation.
131. H. Kjellman ed., *La vie Seint Edmund le Rei, poème anglo-normand du XIIe siècle, par Denis Piramus*, Gothenburg, 1935, lines 35–48.
132. See above, p. 146. The text was edited by M. Wilmotte, Paris, CFMA, 1927.
133. ed. E. Löseth, Paris, SATF, 1903.
134. ibid., xlvii.
135. *DLF*, 641.
136. ed. A.-C.-M. Robert, Paris, 1834; and J. Gildea, Villanova, Pennsylvania, I, 1967; II, Part 1, 1968.
137. ed. M. M. Pelan, Paris, 2nd ed. 1956.
138. See below, pp. 207–8.
139. ed. G. Perrie Williams, Paris, CFMA, 1929.
140. ibid., xi.
141. The former has been edited by E. Kölbing and E. Koschwitz, Breslau, 1890; the latter by F. Kluckow, Göttingen, 1924.
142. M. K. Pope ed., *The Romance of Horn by Thomas*, 2 vols., Oxford, 1955–64, vol. II revised and completed by T. B. W. Reid. The suggestion has inevitably been made that this is the Thomas who composed one of the extant versions of the *Tristan* legend.
143. ed. C. Brunel, Paris, SATF, 1943; also by R. Lavaud and R. Nelli in *Les Troubadours*, 2 vols., Bruges, 1960–66, vol. I.
144. ibid., 34–5. In the course of a curious opening scene Arthur is carried away by a monstrous goat, suggesting that the author had access to traditions unknown to Geoffrey and Wace.
145. A. Hilka ed., *Dolopathos sive opusculum de rege et septem sapientibus*, Heidelberg, 1913.
146. J. Misrahi ed., *Le Roman des Sept Sages*, Paris, 1933.
147. G. Paris ed., *Deux Rédactions du Roman des Sept Sages de Rome*, Paris, SATF, 1876, reprinted New York, 1966.
148. The best and most recent study of the legend and the various forms it took in French literature of the twelfth and thirteenth centuries is provided by L. Thorpe in the first volume of his edition of *Le Roman de Laurin*, Cambridge, 1950–58, chapter v, 89–117.
149. Brunel, ed. cit., viii.

Chapter 6

THIRTEENTH-CENTURY LYRIC POETRY

I. THIBAUT DE CHAMPAGNE

OUTSTANDING among the second generation of *trouvères* was Thibaut de Champagne (1201–53), grandson of Marie de Champagne.[1] An account of his life reads like a somewhat bowdlerised version of that of his ancestor Guillaume IX. Like Guillaume he was not a distinguished soldier: on one occasion he helped Louis VIII in his siege of Avignon for the required number of days, but he ignored the king's entreaties to stay longer, and returned home. He participated in the sixth crusade, in which the Christian army was defeated at Gaza. Thibaut's help would have been crucial, but he arrived too late on the scene to be of any use. No more outstanding as an administrator, the subjects of his kingdom of Navarre, which he had inherited through his mother, stipulated that they would not accept his son and heir as sovereign unless he swore to observe their privileges, neglected by his father. Rumour had it that Thibaut poisoned Louis VIII and was the lover of his wife, Blanche of Castile, and although they were unfounded, such rumours show that he was an unpopular figure regarded with suspicion, perhaps jealousy also, by his contemporaries. He was a faithful scion of the family in that his best characteristic was his devotion to poetry. Several witnesses affirm that some of his verses were painted on the walls of his castles at Troyes and Provins,[2] an interesting testimony to the pride he took in them.

The idea that courtly love-poetry was already becoming effete in Thibaut's day finds little support in his poems. Uneven though so substantial an output was bound to be,[3] his best poems are characterised by a liveliness and freshness, drawing their effect from the versification as well as from the contents:

Por conforter ma pesance	To quieten my grief
Faz un son.	I compose a song.
Bons ert, se il m'en avance,	It will be good if it advances my
Car Jason	cause, for Jason who gained
Cil qui conquist la toison,	the fleece never felt such
N'ot pas si grief penitance.	grievous penitence.
E! é! é!	Oh! Oh! Oh!

Je meïsmes a moi tence,	I scold myself
Car raison	for reason tells me
Me dit que je faz enfance,	that I am acting childishly
Quant prison	since a prison holds me
Tieng ou ne vaut raençon;	[lit. I hold] in which a ransom is
Si ai mestier d'alejance.	useless.
E! é! é![4]	And I need some comfort.
	Oh! Oh! Oh!

It is true that Thibaut's attitude remains conventional, for he is the 'fins amis obedianz (II, line 8) (the true obedient lover), much of whose time is spent in 'vivre et atendre et languir' (XII, 20) (living and waiting and languishing). He is '. . . toz jorz a parole menez' (XX, 8) (always led along by words) as he sings of love's 'douces dolors' (sweet pains) and 'mal plesant' (pleasant ache) (XXXI, 1–2). He promises the lady the traditional discretion:

Aucuns i a qui me seulent blasmer,	Some there are who are accustomed
Quant je ne di a qui je sui amis,	to blame me, since I do not say
Mes ja, dame, ne savra mon penser	whose lover I am, but never, lady,
Nus qui soit nez, fors vous . . .	will anyone alive know my thoughts,
(XIII, 28–31)	save you alone . . .

but what was very necessary in the troubadour verse because of its sensuality was less so here, in this almost disembodied passion which allows itself no more than a discreet reference to the lady's complexion or the colour of her hair and eyes. Very French already is this delightfully civilised, highly polished *badinage* which reaches beyond courtly mannerisms to a flirtation that is at once tender and witty:

Dame, merci! Une riens vos demant,	Lady, mercy! One thing I ask of
Dites m'en voir, se Deus vous beneïe:	you, tell me the truth, may God bless
Quant vous morrez et je – mès	you. When you die and I – but that
c'iert avant,	will be first, for after you I could not
Car après vous ne vivroie je mie –,	live – what will become of Love, that
Que devendra Amors, cele esbahie,	fool, for you have so much sense and
Que tant avez sens, valor, et j'aim	worth, and I love so much, that I
tant	really believe that after us Love will
Que je croi bien qu'après nous ert	be no more.
faillie?	
– Par Dieu, Thiebaut, selonc mon	In God's name, Thibaut, in my view
escïent	Love will never perish because of
Amors n'iert ja pour nule mort perie,	anyone's death, and I do not know if
Ne je ne sai se vous m'alez guilant,	you are teasing me, for you are not
Que trop megres n'estes oncore mie.	too thin as yet. When we die (God
Quant nos morrons (Deus nos dont	grant us a good life!) well do I
bone vie!),	believe that Love will suffer greatly,
Bien croi qu'Amors damage i avra	but Love's true worth will still
grant,	endure.
Mès toz jorz ert valors d'amors	
complie,[5]	
(XLVII, 1–14)	

French too is his attempt to give a rational, psychologically valid explanation of the *amour lointain* theme:

Plus tost aime on en estrange
  contree,
Ou on ne puet ne venir ne aler
Qu'on ne fet ce qu'on puet toz jorz
  trouver;
Issi est bien la folie esprouvee.

It is easier to love someone far away in a land to which one cannot go, rather than someone one can meet every day. So is love's folly clearly revealed.

(IX, 37–40)

A certain preciosity, the effect of a refined courtly tradition which already had a long history, can be felt in his imagery, which sometimes takes its root in medieval legend:

Ausi conme unicorne sui
Qui s'esbahist en regardant,
Quant la pucele va mirant.
Tant est liee de son ennui,
Pasmee chiet en son giron;
Lors l'ocit on en traïson.
Et moi ont mort d'autel senblant
Amors et ma dame, por voir:
Mon cuer ont, n'en puis point
  ravoir.[6]

I am just like the unicorn which loses its senses when it gazes on the maiden. So happy is it in its suffering that it falls fainting in her lap. Then it is treacherously put to death. So have Love and my lady killed me in like manner, in truth. They have my heart and I cannot retrieve it.

(XXXIV, 1–9)

His *jeux-partis* reflect this preciosity in the very nature of their debates: for example, two lovers love the same girl, one for her *courtoisie*, the other for her beauty. Which is the better love? Thibaut opts for beauty (arguing that anything a beautiful girl says is bound to be courteous!), whereas his opponent, Baudouin (identity unknown), supports *courtoisie* and each argues his case with zest. Such poems, inherited as we have seen from the Provençal tradition,[7] are interesting for the attitude towards literature which they reveal: it was a game, a tournament with words, one of the skills which a knight was required to master. The same qualities and attitude are revealed in Thibaut's very use of words: in one poem the word ending one stanza must begin the next, and in another, the words ending the last two lines have to be grammatically linked: *partir:partie, faillir:faillie, ami:amie*, etc.[8] Such playing with words grew more fashionable in the later thirteenth century, but did not reach its height until the end of the Middle Ages and the early Renaissance.

Thibaut was not in truth a great poet, and certainly not original as regards his basic material, but so much versatility within so narrow an orbit is remarkable, and the sheer zest and conviction with which he sings of the happiness love can bring leave an abiding impression:

Por mau tens ne por gelee	Not for the bad weather, not for the
Ne por froide matinee	frost
Ne por nule autre riens nee	Not for the morning chill
Ne partirai ma pensee	Not for any creature born
D'amors que j'ai,	Will I give up thinking
Que trop l'ai amee	Of my love
De cuer verai.	For I have loved her greatly
Valara!	With true heart
(VIII, st. i)	Heigh-ho!

II. COLIN MUSET

Colin Muset was born about 1210 in what is now the department of the Haute-Marne, on the confines of Champagne, Burgundy, and Lorraine. This wandering minstrel of humble origin provides a marked contrast with Thibaut de Champagne.[9] Although the elements of courtly love are present in certain of his poems: 'Ma tres douce dame honoree' (VIII, line 17) (my very sweet and noble lady) and the 'felon mesdisant losengier' (VI, 24) (treacherous lying slanderers) who threaten the poet's love, they do not form the central core of his work and seem to be there mainly to humour his aristocratic audience. Colin Muset is a specialist of the diminutive, which imparts a tone of familiarity and of bantering to the delightful charms of his refreshing love-songs set in the minor key:

Sospris sui d'une amorette	I have fallen in love
D'une jone pucelette:	with a fair young maid.
Bele est et blonde et blanchette	She is lovely and fair,
Plus que n'est une erminette,	whiter than an ermine,
S'a la color vermeillette	and as crimson
Ensi com une rosette. (III, 1–6)	as a rosebud.

His heart is not *amoros*, but *amoroset*.[10] Accompanied by a smile rather than a sigh, this love lacks the soulfulness of the more traditional *fin' amors* poetry, though this does not prevent him from declaring gallantly that he will die for his 'blondette' (VI, 7; pretty little blonde), an even more obvious hyperbole than such declarations by other *trouvères*. Whereas Gace Brulé's thoughts moved quickly from his lady to his noble and elevated intentions as a crusader, Colin Muset was ever ready to peer greedily over the shoulder of his charming 'pucellette' at the sumptuous feast that always seemed to be spread out somewhere in his immediate vicinity:

L'en m'apele Colin Muset,	My name is Colin Muset,
S'ai mangié maint bon chaponet,	and I have eaten many a fine capon,
Mainte haste, maint gastelet	many a roast joint, many a cake
En vergier et en praelet,	in orchard and in meadow,
Et quant je puis l'oste trover	and when I can find an innkeeper
Qui veut acroire et bien prester,	willing to give me credit,
Adonc me preng a sejorner	then I settle down
Selon la blondete au vis cler.	with the bright-faced fair young
(IV, 33–40)	thing.

This is the idea of the good life: a mouth-watering repast (there is far more attention paid to good food in the fifteen short poems attributed to him than there is in all the romances of Chrétien de Troyes), an innkeeper willing to give credit, and a fair-haired, bright-faced wench. As for his happy-go-lucky philosophy of life, marked by an obvious self-interest, it can all be summed up in two lines:

Ke valt avoirs en fardel,
s'on nel despent a honor?

What is the point of piling up money
and not spending it well?

(IX, 47–8)

Best of all for this epicurean lover is a flirtation in the summer meadows, with rich food spread out on the grass, and young gallants and damsels all crowned with garlands of flowers:

Quant je la tieng ou prael
Tout entor clos d'arbrissels
En esté a la verdur
Et j'ai oies et gastel,
Poissons, tartes et porcel,
Buef a la verde savor,
Et j'ai le vin en tonel,
Froit et fort et friandel
Por boivre a la grant chalor,
Miels m'i aim k'en un batel
En la mer en grant poour.
Triboudainne, tribondel!
Plus aim le jeu de prael
Ke faire malvais sejor.[11]

When I hold her in the meadow,
with bushes growing all around
in summer's greenery,
and I have geese and a cake,
fish, tarts, and sucking-pig,
beef in green sauce,
wine drawn from the wood
cool and strong and tasty
to drink in the great heat,
I am far happier there than in a boat
full of fear on the open sea,
Fiddle-dee-dee, Fiddle-dee-daa.
I like playing in the meadow
better than staying in some unhappy house.

(IX, 49–62)

The noise and merriment of springtime revelries are beautifully caught in this richly alliterative poem. The troubadours' *joi*, that rather mysterious ecstasy which fired their love-poetry, is here replaced by a more recognisable, down-to-earth *joie de vivre*. Only one matter caused Colin Muset any strong feeling: the avarice of some of the rich on whom such as he depended:

Kant plus ont or et argent,
Vair et gris et dras de soie,
Tant sont moins large metant . . .

(VII, 29–31)

The more gold and silver they possess,
furs and silken robes,
the meaner they are . . .

A note of bitterness and disillusionment crept in as he reflected on the meanness and decadence of the whole age:

Cist siecles faut et desvoie
Chascun jor trop malement,
Et kant plus vos en diroie,
Je n'i voi home joiant,
Et si muerent alsiment
A tot mil mars en monoie
Come cil qui n'a neient;
Trop se mainent folement.

(VII, 33–40)

This age gets worse with
every day that passes,
and what more could I say,
for I see nobody happy,
and yet those with a thousand
pounds saved up die
just like those who are penniless.
Everybody behaves in a very foolish fashion.

Bitterly he reproaches the count who had listened to his playing and had given him nothing:

Sire cuens, j'ai vïelé	My lord count, I have played my
Devant vous en vostre ostel,	viol in your presence, in your own
Si ne m'avez riens doné	abode, yet you have given me noth-
Ne mes gages aquité:	ing, not even my wages.
C'est vilanie!	Now that is villainous!
Foi que doi sainte Marie,	By the faith I owe St Mary, I shall
Ensi ne vous sieurré mie.	follow you no longer. My scrip is
M'aumosniere est mal garnie	badly furnished, and my purse badly
Et ma boursse mal farsie	stuffed.

(XII, 1–9)

Such admonitions were commonplace. He goes on to relate how, when he returns from his visits to the seigneurial Courts with his bag 'de vent farsie' (stuffed with wind), he is greeted by his wife's sarcasms, but if it is bulging with good things through the nobles' generosity, she flings her arms round his neck, unpacks his bag, while the maid (so he was not so poor after all, unless he is indulging in make-believe) kills two capons and prepares a garlic sauce:

Lors sui de mon ostel sire	Then I really am master of my own
A mult grant joie sanz ire	home, in great joy without any
Plus que nuls ne porroit dire	sadness, more than anyone could tell.

(XII, 46–8)

Even this poem, which begins so bitterly, has a happy ending, for generous patrons could still be found, and a poet's lot could still be enviable. Of all the lyric poets of medieval France, Colin Muset was the lightest, the gayest, the most carefree, save in those revealing moments when the harsher realities of life made themselves felt.

III. THE POETS OF ARRAS: JEAN BODEL, BAUDE FASTOUL, ADAM DE LA HALLE

Of particular interest are the poets of Arras, whose varied literary output spans most of the century. A prosperous centre for international trade, commerce, and banking, at its heyday from the late twelfth to the early fourteenth centuries, Arras saw the early emergence of the bourgeoisie whose literary patronage is reflected in the *Confrérie des Jongleurs et Bourgeois d'Arras*. The names of Gautier d'Arras and Conon de Béthune have already been mentioned, but the first poet to refer frequently to his native Arras was Jean Bodel, who was born about 1165 and died in 1209 or 1210. He is the first bourgeois *trouvère* of the thirteenth century, heralding an important development in the literature of the times. He tried his hand at most genres, apart, significantly enough, from love-poetry. He has left us nine *fabliaux*, a *chanson de geste*, a miracle play, much of whose action takes place in an Arras tavern, five *pastourelles*, and the *Congés*, this last-named providing the reason for his inclusion in this chapter. In 1202 it had been Bodel's intention to take part in the fourth crusade, but he contracted leprosy and had to live the rest of his days in a neighbouring leper colony, that of the Grand Val de Beaurains. In the *Congés* he takes leave of his friends, many of whom are named. Whether or not he was the first poet to write a work of this kind is not known,[12] but he was followed, as we shall see, by two other Arras poets. The very situation provides the *Congés* with a ready-made pathos. Bodel was an active man who enjoyed life and was full of the deepest regret at leaving the society 'que tant amer sueil' (line 246) (which I am wont to love so much). Some 43 friends and acquaintances, among them the mayor of Arras, are mentioned in the course of the 540 lines of the poem, divided into 45 stanzas. Usually each refers to one individual, occasionally two:

Congié demant tout premerain	I take my leave first of all of the
A celui qui plus m'est a main	man who has always been close to
Et don je miex loer me doi:	me and with whom I am most
Jehan Boschet, a Dieu remain!	pleased: Jean Boschet, farewell!
Plorant recor et soir et main	Weeping I record morning and
Les biens que j'ai trouvez en toi.	evening all the good qualities I found
Se je plor souvent en requoi,	in you. If I often weep on the quiet,
Assez y a raison pour quoi,	there is very good reason, today
Auques ennuit et plus demain.	already and more tomorrow.
(13–21)	

Descriptions of his physical state as a leper are discreet, the grimmest being the single line 'Moitié sain et moitié porri' (line 60) (Half healthy and half rotten). The greatest impact of this very topical poem must clearly have been immediately after its composition when those mentioned could read their friend's sad farewell for themselves. None the less, the poignancy can still be felt, as the joy that the very thought of his friends aroused mingled in his mind with the sadness of the occasion:

...Doubles pensers qui me court seure	The twofold thought assailing me nourishes both joy and grief in my
Joie et doleur en mon cuer neure;	heart. I laugh and sigh, I sing and
Ri et souspir, et chante et pleure.	weep. In my own mind I am both up
A mon sens et a mon esgart	and down. My body is leaving, my
Sui je et desouz et deseure:	soul stays behind. Thus do I stay,
Li cors s'en va, l'ame demeure;	thus do I depart.
Ainsi demeure, ainsi m'en part.	
(450–6)	

Surprisingly enough, it is not a work of unrelieved melancholy; the occasional quip, showing humour in adversity, has evoked comparisons with several later poets:

Ce courage souriant, qui permet à Bodel de plaisanter au milieu de sa souffrance, c'est celui qui animera Rutebeuf en pleine maladie, et en pleine misère; c'est celui qui fera plaisanter Villon, menacé du gibet; c'est celui qui, de Marot à Verlaine ou à Jules Laforgue, mêle le rire aux instants les plus pathétiques.[13]

Part of the work's fascination for the modern reader lies in its contrast with so much medieval lyric poetry, so often devoted to a literary theme, an abstraction. What could be more solidly down-to-earth, closer to the harsh realities of medieval life, than the *Congés* of Jean Bodel?

Seventy years later, in 1272 or 1273, another Arras poet, Baude Fastoul, in the same circumstances, wrote a *Congés* in imitation of Jean Bodel. He made more allusions to the horrors of leprosy, possibly because his symptoms were more advanced:

. . . Quant je n'arai ne pié ne main,	When my feet have gone, and my hands, my mouth, and nose, and
Bouce ne nés, fors le cuer sain . . .	only my heart is healthy . . .
(lines 82–3)	

However, like Bodel, he remained discreet, disdaining to play too easily on his readers' emotions, intent above all on bidding a sad farewell to his many friends.

The third and last of the Arras *Congés*, by Adam de la Halle, was written in 1276 or 1277. The circumstances were quite different, for there was no question of the poet's illness. Suggestions that he was leaving 'à la suite de conflits municipaux'[14] have recently been contradicted.[15] It seems that he wished to pursue his studies and was leaving his native Arras, possibly for Paris, with that end in view, his imminent departure being alluded to also in one of his two plays, *Le Jeu de la Feuillée*.[16] A poet of considerable force and talent, he begins by expressing his sense of guilt at having dallied so long because of love, but in the next stanza he makes a sudden, somewhat inconsequential, attack on Arras as a corrupt, money-grabbing city:

Arras, Arras, vile de plait	Arras, Arras, town of litigation,
Et de haïne et de detrait,	hatred, and calumny, which once
Qui soliés estre si nobile,	were so noble, they say you are
On va disant c'on vous refait,	being reformed, but if God does not
Mais se Diex le bien n'i ratrait,	restore your virtue, I see no one who
Je ne voi qui vous reconcile.	can. The people there are too fond
On i aime trop crois et pile.	of cash.
(lines 13–19)	

None the less, he had good, kind friends there of whom he was reluctant to take leave, his lady-love above all:

Bele tres douche amie chiere,	My fair lady-love, so dear and sweet,
Je ne puis faire bele chiere,	I cannot be of good cheer, for I am
Car plus dolans de vous me part	sadder at the thought of leaving you
Que de rien que je laisse arriere.	than of leaving anybody else. You
De mon cuer serés tresoriere	shall be treasurer of my heart, and
Et li cors ira d'autre part	my body alone shall depart to seek
Aprendre et querre engien et	knowledge and skill . . .
art . . .	

(61–7)

Like Jean Bodel, Adam de la Halle was a versatile writer, but a more truly lyric poet. Apart from his *Congés*, Bodel shows lyricism of a kind only in his five *pastourelles* which follow the traditional pattern, though they have been praised for their sense of drama and psychological realism.[17] Adam de la Halle, on the other hand, perhaps even more talented as a musician than as a poet, is the author of love-songs and motets at least equal in quality to the songs of Thibaut de Champagne.[18] He provides us with a useful reminder that love-poetry did not suddenly disappear in the course of this century. It was no longer the monopoly of the Courts, but was successfully practised in bourgeois *milieux* in this century which saw a great diversification of the lyric genre. Love, Adam declares, is not a matter of fine clothes and distinguished accent:

. . . behours, robe envoisie,	merrymaking, attractive clothes,
Biaus canters, langue polie,	fine singing, a smooth tongue
Ne saulers agus,	pointed shoes
L'amour pas ne senefie,	do not constitute love,
Mais fins cuers loiaus, repus,	but a true heart loyal and discreet
C'on n'en mesdie.	so that no gossip ensues.

(xxviii, 6–11)

Almost half the lyric poetry of the thirteenth century originated from Arras and its region. Many names have survived, though for some of them only two or three poems are extant: Moniot d'Arras, Adam de Givenchy, Jean Bretel who was 'Prince' of the 'Puy' of Arras in the second third of the century,[19] Gillebert de Berneville, Simon d'Authié, Perrin d'Angicourt, Jean Erart, Thomas Herier, Colart le Bouteillier. Among those from other districts of northern France the following deserve mention: Gilles des Vieux-Maisons, Guillaume de Ferrieres, both of whom wrote in the late twelfth and early thirteenth centuries, Richard de Semilli, Robert de Reims, Auboin de Sézanne, Richard de Fournival, Gilles and Guillaume le Vinier, Messire Jacques de Cysoing, Moniot de Paris, Hue de Lusignan comte de la Marche.[20]

IV. RUTEBEUF

What Paris lacked in numbers it made up in quality. The moment has not yet come to speak about Jean de Meun, author of the second part of the *Roman de la Rose*, but the capital can claim one lyric poet of considerable talent in the person of Rutebeuf, author of 56 extant works written between 1248 and about 1277. He seems to have originated in Champagne, but lived most of his life in Paris. Lyric poetry formed only one part of his literary output, which includes two saints' lives, a miracle play, religious, moral, and didactic verse, *fabliaux*, polemic on contemporary topics, including the crusades, and social satire.[21] A surprising absence, on the other hand, is any mention of love; also, and the two factors are not disconnected, this verse was not designed to be set to music. Very little is known about him except what can be culled from his works, but he makes it abundantly clear that he was a poor man, this *Rude boeuf* (rustic ox) as he calls himself, echoing perhaps the nickname given him by his fellow scholars in Paris, though this may well not have been the true etymology of his name but a deformation of one whose source was quite different.[22] If he was of country origin as seems likely, such a nickname would have had greater point. Only his lyric verse will be considered within the confines of this chapter. It is a lyricism with a background totally different from that of the Court poets, for it is that of the *Goliardi*, clerics who had been through the schools but had not found employment within the Church, or literary patronage at Court, and who complained in their Latin verse of the sordidness of their existence, or evoked in pathetic terms their fleeting joys and lasting hardships. It is necessary to point this out, otherwise Rutebeuf's personal poetry would appear far more original than it was in fact. The true nature of medieval creativity, so it has been said, was 'a perpetual renewal of pre-existing structures',[23] a matter to which we shall return in the conclusion to this chapter. The following paragraphs are taken up with analyses and appreciations of certain of Rutebeuf's personal poems, the *Poèmes de l'Infortune* as they have been called.[24]

La Griesche d'Iver (Winter Dice)[25]

The poem is set in early winter when leaves fall and branches are bare. It is in that season that the poet feels the full effects of his poverty:

Povre sens et povre memoire	A wretched mind, a wretched
M'a Diex doné, li rois de gloire,	memory has God, king of glory,
Et povre rente,	given to me, and a wretched income,
Et froit au cul quant bise vente.	and a chilly backside when the North
(lines 10–13)	Wind blows.

The following lines with their persistent use of Rutebeuf's favourite rhetorical device known as *annominatio* (paronomasia), show him as a juggler with words and syllables:

Li vens me vient, li vens m'esvente
  Et trop sovent
Plusors foïes sent le vent.

The wind assails me, the wind blows around me, and all too often and many a time I feel the wind.

(14–16)

It transpires that his poverty is owed to his gambling with dice:

  Li dé m'ocient,
Li dé m'aguetent et espient,
Li dé m'assaillent et desfient,
  Ce poise moi.

The dice are killing me, the dice lie in wait for me and spy on me, the dice attack me and challenge me, this weighs me down.

(54–7)

It is therefore a self-created misery of which he tells in this taut, rasping phraseology beneath which flows an undercurrent of bitterness and bewildered frustration as he laments over this poverty of his own making. Gambling has taken a firm hold on him and he is powerless to escape. From the first person the poem slides surreptitiously to the third, and it is the hopeless state of the gambler in general, always his own victim, that is depicted:

Du duel son voisin ne li membre,
  Més le sien pleure.
Griesche li a coru seure,
Desnué l'a en petit d'eure,
  Et nus ne l'aime.

He does not remember his neighbour's affliction, but weeps over his own. Gambling has seized hold of him and stripped him bare in a short time, and nobody loves him.

(83–7)

He is isolated, driven in upon himself, destitute, and mocked, a penniless figure of fun.

This strange mixture of the pathetic and the grotesque, a caricature that excites pity and laughter at the same time, is developed further in the following poems. Also of interest is the structure, two octosyllabic lines followed by a hemistich.[26] The short line usually rounds off and completes the meaning of the preceding couplet (27 cases), though sometimes it links up with the following one (9 cases), whereas its rhyme always announces that of the following couplet.

La Griesche d'Esté (Summer Dice)

After only twelve lines on the subject of his 'grant folie' (1) (great madness), he slides once more into the third person as his own torment as a gambler leads him to speak of that of others in like circumstances. There is no escape once caught, and everybody loses. The gambler's plight is presented in bitingly ironical terms:

La griesche est de tel maniere
Qu'ele veut avoir gent legiere
  En son servise:
Une eure en cote, autre en chemise.

Gambling is such that it wishes the people in its service to be lightly clad: one hour in tunic, the next in shirt-sleeves [the tunic having been gambled away].

(34–7)

But gamblers are incurably optimistic, and hope springs eternal in their breast:

Esperance les sert de lobe
Et la griesche les desrobe:
  La borse est vuide

Hope deceives them and gambling strips them. Their purse is empty.

(55–7)

But soon hope fades away, and gambling leads to other disorders (the poem avoids moralising words such as 'vice'). Any winnings are soon spent:

Au tavernier font du vin trere,
  Or entre boule;
Ne boivent pas, chascuns le coule.

They get the innkeeper to draw wine, and now debauchery comes on the scene. They do not just drink wine, each gulps it down in torrents.

(77–9)

In the summer months, when even their clothes have been gambled away, sadness can yield to a brief season's mirth:

Ez vous la joie!
N'i a si nu qui ne s'esjoie;
Plus sont seignor que ras sus moie
  Tout cel esté.

Just look at their merrymaking! None, however stripped bare, fails to rejoice. They lord it more than the rat on the haystack, all summer through.

(108–11)

All have learned to go barefoot.

Together these two caustically worded poems form a marvellous portrait of the gambler which is as true now as when it was written. They show a remarkable understanding of the weaknesses of human nature, an understanding which, as the introduction to both poems reveals, has its starting-point in the poet's self.

Le Dit des Ribaux[27] de Greive (Poem on the Dockers of the Place de Grève)

This short poem is here quoted in full:

'Ribaut, or estes vos a point:
Li aubre despoillent lor branches
Et vos n'aveiz de robe point,
Si en avreiz froit a voz hanches.
Queil vos fussent or li porpoint.
Et li seurquot forrei a manches!
Vos aleiz en esté si joint
Et en yver aleiz si cranche!
Votre soleir n'ont mestier d'oint:
Vos faites de vos talons planches.
Les noires mouches vos ont point,
Or vos repoinderont les blanches'.

'Dockers, now you are in a fine mess. The trees are stripping their branches and you have no clothes and you will feel the cold on your ribs. How precious for you now would be the rich man's doublets and overcoats with fur-lined sleeves! In summer you are so carefree, so careworn in winter. No need for grease on your shoes: your bare heels must serve to walk on. The black flies have stung you, now the white ones [i.e., hail and snow] will sting you in their turn'.

This grim, poignantly ironical picture of the miseries of these labourers does not openly express sympathy for them but very clearly implies it in every line. The use of direct speech throughout adds greatly to its impact and effectiveness. The poet's attitude can be judged by his use of the same metaphors to express their suffering that he had used in the *Griesche d'Iver* to express his own:

Noire mousche en esté me point   Les noires mouches vos ont point,
  En yver blanche   Or vos repoinderont les blanches.

(32–3)

Medieval French poetry has very little to offer us of this type. Its presence here is a remarkable testimony to its author's feeling for the sufferings of others, and justifies the comparison so often made between him and that other Parisian poet, François Villon.

Le Mariage Rutebeuf

The poet bewails the wretched material circumstances of his life, above all his marriage to a withered and dried-up woman of fifty who has brought him nothing but poverty:

Tel fame ai prise   Such a wife have I taken that no-
Que nus fors moi n'aime ne prise,   body apart from me loves her or
Et s'estoit povre et entreprise   esteems her, and she was poor and
  Quant je la pris.   distressed when I married her. A fine
A ci mariage de pris,   marriage this is, for now I am
C'or sui povres et entrepris   equally poor and distressed. Nor is
  Ausi comme ele!   she good-looking or beautiful. She
Et si n'est pas gente ne bele;   has got fifty years in her bowl, and
Cinquante anz a en s'escuele,   she is thin and withered. There is
  S'est maigre et seche: no danger of her deceiving me.
N'ai pas paor qu'ele me treche.

(28–38)

Life has treated him harshly and God loves him only from a distance. His best years are gone, and he has nothing to show for their passing. He cannot earn a living as a labourer: 'Je ne sui pas ouvriers des mains' (98) (I am not a workman), often he returns home penniless and can only feed on hope:

L'esperance de l'endemain,   Hope of a better tomorrow is what I
  Ce sont mes festes   feast on.

(114–15)

On seeing him in the streets, people cross themselves.

Doubts have been expressed as to the veracity of this portrait of the sorry pair.[28] Was it darkened deliberately as a means of soliciting help from wealthy patrons, of whom there is, however, no mention? This would indeed seem to be the case when the poem is considered along with the one following.

La Complainte Rutebeuf

This lament develops that of the *Mariage*:

... bien avez oï le conte   ... well have you heard the tale in
En quel maniere   what manner I married my last wife.
Je pris ma fame darreniere

(3–5)

Now the personal note is reinforced: he has lost the sight of his right eye, his wife has had a baby (at the age of fifty?), his horse has broken its leg, the baby's nurse is clamouring for her wages. He does not know how they can face the winter, all his possessions are pawned, he has been ill for three months, and for a month after the birth of the baby his wife was at death's door. When troubles rained down on them from all sides, their friends stayed away:

Li mal ne sevent seul venir;
Tout ce m'estoit a avenir
    S'est avenu
Que sont mi ami devenu
Que j'avoie si pres tenu
    Et tant amé?
Je cuit qu'il sont trop cler semé;
Il ne furent pas bien femé,
    Si sont failli.
Itel ami m'ont mal bailli,
C'onques, tant com Diex m'assailli
    En maint costé,
N'en vi un seul en mon osté.
Je cuit li vens les a osté,
    L'amor est morte:
Ce sont ami que vens enporte,
Et il ventoit devant ma porte
    Ses enporta.

Troubles simply cannot come singly. All this had to happen to me, and it has happened. What has become of my friends whom I had kept so close, and loved so dearly? I think they were too thinly sown. I did not spread enough manure around them and they have come to nothing. Such friends have brought me trouble, for never, as long as God assailed me on many a side, did I see a single one of them in my abode. I think the wind has carried them off, Love is dead. They are the sort of friends the wind blows away. And it blew in front of my door, and swept them away.

(107–24)

These lines are among the most poignant that Rutebeuf wrote and can with justice be set beside the confessions of François Villon. The purpose of the poem, and possibly that of its companions, is made clear in the conclusion: it was to be sent to 'the good count of Poitiers and Toulouse', who had already helped him in the past and who well understood his needs. This count is known to have been fond of gambling with dice. Is this why Rutebeuf wrote for him, feeling that the mentality he describes in the *Griesche* poems was certain to command the count's sympathy?[29]

La Poverté Rutebeuf

Rutebeuf appeals directly to the king to help him in his dire poverty:

Por Dieu vos pri, frans rois de France,
Que me doneiz queilque chevance,
Si fereiz trop grant charitei.

In God's name I beg you, noble king of France, to give me some resources, and you will be acting in a very charitable way.

(4–6)

Generosity has fled and times are hard. The crusades have made matters worse because they involved the departure of wealthy patrons. Now all the poet's hopes are in the king, and he makes a liberal use of *annominatio* in his bid to enlist his sympathy and help:

Granz rois, s'il avient qu' a vos faille,
A touz ai ge failli sanz faille.
Vivres me faut et est failliz . . .

Great king, if it comes about that I fail with you, I have failed with all without fail, sustenance fails me and has failed.

(25–7)

It is probable that this type of pun, which is not likely to command much respect nowadays, was then considered a clever contribution to a text's effectiveness, and indeed it appears in the most serious religious works, including Rutebeuf's *Miracle de Théophile*. It was clearly intended as something more than mere embellishment.

As in the twelfth- and thirteenth-century Latin verse of the *Goliardi*, difficult material circumstances, hardship and suffering of a kind unknown to the court poets, brought Rutebeuf's work closer to the exigencies of daily living. The concern here is not with relationships between the sexes, which receive only ironical treatment from Rutebeuf, but between man and his fellows, between rich and poor, noble and bourgeois, one social class and another. The sophistication and refinement, the aesthetic achievement, which are the high hallmarks of the court poets' verse, allied to their skill as musicians – all this is quite foreign to Rutebeuf as to the *Goliardi*, but in its place they provide a telling comment on the hopes and fears of medieval man. This non-courtly lyricism is likely to have a greater impact on the modern reader than is thirteenth-century love-poetry, for however perennial the love theme may be, the court poets' treatment of it became increasingly narrow and repetitive. We cannot in any case so easily share the games and social embellishments of the vanished world of the medieval Courts, but inasmuch as the complaints of a Rutebeuf strike at the foibles of human nature or at the foundations of society, we can even now listen to and sympathise with this verse, written though it was a full seven hundred years ago.

However far-reaching his reflections on humanity may be, Rutebeuf's basic concern was with himself, and the inevitable question is: does his personal poetry give us a true self-portrait, or is there a measure of fiction in these lines? The 'sincerity' of any poet as he sets pen to paper is so often an incommensurable quality. The most we can say is that his work is characterised by an aura of sincerity, for this is a pronouncement relating to his art as a poet, not to his true feelings and circumstances, whatever they may have been. It has been suggested, for example, that Rutebeuf's allusion to the failing sight of his right eye was a mere pretence:

La pitié vient plus vite au cœur lorsqu'un sourire l'accompagne. Imaginons un instant notre poète, parfaitement versé dans l'art de la jonglerie, fermant son œil droit au passage en question, au cours de sa récitation.[30]

For such matters we usually have to rely on the text alone, and frequently no firm conclusion is possible. In this particular instance it is noteworthy that Rutebeuf makes a second reference to this affliction, brought on him, he says, by God, and he expresses the hope that God would count it as a penitence.[31] That this was a pretence seems unlikely. It is often claimed, not without justice, that medieval lyric poetry was largely a matter of *topoi*, of loyalty to set themes – particularly in the love-poetry practised by the Courts, but also, surprisingly enough, in the apparently personal confessions of a Rutebeuf[32] – and that the 'poetic I' was a façade hiding what may have been a very different reality. Attitudes in medieval times were not what they are nowadays; no premium was set on originality, there was no copyright and no shame in plagiarism; but even so, in most instances there were close links between the 'poetic I' and the poet's real personality, as the contrasts between the different *trouvères* reveal. To some extent such contrasts reflect literary ability, but the choice of mask is already very different – that of Thibaut de Champagne bears no resemblance to that of Rutebeuf – and the manner of wearing it betrays to some extent the personality behind it. Gace Brulé strikes a different posture from that of *trouvères* treating the same themes: Guiot de Provins or Conon de Béthune, and Rutebeuf, could not be taken for a Jean Bodel or an Adam de la Halle. The problem is a delicate one, but the following assertion concerning Rutebeuf has in the end to be accepted, the more so since we have only his poetry to guide us: 'His poetic success must be measured not through our discovery of his inner soul but through our discovery of his poetic art'.[33] Is this not true to some extent of all lyric poetry, whatever its period of composition?

NOTES

1. For Marie de Champagne, see above, p. 121.
2. A. Wallensköld ed., *Les Chansons de Thibaut de Champagne, Roi de Navarre*, Paris, SATF, 1925, xvii, note 3.
3. The certain attributions to him include 36 love-poems, 14 *jeux-partis* on love, two *pastourelles*, three crusading songs, six religious poems.
4. First two of the five stanzas of this refrain-song (Chanson 1, Wallensköld, ed. cit.) whose structure foreshadows that of the *ballade*, which enjoyed immense popularity in the later Middle Ages.
5. It is probable that Thibaut wrote the lady's words as well as his own, cf. ibid., 165–6.
6. The reference is to a legend, well known in medieval times, concerning the unicorn entranced by the charms of a beautiful girl, and killed in her lap by hunters. ibid., 115.
7. See above, p. 119.
8. Chansons XXVI, XXVIII.
9. J. Bédier ed., *Les Chansons de Colin Muset*, Paris, CFMA, 1912, new ed. 1938.
10. VI, 3. This diminutive defies translation, but it could only be used of a playful, not-too-serious dalliance; in the poem it is coupled to the word 'gai'.
11. The onomatopoeic last line but two occurs in this place in each stanza. It is there above all for the gaiety of the sounds, but *triboudainne* apparently meant a song, so that if the line had to be translated literally, it could perhaps be rendered as 'Dithyrambs and ditties'.
12. P. Ruelle ed., *Les Congés d'Arras*, Liège, 1965, 71.

13. C. Foulon, *L'Œuvre de Jean Bodel*, Paris, 1958, 753.

14. *DLF*, 27.

15. Ruelle, ed. cit., 70.

16. See below, p. 255.

17. Foulon, op. cit., 160.

18. J. H. Marshall ed., *The Chansons of Adam de la Halle*, Manchester, 1971.

19. A *pui* was an association of poets which held periodical poetry-readings and distributed prizes. The *pui* was presided over by a 'Prince' – cf. the habit of addressing a *ballade* to a 'prince'.

20. Neither list is complete. Information on these poets, together with a short bibliography, is provided under their respective names in the *DLF*. Some of the poems can be read in the comprehensive anthology of G. Toja, op. cit.

21. The best edition is by E. Faral and J. Bastin, *Œuvres complètes de Rutebeuf*, 2 vols., Paris, 1959–60.

22. ibid., I, 33.

23. N. F. Regalado, *Poetic Patterns in Rutebeuf: A Study in Noncourtly Modes*, New Haven, 1970, 4.

24. Faral and Bastin, ed. cit., I, 519–80.

25. *La griesche* was a game played with dice, practised in the Courts as well as in the taverns; ibid., I, 521.

26. cf. *Pyramus et Thisbé*, and one of Thibaut de Champagne's poems, above, pp. 180–1.

27. 'Ribaut' (the same word as English 'ribald') had various meanings, mostly pejorative: vagabond, layabout.

28. Faral and Bastin, ed. cit., 546.

29. ibid., I, 520–1.

30. A. Serper, *Rutebeuf poète satirique*, Paris, 1969, 53.

31. *La Paix de Rutebeuf*, 39–42; Faral and Bastin, ed. cit., I, 568.

32. ibid., I, 519.

33. Regalado, op. cit., 270.

Chapter 7

THIRTEENTH-CENTURY ROMANCE

I. THE CONTINUATION OF CHRÉTIEN DE TROYES'S 'CONTE DU GRAAL'

THE enormous success of Arthurian romance from the late twelfth century onwards owed a great deal to Chrétien de Troyes. Several continuations of his *Conte du Graal* were composed.[1] The first, referred to as the *Continuation Gauvain*,[2] deals mainly with the exploits of that mundane adventurer, to the exclusion of Perceval. Realism there is in plenty in the form of tournaments and bloody hand-to-hand encounters, but also magic and folklore, for example the drinking-horn that spilled over whenever a cuckolded husband put it to his lips (Arthur himself was not spared); the decapitated knight who recovered his head and promised to return a year later to exact his revenge (cf. *Sir Gawain and the Green Knight*); the broken sword whose pieces would knit together in the hands of the perfect knight who would then heal the Fisher King and so bring the Grail quest to an end. The many episodes are told chiefly for their entertainment value, which is considerable. There is no interconnecting psychological motivation of the type so skilfully developed by Chrétien. The Grail episodes take up only some 1,200 of the 22,000 lines.[3] In Chrétien's last romance Gauvain had sworn to seek the 'lance qui saine' (line 6198) (the lance which bleeds). Twice, in the course of the first continuation, he entered the Grail castle and each time saw the enigmatic objects first described by Perceval in Chrétien's last work. On the second occasion the Grail moved rapidly through the hall of its own accord: '. . . ore est la, et ore est chi' (13302) (. . . now it is here, now it is there) and served a seven-course meal to the entire assembly, much to Gauvain's astonishment. Although not destined to end the quest, he learned that the lance was that of Longinus and would continue to bleed until the Last Judgement; the Grail had been used by Joseph of Arimathea to collect Christ's blood at the Crucifixion; it had been brought to England and had always belonged to a descendant of Joseph.

The story is carried further by a second instalment, some 13,000 lines in length, the *Continuation Perceval*.[4] The change of heroes did not affect the nature of the adventures until the very end. In the Grail castle Perceval proved his superiority to Gauvain by partially uniting the broken sword, but the joint remained visible and the quest, though clearly nearing its end, was still not over. A third successor, Manessier (the first two are anonymous), concluded the quest after another 10,000 lines. The broken sword was made completely whole and Perceval succeeded his uncle, the Fisher King.

Two manuscripts contain an interpolation of 17,000 lines between the second continuation and Manessier's conclusion. This was owed to Gerbert de Montreuil, author of the *Roman de la Violette*.[5] This interpolation may at one time have had its own conclusion to the Grail quest, but if so, this has been suppressed in the extant manuscripts in favour of Manessier's version. That the quest was not completed until many thousands of lines had been added by various writers is not necessarily proof of the difficulties experienced in finally resolving it. The quest became rather the ultimate *raison d'être* of the many adventures, for however remote they are from it, the reader or audience inevitably feels that at the end will come the solution to this most enigmatic of the countless episodes. As long as the quest continued, adventure could follow adventure, nor was it deemed necessary to mark any specific progression or mounting scale of difficulty, not, at any rate, in these octosyllabic appendages to Chrétien's *Conte du Graal*.

At the end of the twelfth century Robert de Boron, whose piety far surpassed his poetic capacities, composed a series of romances centred on the Grail. The first, the *Roman de l'Estoire dou Graal*, also known as *Joseph d'Arimathie*,[6] a work of comparatively modest dimensions (3,514 octosyllabic lines), was intended to integrate the Grail into the early history of Christianity. The *Continuation Gauvain* may have been indebted to this work for the role allotted to Joseph of Arimathea, unless the two derived from a common source.[7] Whatever his literary debts, Robert's first and principal source was the Bible, for he began with an account of the Fall of Man, the birth of Christ, the origins and significance of baptism and confession, Judas's betrayal of Christ in the house of Simon the leper where there was

... un veissel mout gent   ... a very beautiful vessel in which
Ou Criz feisoit son sacrement   Christ enacted his sacrament
                (lines 395–6)

– the first and incidental mention (not yet by name) of the Grail. It came into the hands of Joseph of Arimathea.[8] When Christ's tomb was found empty, the Jews blamed Joseph and imprisoned him. Pilate gave him the vessel whose brightness lit up his cell. Christ came to comfort Joseph and explained to him the significance of the vessel which would belong to three people, symbolising Father, Son, and Holy Ghost. He also explained the meaning of the bread and wine of the Last Supper.[9] Joseph, miraculously kept alive with food and water supplied by the vessel, was freed many years later by the emperor Vespasian, who, according to Robert de Boron, had been converted to Christianity because he was miraculously cured of leprosy by the towel with which Veronica had wiped Christ's face and which bore its imprint. Joseph joined his sister Enyseus and his brother-in-law Bron or Hebron (both forms appear in the text). Misfortune befell them and their followers because of sinners in their midst. The Holy Ghost ordered Joseph to make a table resembling that used in the Last Supper and to place on it the holy vessel along with a fish caught by Bron, later to be referred to as 'li Riches Peschierres' (3431) (The Rich Fisher, i.e., the Fisher King). Those who sat down at the table, at which only one place, 'le liu Judas' (2528) (Judas's place), stayed empty would receive divine grace, the others would be damned. This seat would later be occupied by Bron's son (2527–34).[10] The vessel whose importance to Christian doctrine has now been so thoroughly established is at last named by one of the assembly: it was called the 'Graal' (Grail) because 'a touz agree et abelist' (2663) (it gives pleasure to all).[11] The Grail was entrusted to Hebron, who departed, following his son Alain 'es vaus d'Avaron' (3123) (to the vales of Avalon), a probable reference to Glastonbury.[12]

It has been pointed out that Hebron is a name occurring in the Book of Numbers[13] as the third son of Kohath, one of those whose 'charge shall be the ark, and the table, and the candlestick, and the altars, and the vessels' (3:31). The Grail was thus equated with the instruments of the tabernacle, and the name Hebron was chosen and shortened to Bron because Robert (or his source) was familiar with the Celtic legend of Bron, the Fisher King. By fusing the two he Christianised an originally pagan story or added further Christian elements to a partly evangelised legend.

A difficult question to answer is whether or not Robert was familiar with Chrétien's *Conte du Graal*. If so, he has made numbers of changes, for he concentrates on the Grail to the exclusion of all else. The Grail, moreover, contains Christ's blood, not the sacred Host, and the Fisher King's enigmatic title is given quite a different explanation. Were these deliberate changes, or were they owed to different sources? The modern scholar's search for an understanding of the many complexities and contradictions of this strangest of medieval legends seems no less arduous than the quest itself. Unlike Perceval, we can at least ask the right questions, but they either remain unanswered, or receive several conflicting answers.

Only 502 lines of Robert's second poem, *Merlin*, have survived, but as also for his *Roman de l'Estoire dou Graal*, a complete prose version is extant. The gradual incursion of prose into what for so long had been the domain of narrative verse is an important development in the thirteenth century, and suggests that reading in private was beginning to rival recitals in public. The change was all the more justifiable in that the poetic worth of the works of a Robert de Boron was much inferior to that of Chrétien de Troyes's romances or Marie de France's lays. Robert's *Merlin* owes much to Geoffrey of Monmouth's *Historia Regum Britanniae* and *Vita Merlini*. Intended to bridge the chronological gap between the early history of the Grail and the crowning of Arthur, it deals with the birth and early accomplishments of Merlin and the exploits of Arthur's father, Uterpendragon, who led the Britons against the Saxons. Uterpendragon was also responsible for the founding of the Round Table, modelled on that made by Joseph of Arimathea to hold the Grail, in its turn a copy of the table used at the Last Supper. The three symbolised the Trinity. *Merlin* ends with Arthur's succeeding to his father's throne.

A third prose work, the *Didot Perceval*, so called after a former owner of one of the manuscripts, may have been based on a third verse romance by Robert, but it is possible that the *Didot Perceval* was composed directly in prose by an anonymous writer who wished to complete the trilogy begun by the *Joseph* and the *Merlin*. There are two versions, varying according to the manuscript, but the basic story is the same. It has affinities with Chrétien de Troyes's *Conte du Graal*, also with the *Continuation Gauvain*, though it is more specific about Perceval's ancestry and includes what Chrétien possibly intended had he lived to complete the story, a second visit to the Grail castle, successfully ending the quest.

II. THE VULGATE CYCLE

The ever-increasing popularity of the Arthurian legends, particularly in the new form of prose sequences and in the new evangelising spirit, is shown by the composition between 1215 and 1230 of a much-enlarged group of five branches, covering some 3,000 quarto-size pages of modern print, known as the Vulgate cycle.[14] The first branch, the *Estoire del Saint Graal*, is an expanded version of Robert's *Joseph* and bridges more thoroughly the period of some 400 years between the time of Joseph and that of Uterpendragon. The second, the *Estoire de Merlin*, consists of the prose version of Robert's *Merlin* followed by a sequel covering the early years of Arthur's reign. The third, *Lancelot del Lac*, consists of the sections

dealing with that hero, the middle one being a considerably modified prose rendering of Chrétien's *Chevalier de la Charrete*.[15] The
fourth is the *Queste del Saint Graal*,[16] which gives a new version
of the end of the quest, and the fifth *La Mort le Roi Artu*,[17] which
tells of the deaths of Arthur and the knights of the Round Table.
Although the Arthurian theme continued to attract attention in
the thirteenth century and indeed throughout the Middle Ages, the
next stage being a vast prose *Tristan* in which the Tristan legend
became linked with the Lancelot and Guenièvre story and the
Grail theme, this brief survey will conclude with some remarks on
the last two branches of the Vulgate cycle, remarkable works in
their own right, the differences between them revealing the varying
attitudes towards the Arthurian material and the differing characteristics possessed by thirteenth-century writers.[18]

III. THE 'QUESTE DEL SAINT GRAAL'

The hero of the *Queste del Saint Graal*, Galahad, is spoken of
almost as a second Messiah:

Et tot ausi come il envoia son filz qu'il avoit devant le comencement dou
monde, tout einsi envoia il Galaad come son esleu chevalier et son esleu
serjant...[19] (And just as he sent his son whom he had before the world
began, in the same way he sent Galahad as his chosen knight and his chosen
servant...).

His very name was one of the mystical appellations of Christ.[20] He
was of the lineage of Solomon, as also was the Virgin Mary;[21] his
parents were Lancelot and the Fisher King's daughter. Great emphasis is laid on Galahad's absolute purity of heart and spotless
virginity. This latter does not mean a mere lack of sexual intercourse
– referred to, for both sexes, as 'pucelage'[22] – it means complete lack
of interest in sexual matters. In the Garden of Eden Eve had known
true virginity; only after the Fall did God order Adam and Eve
to copulate, but in His mercy he enveloped them in darkness in
order to conceal their shame.[23] This austere and puritanical text
reflects the doctrine of St Bernard.[24] With its numerous references
to 'moines blans' (white monks) or to a 'prestres ... vestuz de robe
blanche' (a priest wearing a white robe), and the whole nature
of its outlook, ascetic and mystical, stressing that the heroes must
be in a state of grace, this is either the work of a Cistercian monk
or of a cleric sympathetic to their doctrine. Cured at last by
Galahad, the Fisher King 'se rendi en une religion de blans moines'[25]
(entered a Cistercian monastery). The story concerns the fortunes
of the principal Arthurian knights in the Grail quest, varying

according to how far they could match these lofty Cistercian ideals:

C'est exactement le roman de la grâce ou, si l'on veut, la vie de la grâce dans l'âme chrétienne racontée sous forme de roman. Depuis l'appel initial du Graal jusqu'à l'extase finale de Galaad, nous en reconnaissons tous les degrés: la réprobation de Gauvain, qui ne recourt pas aux sacrements, sources de la grâce; ceux qui meurent au cours de la quête, mais en état de grâce et réconciliés avec Dieu, comme Yvain; ceux qui s'élèvent jusqu'à une mystique imparfaite, mais au prix d'une dure pénitence, comme Lancelot; ceux que la grâce a mis une fois pour toutes hors de péril ou sauvés à l'heure critique de la chute, comme Bohort et Perceval; celui qu'elle a comblé de ses dons au point de lui laisser ignorer jusqu'au péril, comme Galaad. Leurs aventures sont les aventures de la grâce négligée, perdue, retrouvée, conservée, accrue, sous toutes les images qu'un roman de la Table Ronde pouvait offrir à l'auteur d'une telle transcription.[26]

Galahad, veritable monk in knight's clothing, outshone all. The more sinful the knight, the less interesting he became, for only the pure in heart deserved adventures. When Gauvain complained to a hermit of the emptiness of his life, he was told:

Les aventures qui ore avienent sont les senefiances et les demostrances dou Saint Graal, ne li signe dou Saint Graal n'aparront ja a pecheor ne a home envelopé de pechié[27] (The present adventures concern the meaning and power of the Holy Grail, the symbols of which will never appear to a sinner or any man steeped in sin).

In this way attention was centred on the three most virtuous knights, Galahad, Perceval, and Bohort, while Lancelot is frequently and bitterly reproached for his adultery with the queen: 'contre virginité et chastée herberjas tu luxure' (p. 126) (against virginity and chastity you harboured lechery). He put on a hair-shirt, realised that he was 'plus pechierres que nus autres' (a greater sinner than any other), and confessed his sins. His repentance had its effect and he was 'garni de la grace dou saint Esperit' (p. 250), but it soon becomes apparent that even though he had earned God's forgiveness, he had not earned that of the Cistercians. In an ecstatic dream[28] Lancelot was allowed a glimpse of the Grail, but was promptly struck blind, deaf, and dumb, remaining 'come une mote de terre' (p. 256) for 24 days, one for each year that he had served the devil. The work is replete with symbolism of this kind: every dream, every adventure, has its 'senefiance', and every 'senefiance' illustrates some aspect of Christian doctrine: Galahad had to fight seven knights who represented seven deadly sins; when a voice proclaimed that Lancelot was 'harder than stone, more bitter than wood, more barren than a fig-tree', a wise hermit – the text abounds in them – was soon at hand to explain these comparisons, representing the stubbornness, the bitterness, and the sterility of the sinner's life. The Round Table has 'grant senefiance', quite literally, representing la reondece del monde et la circonstance des planetes et des elemenz el firmament; et es circonstances dou firmament voit len les estoiles et mainte autre chose; dont len puet dire que en la Table Reonde est li mondes senefiez a droit (p. 76) (the roundness of the world and the nature of the planets and the elements in the firmament; and in the nature of the firmament can be seen the stars and many another thing, hence it can be said that the Round Table truly symbolises the world).

When the three chosen heroes entered a mysterious boat, they found on it a sign proclaiming 'Je ne sui se foi non' (p. 201) (I exist only as faith) and were warned that non-believers would be cast into the sea. All the 'chevalier plein de povre foi et de male creance' (p. 151) (knights full of poor faith and bad beliefs) were eliminated in the course of the quest apart from the repentant Lancelot for whom, as we have seen, a specially cruel fate was reserved, rather as though he had sneaked into Paradise through a back door and was swiftly ejected. At the end of the story Galahad, having gazed at the Grail, died in ecstasy, Perceval became a hermit and died a year later, and Bohort carried the news back to Arthur that the quest was over.

The metaphysical nature of the *Queste del Saint Graal* has reduced the customary jousting to a minimum, reflecting the Cistercian dislike of violence.[29] The stern Christian exegesis which inspires the entire work makes it difficult reading, but the intricacy of the symbolism is interesting, and the constant reaching beyond the ordinary things of this world to a deep and mystical significance is not without an austere beauty epitomised in the character of the peerless Galahad. Lancelot has admittedly a more lively personality, as the editor points out.[30] A character in whom there is both good and bad is inevitably more convincing than one who is all virtue. The difficulty is one that we have observed already in the Lives of the Saints. Perfection makes monotonous reading. Lancelot is to some extent a foil to Galahad, and at times comes near to stealing the show. That he does not do so is because the author's sympathies were chiefly with Galahad, in whom the virtues of St Bernard, and so many Cistercian ideals, were represented.

IV. 'LA MORT LE ROI ARTU'

While the *Queste* has a metaphysical bias, *La Mort le Roi Artu* has a psychological one. Back at Arthur's Court after his failure in the quest, Lancelot renews his adultery with the queen. He is neither condemned nor condoned, for here there is no moralising, no excuse. This is a human situation which, however much it is deplored, is accepted as such. The king's suspicions are allayed for a time, but he finally discovers the truth. Lancelot and his relatives flee from Court and rescue the queen under sentence of death. War breaks out between Arthur and Lancelot despite their attachment to each other. Arthur, urged on by Gauvain whose brother Gaheriez has been killed by Lancelot (the latter having failed to recognise him), pursues Lancelot to his kingdom of Banoïc in western Gaul, leaving his own kingdom of Logres (England) in charge of Mordret, the son of his incestuous relationship with his sister Morgain. Mordret usurps Arthur's throne and bribes his vassals to turn against him. Guenièvre refuses Mordret's advances and is besieged with a small company of faithful knights in the Tower of London. Arthur returns, and in a bloody encounter with the usurper on Salisbury Plain, the flower of his knights perish. Arthur kills Mordret, but is mortally wounded by him. He orders Girflet to throw his sword Escalibor into the lake; a hand rises above the surface, grasps the sword, brandishes it three times, and draws it under. Arthur sails away with Morgain and her retinue and is later buried at the Noire Chapele. Lancelot returns to Britain, fights and kills Mordret's sons in the Battle of Winchester, and ends his days as a hermit, as also does Bohort. The last sentence stresses that this is the true and definitive end of the knights of the Round Table. Later versions differing from this one would not be authentic.

The *Mort Artu* is a well-developed story which can be summarised in a way not possible with the *Queste*. Both use an interlocking technique whereby an episode concerning a particular hero is interrupted, often at a critical point, and completed at a later stage, but whereas the *Queste*'s action is further broken up by many visions and lengthy interpretations of them, the *Mort Artu* unfolds its action continuously as the storm-clouds of jealousy, anger, and hatred slowly gather in this Twilight of the Gods. As though the author were determined to avoid the diffuse nature of so many Arthurian romances, all here is straightforward. With truth has it been said that no other prose romance of the Middle Ages offers a texture so tightly woven as the *Mort Artu*.[31]

In its tragic intensity the *Mort Artu* recalls two masterpieces of the preceding century: *Tristan* in that the hopelessness of an adulterous love is the starting-point of all the action, the *Chanson de Roland* in that Arthur, hopelessly outnumbered in the battle on Salisbury Plain, had only to summon help from Lancelot, as Gauvain pointed out, for all to be well again, since Lancelot had given clear indications that, despite Arthur's attack, his affection for him was unchanged. Human nature being what it is, Lancelot's love for the queen would not yield to reason, and Arthur's pride would not give way to expediency. The author certainly knew both works – resemblances to Béroul's *Tristan* are particularly close,[32] and his drawing from them shows medieval literature acquiring a tradition of its own.

The sombre prose of the *Mort Artu* moves through a range of emotions: the poignancy of the love scenes when Lancelot and Guenièvre snatch a hurried meeting, oblivious to repeated warnings of the dire consequences; Lancelot's anguish as he is compelled to fight the king he has not ceased to love; Arthur's despair, for he hates Lancelot because of his adultery with the queen he has not ceased to love, yet respects him still as a knight of unmatched 'cortoisie';[33] Gauvian's hatred of Lancelot, gradually undermined by the realisation that Lancelot had not killed his brother intentionally; the pathos of the bloody encounter on Salisbury Plain, the climax of the entire work, a battle scene as vivid and as intense as any in *Roland*:

> ... la poïssiez veoir a l'assembler meint biau coup de lance et meint bon chevalier a la terre verser, et meint bon cheval corre tout estraié parmi le champ, qu'il n'estoit qui les retenist; si poïssiez veoir en poi d'eure la terre couverte de chevaliers dont li un estoient mort et li autre navré. Einsi commença la bataille es pleins de Salebieres, dont li roiaumes de Logres fu tornez a destrucion, et ausi furent meint autre, car puis n'i ot autant de preudomes comme il i avoit eu devant ... (p. 232) (... there you would have seen as they clashed many a fine lance-thrust and many a good knight tumbling to the ground, and many a fine horse galloping riderless over the fields, for there was no one to hold them back; you would have been able to see in a short time the ground covered with knights, some dead, some wounded. So began the battle on Salisbury Plain, as a result of which the kingdom of England faced destruction, as also did many another, for afterwards there were not as many valiant men as there had been before ...).

At the end comes a poetry of a strange, haunting kind as, in one of the few supernatural scenes, Arthur's sword is drawn under the water by a hand, a counterpart to the hand which in the *Queste* descends from heaven and carries aloft both Grail and lance. The simplicity of the description is faithfully reflected by Malory in his *Morte d'Arthur*: '... and there came an arm and an hand above the water and met it, and caught it, and so shook it thrice and brandished, and then vanished away the hand with the sword in the water'. Tennyson's account is inevitably more flowery, but this symbol of the end of the Arthurian world has lost none of its beauty:

> The great brand
> Made lightnings in the splendour of the moon,
> And flashing round and round, and whirl'd in an arch,
> Shot like a streamer of the northern morn,
> Seen where the moving isles of winter shock
> By night, with noises of the Northern Sea.
> So flash'd and fell the brand Excalibur:
> But ere he dipt the surface, rose an arm
> Clothed in white samite, mystic, wonderful,
> And caught him by the hilt, and brandish'd him
> Three times, and drew him under in the mere.[34]

Medieval Arthurian romance enjoyed an invigorating dawn in the romances of Chrétien de Troyes, the serenity of which was barely disturbed by the few quickly passing clouds; the legend's midday hours, as represented by Chrétien's successors, were long-drawn-out, for knightly adventures had to give way to ascetic preachings which made the entire world undergo a cosmic transubstantiation. At the end, visions and ideals faded away, the euhemerised gods were only too mortal, and the Bretons' belief that Arthur would one day return from Avalon was evinced only in the stories and legends that continued to accumulate around his name.

V. NON-ARTHURIAN ROMANCES OF THE THIRTEENTH CENTURY

However great their popularity, the Arthurian legends by no means monopolised thirteenth-century romance. The many works extant illustrate a variety of trends to which full justice cannot be done here. Not only are neat patterns of evolution almost invariably illusory in any history of literature, in this instance they are altogether impracticable since many texts can only be dated approximately. We may say, *grosso modo*, that while so much Arthurian romance tended towards greater mysticism, non-Arthurian romance remained mainly secular and showed a preference for realistic themes in a contemporary setting. Realism occasionally spilled over into the horrific, as it is inclined to do in any age. Whereas Chrétien de Troyes and his successors idealised the remote past, however much they drew on contemporary institutions:

... or parlons de cez qui furent, si leissons cez qui ancor durent...[35]

...now let us speak about those who lived in the past, and ignore those who live in the present ...

thirteenth-century non-Arthurian romances are often set avowedly in the present and sometimes make topical allusions. To some extent this reflects the growing confidence of a literature beginning to lose its inferiority complex by the side of Latin, that too of a civilisation finding its own feet and developing a belief in its own intrinsic qualities. Of great significance, too, was the gradual undermining of the near-monopoly held by courtly circles and the steady rise of bourgeois influences, parallel to that in the field of lyric poetry.[36] A poet such as Jean Renart[37] was able to move easily from the one domain to the other, whereas Jean de Meun towards the end of the century was quite out of sympathy with courtly attitudes.

VI. 'AUCASSIN ET NICOLETE'

Occupying a place apart is *Aucassin et Nicolete*, composed some-time in the first half of the thirteenth century.[38] In many ways the most delightful of all medieval French works, it is variously spoken of nowadays as a parody, a satire, an 'anti-roman', but it was above all an entertainment pure and simple. Called by its author a 'chante-fable', it consists of alternating passages of heptasyllabic verse, between 10 and 42 lines in length, and prose passages of rather greater length. It was in effect a mime, performed by one actor, possibly several, and giving many opportunities for amusing changes of tone.

Aucassin, son of Count Garin de Beaucaire, loves a Saracen slave girl, Nicolete. His father opposes the marriage; Nicolete is imprisoned, Aucassin likewise when his father despairs of ridding him of his infatuation. Nicolete escapes and arranges a meeting with Aucassin in a nearby forest. They elope, set sail with merchants, and are driven by a storm to the kingdom of Torelore, where they stay for three years. They are then carried off by Saracens, Aucassin's boat being wrecked near Beaucaire where, his father having died, he becomes lord and master. Nicolete lands in Carthage, the sight of whose walls makes her remember that she is in fact the king's daughter! Disguising herself as a minstrel, she goes to Beaucaire, and after teasing Aucassin by singing, unrecognised, in his presence the story of Aucassin and Nicolete, she reveals her identity, and all ends happily with their marriage.

Everything is scaled down in this lighthearted story of 'deus biax enfans petis' (two lovely little children) who readily address strangers as 'Bel enfant'. All is directed towards the creation of an atmosphere of charm and delight. It is a tale of a tender, innocent, wide-eyed love, both touching and amusing as only young love can be, a natural growth, not the hothouse plant so assiduously tended by an experienced knight such as the hero of the *Lai de l'Ombre*, making his subtle and persistent advances to a married court lady.[39] Its naïve nature is exemplified by Aucassin's comparing Nicolete to a bunch of grapes and to 'soupe en maserin' (xi, 14–15) (bread-sops in a wooden bowl). A charming portrait of Nicolete is painted:

Ele avoit les caviaus blons et menus recercelés, et les ex vairs et rians, et le face traitice, et le nes haut et bien assis, et lé levretes vremelletes plus que n'est cerisse ne rose el tans d'esté, et les dens blans et menus; et avoit les mameletes dures qui li souslevoient sa vesteure ausi con ce fuissent deus nois gauges; et estoit graille par mi les flans qu'en vos dex mains le peusciés enclorre... (xii, 19–25) (She had fair hair tightly curled, bright laughing eyes, a lovely face, the nose high and well set, lips redder than cherries or roses in summer, tiny white teeth; her small firm breasts raised up her blouse as though they were two walnuts and her waist was so slim that you could have imprisoned it within your two hands).

An extraordinary feature is that the author seems intent on standing so many conventional aspects of medieval romance on their heads: the French hero has a name the origin of which may be Arabic (Al Kassim), the Saracen heroine has a French name; on the other hand, this may have been intended to mark the fact that the heroine is really the hero, for she leads and decides the action while Aucassin spends much of his time moping for 'me douce amie que je tant aim' (VIII, 23–4) (my little sweetheart whom I love so much); Aucassin declares that he would much rather go to hell than heaven, for whereas heaven is full of old priests, cripples, and beggers, hell receives the handsome, dashing knights and the beautiful ladies who have a husband and several lovers besides; the wild forest where Nicolete hides after her escape from prison contains a monstrously ugly herdsman (resembling the one in Chrétien's *Yvain*), who is exquisitely polite and a very attractive personality, and shepherds who carefully spread their cloaks over the grass before sitting down to eat their bread; in Torelore Aucassin finds the king in bed declaring he is about to have a baby, and a fierce battle raging in which rotten apples and soft cheeses serve as ammunition; when Aucassin begins to fight in a more conventional way, he is quickly stopped and told that such was not the practice there; finally the heroine departs in search of the hero and through her efforts a happy ending is brought about. In some respects all this may have been an oblique comment on the follies of the world, but above all it is innocent and amusing fun, and it would be doing it a disservice to try to discover any particular 'message'.

VII. 'LA CHASTELAINE DE VERGI'

A work of a wholly different kind is *La Chastelaine de Vergi*,[40] one of the few tragic love stories of the Middle Ages not based on legendary material. It consists of 958 octosyllabic lines composed by an unknown author sometime between 1203 and 1288. It is told with an economy of words rare at the period, and is undoubtedly one of the masterpieces of the genre.

The Châtelaine de Vergi grants her love to a knight, but warns him that it will last only as long as he keeps it secret. He will know it is safe to visit her whenever her little dog is in the orchard. The duchess of Burgundy falls in love with the same knight, but when he rejects her advances, she spitefully tells the duke that he has tried to seduce her. The duke accuses the knight, but his suspicions are allayed when the knight feels compelled to reveal his love for the *châtelaine*. The duke accompanies the knight to one of his rendezvous and learns of the role played by the little dog. He swears to tell nobody, but when his wife sees the knight go unpunished, she gets the truth out of her husband and soon knows all about the knight's love for the *châtelaine.* The duke swears that if she lets the secret out, he will kill her. Piqued because the knight prefers a lady whose rank is inferior to hers, the duchess slyly remarks to the *châtelaine* that her little dog is well trained. In despair, believing that her lover has betrayed her, the *châtelaine* dies broken-hearted. The knight finds her and learns from her maid the cause of her death. He draws his sword and falls dead across her body. The duke, true to his oath, puts the duchess to death.

The story has affinities with Marie de France's *Lanval* and reflects *amour courtois* conventions, particularly the importance of keeping love secret:

... par cest example doit l'en s'amor celer par si grant sen c'on ait toz jors en remembrance que li descouvrirs riens n'avance et li celers en toz poins vaut.	This example shows the great wis- dom of keeping love secret and the importance of remembering always that revealing it is of no avail, and concealing is always sound.

(lines 951–5)

The situation, it has been said, is artificial, the assumptions on which the story is based being 'scarcely more rational than those in a folk-tale'.[41] Why, it has been asked, does the *châtelaine* conclude so hastily that her lover has betrayed her? Why was there no communication between the hero and heroine concerning the duchess's importunities? These are said to be weaknesses which undermine the psychological value of the story,[42] but is this really so? Is the behaviour of lovers necessarily *rational*? Would they necessarily follow what to a dispassionate observer seems the obvious course? Our medieval author knew already that 'Le coeur a ses raisons que la raison ne connaît pas'. His analysis of the emotional conflict of each of his protagonists – the *châtelaine* and the knight, the duke and duchess – is admirable. Particularly well described is the knight's dilemma as a result of the duchess's false accusation. He swears, rather rashly, to tell the duke whatever he wants to know, and when the duke asks him to name the woman he loves, the knight has to break one of two promises: that to the *châtelaine*, or that to the duke:

Cil ne set nul conseil de soi, que le geu a parti si fort que l'un et l'autre tient a mort; quar, s'il dit la verité pure, qu'il dira s'il ne se parjure, a mort se tient, s'il mesfet tant qu'il trespasse le couvenant qu'a sa dame et a s'amie a, qu'il est seürs qu'il la perdra s'ele s'en puet apercevoir; et s'il ne dit au duc le voir, parjurés est et foimentie, et pert le païs et s'amie ...	He does not know what course to take, for so great is the dilemma that he sees death in either outcome, for if he speaks the whole truth, which he will unless he perjures himself, he feels he must die if he acts so badly that he breaks the oath he made to his lady-love, for he is sure he will lose her if she finds this out, and if he does not tell the duke the truth, he has committed perjury and broken his promise, and is exiled from the country and from his love.

(268–80)

The ending is admittedly melodramatic, but in a tragedy of love and passion is not out of place. This story, which frequently receives high praise, has been hailed as 'une des plus parfaites réussites de la littérature narrative du Moyen Age'.[43]

VIII. THE ROMANCES OF JEAN RENART

Several works have survived by Jean Renart, born at Dammartin near Senlis about 1180. He frequented the Courts of Flanders and Champagne, but was not a court poet after the fashion of Chrétien de Troyes.[44] He died about 1250.

The earliest extant of Jean Renart's works is *L'Escoufle* (= modern French 'milan', 'kite'), a *roman d'aventure* of 9,102 octosyllabic lines composed about 1200.[45]

Richard, count of Montivillier, rules over much of Normandy. He is held in high esteem by his vassals, who are grieved when he departs on a crusade. He leads the Christian armies to victory against the Saracens. Returning home through Italy, he gives his services to the emperor of Rome in his struggle against rebellious vassals. Reluctant to let Richard depart, the emperor arranges his marriage to the lady of Genoa. On the very day their son Guillaume is born, the empress gives birth to a daughter, Aelis. They grow up together, and it is agreed they should be married. However, after Richard's death, the emperor's counsellors advise against this union and the lovers are separated. They decide to elope and to make for Normandy. Aelis carries her jewels in an alms-purse of red leather. One day when they are relaxing near a spring, a kite, mistaking the purse for a piece of red meat, swoops down and carries it off. Guillaume chases the bird, leaving Aelis asleep on the grass. Waking up and finding both Guillaume and her jewels gone, Aelis despairs, thinking that he has abandoned her and left for Normandy on his own. Guillaume meantime recovers the purse and returns to find Aelis gone. While she continues the journey to Normandy to look for him there, Guillaume retraces the journey they had covered together in an effort to find her. After many dramatic adventures they are reunited and happily married, eventually becoming emperor and empress of Rome.

This adventure story, rich in lively, colourful scenes, was written by a keen observer of the life around him. Among the many vivid descriptions, the following portrait of Richard's three-year-old son is remarkable, since comparatively little attention is paid to young children in most medieval romances:

Il savoit ja si bel porter
Ses bras as cols des chevaliers;
As serjans et as escuiers,
Devenoit baus et esraisniés.
Mout par en est joians et liés
Li bons quens et sa bone mere.
De sa teste qui si blonde ere
Resambloit il un angelot.

(lines 1808–15)

He could already put his arms round the knights' necks. With the servants and squires he grew lively and full of chatter. The good count and his good mother were very happy and joyful because of him. His head that was so fair made him look like an angel.

The central episode, the carrying-off of the jewels by a bird of prey, appears to be a borrowing from the *Arabian Nights*,[46] and the theme of the separation of lovers (or of a family), who undergo many perils before they are reunited, was a much-exploited one which we have encountered already in *Guillaume d'Angleterre* and in *Aucassin et Nicolete*.

Some ten years later Jean Renart wrote a second romance, the *Roman de la Rose*, now usually known as the *Roman de Guillaume de Dole* in order to distinguish it from the work by Guillaume de Lorris and Jean de Meun.[47] It contains 5,655 octosyllabic lines in the usual rhyming couplets. Jean Renart's introduction points out that a novel feature is the inclusion of several songs which would add to the entertainment value of the story.

An emperor of Germany called Conrad is unmarried and leads a gay life at Court. One day he learns from his minstrel Jouglet about a distinguished knight, Guillaume de Dole, and his beautiful sister Liénor. So successfully does Jouglet apply himself to the task of describing Liénor that the emperor falls in love with her, although he has never seen her. He invites Guillaume to Court, becomes friendly with him, and eventually tells him of his love for Liénor. The emperor's seneschal, a spiteful and scheming character, visits Dole and in a conversation with Guillaume's mother, learns that Liénor, whom he has not met, has a birthmark on her thigh resembling a red rose. Back at Court, he pretends he has had relations with Liénor, and describes her birthmark. Both the emperor and Guillaume are in despair. Liénor hears about the false accusation and decides to intervene. She sends the seneschal some jewels with a message that they are a present from a woman he once loved; he is to wear them under his clothes. Mystified but flattered, he obeys. At Court, where she is unknown, Liénor tells the emperor that the seneschal has raped her and stolen her jewels, which are found hidden under his clothes. He undergoes a trial by ordeal which establishes his innocence. Liénor then reveals her identity, naming herself as 'la pucele a la rose' (line 5040) (the girl with the rose), and is able to proclaim that the seneschal has never touched her. His innocence is hers also, and the emperor has therefore no reason not to marry her. The wedding takes place, the seneschal is pardoned, and all ends happily.

Despite the romantic touches which give it great charm – such as the emperor's falling in love with Jouglet's description of Liénor – this is a realistic enough tale with a neat, well-turned plot. There is no magic to distract attention from the characters and their feelings which determine the action. The atmosphere is delightfully 'authentic', relaxed and carefree for the most part, but with a skilfully contrived dramatic climax as the tables are turned on the seneschal and it is his turn to face a false charge. Above all, this is 'un roman de mœurs suivant une formule déjà moderne, mœurs d'une société aristocratique avec tous les personnages qui la composent, grands seigneurs, bourgeois et serviteurs'.[48] This story was imitated by Gerbert de Montreuil in his *Roman de la Violette*,[49] in which the heroine's birthmark resembled a violet. The influence of

Jean Renart is also shown by the introduction of songs into the text, which became something of a fashion.[50]

The story, told in the 518 lines of Marie de France's *lai Le Fresne*, is expanded to no fewer than 7,800 lines in *Galeran de Bretagne*, the attribution of which to Jean Renart is no more than probable.[51]

Madame Gente lives up to her name (gent(e)=beautiful, pleasing) in appearance only, for she is spiteful, ever ready to give free rein to 'le cheval de sa langue' (line 37) (her horse of a tongue). She accuses Marsile, mother of twins, of having lain with two men, but is the victim of her own slander when she herself bears twins. She abandons one of them, who is found by nuns in a cradle hanging from a tree-branch – hence the name they gave her: 'Fresne' (Ash). She grows up with the abbess's nephew Galeran, son of the comte de Bretagne, and they fall in love. When Galeran's father dies, the abbess forbids them to meet or to correspond, for it is inconceivable that the comte de Bretagne should wed a mere foundling. Fresne quarrels with the abbess and flees to Rouen, where she makes a living out of her embroidery. Galeran tries in vain to find her. Eventually, forced to marry to ensure the succession, his choice falls upon Fresne's twin sister, who looks so much like her. News of the impending marriage reaches Fresne in Rouen, and she comes to Galeran's castle disguised as a minstrel. Galeran recognises her, and when her mother confesses the truth, Fresne takes her sister's place and the lovers are happily married.

Like *Escoufle* and *Guillaume de Dole*, this tale is a mixture of courtly refinement and a bourgeois realism that was rare in the preceding century. The author describes a whole variety of *milieux* which he appears to have known at first hand, as though it is a tale of real people, in real settings. He has an eye for precise material details: a nurse's care of a baby:

La dame, pour ce qu'il se taise,	In order to quieten him, the lady
De l'aleter se met en grant	sets about feeding him, and just as
Et, ainsi com endort l'enfant,	the child is falling asleep, she picks
Le lieve et baigne doulcement	him up, baths him gently, and pops
Et le recouche nectement,	him back into bed all clean and in
Com celle qui bien l'a apris.	expert fashion.
(748–53)	

the game that could be hunted in the countryside:

. . . maint bon porc sauvage,	. . . many a fine wild pig, hind and
Biches et cerfs et dains et ours,	deer and buck and bears, which dogs
Que chiens prennent souvent au cours;	often take in the hunt, and there are rabbits and squirrels, foxes and hares
Si a counins et escureuz,	and roebuck, that are often caught
Goupiz et lievres et chevreuz	with great patience.
Qu'on prent souvent par grant atente.	
(830–5)	

the coats of arms carried by knights in a tournament, representing a very different range of beasts:

Cil un lyon, cil un cenglier,	One a lion, one a boar, one a leo-
Cil un liepart, cil un poisson;	pard, one a fish, and one carries on
Cil porte sur son heaulme en son	the top of his helmet a beast or a
Beste ou oisel ou flour aucune...	bird or some flower or other.

(5910–13)

the food and wine consumed in banquets:

...on y aporte et amaine,	On carts, big and small, they bring
Et sur charretes et sur chars,	deer and boar and other meat, and
Cerfs et cengliers et autres chars,	on the packhorses fish. There would
Et sur les sommiers lé poissons;	be no point in being in Soissons since
Pour nïent seroit a Soissons,	wine comes strong and pleasant here,
Que vin y vient fort et plaisant;	and there is many a swan and many
Si a maint cygne et main faisant,	a pheasant and an abundance of
Et foison de pain beluté,	bread made with sifted flour, whiter
Plus blans que n'est lis en esté;	than the lily in summer; fodder and
Feurre et avaine y a assez.	oats are there in plenty.

(6782–91)

In particular, the lives of ordinary people – cooks, midwives, minstrels – have not escaped his attention.

The slightest, but most charming, of Jean Renart's works is the *Lai de l'Ombre*.[52]

A knight endowed with all the courtly virtues confesses his love to a married lady, who gently but firmly discourages him. As a token of his feelings he slips his ring on to her finger without her noticing, and departs. She recalls him, and sitting apart from other members of the Court on the edge of a well, returns it to him. He then offers it to his 'douce amie' who will not spurn it, that is, to the lady's reflection in the water, and drops it into the well. So touched is the lady by his gesture that she offers him her own ring, and with it her love.

The interest of this delicate trifle lies in the analysis of the knight's growing love, in the subtlety of the dialogue and the carefully graduated stages in which the lady's affection is won. The situation has all the ambiguity of courtly love, for it carries a hint of adultery; but over the whole relationship is cast a cloak of good manners and *savoir-vivre*, for both knight and lady follow the recognised and accepted code of behaviour. This elegant *marivaudage* reflects the sophistication of contemporary court circles.

IX. 'LA FILLE DU COMTE DE PONTIEU'

The first short story extant in French prose is the anonymous *La Fille du Comte de Pontieu*, written possibly in the first half of the century.[53]

Thibaut de Domart and his wife, daughter of the comte de Ponthieu, set off on a pilgrimage to Saint-Jacques de Compostelle. On their way they are attacked by robbers, the husband is tied up and his wife raped. When they have gone she tries to kill her husband with a sword, but only succeeds in wounding him slightly and in cutting through his bonds. He leaves her in a nunnery until his return, when he tells the count what has happened. Appalled at his daughter's behaviour, he has her fastened in a barrel and cast into the sea.[54] Saved by Flemish merchants, she is sold to the sultan of Almeria, who marries her. Remorsefully, the count and his son-in-law take the Cross, but are shipwrecked at Almeria. They are rescued by the sultana, who recognises them and asks them to tell their story. When she hears that Thibaut's wife tried to kill him, she explains that this was evidently caused by the shame she felt. Thibaut replies that her humiliation at the hands of the robbers would not have destroyed his love for her. The sultana reveals her true identity and succeeds in departing with them, leaving behind a daughter from whom was descended Saladin.

The style of this early prose work is dry, clipped, and awkward, but with greater economy of wording than in most contemporary verse romances.

X. THE 'ROMAN DE MARQUES DE ROME' AND THE 'ROMAN DE LAURIN'

Two prose works dating from the 1250s or 1260s were sequels to the highly successful legend of the Seven Sages of Rome:[55] *Le Roman de Marques de Rome*[56] and *Le Roman de Laurin*.[57] The latter in particular, as its editor points out, is a rich source of details concerning the daily life of the nobility in the thirteenth century:

The plenary court, the life of the noble envoy hastening on some great leader's urgent business, the living conditions of marauding knights in their mountain strongholds and of the women who live with them in enforced concubinage, the siege, the *table ronde*, the tourney, the quintain, the *combat-à-deux* with lance and sword, the armour and the weapons of the time ...[58]

Later in the century further sequels followed: *Le Roman de Cassidorus*,[59] *Le Roman de Pelyarmenus*, and *Le Roman de Kanor*.

XI. THE 'ROMAN DU CASTELAIN DE COUCI'

Towards the end of the century, a certain Jakemes wrote a tale of love and adventure, *Le Roman du Castelain de Couci et de la Dame de Fayel*,[60] a work of 8,266 octosyllabic lines which, like *La Fille du comte de Pontieu*, contains some horrific scenes.

Renaut, châtelain de Coucy, falls in love with la dame de Fayel. For her sake he distinguishes himself in tournaments and writes several songs included in the text.[61] The lady's husband becomes suspicious and pretends that both he and his wife will take part in the next crusade. Hearing this, Renart takes the Cross, but the seigneur de Fayel and his wife stay at home, the husband feigning illness. Renart dies of his wounds in the Holy Land, and asks that his heart should be cut out, embalmed, and presented to the lady. The husband learns of this, takes the heart to the kitchen, and orders that it should be cooked and served to his wife. She finds it a tasty morsel, but on hearing the truth, dies of grief shortly afterwards.

The legend of the eaten heart was a well-known one and several medieval versions have survived in a variety of languages.[62]

XII. THE ROMANCES OF PHILIPPE DE RÉMI

Philippe de Rémi, sire de Beaumanoir, who lived in the second half of the thirteenth century, is well known for the *Coutumes de Beauvaisis*, an important book on French common law. Between 1270 and 1280 he also wrote two romances, *Manekine* and *Jehan et Blonde*.[63]

Manekine, a romance of 8,590 octosyllabic lines, is a version of a widespread legend about a king who, after his wife's death, falls in love with his own daughter. His barons, having sought in vain a suitable spouse to bear him a son, suggest that he should marry his daughter. She declares that she would rather die, but he ignores her entreaties, since '... pensés de feme c'est vens' (line 628) (Woman's thought is a puff of wind). In an effort to dissuade him she cuts off her left hand. The king sentences her to be burned. The seneschal takes pity on her and casts her off in a boat. She lands in Scotland, where the king of that country marries her, against his mother's wishes. While he is away in France, the queen, whom they call Manekine because she has only one hand, gives birth to a son. Her mother-in-law writes to the king saying that his wife has been delivered of a monster. The king orders that his wife and child should await his arrival, but the mother-in-law substitutes a letter for this reply ordering the seneschal to burn mother and child. Once more she is spared and cast adrift with her child:

Qui encor pas deus mois n'avoit   who was not yet two months old and
Et rioit ou giron sa mere   laughed in his mother's lap.
         (4810–1)

The king learns the truth on his return and has his mother walled up in the tower and fed on bread and water. Several years later he finds his wife in Rome, and they are happily reunited. The father has also gone to Rome to beg forgiveness of his sins, and the three are reconciled. Her hand is miraculously restored. The moral of this tale is that no matter how harsh one's life is, one should never give way to despair, but should trust in God.[64]

Jehan et Blonde, usually considered the better of Philippe de Rémi's two romances, is a pleasant idyll in which a French boy meets an English girl. The Channel, disparagingly referred to as 'le ruisseau', does nothing to hinder their romance.

Jehan, twenty-year-old son of a French knight, sails for England where he meets the earl of Oxford on his way to a session of parliament. He becomes a squire in the earl's service and falls in love with his daughter,

Blonde. Two years later Jehan is recalled to France on the death of his mother. During his absence it is arranged that Blonde should marry the duke of Gloucester. She obtains a delay of four months. Jehan arrives a few days before the wedding and joins the duke's cortège on its way to Oxford. The lovers are eventually reunited and escape together. After various adventures they are married and are reconciled with the earl of Oxford, to whom Jehan eventually succeeds. All ends happily: 'Car a bon port vient qui bien nage' (line 6246) (The good swimmer gets to a good port).

The lovers are reunited . . . this expression has occurred several times in the preceding analyses. Decidedly, however tragic its legends, the Middle Ages expected its run-of-the-mill entertainment-literature to provide happy endings, long and arduous though the adventures separating hero and heroine may be. From this point of view, *La Chastelaine de Vergi* is exceptional. In quite another respect also, *Jehan et Blonde* resembles other romances of the century, particularly those of Jean Renart:

Ce roman nous reflète fidèlement la vie chevaleresque de l'époque; il ne contient rien de surnaturel ni d'invraisemblable, et il nous peint mieux peut-être que de savantes discussions, les détails de la vie privée au XIIIe siècle.[65]

XIII. THE 'ROMAN DE LA ROSE'

The most influential of all medieval romances, around which was to centre the first literary 'quarrel' in French literature, was the *Roman de la Rose*.[66] The first 4,000 lines were written between 1225 and 1230 by Guillaume de Lorris, while a further 18,000 lines were added to the unfinished work, some forty years later, between 1269 and 1278, by Jean de Meun. Whereas this is the sole poem extant by Guillaume de Lorris, several other works by Jean de Meun have survived: translations into French of the *De re militari* of Vegetius, the letters of Abelard and Heloïse, and the *Consolatio Philosophiae* of Boethius. Two other poems are attributed to him: the *Testament maistre Jehan de Meun*, and the *Codicile maistre Jehan de Meun*.[67] No information has survived on the lives of these poets, both of whom are known solely through their writings. The prodigious success of the *Roman de la Rose*, which lasted into the sixteenth century and even beyond, is attested by the large number of manuscripts to have survived, some three hundred altogether, and by its widespread influence on many poets, foremost among whom was its English translator Geoffrey Chaucer, 'through whose works Jean's old poem echoes and re-echoes'.[68]

Summary of Guillaume de Lorris's section (lines 1–4028)[69]

In his twentieth year the poet has a dream about love.[70] One May morning he follows a stream and comes to a walled garden. On the outside of the wall are pictures of various allegorical characters: Haine, Felonie, Vilenie, Convoitise (Covetousness), Avarice, Envie, Tristesse, Vieillesse, Papelardie (Religious Hypocrisy), Pauvreté.[71] Each is vividly portrayed. The poet knocks on a little door, opened for him by a charming girl called Oiseuse (Idleness), friend of Deduit (Pleasure), the garden's owner, whom the poet finds in the company of Leece (Happiness). Courtoisie, another lady, invites the poet to join their dance. Amour is followed by a young man, Doux Regard, who carries Amour's bows, one of rough black wood, the other elaborately carved. Each bow has five arrows, iron for the former (each has a name: Orgueil, Vilenie, Honte, Desesperance, Nouveau Penser), gold for the latter (respectively they are Beauté, Simplece, Franchise, Compagnie, Beau Semblant). Several of the dancers are named and described at length: Beauté, Richesse, Largesse, Franchise, Jeunesse. The poet discovers the fountain at which Narcissus had met his death. The story of Narcissus is then told as a warning to *ladies* not to spurn their suitors.[72] At the bottom of the fountain the poet perceives two 'pierres de cristal',[73] each of which reflects half the garden. No man can look into this *Fontaine d'Amour* without succumbing to love. The poet's attention is caught by a reflection of 'rosiers chargiez de roses' (1614). Overcome with folly, he would have plucked a crimson bud had it not been for the thorns. Amour chooses this moment to shoot the golden arrow of Beauté through the poet's eye, followed by the four others. Henceforth completely in love's thrall, the poet promises to obey his ten commandments: to commit no villainy; to speak no evil of others; to treat others with politeness; to utter no coarse words; to respect women and to defend them against their revilers; to show no pride; to pay attention to personal appearance and hygiene; to be always joyful; to exploit natural talents, whether for dancing, singing, horse-riding, or jousting; to shun avarice. Obedience will not ensure peace of mind, for he will be tormented by the absence of his love and even by her presence, which will only increase his desire. He will, however, have his allies: Esperance, Doux Penser, Doux Parler, Doux Regard, in addition to Bel Accueil, Courtoisie's son, who helps him approach the rose he so desires to pluck. They find it guarded by Danger,[74] who, aided by Male Bouche (Slander), Honte, and Peur, drives Bel Accueil away and forces the poet to retreat. Raison, created by God in His own image, warns the poet of the folly of being friendly with Oiseuse, and counsels him to eschew this 'torment called love, in which all is madness' (3025–6). Undeterred, the poet finds a new confidant in Ami, who advises a more diplomatic approach: Danger must be flattered. With support from Venus, the lover is at last allowed to kiss the rose, but more perils ensue. Male Bouche and Jalousie again drive Bel Accueil away. Jalousie decides to build a castle round the roses and to shut Bel Accueil away in a tower watched over by an old woman. The lover despairs and fears that he has lost Bel Accueil's support for ever. Guillaume's section breaks off at this point.

In the absence of Guillaume's conclusion, in which he intended to give 'dou songe la senefiance' (2070), the full meaning of the dream is a matter for surmise. However, in a reference anticipating his conclusion, Guillaume reveals that the God of Love himself finally took the castle by storm,[75] so proving himself a more effective ally than Venus.[76] It appears therefore that Guillaume's intention was that the lover should eventually be successful in his quest. His story is concerned with the development of the courtship of a wealthy, leisurely, aristocratic young lover with a girl of the same social class. We are shown the young man's awakening to notions of love and see him pass from an embryonic desire, through an impetuous and clumsy passion, to what presumably, had Guillaume completed the story, would have been an understanding of true love as conceived by courtly traditions. We see also the conflict of feelings that his attentions awaken in the heart of the girl, and the antagonism of her entourage to the lover's attentions.[77] Not until the lover understands the girl's reactions, modulates his behaviour accordingly, and learns not to excite jealousy in others can his suit succeed.[78]

In Jean de Meun's section the allegorical characters become more loquacious, and far more space is devoted to their words than to their deeds. Whereas Guillaume de Lorris had based his story on the traditional tenets and outlook of the courtly creed, Jean de Meun employed the method of the scholastic *disputatio*, setting the doctrines propounded by the many personifications in opposition to one another. The Garden of Love becomes, as it were, a tangled forest of lengthy argument and counter-argument through which the hapless young lover doggedly gropes his way. The many ideas, centred only loosely on the subject of love, are related specifically to the nature of the allegorical character speaking. It is in consequence an elementary (though often committed) error to assume that all inevitably reflect Jean de Meun's personal views. Moreover, it must not be overlooked that in the medieval scholastic method of argument, to formulate an idea was not necessarily to hold it as one's own.[79]

Jean de Meun's section (lines 4029–21750)

Since a full summary of this vast compendium would demand more space than can be allotted to it here, the following account picks out some salient features and illustrates them where expedient with quotations.

In a long discourse (4199–7118) Raison tries once more to turn the young man against love:

Amors se bien sui apensee, c'est maladie de pensee antre. II. persones annexe franches entr'els, de divers sexe, venanz a genz par ardeur nee de vision desordenee, pour acoler et pour besier pour els charnelment aesier . . .[80]	Love, if I am right about this, is an illness of the mind affecting two persons associating freely and of different sex, arising from a passion born of a disorderly vision, making them hug and kiss and seek carnal satisfaction.
(4347–54)	

Whatever pleasure love brings has to be paid for:

maint i perdent, bien dire l'os, sens, tens, chatel, cors, ame, los.	Because of love many men lose – I do not hesitate to say this – sense,
(4597–8)	time, chattels, body, soul, reputation.

More important, in human relationships, is friendship. Like friendship, happiness depends not on wealth, but on an attitude of mind. Even the dockers of the *Place de Grève* are rich in this respect:

maint ribaut ont les queurs si bauz,
portanz sas de charbon an Greve,
que la peine riens ne leur greve,
s'il en pacience travaillent,
qu'il balent et tripent et saillent
et vont a Seint Marcel aus tripes
ne ne prisent tresors trois pipes,
ainz despendent en la taverne
tout leur gaaign et leur esperne,
puis revont porter les fardeaus
par leesces, non pas par deaus . . .
(5018–28)

Many dockers carrying sacks of charcoal on the *Place de Grève* are so lighthearted that the toil grieves them not at all, they suffer it gladly and dance and trip and leap about and go to *St Marcel* [the butchers' district in medieval Paris] for their tripe, and care nothing for hoarded treasure, but spend in the tavern all their earnings and savings, then back they go to carry their loads, quite happily, without moaning . . .

Wisdom consists in rejecting temporal pleasures dependent on Fortune and in realising that in all happiness there is a grain of sadness, and in all unhappiness a grain of comfort:

Ne ja nus si liez ne sera
quant il bien se porpensera,
qu'il ne truisse en sa greigneur ese
quelque chose qui li desplese;
ne ja tant de meschief n'avra
quant bien porpenser se savra
qu'il ne truisse en son desconfort
quelque chose qui le confort
(6805–12)

There is none so happy who, if he gives it a thought, cannot find in his greatest contentment, something to displease him, and never will he suffer so much misfortune that, when he thinks about it, he cannot find in his misery a grain of comfort.

Still the would-be lover is not to be discouraged. He takes Raison to task for using a coarse word: 'Coilles' (testicles). These are the organs of generation, made by God, retorts Raison. God made them but not the name, replies the lover. But if I called testicles relics, and relics were to be called testicles, relics would be a dirty word, and testicles a respectable one, Raison rejoins. There can be no harm in the proper term, and all substitutes are useless. So saying, Raison departs. The young man next listens to the advice of Amis (7253–9972),[81] who tells him that he must show a friendly countenance to all and be an opportunist in relations with others. But once the lady is won, what then? Jealousy can so easily ruin their relationship, and all men, declares Amis, end up regretting marriage. Virtuous women are rarer than the phoenix. Their finery does not make them beautiful: a dung-heap covered with a silken cloth is still a dung-heap. The sole consolation, as Juvenal says, is that debauchery is the least of women's crimes; they willingly resort to many other devilish tricks. To escape all this a husband must avoid treating his wife like a possession. She must have her freedom and there must be no recriminations:

Amor ne peut durer ne vivre
s'el n'est en queur franc et delivre.
(9411–12)

Love can only subsist in a free and candid heart.

The lover renews his vows to Amour, who decides to attack Jalousie's castle with all the help he can muster, including that of Faux Semblant (Deceit),[82] who delivers the next discourse. His favourite haunt is among monks who preach humility although they are full of pride: 'la robe ne fet pas le moine' (11028). The Church itself is menaced by such hypocrites. The begging practised by the mendicant orders found no precedent in the life of Christ and His disciples. Man is made to work, not beg.

The attack on Jalousie's castle proceeds, and the old woman, guardian of Bel Accueil, is captured. She agrees to give Bel Accueil a present from the lover, and with it she proffers much advice (12710–14516).[83] Fidelity in love is, according to the old hag, folly. Men are deceivers ever, and must be treated likewise. One must make oneself as attractive as possible to the opposite sex, and woman's prime purpose in love must be to make as much money as possible:

Fole est qui son ami ne plume	Foolish is the woman who does not
jusqu'a la darreniere plume.	strip her lover of every penny.
(13667–8)	

Women are born free and are everywhere in chains. This has been brought about by law, but nature's rule is 'toutes por touz et touz por toutes' (13856) (all women for all men, all men for all women). Much advice ensues on how to hold a lover's attentions and how to deceive a suspicious husband with drink or drugs.

The lover enters the castle and meets Bel Accueil, but is still prevented by Danger from plucking the rose, and Bel Accueil is again imprisoned. Love appeals for help to his mother Venus, who quickly joins the fray. Nature has not so far taken part, since she has to work incessantly at her forge to ensure the continuation of species, constantly threatened by Death.[84] She is admired by Art, whose imitations remain lifeless. After listening to an address by her chaplain, Genius, on the deceitful nature of women, Nature begins a long complaint (16699–19375) in which the creation of the entire universe is passed under review. Only man causes her undue worry, for it is difficult to bring him to his natural end because of the many types of death which he brings on himself. This is not to be shrugged off as destiny, for man has the power of controlling his own fate. The problem of free will and predestination is then examined at length in relation to God's omniscience. Reflections on a wide variety of natural phenomena lead Nature back eventually to her main and most troublesome preoccupation, mankind. However, despite all the difficulties that mankind has caused, Nature will support Amour and Venus in their onslaught on Jalousie's castle, and will excommunicate all their enemies. Genius carries this message to Amour and delivers a long address (19475–20637) on the importance of making generous and proper use of the sex organs in order to ensure the continuation of the species. The attack on the castle begins when Venus shoots an arrow through a loophole, setting fire to the interior. The lover, in the guise of a pilgrim, is at last free to approach the sanctuary. He pushes his staff (Nature's gift) between the two pillars, penetrates with difficulty into a narrow passage which none had taken before him (and which, so he hopes, none would take after him), and gently plucks the rose:

Atant fu jorz et je m'esveille.	Then day broke and I woke up.
(21750 – the last line)	

Certain writers of the fourteenth and fifteenth centuries saw Jean de Meun as a rabid anti-feminist,[85] while others denied this. Our own times have presented him as a freethinker, a thirteenth-century Voltaire, a view which has recently been challenged.[86] So skilfully and cogently presented are Jean de Meun's many arguments that it is difficult to avoid looking on them as his personal opinions, but it is precisely this ability to sound convincing and forceful that has proved so misleading. It has resulted in the conflict of views among his characters being transposed to his readers, and the 'Querelle du Roman de la Rose' is not yet over.

What, in the first place, was Jean de Meun's attitude towards the central figure of the lover? Did he, as has been maintained,[87] look on him as a 'cad and a fool', an 'intellectual rake', or did he view him as a sort of archetypal lover who, as all young men are wont to do, ignores reason, behaves foolishly, and follows bad advice in his insatiable desire to discover what love is all about? If this is not the story of a special individual, this can only mean that Jean de Meun was a moralist bent on exposing the follies of youth, though this did not prevent him from including much broader issues. A twenty-year-old's interest in love he sees as devoid of all idealism, a desire above all for sexual gratification, and hence his conclusion is a thinly disguised, thoroughly scurrilous, description of sexual intercourse. That this was his own outlook does not necessarily follow, and that it was that of Guillaume de Lorris is even less likely.

In the second place, amidst the strongly held contentions of his allegorical characters, where (if anywhere) does Jean de Meun himself stand? That he was at least sympathetic to the voice of Raison, as doubtless were many of his readers, seems probable, but he has not made a great deal of this character who takes no part in the last eleven thousand lines. Would he have wished to be associated with Amis's advocacy of venality and hypocrisy, or with the old woman's cynical views on love which owe much, as he is at pains to explain, to classical literature (15185–98; elsewhere Ovid and Juvenal are several times referred to), or with Genius's mock-sermon (in bishop's raiment!) in praise of sexual intercourse? On the other hand, surely he was incensed by the hypocrisy of the religious orders revealed by Faux Semblant and attacked by other thirteenth-century writers? Further studies of his many debts to contemporary and classical Latin sources, and analyses of the structures and patterns of his work, may help to provide answers to these questions.[88] It may be that his ultimate aim was above all to stimulate discussion and reflection on the human condition, and in this respect, even today, his work retains its relevance and significance.

Finally, one cannot but be struck by the contrast between the two poets: Guillaume de Lorris genteel, refined, showing the subtlety and mannerisms of a court poet; Jean de Meun a thinker and a scholar who did not shrink from dealing in a forthright manner with sexual matters. Together they reflect the evolution of medieval literature, as the studied conceits and conventions of the courtly outlook yielded to more hard-headed attitudes. Literature becomes less of a distraction, less of a dalliance with Idleness in Pleasure's Garden of Love, and more of a comment on what life is all about.

NOTES

1. Altogether there are six additions, two of which are prologues. See A. W. Thompson, 'Additions to Chrétien's *Perceval* – Prologues and Continuations', *ALMA*, 206–17.

2. W. Roach ed., *The Continuations of the Old French Perceval of Chrétien de Troyes*, 3 vols., Philadelphia, 1949–52. Vol. II was edited by W. Roach and R. H. Ivy, Jr.

3. Both numbers vary considerably according to the manuscripts, of which there are eleven.

4. For details of edition see *ALMA*, 207.

5. See below, pp. 211–12.

6. ed. W. Nitze, Paris, CFMA, 1927.

7. Robert refers (as does Chrétien in the *Conte du Graal*) to his source:

le grant livre . . .   the great book in which the stories
Ou les estoires sunt escrites   written by the great clerics are copied
Par les granz clers feites   out.
et dites

(lines 932–4)

8. The account here is substantially the same as in the *Continuation Gauvain*.

9. The doctrine of transubstantiation had been widely discussed in the twelfth century and was accepted at the Lateran council of 1215.

10. It was actually occupied by his grandson Perceval, son of Bron's twelfth child, Alain.

11. 'Graal' in fact derives from medieval Latin *gradalis* or *gradalus* (dish, platter), and 'agreer' from quite a different root, *gratus* (pleasing).

12. *ALMA*, 65–7; also R. S. Loomis, *The Grail from Celtic Myth to Christian Symbol*, Cardiff–New York, 1963, 249–70.

13. 3:19.

14. H. O. Sommer ed., *The Vulgate Version of the Arthurian Romances*, New York, 8 vols., 1969.

15. *ALMA*, 300.

16. Also ed. A. Pauphilet, Paris, 1949.

17. Also ed. J. Frappier, Paris, 1936; 3rd ed. Paris–Geneva, 1964.

18. Not all the romances omitted from this chapter are of secondary importance. Particularly interesting is *Perlesvaus*, a prose romance of the late twelfth or early thirteenth century reflecting the fashionable tendency to Christianise the legend. See W. A. Nitze, 'Perlesvaus', *ALMA*, 263–73. A useful survey, which includes most of those not mentioned here, is A. Micha, 'Miscellaneous French Romances in Verse', *ALMA*, 358–92.

19. Pauphilet, ed. cit., 55; cf. 38, 78.

20. *ALMA*, 305.

21. ibid., 220–1.

22. ibid., 213.

23. ibid., 215.

24. E. Gilson, *Les Idées et les lettres*, Paris, 1932, 79–91.

25. ibid., 272. Founded in 1098, tremendously dynamic in the period 1134–1342, owing its success largely to St Bernard's influence, the Cistercian order was dedicated to the strict observance of the rule of St Benedict, and both the monks and the lay brothers who served them led simple, ascetic lives. They were mystics, believing that God can only be known through love.

26. ibid., 84–5.

27. Pauphilet, ed. cit., 160–1.

28. An inferior form of the mystical life according to St Bernard; ibid., 79–81.

29. *ALMA*, 269.

30. Pauphilet, ed. cit., xi.

31. *ALMA*, 308.
32. Frappier, *Mort Artu*, xiv.
33. ibid., 152. Lancelot had spared the king's life on the battlefield.
34. *The Passing of Arthur*.
35. *Yvain*, lines 29–30.
36. See above, p. 185.
37. See below, pp. 210–13.
38. ed. M. Roques, Paris, CFMA, 1925, 2nd ed. 1936.
39. See below, p. 213.
40. ed. F. Whitehead, Manchester, 2nd ed. 1951; reprinted 1961.
41. ibid., xix.
42. ibid., xviii–xix.
43. *DLF*, 177. Throughout the Middle Ages it was frequently revised. In the sixteenth century Marguerite d'Angoulême included it in her *Heptameron*, and new versions of the story appeared as late as the eighteenth century. See G. Raynaud, 'La Chastelaine de Vergi', *R*, XXI, 1892, 145–193, esp. 155–65.
44. See above, pp. 145–6.
45. ed. H. Michelant and P. Meyer, Paris, SATF, 1894, reprinted New York, 1968.
46. *Tale of Kamar al-Zaman*, 207th Night.
47. See below, pp. 216–21. There are two good modern editions of *Guillaume de Dôle*: one by R. Lejeune, Paris, 1936; the other by F. Lecoy, Paris, CFMA, 1962.
48. Lejeune, ed. cit., xii.
49. ed. D.-L. Buffum, Paris, SATF, 1928.
50. cf. *Le Roman du Castelain de Couci*, below pp. 214–15.
51. ed. L. Foulet, Paris, CFMA, 1925, v–viii.
52. There are two good modern editions: J. Bédier, Paris, SATF, 1913; and J. Orr, Edinburgh, 1948.
53. ed. C. Brunel, Paris, CFMA, 1926.
54. 'Molt en fu mesire Tiebaus dolans . . .' (p. 16) (Thibaut was most upset).
55. See above, p. 173.
56. ed. J. Alton, Tübingen, 1889. Strictly speaking this is not so much a sequel as a rehash, with the introduction of several different stories and characters.
57. ed. L. Thorpe, Cambridge, 2 vols., 1950–58.
58. ibid., II, xiii.
59. ed. J. Palermo, Paris, SATF, 2 vols., 1963–64.
60. ed. J. E. Matzke and M. Delbouille, Paris, SATF, 1936.
61. They are those of the actual *trouvère* known as Le Chastelain de Coucy, see above, p. 127.
62. Matzke and Delbouille, ed. cit., xlvi–lxiii.
63. H. Suchier ed., *Œuvres poétiques de Philippe de Remi Sire de Beaumanoir*, Paris, SATF, 2 vols., 1884–85.
64. For a slightly later version of this well-known legend, see below, p. 333. Observe also the parallel with *Guillaume d'Angleterre* and the *Vie de Saint Brendan*, see above, pp. 171–2, 34–42.
65. Suchier, ed. cit., I, ci.
66. The most recent edition is by F. Lecoy, Paris, CFMA, 3 vols., 1965–1970. Details of the 'Querelle du *Roman de la Rose*' are given in vol. I, xxviii–xxxi.
67. Bibliographical information on all these works is given ibid., I, ix–x.
68. J. V. Fleming, *The Roman de la Rose. A Study in Allegory and Iconography*, Princeton, 1969, 47.
69. Fuller summaries of both sections are provided in the introductions to the three volumes of Lecoy, ed. cit.
70. The first person is used throughout: In my twentieth year, etc., and is continued by Jean de Meun.
71. These are all essentially anti-courtly attributes. They represent, broadly speaking, the very opposites of the allegorical characters the poet is soon to encounter inside the garden.

72. A 'splendid non-sequitur' as Fleming observes (op. cit., 96). Was Guillaume in fact sounding a warning, as Fleming believes (ibid.), concerning the dangers of auto-eroticism?

73. Line 1536. Do they represent his own eyes, or those of his future lady-love? The poet does not say, and both interpretations have been proposed, see Fleming, ibid., 93.

74. On the whole the most difficult of Guillaume's allegorisations to understand. The word 'danger' originally meant 'power', 'dominion', hence Danger's alliance with Slander and Jealousy suggests that the reference is to the social forces which (as in so many courtly works) form a barrier to love: husband, parents, and indeed all those who know about the affair. This interpretation has been strenuously denied in favour of a more psychological interpretation; see Lewis, op. cit., 123–5; and Fleming, op. cit., 188–9.

75. 3485–6. See D. Kelly, ' "Li chastiaus . . . Qu'Amours prist puis par ses esforz": The Conclusion of Guillaume de Lorris' *Rose*', *Humanistic Studies*, XLII, 1972, 61–78.

76. Who, according to Kelly, ibid., 75, represented 'sexual activity wherein "love" as such plays no part'.

77. On the characters Danger, Male Bouche, and Jalousie, see above, p. 217. Honte, Peur, and Bel Accueil (possibly Danger as well) appear to represent the lady's (or girl's) reactions. In Jean de Meun's section, the old woman's advice to the younger woman on how to treat her lovers is addressed to Bel Accueil.

78. Fleming (op. cit., 100–1) suggests that Guillaume has portrayed the first four of the traditional five 'steps of love': *visus* (seeing), *alloquium* (speaking to), *contactus* (touch), *osculum* (kiss). Jean de Meun added the fifth and last stage, *factum* (intercourse), so completing the work, whose two sections prosecute, in Fleming's view, 'a single and unified action' (ibid., 104).

79. The warning that the views of Jean de Meun's characters may not be his own is sounded at length, with important results, by Fleming, ibid.

80. This definition is taken from Andreas Capellanus's *De Amore* (Book I, chapter 1). See above, pp. 129–30.

81. Fleming, op. cit., sees Jean de Meun's Amis as 'a miserable comforter and cynical advisor' (139–40), one of the most complex and shifting of his characters. He points out that in manuscript illuminations, Amis and Raison stand on opposite sides of the lover (140).

82. In Faux Semblant, Jean de Meun illustrates, as Fleming points out, 'the hypocrisy which uses the external manifestations of religion to disguise carnal attitudes' (ibid., 162).

83. The *Vetula* was a stock character who made frequent appearances in medieval French literature. Her blatant cynicism owed much to the principal classical source of this figure: Ovid's *Ars Amatoria*, ibid., 171–84.

84. Nature represents, according to Fleming (ibid., 194–6) 'natura post peccatum Ade', that is, nature as she is in consequence of Adam's sin, with death as her perpetual enemy. Genius, her chaplain, is 'an aspect of Nature', representing above all 'natural concupiscence' (ibid., 194).

85. See below, pp. 272–4.

86. Fleming, op. cit.

87. ibid., 107, 143.

88. The most far-reaching attempt so far made to define the real meaning and intent of the *Roman de la Rose* is provided by Fleming, ibid. See also his article, 'Hoccleve's "Letter of Cupid" and the quarrel over the *Roman de la Rose*', *MAe*, XL, 1971, 21–40. Both authors borrow frequently from Ovid, particularly from the *Metamorphoses* and the *Ars Amatoria*. Among Jean de Meun's many sources, the following names, sometimes quoted by him, are noteworthy: *classical*: Cicero, Claudian, Horace, Juvenal, Livy, Sallust, Suetonius, Vergil; *medieval*: Alanus de Insulis, Boethius, Guillaume de Saint-Amour, John of Salisbury.

Chapter 8

FABLES, *FABLIAUX*, AND THE *ROMAN DE RENART*

I. PROVERBS AND FABLES

THAT so much medieval literature reveals a strong penchant for moralising and edification must not be attributed entirely to the influence of the Church. It may seem fanciful to conjure up a notion as vague as 'the wisdom of the people', and yet the popularity of proverbs and fables, whose origins stretch back to antiquity and beyond, testifies to a sort of earthy commonsense, a hard, practical outlook reflecting the experience of countless generations, a philosophy running at a lower level than that of a Jean de Meun, but certainly more within reach of the illiterate majority.[1] Thousands of medieval proverbs have survived,[2] many of which aptly sum up the character or behaviour of certain types of individual, or apply appropriately to certain recurring circumstances: 'Nature passe norreture' (Mor. 1328; lit. 'Nature surpasses education'), reflecting a belief that inborn characteristics are of greater consequence than acquired ones;[3] 'De mauvés arbre mauvés fruit' (Mor. 520; lit. 'From a bad tree bad fruit'); 'De grant vent petite pluie' (Mor. 506; lit. 'From a strong wind little rain' – cf. English 'Much ado about nothing'); 'Les vieilles voyes sont les meilleures' (Mor. 1052; lit. 'Old paths are the best'); 'Li mestiers duit l'omme' (Mor. 1096; lit. 'The trade fashions the man'); 'Chascun prestre loe ses reliques' (Mor. 360; lit. 'Each priest praises his relics'); 'Chantés a l'asne, il vous fera des pés' (Mor. 340; lit. 'Sing to the donkey, he'll blow you farts'). Some reflect popular superstitions: 'Paques pluieuses sont froumenteuses' (Mor. 1605; lit. 'A rainy Easter brings a bountiful harvest') or simple observations of nature; 'Plaine lune, mer au grant' (Mor. 1641; lit. 'Full moon, high tide'). An antifeministic bias is often in evidence, as in the following doggerel:

Femme se plaint, femme se deult	Woman groans, woman wheezes,
Femme est malade quant el veult.	Woman is ill whenever she pleases.
(Mor. 739)	

Certain proverbs seem already to be fables in miniature: 'Femme qui parle come home et geline qui chante come coq ne sont bonnes a tenir' (Mor. 737; lit. 'A woman who speaks like a man and a hen that sings like a cock are not good to keep').[4]

Fables, which may be looked upon as embellished, or expanded, proverbs, apologues in which animals, with appropriate characteristics, talk and behave like human beings, began to appear in French, according to extant evidence, in the twelfth century, but had existed for centuries before that in Latin, and much earlier still in Greek. Aesop, who lived in the sixth century B.C., is traditionally (but wrongly) thought of as the father of the genre.[5] His name was at least known in medieval times, as the title *Isopet*, often given to collections of fables in the vernacular, reveals,[6] but not so that of Phaedrus, the first to write fables in Latin verse meant to be read consecutively as literature rather than to be used as a fund of anecdotes by moralists and preachers. None the less, this latter use was continued by the Christian Church for centuries in the *exempla*, short moralising tales resembling the fables in their aims.[7] Phaedrus's collection, based on earlier sets, now lost, originating for the most part in those of Aesop, to whom frequent reference is made, was used by later writers, but not before the sixteenth century was the correct text established under his name. The earliest surviving examples of fables in French appear to be those ascribed to Marie de France and supposed to have been written towards the end of the twelfth century, but the dating is as uncertain as the attribution.[8] They are written in octosyllabic rhyming couplets, the shortest having less than 20 lines, the longest well over a hundred. They enjoyed considerable popularity, judging from the relatively substantial number of manuscripts that have survived (23 altogether). The following examples, chosen from the shorter specimens, give some idea of their nature:

Del prestre e del lu (The priest and the wolf)

Un prestre volst jadis aprendre
A un lu lettres fere entendre.
'A' dist le prestre, 'A' dist li lus,
Que mut ert fel e enginnus.
'B' dist le prestre, 'di od mei!'
'B' dist li lus 'e jo l'otrei'.
'C' dist le prestre, 'di avant!'
'C' dist li lus, 'a i dunc tant?'
Respunt le prestre: 'Or di par tei!'
Li lus li dist: 'Jeo ne sai quei'.
'Di que te semble, si espel'.
Respunt li lus, il dit 'Aignel!'
Le prestre dit que verté tuche:
Tel en pensé, tel en la buche.

Once upon a time a priest wanted to teach a wolf to understand letters. 'A' said the priest, 'A' said the wolf, who was very shy and cunning, 'B' said the priest, 'say it with me!' 'B' said the wolf, 'I agree'. 'C' said the priest, 'say it now!' 'C' said the wolf, 'is there really so much?' The priest replies: 'Now say it alone'. The wolf said: 'I cannot'. 'Tell me what you make of it, and spell it out'. The wolf replies 'Lamb'. The priest says that he is touching on the truth of the matter: what is in the mind

De plusurs le veit hum sovent:
Cel dunt il pensent durement
E par lur buche est cuneü,
Ainceis que seit d'autre sceü;
La buche mustre le penser,
Tut deivë ele de el parler.[9]

comes into the mouth. We often find this with many men: what is on their mind is revealed by their tongue before it is actually known to others. The tongue betrays the thought even though it is supposed to be speaking about something different.

As with certain other fables, there is really much more to this one than meets the eye. The reflection on human nature which it embodies has, in more sophisticated forms, been carried much further in modern times.[10] The collection also contains an example of the well-known 'moonraker' theme, found in various forms in most collections of fables:

Del gupil e de l'umbre de la lune (The fox and the reflection of the moon)

D'un gupil dit që une nuit
Esteit alez en sun deduit.
Sur une mare trespassa;
Quant dedenz l'ewe regarda,
L'umbre de la lune ad veü,
Mes ne sot mie quei ceo fu.
Puis ad pensé en sun curage
Qu'il ot veü un grant furmage.
L'ewe comencë a laper;
Tresbien quida en sun penser,
Si l'ewe de la mare ert mendre,
Que le furmage peüst prendre.
Tant ad beü që il creva;
Ileoc cheï, puis ne leva.
   Meint humme espeirë, utre dreit
E utre ceo qu'il ne devreit
Aver tutes ses volentez,
Dunt puis est morz e afolez.[11]

The story is told of a fox on the prowl one night for his distraction. He came to a pond, and when he looked into the water, he saw the reflection of the moon but did not realise what it was. Then he thought to himself that he had seen an enormous cheese. He begins to lap up the water, thinking that if there is less water in the pond, he would be able to get the cheese. He drank so much that he died. He dropped dead on the spot, and never rose again.
   Many a man hopes, beyond what is right or reasonable, to satisfy all his wishes, and is killed as a result.

At least five *Isopets* are extant from the thirteenth and fourteenth centuries,[12] and fables sometimes appear in unexpected forms and places.[13]

II. THE FABLIAUX

The relationship of the *fabliau* to the fable is not as close as the name would appear to imply (fable<*fabula*; *fabliau* is the Picard form of the diminutive *fableau*<*fabulellum*, this genre having been popular in Picardy). Like so many medieval generic terms, *fabliau* was used rather loosely, and it is impossible to produce a simple definition embracing all works which medieval writers called *fabliaux*. Most are concerned, not with animals, but with people, usually of the lower orders, countryfolk especially, and conform to

Bédier's definition 'des contes à rire en vers'.[14] Large numbers end
with a moral,[15] as do the fables, and though not all involve humour,
most are jokes, often bawdy,[16] provoking a ribald belly laugh, dealing in hearty, *gaulois* fashion with one or more of those perennial
and ever-fascinating topics, the Seven Deadly Sins. Even the moral
of the *fabliau* may contain a jesting element, parodying those of the
fables. Some 150 of these tales have survived, their length usually
exceeding that of the fables without attaining that of the romances;
most contain between two and five hundred of the ubiquitous octo-
syllabics in rhyming couplets. Their authors, anonymous for the
greater part, were 'a motley collection of jongleurs and wandering
clerks as well as professional poets of higher station and the
occasional laughter-loving amateur'.[17] The lively tales they tell
reflect the realities of daily life:

The people are not mere literary conventions. They are human beings seen
with a human eye: the orphan brothers driven by starvation to petty theft;
the priest going to market mumbling his prayers, but with a ready eye for
choice blackberries in the hedgerow; the merry, roving students with their
thoughts on more than books; the sleepy knight, the sharp-eyed little cob-
bler's daughter, or Brifaut's waspish wife. And the scenes are set with realistic
detail: here an interior with a box bed beside the fire, there a storeyed house
by a canal; a market scene, or a street fragrant with the smell of spices from
the grocers' shops; a countryman ploughing his fields, or a fisherman at his
nets on the sea. It is from the fabliaux that much of our knowledge of life
in thirteenth-century France has been gleaned.[18]

Among the better-known examples are the following:

Du Vilain Asnier (The Peasant Donkey-man)

A peasant loads his donkeys with dung. When he passes in front of the
spice-merchant's shop, the strong smell of the spices makes him faint. A
passer-by revives him by holding a forkful of dung under his nose. The
moral of this tale is: to each his own.[19]

D'un Preudome qui rescolt son compere de noier (The worthy man who rescued his companion from drowning)

In rescuing a drowning man with his boathook, a fisherman accidentally
blinds him in one eye. The man who has been rescued complained about
the loss of his eye and the fisherman is had up in court. It is suggested that
the man be returned to the sea, and if he can save himself without the fisherman's help, the latter should pay compensation. The thought of being put
back into the sea is too much, and the fisherman is set free. The moral is:
'... son tens pert qui felon sert' (Saving a scoundrel is a waste of time).[20]

Estula (Areyouthere)

One dark night two poor, starving brothers set out to rob a rich man's
farm. While one steals some cabbages, the other enters the sheep pen. Hearing a noise, the farmer asks his son to call in their dog Estula (Areyouthere).
Thinking his brother is calling him, the thief in the sheep pen replies 'Yes,

I'm over here!' The farmer's son rushes indoors and tells his father the dog is talking. The farmer tries out the miracle for himself and finds that it is true. The son dashes off to get the priest and, finding him in his stockinged feet, carries him home on his back. The thief who has stolen the cabbages mistakes him for his brother carrying a sheep and tells him to throw it down and cut its throat. Greatly alarmed, the priest jumps down and scampers off shoeless into the night, leaving his surplice caught on a post. The farmer's son runs off in pursuit. The other thief then appears carrying a sheep. Back at home the brothers find that they have acquired a sack of cabbages, a sheep, and a priest's cloak. The moral of this tale is:

En pou d'eure Deus labeure	God works in a lightning way, You
(Mor. 679)	can weep in the evening and laugh
Teus rit au main qui au soir plore	the next day[21]
(Mor. 2368)	

Del Couvoiteus et de l'Envïeus (The Greedy Man and the Jealous Man)

St Martin invites one of this pair to wish for anything he wants. It will at once be granted him, and the second will have twice as much. The greedy man, wishing to be the second, remains silent, and the other, who will die of jealousy if the other gets more than he does, also remains silent. The jealous man solves the dilemma by asking that he be made blind in one eye. The greedy man is completely blinded. The story is its own moral: be neither greedy, nor jealous.[22]

Du Provoire qui menga les mores (The Priest who ate blackberries)

As he rides to market mumbling his prayers, a priest spots some lovely blackberries in the hedgerow. Since the best are out of his reach, he stands on his saddle and eats his fill. He looks down at his mare in amusement, and thinks to himself: 'Supposing someone says Gee-up!' He not only thinks it, he says it aloud, off goes the mare, and the priest topples over into the brambles where he is held fast. The mare trots home, whereat the priest's 'wife' faints and his servants set out to look for him. They hear his cries for help and release him. The moral of this tale is: 'Cil ne fait mie savoir, Qui tot son pensé dit et conte' (He who expresses all his thoughts does not act wisely).[23]

Des Deus Anglois et de l'Anel (The Two Englishmen and the Donkey)

An Englishman recovering from a fever addresses his compatriot in a weird mixture of French and English:

Mi have tote nuit soué	I have been sweating all night,
Mi ave, ge cuit, plus soé	I have, I think, been sweating even
Si cuit vueil mengier un petit.	more, and think I want to eat a little.

He adds, in his Pidgin-French:

Se tu avez un anel cras	If you have a plump lamb [but see
Mi porra bien mengier, ce croi	below] I shall be able to eat, I believe.

'anel' is intended for 'agnel' (lamb), but sounded more like 'asnel' (young donkey). Off goes his companion to the shop, where his French, equally strange, is received with consternation:

'Que vas tu', fait il, 'fastroillant?'   'Whatever are you jabbering about', says he.

Finally, believing he is asking for a young donkey, the shopkeeper sells him one. The Englishman takes it home, skins and cooks it, and serves a leg to the convalescent. The latter eats it with relish, but then looks at the huge bone in astonishment: 'Quel beste m'as tu ci porté?' (What is this animal you have brought me?) He finally understands that he has eaten, not the son of a *baa*, but the son of a *hee-haw*. Both have a good laugh, and the tale ends there.[24]

Du Prestre qui ot mere mal gré sien (The Priest who acquired a mother despite himself)

A priest refuses to do the bidding of his cross-grained old mother, who complains to the bishop. It is arranged that the latter should interview the priest in his mother's presence. While waiting for him to arrive, the bishop tells the priest's mother that her son may be suspended. The mother panics since she confuses in her mind 'soupendre' (to suspend) with 'pendre' (to hang) and assumes that her son is about to be put to death. When a fat priest comes waddling in before her son's arrival, she at once exclaims: 'That's him, that fat priest is my son!' The bishop threatens him with suspension and orders him to take his 'mother' home on his palfrey. The astonished priest does not dare disobey. On their way they meet the real son, who, highly amused, finally agrees to take his mother off the other's hands in return for the sum of £60. There is no moral, nor is it easy to see what moral or proverb could be tacked on here.[25]

Du Vilain qui conquist Paradis par plait (The Farm Labourer who argued his way into Paradise)

On his death the farm labourer's soul does not know where to go, but, seeing the archangel St Michael conveying another soul to heaven, he tacks on behind. When St Peter refuses to allow him in, the labourer's soul reproaches him with denying Christ three times. St Peter ruefully withdraws and fetches St Thomas. The latter in his turn receives short shrift from the labourer's soul, and turns to St Paul for help. St Paul suffers likewise, and it is finally decided that the best course is to admit the soul. The moral of this tale is 'Mielz valt engien que ne fait force' (Cleverness is worth more than force).[26]

De la Male Honte (These words have a double meaning, on which the whole tale depends: i. Foul shame; ii. Honte's bag)

Since he has died without heirs in England, Honte's possessions are to pass to the king, as is the custom. He has had them loaded into a bag, and after his death his friend takes them to the king. He finds him in London and says to him 'La male Honte vos aport' ('I've brought you Honte's bag', though the more immediately apparent meaning is 'I've brought you foul shame!'). The king at once orders him out of his presence. The same thing happens when he tries again in church. On the third attempt the enraged king orders him to be put to death, but an investigation is held on the advice of a counsellor, and when the king learns the truth, he laughs heartily, slaps his thigh, and tells him to keep his 'foul shame'.[27]

Du Vilein Mire (The Peasant Doctor)

A peasant is afraid of being deceived by his wife, who is the daughter of a knight. Accordingly, each morning before leaving for work, he gives her a beating so that her face will be tear-stained and unattractive throughout the day. One morning as she ponders revenge, two of the king's servants arrive and tell her they are looking for a doctor to cure the king's daughter who has a fishbone lodged in her throat. She directs them to the field where her husband is working and claims that he is a marvellous doctor, but that he will treat no one unless he is first given a sound beating. They find him, and when he denies all knowledge of medicine, shower him with blows. He soon gives way, is taken to Court, given another beating, and ordered to cure the king's daughter. He performs strange antics which make her laugh, so coughing up the fishbone. He is then ordered to cure a whole roomful of people and is duly given the prescribed beating. The peasant, having ordered the king out of the room, tells them that he can cure them but that he will first have to kill and burn one of their number who is very ill. He will make a powder from his remains which will cure the others. He picks out one, saying 'You look very feeble, you'll do'. The invalid replies 'No, I'm quite all right really'. He is accordingly asked to leave, and assures the king as he does so that he has been cured. So with a second, a third, and eventually all in the room. The peasant becomes a famous doctor, loved and cherished by his wife.[28]

The most famous version of this story nowadays is Molière's *Le Médecin malgré lui*, whose direct source was not here, but in an Italian farce based on the same idea. The ultimate source of this theme may have been the East, but the question of the oriental origins of the *fabliaux* is received nowadays with more caution than was at one time the case. Their origins were many and various, and no single source, no single theory, however all-embracing, can account for all of them:

On peut rechercher l'origine et la propagation d'un conte au cas et au cas seulement où ce conte, réduit à sa forme organique, renferme sous cette forme des éléments qui en limitent la diffusion dans l'espace ou la durée. Au contraire, si cette forme organique ne renferme que des éléments qui ne supposent aucune condition d'adhésion spéciale – sociale, morale, surnaturelle – la recherche de la propagation et de l'origine de ce conte est vaine, et c'est le cas de tous ceux pour lesquels se bâtissent les théories.[29]

On this principle, of those outlined above, *La Male Honte, Estula*, and *Des Deus Anglois et de l'Anel* may be regarded as medieval French tales, depending on untranslatable puns (though the last named could conceivably have originated in England), and because of its theme *Du Vilain qui conquist paradis par plait* is at least of Christian origin, whereas others featuring priests – quite often the victims of these tales – could simply be transpositions of earlier tales in which dignitaries of whatever kind were made to come a cropper.

The relaxed style of the *fabliaux*, from which no word or expression was barred on moral grounds, contrasts sharply with the relatively refined nature of most of the courtly romances:

Dans le style noble se trouve concentré tout ce que les nobles courtois considéraient comme caractéristique de l'élégance et des qualités aristocratiques:
noblesse, courage, esprit, intelligence, sentiments sublimes, beauté physique.
Le style bas est l'essence de tout ce qui était considéré comme étranger à la
noblesse et propre aux roturiers: vulgarité, paillardise, lourdeur, bêtise, bas
instincts, laideur et saleté.[30]

It would, however, be wrong to think of the two as belonging to
entirely different *milieux*, providing evidence of a strongly stratified
society. So many medieval authors and texts bear witness to the
dichotomy of the medieval mind which could switch so easily from
one extreme to another:

... il faut compter sur l'existence d'un côté bas, tant en littérature que dans
la façon de penser, dans les cercles lettrés du moyen age: on n'y était pas
seulement capable de s'exalter en écoutant des aventures galantes ou des
exploits grandioses; on était également capable de s'esclaffer en écoutant un
conte d'un comique élémentaire ou grossier.[31]

That the courtly *milieux* were able on occasions to relax over a
bawdy joke, or to poke fun at the foibles of human nature, is significant, for it betokens a society a good deal more healthy and open-
minded than is sometimes supposed.

III. THE 'ROMAN DE RENART'

The popularity of the numerous tales concerning Reynard the Fox
in England as well as on the continent is demonstrated by the many
surviving church carvings and manuscript illuminations depicting
his escapades.[32] It has been said that the success of these stories,
known collectively as the *Roman de Renart*, was equalled by only
two other works, the *Roman de Tristan* and the *Roman de la Rose*,
and that even so the *Roman de Renart* was closer to people's hearts
than were these exceptional works.[33] Towards 1175 a Frenchman,
about whom nothing is known apart from his name, Pierre de Saint-
Cloud, wrote a poem about Reynard the Fox and Isangrin the Wolf.
As his basis he used certain fables, and a Latin poem *Isengrimus*,
composed in 1149[34] by a certain Nivardus, who in his turn made
use of earlier Latin sources. This was the start of a vogue which
reached its peak about 1200, though it was to last well on into the
fourteenth century. Various poets, mostly anonymous, composed
many 'branches'[35] of this story which lent itself admirably to
episodic treatment. The manuscripts (some 20 in all) can be divided
roughly into three groups according to the number and order of the
branches, of which 28 have survived, exceeding 25,000 lines in total
length. In most cases the branches were not designed specifically to
follow on one from another, and a confused state of affairs was

bound to arise. It is no surprise to find that the first branch alludes to episodes occurring in the second branch as though they had already taken place, and apparently owes its position at the head of the collection to the success it enjoyed, recounting in vivid style Reynard's trial for crimes committed earlier. The second branch is that of Pierre de Saint-Cloud and is doubtless the original one. His audience had heard many stories telling how Paris carried off Helen, they had heard 'fables' and 'chançons de geste' about Tristan, but

. . . onques n'oïstes la guerre,	. . . never did you hear of the war,
qui mout fu dure de grant fin,	which was extremely bitter, between
entre Renart et Isengrin	Reynard and Isengrin, which went
qui mout dura et mout fu dure.[36]	on for a long time and was very fierce.

The author describes how a traditional rivalry (recalling a little that between Roland and Ganelon) became an open war. Its repercussions were to last throughout all the remaining episodes and provided a hub around which all could revolve. Here is a summary of Pierre de Saint-Cloud's tale.

Chanticleer the cock scornfully dismisses his wife Pinte's fears of Reynard the fox, but has a foreboding dream about an animal with a red fur cloak which Pinte has no difficulty in interpreting. The dream soon comes true, for the prowling Reynard tries to grab Chanticleer as he is dozing off, but misses. He then persuades Chanticleer to sing, hinting that he is unable to match the voice of his father, the late Chanteclin:

lors chanta Chantecler un vers;	then Chanticleer sang a verse, one
un oil ot clous et l'autre overt,	eye closed and the other open, for
car mout forment cremoit Renart;	he was very much afraid of Reynard
sovent regarde cele part.	and often looks towards him. 'That
'Ce, dit Renart, ne fait neant.	is nothing', says Reynard, 'Chante-
Chanteclins chantoit autrement,	clin sang differently, in one long
a un lonc trait, a ieuz clingniez;	breath and with his eyes closed. He
l'on l'oïst bien de .xx. plaissiez'.	could be heard twenty farmyards
Chanteclés quide que voir die;	away'. Chanticleer believes him, and
lors lait aler la melodie,	with his eyes closed, gives full throat.
les iauz clingniez, par grant aïr.	Then Reynard was unwilling to wait
Lors ne vost plus Renart soufrir:	a moment longer. Jumping over a
par dedesus un roige chol	red cabbage, he grabs him by the
le prant Renart par mi le col;	neck and runs off with him, rejoi-
fuient s'en va et fait grant joie	cing greatly to have found some
de ce qu'il a encontré proie.	prey.

(lines 4383–98)

Reynard's triumph is short-lived, for, in tit-for-tat fashion, Chanticleer persuades him to shout defiance at his pursuers, and flies off as soon as the fox opens his mouth. The starving Reynard next devotes his attentions to a tomtit, inviting him to fly down from the oak-tree to kiss him. He offers to close his eyes, and the tomtit proceeds to tickle his moustache with a bunch of moss and leaves, which is all that was left to Reynard when he made his grab. At that moment the hunters come in view, and up goes the cry 'Vez le gorpil! Vez le gorpil!' (4561) (See the fox! See the fox!). Reynard, hastily

declining the tomtit's taunting invitation to kiss him in return, outruns the
hounds and after further perils collapses into a ditch. Along comes Tibert
the cat, but there is no chance of a meal here for the ever hungry fox.
Tibert agrees to become Reynard's 'soldier', but as they go off together
Reynard tries to push him into a trap. Tibert turns the tables on him and
the fox is caught just as a peasant arrives with two dogs. The peasant swings
his axe and Reynard narrowly escapes losing his head. Once more he breaks
away and makes off. As he prepares to enjoy a well-earned rest, he spies
Tiecelin the crow sitting on a beech-tree with a soft cheese clutched in his
right claw. Reynard is at once up to his old tricks again. He asks Tiecelin if
he is as good a singer as his father Rohart. In his demonstration, the crow
loosens his grip on the cheese, and down it falls in front of Reynard. Resist-
ing the temptation to pounce on it, the fox invites the crow to come down
and remove this foul-smelling object from under his nose, at the same time
making himself appear as harmless as possible by trailing his wounded leg.
Tiecelin is deceived, Reynard grabs at him, but only gets four feathers. He
has to make do with the cheese. On his way once more, he chances upon
Isangrin's den, and finding the master out, makes advances to his wife
Hersent, who receives him favourably. Fearing Isangrin's arrival, Reynard
does not tarry, but before leaving he soils the four wolf-cubs and eats up all
the food supplies. On his return Isangrin is not unnaturally furious, and
declares that henceforth Reynard had better be on his guard. One day they
find him in a field from which the crop of peas has just been cleared. The
chase to Reynard's den begins; Hersent, being lighter than her husband,
outdistances him, rushes into the fox's den immediately behind the quarry,
but gets firmly stuck in the entrance. Reynard promptly emerges from
another entrance, lifts Hersent's tail, and copulates with her with enormous
vigour:

Sire Renart tel li redone   Sire Reynard gives it to her in such
que toute la fouse en estone.   a way that the whole den resounds.

                    (5959–60)

Isangrin comes panting up in time to see what is going on. He has to dig
away some earth in order to rescue his spouse, and, in his helpless rage, is
reduced to insulting her:

'Haï!' fait il, 'pute orde vivre,   'Ah!' says he, 'you stinking horrid
pute serpant, pute coleuvre,   viper, you stinking serpent, you
bien ai veüe toute l'euvre . . .'   stinking grass-snake, I saw the whole
                    (6070–2)   affair'.

The remaining branches of this vast compilation vary in quality,
but the spirit of the best of them reflects that of this seminal tale
which so obviously invited imitation and development. Indebtedness
to Latin fables, as well as to the *Isengrimus*, is particularly evident
in certain episodes of Pierre de Saint-Cloud's work; that, for example, concerning Chanticleer, or that concerning Tiecelin the crow
and his cheese. The basic theme which ensured the story's success is
found also in certain fables and *fabliaux*: the duper duped. Usually
the slyness of the fox was thwarted at the last moment if he was
hoping to make a meal of his intended victim (though he did manage
to wreak havoc among the poultry. In the first branch Pinte,
Chanticleer's wife, reveals that Reynard had gobbled up her five
brothers and five sisters!), whereas the tricks he was fond of playing

on those mightier than himself, such as Isangrin the wolf, Bruin the
bear, were often cruelly successful.

The *Roman de Renart* achieved a better harmony between its
subject-matter and the octosyllabic rhyming couplets than did most
romances. With no pretensions to psychological finesses or philosophical discourses, this quick-moving narrative, in which one 'fole
aventure' follows hard on the heels of another, is admirably suited
to this light, skipping measure. The fact that animals, not human
beings, are the protagonists enables the story to range lightheartedly
and uninhibitedly over the whole range of bodily functions, which are
to the *Roman de Renart* what emotions are to the courtly romances.
As in the *fabliau*, words such as *foutre, pertuis, pet, etc.*, are used
with a readiness which would have made a Chrétien de Troyes
throw up his arms in horror. Along with this go physical descriptions
of the countryside and cultivated land, a literally down-to-earth
realism providing a fascinating backcloth to this world of fantasy in
which animals are made to speak and reason like human beings. It is
a paradox that this imaginative fiction, a sort of country-dwellers'
Otherworld created principally by clerics, numbers of whom would
have been of peasant stock,[37] should be so much closer to the lives
of the people than were the human dramas of the court poets. In
some other branches, human beings, particularly the 'villeins', appear
more frequently, and two parallel worlds are created which react on
each other and seem to be governed by much the same self-interested
motives. The peasants themselves are often rather mischievously
portrayed, less so, however, than the priests, monks, and pilgrims,
while the bourgeois are absent largely because of the rural settings
of these tales, but in most instances the mockery stops short of satire.
It is above all a matter of an irreverent fun, a bawdy, carefree, uninhibited amusement admirably illustrated by the unfortunate priest
shorn of a testicle by the sharp teeth of Tibert the cat, who gleefully
commented: 'Ne sonera mes c'une cloche' (928) (He will only ring
one bell now). The portrayal of the peasants can be very vivid, as in
this description of a mob in hot pursuit of Bruin the bear. Their
extraordinary nicknames may not be mere literary fantasy:

Qui lors veïst vilains venir	You should have seen the swarm of
et fremïer parmi la rue!	peasants coming along the street,
Qui porte hache, qui maçue,	some carrying hatchets, some clubs,
qui flael, qui baston d'espine:	some flails, some thorn-sticks, and
grant poor a Bruns de s'eschine.	Bruin greatly fears for his back. Up
Devant lui vient Hurtevilain	to him comes Hurtevilain [Shove-
et Joudoïn Trouseputain	peasant] and Joudouin Trouseputain
Et Baudoïn Porteciviere	[Whoremonger] and Baudouin Porte-
qui fout sa fame par derrieres	civière [Stretcherbearer] who copu-
Girout Barbete qui l'acole	lates with his wife from the rear,
et un des fiuz sire Nichole . . .	Girout Barbete who holds her in his
(652–62)	arms, and one of sire Nichol's sons . . .

META8.META

Occasionally, however, a bitter reflection breaks the surface and betrays the author's feelings, as in the following diatribe by Reynard on the sharp contrast between the rich and the poor, the more significant as it is by no means essential to the story:

l'en dit a cort 'Sire, lavez'
au riche home, quant il i vient.
Gariz est qui ses manches tient:[38]
de premier dou buef a l'egrés
aprés vienent li autre mes,
qant li sires en viaut avoir.
Mes povres hom qui n'a avoir
fu faiz de la merde au deauble:
ne siet a feu, ne siet a table,
einz menjue sus son giron.
Li chien li vienent en viron
qui li tolent le pain des mains...
(526–37)

At Court they say 'Sir, wash' to the rich man when he comes in. Merely to hold his sleeves brings salvation. First of all comes beef in sour sauce, then the other dishes, whatever the master feels like having. But a poor and penniless man might as well be made of devil's shit. He does not sit round a fire or at table but eats from his lap. The dogs come all around him and snatch the bread out of his hands.

Brute force, conceit, arrogance, slyness, cunning, all are made to come a cropper, the best-laid schemes of beasts and men 'gang aft agley', and it is one of the delights of the theme that the tomtits of this world are allowed to triumph. Despite its many antecedents in the long line of Greek and Latin fables, the *Roman de Renart* is undoubtedly one of the most astonishing literary inventions of the Middle Ages, a distorting mirror held up to all living society, a rich source of wit and laughter.

IV. 'RENART LE BESTOURNÉ' OF RUTEBEUF

The passage quoted above shows how easily this literature could develop in the direction of social satire, and this is what eventually happened in the later thirteenth century. That Reynard could so readily become the very embodiment of evil suggests that, for all his popularity, he was looked upon without sentimentality or affection. There was some hesitation between Reynard as the denouncer of injustice (as in the above passage) and Reynard as the embodiment of it, but the latter eventually prevailed. Rutebeuf's *Renart le Bestourné* (Reynard the Hypocrite)[39] is written in that poet's usual caustic, vigorous style:

Renars est mors: Renars est vis!
Renars est ors, Renars est vils:
Et Renars regne![40]

Reynard is dead – Reynard is alive!
Reynard is horrid – Reynard is vile:
And Reynard reigns!

Reynard has here assumed a very special meaning[41] which for long escaped commentators of this difficult poem: he represents the friars, the mendicant orders who had established a powerful hold on the kingdom of France, and on King Louis IX in particular. In 1261 the king had decided to abolish the luxuries of court life which he came to believe were offensive in the eyes of God. Among the measures taken were several which had a dire effect on the lives of *trouvères* like Rutebeuf, such as their exclusion from the palace at mealtimes. Like his lyricism[42] Rutebeuf's satire only developed fully under the goad of his own involvement and suffering. It may well be that he made the mendicant orders scapegoats for economic circumstances whose root causes lay far deeper than he suspected. In this vicious attack, the king, in the person of Noble the lion, is accused of avarice, and his ministers, represented by Reynard the fox, Bernard the donkey, Roneau the dog, and Isangrin the wolf, of ruthlessness and dishonesty. Compassion, pity, charity, friendship, all have been flung out, and the king's palace resembles a hermitage. Other thirteenth-century poets complain in like manner of these economic stringencies which had such a disastrous effect on their lives.[43] It may well be that they did indeed have a far harder time than their predecessors of the late twelfth and early thirteenth centuries, hence the radical change in tone of the Reynard tales.

V. LATER TALES OF RENART

Rutebeuf's diatribe contains a mere 163 lines, while other late thirteenth-century poems developed this harsh satirical vein at far greater length. The anonymous *Couronnement de Renard*, a work of 3,398 octosyllabic lines composed sometime between 1251 and 1288, shows the triumph of all the vices when Reynard is crowned king in place of the ageing Noble the lion.[44] *Renart le Nouvel*, written by Jacquemart Gielee about 1288 and revealing a knowledge of the *Couronnement*, makes Reynard a personification of the Devil.[45] Among the targets for satirical abuse the mendicant orders once more hold a prominent place. The last medieval metamorphosis of these animal tales was the fourteenth-century *Renart le Contrefait* which, in its fullest development, contained more than 60,000 lines.[46] The anonymous author, a cleric of Troyes defrocked because he had lived with a concubine, presented himself in the guise of Reynard

| Pour dire par escript couvert | In order to say covertly |
| Ce qu'il n'osoit dire en appert. | What he dared not say overtly. |

(lines 121–2)

He too satirised contemporary society, particularly the nobility, the Church, and the friars, but this vast encyclopedic hotch-potch, into which the author has piled reminiscences of all his reading, also involves much edifying material. The resulting jumble produces some peculiar associations, as when Reynard, on his way to confession, meets the allegorical figures Peur, Nature, and Raison. Quite lost are the simple, naïve humour, the good-natured laughter, the entire spirit of the original, save in rare passages of direct imitation. It is sad that the earliest printed tales of Reynard in French showed no knowledge of the work of Pierre de Saint-Cloud and his immediate successors, but were based on these later works, particularly on *Renart le Nouvel*. In other spheres too the Renaissance did not know medieval works in their finest forms, but only in late, expanded versions which had lost many of the earlier qualities.

NOTES

1. This is not an attempt to revive the old-fashioned notion that 'popular' genres were composed by the masses in a sort of composite and accumulative fashion. They were the work of individuals, some of whom may well have been erudite.

2. J. Morawski, *Proverbes français antérieurs au XVe siècle* (Paris, CFMA, 1925) lists 2,500. (Mor.=Morawski.)

3. One manuscript reverses the proverb: 'Norreture passe nature' (Mor. 1399), possibly showing a different point of view on this evergreen topic. Theoretically 'nature' may still be read as the subject, but this is doubtful since, unlike many masculine nouns, feminine nouns give no morphological indication of their function.

4. A useful bibliographical note listing some studies of French proverbs is given by J. Bédier, *Les Fabliaux*, 6th ed. Paris, 1964, 283, note 1.

5. It has even been doubted whether there ever was such a figure as Aesop, but the evidence provided by Herodotus seems to find credence nowadays, cf. *Esope, Fables*, edited and translated by E. Chambry, Paris, 1960, ix–xvii.

6. *Avionnet* was another such title, from Avianus, a fourth-century composer of Latin fables.

7. Particularly important in this sphere is the *Disciplina Clericalis* of Petrus Alphonsus, translated into the vernacular as the *Castoiement d'un père à son fils*. See A. Hilka and W. Söderhjelm eds., *Petri Alphonsi Disciplina Clericalis*, Annales Soc. Scient. Fennicae, XLIX, 4, Helsingfors, 1922.

8. See above, p. 167.

9. Quoted Ewert and Johnston, ed. cit., Fable no. 38.

10. Compare the following passage from Valéry's *Variétés*: 'L'homme vit et se meut dans ce qu'il voit; mais il ne voit que ce qu'il songe. Au milieu d'une campagne, essayez divers personnages. Un philosophe vaguement n'apercevra que phénomènes; un géologue, des époques cristallisées, mêlées, ruinées, pulvérisées; un homme de guerre, des occasions et des obstacles . . .'. Valéry's idea is not fundamentally different from that of the medieval fable, but the pictorial, anecdotal, allegorical, edifying presentation so characteristic of the Middle Ages has given way to the more intellectual and abstract approach of modern times, a difference that has its roots in the social and educational characteristics of the different epochs and in the different levels at which the medieval fabulist and the modern scholar were functioning. The Middle Ages knew all about what is nowadays termed the 'Freudian slip'.

11. Ewert and Johnston, ed. cit., no. 31.

12. J. Bastin ed., *Recueil général des Isopets*, Paris, SATF, 2 vols., 1929–1930.

13. Such as the delightful *ballade* by Eustache Deschamps on the well-known theme of belling the cat, see the marquis de Queux de Saint-Hilaire and Gaston Raynaud, *Œuvres complètes de Eustache Deschamps*, Paris, SATF, 11 vols., 1878–1903, vol. I, Ballade LVIII, 151–2.

14. *Les Fabliaux*, 30–40, esp. 36.

15. Some 75 per cent according to R. C. Johnston and D. D. R. Owen, *Fabliaux*, Oxford, 1957, xiv.

16. It would be a misrepresentation of the genre not to mention this erotic element, as evinced in some Freudian-type tales, e.g., Jean Bodel's *Mad Desire (Li souhaiz desvez)*, in which a woman, having been refused intercourse by her husband, dreams of a market in which the only goods for sale were male sex organs. She decided to buy one of extraordinary dimensions, but when she and her husband woke up, she was soon able to compare her dream with reality (Foulon, op. cit., 31). This may be compared with the anonymous fable of the monk who, sexually aroused, dreamt of a market, besieged by monks, where only female sex organs were sold. Having spurned several old, skinny, withered ones, he finally bought a plump, sweet-smelling English specimen, with hair as soft as wool. (*R*, XLIV, 1915, 560-3.) Proverbs too made free mention of sex organs: 'Vit red ne porte fei' (Mor. 2494).

17. Johnston and Owen, ed. cit., vii. For more details of the authors of *fabliaux*, see Bédier, *Les Fabliaux*, 386-435.

18. Johnston and Owen, ed. cit., xii–xiii.

19. ibid., 4; T. B. W. Reid ed., *Twelve Fabliaux*, Manchester, 1958, 1.

20. Johnston and Owen, ed. cit., 1; Reid, ed. cit., 3.

21. Johnston and Owen, ed. cit., 6.

22. Reid, ed. cit., 5.

23 Johnston and Owen, ed. cit., 36; Reid, ed. cit., 8.

24. ibid., 11.

25. ibid., 14.

26. ibid., 19.

27. Johnston and Owen, ed. cit., 51.

28. ibid., 56.

29. Bédier, *Les Fabliaux*, 281.

30. P. Nykrog, *Les Fabliaux, étude d'histoire littéraire et de stylistique médiévale,* Copenhagen, 1957, 235.

31. ibid., 237.

32. K. Varty, *Reynard the Fox, A Study of the Fox in Medieval English Art*, Leicester, 1967. His popularity in France is further attested by the substitution of the name Renard for the ordinary term 'le goupil', which derived from a diminutive of Latin *vulpes*.

33. L. Foulet, *Le Roman de Renard*, Paris, 1914, 534-5. See also J. Flinn, *Le Roman de Renart dans la littérature française et dans les littératures étrangères au moyen âge*, Paris, 1963, 1-2.

34. ibid., 3.

35. A term used by the authors themselves.

36. Quoted from the most easily available edition, that of Mario Roques, Paris, CFMA, 1951, lines 3742-5. Altogether this edition covers six volumes of the CFMA series. The best edition is still that of E. Martin, 3 vols., Strasbourg–Paris, 1881-87.

37. That the authors were mostly clerics is shown by Foulet, op. cit., 566–567. See also R. Bossuat, *Le Roman de Renart*, Paris, 2nd impression, 1967, chapter 7.

38. On the meaning of this strange line, see F. Lyons, 'Pour le commentaire de *Renart*', *R*, LXXI, 1950, 238-40.

39. Literally 'turned round', in the sense of a criminal who became master of a kingdom.

40. Faral and Bastin, ed. cit., 537-44. The first line alludes to Branch XIII, in which Reynard was allegedly dead but very much alive in fact.

41. Admirably explained ibid., 532-7.

42. See above, pp. 189-95.

43. Faral and Bastin, ed. cit., 534, note 1.

44. ed. A. Foulet, Princeton, 1929.

45. ed. H. Roussel, Paris, SATF, 1961.

46. ed. G. Raynaud and H. Lemaître, 2 vols., Paris, 1914.

Chapter 9

MEDIEVAL THEATRE

I. THE BEGINNINGS OF MEDIEVAL DRAMA

ALMOST all verse works of the twelfth and thirteenth centuries constituted dramatic entertainment inasmuch as they
were designed to be presented by a jongleur before an
assembly. The high proportion of dialogue even in many lives of
saints and *chansons de geste* would surely have invited the jongleur
to modulate his voice according to the character speaking. There is
no indication in such instances that different roles were interpreted
by different characters, although the 'chantefable' *Aucassin et
Nicolete* poses particular problems, as we have seen.[1] This dramatic
element present in varying degrees in most early medieval literature
clearly did not constitute theatre in the full sense. The question of
when and how the first French plays were composed and performed
plunges us yet again into the mist-shrouded region of *Origins*, to
which the early history of the *chansons de geste*, of lyric poetry, of
amour courtois, of the romances, of fables and *fabliaux*, inevitably
leads the inquisitive scholar. Is it possible to speak of a continuity of
tradition linking the Roman theatre to the earliest French theatre?
Is the debt to classical sources, so evident in outstanding playwrights
of later centuries – Corneille, Racine, etc. – to be found already in
the first French plays extant? To such categorical questions the
answer can only be a firm no, but even so it needs to be hedged about
with qualifications. We do not know what forms of public entertainment subsisted in the centuries following the collapse of the Roman
Empire, but however turbulent that epoch of invasions and migra-
tions of Germanic tribes across the face of Europe, it is inconceivable
that all dramatic representation should have ceased for several
hundred years. The 'mimi' of Roman times continued to flourish
even though the classical Roman theatre died out and the very
terms 'comedy' and 'tragedy' were no longer understood in their
full and original sense.[2] The 'mimi' were certainly the authentic
ancestors of the 'jongleurs', a term which began to oust the older
one in the ninth century.[3] The argument, such as it is, soon turns
circle, for we have to confess that we simply do not know whether

the 'mimes' and their descendants produced entertainment to which words like 'theatre' and 'play' could fairly be attached, but when scenes of comedy and horseplay began to appear in certain religious plays, when gleeful devils escorted sinners into the jaws of hell, these were not brand-new inventions, but adaptations of the jongleurs' antics.[4]

If this popular tradition is doomed to remain for ever a mystery, is it not possible to turn to more erudite sources for information, and in any case would not the sophisticated theatre of classical antiquity have depended on such sources for its survival? The missing link appears to be provided by the six Latin plays of the tenth-century Benedictine nun of Gandersheim in Saxony, Hrotsvitha.[5] They deal with the lives of certain early Christian martyrs, but their literary model, so the author claims in her preface, was Terence, whose works were frequently copied in medieval *scriptoria*. The dialogue of these remarkable plays is crisp and lively, and they are by no means as solemn and ascetic as their subjects suggest, as when Dulcitius, governor of Thessalonica, in the play bearing his name, thinks he is embracing some beautiful Christian girls, but through a strange delusion is passionately clutching saucepans, frying-pans, and kettles to his bosom, emerging as black as soot from this culinary dalliance.[6] Only one minute stage direction in one manuscript has survived to suggest that these plays were actually performed.[7] The likelihood is that they were normally read in private, as also were the plays of Terence. Only one manuscript of Hrotsvitha's complete works has survived, and she appears to have had no predecessors or imitators. It may be that certain crucial manuscripts have long since disappeared, but if this was part of an active, living theatre, it is likely that some references at least to Hrotsvitha and her plays would have survived, but this is not the case.[8] A few other medieval Latin works with antecedents in classical comedy have been preserved, but only sporadically. The misunderstandings of the theatre of antiquity which they betray lead to the conclusion that there was no clear and continuous line of development.

II. THE EARLIEST MEDIEVAL DRAMATIC WORK EXTANT

It is not without irony that the Christian Church, that inexorable enemy of the theatre, should eventually have given rise to a new theatre; ironical too that that theatre should have accepted comic scenes from the jongleur's repertoire which were the fore-runners of later independent comic productions. From an early age, parts of a sermon entitled *Contra Judaeos, Paganos et Arianos sermo de symbolo*, written apparently in the fifth or sixth century and falsely attributed to St Augustine, used to be read at the Christmas matins. A separate voice was assigned to each of the various prophets who foretold the coming of Christ, and from the thirteenth century onwards, rubrics indicate that characters wore appropriate costume and disguise, e.g., *Johannes Baptista: pilosa veste et longis capillis, barbatus, palmam tenens*[9] (John the Baptist, wearing a shaggy garment, with long hair, bearded, holding a palm). Particular attention is usually drawn nowadays to the *tropes*, embellishments of particular aspects of the liturgy, which from their beginnings were already plays in miniature. The simplest, preserved in a manuscript of St Gall, dates from the middle of the tenth century and was sung antiphonally before the Introit of the Mass for Easter morning:

Item de Resurrectione Domini

Concerning the resurrection of the Lord

Interrogatio:
Quem queritis in sepulchro, Christicole?
Responsio:
Iesum Nazareneum crucifixum, o caelicolae.
Non est hic, surrexit sicut predixerat; ite, nuntiate quia surrexit de sepulchro.
Resurrexi.[10]

Question:
Whom seek you in the tomb, followers of Christ?
Response:
Jesus of Nazareth who has been crucified, oh dwellers in heaven.
He is not here, He has arisen as He had foretold: go forth, announce that He has arisen from the tomb.
I have arisen.

The opening question is asked by angels standing before the empty sepulchre, and the reply is given by the Marys. Many versions expanded this primitive form, and strove to moderate the abrupt switch from the declaration of the angel: 'Non est hic, surrexit', etc., to the words of Christ Himself: 'Resurrexi', etc.[11] By the eleventh century, elementary 'stage directions' were being added, e.g., *Indutus presbyter sacris vestibus stet post altare, et dicat alta voce* (Let the priest wearing holy robes stand behind the altar, and let him say in a loud voice):

Quem queritis in sepulchro, Christicole? . . .

Whom seek you in the tomb, followers of Christ?

Another version places the altar between the 'angel' and the 'Marys', thus incorporating it very clearly into the setting. Clearly the seeds of drama were sprouting here, although there was as yet no attempt actually to *impersonate* the characters represented. Transference of the *trope* to the end of the early morning service of matins – a suitable place for a dialogue represented as taking place in the early morning[12] – by severing it from the context which had brought it into being, gave it an independent existence, so allowing a freer development in which full dramatic representation was possible. The popularity of this Easter play, the *Visitatio Sepulchri*, is shown by its having survived in over 400 manuscripts whose dates span the whole of the Middle Ages.[13]

The Easter *trope* served as a model for the earliest Christmas play, the *Officium Pastorum*:

Quem queritis in praesepe, pastores, dicite?	Whom seek you in the stables, shepherds, say?

Transference from the Introit of the High Mass on Christmas Day to matins enabled this *trope* to develop along the lines of the Easter prototype. In this way early Nativity plays evolved of a type whose popularity was to last down the centuries, though fewer versions have survived from medieval times than of the *Visitatio Sepulchri*.

Transition from Latin to the vernacular is clearly revealed in certain plays in which both languages are used. The earliest extant in which the vernacular begins to appear prominently is the *Sponsus*, a dramatisation of the parable of the Wise and Foolish Virgins, dating, like the *Chanson de Roland* and the poems of Guillaume IX, from the end of the eleventh century.[14] Nearly half the play is in French.[15] The symbolical value of the story, with its warning to humanity not to drift into idle, sinful ways, is admirably exploited. The whole play was set to music, which has survived. Particularly dramatic is Gabriel's warning to the Virgins to remain vigilant as they await the coming of the Lord:

Oiet, virgines, aiso que vos dirum! Aiseet presen que vos comandarum! Atendet Sponsum! Jhesu salvaire a nom Gaire noi dormet! aisel espos que vos hor atendet.	Listen, virgins, to what we shall tell you! Leave as soon as we order you to do so! Await the bridegroom! Jesus the Saviour He is called (sleep but a little), that bridegroom whom you now await.
Venit en terra per los vostres pechet, de la virgine en Betleem fo net, e flum Jorda lavet e bateet Gaire noi dormet aisel espos que vos hor atendet. (lines 21–30)	He came to earth because of your sins, of the Virgin was He born in Bethlehem, in the River Jordan washed and baptised (sleep but a little), that bridegroom whom you now await.

The lamentations of the Foolish Virgins, which take up nearly a third of the play, are in rhymed decasyllabic Latin verse, each stanza of four lines ending in the vigorous and poignant refrain in the popular idiom 'Dolentas, chaitivas, trop i avem dormit' (Grieving wretches, too long have we slept) (later counterbalanced exactly in the Wise Virgins' reproaches in which *avet*, second person plural, takes the place of the first person plural *avem*). Their request to the Wise Virgins to give them some of their oil, the reply directing them to the merchants, the latter's refusal to help, all are couched in the vernacular, whose peculiarities are owed to a revision of the original French text by a scribe from the Limousin region.[16] All the crucial aspects of the play are expressed in a language which the ordinary people could understand. Latin is retained for the static moments of the action and so seems to be withdrawing gradually into the background. As a play it is very slight and relies heavily on its source, and yet its artistic merit is considerable, sufficiently so to prevent our thinking of the growth of religious drama as a simple vegetative process, moving progressively from threadbare origins to a splendour not achieved before the later Middle Ages. The *Sponsus* has been hailed as 'l'un des drames les plus artistiques et, en même temps, l'un des plus poignants que nous ait légués le Moyen Age'.[17]

III. THE 'MYSTÈRE D'ADAM'

It is not inappropriate that the earliest extant play whose spoken parts were entirely in the vernacular, the *Mystère d'Adam*,[18] should be concerned principally with Adam and Eve. Significantly enough, however, the stage directions are still in Latin, for they are addressed to the clergy who would have provided the actors. Dating from about the middle of the twelfth century, this may be the first religious drama surviving to have been performed outside the Church.[19] The general subject, redemption made necessary by sin, was intended for the liturgy of Septuagesima Sunday[20] as a preparation for Lent. The three sections of the play, the expulsion of Adam and Eve from Paradise, the killing of Abel by Cain, the procession of the prophets, are united in looking forward to the coming of the Saviour, a theme which emerges more clearly as the play proceeds. The Latin *didascalia* describe accessories and costumes in some detail, stage-settings and scenery rather more generally. Paradise is to be in a fairly high place, surrounded by curtains, so that those inside can only be seen from the shoulder upwards. Adam wears a red tunic, Eve a white garment. Near the forbidden tree an artificial serpent is to rise up, and Eve must appear to listen to it. After the Fall, they are driven from Paradise, and, in humbler garb, cultivate some land while the Devil plants weeds. Noisy demons take them off to hell from which rise clouds of smoke. In the next scene Cain and Abel, the former in red, the latter in white, till the soil. Two large stones represent the altars at which they offer sacrifices. In the procession of prophets announcing the coming of Christ, the appearance of each is carefully described.

A striking feature is the vivid character portrayal, nowhere more effective than in the Devil's temptation of Eve:

Diabolus
Eva, ça sui venuz a toi.

Eve, I have come to see you.

Eva
Di moi, Sathan, e tu pur quoi?

Tell me, Satan, why?

Diabolus
Jo vois querant tun pru, tun honor.

I am seeking something to your advantage, that will bring you honour.

Eva
Ço dunge Deu!

God grant it!

Diabolus
N'aiez poür!
Molt a grant tens que jo ai apris
Toz les conseils de paraïs:
Une partie t'en dirrai.

Fear not!
A very long time ago I learned all the secrets of paradise.
I shall tell you some of them.

Eva
Ore le comence, e jo l'orrai.

Now begin and I shall listen.

Diabolus
Orras me tu?

Will you?

Eva
Si frai bien,
Ne te curcerai de rien.

Yes indeed, I shall not vex you in any way.

Diabolus
Celeras m'en?

Will you keep the secret?

Eva
Oïl, par foi.

Yes, in faith.

Diabolus
Iert descovert!

It will be revealed!

Eva
Nenil par moi.

Not by me.

Diabolus
Or me mettrai en ta creance,
Ne voil de toi altre fiance.

Now I shall put my trust in you.
I want no other assurance from you.

Eva
Bien te pois creire a ma parole.

You can take my word for it.

Diabolus
Tu as esté en bone escole.
Jo vi Adam, mais trop est fols.

You have been well taught.
I saw Adam, but he is very foolish.

Eva
Un poi est durs.

He is a little stubborn.

Diabolus
Il serra mols.
Il est plus dors que n'est emfers.

He will soften up.
He is harder than hell.

Eva
Il est mult francs.

He is very independent.

Diabolus
Ainz est mult serf.
Cure nen voelt prendre de soi;
Car la prenge sevals de toi.
Tu es fieblette e tendre chose
E es plus fresche que n'est rose;
Tu es plus blanche que cristal,
Que nief que chiet sor glace
   enval;
Mal cuple em fist li criator:
Tu es trop tendre e il trop dur;
Mais neporquant tu es plus sage,
En grant sens as mis tun
   corrage . . .

On the contrary he is very much of
a slave. He does not want to look
after himself. At least look after
yourself. You are weak and tender,
fresher than a rose, whiter than crys-
tal, than snow falling on ice in the
valley. The Creator made an ill-
matched couple: you are too tender
and he is too hard. But nevertheless
you are wiser, and have acted very
sensibly.

(lines 205–34)

Eve is coy, prone to flattery, the Devil a skilled seducer in the courtly tradition. The play counts among the best dramatic productions of the French Middle Ages.

Rather like the stained glass and stone carvings of medieval churches, contemporary religious drama was essentially edifying in its basic aims and spirit, and the considerable artistic value attained was not an end in itself. This early theatre was clearly not conceived primarily as entertainment, though one wonders what amount of horseplay accompanied the final demise of the Foolish Virgins in the *Sponsus*: 'Modo accipiant eas demones, et precipitentur in infernum'[21] (Now let the demons receive them and hurl them into hell). The descent of Adam and Eve into hell was an even noisier and more fearsome occasion according to the extraordinarily detailed stage directions.[22]

IV. 'COURTOIS D'ARRAS'

The twelfth and thirteenth centuries have not bequeathed us many French plays on biblical subjects. *Les Trois Maries*, *La Sainte Resurreccion*, and *Courtois d'Arras*[23] are the most notable ones. The last named, based on the parable of the prodigal son, deserves attention because of its bold adaptation to a contemporary setting, no doubt imitating in this respect the most outstanding miracle play of these centuries, *Le Jeu de Saint Nicolas*,[24] originating from the same town, Arras. Composed in the early thirteenth century, *Courtois d'Arras* contains 652 octosyllabic lines, all but nine of which consist of dialogue. It is possible that this was in fact intended as a dramatic monologue for recital by a single jongleur (there are no stage directions), but with its total of nine characters it could well have been presented as a play. The treatment of the biblical source is freer and more imaginative than in the *Mystère d'Adam*, and the element of local colour very strong indeed.

Courtois, the prodigal son, is attracted to a tavern by the cries of the innkeeper's lad:

Chaiens est li vins de Soisçons!	There is wine from Soissons in here!
Sor l'erbe verde et sor les jons	On the green grass and on the rushes
on i boit a hanap d'argent;	you can drink from a silver goblet.
çaiens boivent tote la gent,	Everybody drinks in here, both fools
chaiens boivent et fol et sage,	and wise men, and nobody leaves a
e se n'i laisse nus son gaje!	pledge. All you need do is chalk up
Ne l'estuet fors conter la dete . . .[25]	your debt.

Two hussies, Manchevaire and Pourette, in league with the innkeeper, soon make the poor innocent[26] drunk and steal his money. To pay his debts to the innkeeper Courtois has to leave him his tunic and breeches. After a miserable existence as a swineherd, the once boastful Courtois returns meekly home and is heartily welcomed by his father. The play ends with the singing of the *Te Deum*.

V. THE 'JEU DE SAINT NICOLAS' OF JEAN BODEL

Apart from the Bible, miracles wrought by saints were to provide a fertile source for drama. These stories, popular in monasteries and church schools, were told and dramatised in Latin before adaptations into French had introduced them to the masses. Vernacular versions tended on the whole to be bolder and more ingenious, none more so than Jean Bodel's astonishing *Le Jeu de Saint Nicolas*,[27] far surpassing in length and inventiveness the Latin play which had preceded it by some 50 years, the *Ludus super iconia Sancti Nicholai* by Hilarius.[28] That the first French miracle play is about St Nicholas is no less appropriate than the beginning of biblical drama with the story of Adam and Eve, for St Nicholas, largely an accretion of legend but with some basis in history, was a very popular saint, friendlier, more approachable as it were, than most. In England alone more than 400 churches are dedicated to him. Many tales were told about him, including his saving of three sisters from a shameful life by throwing bags of gold down their chimney on three successive nights – hence the origin of the Santa Claus myth.

Writing between the third and fourth crusades about the year 1200,[29] in the days of Richard Cœur-de-Lion, Jean Bodel deemed it wise to connect the legend with the wars against the Saracens. The story, as he told it, is as follows:

A Christian army which has invaded Saracen territory, is annihilated. Only one Christian, a 'prud'homme' (a man of noble character), found kneeling in prayer before a statue of St Nicholas, is spared. Questioned about the statue, he tells the Saracens of St Nicholas's power to guard treasure. The Saracen king puts this to the test, but when the treasure is stolen, orders the Christian to be put to death. The treasure is restored just in time (as in Hilarius's version) and the Saracens are so impressed that they are converted to the Christian faith.

So bare a summary does no justice to the zest and skill which Bodel displayed in this, the longest and richest play of the times, containing over 1,500 lines of varying lengths, the majority octo-syllabics. Tavern scenes which introduce us to the thieves who stole the unguarded treasure, but restored it when St Nicholas appeared to them in a dream, take up very nearly half the play.[30] These scenes could have been far more succinct without detracting from the basic plot, and it is clear that their purpose – like that of the much shorter tavern scenes of *Courtois d'Arras* – was simply to entertain. Details of the wines drunk in the taverns (both wines and inn are unashamedly, delightfully French and of the Arras region, though we are supposed to be in the land of the Saracens!); the debts carefully chalked up by the innkeeper and his lad; the dice-games played so heartily (with none of the ruefulness displayed by Rutebeuf); the racy, popular, realistic idiom of the gamblers, all indicate that Bodel was drawing on personal observations if not direct experience.[31] In the following lines the Saracen king's messenger stops for a quick throw of the dice before departing on his mission to summon the Saracen armies to help stem the Christian invasion:

Auberon (king's messenger)
Giete as plus poins, sans papetourt.

Throw for the highest number of points, and no cheating.

Clikés (gambler)
Il s'en vont, n'en ai nul assis . . .

They're off, I haven't stopped any of them.

Auberon
Par foi! tu n'as ne cinc ne sis;
Ains i a ternes et un as.

I'faith, you've got neither five nor six, but two threes and a one.

Clikés
Che ne sont que set poins, elas!
Con par sui mesqueans a dés!

That only makes seven points, alas!
How unlucky I am at dice.

Auberon
Toutes eures giet jou aprés . . .
Biaus dous amis, coi que tu aies,
Tu n'en goutas et si le paies:
J'ai quaernes, le plus mal gieu.

Anyway I throw next . . . My fine, fair friend, whatever you may have, you didn't taste any, but you're paying. I've got double fours for the worst part of my throw.

Clikés
Honnis soient tout li courlieu
Car tous jours sont il a le fuite.

A plague on all messengers, they're always a fly lot.

Auberon
Biaus ostes, chis vassaus m'acuite;
Il me dist lait, mais nequedent.

Fair host, this young gentleman pays for me. He insulted me, but no matter.

Innkeeper
Va, va, mar vit li piés le dent.
                (lines 300-14)

Away with you, and woe that the messenger met the thief.

Similar games are described later in greater detail, amidst much excitement, quarrelling, shouting, and drinking. The play, more entertaining than edifying, is a fascinating mixture of reality and fantasy. Scenes of daily life alternate with descents of angels and mysterious apparitions of St Nicholas; certain characters drawn from the author's imagination (e.g., those of the Saracen kings) are only vaguely delineated, whereas the rascally thieves who frequented the inns are given their individual traits and are fully rounded personages. The heroism of the Christian army, facing certain death, is evoked in a short but vivid scene strongly reminiscent of the *chansons de geste*: a young knight shows that he has 'grant cuer en cors petit' (409) (a great heart in a small body) and an angel assures them of salvation. The rich invention and sheer creativity of this play have led to the suggestion that it was in the domain of the theatre that medieval literature, so respectful elsewhere of traditional style and rhetoric, achieved its greatest originality. At the very least, it has been claimed, Jean Bodel may be deemed 'un individu qu'on ne peut confondre avec aucun autre'.[32]

VI. THE 'MIRACLE DE THÉOPHILE' OF RUTEBEUF

The second surviving French miracle play, like the *Jeu de Saint Nicolas*, is by an author whose name we have met elsewhere: the *Miracle de Théophile*, written by Rutebeuf, probably in 1261. The play recalls the Faust legend, for Théophile, embittered at having been passed over for promotion and left destitute by his bishop, rebelled against the Church and sold his soul to the Devil. This new allegiance enabled him to regain his lost offices, but he fell prey to despair when he realised the enormity of his sins. His long, fervent prayers to the Virgin Mary secured his salvation. Needless to say, this solemn work has none of the knockabout boisterousness of Bodel's play. Its most striking characteristic is a note of lyrical intensity, particularly in Théophile's lamentations over his poverty, couched in terms so similar to those Rutebeuf used to describe his own miseries that he evidently identified with his hero:

Ahi! Ahi! Diex, rois de gloire,
Tant vous ai eü en memoire
Tout ai doné et despendu
Et tout ai aus povres tendu:
Ne m'est remez vaillant un sac.
Bien m'a dit li evesque 'Eschac!'
Et m'a rendu maté en l'angle:
Sanz avoir m'a lessié tout sangle.
Or m'estuet il morir de fain
Se je n'envoi ma robe au pain.
Et ma mesnie que fera?
Ne sai se Diex les pestera . . .[33]

Oh! Oh! God, King of Glory, so much have I had you in mind, I have given everything away and offered it all to the poor. Nothing to the value of a single halfpenny is left to me. With good reason the bishop has said to me 'Checkmate' and has defeated me in a corner of the board. He has left me without money, quite destitute. Now I shall have to die of hunger unless I sell my robe for bread. And what will my household do? I know not if God will feed them . . .

In depicting Théophile's degradation, Rutebeuf could have introduced harlots as in *Courtois d'Arras* and gambling and drinking as in the *Jeu de Saint Nicolas*, but he eschewed all such ornaments, concentrating instead on the subtle changes in Théophile's character as he became the Devil's vassal and vented his spite on his fellow clergy. His repentance, which takes up nearly a quarter of the play, was the occasion for Rutebeuf to display his skill in handling varying and complex verse measures, lines of four, six, eight, and twelve syllables all being used. The metaphors referring to the Virgin Mary, though not original, have a lyrical beauty of their own:

Si comme en la verriere
Entre et reva arriere
Li solaus que n'entame,
Ainsinc fus virge entiere
Quant Diex, qui es ciex iere,
Fist de toi mere et dame.
(lines 492–7)

Just as the sun shines through the glass window without breaking it, so you were a virgin most pure, when God in heaven made of you a mother and a lady.

Though not lacking in dramatic quality, this is the work of a poet more than of a playwright. Like the otherwise very different *Courtois d'Arras*, the *Miracle de Théophile* would have lent itself to recitation by a single jongleur, though it could equally well have been acted as a play.

VII. THE FOURTEENTH-CENTURY 'MIRACLES DE NOTRE DAME'

From the fourteenth century a collection of forty *Miracles de Notre Dame*, each consisting on average of approximately 2,000 lines, has survived.[34] Recent study of the sole extant manuscript has shown that these plays were performed at the annual meetings of the Paris Guild of Goldsmiths from 1339 to 1382, with a gap in 1354 and 1358–60, possibly owed to the popular insurrections of those years.[35] Each tells of a miracle wrought by the Virgin Mary, who rescues a repentant sinner, or intervenes in person to right some grievous wrong or dreadful calamity. Apart from the traditional Marian literature such as Gautier de Coinci's non-dramatic *Miracles de Notre Dame*, themselves drawn from abundant Latin sources, their sources were many and varied, so much so that the collection has been described as 'a hoard of medieval legends'.[36] The *Dramatis Personae*, usually listing about 25 characters, but rising in one instance to as many as 46, contain some interesting and significant juxtapositions: Bailiff, Porter, Cochet the Executioner, God, Our Lady, Gabriel, Michael, First Poor Man, Second Poor Man, Third Poor Man, Saint John, First Nun, Second Nun . . .[37] Rich and poor, earthly and heavenly, all rub shoulders in an easy familiarity. Nothing, it has been said, is more natural in these plays than the supernatural.[38] The following summaries of two of the miracles will give some idea of their nature.

Miracle vii: 'Cy conmence un miracle de Nostre Dame, d'une nonne qui laissa son abbaie pour s'en aler avec un chevalier . . .' (Here begins a miracle of Our Lady, concerning a nun who left her abbey and absconded with a knight).

A knight finds the nun with whom he is in love praying to a statue of the Virgin Mary. She finally agrees to yield to his entreaties only if he will marry her. The Virgin, accompanied as always by Gabriel and Michael, decides to warn the nun of her folly. Saying a last prayer in chapel, the nun finds the doorway blocked by the statue of the Virgin. The following night the same thing happens, and on the third she neglects her prayers and steals away. There is consternation next day when it is discovered that she is missing. In the next scene they have been happily married for some years, and have two sons. The Virgin decides to intervene to call her former servant back from sin to grace. Remembering the warning she has received many years ago, the former nun persuades her husband to take her back to the abbess. Their squire places their sons in the care of an uncle. The wife is received back in the nunnery, and the husband becomes a monk.

Miracle xxvi: 'Cy conmence un miracle de Nostre Dame, conment elle garda une femme d'estre arse' (Here begins a miracle of Our Lady, how she saved a woman from being burned).

Guibourc, infuriated by false rumours that she has slept with her son-in-law Aubin, decides to put an end to them once for all by having Aubin put to death. She has him strangled, and tries to make it appear that he has died in his sleep. The bailiff examines the body, finds bruises on the neck, and arrests the whole family. To save the others Guibourc confesses and is sentenced to be burned at the stake. She prays fervently to the Virgin Mary. Just as the burning is to begin, God (=Christ) appears and orders His mother to rescue Guibourc. Gabriel and Michael descend, singing a rondel in praise of God's mercy. Guibourc is saved, gives away her possessions to the poor, and amid scenes of prayer and devotion, becomes a nun.

Despite their subject, there is little mysticism in these plays. All is cosily matter-of-fact and realistic. Christ, the Virgin, and the angels are creatures of flesh and blood, though in an actual performance the singing of rondels by the angels as they descended from heaven may have served adequately to distinguish them from common mortals. As plays they are often touching in their sincerity and extremely naïve faith, but it is as tableaux of life and beliefs in fourteenth-century France that they have considerable importance.

VIII. THE 'PASSION DU PALATINUS'

Although no stage directions have survived with the miracle plays, it is likely that they used a number of juxtaposed stage settings out of doors, the action moving to the appropriate setting or 'mansion'.[39] It seems that the average miracle needed some eight sets,[40] whereas the passion plays which began to appear in the thirteenth century or earlier, and acquired mammoth proportions in the course of the fourteenth and fifteenth centuries, required many more. Some of the action could have taken place in a neutral foreground.[41] The earliest extant passion play is the fourteenth-century *Passion du Palatinus*, a work of nearly 2,000 lines.[42]

In the opening lines Jesus expresses His wish to eat with His disciples. 'Ainz que ma vie soit pour le pueple finee' (line 4) (Before my life is finished for the sake of the people). Peter and John go ahead to make the arrangements while children sing songs of welcome. On His arrival Mary Magdalen anoints Christ's feet and Jesus forgives her her sins. The story of the Last Supper as told in the gospels is followed closely. Much is made of Judas's betrayal, and in a lively scene he protests to the Jews that he has only been given 28 pieces of silver. Much is made also of Pilate's reluctance to condemn Jesus, and the responsibility of the Jews in this respect is heavily insisted upon. A gruelling scene describes the scourging of Jesus, which stops only when His tormentors are weary, and later the fashioning of the nails for the crucifixion by the blacksmith's wife, her husband's hands having been miraculously paralysed. (At least we are not told, as in later passion plays, that the nails were deliberately made blunt in order to cause greater pain when they pierced Christ's flesh.[43]) By the time the play is little over half-way through,

Christ has already been crucified. The passion is not the climax of the play. This is revealed after the harrowing of hell in which a little light relief is provided by the bickering of an allegorical figure named Enfer and Satan, both fearful of the coming of Christ. The last scene takes us to the tomb where the three Marys lament over Christ's death, but even here a little distraction is provided by the introduction of a spice-merchant who boasts of the magical properties of his herbs with almost as much extravagance and effrontery as is found in the most outstanding extant poem on this subject, the *Dit de l'Herberie* by Rutebeuf:[44] they will restore lost youth, the power to make love, etc. At the end the tomb is found to be empty, Christ has risen from the dead, and because of His sacrifice, the way to Paradise is open to all of us. As with so many religious plays the *Te Deum* was sung at the end.

The original aspects of this early passion play point all in the same direction, towards an earthy, matter-of-fact realism, marked by a touch of sadism and a little humour at times. The very nature of the enterprise cannot have favoured a more mystical approach, the whole point being to bring to life before the eyes of the people the passion of Our Lord, and to present it in human terms that they could understand. Here, as in the miracle plays, something of the mentality of the age is revealed.

IX. THE FIFTEENTH-CENTURY PASSION PLAYS

In the fifteenth century the picture was broadened further and passion plays appeared in ever-increasing numbers and dimensions: *La Passion de Sémur* (anonymous); *Le Mystère de la Vengeance Jhesu Crist* and the *Mystère de la Passion*, both by Eustache Marcadé, all three belonging to the first third of the century: *Le Mystère de la Passion* by Arnoul Gréban, written about 1450 and generally acknowledged as the masterpiece of the genre; *La Passion d'Autun* (anonymous) belonging to the later fifteenth century; and the *Mystère de la Passion* by Jean Michel, a revision of Gréban's work which appeared in 1486. They dealt with the whole span of Christ's life from the Nativity onwards. A favourite introduction was provided by an allegorical debate in Paradise in which Miséricorde convinced Justice of the necessity of a redemption for mankind, so paving the way for the coming of Christ. Ambitions soared in these cosmic creations, ten to fifteen and more times the length of the *Passion du Palatinus*, involving as many as 400 roles and taking several days to produce.[45] Not only was the chronological scope widened, but the intellectual one as well. These plays could be appreciated in different ways, at different levels, according to the mental capacities of the spectator. The entire medieval concept of man and his place in the universe was implicated, Manichean doctrines were exposed and attacked, the works of the greatest medieval theologians were quoted by these most enterprising, diligent, and erudite of play-wrights. Special companies of actors came into being, the famous *Confréries de la Passion*, the formation of which went back at least to the late fourteenth century.[46] On occasions whole towns might be involved in this industry devoted to reliving the most striking and dramatic moments in the history of the Christian world. So daunting is the size of the mysteries that even today not all have been properly edited, and information on the customs and outlook of the later Middle Ages remains to be gleaned from their pages. In aims and dimensions they are the most impressive works of the times, and if medieval literature began with works which are epic in quality, it may be said to have ended with works which are epic in quantity. What of their literary and dramatic character-istics? Dramatically centred on the scourging and crucifixion of Christ, frequently treated with macabre realism surpassing that of the *Passion du Palatinus*, they end none the less with the Resurrec-tion and hence with a ray of hope and optimism sometimes lost sight of in histories of literature anxious to underline the beauties of the Renaissance dawn by dwelling on the intense gloom of the night preceding it.[47] It remains true, however, that no authors of passion plays could match in the quality of their writing the aspirations they set themselves. There is immense talent in these works, much drama, at times (particularly in Gréban) truly poetic and imaginative touches, but in the end they impress by the in-dustry they display, not by any genius. It was as though the hero who towered over all others in the Christian universe, archetype of countless martyrs, eluded these ambitious playwrights at the end, for concrete details of the Passion were inevitably so much easier to depict on the stage than its spiritual significance. But this, of course, is no more than the literary judgement of a twentieth-century manual. For thousands of spectators these plays may well have constituted a unique and intensely moving occasion, an utterly convincing asseveration of the faith by which they lived and died. On the other hand, the fact that the later Middle Ages evidently felt the need of some such reassurance has another kind of significance.

X. COMIC THEATRE OF THE THIRTEENTH CENTURY: 'LE GARÇON ET L'AVEUGLE', 'LE JEU DE LA FEUILLÉE', 'LE JEU DE ROBIN ET MARION'

That the secular theatre has left far fewer traces may merely mean that there was less incentive or less money to devote to the recording of it. As Faral has observed: 'Tout donne à penser qu'une production comique, intense même, a pu exister, sans que rien en ait survécu'.[48] The earliest farce extant, *Le Garçon et l'Aveugle*, a short piece of 265 lines, was written sometime between 1266 and 1282.[49] A young lad plays tricks on a blind man while pretending to help him with his begging, and eventually makes off with his savings. The humour may appear crude and heartless, but the blind man is exposed as a lecherous, lying old hypocrite with plenty of money hidden away, so no element of sympathy or compassion can intervene to spoil the comic effect. The theme reappears later, even in the passion plays,[50] and, in a general sense, is that of the *Roman de Renart* and so many *fabliaux*: the wily villain who has met his match.[51]

From the late 1270s and early 1280s have survived two remarkable plays by the Arras poet and musician Adam de la Halle: *Le Jeu de la Feuillée* and *Le Jeu de Robin et Marion*.[52] The former is a local revue, almost 1,100 lines in length, full of topical allusions, composed on the occasion of Adam's departure for Paris to continue his studies there. Clearly intended solely for the townsfolk of Arras, the play contains much lighthearted banter at the expense of various named individuals. Significant is the presence of a 'fool' whose prattlings hide a sharp wit.[53] The action apparently takes place at Pentecost, when the women of Arras believed that fairies were wont to appear, and the shrine of Our Lady was exposed in the Petit Marché under a *feuillée*, a canopy of green foliage.[54] The dialogue contains a good deal of barbed wit which doubtless hit its target on numerous occasions, as when the physician declared that Henri, Adam's father, suffered from 'uns maus c'on claime avarisse' (line 203) (an illness called avarice) and went on:

Je sui maistre bien acanlés,	I am a doctor with plenty of
S'ai des gens amont et aval	patients, and I have got people up
Cui je garirai de chest mal;	hill and down dale whom I shall
Nommeement en cheste vile	cure of this illness; in this town
En ai jou bien plus de deus mile	especially I have more than two
Ou il n'a respas ne confort.	thousand for whom there is no cure
Halois en gist ja a le mort,	or relief. Halois is at death's door
Entre lui et Robert Cosel,	because of it, also Robert Cosel, and
Et che bietu le Faverel;	Faverel [bietu=?] and all their
Aussi fait trestous leur lignages.	kinsfolk.

(206–15)

Le Jeu de Robin et Marion is a dramatisation of the favourite *pastourelle* theme: a knight makes love to a shepherdess and attempts to carry her off. In this instance she escapes, rejoins her beloved Robin, and shepherds and shepherdesses cavort merrily on the green meadows. Marion, not unlike Nicolete in this respect,[55] has a firmer and more resolute character than her lover. Robin is an amusing braggart whose courage is great only when danger is remote, but in singing and dancing he excels, and distinguishes himself by rescuing a lamb from the wolf, though his clumsy handling of it horrifies Marion. The peasants feast on bread, cheese, apples, and water, and play a variety of games together, fully described. The threat posed by the burlesque 'chevalier' soon passes, and its gay, carefree, comic-opera atmosphere, enlivened by the sprightly melodious tunes, makes this the most charming of the medieval French texts written solely for amusement and entertainment.

XI. THE 'ESTOIRE DE GRISELDIS'

The first surviving non-religious play that is wholly serious in its basic theme (though there are moments of comic relief) is the *Estoire de Griseldis*.[56] This dramatisation of a well-known medieval tale dates from 1395.

> The reluctant marquis de Saluce is persuaded by his barons to marry in order to ensure his succession. He chooses a humble peasant girl, but since the Court despises her on account of her origin, the marquis puts her constancy and obedience to the test by making her undergo all manner of tribulations, such as depriving her of her children, pretending to have their marriage annulled and to be intending to remarry. At last, having demonstrated to his satisfaction that Griseldis is in fact the ideal wife, he drops the pretence and all ends in feasting and merriment.

The story of Griselda (familiar to readers of Chaucer's *Clerkes Tale*) first appeared in 1353 as the last *novella* in Boccaccio's *Decameron*. It certainly had earlier sources, possibly in folklore, but these are unknown. It was retold in Latin (the name becoming Griseldis) by Petrarch in 1373, translated into French between 1384 and 1389 by Philippe de Mézières, tutor of the future Charles VI and author of numerous religious and didactic works in Latin and French, and incorporated by him into a work on marriage, *Le Livre de la Vertu*,[57] written between 1384 and 1389. This is the direct source of the French play, and it is not impossible that Philippe de Mézières wrote the play also or at least had a hand in its composition. The staging of the play must have presented difficulties, since some 25 changes of scene are involved in a total length of 2,609 lines. Use was very likely made of the simultaneous stage-settings, the *mansions* of the type so necessary in the passion plays. However extreme the marquis's treatment of his wife appears, the play is realistic inasmuch as it contains no allegorisations, no sermons, no divine intervention, and is interesting for its undoubted success in dramatising the basic story.

XII. THE FIFTEENTH-CENTURY SECULAR THEATRE: THE 'FARCE DE PIERRE PATHELIN'

In the fifteenth century the secular theatre was extremely active. Professional companies existed, bearing names such as *Les Enfants sans souci*, *Les Clercs de la Basoche*, etc.[58] Their shows consisted of a series of short plays, usually in a particular order. First would come the *sottie*, a curtain-raiser in which the 'fools' wore a special costume, a fool's cap with donkey's ears, particoloured dress with bells on their legs, carrying the bauble, mock symbol of office, in their hands. These actors belied their names, for they had to be nimble in both mind and body, masters of quick repartee, of puns, of jests satirical or obscene, concerned often with topicalities, clowns whose contortions and antics attracted the crowd and kept it amused.[59] The *sottie* would be followed by a monologue, known as a *sermon joyeux*, a mock sermon dealing with any one of a variety of scurrilous subjects.[60] A morality play, pointing to a lesson of some kind, would follow.[61] Finally would come a farce, dealing with such matters as quarrels between deceiving or bullying husbands and wives, or the perennial theme of the duper duped. About 150 farces have survived, a considerable number belonging to the sixteenth century, when they remained very popular. Some reached beyond the level of slapstick, notably the best known of those extant, the *Farce de Pierre Pathelin*, composed by an unknown author about 1465,[62] in truth more of a comedy than a true farce,[63] the sole medieval play still performed frequently at the present day.

Pathelin, a penniless lawyer, buys some cloth from a draper, whom he invites to his house to collect the money at a later date. When he does so he finds Pathelin apparently desperately ill in bed, prattling away in a mixture of foreign tongues:

> Vuacarme, lief gode man;
> Etlbelic boq iglughe golan;
> Henrien, Henrien, conselapen;
> Ych salgneb nede que maignen
> Grile, grile, schohehonden
> Zilop, zilop en mon que bouden . . .
> (lines 863–8)

The draper retires baffled. He accuses his shepherd of stealing some of his sheep, and has him up in court. The shepherd chooses Pathelin to defend him and is advised by Pathelin to play the simpleton and reply 'baa' to all questions. In court the draper is amazed to find Pathelin alive and well, and becomes hopelessly confused over his cloth and the stolen sheep, hence the judge's reiterated 'Revenons a ces moutons!' (Let us get back to those sheep!). The shepherd is eventually declared innocent, but when Pathelin asks him for his fee, the only reply he can get is 'Baa!' Pathelin ruefully confesses at the end that he, the duper, has been outwitted:

Or cuidoye estre sur tous maistre,
De trompeurs d'icy et d'ailleurs,
Des fort coureux et des bailleurs
De parolles en payement
A rendre au jour du jugement,
Et ung bergier des champs me
passe!

(lines 1588–92)

I thought I could outwit everybody,
tricksters from here and elsewhere,
bold adventurers and those who give
words as payment, to be settled on
Judgement Day, and a mere rustic
shepherd outdoes me!

The characters are vividly and amusingly portrayed: Pathelin with his ready wits and quick tongue, the draper naïve and avaricious, the shepherd a sly peasant who gets the better of them all, the judge a well-meaning magistrate hopelessly at sea amidst the subterfuges of Pathelin and his client.

The comic theatre of the late Middle Ages, more than the passion plays, pointed the way to future developments, and many are the similarities between the fifteenth-century farces and the theatre of Molière.[64]

NOTES

1. See above, pp. 207–8.
2. K. Young, *The Drama of the Medieval Church*, 2 vols., Oxford, 1933, I, 6–7.
3. E. Faral, *Les Jongleurs en France au Moyen Age*, Paris, 1910.
4. ibid., 31, 226–30.
5. H. Homeyer ed., *Hrotsvithae Opera*, Munich–Paderborn–Vienna, 1970.
6. For the symbolism of these utensils, see S. Sticca, 'Hrotswitha's Dulcitius and its spiritualis significatio', in *Hommages à M. Renard*, Brussels, 1969, vol. I, 700–6.
7. *Callimachus*, Scene viii: To the Spectators. This necessitates the reading *Expavete* in place of the more usual *Expaveo*.
8. Young, op. cit., I, 6–7.
9. ibid., II, 145.
10. ibid., I, 201.
11. ibid., I, 206.
12. For further reasons for this placing see ibid., I, 233.
13. See the very full treatment of the many additions and variations ibid., I, 239–410.
14. L.-P. Thomas ed., *Le Sponsus, Mystère des vierges sages et des vierges folles*, Paris, 1951.
15. To be precise, 45 out of the total of 105 lines.
16. Thomas, ed. cit., 76–113.
17. ibid., 50.
18. The most recent edition is that of W. Noomen, *Le Jeu d'Adam*, Paris, CFMA, 1971. The footnotes on pp. 5–6 of this work give details of other editions and studies of this text.
19. Doubt has recently been cast on this widely-held view, see W. Noomen, '*Le Jeu d'Adam*. Etude descriptive et analytique', *R*, LXXXIX, 1968, 145–193, esp. 190–3.
20. Noomen, ed. cit., 7–11.
21. Thomas, ed. cit., 186.
22. P. Studer ed., *Le Mystère d'Adam*, Manchester, 1918, reprinted 1928, 1949, 29.
23. *Les Trois Maries*, surviving only in a fragment of forty lines, has been edited by P. Meyer in *R*, XXXIII, 1904, 239–45; *La Sainte Resurreccion*,

also known as *La Résurrection du Sauveur*, surviving in a fragment of 372 lines, has been edited by J. G. Wright, Paris, CFMA, 1931; and *Courtois d'Arras* by E. Faral, Paris, CFMA, 1922.

24. See below.

25. Faral, ed. cit., lines 103–9.

26. Courtois seems an ironical choice of name for such a country bumpkin.

27. ed. F. J. Warne, Oxford, 1951, and A. Henry, Paris–Brussels, 1962.

28. Details of other works on St Nicholas which preceded Bodel's play are given by Warne in his excellent introduction.

29. Henry, ed. cit., 7, 181.

30. To be precise, 728 out of a total of 1,538 lines, more than half the play if we discount the 114 lines of the prologue, apocryphal in the view of Henry, ibid., 9–15.

31. Foulon, op. cit., 637–8.

32. Henry, ed. cit., 44.

33. Faral and Bastin, ed. cit., II, 179, lines 1–12.

34. ed. G. Paris and U. Robert, 8 vols., Paris, SATF, 1876–93.

35. G. Runnalls, 'The Miracles de Nostre Dames par personnages: Erasures in the MS, and the Dates of the Plays and the "Serventois" ', *PQ*, XLIX, 1970, 19–29.

36. ibid., 19.

37. This is part of the *Dramatis Personae* of the 26th Miracle, see below.

38. This remark by Petit de Julleville is quoted by G. Frank, *The Medieval French Drama*, Oxford, 1954, 121.

39. On the simultaneous stage settings used in medieval plays, see ibid., 90–1, 269–70.

40. G. Runnalls, 'A Newly Discovered Fourteenth Century Play? Le Mystère de Saint Christofle', *RPh*, XXIV, 1970–71, 473.

41. Frank, op. cit., 128–9.

42. G. Frank ed., *La Passion du Palatinus*, Paris, CFMA, 1922.

43. D. Poirion, *Le Moyen Age II: 1300–1480*, Paris, 1971, 180 (part of the series *Littérature française*, general editor C. Pichois). It is likely that such traits were borrowed from narrative, non-dramatic poems such as the early fourteenth-century *Livre de la Passion*, ed. G. Frank, Paris, CFMA, 1930; or from the *Passion des Jongleurs*, earliest extant poem of this type, dating from the end of the twelfth century or the beginning of the thirteenth. This work has been edited partly by H. Theben, *Die altfranzösische Achtsilbnerredaktion der Passion*, Gréifswald, 1909, completed by E. Pfuhl, *Die weitere Fassung der altfranzösischen Dichtung . . . über Christi Höllenfahrt*, Greifswald, 1909.

44. Faral and Bastin, ed. cit., II, 266.

45. Four days in the case of Gréban and Michel. The record appears to be eight, see Poirion, op. cit., 175.

46. Frank ed., *Passion du Palatinus*, 111.

47. Poirion, op. cit., 178–81, challenges this conventional view of fifteenth-century French literature so brilliantly, but misleadingly, given by J. Huizinga in his famous *Waning of the Middle Ages*, of which several English editions have appeared since 1924, the latest being London, 1967.

48. *Les Jongleurs en France au Moyen Age*, 228.

49. ed. M. Roques, Paris, CFMA, 1921.

50. J.-M. Richard ed., *La Passion d'Arras*, Arras, 1891, lines 8431–60; E. Roy ed., *La Passion de Sémur*, Dijon–Paris, 1903, lines 7283–344.

51. cf. too the *Farce de Pathelin*, see below, pp. 257–8.

52. E. Langlois ed., *Le Jeu de la Feuillée*, Paris, CFMA, 2nd ed. 1951; K. Varty ed., *Le Jeu de Robin et de Marion*, London, 1960.

53. Precursor of the 'fools' in the *sotties*, perhaps already a stock figure in Adam's day. See below, p. 257.

54. Frank, *The Medieval French Drama*, 227.

55. See above, pp. 207–8.

56. ed. B. M. Craig, Lawrence, Kansas, 1954, and by M. Roques, Geneva–Paris, 1957.

57. The full title of which is *Le Livre de la vertu et du sacrement de*

mariage et du reconfort des dames mariées. A study of this work (*Etude sur . . .*) was published by E. Golenistscheff-Koutouzoff, Sofia, 1937.

58. Information on these companies is given by Frank, *The Medieval French Drama*, 249–50. See also DLF, 705–6; and R. Lebègue, *Le Théâtre comique en France de Pathelin à Mélite*, Paris, 1972.

59. They are represented by works such as *Les Menus Propos*, *Les Sobres Sots*, *Les Sots Ecclésiastiques*, *Les Vigiles de Triboulet*, etc. Frank, *The Medieval French Drama*, chapter xxiv.

60. Among the best known are *Sermon des maux que l'homme a en mariage*; *Le Franc Archier de Bagnolet*; *Monologue de la Botte de Foin*, the last-named by Guillaume Coquillart.

61. e.g., *La moralité de l'Aveugle et du Boiteux*; *Le Chevalier qui donna sa femme au diable*; *L'Homme juste et l'homme mondain*; *La Condamnation de Banquet*.

62. The most recent edition is by C. E. Pickford in the Classiques Bordas series, Paris, 1967.

63. In the Middle Ages 'comedy' meant neither what it meant in classical times nor what it means in modern times (see above, p. 240). It denoted a poem whose beginning was sad, but which had a happy ending. The explanation of how the term 'farce' originated is not altogether clear. It meant in the first place 'stuffing' (<Latin verb *farcire*). Did its use arise because these plays provided short, amusing interludes in the course of the long religious dramas, or was it used simply because they contained a mixture of many ingredients? In any case, generic names like 'farce' and 'sottie' were not used very precisely in the Middle Ages, and a play could be referred to as a 'farce et sottie' – cf. the remarks above, pp. 227–8, on 'fabliau'.

64. Pickford, ed. cit., 5–6.

Chapter 10

MORAL AND DIDACTIC LITERATURE

I. THE BESTIARIES

MUCH medieval literature had a didactic aim, but whereas with some works the didacticism is on the surface and constitutes their whole purpose, with others it is buried deep inside the text and is only incidental. Many have a religious colouring, obvious examples being the lives of the saints and numerous *chansons de geste*; while this may be true of certain courtly romances, their didacticism, often expressed symbolically, is concerned rather with many aspects of society. As we have seen, the *Roman de la Rose* is remarkable in its grafting of an enormous many-branched tree of moral and didactic material on to the slender stock of an art of love.[1] As so often the case, distinctions between genres (in this instance between what did and what did not constitute didactic literature) were far less sharply marked in medieval times than is suggested by a categorical analysis of the type being undertaken here. This chapter is concerned with a few of the many texts in which the moral or instructive intent was paramount. Contrary to what one might expect, some of the most forceful and compelling medieval literature is to be found among such works.

The medieval propensity for seeing all creation in terms of God, Man, and the Devil[2] is admirably displayed in the bestiaries, the earliest extant French version of which, owed to Philippe de Thaon, was composed between 1121 and 1135.[3] This appears to be the oldest surviving Anglo-Norman text. When Philippe was writing, the genre had been in existence for about a thousand years, since the prototype was the *Physiologus*, an anonymous Greek work of the second century A.D., translated several times into Latin, the latest about 1100, and thence into numerous vernaculars. There is a certain charm, a naïve ingenuity, in the description of the animals in Philippe's version, and in the symbolism and superstitions associated with them. Some thirteen are said to represent Christ, among them the lion, king of animals, the 'monosceros' (i.e., the unicorn), and the deer; eleven, varying in size from the ant to the elephant, depict Man, while among the seven standing for the Devil are the fox, the hedgehog, and the monkey. To Philippe's bestiary is attached a lapidary in which the diamond and the twelve stones of the Apocalypse symbolise Christian virtues or particular aspects of the faith:

Jaspe ruge demustre amur,
La verte, fei, blanche, dulçur;
Saphires mustre ki fei at
Que ensemble od Dé regnerat;
Chalcedoines, ki est fuïn,
Mustre qu'od Dé serum veisin . . .
(lines 2981–6)

Red jasper stands for love, green for faith, white for gentleness. Sapphire shows that whoever has faith will reign along with God. Chalcedony, which is fiery in colour, shows that with God we shall be neighbours.

II. THE 'LIVRE DES MANIÈRES' OF ETIENNE DE FOUGÈRES

A particularly early 'état du monde', reminding men of all ranks, from kings to peasants, of their duties, and attacking them for their many failings, is *Le Livre des Manières*, a poem of 1,344 octosyllabic lines, by Etienne de Fougères, bishop of Rennes, who died in 1178.[4] The basic theme, echoed in numerous works of this type, is that '. . . tot le siecle est vanité' (line 410) (. . . all the world is vanity). A king must remember: 'Reis n'est pas son' (161) (A king does not belong to himself alone) and must never neglect Holy Church. Evil priests are roundly condemned, particularly those who live with concubines and have families. Of such a man he exclaims:

E Dex! que feiz o ton toneire?
Por quei nel tues tot en eire?
(229–30)

Oh God! What are you doing with your thunder? Why do you not kill him immediately?

Knights are attacked for their love of pleasure:

Haut ordre fut chevalerie
Mais or est ce trigalerie.
Trop aiment dance et balerie
Et demener bachelerie.
(585–8)

Chivalry was a high order, but nowadays it is all debauchery. They are too fond of dancing and merry-making and leading a wild life.

The work is remarkable for the detailed and sympathetic portrait it paints of the hard life of the peasant:

Terres arer, norir aumaille,
Sor le vilain est la bataille;
Quar chevalier et clerc sanz faille
Vivent de ce que il travaille.

Ploughing the land, feeding the cattle, the battle depends on the peasant, for knights and churchmen all live on the sweat of his brow.

Moult a travail et moult a peine
Au meilor jor de la semaine.
Il seinme seigle, il here aveine,
Il fauche prez, il tose leine.

He has much travail, much torment even on the best day of the week. He sows rye, he tills the oats, he mows the meadows, he shears wool.

Il fet paliz, il fet meiseires,
Il fet estanz par ces rivieres,
Primes corvees, peis preieres
Et peis cent choses costumieres.

He builds straw ricks, he builds dry
walls, he makes ponds along the
rivers, first one imposition then
another, then a hundred traditional
burdens.

Ne mengera ja de bon pain;
Nos en avon le meillor grein
Et le plus lies et le plus sein;
La droe remeint au vilain.

He will never eat good bread. We
have the best corn, the finest and the
most healthy. All that is left for the
peasant are the tares.

(677–92)

However hard his lot, even the peasant has no right to show God
any resentment. The author ends his poem with a confession of his
own sins, and laments the absence of good works from his life:

Nule bone! tante malveise!...
Tante malveise! nule bone!

No good work, so many bad ones!
So many bad works, no good one!

(1265, 1269)

III. THE 'VERS DE LA MORT' OF HÉLINANT

An outstanding work in this domain is *Les Vers de la Mort*, composed between 1194 and 1197 by Hélinant, a Cistercian monk at
the monastery of Froidmont in the diocese of Beauvais.[5] He is also
the author of a collection of Latin sermons, two ascetic treatises, and
a chronicle; his teacher Raoul had studied under Abelard. *Les Vers
de la Mort* became well known in the thirteenth and fourteenth
centuries and were imitated not only in subject-matter, but also in
their distinctive form, each stanza containing twelve octosyllabic
lines based on the intersecting rhyme pattern *a a b/a a b/b b a/
b b a*. The theme is that death stalks each of us, high and low,
'comme lerres par nuit' (xxiii, line 10) (like a thief in the night),
and there can be no escaping. Such a subject risks being droningly
monotonous, but the terse, hard-hitting phraseology of this Cistercian monk, enlivened by original, vivid metaphors, attains at times
a rare kind of monastic lyricism:

Morz, crie a Romme, crie a Rains
'Seigneur, tuit estes en mes mains,
Aussi li haut comme li bas.
Ovrez voz ieuz, ceigniez vos rains,
Ainçois que je vos praigne as frains
Et vos face crier Hé las!
Certes je queur plus que le pas,
Si aport dez de deus et d'as
Por vos faire jeter del mains.
Laissiez voz chiflois et voz gas!
Teus me cueve desoz ses dras
Qui cuide estre haitiez et sains'.

(xv)

Death, cry out in Rome, cry out in
Rheims: 'Lords, you are all in my
hands, the mighty as well as the
humble. Open your eyes, gird your
loins, before I take you by the bridle
and make you cry out: "Alas!" In
truth I run fast and bring dice
marked with twos and ones to make
you throw the lowest scores. Give up
your mocking and jesting. A man
may be harbouring me under his
clothes who thinks he is hale and
hearty'.

A climax is reached in a splendid passage of some 30 lines, each of which hammers the lesson home:

Morz fait a chascun sa droiture,	Death gives each his rightful due,
Morz fait a toz droite mesure,	Death gives each his proper measure,
Morz poise tot a juste pois,	Death weighs all with a fair weight,
Morz venge chascun de s'injure ...	Death avenges each man's insult.
(XXXII, 1–4)	

This is no servile mind, meekly doling out the well-worn Christian message: watch and pray, for we know not when our hour cometh. Independent and outspoken, a sharp-tongued censurer of human vanity and greed,[6] he did not hesitate to give even Rome a lashing:

Romme est li mauz qui tot asomme,	Rome is the evil that crushes every-
Romme nos fait de siu chandoile:	thing, Rome makes our candles of
Car son legat vent por estoile,	tallow [instead of wax, i.e., imposes
Ja tant n'ert tainz de noire gomme.	harsh conditions] for it sells its legate
(XIII, 9–12)	as a veritable star, however stained
	with black pitch he may in fact be.

This insistence on the frailty of all human things meant in theory that the moral lesson could easily be swept aside, for if we are bound to die, and always sooner than we think, why not have a good time while yet we may? Hélinant anticipates such arguments in terms which have been said to lack subtlety, but it is probable that he was not addressing particularly subtle people. Remarkable is his putting into his interlocutor's mouth words denying the continuation of any form of life after death:

'Morz est la fins de la bataille	Death is the end of the battle, and
Et ame et cors noient devient'.	body and soul become nothing.
(XXXIV, 11–12)[7]	

Could it be that even the twelfth century had its freethinkers and libertines? Hélinant's rejoinder is as crude and direct as any anti-Christian argument:

... s'il n'est autre vie,	... if there is no other life, between
Entre ame a homme et ame a truie	a man's soul and that of a pig there
N'a donques point de diference.	can be no difference.
(XXXV, 10–12)	

So many saints, so many martyrs have given witness to the truth of God's message that it must be accepted as self-evident. Those non-believers who are slaves to the sins of the flesh will suffer everlasting torment. The conclusion is as forthright and personal as the whole poem: 'Away with you, Greed! Away with you, Luxury! I have no care for your dainty morsels. I would rather have my peas and mash'. Imitations, some even with the same title, continued to appear throughout the Middle Ages, and the *Dies Irae* attitude of mind, fundamental to the whole period, crops up in many places, in Latin as in the vernacular, both before and after it was given this particularly vigorous and poetic expression.

IV. THE 'POÈME MORAL'

The same theme, the vanities of this world and the joys of Paradise, provides the basis of *Le Poème Moral*, an anonymous work containing 3,796 alexandrine lines written in the Walloon region about 1200.[8] What is interesting here is that broader issues are raised which have haunted the Christian conscience down the ages, such as: Why does God allow the good and the just to suffer so much? The answer given is that evil men may indeed have some joy in this world, but they may be certain that in the next they will have none, whereas the greater the tribulations of just men on earth, the more can they be certain of Paradise after death. For this reason it is wrong to say of the prosperous man: 'Cestui at Deus aidiet' (line 319) (God has helped this man) and of the seemingly wretched: 'Tot l'ait Deus obliiet' (320) (God has quite forgotten him). Misfortune can have a beneficial effect in that it makes a man renounce the foolish pleasures of this world. To illustrate his doctrine the author tells at some length the stories of two saints, both sinners in their early years before they became followers of Christ: St Moses the Black and St Thaïs of Egypt. He apologises, naïvely but charmingly, for the discursive nature of his text:

Pusc'estre qu'il vos grievet et nos
vos anoiomes
De ce ke, si sovent, de nostre voie
eissomes;
Mais or ne vos anuit, car tost i
revenromes;
Un poi irons avant, puis si
returneromes.

Perhaps you are irritated and bored by our continual digressions, but let it not trouble you, for we shall quickly return to our subject. We shall proceed a little further, then return to the subject.

(1361–4)

He then goes on to deal with the proper use and distribution of goods in this world. To the poor one must give generously, but never to the jongleurs for whom the author has abundant scorn and hatred:

Ceaz qui sevent les jambes
encontremont jeter,
Qui sevent tote nuit rotruenges
canteir,
Ki la mainie funt et sallir et
danceir . . .

Those who can throw their legs in the air, sing ditties the whole night through, and set the entire household leaping and dancing.

(2065–7)

They are a noisy lot who spread corruption in all they say and do:

Or sallent, or vïelent, or braient et
or crient.
Trestot turne a pechiet, cant k'il
funt, cant k'il dient . . .
Ki a teil gent donent, n'ont ne sens
ne savoir.

(2074–5, 2089)

Now they dance, now they fiddle, now they bray, now they shout. Everything turns to sin, whatever they do or say. Those who give to such people are devoid of sense and knowledge.

The end of this long diatribe shows the hapless Christian constantly assailed by Satan's army of vices, and paints a terrifying picture of hell and the Last Judgement.

V. THE 'BIBLE' OF GUIOT DE PROVINS

More personal is the *Bible* of Guiot de Provins,[9] a poem of 2,686 octosyllabic lines completed probably in 1206. In his early years Guiot appears to have travelled widely from Court to Court as a professional poet,[10] but at the time of writing his *Bible* he had been a Benedictine monk for twelve years. He had participated in the third crusade (1189–92) and on his return had found the seigneurial Courts greatly impoverished as a direct result of the holy wars, while the monarchy had extended its domains: Philip Augustus in particular had seized lands belonging to Richard Cœur-de-Lion in Normandy, Anjou, and Limousin. There is a strong 'those were the days' flavour about Guiot's survey of society, as he harks back to the good old times and contrasts them with the wretchedness he sees all around him in the present. Gone is the generosity of the past, and all now is meanness and penny-pinching:

Aï France! Aï Borgoigne!
Certes, con estes avuglées!
Con vos vi de gent honorées!
Or plorent les belles maisons
les boins princes, les boins barons
qui les grans cors i assembloient
et les biaus avoirs i donoient.

(lines 112–18)

Oh France! Oh Burgundy! In truth how blinded you are! How once I saw you honoured by your people! Now the noble houses mourn for the good princes, the good barons who assembled great Courts and gave away fine possessions.

He lists no fewer than 86 of his former benefactors, all now dead. Those who had replaced them had none of their sterling qualities:

Que sont li prince devenu?
Deus, que vi je, et que voi gié!

(282–3)

What has become of the princes? Oh God! what once I saw, what now I see!

The religious orders, each in turn, come in for harsh satire, possibly the earliest of many such attacks in which hypocrisy is a constantly recurring word, but it is on doctors that he is most effective. In this respect he shows himself to have been a worthy predecessor of Molière, whom he reflects in his caustic comments and sly digs. Once in a doctor's clutches trying to get away is as hard as breaking out of prison. They mesmerise their patients with big words and always manage to find symptoms of some shocking ailment:

En chescun home truevent toche:	In every man they find an ailment.
se il ait fievre ou toz soiche	If he has a fever or a dry cough,
lor dïent il qu'il est tesiques	they say that he is phthisical, catar-
ou enfunduz, ou ydropiques	rhous, or dropsical, bilious, condylo-
melancolious, ou fïous,	matous, pulmonic or paralytic ...
ou corpeus, ou palasimous ...	Their works are too recondite and
Trop per sont lor oevres repotes	their words so involved that there is
et lor parolles si enpotes	nothing save villainy in them.
n'i ait se viloignie non.	

(2565–70, 2575–7)

As for their medicines, Guiot observes cryptically that he would rather have a fat capon. He admits that a few good doctors can be found, and when he is ill, he is anxious enough to see one of them, but as soon as he is better, the doctor can go to Salonica, 'lui et toute sa fisique' (2684) (he and all his physic), and never return. This last comment brings to an end this most personal and lively of the moral treatises examined in this chapter.

VI. THE 'BIBLE AU SEIGNEUR DE BERZÉ'

Rather more general, and gentler, is the *Bible au Seigneur de Berzé*,[11] a poem of 1,028 octosyllabic lines composed sometime in the first half of the thirteenth century. The author, at pains to point out that he is neither a cleric nor a man of letters, has neither the moral severity of an Etienne de Fougères (he does not accept that a life of torment and tribulation is a necessary prerequisite to Paradise) nor the literary pretensions of a Guiot de Provins. His moral outlook, pessimistic but relatively tolerant, is drawn as much from his own experiences as from the Church's teaching. At Constantinople, on the fourth crusade, he had seen the deaths of no fewer than four emperors. Where they fell

... n'ot a aus sevelir	That day there was no priest, no
Le jour provoire ne clerçon,	cleric to bury them, but they were
Ains les mengierent li gaignon	devoured by the dogs, the crows,
E li corbel e les corneilles.	and the rooks.

(lines 438–41)

Had they been told on the morning of their death that such was their destiny, they would have been astonished and dismayed, 'Mais Diex le volt ainsi soufrir' (445) (But God wished to suffer it thus). Those who survived and eventually triumphed won great riches, but they forgot God, and He forgot them. Their demise could theoretically have been given a purely secular explanation: discipline was undermined when they acquired booty, but the seigneur de Berzé remains firm in his Christian explanation.

Tant com nous eümes creance	For as long as we had our belief, our
Nous dura la bone cheance,	good fortune prevailed, and when
E quant la creance failli	our belief failed, so did our good
E la bone cheance aussi.	fortune.

(495–8)

God taught them the vanity of riches and the dreadful uncertainty of life. In the same way death awaits all of us, we know not when. We cannot be certain of a single day of life, and must be constantly prepared for the Day of Judgement.

VII. THE 'ENSEIGNEMENT DES PRINCES' AND THE 'CHASTOIEMENT DES DAMES' OF ROBERT DE BLOIS

Writing towards the middle of the century, Robert de Blois, author of two romances, *Beausdous* and *Floris et Lyriopé*,[12] also composed two didactic poems: *L'Enseignement des Princes* and *Le Chastoiement des Dames*.[13] The former, comprising 1,404 octosyllabic lines, includes a vigorous denunciation of the vices liable to afflict the ruling classes, with a particular insistence, as in the works of other *trouvères* of this century, on the dangers of avarice. The latter, a shorter work of 757 lines, is an astonishingly practical code of conduct for ladies, dealing with their behaviour in the street, in church, in society, at table. With an owlish solemnity Robert assures ladies that the purpose of brooches is to prevent men from plunging their hands into their bosoms to feel their naked flesh – a practice, he says, which soon leads to other things which are the husband's sole prerogative. In church, she who has a fine voice may sing by all means, but not too lustily. At table she must not seize the daintiest morsel for herself, and should remember that the tablecloth is not there for her to wipe her mouth or to blow her nose on. If a would-be lover makes advances to her, she should not yield too precipitately, but if he is persistent in the face of her vigorous and reiterated protests of loyalty to her husband, she may eventually accept him if she so wishes.

VIII. THE 'DOCTRINAL SAUVAGE' AND PHILIPPE DE NOVARE'S 'DES QUATRE TENZ D'AAGE D'OME'

Towards the end of the thirteenth century appeared two works, the *Doctrinal Sauvage*[14] and Philippe de Novare's *Des Quatre Tenz d'Aage d'Ome*.[15] The former is laboured, repetitive, and short. A didactic treatise of 280 alexandrine lines, it is full of finger-wagging admonitions, often of an undeniably sensible kind: kings, dukes, counts, princes, bishops, and archbishops must be just and merciful and must not stray from the paths of righteousness through some relative's influence. All men, rich and poor alike, must support Holy Church according to their capabilities:

Et li riche et li povre, tuit devons Dieu servir.	Both rich and poor, we must all serve God.

(p. 160)

Philippe de Novare's prose treatise is far more wide-ranging, and far more interesting. His opening remark: 'Cil qui fist cest conte avoit LXX anz passez . . .' (the one who wrote this tale was over seventy . . .) alerts the reader to the possibility that his views may not represent those prevailing at the time (the 'generation gap' is not a new phenomenon, though it was certainly much narrower then than now). However, he is well aware of the accusations usually levelled against those in their dotage, that they 'sont revenu en anfance' (p. 22) (have returned to childhood), and he shows that he has the wisdom of his years without the senility. A man of wide experience – soldier, jurist, diplomat, poet – he served in Cyprus for a long period and lived most of his life in the East. Only in the repetitive nature of his *Four Ages of Man* does he show his age, as when he returns to his adage that childhood is 'li fondemenz de vie' (12, 18) (the foundation of life), but at least his main points emerge clearly as a result. The following résumé lists a few of them.

A child's upbringing is a matter of reason 'car volantez ne doit mie chevauchier raison' (p. 6) (for whim must not override reason). Tears must not discourage parents from punishing their child when the need arises: better a child should weep for its own good than parents for the trouble it causes. Learning should begin at an early age, particularly for the clergy and knighthood. The former is an excellent vocation, since it breaks through social barriers; a poor man may become a great prelate, even 'peres et sires de toute crestiente' (11) (father and lord of all Christianity). A man may also serve God by becoming a knight, and may prosper as a result. The sons of the rich should be taught to be generous and to have a proper sense of their responsibilities. It should always be remembered that 'Tuit trop sont mal' (14) (all excesses are bad). Girls have to be taught obedience, for in adult life they will have to obey either a husband or a mother superior. Their education is a simpler affair than for boys; they must learn to spin and sew, but 'A fame ne doit on apanre letres ne escrire, se ce n'est especiaument por estre nonnain; car par lire et escrire de fame sont maint mal avenu' (16) (A woman must not be taught how to read and write, except to become a nun, for through the reading and writing of woman much evil has come about). To hold her head high it is enough for a woman to remain virtuous.

Youth is the most perilous of the four ages, for then reason often yields to temptation. Young people think they know everything, but 'cuidier n'est pas savoir' (22) (presumption is not knowledge). They are too impatient: '. . . la conscience des jones genz est ausis comme une grant vecie anflee de volanté, et qui a droit la fiert, de legier crieve' (24) (The conscience of young people is like a great bladder inflated with whims, and whoever gives it a good blow, it easily bursts). Their judgement is not yet sound, they are reckless and imagine that death is only for the aged. The very word Jovanz (<Latin *juventus*, 'youth') is made up of 'Joie' and 'vent'. However, the sins of a young man are more easily forgiven than those of an older one, and youth is no time for sadness. A young man must remember that marriage is a 'morteus bataille ou covient morir l'un des deux' (45) (a mortal battle in which one or the other must perish), but whatever troubles it brings, the good outweighs the bad. It is the best arrangement for human society, and an essential one.

Middle age is the time of maturity when above all one must learn to know oneself and to make one's peace with God. At this time of life a man must set his house in order, look after his dependants, and provide for his old age. He must allow others to benefit from his wisdom. This is the time to go over one's works, to sort out the good from the bad, and to ensure that they will survive after one's death. He is clearly thinking of written works, since he goes on: 'Et cil qui ne sevent les escritures . . .' (67–8) (and those who cannot write . . .). Always remember that the time is now at hand when, one after the other, the leaves will fall and the very tree will die and rot away. There are those who say that after this life there is no other,[16] but God is not to be mocked in this way. A man can model one of God's creatures in wood or stone, but not all the men in the world can breathe life into it. There can be no sense in scepticism, for in this world the good are often persecuted and evil men triumph,[17] but even the Arabs agree that God is just and omnipotent: 'donc i a il autre siecle en quoi il fornist droiture et as bons et as maus, de ce dont ele n'est fornie en cest siecle' (82) (therefore there is another world in which He dispenses justice to the good and the bad, since it is not so dispensed in this world). A man must confess his sins and say his prayers regularly, and not sneak out of church before the end of the service. One should always be busy throughout the day, except that an hour's rest is permissible after the midday meal.

Old people should remember that they stand on the brink of their tomb and that they will be judged according to what they are when they fall in. They must now despise the world, for they have suffered enough of its tribulations and sorrows. Some old women try to recapture their youth by plastering their faces and dyeing their hair – a vain enterprise. Old men must realise that the time to frequent women has passed away. May God bring all Christians to a good end.

IX. THE 'ROMAN DE FAUVEL' OF GERVAIS DU BUS

A far more embittered criticism of society forms the basis of the *Roman de Fauvel*, composed between 1310 and 1314 by Gervais du Bus who, like his contemporary Jehan Maillart, was a notary at the royal chancellory in Paris. This work of 3,280 octosyllabic lines owes much to Jacquemart Gielee's *Renart le Nouvel* and Jean de Meun's *Roman de la Rose*. It is a twofold satire, of contemporary institutions and figures (not actually named) on the one hand, of all human life and nature on the other. Fauvel (from *fauve*, which the medieval mind tended to associate with *faux*, hence with ideas of hypocrisy) is ingeniously explained by the author as consisting of the initials of Flatterie, Avarice, Vilenie (v=u), Variété, Envie, Lâcheté.[18] All people, from the highest to the lowest, make haste to do him homage. His Court is made up of all the human vices, no fewer than forty-five allegorical characters (drawn largely from the *Roman de la Rose*). Among the numerous remarkable features of this caustic poem are the two large wheels of Fortune, within each of which are set two smaller wheels turning in the opposite directions. These signify that there is no prosperity without its share of adversity and that no happiness, however great, is complete.[19] The author lashes out frenziedly in all directions, seeing the whole of human society as wicked and degenerate:

Puis que les rois sont menteours	Since kings are liars
Et riches hommes flateours,	and rich men flatterers,
Prelas plains de vainne cointise,	prelates full of empty knowledge,
Et chevaliers heent l'Yglise,	and knights hate the Church,
Clergié est example de vices,	the clergy is an embodiment of vices,
Religious plains de delices,	monks are full of lechery,
Riches hommes sans charitei,	rich men without charity,
Et marcheans sans veritei,	merchants without honesty,
Labourëurs sans lëautei . . .	farm-labourers without loyalty,
Je conclu par droite reson	I conclude with good reason
Que près summes de la seson	that we are close to the time
En quoi doit definer le monde . . .	when the world will end.
(lines 1131–9, 1163–5)	

X. THE 'LIVRE DE LA MUTACION DE FORTUNE' AND OTHER DIDACTIC WORKS BY CHRISTINE DE PISAN

One of the most prolific of medieval French poets was Christine de Pisan. Born in Venice in 1365, she was brought up in France from the age of three or four and spent her life in that country, dying about 1430. Writing in the later years of the fourteenth century and in the first decade of the fifteenth, she produced some charming love-poetry[20] and longer narrative poems, of which the most ambitious is *Le Livre de la Mutacion de Fortune*,[21] a vast compilation of 23,636 octosyllabic lines incorporating a short passage in prose written when she was ill and unable to 'rimer'. Its complexity and prolixity make it a most difficult work to summarise or classify. Beginning as an autobiography, it becomes many things in the course of its development: a moral treatise, an encyclopedia, a chronicle, an anthology of legends, a history of mankind. Centred on the castle of Fortune and its occupants, it enables the author to develop her views on the world past and present, on evil and good, poverty and wealth, philosophy and theology, following a mass of sources classical and medieval, including sections of Dante's *Purgatory*. What is lacking is a vision lifting it above the sum of its many disparate parts. This could have been one of the finest of all medieval works, but the author's talent, it must be said, was simply not of this scale. Her didacticism appears to much better effect in shorter works in which she took up a stern moral stance, condemning what she regarded as the depravity of the age, and also, ardent feminist that she was, opposing that misogyny which was such a deep-rooted feature of the medieval outlook. Particularly worthy of note is *L'Epistre au Dieu d'Amours*,[22] a lucid, eloquent diatribe protesting vigorously against the Ovidian anti-feminist cynicism that had held sway for so long. It is a plea set in the mouth of Cupid (the only bit of literary fantasy in an otherwise realistic, hard-hitting polemic), defending 'Gentilz femmes, bourgoises et pucelles' (gentle women, bourgeoises and maidens); and indeed 'toutes femmes generaument' (lines 12–13) (all women generally). The author (for the Cupid disguise is diaphanous) roundly condemns the hypocritical pretence put up by so many knights and squires to be true lovers. They are full of deceit, interested solely in their selfish pleasures. They meet in private to boast of their conquests and gossip on the women they have possessed. Decent men do admittedly exist, as also do deceitful women, but both are tiny minorities. Ovid's works have enjoyed popularity for far too long, in particular the *Remedia Amoris* and the *Ars Amatoria* which could more appropriately be named *L'Art de grant decevance* (377). What can be said about Jean de Meun and his *Roman de la Rose*?

Et Jehan de Meun ou Romant de la Rose,
Quel long procès! quel difficile chose!
Et sciences et cleres et obscures
Y met il la et de grans aventures!
Et que de gent soupploiez et rovez
Et de peines et de baraz trouvez
Pour decepvoir sanz plus une pucelle.

(389–95)

And Jean de Meun in the *Roman de la Rose*. What a long-drawn-out business! What a difficult affair! He has compiled it of science both clear and obscure, and mighty adventures! What a lot of supplications and requests, of trouble and trickery, all that just to deceive a girl.

Why do men find it necessary to devote so much cunning, so much effort, so much of their time, to tricking

Une ignorant petite femmellette?	An ignorant little woman.
(550)	

Man's brutality finds no counterpart in women

Car nature de femme est debonnaire	Woman's nature is noble.
(672)	

Man owes woman respect and each should remember

C'est sa mere, c'est sa suer, c'est s'amie	She is his mother, his sister, his sweetheart.
(733)	

This poem of 826 octosyllabic lines, dated May 1399, was written at a time when the 'courtly' movement of the past was enjoying a brief revival in Paris, where a gathering of noblemen and poets founded *La Cour Amoureuse* devoted to the composition of poetry honouring 'toutes dames et demoiselles'[23] (all ladies and damsels). The aim was partly to find an escape from the rigours of the times, not merely the long-drawn-out conflict with England, but also the struggles with that even more pernicious and persistent enemy, the plague. At one time this society, so full of good intentions, contained over 600 members, including the king himself, but many of its romantic company fell at Agincourt in 1415, and the courtly spirit did not survive long into the fifteenth century. Christine de Pisan's *Epistre au Dieu d'Amours* soon took its place in a literary quarrel, the first in French literature, which has come to be known as the *Querelle du Roman de la Rose*. Several scholars took up the cudgels in defence of Jean de Meun, while Christine attracted some powerful allies, among them Martin Le Franc, one of the pope's secretaries,[24] and Jean Gerson, theologian, Chancellor of the University of Paris, most of whose writings, the moral tone of which is elevated and noble, were composed in Latin. Like many a man of his stamp in our own day, Gerson was a bitter opponent of the lax morals and sexual permissiveness that marked the war-ridden age in which he lived. Both he and Christine de Pisan were shocked by certain passages of the still very fashionable *Roman de la Rose*, particularly those bearing the Ovidian imprint.

XI. THE 'TRACTATUS CONTRA ROMANTIUM DE ROSA' OF JEAN GERSON

In his *Tractatus contra Romantium de Rosa*, Gerson brought all his rhetorical training to bear against this work which 'reprehendit omnes, vilipendit omnes, contemnit omnes sine ulla exceptione'[25] (reprehends everybody, vilifies everybody, spurns everybody without a single exception). Love is the source of so many disasters

Quis succendit magnam Trojam igni et flamma? Stultus amator. Quis tum interire fecit plures quam centum mille Nobiles: Hectorem, Achillem, Priamum, et alios? Fatuus amor. Quis expulit urbe Tarquinium Regem et ejus sololem? Fatuus amator. Quis decipit per fraudes et perjuria illegitima filias honestas, et virgines Deo sacras, atque Religiosas? Stultus amor . . .[26] (Who set fire to mighty Troy? A stupid lover. Who brought death to more than a hundred thousand nobles: Hector, Achilles, Priam, and others? Fatuous love. Who drove out from the town of the Tarquins the king and his sister? A fatuous lover. Who deceives through fraud and unlawful perjury honest maidens, virgins sacred to God, and nuns? Stupid love . . .).

In fact neither Christine de Pisan nor Jean Gerson nor Martin Le Franc did Jean de Meun full justice. They failed to make allowance for his own apologia, and, waxing indignant over certain details, ignored the broad and tolerant view of human society, somewhat detached and ironical it is true, which emerges from the totality of his work. But, of course, it is all too easy for the present writer to pass judgement; there were no doubt cogent arguments, and much right, on both sides.

XII. THE 'LIVRE DES FAIS D'ARMES ET DE CHEVALERIE' OF CHRISTINE DE PISAN

It is surprising to find that Christine de Pisan, this ardent feminist, was also the author of a military treatise, *Le Livre des fais d'armes et de chevalerie*, based on Latin sources such as Vegetius's *De re militari*, possibly indirectly through the fourteenth-century translation of Jean de Vignai. Dealing with such matters as the duties of kings, princes, and captains in wartime, the qualities most to be desired in 'gens d'arme', the many problems involved in commanding an army, varying according to the vicissitudes of fortune, this work was printed several times in modified forms in the early sixteenth century, and an English translation, *The Book of Fayttes of Armes and of Chyvalrye*, was published by Caxton in 1489, in which the subject is defined as 'the right honorable offyce of armes and of chyvalrye'.[27]

XIII. THE 'QUADRILOGUE INVECTIF' OF ALAIN CHARTIER

One of the most eloquent and forceful of medieval French writers, Alain Chartier, was born in Bayeux in or about 1385. He studied in Paris and became secretary to Charles VI and later to the Dauphin (Charles VII). He was appointed canon of Paris in 1420, and of Tours in 1427. Like Christine de Pisan, he wrote in verse and

prose on a wide variety of subjects. He died in Avignon towards
1435. His *Quadrilogue Invectif*, sometimes spoken of as his masterpiece,[28] was written in 1421, six years after Agincourt,[29] when the
fortunes of France, in her interminable struggles with England, had
reached their lowest ebb. Henry V, whose claims to large areas of
western France originated in Aliénor d'Aquitaine's marriage to
Henry II in 1152,[30] had gone from triumph to triumph. Normandy
had become an English colony, and the Dauphin (Charles VII) had
been compelled to seek refuge south of the Loire. True Frenchman,
ardent patriot, staunch supporter of the Dauphin, Alain Chartier
was bitterly critical of all aspects of French life, which he considered
responsible for the present degradation. He wrote with tremendous
force, conviction, and eloquence. With such a spirit abroad in the
years immediately before the emergence of Joan of Arc, there can
be little wonder that France eventually triumphed over her perennial
foes. The *Quadrilogue* tells how, in a dream, the author heard
France haranguing her sons, reproaching them with their failure
to defend their homeland:

Mes anciens ennemis et adversaires me guerroient au dehors par feu et par
glaive, et vous par dedans me guerroiez par voz couvoitises et mauvaises
ambitions (p. 11)...Vous grevez et guerroiez voz ennemis de souhaiz.
Vous desirez leur desconfiture par prieres et parolles, et ilz pourchacent la vostre
par entreprinse de fait. Vous conseillez de les dechacer, et ilz besoignent
en vous dechaçant; leur travail et songneux desir de conquerir esbahit voz
couraiges et vostre negligence de defendre enhardist leurs voulentez (12)...
Qu'est devenue la constance et loyauté du peuple françois, qui si longtemps
a eu renom de perseverer loial, ferme et entier vers son naturel seigneur
sans querir nouvelles mutacions? (ibid.)...Plusieurs de la chevalerie et des
nobles crient aux armes, mais ilz courent a l'argent; le clergé et les con-
seilliers parlent a deux visaiges et vivent avecques les vivans; le peuple
veult estre en sceurté gardé et tenu franc, et si est impacient de souffrir
subgection de seigneurie (ibid.)...Endormez vous comme pourceaux en
l'ordure et vilté des horribles pechiez qui vous ont mis si pres de la fin de
voz bons jours! Estoupez voz oreilles a toutes bonnes amonicions, mais ce
sera par tele condicion que tant plus y demourrez et plus approuchera le
douloureux jour de vostre exterminacion (14)...Quelles gens estes vous, ne
quelles durtez avez vous en voz couraiges, qui ainsi vous laissez perdre a
vostre escient, sans vouloir delaisser ce qui vous meyne a perdicion et vous
tire a perdicion les bras au col (ibid.)...Les ennemis ne sont de fer immor-
telz ou indiviables ne que vous, ilz n'ont glaives ne armeures que vous n'ayez
les pareilles, ne ne sont en si grant nombre que ne soiez autant ou plus
(17)[31]...
(My enemies and adversaries of old wage war on me from outside with fire
and sword, and you wage war on me from inside with your greed and evil
ambitions...You attack your enemies and wage war on them with wishes.
You desire their discomfiture in prayer and words, and they seek yours in
deeds. You suggest that they should be pursued, and they set about pursuing you. Their efforts and keen desire to conquer terrify you, and your
negligence in defence strengthens their resolve...What has become of the
steadfastness and loyalty of the French people, who for so long had the

reputation of persevering loyally, firmly, wholeheartedly in service of their rightful lord without seeking new changes? Many knights and nobles cry to arms, but they run to money. The clergy and councillors speak with two faces and live with the living. The people want to live securely and in freedom, and yet are impatient to suffer domination ... Fall asleep like swine in the filth and vileness of your horrible sins which have brought you near to the end of your good days! Block up your ears to all admonitions, but the result will be that the more you stay in this condition, the closer will come the terrible day of your extermination. What sort of people are you, and what sort of resistance do you offer when you knowingly go to your ruin without wishing to cast off the cause of it which drags you to your perdition with your arms clasped at your necks? The enemy are not made of iron, they are no more immortal than you, they have no swords or armour without your having the equivalent, they are not in such great numbers that you have not as many or more . . .)

The people, the clergy, and the nobility each then speak in turn and each blames the other two.

That the outstanding moralists of the early fifteenth century – Jean Gerson, Christine de Pisan, Alain Chartier, and others – should have written so ardently in defence of the French cause is significant and important. The spark of patriotism which they helped to ignite became a raging fire which drove their enemies from French soil, bringing the Hundred Years War to an end and leaving the English in a sorry state of disarray culminating in the Wars of the Roses. These moralists were not, however, wholly successful. Such absolute idealists rarely are. The second half of the century, aftermath of a long and bitter war, went through a period of permissiveness similar to those which our own century has seen. The morals of the age were severely censured in Jean Meschinot's *Les Lunettes des Princes*,[32] composed in or about 1460, seeing everything as bad today and worse tomorrow, reminding princes of their moral duties, reading to them from the book of Conscience with the aid of spectacles of which one lens is inscribed Justice, the other Prudence. Both the moral rectitude so sternly defended by Gerson, Meschinot, and others, and the balanced relationship between the sexes, free from the taint of misogyny, so ardently advocated by Christine de Pisan, eluded the declining Middle Ages, even though their waning was not as lugubrious and nihilistic as has so often been claimed.

NOTES

1. See above, pp. 216–24.
2. This is seen too in the iconography of moral themes, displayed in countless sculptures, paintings and stained-glass windows of medieval churches and cathedrals, and in manuscript illuminations. This alone is an immense subject, and although it is frequently closely related to literary texts, and helps to elucidate them (see, for example, Fleming, op. cit.: above, p. 223), no space can be allotted to it here. It has been given a thorough treatment in the several works of E. Mâle: *L'Art religieux du XIIe siècle en France*, Paris,

3rd ed., 1928; *L'Art religieux du XIIIe siècle en France*, Paris, 6th ed., 1925 (translated into English by D. Nussey as *The Gothic Image. Religious Art in France of the Thirteenth Century*, London, 1961); *L'Art religieux de la fin du Moyen Age*, Paris, 4th ed., 1931.

3. E. Walberg ed., *Le Bestiaire de Philippe de Thaün*, Paris, 1900.

4. J. Kremer ed., *Le Livre des Manières d'Etienne de Fougères*, Marburg, 1887.

5. Fr. Wulff and E. Walberg eds., *Les Vers de la Mort par Hélinant, moine de Froidmont*, Paris, SATF, 1905.

6. cf. Guernes de Pont-Sainte-Maxence, above, pp. 42–50.

7. Compare Philippe de Novare's arguments against sceptics. See below, p. 270.

8. A. Bayot ed., *Le Poème Moral, Traité de vie chrétienne, écrit dans la région wallonne vers l'an 1200*, Brussels, 1929.

9. *Bible* in this sense has been defined as: 'toute composition qui prétendait donner en quelque sorte un tableau du monde – un *speculum mundi* en vulgaire', see J. Orr ed., *Les Œuvres de Guiot de Provins*, xxiv.

10. See above, p. 121.

11. F. Lecoy ed., *La 'Bible' au Seigneur de Berzé*, Paris, 1938.

12. ed. J. Ulrich, 2 vols., Berlin, 1889–95.

13. ed. J. H. Fox, in *Robert de Blois, son œuvre didactique et narrative*, Paris, 1950.

14. Published by A. Jubinal in *Nouveau Recueil de contes, dits, fabliaux et autres pièces inédites des XIIIe, XIVe et XVe siècles*, Paris, 2 vols., 1839–1842, vol. 2, 150–61.

15. M. de Fréville ed., *Les Quatre Ages de l'Homme. Traité Moral de Philippe de Navarre*, Paris, SATF, 1888.

16. See above, p. 264.

17. See above, p. 265.

18. A. Langfors ed., *Le Roman de Fauvel*, Paris, SATF, 1914–19. It is interesting to note that the expression *correer* (lit. to make ready, to equip, to look after) *Fauvel* gave English 'to curry favour'.

19. See above, p. 219.

20. M. Roy ed., *Œuvres poétiques de Christine de Pisan*, Paris, SATF, 3 vols., 1886–91, reprinted New York, 1965. See below, pp. 302–3.

21. S. Solente ed., *Le Livre de la Mutacion de Fortune*, Paris, SATF, 4 vols., 1959–66.

22. Roy, ed. cit., II, 1–27.

23. A. Piaget, 'Un manuscrit de la Cour Amoureuse de Charles VI', *R*, XXXI, 1902, 602.

24. See below, p. 326, note 33.

25. Quoted from the 1706 edition of his works, vol. 3, 303.

26. ibid., 302.

27. At the time of writing this translation is more readily available than the French original, having been edited for the EETS by A. T. P. Byles in 1932, re-edited 1937. Also worthy of mention is Ramon Lull's *Le Libre del Orde de Cavayleria* (ed. M. Aguiló y Fuster, Barcelona, 1879, and J. Ramón de Luanco, Barcelona, 1901), whose Catalan was soon translated into French. An English version, translated and printed by Caxton in 1484, has been edited for the EETS by A. T. P. Byles, under the title *The Book of the Ordre of Chyvalry*, London, 1926. Such treatises, popular in their day, represent an important aspect of medieval literature to which modern scholarship has, as yet, devoted comparatively little attention.

28. ed. E. Droz, Paris, CFMA, 1923.

29. Earlier, Chartier had written a poem lamenting this defeat: *Le Livre des quatre Dames*.

30. See above, p. 121.

31. It is no mere chance that this work was re-edited in 1944 (by R. Bouvier, Paris). The editor, in those equally distressing years, wrote (p. 9): '. . . certaines pages [in the *Quadrilogue Invectif*] sont d'une impressionnante actualité. Elles pourraient littéralement être intégrées aujourd'hui dans un article de revue ou de journal. Ainsi, des circonstances analogues, à cinq

siècles de distance, peuvent inspirer les mêmes réactions, les mêmes cris de
détresse et d'espoir'.

32. ed. O. de Gourcuff, Nantes, 1891. A more recent ed., for a Paris
doctorate, is by C. Martineau-Genieys, Paris, 1969 (typed thesis). Most
recent of all is the edition by B. Toscani, Paris, 1971.

Chapter 11

CHRONICLES AND MEMOIRS

1. THE EARLIEST CHRONICLERS EXTANT

NO scientific attitude towards the writing of history, whether of times remote or recent, existed in the Middle Ages.[1] Not that the chroniclers knowingly distorted the truth. What *was* the truth for people living in an age when myth and legend blended so smoothly with fact and fiction, or when writers were usually dependent on one social class or faction in such a way that impartiality was unrealisable? Subjective always, many none the less made an honest endeavour to present the facts, and some limited themselves to what they had seen with their own eyes, or to eye-witness accounts by people they met. The results were often closer to historical novels than to the writing of history as we know it, reflecting the medieval mentality more faithfully than the events of the age. However, in this domain generalisations are of even less value than elsewhere, for there was much variety among the chroniclers,[2] reliability differing from one to the other. A tendency to prolixity is the most obvious feature they had in common, though this was by no means limited to the chronicles. Their works, many published by the Société de l'Histoire de France, fill a large number of substantial volumes. Only the most notable chroniclers will be mentioned here.

The earliest extant chronicles concerned with the history of medieval France were the work of clerics writing in Latin. Not until the early twelfth century did the first vernacular chronicles appear. An important figure in that century was the Anglo-Norman poet Wace, who was born in Jersey in the early 1100s and studied in Caen and Paris. Towards 1165 he became canon at Bayeux. He is the author of three hagiographic works adapted from Latin sources,[3] and two chronicles, the *Roman de Brut*, named after the legendary founder of the British race, of which this is a history,[4] completed in 1155 and offered, so his English counterpart Layamon informs us,[5] to Aliénor d'Aquitaine, and the *Roman de Rou*, a history of the dukes of Normandy,[6] interrupted and left incomplete about 1174, doubtless because Henry II had invited Benoît de Sainte-Maure[7] to write on the same subject. The principal source of Wace's *Brut* is

Geoffrey of Monmouth's famous *Historia Regum Britanniae*[8] completed twenty years earlier. As a chronicler Wace has acquired a reputation for honesty,[9] owed no doubt to his impatience with Breton superstitions[10] and cautious remarks of which he is fond, such as 'Ne sai se c'est veir' (I know not whether it is the truth). This reputation has not prevented the modern editor of *Brut* from suggesting that on occasions Wace made up certain names,[11] a practice which modern historians might view a little more sympathetically were they too constrained to write in octosyllabic rhyming couplets. Like Geoffrey of Monmouth, Wace was more a writer of romance than a historian, and it is his literary talent, despite a style at times heavy and monotonous, that tends to attract attention nowadays:

... ce qui importe, c'est son talent de peintre et de conteur, joint à un vocabulaire d'écrivain de métier, par lequel il réussit à recréer le détail d'un événement, à lui donner du relief; de ce point de vue, il est admirable, et il ne semble pas qu'on puisse trouver, parmi les auteurs de son siècle, de meilleur technicien dans l'art de la description.[12]

None the less, the attraction of the past was his principal reason for writing chronicles, as he declares in the opening lines of the *Rou*:

Por remembrer des ancesurs
les feiz e les diz e les murs.
(lines 1–2)

To remember the deeds, the words, and customs of our ancestors

Writing alone saves men's deeds from oblivion. Like the moralists of the age, Wace dwells on the ephemeral nature of all earthly things:

Tute rien turnë en declin,
tut chiet, tut moert, tut trait a fin;
tur funt, mur chiet, rose flaistrist,
cheval trebuche, drap viescist,
huem moert, fer use, fust purrist,
tute rien faite od mein perist.
(lines 131–6)

Everything passes away. Everything collapses, everything dies, everything goes to its end. Man dies, iron wears out, wood rots, towers crumble, walls fall down, roses wither, horses stumble, clothes grow old, all work of the hands perishes.

The principal sources of the *Rou* were the eleventh-century Latin chronicles of Dudon de Saint-Quentin, *De moribus et actis primorum normanniae ducum*, and Guillaume de Jumièges, *Gesta Normannorum ducum*. Unlike the *Brut*, *Rou* contains long passages in alexandrine verse, much of which has a ponderous didactic ring about it:

Li païz ke Normanz unt porpriz e
poplé
De Normanz Normandie a cest non
recovré;
Newstrie aveit non es tems
d'antiquité

The region which the Normans have occupied, from the Normans has acquired the name Normandy. In ancient times it was called Neustria, but the new occupants have changed the name. The ancestors'

Mez por la gent novele ont le non
 remué;
Li non as ancessors a bien as hers
 duré,
Normant sont, Normant furent,
 Normanz ont esté;
cen conte Maistre Vacce qui escript a
 trové.

name has endured with their descendants. Normans they are, Normans
they were, Normans they have been.
So says Master Wace who found it
written down.

(437–43)

Benoît de Sainte-Maure's *Chronique des Ducs de Normandie*[13] covers the same ground in a more fluid style in which meaning spills over from one rhyming couplet to the next more readily than in Wace's *Rou*. Written throughout in octosyllabic verse, totalling 44,544 lines, it begins with the death of a duke, unnamed, and the succession to the title of his elder son, Rollon (Rou) 'Qui unc ne fu mauvais ne fous' (line 2412) (Who never was evil or mad), and ends, ten dukes later, with the death of Henry I, fourth son of William the Conqueror, in 1135, and his burial at Reading.

II. THE 'CONQUESTE DE CONSTANTINOPLE' OF GEOFFROI DE VILLEHARDOUIN

Totally different in style and conception is Geoffroi de Ville-hardouin's *Conqueste de Constantinople*.[14] This account of the fourth crusade (1202–04) was written shortly after the events it describes by one who was not merely an eyewitness but who, as marshal of Champagne, was among the leaders of what has been termed the most extraordinary adventure of the Middle Ages. We may therefore expect to find less legendary material than in the works of a Wace or a Benoît de Sainte-Maure, but a distortion of a more subtle kind soon becomes apparent. Villehardouin set out to explain how it was that a crusading army was turned aside from its true purpose, to free the Holy Land from the infidel, and ended up by attacking Constantinople, capital of Eastern Christianity, an astonishing change of plan for which Villehardouin shared respon-sibility. His work, objective in appearance, is based in fact on a well-argued thesis which he himself doubtless saw as the whole truth: that the very nature of events led to the sacking of Constantinople, and that at no time were the crusaders free to make a choice between the conquest of Constantinople and the recapture of Jeru-salem. Villehardouin believed that Constantinople would serve as a base for future expeditions to regain the Holy Land 'if ever it is regained'. Quite apart from its historical importance, Ville-hardouin's *Conqueste* occupies a prominent place in French litera-ture, being one of the earliest prose works to have survived. The following passage relates how the crusaders, unable to pay the Venetians the enormous sums they demanded in order to convey the army by sea to the Holy Land, agreed to help them recapture Zara, a town in Dalmatia, from the king of Hungary, who had taken it in 1186. This was the vital decision in the deflecting of the crusade from its true purpose:

Lors parla li dux a sa gent et lors dist: 'Seignor, ceste genz ne nos puënt plus païer. E quan qu'ele nos ont païé, nos l'avons tot gaaignié por la convenance que il ne nos puënt mie tenir. Mes nostre droiz ne seroit mie par toz contez, si en recevriens grant blasme, et nostre terre. Or lor querons un plait. Li rois de Ungrie si nos tost Jadres en Sclavonie, qui est unes des plus forz citez del munde. Ne ja, par poöir que nos aïons, recovree ne sera, se par ceste genz non. Querons lor qu'il le nos aïent a conquerre, et nos lor respiterons les **XXX** M. mars d'argent que il nos doivent trosque adont que Diex les nos laira conquerre ensemble, nos et els'. Ensi fu cis plais requis. Mult fu contraliez de ceus qui volsissent que l'ost se departist, mes totes voies fu faiz li plaiz et otroiés.[15]
(Then the duke spoke to his men and said: 'Lords, these people can no longer pay us. And whatever they have paid us already, we have earned absolutely through the agreement which they cannot respect. But our right would not be respected by everybody, and we and our land would receive great blame. Now let us seek a settlement with them. The king of Hungary took from us Zara in Sclavonia, one of the strongest cities in the world. Never through our own efforts will it be recovered, unless these people help us. Let us ask them to help us conquer it, and we will let them off paying the thirty thousand silver marks that they owe us until God allows us to earn them together, us and them'. This was agreed. Those who wanted the army to disband were very vexed, but the agreement was made and accepted.)

Early though this prose is, the style is clear and straightforward, possessing an almost classical sobriety rare among early medieval prose-writers.

III. THE 'CONQUESTE DE CONSTANTINOPLE' OF ROBERT DE CLARI

A less remarkable stylist, but a writer capable of a gripping narrative and vivid description, was Robert de Clari, a knight of modest means, who took part in this same crusade and wrote an account of his experiences,[16] devoting less attention than Villehardouin to diplomatic manœuvres, and more to actual events. When he attempts to explain developments, he can be superficial and erroneous,[17] but his story is invaluable in that it records the preoccupations and attitudes of the mass of the crusaders. Here is part of his description of the departure of the fleet of ships from Venice, as they set off to attack Zara:

... ch'estoit le plus bele cose a eswarder qui fust tres le commenchement du monde, car il y avoit bien chent paire de busines, que d'argent que d'arain, qui toutes sonnerent a l'esmovoir, et tant de tymbres et tabours et autres estrumens, que ch'estoit une fine merveille. Quant il furent en chele mer et il eurent tendu leur voiles et leur banieres mises haut as castiaus des nes et leur enseingnes, si sanla bien que le mers formiast toute et qu'ele fust toute enbrasee des nes qu'il menoient et de la grant goie qu'il demenoient (p. 13).
(... it was the finest sight since the world began, for there were quite a hundred pairs of trumpets, both silver and bronze, which all sounded as they moved off, and so many drums and tabors and other instruments that it was an absolute marvel. When they were at sea and had hoisted their sails and raised their flags and banners high on the poops, it seemed that the sea was quite swarming and all alight with the ships they were taking and the great joy they were showing.)

IV. THE 'HISTOIRE DE GUILLAUME LE MARÉCHAL'

More impartial than Villehardouin and Robert de Clari is the *Histoire de Guillaume le Maréchal*,[18] who was regent of England from 1216, when Henry III acceded to the throne at the age of nine, to his death in 1219. The chronicle in fact covers a much wider period, devoted as it is to the career of this brilliant soldier and powerful knight (who overcame some 500 rivals in tournaments) during the reigns of Henry II, Richard Cœur-de-Lion, John Lackland, and Henry III. So prominent was the role he played that numbers of the essential features of English and indeed European history of the times are reflected in these pages, which are at their most accurate and reliable for the years 1186–1219, since for those years the anonymous poet worked from eyewitness notes supplied to him by Guillaume's devoted squire, Jean d'Erlee. This poem of 19,214 octosyllabic lines was composed between 1219 and 1226 at the request of Guillaume's eldest son, prompted possibly by Jean d'Erlee. Filled with accounts of campaigns on the continent, in England and Ireland, the chronicle reaches a culminating point in the Battle of Lincoln in 1217, where Guillaume put to flight the young king's adversaries and so secured the succession for him. As an actual historical document, there is no French chronicle of the thirteenth or fourteenth century superior to this one.

V. THE 'HISTOIRE DE SAINT LOUIS' OF JOINVILLE

The seventh crusade (1248–54) plays an important part in Jean de Joinville's *Histoire de Saint Louis*,[19] completed in 1309 when its author was 84 years of age. This is more of a biography than a history; Joinville, seneschal of Champagne, close confidant of Louis IX for many years, having been asked by Queen Jeanne de Navarre, wife of Philip the Fair, to write a book 'on the holy words and good deeds' of St Louis. Joinville had taken part with the king in the seventh crusade, but refused to accompany him on the eighth sixteen years later, during which the king met his death. In 1282 Joinville gave evidence at the inquiry leading to the king's canonisation. Written as it was in extreme old age, fifty years and more after the events it portrays, this work is inevitably somewhat jumbled, part biography of the crusading king, part autobiography, and the years may well have put a golden gloss on much of what actually occurred; yet it is full of lively scenes and skilfully etched portraits, a true masterpiece in the detail, if not in the overall plan (rarely the *forte* of any medieval writer in France). At times a very dry humour – or what may be taken for such – peeps through. When the king asked Joinville if he would rather be a leper or a sinner, Joinville – 'je, qui onques ne li menti' (I, who never lied to him) – replied that he would much rather be a sinner, and when the king asked him if he had ever washed the feet of the poor, Joinville replied very firmly that never would he do any such thing. On both occasions he earned the king's remonstrances. Many such dialogues are recorded reflecting Louis's piety and love of justice. On the other hand, Joinville's accounts of his numerous skirmishes with the Turks yield nothing in realism to the battles evoked by Robert de Clari or Villehardouin, or the countless hand-to-hand encounters so gorily portrayed in the *chansons de geste*:

Je et mi chevalier ferimes des esperons, et alames rescourre monsignour Raoul de Wanou, qui estoit avec moy, que il avoient tirié à terre. Endementières que je en revenoie, li Turc m'apuièrent de lour glaives; mes chevaus s'agenoilla pour le fais que il senti, et je en alai outre parmi les oreilles dou cheval, et me resdreçai, au plus tost que je peu, mon escu à mon col et m'espée en ma main; et mes sires Erars de Severey (que Diex absoille!), qui estoit entour moy, vint à moy et nous dist que nous nous treissions emprès une maison deffaite, et illec atenderiens le roy qui venoit. Ainsi comme nous en aliens à pié et à cheval, une grans route de Turs vint hurter à nous, et me portèrent à terre et alèrent par dessus moy, et firent voler mon escu de mon col; et quant il furent outre passei, messires Erars de Syverey revint sur moy et m'emmena, et en alames jusques aus murs de la maison deffaite .. [20]

(I and my knights pricked with our spurs and went to the rescue of my lord Raoul de Wanou who was with me, whom they had dragged to the ground. While I was coming back, the Turks pressed on me with their swords. My horse stumbled because of the weight and I went clean over the horse's ears and got up again as fast as I could, my shield hung from my neck and my sword in my hand; and my lord Erart de Severey (God bless him!) who was nearby, came to me and told us to withdraw to the vicinity of a ruined house, and there to await the king's arrival. While we were going off on foot and on horse, a great band of Turks came at us headlong, and bore me to the ground and went right over me, causing my shield to fly from around my neck; and when they had passed, my lord Erart de Syverey came back to me and took me off to the walls of the ruined house . . .)

Many such scenes are described in this colourful work which breathes new life into several genres: hagiography, *chanson de geste*, chronicle. Above all, Joinville reveals something of the life and outlook of a French nobleman towards the end of the epic era of the crusades.

VI. THE 'GRANDES CHRONIQUES DE FRANCE'

Begun in the thirteenth century, possibly at the instigation of St Louis, was the vast compilation known as *Les Grandes Chroniques de France*.[21] Originating in the abbey of Saint-Denis, they were written 'pour fere cognoistre aux vaillanz genz la geste des rois [de France] et pour mostrer a touz dont vient la hautece dou monde' (I, 3) (to let worthy people know the history of the kings of France and to reveal to all the source of the world's nobility). The early parts, based on Latin chronicles, are largely mythical, tracing the descent of the French from the Trojans, but the later parts are more trustworthy, based on eyewitness accounts or on actual historical documents available to the abbey of Saint-Denis, whose abbot was a member of the king's council. The monks of that important and influential centre continued to produce the chronicles to cover the history of France up to the death of Philip VI of Valois in 1350, after which further instalments were added by secular writers into the sixteenth century. Their blending of myth and reality has earned for the *Grandes Chroniques* the not inappropriate title of 'La Bible de France'.

VII. THE 'RÉCITS D'UN MÉNESTREL DE REIMS'

A sharp contrast is provided by a thirteenth-century prose work, the *Récits d'un Ménestrel de Reims*,[22] which covers much of the twelfth and the beginning of the thirteenth, but in quite a different spirit. This was primarily an entertainment, designed – despite being written in prose – to be listened to rather than read[23] and it was doubtless to this end that a substantial part was written in dialogue form. Witty and lively, its aim was to surprise and arouse, for this is 'une oeuvre d'imagination aussi dénuée de vérité que de vraisemblance historique' (p. ix). Its editor sums up its historical worth by observing that in these pages truth is 'un accessoire de la fiction' (ibid.). The most famous of its numerous colourful anecdotes concerns the minstrel Blondel and his discovery that Richard Cœur-de-Lion was held captive in an Austrian castle. Blondel stayed there for some time, suspecting that the mysterious prisoner he was never allowed to see might be his master. One day Richard caught a glimpse of the minstrel in the garden below his tower and began to sing a song which they had composed together:

Si commença a chanteir le premier mot haut et cler, car il chantoit très bien; et quant Blondiaus l'oï, si sot certainnement que ce estoit ses sires. Si ot en son cuer la graingneur joie qu'il eust eü onques mais nul jour' (p. 43). (And he began to sing the first word loud and clear, for he sang very well; and when Blondel heard him, he knew for sure that it was his master. And he felt the greatest joy he had ever felt in his life.)

According to this account Blondel took the news back to England of the king's whereabouts, and his ransom was duly arranged.

VIII. THE CHRONICLES OF JEAN FROISSART

Well known as a chronicler of the fourteenth century is Jean Froissart, the four books of whose chronicles cover most of the century from 1325 onwards, that is, rather more than the first half of the Hundred Years War.[24] Born in Valenciennes in or about 1337, the very year which saw the start of the Hundred Years War, when Edward III put forward his claim to the French throne, Froissart spent much of his time attached to various courts in England and on the continent. In 1361 he was appointed secretary to the queen of England, Philippa of Hainaut, wife of Edward III. After her death in 1369 he had a succession of patrons: Wenceslas of Bohemia, Albert of Bavaria, Guy de Blois. Consequently, in his abundant writings – lyric poetry, romances, chronicles – he reflected the tastes and outlook of the aristocracy. The year of his death is unknown, but cannot have been much beyond the end of the fourteenth century. Travelling widely on the continent, also in England and Scotland, his alert, inquisitive mind observed the habits and customs of different peoples, particularly in the matter of waging war. Like a modern news-reporter, he spoke to many who had taken part in the military engagements of the day. He also made use of chronicles written by eyewitnesses, notably Jean le Bel,[25] large sections of whose history of Edward III's campaigns were incorporated by Froissart into his own work. He may have been invited, possibly by Queen Philippa, to continue Jean le Bel's chronicle where it had been left off. In his prologue he acknowledges his indebtedness to Jean le Bel, though he gave no hint of its extent.[26] Froissart's method, and particular interests, made his chronicles strong on the description of actual events, but a good deal less effective on the forces which led up to them. He had no single hero to build his chronicle around, yet a particular attitude of mind influenced all that he wrote, and there is no more impartiality here than in his predecessors. Like Jean le Bel, he was a fervent admirer of the warring nobility, whether engaged in tournaments, which he describes at inordinate length, with all the enthusiasm of an *aficionado* of the bullring (not that he is alone in this. Other chronicles, such as the *Histoire de Guillaume le Maréchal*, also devote much space to tournaments, whose importance loomed large in the life of the nobility), or in actual battles.[27] Valiant feats of arms and glorious chivalry, such was the very stuff of history. Master of the picturesque phrase, the little details that bring a whole scene to life, he evoked the battles of the fourteenth century in vivid Technicolor, delighting, for example, in describing the exact colours and insignia of the coats-of-arms borne by his many heroes of different nationalities. Froissart was a romantic who kept alive the ideals, and illusions, of chivalry, one of the last really great writers to do so.

IX. THE CHRONICLES OF ENGUERRAN DE MONSTRELET

In the first half of the fifteenth century Enguerran de Monstrelet[28] set out to continue the work of the one he called 'ce prudent et très renommé historien, maistre Jean Froissart' (I, 5) (this wise and very renowned historian, master Jean Froissart). He too was a fervent admirer of 'les très dignes et haulx fais d'armes' (I, 2) (very worthy and noble feats of arms), but, talented writer and conscientious historian though he was (his chronicles are among the most reliable for the period), his account was duller and more plodding than that of his illustrious predecessor. Glorification of feats of arms had become almost an anachronism by the fifteenth century, though Monstrelet was not quite alone, for something of this attitude lingered on still in the Burgundian chroniclers Georges Chastellain, Jean Molinet, and Olivier de la Marche.[29] On the whole they were less sycophantic and more objective than their predecessors,[30] but the last-named in particular was intent still on fanning the embers of Burgundy's dying glory, even after Louis XI, the 'universal spider', had made the once proud and immensely rich duchy a part of his kingdom in 1482.

A new spirit was to pervade the later fifteenth century, wearied no doubt by the long-drawn-out, destructive warfare. Glamour seems to have worn itself out in the defeats of the fourteenth century, and the victories of the fifteenth produced a more hard-headed, realistic outlook. War was not a game after all, and it was not so much the bloodshed and death that pointed this lesson, but the grim economic consequences affecting the entire nation. Did this mark the end of an age of heroes, or was it not more simply that the persistent voice of reality could be ignored no longer? This radical change of outlook owed much to the rise of the bourgeoisie at the expense of the nobility, a development which gathered impetus from the thirteenth century onwards. Jean le Bel praised Edward II for having nobles as counsellors – hence, he maintained, the English monarch's successes against the French – whereas the French king surrounded himself with lesser men, and paid the penalty. This is a prejudiced view, and the French, after all, were to have the last laugh. Their ultimate and decisive victories owed more to popular movements and feelings – witness the triumphs of Joan of Arc — than to the nobility's 'glorious feats of arms'. Froissart's counterpart in the later fifteenth century, Philippe de Commynes, had an utterly different outlook, seeing as much cowardice as heroism in warfare, only too well aware of the sordid intrigues and underhand motives behind what he called 'la bestialité des princes', an expression which Froissart could never have used in so all-embracing a fashion.

X. THE 'JOURNAL D'UN BOURGEOIS DE PARIS'

The true meaning of warfare is well illustrated in the grim but fascinating pages of the anonymous *Journal d'un bourgeois de Paris*[31] which covers life in the capital, diary-fashion, between 1405 and 1449. We follow closely the harsh living conditions of the ordinary people of Paris as they are menaced by one enemy after another. Whenever hostile forces approach the gates of the capital, the price of bread rises steeply (price changes are recorded with great precision) and foods like cheese and eggs become prohibitively dear. The bitterness and miseries of civil war often colour the comments. The account of a clash between Parisian forces and the Armagnacs is concluded thus:

Dont c'est grant pitié et d'une part et d'autre, que fault que chrestienté tue ainsi l'un l'autre sans savoir cause pourquoy, car l'un sera de cent lieues loing de l'autre, qui se vendront entretuer, pour gaigner ung pou d'argent ou le gibet au corps ou enfer a la pauvre ame (p. 233).
(Wherefore it is a great pity on both sides that Christians have to kill each other without knowing why, for one will be a hundred leagues away from the other, and they will come together to kill each other, to earn a little money, or the gibbet for their bodies and hell for their wretched souls.)

Even Joan of Arc is not presented in romantic or sentimental fashion: some said that she was a martyr, some that she should have been put to death sooner, 'mais quelle mauvestie ou bonté qu'elle eust faicte, elle fut arse celui jour' (269–70) (but whatever evil or good she had done, on that day she was burned). Natural calamities are also recorded: harsh frosts in winter, plagues of cock-chafers in the summer (1422, 1425, 1428, etc.).

XI. THE 'CHRONIQUE SCANDALEUSE'

Equally forthright and down-to-earth is the *Journal de Jean de Roye*,[32] which covers the years 1460–83, again with particular reference to living conditions in Paris. Already in the sixteenth century it was known as the *Chronique scandaleuse* 'à cause qu'elle fait mention de tout ce qu'a fait le roi Louis XI et récite des choses qui ne sont pas trop à son advantage'.[33] Pestilence, crime, immorality, warfare provide a grimmer and more convincing justification for this second, and very apt, title. Decidedly, the age of glorious chivalry, of high-flown encomia, was dead.

XII. THE 'MÉMOIRES' OF PHILIPPE DE COMMYNES

Most outstanding of the fifteenth-century chroniclers was undoubtedly Philippe de Commynes, who was born about 1447 and died in 1511. In 1464 he began his career in the service of Charles, comte de Charolais, who became duke of Burgundy on the death of his father, Philip the Good, in 1467, and whose temperament and actions earned for him the nickname le Téméraire (the Rash). In 1472 Commynes changed allegiance and soon became a trusted confidant of Louis XI. The eight books of his *Mémoires*[34] cover the years 1464–98, that is, all but the first three years of Louis XI's reign (1461–83) and that of his successor, Charles VIII (1483–98), and end with the coronation of Louis XII. Commynes deals above all with the events, military and political, in which he himself had been involved, hesitant only when 'je n'estoie point sur les lieux' (I, 89) (I was not on the spot), but he also summarises developments such as the rivalry in England of the houses of Lancaster and York. True man of the fifteenth century in his realistic attitude towards human affairs, knowing men and their motives too well to impute to them high-minded, dispassionate ideals, he saw them as they are, not as he would have liked them to be. The Battle of Montlhéry between the forces of the duke of Burgundy and the king he depicts as a confused struggle between different groups, with men running away on both sides. In the half-light of early day horsemen approach an enemy group gingerly and prepare to attack, only to discover that the enemy was in fact a clump of tall thistles. Subsequent parleys were equally confused, with three meetings held simultaneously in the same chamber (I, 77). Always Commynes keeps a cool, ironical eye on men's behaviour:

Tel perdit ses offices et estatz pour s'en estre fuy, et furent donnéz à d'autres qui avoyent fuy dix lieues plus loing. Ung de nostre costé perdit auctorité et, privé de la présence de son maistre, ung moys après eut plus d'auctorité que devant (I, 34–5).

(One man was deprived of his duties and estates because he ran away, and they were bestowed on others who had fled ten leagues further. One of our side was stripped of his authority, and, after his master's departure, one month later he had more authority than before.)

Whether on the field of battle or in council chamber, he finds that men are a mixture of good and evil, and tends to see everything and everybody in terms of opposites:

Au fort, il me semble que Dieu n'a créé en ce monde ny homme ny beste à qui il n'ayt fait quelque chose son contraire pour le tenir en humilité et en craincte (II, 207–8) (In the end it seems to me that God has created no man or beast without making also his opposite to keep him in humility and fear).

He makes many observations on princes, their temperaments and ways, their understanding, or more frequently misunderstanding, of the realities of history. He remarks that one prince with 10,000 men is more to be feared than ten with six thousand each, since it would take them too long to agree among themselves. The sharp cutting edge of his satirical observation is blunted slightly only in his portrait of Louis XI, but even here his admiration stopped short of adulation. Commynes was no Joinville, and only in a world where political intrigue was elevated to a religion could Louis XI ever have been a saint. Commynes, however, explained away the suffering Louis XI had caused so many (Commynes himself spent eight months in one of the infamous iron cages at Loches) in one of those generalisations on human nature of which he was so fond:

... il n'est nul homme, de quelque dignité qu'il soit, qui ne souffre ou en son secret ou en public, et par especial ceux qui font souffrir les autres (II, 321–322) (there is no man, no matter how great his dignity, who does not suffer either in secret or in public, particularly if he makes others suffer).

For every single day of pleasure in the king's life there had been at least twenty of toil and misery.

It has been argued that Commynes deliberately painted humanity in the blackest colours in order to make his desertion of the duke of Burgundy appear a trivial affair.[35] It seems more likely, however, that his tendency towards a universal pessimism is a bias reflecting, partly the intellectual climate of the age, but mainly Commynes's own temperament, cynical, disillusioned, destructive, a temperament which accounts in the first instance for his change of loyalty and which can be felt in almost all that he wrote, for example, his seeing on the battlefield at Montlhéry as many cowards as heroes, and his dwelling on the fact. It is in any case clear that a change from the Burgundy camp to the French one was not so extraordinary as to engender such a large and important book. Commynes depicted men as he genuinely felt them to be.

Intended ostensibly to serve as material for a larger work to be written in Latin by Angelo Cato, archbishop of Vienne,[36] Commynes none the less clearly hoped that his memoirs would be read and consulted, since he makes so many personal observations on the behaviour of others, particularly those in authority. It is for his ability to look beneath the surface of events and to penetrate the secret motives of even the greatest men that he has sometimes been referred to as the first real historian,[37] rather as his contemporary François Villon has been called the first modern poet. Knowing neither Greek nor Latin, he wrote a simple, clear, direct French in this age when the language had reached maturity and was not yet cluttered up with erudite expressions, or grown self-conscious about the need for clarity: free-flowing, natural still, already a wonderful instrument in the hands of gifted writers like Chartier, Gerson, and Commynes.

NOTES

1. An excellent account of the medieval conception of history and of its domination by religious doctrines is given by G. W. Coopland in his introduction to *The Tree of Battles of Honoré Bonet*, Liverpool, 1949, 38–47.
2. On this subject see Payen, op. cit., 86–91.
3. See above, p. 51.
4. I. Arnold ed., *Le Roman de Brut de Wace*, Paris, SATF, 2 vols., 1938–1940.
5. G. L. Brook and R. F. Leslie eds., *Layamon: Brut*, Oxford, EETS, 1963, vol. I, lines 20–3.
6. The latest edition is in the SATF series by A. J. Holden. Vol. I was published in 1970, vol. II 1971.
7. See above, pp. 121, 134, 137, 138.
8. See above, pp. 146–7.
9. Arnold, ed. cit., I, LXXXI.
10. See above, p. 148.
11. Arnold, ed. cit., I, LXXXII.
12. ibid., LXXXVII.
13. ed. C. Fahlin, Uppsala, 2 vols., 1951–54.
14. ed. Paulin Paris in 1838 for the Société de l'Histoire de France; a more recent edition is that of J. E. White, New York, 1968.
15. ibid., 45–6.
16. P. Lauer ed., *La Conqueste de Constantinople*, Paris, CFMA, 1924.
17. ibid., viii–ix.
18. P. Meyer ed., *Histoire de Guillaume le Maréchal*, Société de l'Histoire de France, Paris, 3 vols., 1891–1901.
19. Natalis de Wailly ed., *Histoire de Saint Louis par Jean, Sire de Joinville*, Société de l'Histoire de France, Paris, 1868, reprint New York, 1965.
20. ibid., 78–9.
21. J. Viard ed., *Les Grandes Chroniques de France*, Société de l'Histoire de France, Paris, 10 vols., 1920–53.

22. Natalis de Wailly ed., *Récits d'un Ménestrel de Reims*, Société de l'Histoire de France, Paris, 1876.

23. ibid., vi–viii.

24. ed. S. Luce, G. Raynaud, L. Mirot for the Société de l'Histoire de France, Paris, 13 vols., 1869–1957. For K. de Lettenhove's ed. see below, p. 325. The first book of the chronicles has recently been edited by G. T. Diller, *Froissart. Chroniques. Début du premier livre*, Geneva, *TLF*, 1972.

25. J. Viard and E. Deprez eds., *Chronique de Jean le Bel*, Société de l'Histoire de France, Paris, 2 vols., 1904–05.

26. It is worth noting that Jean le Bel's modern editors place him 'dans les premiers rangs parmi nos écrivains du moyen âge', ibid., I, xxvii.

27. He was delighted by 'notables proesses et merveilleuses aventures, les grandes apertises et les beaulx fais d'armes' (noteworthy acts of prowess and incredible adventures, great deeds of valour and fine feats of arms) and it makes no difference whatever that these are not his own words, but Jean le Bel's (I, xxxi).

28. L. Douët-d'Arcq ed., *La Chronique d'Enguerran de Monstrelet, 1400–1444*, Paris, 6 vols., 1857–62.

29. Kervyn de Lettenhove ed., *Œuvres de Georges Chastellain*, Brussels, 8 vols., 1863–66; G. Doutrepont and O. Jodogne eds., *Chroniques de Jean Molinet*, Brussels, 3 vols., 1935–37; H. Beaune and J. d'Arbaumont eds., *Mémoires d'Olivier de la Marche*, Paris, 4 vols., 1883–88.

30. Here is Chastellain's verdict on the princes of his age, with Louis XI particularly in mind: 'Les princes de notre temps sont corrompus; ils ne craignent point de se voir reprocher le mal qu'ils font, ils recherchent peu la louange que l'on acquiert légitimement en faisant le bien. Tout entiers à leur vanité, ils oublient Dieu et ne vivent plus qu'en eux-mêmes et pour eux-mêmes' (I, xLv) (The princes of our age are corrupt; they do not fear being reproached with the evil they do, they are not after the praise that is the rightful consequence of doing good. Entirely given up to their vanity, they forget God and live only in themselves and for themselves).

31. A. Tuetey ed., *Journal d'un bourgeois de Paris*, Société de l'Histoire de Paris, Paris, 1881.

32. B. de Mandrot ed., *Journal de Jean de Roye connu sous le nom de Chronique Scandaleuse, 1460–1483*, Société de l'Histoire de France, Paris, 2 vols., 1894–96.

33. La Croix du Maine, writing in 1584; ibid., I, xii–xiii.

34. J. Calmette and G. Durville eds., *Mémoires de Philippe de Commynes*, Paris, Les Classiques de l'Histoire de France au Moyen Age, 3 vols., 1924–1925.

35. J. Dufournet, *La Destruction des mythes dans les Mémoires de Philippe de Commynes*, Geneva, 1966, 698.

36. ibid., 697.

37. ibid., 13.

Chapter 12

POETRY OF THE FOURTEENTH AND
FIFTEENTH CENTURIES

I. GUILLAUME DE MACHAUT

INFLUENTIAL in shaping the poetic tastes of the later Middle Ages was Guillaume de Machaut, born in the village of that name in the Ardennes in or about 1300.[1] After studying theology (where is not known) and becoming *maistre-ès-arts*, he joined the clergy of the diocese of Rheims, and was attached for a number of years to the household of Jean de Luxembourg, king of Bohemia. In 1337 he became a canon at Rheims cathedral, and died in 1377. Well known nowadays as the finest musician of his times, he was also a very active writer. He launched two fashions within the sphere of lyric poetry whose success was to last to the end of the Middle Ages and beyond: in form the use of certain genres, whose ultimate origins are obscure, no doubt popular, principally the *ballade*, the *rondeau*, and the *virelai*, and in substance a frequent recourse to allegory of the type so successfully exploited by Guillaume de Lorris. Indeed, Guillaume de Machaut's first work, *Le Dit du Verger*, is a mini-*Roman de la Rose* displaying considerable charm,[2] and an ability to fuse fantasy and reality in an ingenious fashion. The poet dreams of love beneath a tree in an orchard, in the branches of which sat the God of Love. When he flew aloft the tree was shaken and the cold dew showered down on the poet, waking him up!

Two lengthy narrative poems ('dits') by Guillaume consist of debates similar in tone to the 'tensons' or 'jeux-partis' of the twelfth and thirteenth centuries, but much longer. Which is more deserving of pity, a jilted knight or a widowed lady? On this subject Guillaume wrote some 6,000 lines, developing many arguments often of a subtle kind. In the first of these poems, the *Jugement dou Roy de Behaigne*, consisting of 2,079 lines arranged in stanzas of three decasyllabic lines followed by one of four syllables, the decision was left, at Guillaume's suggestion, to his patron, the king of Bohemia. Guillaume led the knight and the widow to Durbuy, a real castle, accurately described. Inside they

293

met the king surrounded by allegorical figures: Richesse, Amour, Biauté, Loiauté, Leesse, etc., presided over by Raison. The king pronounced in favour of the knight whose suffering he considered perpetual, while time would help the lady forget her dead husband. Placing this very real king in the midst of such unreal courtiers is Guillaume's way of implying that the influence of the king's noble mind and character permeated the entire Court. The king is shown in full command of his gallant retinue: he presides over them, lets them discuss among themselves, reminds them of the essential issue when they digress, sums up their arguments, makes the final pronouncement, and rounds everything off with a week's jollities. *The Jugement dou Roy de Navarre*, written probably when Charles II (the Bad) acceded to the throne of Navarre in 1349, returned to the same subject, this time deciding in favour of the young widow. Had the first poem been received unfavourably by the ladies at Court? Did Guillaume feel obliged to write this palinode as a result? This is possible, but there is nothing apologetic about the tone, and Guillaume, no longer the amused bystander, is the principal advocate of the original decision, gradually over-whelmed in a flood of arguments by another set of allegorical characters, all ladies. Only their names are abstractions, for they behave in very convincing fashion, often all talking excitedly at the same time. The central figure is not the king of Navarre, but a lady, herself an allegorical abstraction, Beneurté (Felicity), of whom the allegorical damsels Largesse, Paix, Concorde, etc., are 'embellishments'. Allegory within allegory within allegory, for even Beneurté's clothes have special significance – her blouse is Franchise, her petticoat Simplesse, made of Bienveillance and embroidered with Souffisance. Having listened patiently to the lengthy debate in which many of the favourite love stories of the Middle Ages, classical and medieval, are summarised as support for arguments on both sides (an excellent mirror of courtly reading and interest in the mid-fourteenth century), the king of Navarre reversed the earlier decision, and as punishment for his obstinacy sentenced Guillaume to write three poems: a lay, a *rondeau*, and a *ballade*.

The modern reader is likely to be struck above all by the intro-duction to this poem, which could well have been quite a separate work. In this passage of 430 lines, Guillaume gives a vivid description of the Black Death which swept through Europe in 1348 and 1349. The gruesome details of the plague and its effects correspond with those in contemporary chronicles. Guillaume relates how he shut himself indoors to escape infection, only emerging when it was clearly over. On his first outing he went hunting hares, and then, with that astonishing propensity for blending (more accurately in this case juxtaposing) truth and fiction, relates how he met a lady who challenged him about the verdict in the *Jugement dou Roy de Behaigne*. She took him to her Court, and turned out to be Lady Beneurté. Why this name should have been chosen for the central allegorical figure is not explained, but is clearly important.[3] She is represented as all-powerful, constantly present 'Entre ami et loial amie' (line 3901) (Between a lover and his loyal sweetheart). Therefore she had evidently been present between the lady and her dead husband, but not between the knight and his flighty lady who was not 'loial'. In the first *Jugement*, Guillaume had failed to take account of this difference. Happiness is not so widespread that it can be discounted lightly. The lady's loss was consequently greater than was that of the jilted knight.[4]

Between the *Jugements* Guillaume composed the *Remede de Fortune*, a work of 4,298 lines, mainly octosyllabic, important in that it contains several 'fixed forms':[5] lay, *complainte, chanson royale, ballade, virelai, rondelet, prière, refrain*, all but the last two being provided with a musical accompaniment. The subject is a love affair which Guillaume had had or at least pretended to have had. Both form and subject are treated in a doctrinal manner, as though Guillaume was growing into his role as the eminent poet and songwriter of the day, demonstrating to others how it should all be done. Yet again he reveals his capacity for carrying fantasy into the actual world, making the fantasy realistic and convincing rather than allowing it to bear us off into a world of make-believe.

We have followed Guillaume's literary career from its beginnings to the time when he was established as a successful poet and musician. Space allows us no more than a passing mention of his remaining works: *Le Dit dou Lyon*, a poem of 2,204 octosyllabic lines in which Guillaume is once more cast in his favourite role as a faithful lover, moving still in a world of fantasy, indebted in this instance to the romances of Chrétien de Troyes, witness the lion which befriends the hero, and the miraculous orchard defended by a wall of air. Differences, however, are noteworthy: the author builds the work around himself, no interest is shown in feats of arms, and allegory now plays a prominent role, the lion, for example, representing the perfect lover. *Le Dit de l'Alerion*, containing 4,814 octosyllabic lines, deals outwardly with the poet's interest in birds of prey, but it becomes evident that the real subject is yet again Guillaume's love-life, here presented in metaphorical fashion. Very different is the *Confort d'Ami*, a work of 4,004 octosyllabic lines written as consolation for Charles the Bad (for whom Guillaume had earlier written the *Jugement dou Roy de Navarre*) at a time when he was held prisoner by John II (the

Good), king of France. *La Fontaine Amoureuse*, containing 2,848 lines, mostly octosyllabic, is also a consolation, written for Jean, duc de Berry, who, newly married in 1360, was compelled under the treaty of Brétigny to go as hostage to England. Guillaume's principal borrowing on this occasion was from the *Ovide moralisé*, an early fourteenth-century adaptation of the *Metamorphoses*. The success of this poem is revealed by the number of imitators it inspired: Froissart, Oton de Granson, Chaucer, Christine de Pisan.

In his last *dit*, devoted appropriately enough to the dominant subject of his abundant verse, Guillaume gives the impression of wanting to batter down the walls of Incredulousness and to carry the Castle of Truth by storm. Indeed nothing is more convincing than *Le Voir Dit*[6] – The True Tale (were the others fictions after all?) – a voluminous exchange of letters (in prose) and poems between the ageing poet and musician and a tender young admirer whose name is given in an anagram: Peronne d'Armentières.[7] The slow progress of their love is followed from its innocent beginnings to the time when Guillaume slept with her, though the good canon was at pains to behave, he assures us, 'plus simplement qu'une pucelle' (line 3470) (more simply than a maiden). Whether this affair took place solely in the poet's fertile imagination, or in actual fact, or was an idealised version of a real affair, it is undeniable that some of Guillaume's finest love-poetry is to be found here. All his versatility as a writer of prose, of narrative verse, of *ballades*, rondels, and *virelais* with accompanying music, all his culture steeped in classical mythology, are fully deployed in this delightful composition. Guillaume's love of music seems on occasions to have affected the very choice of words. In the soft, caressing vowel sounds of the following passage, rounded off each time by the rolled *r*, the poet has transformed himself into a turtle-dove:

Mon cuer, ma suer, ma douce amour	My heart, my sister, sweet my love,
Oy de ton ami la clamour.	Hear your lover's lament,
Mon cuer, ma suer, ma douce amour	My heart, my sister, sweet my love,
Voy comment je pour toy demour;	See how I linger here for you.
Fay tant qu'o toy soit mon demour.	Bring it about that my abode be with you,
Mon cuer, ma suer, ma douce amour	My heart, my sister, sweet my love,
Oy du grand desir la rumour	Hear the murmur of this keen desire
Qui fait en mon cuer son demour . . .	Which makes its abode in my heart.

This particular poem contains 51 lines, 24 of which consist of the refrain (lines 4412–63).

Guillaume de Machaut's well-merited fame as a musician, particularly as the composer of one of the earliest polyphonic masses,

written possibly for the coronation of Charles V, should not be
allowed to overshadow his very substantial achievements as a poet
and as a vital formative influence on many writers of the fourteenth and fifteenth centuries.

II. EUSTACHE DESCHAMPS

When Machaut died in 1377, his admirer and imitator Eustache
Deschamps, thirty-one years of age at the time, wrote a *ballade*
honouring the poet and musician who had been partly responsible
for his upbringing and who, according to a later work, was his
uncle.[8] Deschamps occupied a variety of posts at the Court of
Charles V. He was a protégé of Louis d'Orléans, father of the
prince-poet. In 1389 he became bailiff of Senlis. He died in 1407.
Deschamps was the most fertile *ballade*-monger France has ever
known, with a total of 1,017 *ballades* to his credit and a considerable, though lesser, number of *rondeaux* and *virelais*. Like Machaut
he composed over 80,000 lines of verse, ranging widely over a
variety of topics, and several prose works, among which is his
Art de Dictier composed in 1392,[9] the first treatise on the composition of poetry to have been written in French. Much of this
pioneering work is taken up with examples of the different types
of 'fixed forms',[10] but this introduction, after describing briefly
the seven liberal arts, comments significantly on the nature of
poetry. No musician, Deschamps defends poetry as a genre in its
own right, calling it a 'musique naturelle' on the grounds that it
is a gift which one either does or does not possess. The technique
of composing *ballades* can be acquired, but only by those endowed with the poetic instinct. It does not occur to Deschamps
that the same remarks could be made about music, which he dubs
'musique artificielle'. The very sounds of the language can have a
musicality of their own, a 'musique de bouche'. Written at a
time when poetry and music were beginning to go their different
ways, this treatise is in effect a justification of this development.[11] Theorists of the following century, in their 'arts de seconde
rhétorique', were to concentrate their attention more and more on
the organisation of the word matter in various complex versification patterns, a trend which the very liberation from music did
much to encourage.

Deschamps was a most versatile 'maker', but particularly striking
in his work is a preoccupation with daily life, at a more mundane,
trivial level than Guillaume de Machaut. He shows an earthy
realism, a wry, at times scurrilous, humour as he comments on
conditions at Court, at home, or in the course of his travels: cold,

draughty rooms at Court, the mud in Flanders, lice, fleas, stink, and pigs in Bohemia, the miseries of a cold winter, of being sea-sick on a cross-channel voyage, of walking in streets cluttered up with beggars ('Take 'em, hang 'em and good riddance' is his robust and heartless refrain here, Ballade 1299), of riding on a lame and tired horse, of being tricked by thieving valets, of sleeping two in a bed, of badly cooked food in Bohemia, of wineless meals in England, of always having tripe and onions for lunch, of meals where everything is served with mustard.[12] The culinary pre-occupation alone of this poet would fill a volume. He painted a charming picture of his native town, Vertus:

... Bons vins a, fromens, soille, avaine,
Moulins, jardins, riviere saine
Et qui court contre le souleil,
Sanz tarir vient de vive vaine:
Chascun le puet veoir a l'ueil ...

(Ballade 1339, lines 6–10)

It has good wines, wheat, rye, oats, mills, gardens, a clean river flowing towards the sun, without drying up, since it rises from a never-ceasing spring. Anyone can see this for himself.

He wrote several *ballades* on the unsurpassed beauty of Paris. Occasionally he gave proof of having the eye of a poet, if not his pen, as when he saw the sun glistening on dew-drops in a wood in early morning. He wrote about love, delightfully in his early verse, but mostly sceptically in his mature years, about marriage dis-paragingly, about parentage worriedly – 'Qui fille a n'est pas a repos' (He who has a daughter is not at ease), about the young generation despairingly:

Li jeune enfant deviennent rufien
Joueurs de dez, gourmans et plains d'ivresse

(Ballade 933, lines 9–10)

Youngsters become ruffians, Dice-players, greedy drunkards ...

about old age resignedly, about death moralisingly. It is a poetry of physical impressions, taken up with what strikes his ever-observant eye, often content to stop at the surface appearance of things. It is a poetry that never takes wing; his Muse wore hob-nailed boots. A skilful caricaturist, he looks round the banqueting table and describes the facial contortions of the guests chewing away at their food. In the twentieth century he would surely have been a newspaper or television reporter drawing amusing and vivid descriptions of 'Deschamps's world'. To sum up, a robust, matter-of-fact Champenois personality with an ironical sense of humour, somewhat cynical and disillusioned, uninterested in literary ideal-isms and airy-fairy notions, endowed with a practical philosophy for daily living, a ready though superficial pen, a fertile versifier, a mediocre poet.

III. THE POETRY OF JEAN FROISSART

On his arrival in 1361, at the age of twenty-four, at the English Court of his compatriot Queen Philippa of Hainaut[13] Froissart's future career as poet and chronicler was foreshadowed in the poem he presented to her (now lost) on the Battle of Poitiers (1356). A traditionalist who believed that

... toute joie et toute honnours Viennent et d'armes et d'amours ...[14]	All joy and all honour Come from arms and love ...

Froissart paid homage to the former in his chronicles and to the latter in a series of poetical works strongly influenced by Machaut, whose ability to depict scenes of actual life Froissart has been held to surpass.[15]

A particularly charming poem is the *Espinette amoureuse*,[16] an autobiographical (or pseudo-autobiographical) work of 4,198 lines, mostly octosyllabic, composed in 1369. Froissart begins by recalling the carefree years of his childhood. When still a 'puchiaus' (young lad) not twelve years of age, he would give presents to the 'pucelettes' (young lasses) – pins, an apple, a pear, a glass ring – and wonder when the time for love would come. Meantime he was happy in his pursuits:

Je faisoie bien une escluse En un ruissot d'une tieulette, Et puis prendoie une esculette Que noer je faisoie aval; Et s'ai souvent fait en un val D'un ruissot ou d'un acoulin Sus deus tieulettes un moulin; Et puis jeuiens aux papelotes Et ou ruissot laviens nos cotes, Nos caperons et nos cemises; Si sont bien nos ententes mises A faire voler aval vent Une plume ...	I would make a dam in a stream with a small tile, then I would take a little bowl and float it downstream, and in the valley of a stream or rivulet I have often made a mill on two little tiles. And then we would play with mud-pies and wash our tunics, our cloaks, and shirts in the stream. And we have spent our time flying a feather down the wind.

(lines 152–64)

He was more interested in making mud-pies than in playing chess! He names over forty children's games on which he loved to spend his time. At school he was a refractory child, often smacked by his parents for tearing his clothes, but

On y perdoit sa painne toute Car pour ce ja mains n'en feïsse (266–7)	It was an utter waste of time, for never would I take the slightest notice.

In winter he read love stories and so formed a taste which stayed with him in adult life. Like Guillaume de Lorris and Machaut, he awoke to love through nature. He describes a moment of ecstasy early one morning in a small garden:

Je me tenoie en un moment	I stood still for a moment, and re-
Et pensoie au chant des oisiaus,	flected on the birdsong, as I looked
En regardant les arbrissiaus	at the young trees growing in pro-
Dont il y avoit grant fuison . . .	fusion.
(380–3)	

In this propitious setting allegorical figures inevitably appear, drawn from the classical legends in which these fourteenth-century writers were so well versed. Mercury introduces the poet to Juno, Venus, and Pallas and asks him if Paris had been right to give the golden apple to Venus. The story of Helen and the sack of Troy is then recalled, albeit briefly. After some hesitation Froissart approves of Paris's verdict and Mercury departs in a huff, exclaiming: 'I knew you'd say that. All lovers tread that path' (523–4). Venus expresses her pleasure and promises to introduce the poet to love. What follows is a leisurely account of a flirtation with a lovely girl whom Froissart finds engrossed in reading a courtly romance, *Cleomadès*, by Adenet le Roi. The earnest novice composes numbers of *ballades*, *virelais*, and *rondeaux* in honour of his new-found love – pleasant ditties rarely rising above the level of

> A drink! A drink! There's a fire in my heart
> For it's been smitten by a smouldering dart.
> (1556–7)

Not surprisingly, he made little impression on the lady, and accordingly sought solace in foreign travel, spending a long period in the country 'which hates peace more than war' (i.e., England, 2546), consoled by a magic mirror which, formerly the property of the girl, reflected her image whenever he looked into it. Her reflection obligingly produces a series of poems headed 'The Lady's Consolation', a counterpart to his earlier lament. On his return he is at last favourably received by her. In an idyllic scene love burgeons amidst nature's beauties:

Diex! que li tamps estoit jolis,	God! how lovely the weather was,
Li airs quois et clers et seris!	the air peaceful, bright, and serene.
Et chil rossegnol haut chantoient,	And the nightingales sang loud,
Qui forment nous resjoïssoient.	bringing us great joy.
(3654–7)	

They picnic beneath a white-flowering hawthorn – the 'espinette' of the title. Their embryonic and wholly innocent relationship ends when Male Bouche (Nasty Mouth), that spoilsport from the *Roman de la Rose*, appears on the scene and sours the lady's feelings for him. In their final encounter she tauntingly exclaims: 'Point d'amie chi pour vous' (3783) (No sweetheart for you here), gives his hair a violent tug, and trips off. This, he decides cheerfully, is a token of affection, and pens a *ballade* accordingly. So the story concludes.

The *Espinette amoureuse* represents only a very small part of Froissart's courtly verse.[17] At times ingenious, indeed far-fetched, as in the detailed comparison of a lover with a clock, in *L'Orloge amoureus*; at times witty and original, as in *Le Dit dou Florin*, in which he has a long discussion with his one remaining florin; at times vivid with scenes of court life and festivities, as in *La Prison amoureuse*; usually autobiographical, though his love-life is often pushed into the background to make way for a series of digressions, as in *Le Joli Buisson de Jeunesse*; Froissart's poetry is invariably pleasant, and often surprisingly fresh and sparkling, provided that the reader can accept a leisurely pace and numerous incursions into classical legends or moralising discourses; provided also that he will not tire of the rhyming octosyllabic couplets favoured still by Froissart, a pattern varied occasionally by the insertion of *ballades, rondeux,* or *virelais*. Superficial as in his chronicles, merely trifling with life and love, titillating the emotions but rarely stirring them, Froissart, in common with other French poets of his century, made no pretence at philosophical implications, and precious little at aesthetic achievement beyond the outward poetic forms and conventions, contrasting in this respect with his more ambitious and gifted Italian contemporaries. There is a quality of gentlemanly amateurishness about his poetry, oddly at variance with the lofty concept of love, which Froissart repeated too glibly after so many others, as the fount of all goodness and virtue. Perhaps the superiority of a Petrarch was owed in no small measure to his facing up to that traditional concept, to his renewing it and giving it the whole of his mind and attention in poetry far more complex, more subtle, more profound than that of his French counterparts, and inevitably more removed from the practicalities of daily existence which Froissart – 'un réaliste-né', as he has been termed[18] – like Guillaume de Machaut and Deschamps, could rarely forget. Since they are unlikely to have been wholly ignorant of Petrarch's work – indeed it is likely that Froissart had met him[19] – since this same interest in the realities of daily living remains a feature of so much fifteenth-century literature, one suspects that these stolid, commonsense, conservative, fundamentally *unpoetic* northerners were reluctant to commit themselves to a literature so esoteric, so ethereal, so serious. The amateurs were not ready to turn professional, and French poets were still something else apart from the wholly dedicated men of letters which their descendants were to become in the sixteenth century.

IV. THE POETRY OF CHRISTINE DE PISAN

Exceptional in certain important respects was Christine de Pisan, not only because she was born in Venice of Italian parents, but also because, left a widow with three children at the age of twenty-five, she made a living by the pen, and in the course of some ten years (1400–10) produced an enormous amount of literature in prose and verse, ranging widely over many topics. Mention has already been made of her feminism and consequent criticism of Ovid and Jean de Meun.[20] As a lyric poet she followed the fashion set by Guillaume de Machaut, writing numerous *ballades*, *rondeaux*, and *virelais* on traditional themes; the *ballades* were sometimes arranged in a sequence in order to tell a love story. A personal note may sometimes be discerned, as in the several poems expressing her grief at the death of her husband.[21] Particularly famous is the *ballade* which emphasises her loneliness and sadness as a widow through the persistent repetition at the beginning of each line of 'Seulete sui . . .', a telling use of the rhetorical device known as anaphora:

Seulete sui, et seulete vueil estre;	Alone am I, and alone I wish to be;
Seulete m'a mon doulx ami laissée;	Alone has my sweet love left me.
Seulette sui, sanz compaignon ne maistre;	Alone am I, without companion or master;
Seulette sui, dolente et courroussiée;	Alone am I, sad and grieving,
Seulette sui, en languour mesaisiée;	Alone am I, unhappy and languishing,
Seulette sui, plus que nulle esgarée;	Alone am I, most forlorn of women,
Seulete sui, sans ami demourée.[22]	Alone am I, without my love remaining.

Elsewhere she makes it clear that her conventional love-poetry is not autobiographical,[23] closely echoing, albeit from a different viewpoint, Machaut's remarks in his prologue on the gap that may exist between the poet's real feelings and those portrayed:

De triste cuer chanter joyeusement . . .	To sing joyfully with a sad heart, this am I frequently compelled to
Ainsi me faut faire communement . . .[24]	do.

Convention demanded that courtly poetry should celebrate adulterous love. Although Christine followed this tradition, she usually showed it leading to unhappiness, particularly for the woman. She has been called '. . . above all, the poetess of love's ending and aftermath rather than of its budding and blossoming'.[25] At heart she certainly felt that love and marriage are compatible, as in her own life. She wrote at least one *ballade* in praise of married life.[26] A remarkable series of *ballades*, written in the first person, tells of the development of a love-affair entirely from the woman's point of view, showing a fleeting happiness quickly yielding to sadness when the lover forsakes her. This is a medieval counterpart of Cocteau's famous *La Voix humaine*. Moral implications are not far beneath the surface: love is not to be trifled with; flirtations, even following the approved fashions of the age, bring unhappiness, at least to the woman. For this same reason her ideal knight is one who treats her sex with respect and is not merely seeking to gratify his own physical desires. Did she realise that, for this selfsame reason, her *bête noire* Jean de Meun had condemned sexual relationships[27] and that he advocated marriage even though he did not view it as an idyllic state or as one that would necessarily ensure happiness? Much of Christine's love-poetry is facile, betraying no doubt the rapidity with which she wrote, but at her best she was able to instil into it a quality of pathos, and to write movingly, often charmingly. Her own widowed state, her keen interest in the emotional life and social status of her sex, made this something more for her than the usual literary pastime of courtly *milieux*, and have encouraged one prominent scholar to hail Christine de Pisan as the first French author in the accepted sense, one, that is, whose life and work may be taken together, each explaining the other.[28]

V. THE POETRY OF ALAIN CHARTIER

Among the several poetic works which Alain Chartier[29] wrote on widely differing subjects, the one which created the greatest stir in his own day was the *Belle Dame sans merci*.[30] Written in 1424 at the height of his career, this poem of 800 octosyllabic lines is composed of stanzas of 8 lines arranged according to the intersecting rhyme pattern *a b a b b c b c*, a pattern adopted by Villon some thirty years later in his main works. A brief summary follows:

The poet (writing in the first person) rides along sadly, his mind full of memories of his mistress who has died recently. His relations with Love are for ever broken. At the end of his ride some friends prevail upon him to join them at a party, where he notices a man looking very preoccupied – 'Ennuyé, mesgre, blesme et palle' (line 99) (Worried, thin, wan, and pale) – his eyes constantly turning towards a certain lady. Amused, the poet thinks to himself: 'Autel fusmes comme vous estes' (120) (I was like that once). Later, he overhears a conversation between the lover and the lady. The former's supplications meet with an icy response:

Beau sire, ce fol pensement	Good sir, will this stupid thought
Ne vous laissera il jamais?	Never leave you?
Ne penserez vous autrement	Will the idea never occur to you
De donner a vostre cuer paix?	To leave your heart in peace?

(221–4)

If I glance at you, she remarks, what of it? 'Les yeulz sont fais pour regarder' (238). The lover persists, swearing homage, loyalty, and submission in accordance with the best courtly tradition, but to no avail. The old formula no longer works its magic. The lady is determined to keep her independence:

Je suy franche et franche vueil estre	I am free and intend to stay that
Sans moy de mon cuer dessaisir	way without parting with my heart
Pour en faire un autre le maistre	so that another can be its master.
(286–8)	

Whereas an obstacle to courtly love-affairs was traditionally provided by the 'losengiers' – the malicious, lying gossips, jealous of lovers, always bent on destroying their happiness – we now find the lady making the astonishing pronouncement 'Amours est cruel losengier' (313) (Love is a cruel deceiver). Love, deceiver ever, is the real enemy, at least from the woman's standpoint, as it appears to Chartier's heroine. As regards the lover himself, he would discover that 'c'est ung mal dont on relieve' (380) (it is an illness that clears up). She makes it quite clear that she does not want him or any other to have her heart which she refuses to abandon 'A courte foy et longue langue (736) (To short faith and a long tongue). She tells the lover 'Riens ne vous nuit fors vous meismes' (763) (You are your own worst enemy). Later, the poet learns of the death of the grief-stricken lover, and in his conclusion warns 'dames et damoiselles' not to model themselves on La belle dame sans merci.

Despite this disclaimer, which showed that he did not side with his heroine, reaction was sharp and swift.[31] Court poets condemned Chartier or the Belle dame, or even tried to bring her back into the courtly fold by claiming that she already had a lover to whom she wished to remain faithful, a possibility expressly denied in the original poem. Chartier was stung into writing a defence, the *Excusacion envers les dames*,[32] a poem of 244 lines. Love accuses him of encouraging ladies to show no pity. Not so, says Chartier, but it is not incumbent on the lady to show pity too readily. Pity is like a fine jewel that should only be displayed occasionally. People had read far too much into his poem:

Mon livre qui vault poy et monte	My book, whose worth is small, has
A nesune autre fin ne tent	the sole aim of telling the tale of a
Si non a recorder le compte	sad, unhappy lover and his com-
D'un triste amoureux mal content	plaints that he is kept dangling too
Qui prie et plaint que trop attent	long and spurned. Anyone who sees
Et comme refus le reboute.	anything else in it either reads too
Et qui autre chose y entent,	much into it or misunderstands it
Il y voit trop ou n'y voit goute.	altogether.
(193–200)	

Besides, a lover's accusing his lady of cruelty is not to be taken seriously (but Chartier had made this very accusation himself at the end of his original poem!). Love departs satisfied with this explanation, but it is unlikely to have satisfied Chartier's opponents. Far from being a palinode, the *Excusacion* is an assertion of the lady's right to reject her suitor's advances, without even showing him any pity, however respectful he may have been of recognised procedures. The old order was undoubtedly justified in feeling itself challenged inasmuch as the heroine's rejection of this conventional courtship was couched in general terms frequently reaching beyond her own particular case. In this respect at least Chartier sounded a new note – the very sharpness of the reactions testifies to its novelty[33] – a hard-headed psychological realism, an impatience with idealised concepts of love, an ironical attitude towards the old traditions, soon to find many echoes in the vernacular literature of the fifteenth century. Not that Chartier, or any of his contemporaries, was an iconoclast. Changes in taste and outlook differed from those of the sixteenth century in being evolutionary rather than revolutionary, and in having no theoretical or doctrinaire background. It is not at all surprising to find Chartier composing *ballades* and *rondeaux* couched firmly in the established idiom:

Loyaument et a tousjours mais,	Loyally and always, for long and
Despieça et plus qu'onques mais,	more than ever, I am yours and
Je suy vostre et vostre me tien,	yours I remain, my joy, my solace,
Ma joie, mon soulas, mon bien,	my treasure, my hope, my desire,
Mon espoir, mon desir, ma paix.	my peace.
Ma volenté, mes diz, mes fais	Such is my wish, such my words, my
Sont tieulz et seront a jamais.	deeds, and always shall be. This is
C'est la leczon que je retien.	the lesson I retain.
Ou que je suy ou que je vais,	Wherever I am, wherever I go,
Quoy que je dis ou que je tays,	Whatever I say or do not say
Vous avez le cuer qui fut mien.	You have the heart which once was
Or nous entramons donques bien,	mine.
Si seront noz plaisirs parfais.[34]	Let us love each other truly, then,
	And our pleasures will be perfect.

VI. CHARLES D'ORLÉANS

Changes occurring within an outwardly unchanging idiom may be observed also in the poetry of Charles d'Orléans,[35] brought about in his case by the tragic circumstances of his life. In 1407, when he was in his thirteenth year, his father Louis, duc d'Orléans, brother of the mad King Charles VI, was assassinated by the duke of Burgundy's men. In 1408 his mother, Valentine Visconti, duchess of Milan, died of grief, having tried in vain to secure condemnation of her husband's murderer. The following year the young duke's wife, Isabelle, widow of Richard II of England, died in childbirth. After eight largely fruitless years attempting to avenge his father's death, Charles obtained satisfaction of a kind, but soon afterwards was captured by the English at

Agincourt in 1415, and held prisoner in England for 25 years, being finally released in 1440 at the age of forty-six. His second wife Bonne d'Armagnac, whom he hardly knew – she was only eleven years of age when they were married in 1410 – died while he was a prisoner. Not long after his release, he led an expedition to Italy in a vain attempt to recapture estates inherited through his mother. His declining years were spent mainly at his castle in Blois, where his favourite pastime was the writing of poetry, as it had been during his long imprisonment in England. He died in 1465.

Charles's poetic career began at the tender age of ten, with the *Livre contre tout péché* (The Book against all sins), a didactic piece of 148 octosyllabic lines, written no doubt with the aid of his tutor, condemning the Seven Deadly Sins. The date of his first major work, *La Retenue d'Amours* (Love's Retinue), is not known, but may have been a year or so before Agincourt. In this poem of 457 lines, mainly decasyllabic, Jeunesse introduces to the God of Love and his Court the young prince

... sailly de la maison de France	... a scion of the house of France
Creu ou jardin semé de fleur de lis.	Grown in the garden sown with lilies.

(lines 166–7)

In a *Lettre de Retenue* parodying legal jargon, Charles swears an oath of allegiance to Love. Some 23 years later, while still held prisoner in England, Charles wrote a counterpart to the *Retenue*, the *Songe en Complainte* (Dream Lament), a poem of 550 lines, in which he asks to be released from his obligation to Love because of the death of his mistress, for whom, in the intervening years, he had composed some 70 *ballades*, many of which have also survived in English adaptations, possibly the work of Charles himself. Who was the lady of the *ballades*? Was she his wife, some other person or persons, English possibly, or was she just a fiction, Charles's homage, as it were, to the courtly creed, a manner of passing the time and of recording something of his unhappiness and enduring patience as a prisoner? Whatever the truth of this much-debated matter, there is about these love-poems an enigmatic dichotomy. It is as though his love, real or professed, for the mistress from whom he was separated, absorbed all the sadness of the present moment, all his hopes for the future, and it is truly astonishing that this prince held prisoner in a foreign land should have bewailed his plight almost entirely in terms of the age-old *Princesse lointaine* theme. His despair on hearing of her death finds an even deeper echo in his solitariness and destitution, separated from the country he loved. He is driven in upon himself, and allegory finds a new psychological reality. A forest reflects his feeling of gloom and boredom, a hermitage represents his mind, a passing cloud his sadness, a game of chess is life and the opponent is Danger, a hard bed is boredom once more, sleep is Nonchalance, representing his growing lassitude and indifference, church candles are sighs and a tomb regrets, while his mind is a swarm of characters, complaining, remonstrating, attacking, occasionally consoling, each according to his nature: Souvenir, Amour, Dangier, Desir, Fortune, Tristesse, Espoir, Confort, Aventure, Mort. Occasionally he spoke openly, and movingly, of his longing to return to France:

En regardant vers le païs de France,	Looking towards the country of
Un jour m'avint, a Dovre sur la mer,	France
Qu'il me souvint de la doulce	One day at Dover on sea,
plaisance	I happened to recall the sweet
Que souloye oudit pays trouver;	pleasure
Si commençay de cueur a souspirer,	I used to find in that country,
Combien certes que grant bien me	And I began to sigh deeply
faisoit	Although to be sure it did me much
De voir France que mon cueur	good
amer doit.	To see France, my heart's true love.

(Ballade LXXV, lines 1–7)

With equal fervour he wrote a *ballade* in favour of peace, and a splendid patriotic poem, echoing Chartier's *Quadrilogue Invectif*,[36] urging the 'Très crétien, franc royaume de France' (Very Christian, noble Kingdom of France) to awaken from her sloth and to recapture her former greatness (Complainte I). In an exchange of *ballades* he cemented a surprising alliance with the duke of Burgundy, son of his father's assassin. This new-found ally helped Charles to secure his longed-for release and gave him in marriage his niece, Marie de Clèves, mother-to-be of the future Louis XII. In this respect, at least, Charles's poetry served a practical purpose and made an unexpected contribution to the course of French history.

Back in France, Charles gave preference to the rondel rather than the *ballade*, writing occasionally on love, more often on festivities, leisurely pursuits, or whatever marked the passing of time: the changing seasons, springtime flowers, May Day festivals, New Year's Day, St Valentine's Day, jousting, sailing on the Loire, hunting. Often a poem will isolate Charles from the surrounding merriment – he is too languid, too nonchalant, too indifferent to join in and plays his favourite role of a casual bystander, mildly interested. The imprint of his earlier life, and verse, is still apparent, for so many of these poems are related to his moods – it all seems to lead inwards, reflecting his all-pervading melancholy. At times he tries to shake it off:

Alez vous ant, allez, alés,	Away with you, away, away
Soussy, Soing et Merencolie,	Care, Worry, and Melancholy.
Me cuidez vous toute ma vie	Do you think you can dominate
Gouverner, comme fait avés? ...	My whole life, as you have done ...

(Rondeau 55, 1–4)

but all too often it is a matter of whiling away the time as best he can:

Tellement, quellement	As well as I may
Me faut le temps passer,	I must pass time away
Et soucy amasser	And troubles amass
Maintesfoiz, mallement . . .	So often, alas!

(Rondeau 157, 1–4)

He was fond of organising poetry competitions among his courtiers, supplying them with the first line, frequently a proverb or some allegorical metaphor: 'L'abit le moine ne fait pas' (The habit does not make the monk), 'De fol juge brefve sentence' (From a mad judge a brief sentence), 'En la forest de Longue Actente' (In the forest of Long Waiting), 'Dedens l'abisme de douleur' (In the abyss of woe). François Villon participated in one of the duke's competitions, in which a *ballade* had to be written with the opening line: 'Je meurs de soif auprès de la fontaine' (I am dying of thirst at the fountain's edge).

Most of Charles's rondels are slight and unpretentious, indeed so unsubstantial that they are usually spoken of condescendingly. None the less, they represent an art-form at its peak. This is verse of exquisite delicacy, and has become part of the French heritage which children learn at school:

Le temps a laissé son manteau	The weather has shed its cloak
De vent, de froidure et de pluye,	Of wind, cold, and rain,
Et s'est vestu de brouderie,	And has put on its finery,
De soleil luyant, cler et beau.	Of sunshine bright and lovely.
Il n'y a beste, ne oyseau,	No beast is there, no bird,
Qu'en son jargon ne chante ou crie:	That in its language does not proclaim:
Le temps a laissé son manteau	The weather has shed its cloak
De vent, de froidure et de pluye.	Of wind, cold, and rain.
Rivière, fontaine et ruisseau	Rivers, fountains, streams,
Portent, en livree jolie,	Decked in pretty livery
Gouttes d'argent d'orfaverie	Wear drops of silver and gold,
Chascun s'abille de nouveau:	Everyone dons garments new;
Le temps a laissé son manteau.	The weather has shed its cloak.

(Rondeau 31)

Les fourriers d'Esté sont venus	Summer's harbingers have arrived
Pour appareillier son logis	To make ready his dwelling place
Et ont fait tendre ses tappis,	And have spread wide his carpets
De fleurs et verdure tissus.	With flowers and greenery woven.
En estendant tappis velus,	Spreading out the deep-piled carpets
De vert herbe par le païs,	Of green grass over the countryside
Les fourriers d'Esté sont venus.	Summer's harbingers have arrived.

Cueurs d'ennuy pieça morfondus,	Hearts for long sad and chilled
Dieu mercy, sont sains et jolis;	Thanks be to God are warm and
Alez vous ent, prenez païs,	merry.
Yver, vous ne demourrés plus;	Away with you, be gone,
Les fourriers d'Esté sont venus.	Winter, you shall tarry no more:
(Rondeau 30)[37]	Summer's harbingers have arrived.

The mood of his later years was a wistful melancholy, a gentle brooding on the life with which he had never quite come to grips. Something had always eluded him, he had been buffeted by Fortune, mocked by Hope, tormented by Souci, Soin, and Mélancolie, for ever 'l'homme esgaré qui ne scet ou li va' (the wanderer who knows not where he goes). This is a verse, like its author, of princely distinction, aristocratic even in its preoccupation with life's trivia, turning the mood of the moment, a passing fancy, a favourite expression, a day's pastime, into a tiny, finely wrought jewel existing for itself alone, to be admired for what it is, or tossed aside. It does not exist to illustrate any humanistic or aesthetic philosophy, it is a poetic impasse leading nowhere, but without which medieval French poetry would be inestimably poorer. One senses in his work the ending of a long tradition, a gradually fading interest in courtly love with no dominant doctrine, no framework of beliefs to replace it, a humdrum poetry ungrandiose yet lacking neither pathos nor beauty. Charles's rondels are the exquisite products of a casual, part-time artist, wayward and gifted; poetry which, for all its triviality, provides a not inglorious climax to the centuries-old literature of the Courts of northern France.

VII. FRANÇOIS VILLON

Of the poets surveyed in this chapter, François Villon is the most scantily represented in surviving manuscripts: one poem of 320 lines, one of 2,023 lines, a handful of *ballades* and miscellaneous poems, and the title of an inextant work, which, if it ever existed, was probably of minor importance – an amount which would have represented no more than a year's output to poets who have left us over 80,000 lines. Furthermore, some two-thirds of what Villon has left us is burlesque verse of a highly topical nature, so that his reputation as a lyric poet rests on a very small quantity of verse, little more than a thousand lines, comprising the first nine hundred or so of the *Testament*, his main work,[38] and several *ballades*. Villon's first extant work, *Le Lais*, is a lighthearted parody of a testament written, as the opening line tells us, in 1456. He was about twenty-five at the time. He professes to be leaving Paris because he has been crossed in love, and, uncertain of his return, makes a series of comical legacies to friends, relatives,

various officials and noteworthies of the capital, giving away
things he did not possess, such as the accoutrements of nobility,
or his favourite taverns, or worthless belongings such as his hair
clippings which he bequeaths to his barber, cobwebs from his
windows for the hospital, all managed in such a way that he pokes
fun, often barbed with satire or larded with eroticisms, at his
legatees. His declaration that he was leaving for Angers was seen
in a new light when documents were unearthed from the Paris
archives in 1873 revealing that Villon had taken part in a robbery
of the Collège de Navarre, one of the colleges making up the
University of Paris, and that he had informed one of his con-
federates that he was going to Angers to reconnoitre possibilities
for a robbery there. It has recently been suggested that this too
was not the real reason for his departure. His real intention was
to visit the Court of René of Anjou to try to establish himself as a
successful court poet, for which end the 120 gold crowns, his share
of the booty, would clearly be useful. This suggestion is a plausible
one, and it may well be that Villon was determined at this time to
turn over a new leaf. Fortune had early smiled on him when, son
of poor parents, he was adopted by Guillaume de Villon, chaplain
of Saint-Benoît-le-Bétourné in the Latin Quarter, and educated
at the university, becoming *licencié* then *maistre-ès-arts* in 1452.
Later confessions indicate, however, that already he did not take
his studies too seriously.[39] What he did in the years immediately
following his graduation is not known, but in 1455 he became
involved in a brawl with a priest, whom he stabbed to death.
It seems rather sinister that the letters of pardon which he was
granted should be in several names: François de Montcorbier,
François des Loges, François Villon. Moreover, to the barber who
dressed his wounds, he gave his name as Michel Mouton. The
following year he took part in the robbery of the Collège de Navarre
and left for Angers, having probably composed the *Lais* shortly
before his departure. In the five years that elapsed between the
composition of the *Lais* and that of the *Testament*, Villon seems to
have travelled widely, visiting (so various allusions in the *Testament*
suggest) in addition to Angers the small towns of Saint-Julien-de-
Vouventes (south of Châteaubriant) and Saint-Generou (near
Parthenay). At Blois he took part, as we have seen, in one of the
duke's poetry competitions. He also wrote a poem of 132 lines
celebrating the birth of Charles's daughter Marie in 1457, though
it may have been composed later, on the occasion of her entering
Orleans in 1460. Is Villon's declaration that he owed her his life a
mere hyperbole, or does it have another significance? Was he in
prison at Orleans, and released with others on her arrival? The
truth is not known. In 1461 he was certainly behind bars at Meung-

sur-Loire on the orders of Thibaut d'Aussigny, bishop of Orleans, as the beginning of the *Testament* reveals. The reason for this imprisonment is unknown, but we should have to be very gullible to believe that Villon was guilty of no misdemeanour, even though miscarriages of justice were more frequent then than now. He was freed along with other prisoners when the new king, Louis XI, passed through Meung-sur-Loire during a journey from Paris to his native Touraine. For a time Villon remained in hiding, no doubt fearing arrest because of his participation in the robbery of the Collège de Navarre. During this period he wrote the *Testament* and a remarkable *ballade*, the *Débat du Cuer et du Corps*. Sure enough, on his return to Paris in 1462, he was arrested, but was released on promising to restore his share of the robbery. In 1463, prison again, this time because of a street brawl. He seems to have been little more than a bystander, but the patience of the authorities was exhausted and he was sentenced to be hanged. It was probably at this time that he wrote the *Epitaphe Villon* (often called the *Ballade des Pendus*) and the quatrain that accompanies it. The sentence was commuted to one of banishment from Paris. Villon wrote a *ballade* celebrating his release, after which all trace of him is lost. How he ended his days is not known.

In the course of his wanderings, Villon endured much hardship,[40] and there is little wonder that at the beginning of the *Testament*, in a passage of some 900 lines, he doffs his usual clown's garb, albeit momentarily. He gives vent to his feelings in an extended 'examen de conscience' that pours out in an untidy stream, apparently unplanned and spontaneous, triggered off in the first instance by his outraged feeling at having been imprisoned and harshly treated by Thibaut d'Aussigny. Having expressed his resentment in the first six stanzas, he devotes the following five to extolling the king whose passing through Meung-sur-Loire had occasioned his release, and then begins to reflect on his sufferings, owed, he maintains, to his poverty and cruel fate more than to his folly, though he confesses that he wasted his time in youth and enjoyed himself when he should have been following more serious pursuits. Nostalgia as he thinks of his early days and pleasant companions long since gone their different ways mingles with remorse and self-pity. In the face of death and old age, he turns his thoughts to women, finding great pathos, but also comfort of a kind, in the fact that even they cannot escape the human condition: the *Ballade des Dames du Temps Jadis* is the climax of his lines on death, the *Regrets de la Belle Heaulmière* the climax of the passage on old age. Each enables him to move beyond his dread and to resign himself to the inevitable. That he should turn to women at such moments is fascinating and strange, an effect partly

of his own psychology, partly also possibly of the age-old courtly
tradition, however much he parodied its outward conventions and
attitudes. Having worked his way through so many feelings and
reflections, back he comes in the second half of the *Testament* to
the comparatively trivial farce of the *Lais* in a longer string of
burlesque legacies with, it is true, a wider and deeper range of
feelings than in the first work: affection in the case of Guillaume
de Villon – 'mon plus que pere' (my more than father) – and his
mother, here mentioned for the first time and for whom he writes
a prayer to the Virgin Mary; deeper hatred for those who had
ordered his arrest and imprisonment; and an occasional interrup-
tion of the satirical vein as a reflection on physical suffering or
death passes fleetingly through his mind. It is not without a certain
air of resignation that he dons the clown's garb once more:

Au moins sera de moi memoire	At least the memory of me shall
Telle qu'elle est d'ung bon follastre.	remain
(lines 1882–3)	Such as it is, of a good clown.

Various works of the fifteenth and sixteenth centuries bear out
this prediction that he would be remembered as a jester. The
Repues Franches, composed in the later fifteenth century by an
unknown author, makes Villon a sort of Robin Hood of the Latin
Quarter, adept at obtaining free food for down-and-outs or those
disinclined to work – a lighthearted, coarse piece of buffoonery.
Rabelais may have found inspiration for Panurge in Villon, and
in two anecdotes tells of farcical tricks that Villon was supposed to
have played, interesting in that they show in what light Villon
was thought of at the time. In the seventeenth century Cotgrave
records the word *villon*, defining it as 'A cousener, conycatcher,
cunning or wittie rogue; a nimble knave; a pleasant theefe (for
such a one was François Villon . . .)', and even in the eighteenth
century the adjectives most frequently applied to Villon's poetry
were 'badin' and 'plaisant'. The serious aspects of Villon's poetry
received scant attention before the nineteenth century. Théophile
Gautier included a study of Villon in his *Les Grotesques* and
interest in him increased steadily throughout the century, reaching
the level of a cult after the discovery in 1873 of the legal documents
concerning him. In our own day attempts to view Villon's poetry
as nothing more than a series of eroticisms, replete with many
allusions to homosexual practices, accompanied by claims that
Villon's 'lyrisme autobiographique' was a veneer, have been pushed
to great lengths.[41] This is far from being the first controversy
that has centred around his name, and for a large number of
readers of many nationalities, he remains one of the outstanding
poets of all French literature. His most poignant lines are those on

death, and for this reason this brief analysis is concluded with the two poems he wrote while under sentence of death. The quatrain illustrates how even in such circumstances he could quip and joke in a facetious manner in what could be considered the first 'sick joke' of European literature:

Je suis Françoys, dont il me poise,
Né de Paris emprès Pontoise,
Et de la corde d'une toise
Sçaura mon col que mon cul poise
(*Poésies Diverses*, XIII)

I am François, and that's a weight on my mind,
Born in Paris in the region of Ponthoise
And with the aid of six feet of rope
My neck will soon know the weight of my arse.

The *Epitaphe Villon*, on the other hand, illustrates his ability to write verse that is intensely moving, beginning at a personal level, but quickly widening the scope to include others whose plight resembled his own. His concept of the common bonds of humanity, in which the responsibility of every individual is engaged, seen within a still firm framework of Christianity, is truly remarkable. This is a humanism of a special kind, arising, not from his studies or his readings, but from his own experiences and from his feelings for others:

Freres humains qui après nous vivez,
N'ayez les cuers contre nous endurcis,
Car, se pitié de nous povres avez,
Dieu en aura plus tost de vous mercis.
Vous nous voiez cy attachez cinq, six:
Quant de la chair, que trop avons nourrie,
Elle est pieça devoree et pourrie,
Et nous , les os, devenons cendre et pouldre.
De nostre mal personne ne s'en rie;
Mais priez Dieu que tous nous vueille absouldre!

Se freres vous clamons, pas n'en devez
Avoir desdaing, quoy que fusmes occis
Par justice. Toutesfois, vous sçavez
Que tous hommes n'ont pas bon sens rassis;
Excusez nous, puis que sommes transsis,
Envers le fils de la Vierge Marie,

Brother men who live after us,
Do not harden your hearts against us,
For if you have pity on us wretches
God will the sooner have mercy on you.
You see us strung up here, five or six.
As for the flesh, which we fed only too well,
For a long time now it has been rotten
And we the bones turn to ashes and dust.
Let no one laugh at our plight
But pray to God that He will forgive us all.

If we call you brothers, do not feel disdain
Although we were killed
By Justice. Yet you know
That all men do not have common-sense.
Ask forgiveness for us, since we are dead,
From the son of the Virgin Mary
Let Her grace not be withered for us,

Que sa grace ne soit pour nous
tarie,
Nous preservant de l'infernale
fouldre.
Nous sommes mors, ame ne nous
harie;
Mais priez Dieu que tous nous
vueille absouldre!

La pluye nous a debuez et lavez,
Et le soleil dessechiez et noircis;
Pies, corbeaulx, nous ont les yeux
cavez,
Et arrachié la barbe et les sourcis.
Jamais nul temps nous ne sommes
assis:
Puis ça, puis la, comme le vent
varie,
A son plaisir sans cesser nous
charie,
Plus becquetez d'oiseaulx que dez a
couldre.
Ne soiez donc de nostre confrairie;
Mais priez Dieu que tous nous
vueille absouldre!

Prince Jhesus, qui sur tous a
maistrie,
Garde qu'Enfer n'ait de nous
seigneurie:
A luy n'ayons que faire ne que
souldre.
Hommes, icy n'a point de
mocquerie;
Mais priez Dieu que tous nous
vueille absouldre!

Preserving us from the thunderbolt
of hell.
We are dead, let no one harry us;
But pray to God that He will forgive
us all.

The rain has soaked and washed us
And the sun has dried and blackened
us.
Magpies, crows have hollowed out
our eyes,
And torn away our beard and eye-
brows.
Never at any time are we still.
Here and there as the wind turns,
It moves us unceasingly as the whim
takes it,
More pecked by birds than the
thimble by the needle.
Do not join our brotherhood, then,
But pray to God that He will for-
give us all.

Prince Jesus, who reigns over us all,
Take care lest hell have dominion
over us.
Let us have nothing to do with it,
nothing to owe it.
Men, here there is no mockery;
But pray to God that He will for-
give us all.

In Villon's humanistic conception of Christianity, no man, dead or alive, however evil, can be denied the privilege of the human condition. However self-interested this appeal no doubt was, it prevents Villon's lyricism from becoming too narrow and maudlin, and continues to win for him many admirers down the generations.

The neatness with which the Charles d'Orléans–François Villon diptych appears to conclude medieval poetry does a disservice to other fifteenth-century poets. For many students of medieval litera-ture the sun has now set, whereas for students of the Renaissance it has not yet risen, and both sides tend to toss no more than the occasional condescending remark into the night separating them. Despite this double-edged prejudice, several poets writing in the second half of the century possessed considerable talent. Only some of them can be mentioned here. It is not always possible to place them or their works in exact chronological perspective, since information on dates of birth and composition is sometimes approximate or inexistent. Questions of literary relationships may remain unanswered for the same reasons or because the subject-matter was mostly conventional, a vast common stock from which all drew.

VIII. GUILLAUME ALEXIS

Guillaume Alexis (or Alecis), who was born about 1425 and who died in 1486 while on a pilgrimage to the Holy Land, was a monk of the abbey of Lyre in Normandy; in his works he refers to himself as 'prieur de Bucy', a priory which has not been identified. He was a prolific writer of religious, moral, and didactic works, some in a mixture of verse and prose.[42] This outspoken enemy of the '... pompes et orgueil du monde'[43] (the world's pomp and pride) possessed a style not lacking in vigour and well-chosen expressions. Characteristic is *Le Blason de Faulses Amours*, a poem of 1,512 lines divided into stanzas of 12 lines, the first 8 lines containing four syllables only, the last 4 eight. This is a debate between a 'gentilhomme' and a monk on the subject of love. The former speaks in praise of love, but the latter overwhelms him in a flood of objections and satirical remarks. At the end, the 'gentilhomme' is quite won over. There are echoes of Villon in the argument that love brings all men to disaster, but this was a well-worn *topos*. The examples quoted, like those in Villon's *Double Ballade*, are taken both from the Bible and from classical literature: no doubt the best known of Alexis's works, it was imitated by La Fontaine in the seventeenth century in his *conte Janot et Catin*.

The refrain 'Bieneureux est qui rien n'y a' (Very happy is he who has nothing to do with it), used by Villon in the *Double Ballade*, serves also in Alexis's *Le Debat de l'Omme et de la Femme*, in which the man attacks love and woman counters with the refrain 'Maleureux est qui riens n'y a' (Unhappy is he who ...). Since this work was written sometime in the 1460s, it is difficult to say whether or not it preceded Villon's poem.[44] Further resemblances in phraseology and theme to Villon are owed principally to the fact that both were dealing with conventional material. It is interesting none the less to observe that the mentality of the monk and that of the vagabond poet had a good deal in common:

Guillaume Alexis

(Aux gloutons) . . . fault querre . . .	Gluttons have to be provided with
Pigment, ypocras ou claré	Mead, hippocras, or claret
Et autre vin cler et paré	And other wines clear and spiced
Pour leur chair qui sera pourrie . . .	For their flesh which will one day be
Helas, quel povre nourriture	rotten . . .
Qui si tost tourne en pourriture!	Alas! what wretched food
(II, 198)	That turns so soon to dust!

François Villon

Aient esté seigneurs ou dames	Whether they were lords or ladies
Souef et tendrement nourris	Softly and tenderly nourished
De cresme, fromentee ou riz,	On cream, frumenty, or rice
Leurs os sont declinez en pouldre	Their bones have turned to dust,
Auxquelz ne chault d'esbatz ne ris.	They are indifferent to merriment
(*Le Testament*, lines 1762–6)	and laughter now.

Needless to say, Alexis quite lacks the intensity of Villon's lyricism, and his feeling for humanity.

IX. HENRI BAUDE

A contemporary of Guillaume Alexis was Henri Baude, who was born in Moulins and became for a time one of Louis XI's tax officials.[45] He was put on trial for fraud in 1467 and stripped of his goods. He seems to have regained his position in later years, and to have been involved in further litigation. He was still alive in 1496, and probably died about the turn of the century. He is the author of humorous and satirical verse with a flavour of Villon 'le bon follastre', but that there was any direct influence of the one poet on the other is unproven. He wrote a debate between a horse and an ox on their respective merits as man's servants, a mule's testament bequeathing its body to the crows, its 'belle voix' to its last owner Barbeau, and its 'song' to the vicar. Its tail will make a fly-whisk, its tongue a shoe-horn, and its ears will serve Bailly.[46] Baude wrote numerous other works, among them a *ballade* satirising life at Court, and a series of short poems intended as commentaries on tapestry scenes, of which the following is representative:

Ung homme de court	*Courtier*
Homme, parle a moy si tu daignes,	Man, speak to me if you will,
que regarde tu en ce bois?	What are you watching in that wood?
Ung homme, regardant dans ung bois, ouquel a, entre deux arbres, une grant toille d'eraigne.	A man, watching a large spider's web in a wood, between two trees.
Je pence aux toilles des eraignes	I am thinking about spiders' webs
qui sont semblables a nos droiz:	which are just like our rights.
grosses mousches en tous endroiz	The big flies are always let through,
passent, les petites sont prises.	The little ones are caught.
Le fol	*Fool*
Les petitz sont subgectz aux loix	Ordinary folk must respect the law,
et les grans en font a leurs guises.[47]	And the high and mighty please themselves.

Whether or not these tapestries even existed is not known, but if they did, their themes, evidently satirical, would have suited a bourgeois milieu more than an aristocratic one. As a genre these rhymed proverbs recall the harsher and cruder *Proverbes au Vilain*[48] and reflect the frequently encountered medieval predilection for apophthegms of this type.

X. JEAN ROBERTET

Another poet whose date of birth is unknown and who died in the opening years of the sixteenth century is Jean Robertet, member of a family which had been in the service of the dukes of Bourbon for at least a century. After studying law and spending a period in Italy, he became secretary to the duke and later to Louis XI. He wrote numbers of *ballades*, *rondeaux*, and *épîtres* of a more learned nature than those of Baude, displaying a knowledge of Italian culture rare in France at the period, and considerable classical erudition. His main work, the *Complainte de la Mort de Chastellain*, written, he tells us, on the last day of April 1476, in Tours, contains 422 decasyllabic lines and two short prose passages. The 'petit escollier' Robertet solicits help for his lamentations from Petrarch, Livy, Justinus, and Boccaccio. Robertet is also the author of the first French adaptation of Petrarch's *Trionfi*, a rondel in praise of Charles d'Orléans, and, along with Villon and others, a *ballade* in the competition organised by the duke on the theme and opening line 'Je meurs de soif auprès de la fontaine'.

XI. GEORGES CHASTELLAIN

A very active literary centre in the later fifteenth century was that of the immensely rich, luxury-loving Court of Burgundy, far outshining in splendour and dynamism those of the dukes of Brittany, Bourbon, and Orléans. A writer attached to this Court who became to this period the doyen of literature that Machaut had been to the early fourteenth century was Georges Chastellain, witness the high respect shown him by Robertet, who probably made his acquaintance through the contacts between the Courts of Bourbon and Burgundy.[49] Born in Flanders in 1415, he studied at the University of Louvain and appears to have led an exciting youth, since he was nicknamed L'Aventureux, later to be known as 'le grand Georges'. He occupied a variety of posts, mainly in the service of Philip the Good, being promoted from pantler to counsellor, and to chronicler from 1455 onwards. A versatile, gifted, and prolific writer, in addition to his chronicles and numerous prose works he has left poetry of various kinds: courtly, lyric, political, didactic. In

Le Pas de la Mort a lament over the death of his mistress soon leads to reflections on the vanity of human things, that favourite medieval *topos*. Like Villon, Chastellain reduces humanity to a common level, but his motivation is a moralising one and lacks Villon's emotional impact, for nothing stifles lyricism so effectively as a tendency to pontificate:

Pensons a nostre humanité	If we think about our human state,
Veons bien nostre povreté,	And see our poverty for what it is,
Et nostre cœur en aura deuil.	Our hearts will be grieved.
Souspirons et plourons de l'oeil	Let us sigh and weep
Contemplant nostre povre vie:	Contemplating our wretched life.
Sage est celuy qui peu s'y fie	Wise is he who places little store by
(Vol. 6, 55)	it.

In *L'Oultré d'Amour* (Love's Victim) the poet dreams of a lover lamenting over the death of his mistress. It is rather as though he takes one of Machaut's protagonists, the widowed knight, and presents him after the fashion of the lover in Chartier's *Belle Dame sans merci*, for the knight debates his feelings, particularly his longing for death, with his squire, in a manner recalling that of Chartier's poem. In vain the squire urges the knight to 'se garnir d'une amour neuve' (vol. 6, 117) (find a new love); the knight refuses, considering that his loyalty and hence his honour are at stake. *Le Throne Azuré* is a poem in praise of the royal house of France at a time when the English are being ejected from Normandy, the last line helping them on their way with a vigorous shove: 'Fuyez-vous-en, que le dyable vous suive!' (vol. 6, 138) (Get out of it and may the devil go with you). A lengthy epistle sings the praises of the duke of Burgundy, and *Le Miroer des nobles hommes de France* exhorts the nobility to remain just and virtuous at a time when corruption was rife (another common *topos*):

Tout et partout gouvernement s'empire;	Everywhere government is deteriorating.
Vertu languit, felicité souspire,	Virtue is languishing, felicity sighing,
Honneur s'estraint, nature trait au pire ...	Honour choking, nature declining...
(6, 208)	

Le Dit de Vérité likewise extols virtue, as indeed does most of Chastellain's verse and prose, inspired by the knowledge that

Rois meurent et nations s'esvanouissent, mais seule vertu suit l'homme en sa bierre et luy baille gloire eternelle[50] (Kings die and nations pass away, but virtue alone follows man into his coffin and confers on him eternal glory).

On the whole Chastellain was more at home in prose than in verse and was constantly apt to be prolix and banal, but even so, his verse is not lacking in moments of pathos and is not marred by that excessive flamboyancy which came to characterise the poets of Burgundy and those influenced by them, sometimes disparagingly referred to as *Les Grands Rhétoriqueurs*.[51]

XII. JEAN MOLINET

On Chastellain's death in 1475, his place as chronicler was taken by his disciple Jean Molinet, twenty years his junior, who followed the tradition of the late medieval chronicler-poets in having a finger constantly on the pulse of contemporary events and attitudes.[52] As a poet Molinet has to live down an unfortunate predilection for toying with words and syllables in a manner all the more astonishing as the more solemn moments of a work, such as the death of a respected figure, are often involved:

Le pere estoit de paix insigne signe	The father was of peace's cymbals a symbol.
Le filz sera des bons la bonne bonne,	The son was of suns the sunniest one.
Le pere es cieux trouve gourdine digne	The father in the heavens finds a heavenly leaven
Le fils querra gloire ains qu'il fine fine ...	The son will seek amends before God sends the end ...

(1, 276)[53]

It is only fair to add that this rhetorical practice, misplaced and run to seed, is encountered only occasionally in Molinet's vast and wide-ranging output. He wrote encomia of the high and mighty, particularly those of Burgundy, epithalamia celebrating marriage between noble families, or the births of royal children, epitaphs for the great, usually praising (often beyond their merits) their military skills. Numbers echo his interests as a chronicler, dealing with contemporary events or the marvels of the age as in his *Recollection des Merveilleuses Advenues* (1, 284–334), a miscellaneous string of topical notes and jottings in rhyme, including the career and martyrdom of Joan of Arc (in a mere 16 lines!), the appearance of several comets, monstrous births, and terrible storms. *Le Voiage de Napples* (1, 277–83) celebrates Charles VIII's Italian expedition of 1494–95 with bombastic lines such as 'France t'amaine ung second Charlemaine' (line 60) (France brings you a second Charlemagne) and no hint at all that the French had much to learn and profit from in their contact with Italy. The contemporary penchant for didacticism is revealed in Molinet's revamped prose work *Le Roman de la Rose moralisé*,[54] whose lengthy symbolical interpretations would no doubt have bewildered the original authors. Occasionally he writes about himself with a certain wry humour, as when he complains about the non-arrival of his salary, or pathetically when he describes his developing blindness in old age. He composes numbers of amusing fables as did Deschamps; he invents a lively debate between April and May, each month vaunting its respective merits; in lascivious vein he rhymes a riotously scabrous complaint of a 'gentleman' to his lady in which the erotic potentialities of words such as *confesse, convys, confort, condescendre, conjoindre, conferme, conserve, convers* are gleefully exploited. He was long-winded and convoluted, a man of many parts, none of them great; but he mirrored, faithfully and skilfully, the events and atmosphere of the *milieux* he frequented. All was grist to this industrious mill, grinding away into the early sixteenth century, quite oblivious to the many changes so soon to sweep through French literature.

XIII. GUILLAUME CRÉTIN

Lettres, allez sans sejourner en place
Que ne soyez es mains de Molinet
Et le gardez que desir mol il n'ayt
A m'escripre, mais vouloir bien
    ample a ce.

Letter come, do not delay,
Go to the hands of Molinet,
To write to me would be no folly, nay,
But let his desire be keen, I pray.

So wrote Guillaume Crétin at the head of a poem addressed to Molinet, in which the complex punning rhymes ('rimes équivoques') and verbal dexterity were intended as a homage and a flattery.[55] Little is known about Crétin's life save that he was born in Paris, occupied various positions in the Church, eventually becoming canon at Vincennes, that he lived for some time in Lyons towards the end of the fifteenth century, and that he died in November 1525. His output, mostly in the form of *ballades, chants royaux,*[56] *épîtres,* and *rondeaux,*[57] is as varied and as related to figures and events of the day as that of his immediate predecessors and contemporaries, except that, conscious no doubt of his ecclesiastical dignity, he wrote nothing coarse, nothing amorous, writing on love, but never – *à la Machaut* – as a lover. Religious and moral verse, liberally sprinkled with proverbs, predominates in his work. However conventional his subject-matter, his vocabulary, abstruse, erudite, obscure on occasions, marks a clear change from poetry of the past,[58] for example his description of the Virgin Mary as 'la simple colombelle Qui le dragon plutonique debelle' (p. 15) (the simple little dove which subdues the plutonic dragon) or the Creator as 'l'altitonant supreme plasmateur' (31) (the high-thundering supreme plasmator). Whatever one makes of Crétin's poetry nowadays – and it is hard to avoid an impression of pedantry, aridity, and heaviness – it is significant that for at least the first half of the sixteenth century a number of writers spoke of him in flattering terms, though the esteem in which he was held doubtless rested on his chronicles as well as on his verse work. Crétin was essentially a poet's poet, a dedicated man of letters likely to appeal above all to others of his type, one whose esoteric language and knowledge of both classical and biblical mythology, displayed in a welter of names and allusions and in constant recourse to allegory, flourished in this age when erudition was already becoming more and more the hallmark of the respected poet. Crétin, moreover, frequently refers to contemporary poets and musicians by name, and however little we may appreciate his poetry and that of others of his time, the impression conveyed is most certainly not of a literary vacuum between one age and the next, but of a bustling, active period which, while retaining the old conventions and subject-matter, had none the less evolved a style and tastes of its own. But what was the ultimate value of that style and those tastes? In bombarding each other with gobbets of word matter where repetition of sounds was the only real 'meaning' – 'Se lourd baston le bastonne, bas tonne' – their undoubted skill and erudition were draining away uselessly into the sands of triviality. What they lacked was to be provided by Renaissance poets: a new motivation, a worthwhile purpose. To leave matters there, however, would be unjust, for an account of Crétin's verse, and that of his fellow rhetoricians, all too easily turns into an indictment. So appalling, to modern tastes at least, is their worst verse that it has become traditional to judge them by it rather than by their best verse, a privilege surely accorded to most poets. By way of retribution, here is a short passage in which Crétin describes festivities at Court:

On chante, on rit, on s'acolle, on se baise,	They sing, laugh, hug, kiss,
De bien longtemps le rire ne s'appaise;	The laughter does not die down for a long time.
Apres cela on tire vers l'hostel	After that they go off to the hostel
Du chevalier, qui a bruict et loz tel	Of the knight who has a reputation
De traicter gens fort bien, pour quelque affaire	For treating people extremely well, Whatever the affair he has in hand.
Qu'il sache avoir a conduyre et a faire.	
Serviteurs vont acoustrer les estables,	Servants go to prepare the stables,
Les ungs au foing, autres dressent les tables,	Some go for hay, others lay the tables,
Maistres d'hotelz courent parmi la place,	Butlers run all over the place,
Paiges sur bout, il faut que tout desplace,	Pages stand ready, everything has to be shifted, Wines are broached, venison larded, Chickens, pigeons, goslings, none are spared, And are straight away put on the spit.

On perse vins, on larde venayson,
Poullet, pigeon ne se saulve, ne
oyson
Que incontinent il ne soit mis en
broche.
 Et ce pendant que viande on
  embroche,
Les amoureux se devisent aux
dames,
Comptent leur cas, jurent Dieu et
leurs ames
Que leur amour tant les tourmente
et nuict
Qu'ilz n'ont repoz la seule heure de
nuyt,
Font des piteux, souspirent et
lamentent;
Mais pour certain je croy qu'en
cela mentent.[59]

While the meat is being spitted,
Lovers chat to the ladies,
Tell them their tale, swear by God
and their souls
That their love torments and hurts
them so much
That they have no rest a single hour
of the night.
They behave piteously, they sigh and
lament,
But I know for sure that they are
lying.

In this lively, colourful, amusing picture, details are well observed and brought to life. The scepticism of the age on the matter of courtly love is there in the closing lines, but is expressed in a delightfully witty, lighthearted manner. In the following century Du Bellay proclaimed: 'Qu'il n'y ait vers où n'apparaisse quelque vestige de rare et antique érudition', but in the view of many readers both he and Ronsard were at their best when they forgot this precept. The latter, after all, is not appreciated above all for the *Franciade*, or even the Pindaric odes. So with Crétin, who was capable of discarding on occasions his own concept of what constitutes erudition. It may be that this poet, like others of his day, has not yet been given his due. It is salutary to remember that for many readers of the nineteenth century François Villon was a lamentably bad poet.

XIV. JEAN LEMAIRE DE BELGES

Since the last poet to be named in this chapter, Jean Lemaire de Belges (Belges being the former name of his birthplace, Bavai), is usually considered as belonging to the vanguard of the Renaissance more than to the rearguard of the Middle Ages (such are the artificialities of literary history), he will be mentioned only briefly here.[60] Born in 1473, he was brought up by his godfather Jean Molinet and encouraged to write not only by him but also by Guillaume Crétin, whom he met in 1498. He was educated at the University of Paris and acquired a broad classical education, although, like his predecessors, he knew Greek works only in translation. Chronicler and poet like Chastellain, Molinet, and Crétin, his historical works showed less preoccupation with actualities and a correspondingly greater interest in antiquity, while his poetry, benefiting no doubt from his visits to Rome, at times imitated the Italian *terza rima*. He declared his intention to

. . . suyvir par noble poësie Le bon Petrarcque, en amours le vray maistre.	. . . follow through noble poetry The good Petrarch, in love the true master.

However, for one born and brought up in the war-torn north, it was no easy matter to change

. . . Mars au noble dieu d'amours Et chant bellicque aux amoureuses larmes.[61]	Mars for the noble god of love And warsong for love's tears.

Clearly, new horizons were beginning to loom up in a fuller, more truly humanistic interpretation of the classics, and in the growing attention paid to Italian models. Jean Lemaire could be as pompous and pedantic as his predecessors, particularly in the allegorical poems lamenting the deaths of the various figures who had been his patrons: *Le Temple d'Honneur et de Vertu* in praise of Pierre, duc de Bourbon, who died in 1503;[62] the *Plainte du Désiré* in praise of Louis de Luxembourg, comte de Ligny, who died the following year;[63] the *Couronne margaritique* written for Marguerite d'Autriche when her husband, Philibert de Savoie, died in 1505.[64] The device which she then adopted – 'Fortune infortune fort une' (Fortune brings great misfortune to one) – reveals the continuing predilection for homonymic puns of the type dear to Molinet and Crétin. It was to amuse Marguerite d'Autriche that he wrote his two *Epîtres de l'Amant vert*,[65] showing that he was capable of a pleasing touch of fantasy. During her absence from her residence at Pont d'Ain, Marguerite's parrot had the misfortune to be eaten by a dog. Jean Lemaire had the Gilbertian notion of presenting this as the suicide of the 'green lover', caused by his despair at the absence of his mistress with whom he was so much in love. Such whimsicality is rare in a considerable volume of poetry most of which is erudite and serious, though not without its wry moments when he speaks of himself. Among his last works special mention must be made of *La Concorde des Deux Langages*, written in 1511, a debate on the merits of French and Italian. The concord that the poet establishes between them is prophetic, rich with promise for the future.

Jean Lemaire's debt to the poets of the later fifteenth century was immense, and his contribution to the development of sixteenth-century poetry considerable. The conventions of literary history obscure the fact that, from what we regard as the end of one age to the beginning of the next, there was a continuity of tradition. There was, in truth, no end, no beginning.

NOTES

1. E. Hoepffner ed., *Œuvres de Guillaume de Machaut*, Paris, SATF, 3 vols., 1908–21; V. Chichmaref ed., *Guillaume de Machaut, Poésies lyriques*, Paris, 2 vols., 1909. The former contains the longer narrative poems, the latter mainly shorter pieces, *ballades*, rondels, and motets in particular.

2. The influence of Guillaume de Lorris's section of the *Roman de la Rose* is also very apparent in Nicole de Margival's *Le Dit de la Panthère d'Amours* (ed. H. A. Todd, Paris, SATF, 1883, reprinted New York, 1966), whose exact date of composition is unknown, but was probably a few years earlier than Guillaume de Machaut's work. In this allegorical extravaganza of 2,665 lines (mostly octosyllabics), Guillaume de Lorris's orchard is replaced by a forest, and the symbol of love is no longer a rose, but an elusive animal worshipped by all: the panther, whose traits are borrowed from the bestiaries. The influence of the *Roman de la Rose* is also discernible, but is rather more indirect, in Jean de Condé's allegorical fantasy *La Messe des Oiseaux*, dating from the early fourteenth century (ed. J. Ribard, Geneva, 1970), and in Charles d'Orléans's first important work, *La Retenue d'Amours* (see below, p. 306).

3. She first appears in Guillaume's work in the *Remede de Fortune*, composed between the two *Jugements* (see below, p. 295) and results from Guillaume's reading of Boethius's *De Consolatione Philosophiae*.

4. For a very different view of this intriguing work, see W. Calin, 'A Reading of Machaut's "Jugement du Roy de Navarre"', *MLR*, LXVI, 1971, 294–7.

5. This convenient term is something of a misnomer, for within a particular framework considerable variation was possible. Details of the various fixed forms can be found in M. Grammont, *Petit traité de versification française*, Paris, 1908 (numerous editions since); also in W. T. Elwert, *Traité de versification française*, Paris, 1965. See also below, note 10.

6. *Le Livre du Voir Dit de Guillaume de Machaut*, Société des Bibliophiles François, Paris, 1875; also Geneva, 1969.

7. Possibly not the first time a French poet ventured to name his lady-love, but it is so to the best of the present author's knowledge. Note, however, that the name is very carefully camouflaged, and that the solution of the anagram is not altogether certain.

8. De Queux de Sainte-Hilaire and Gaston Raynaud, ed. cit., vol. XI, 11, note 4.

9. ibid., vol. VII, 266–92.

10. Deschamps quotes examples and comments briefly on them, but rarely offers definitions, and is frequently muddled and obscure. He quotes the first stanzas only of various of his *ballades*, varying in length and rhyme patterns: the first – 'Balade de .VIII. vers couppez' – contains eight lines in each stanza, of 10 or 11 syllables depending on whether the rhyme is masculine or feminine. (These were not yet required to alternate, though Deschamps does say that no poem should contain all masculine or all feminine rhymes 'car la balade n'en est pas si plaisant ne de si bonne façon'; ibid., 276) (for the *ballade* is not so pleasing as a result nor is it so well composed.) The fifth line in this first example is a hemistich only, hence the term 'vers couppez'. The rhyme pattern is *a b a b c c d d*, so that the structure of the stanza is effectively a bipartite one, though Deschamps does not draw attention to this. Others give the following schemes, often in leonine, that is, rich rhyme. The pattern of the first four lines remains constant, while that of the remainder varies: *a b a b bc bc*; *a b a b b c c d d*; *a b a b b c c d c c*; *a b a b bcc dcd*, etc. Composition becomes a *tour de force*, the poet's attention being concentrated on sounds, in the 'Balade equivoque, retrograde et leonime', where the beginning of a line repeats the syllable that ended the preceding line, with a change of meaning:

Lasse, lasse, maleureuse et *dolente*!	Alas! Alas! unhappy and full of woe.
Lente me voy, fors de soupirs et	Slow do I see myself, save in sighs and
plains.	complaints,
Plains sont mes jours d'ennuy . . .	Full are my days of torment . . .

(277)

A *serventoys* contains five stanzas, formerly without refrain 'mais a present on les y fait' (but nowadays they do have one), often praising the Virgin Mary or the Divinity. A *virelai* is divided into three stanzas like a *ballade* (the first time Deschamps has said this of the *ballade*), each based on two rhymes; there is no repetition in the body of the poem, but the end repeats the beginning. Varieties of the rondel follow, without any description. The first is a short 'rondel sangle':

Cilz qui onques encores ne vous vit	He who never set eyes on you
Vous aime fort et desire veoir.	Loves you dearly and desires to see you.
Or vous verra, car en cest espoir vit	Now he shall see you, for in this hope lives
Cilz qui . . .	He who . . .
Car pour les biens que chascun de vous dit	For because of the good things that each man says of you, he wishes to
Vous veult donner cuer, corps, vie et pouoir:	give you heart, body, life, and power. He who . . .
Cilz qui . . .	Loves you . . .
Vous aime . . .	

(284)

Others follow, divided AB *cd/e f* A B*/g h i j* A B; A *b c/d e* A*/f g h* A; A B*/ c* A*/d e* A B. The lay is 'une chose longue et malaisiee a faire et trouver' (287) (a long affair difficult to compose). It consists of a varying number of stanzas each of a bipartite construction. The last stanza must use the same rhymes as the first, but there is no refrain.

11. K. Varty, 'Deschamps's *Art de Dictier*', *FS*, XIX, 1965, 164–7.

12. So often in its long history, the *ballade* has been applied in witty fashion to the trivia of daily existence. This was also the tendency in late nineteenth- and early twentieth-century English and French poetry.

13. See above, p. 286.

14. A. Fourrier ed., *L'Espinette amoureuse*, with introduction, notes, and glossary, Paris, 1963, lines 53–4. At the time of writing (1972) this is the only one of Froissart's poems available in a modern critical edition.

15. ibid., page 37.

16. See above, note 14.

17. A. Scheler ed., *Œuvres de Froissart. Poésies*, Brussels, 3 vols., 1869–1872. These constitute vols. 26–8 of K. de Lettenhove's 29-volume edition of all Froissart's works, Brussels, 1866–77.

18. Fourrier, op. cit., 36.

19. J. Bastin, *Froissart, Chroniqueur, Romancier et Poète*, Brussels, 1948, 5.

20. See above, pp. 272–3.

21. Mentioned also in the *Livre de la Mutacion de Fortune*, see above, pp. 271–2.

22. K. Varty ed., *Christine de Pisan's Ballades, Rondeaux, and Virelais. An Anthology*, Leicester, 1965, Poem 5, p. 7.

23. ibid., xx.

24. ibid., Poem 45, lines 1–5.

25. ibid., xxvii.

26. ibid., Poem 1. Cf. on this subject Jacques d'Autun's poem, analysed by Dronke, *The Medieval Lyric*, 129–30, reproduced by B. Woledge, ed. cit., 158–60.

27. See above, pp. 218–19.

28. Poirion, op. cit., 206.

29. See above, pp. 274–5.

30. A. Piaget ed., *Alain Chartier, La Belle Dame sans mercy et les poésies lyriques*, Paris, 1945.

31. Poirion, op. cit., 128–30.

32. Piaget, ed. cit., 37–44.

33. Longest and most important of subsequent works in defence of women was Martin Le Franc's *Le Champion des Dames* (ed. A. Piaget, first part, Lausanne, 1968), a poem of more than 24,000 lines composed between 1440 and 1442, in which Franc Vouloir, the ladies' champion, opposes and finally defeats after fierce debates their reviler, Malebouche. Martin Le Franc was not reacting solely against Alain Chartier's poem, but also, and more extensively, against Jean de Meun. From this point of view compare Christine de Pisan's *L'Epistre au Dieu d'Amours*, see above, pp. 272–3.

34. Piaget, ed. cit., *Excusacion*, p. 61.

35. P. Champion ed., *Charles d'Orléans, Poésies*, Paris, CFMA, 2 vols., 1923–27 (several reprints in recent years).

36. See above, pp. 274–6.

37. The structure of Charles d'Orléans's rondels, for long the subject of much controversy, is given careful analysis by G. Defaux, 'Charles d'Orléans ou la poétique du secret', *R*, 1972, XCIII, 194–243. Defaux's conclusion is that, in those composed after 1440, only the first line, not the first couplet, should be repeated in the middle and at the end.

38. Of the many editions currently available, the most scholarly and reliable is still that by A. Longnon, revised by L. Foulet, published in the CFMA series, re-edited several times since 1911 (1914, 1923, 1932).

39. *Le Testament*, stanza XXVI.

40. So he tells us in the *Testament*, stanza XII.

41. Mainly by P. Guiraud in two works: *Le Jargon de Villon ou le gai savoir de la Coquille*, Paris, 1968; *Le Testament de Villon ou le gai savoir de la Basoche*, Paris, 1970.

42. ed. A. Piaget and E. Picot, Paris, SATF, 3 vols., 1896–1908 (reprint ed. New York, 1968).

43. Vol. II, 189.

44. Alexis's editor thinks that this *Débat* was composed shortly after Villon's *Double Ballade*, but this is far from certain. The hypothesis that Alexis's works came first and that Villon had read them at least deserves consideration.

45. J. Quicherat ed., *Les Vers de Maître Henri Baude*, Paris, 1856; A. Scoumanne ed., *Henri Baude, Dictz Moraulx pour faire tapisserie*, Geneva–Paris, 1959.

46. Possibly Jean de Bailly, secretary to King Louis XI, who figures in Villon's *Testament*.

47. Scoumanne, ed. cit., 98.

48. cf. above, chapter 8.

49. For Chastellain's poetry, see vols. 6, 7, and 8 of his complete works, referred to above, p. 292.

50. Contrast Villon's conviction, inspired possibly by the teachings of men such as Guillaume de Villon, that death effaces all except sin. One might hazard the generalisation that Villon's lyric verse had a moral foundation – an idea promulgated by Siciliano long ago – whereas Chastellain wrote moral verse with a lyric foundation.

51. On the amorphous, unsatisfactory nature of the literary historians' term *Grands Rhétoriqueurs*, whose authenticity as a medieval term is roughly on a par with that of *amour courtois*, see the excellent article by V.-L. Saulnier in *DLF*, 634–5.

52. N. Dupire ed., *Les Faictz et Dictz de Jean Molinet*, Paris, SATF, 3 vols., 1936–39.

53. The medieval attitude towards word-play was different from ours. It was evidently looked upon as conferring dignity and grace to a text, witness certain passages of Rutebeuf's *Miracle de Théophile* (lines 412–19, 528–36), the religious sincerity of which cannot be questioned (see above, pp. 249–50).

54. This work was last published in the sixteenth century.

55. K. Chesney ed., *Œuvres poétiques de Guillaume Crétin*, Paris, 1932, 320.

56. The *chant royal* was an extended *ballade* containing five stanzas instead of the customary three.

57. The last-named differ in form from those of Charles d'Orléans in that now only the first words of the first line are repeated, not the whole of the first line or couplet. In the fifteenth century, however, it is not always clear whether such abbreviations were intended by the poet or were owed to the copyist's not troubling to rewrite the whole line or couplet three times. Some, such as those of Villon, can in fact be read either way.

58. It has affinities, however, with the learned, pedantic jargon used by Arnoul Gréban in his *Mystère de la Passion* (see above, pp. 253-4).

59. *Débat entre Deux Dames*, Chesney, ed. cit., 97-8, lines 85-104.

60. J. Stecher ed., *Œuvres de Jean Lemaire de Belges*, Louvain,, 4 vols., 1882-91. Cf. also I. D. McFarlane, *A Literary History of France: Renaissance France, 1470-1589,* London, 1974, 40-5, 49-50.

61. J. Frappier ed., *La Concorde des Deux Langages*, Paris, 1947, lines 5-6, 17-18.

62. ed. H. Hornik, Geneva–Paris, 1957.

63. ed. D. Yabsley, Paris, 1932.

64. Stecher, ed. cit., vol. 4, 15-167.

65. ed. J. Frappier, Lille–Geneva, 1948. Photographic reproductions of sixteenth-century editions of these poems, along with *La Concorde des Deux Langages*, have been published by M. Françon, Cambridge, Mass., 1964.

Chapter 13

MISCELLANEOUS NARRATIVE WORKS OF THE FOURTEENTH CENTURY

I. FOURTEENTH-CENTURY 'CHANSONS DE GESTE'

STORIES of derring-do and single combats between valiant knights retained their popularity in the fourteenth century. The formula developed by authors from the twelfth century onwards still held good:

One knight, 'A', tilts at another, 'B'. Such was the fury of that charge that A's spear (or battle-axe, sword, mace) was bent (broken, splintered, torn from his grasp), and B's helmet (breastplate, arm, leg, shoulder, steed) was grazed (gashed, pierced, crushed, cloven, broken), and B or (and) A was (were) flung to the ground. And hard would it have gone with B or (and) A, had it not been that C, a friend, came galloping up, or that D, a foe, fighting nearby, was unable (unwilling) to intervene, whereupon C engaged D ... and so *ad infinitum*.[1]

This pattern is found not only in continuations of romances, but also in descendants of the *chansons de geste*, whose authors, familiar with the vast corpus of tales of legendary heroes and their adventures inherited from the twelfth- and thirteenth-century romances, made no attempt to recapture the spirit of the early epic literature. It was henceforth no more than a tainted tradition, even though the basic theme remained that of the crusades. Thus the *Entrée d'Espagne*, an early fourteenth-century poem of 7,976 decasyllabic lines written in northern Italy, as also was its continuation, the *Prise de Pampelune*, sets out to relate what happened during the first seven years of Charlemagne's Spanish campaign;[2] but after a time the author could not resist whisking Roland off to the Orient for a long episode in which he accomplishes marvellous feats in honour of a beautiful Saracen princess and undergoes a whole array of adventures on land and sea, with miracles wrought by God in his favour. While the *Entrée d'Espagne* and the *Prise de Pampelune* seem to have been unknown in France, but popular in north Italy where they were to play a part in leading to such works as *Orlando Furioso*, in France too the epic tradition lingered on, even quite late in the fourteenth century, in tales such as

Baudouin de Sebourc, the work of a Flemish poet, and *Li Bastars de Bouillon*,[3] epic still in that the heroes fight the enemies of Christianity, but with all the richly varied episodic adventures, now realistic, now fantastic; with the bewildering changes of heroes as well as of settings, inherited from the later romances; and with moralising and satirical material added for good measure. In their heterogeneity, in the superficiality of their puppet-like characters, in their outworn artistry, in their feverish search for variety within the well-worn themes, such works herald a decline. This, however, was not a contemporary view, and it is as well to record that what may strike the modern reader as far-fetched, even absurd, did not necessarily have such an effect in those times.

II. THE 'VOEUX DU PAON' OF JACQUES DE LONGUYON

Certain works reflected contemporary notions of chivalry, such as the *Voeux du Paon*, a romance of 8,784 alexandrine lines by Jacques de Longuyon,[4] an early fourteenth-century continuation of the adventures of Alexander the Great, adventures which had been developed in at least four 'branches' over the two preceding centuries. The work is so called because the heroes made vows to a roasted peacock that they would accomplish certain deeds. In substance their vows bear a slight resemblance to those made by the Saracens in the *Chanson de Roland* before the Battle of Roncevaux, and a rather closer one to the 'gabs' of the *Pèlerinage de Charlemagne*:[5] one knight swears that in the coming fray he will dismount and fight with the foot-soldiers; another will snatch Alexander's sword from his grasp, which prompts another knight to swear that he will remove this knight's helmet in the battle 's'il ne tient a cyment' (line 4098) (unless it is cemented on); while a lady swears that, once the war is over, she will make a golden image of the peacock and set it on a pillar of pure gold, a boast which gave a later poet, Jean de Court, the subject of yet another continuation, *Le Restor du Paon*, a poem of 2,691 alexandrine lines completed about 1325, continued in its turn by the *Parfait du Paon*, written by Jean de la Motte about 1340.[6] The strange notion that such vows should be made to a peacock was apparently owed by Jacques de Longuyon to Bishop Thiébaut de Bar, who is named in the concluding lines. This same bishop encouraged another poet to develop the same theme in the *Voeux de l'Epervier*,[7] while in 1306, King Edward I, who also knew Bishop Thiébaut, swore to two swans, brought to him on a large platter and covered with a network of gold, that he would march into Scotland to chastise Robert Bruce, so instigating the expedition so soon to lead to his death. A Picard poem, the *Voeux du Héron*, an anonymous work of 440 alexandrine lines, claims that in 1338 Robert of Artois brought a heron to Edward III, declaring that since it is the most fainthearted of birds, it should be given to the king who had lost France.[8] Stung by this taunt, the king vowed to the heron that he would ravage France, and so, if this extravagant tale can be believed, began the Hundred Years War![9] Whatever the truth of the matter, it is clear that such vows were not mere literary fantasies, but were believed in and acted upon still in the early fourteenth century. Jacques de Longuyon, it has been pointed out, merely brought the knights of Alexander into line with the most recent practice of chivalry.[10] Another feature which reached beyond the pages of romance is provided by this same author's *excursus* on the Nine Worthies. This idea of listing the noblest men and women who ever lived was very old, but Jacques de Longuyon gave it a clear form, and for centuries afterwards it was to retain its popularity.

III. 'PERCEFOREST'

Longest of all medieval romances in French is *Perceforest*, also written in the early fourteenth century, a work mostly in prose but with some verse intercalations,[11] whose 531 chapters would, it has been calculated, fill about 7,000 sides of modern print.[12] It has survived in four fifteenth-century manuscripts, of which the sole complete one belonged to the duke of Burgundy, and in two printed editions, one of 1528, another of 1531. Not surprisingly, it has found no editor since the sixteenth century. It owes much to the *Voeux du Paon*, its action taking over from the end of that work. A vast preamble of fourteen chapters deals with the geography and early history of Britain, borrowing from many Latin authors, classical and medieval, principally from Geoffrey of Monmouth.[13] The story begins in earnest when Alexander, borne by a tempest to the shores of Britain, gave Scotland to Gadifer and England to Betis, soon to be called Perceforest because of his triumph in penetrating a dense forest, where he killed Darnant the evil magician. The work is an attempt to tie many loose strands together, a sort of Alexandro-Arthurian, pagano-Christian, Graeco-Romano-Celtic romance-epic, a prehistory of chivalry (already the *Voeux du Paon* referred to Alexander as 'the father of chivalry'; line 1184) depicting a series of civilisations in Britain rising and falling before the dawn of the Arthurian era, but with a tradition of chivalry handed down and evolving from one age to another. The chivalric Ordre du Franc Palais, which appears in *Perceforest* as the ancestor of that of the Round Table, is said to have inspired the numerous orders of chivalry which sprang up in the fourteenth century, of which the Order of the Garter was but one. The Middle Ages had immense respect for institutions of ancient origin. To create the impression that the knights of the fourteenth century were following in the footsteps of their remote ancestors (cf. the purpose of the *Chanson de Roland* some three centuries earlier),[14] to invent new adventures for well-loved and venerated figures, these were the aims of which these basically conservative writers never wearied, reflecting in this the psychology of their age.

IV. 'BERINUS ET AIGRES'

From about the middle of the fourteenth century is extant a prose romance called *Berinus et Aigres*, a revision of a thirteenth-century story in verse which has been lost except for a few fragments, but which is believed to have contained between thirteen and fourteen thousand lines.[15] This is another rambling, episodic tale, describing the incredible adventures firstly of Berinus, son of a rich Roman citizen forced to leave home because of a quarrel instigated by his stepmother; secondly of his son Aigres, who, having slaughtered a band of twelve robbers, rescued the beautiful young Balbine from the clutches of the villainous Maligan, having been cast into a den of enraged lions, and been abandoned at the bottom of a deep well, emerges unscathed; and after further amazing happenings, in the course of which he kills his father Berinus, stuck fast in a vat of pitch, he returns to Rome to marry the emperor's daughter, departs on a pilgrimage to the Holy Land to expiate his patricide, and at length returns home to mount the throne and live happily ever after. A skilful blending of disparate elements of both Eastern and Western origin, *Berinus* owes much to the ever-popular legend of the Seven Sages of Rome.[16] Some nautical adventures reveal the influence of the story of Sinbad the Sailor; Aigre's exploits are indebted to certain *chansons de geste* of the thirteenth century; the several love stories, courtly in tone, resemble those of twelfth-century *romans courtois*, while numerous hand-to-hand combats follow the time-honoured formula.

V. ARTUS DE BRETAGNE

Dating from the same period, *Artus de Bretagne* (also known as *Petit Artus de Bretagne*) is a tale of adventure, enchantments, and magic. The hero (who is not King Arthur, but a descendant of Lancelot du Lac) survives numerous perilous encounters, with, for example, an awesome giant, a lion, a burning spear, a revolving castle. This romance has survived in ten manuscripts, and evidently retained its popularity over a long period, since it was edited thirteen times between 1493 and 1584, while an English translation went through three editions. Such a work has much to reveal about literary tastes of the later Middle Ages and the Renaissance, and it is unfortunate that no modern edition is at present available.[17]

VI. 'MÉLIADOR' OF FROISSART

It will come as no surprise to whomsoever has read the preceding chapters that the indefatigable Jean Froissart composed a romance, and that it is a substantial work of some 31,000 lines (the surviving copy is incomplete).[18] There is a historical colouring about this romance, just as there is a romantic colouring about his historical writings. Dating from 1384 and concerned basically with royal dynasties and marriages, *Méliador* tells how Hermondine, heiress to the throne of Scotland, agrees to marry the most valiant of her suitors.[19] Young nobles from far and wide – Méliador from Cornwall, Agamanor from Normandy, Gratien from Italy, Hermonicet from Carthage, and many others – distinguish themselves in countless single combats and tournaments, the vanquished being required to report back to Arthur's Court according to the formula of Arthurian romance. Love is served mainly by the sword, but also by the arts, painting, singing, dancing, and above all poetry in the shape of *rondeaux* and *virelais*, composed not by Froissart but by his patron at the time, Wenceslas of Bohemia, duke of Luxembourg and Brabant, incorporated in the text as a tribute to him. The work benefits from its author's experiences as a chronicler and from his extensive travels, in that its geography is a good deal more accurate than is that of most works of this nature, many names and positions of towns and rivers in England, Wales, Scotland, and Ireland being correctly given. Names of characters are taken, sometimes from earlier romances, sometimes from contemporary history. It is a world of gentlemen, gallant alike in victory and defeat, and of beautiful ladies who inspire their deeds of valour. Froissart persists in painting men as they ought to be, according to the chivalric code in an age increasingly conscious of men as they actually are, for by this time the Hundred Years War had run almost half its span, and the main battles had been won, not by the haughty knights, but by the humble and despised archers. After five years of adventure and romance, *Méliador* concludes with a magnificent tournament involving 1,566 knights-errant, a grand finale, a Cup Final of the Arthurian world. Méliador, already triumphant in numerous encounters, emerges as the victor and marries the princess of Scotland. That Froissart's romance had many readers is doubtful. He had greater success as chronicler and lyric poet. He was a writer at his best in depicting particular events and individual details, but who persisted in undertaking vast frescoes, frescoes, moreover, of a type which by the end of the century was becoming old-fashioned.

VII. THE 'ROMAN DU COMTE D'ANJOU' OF JEHAN MAILLART

Fourteenth-century romance was not always of this type. Jehan Maillart's *Le Roman du Comte d'Anjou*,[20] of which the year of composition, 1316, is quoted in its conclusion, is a story of 8,156 lines in the usual octosyllabic rhyming couplets, giving a version of the legend told in the preceding century in Philippe de Beaumanoir's *Manekine*.[21] It is noteworthy that the most extravagant elements of the earlier version, such as the daughter's cutting off her hand and its miraculous restoration, are avoided. The author, a notary at the royal chancellory in Paris,[22] insists that this is a true tale, and whatever we make of this assertion, it is certainly a story limited to what could theoretically happen. It has a factual, realistic atmosphere, a convincing psychological basis, of the type associated with bourgeois *milieux* and attitudes, and is written in what its modern editor calls 'ce vif et goguenard langage du bourgeois ou du clerc parisien, mis en œuvre au siècle suivant par Villon'.[23] Not that the language is coarse or unrestrained. It is often frank and open, but the author could exercise tact when the need arose, as in the following lines describing the wedding-night of the hero and heroine:

Quant li quens sa fame regarde,	When the count looks at his wife,
Molt li demeure et molt li tarde	he longs to be in bed with her. He
Qu'il soit avecques li couchiéz;	came to the bedside and without
Vers le chevéz s'est aprouchiéz,	more ado goes to bed. He finds his
Si se couche sanz pluz atendre;	wife white and tender, and when he
Sa feme trueve blance et tendre,	feels her hard breasts, he makes a
Et quant sent la poitrine dure,	belt around her with his two arms.
De ses deus bras li fait chainture;	Then he kissed her full on the mouth
Puis la baisa droit en la bouche,	and his body touches hers. About the
A tant son cors au sien atouche.	rest I could not tell you, but no
Du seurplus parler ne saroie;	man could experience such great
Mez nus ne pourroit si grant joie	joy . . .
Avoir . . .	

(lines 2935–47)

VIII. THE 'ROMAN DES DEDUIS' OF GACE DE LA BUIGNE AND THE 'LIVRE DU ROY MODUS ET DE LA ROYNE RATIO' OF HENRI DE FERRIERES

Certain works of the later Middle Ages defy any simple description or definition, and could be classified under several headings. Fiction and non-fiction, characters real and allegorical, practical advice, moral reflections, all may be found within a single work. This is true of two late fourteenth-century texts both of which deal basically with hunting: Gace de la Buigne's *Le Roman des Deduis*, begun in 1359, completed after 1370, and Henri de Ferrieres's *Livre du Roy Modus et de la Royne Ratio*, composed about the same time.[24] Gace de la Buigne wrote his treatise on 'deduits' (a word meaning 'pleasures', 'sports', 'pastimes') for the young Philip, duke of Burgundy, in order that he should avoid idleness and be well educated. A poem of 12,210 octosyllabic lines, it has much to say about the taming and training of falcons and other birds of prey, and later of dogs. It has much to say about noble qualities of the mind, arranging an allegorical debate between them centred principally on the importance to be allotted to the qualities of Pity, Grace, and Mercy. It builds up a story about life presented in terms of a battle between the vices and virtues. However discursive and disjointed, it always returns to the theme of the hunt, the *leitmotiv* running throughout the poem. The moral advice is based not on a religious foundation (though religion is not ignored), but on a practical one: a man who is impetuous or bad-tempered, or gluttonous or a drunkard, will never make a good falconer because he will never have the patience and skill necessary to train a falcon and to work in co-operation with it. The author is very ready to generalise: to be good at your occupation, whatever it is, you must hold it in high esteem and for this end a life of virtue is essential (lines 609–36). He is convinced that

Le mestier de fauconnerie
Requiert homme de honneste vie,
Car ribaut glouton ne puet faire
Chose qui a l'oiseau puist plaire,
Et, se tu ne li fais plaisir,
Nullement n'en pourras joïr.
(1983–8)

The practice of falconry calls for a man of honest ways, for the ribald glutton can do nothing to please the bird, and if you do not please him, you will get no enjoyment out of him.

He is also a great lover of dogs. In ascribing virtues to them, he is aware that he is speaking figuratively ('transomptivement', 5655), for such features belong essentially to men:

Chien est loyal a son seignour,	A dog is loyal to his master,
Chien est de bonne et vraye amour,	A dog is good in love and true,
Chien est de bon entendement,	A dog is good in understanding,
Chien saige a bien vray jugement,	A dog is wise with good sound
Chien a force, chien a bonté,	judgement,
Chien a hardiesce et beauté.	A dog is strong, a dog is kind,
(5659–64)	A dog is bold and beautiful.

The very lengthy debate between *Deduit d'Oiseaux* and *Deduit de Chiens* leaves honours on both sides, and there is surely great charm in the conclusion: may God forgive the author his faults, for he was a great lover of dogs and birds.

The *Livre du Roy Modus et de la Royne Ratio*, a more substantial work written in prose as well as verse, is concerned with explanations of the manner (Modus) and the method (Ratio) of the hunt, given by these allegorical characters. The advice is far more detailed and precise than in the *Roman des Deduis*. In the early part of the work the careful examination of natural phenomena, and the deductions that may be based on them, have a certain scientific quality, apparent already in the opening chapter, in which the author talks about the seasons and the effects of the sun in terms radically different from those of countless medieval poets who used this traditional *exordium*:

Toutes les choses qui ont vie sont gouvernees par la chaleur du soleil, car celle chaleur est propice a toute nature, que rien sanz elle ne puet fructifier, par quoi nous veon que, en l'iver quant le soleil nous regarde de costé et il n'a a plain sur nous son regart, que y gele et fait froit, et la vertu des arbres et des herbes retourne a leur rachines, et pour ce sechent leur fueilles et chïent[25] (All living things are governed by the heat of the sun, for this heat is propitious to all nature. Without it nothing can bear fruit, wherefore we see that, in winter when the sun beholds us from the side and does not look fully on us, there is frost and cold, and the vigour of trees and grass returns to their roots, so that their leaves wither and fall down).

Much of what follows is a practical huntsman's manual, on, for example, the habits of deer; how to judge their condition and size by examining their tracks and droppings; what animals the huntsman can expect to find at particular seasons of the year; how to skin a deer once it has been caught. The hunting of other animals is also dealt with, such as hares, wild boars, wolves, foxes, otters, partridge, and all manner of birds. The relative merits of hunting with falcons and dogs are weighed up and judgement is entrusted to the author's patron, the comte de Tancarville, who pronounces in favour of the latter. In the later part of the work, subtitled *Le Songe de Pestilence*, the author tells of a dream he had in the forest. Although further information is given here on hunting, particularly on falconry, there is once more, as in *Le Roman des Deduis*, much reflection on vices and virtues, with vast mêlées between the two sides[26] and violent single combats between Pride and Humility. Reflections on the actual battles of the times are included; prophecies of pestilence which will infect France where vice has triumphed over virtue; thoughts on the benefits which the influence of the planets can bring; a welter of facts, superstitions, allegorical fantasies, historical events beneath which the hunting theme is at length quite submerged, except that the reader is encouraged to think of hunting as the enemy of sloth. This strange miscellany ends with a *chant royal*[27] in praise of the Virgin Mary.

IX. 'LA CHASSE' OF GASTON PHEBUS

The classical medieval work on the subject of the hunt, *La Chasse*, by Gaston III, comte de Foix (commonly referred to as Gaston Phebus because of his handsome appearance), was written towards the end of the century, between 1387 and 1391.[28] A passionate devotee of the hunt – a passion which cost him his life, since he was killed while hunting bears in the Pyrenees – he has freed the subject from the heterogeneous material of earlier hunting manuals and has given it an extremely thorough treatment. A long study of the various animals that are hunted leads to detailed descriptions of the manner in which each is hunted, killed, and cut up. Some sections are heavily indebted to Henri de Ferrieres's work, while the influence of Gace de la Buigne is more faintly discernible. This treatise quickly became famous, and has survived in forty-one manuscripts. Early in the fifteenth century it was translated into English by Edward of Norwich, second duke of York, who was killed at Agincourt in 1415.

NOTES

1. Quoted from vol. I of R. L. G. Ritchie's edition of *The Buik of Alexander* by J. Barbour, Edinburgh, 1925, xxxii–xxxiii. This edition is in four volumes, and also contains the French texts of which *The Buik of Alexander* is a translation, notably *Li Fuerres de Gadres* and *Les Voeux du Paon*.
2. See the second line of the *Chanson de Roland*, quoted above, p. 72. The *Entrée d'Espagne* has been edited by A. Thomas, Paris, 2 vols., 1913; the *Prise de Pampelune* by A. Mussafia, Vienna, 1868.
3. A new edition of the latter is available, by R. F. Cook, Geneva, 1972. The former does not appear to have been edited since 1841 (by L.-N. Boca, Valenciennes, 2 vols.).
4. Little is known about this author (Ritchie, op. cit., I, xxxv), but the popularity of his work is attested by the fact of its having survived in thirty-nine manuscripts. The library of the dukes of Burgundy contained three copies, one of which is particularly beautiful and may have been prepared for Duke Philip the Bold (1363–1404). ibid., xlviii.

5. Aebischer, ed. cit.
6. The former has been edited by R. J. Carey, Geneva, 1966; the latter by V. Hands for a University of London thesis which has not so far been published.
7. Ritchie, op. cit., xxxviii. This poem has been edited by G. Wolfram and F. Bonnardot in *Jahrbuch der Gesellschaft für lothringische Geschichte und Altertumskunde*, Metz, VI, 1894, and by the same editors as an independent volume, Metz, 1895.
8. This poem has been edited by T. Wright in *Political Poems and Songs . . . from the Accession of Edward III to that of Richard III*, London, 1859, 1–25.
9. It is almost certainly apocryphal, as is shown by B. J. Whiting, 'The Vows of the Heron', *Sp*, XX, 1945, 261–78, though Ritchie points out that it is at least well matched to Edward's character and temperament, op. cit., I, xlvi.
10. ibid., xl.
11. These have been published separately by J. Lods, in *Les Pièces Lyriques du Roman de Perceforest*, Geneva–Lille, 1953. This same author has written a detailed study of the work: *Le Roman de Perceforest*, Geneva–Lille, 1951, but there is as yet no complete modern edition of the work.
12. L.-P. Flutre, 'Etudes sur le Roman de *Perceforêt*', *R*, LXX, 1948–49, 474.
13. See above, pp. 146–7.
14. This same outlook accounts for the 'translatio studii', the idea that 'chevalerie' and 'clergie' went from Greece to Rome, and from Rome to France, as Chrétien de Troyes explained in the prologue to *Cligès* (lines 28–33).
15. ed. R. Bossuat, Paris, SATF, 2 vols., 1931–33.
16. See above, p. 173.
17. For bibliographical information, see *DLF*.
18. *Méliador*, ed. A. Longnon, Paris, SATF, 3 vols., 1895–99.
19. 1384 is the date of the surviving version, but an earlier one probably existed, written between 1365 and 1368. For this information I am indebted to Professor A. Diverres.
20. ed. Mario Roques, Paris, CFMA, 1931.
21. See above, p. 215. It was to turn up later in *Peau d'Ane*, one of Perrault's *contes*.
22. As was his contemporary Gervais du Bus, see above, pp. 270–1.
23. Roques, ed. cit., xvi.
24. The former has been edited by A. Blomqvist, Karlshamn, 1951; the latter by G. Tilander, Paris, SATF, 2 vols., 1932.
25. Tilander, ed. cit., I, 13.
26. This theme was launched by Prudentius (A.D. 348–410?), whose *Psychomachia* depicts the struggle of Christian virtues against pagan vices for the soul of man. This was the first completely allegorical poem in European literature, and its influence on successive generations of writers was immense (Lewis, op. cit., 66–73).
27. See above, p. 327, note 56.
28. ed. J. Lavallée, Paris, 1854. G. Tilander announced that he was preparing a new edition in *DLF*, 1964.

Chapter 14

MISCELLANEOUS NARRATIVE WORKS OF THE FIFTEENTH CENTURY

I. THE 'QUINZE JOYES DE MARIAGE'

OUTWARDLY, literature of the fifteenth century began to assume a more modern appearance, with prose gradually becoming established as the normal narrative medium and with the proportion of anonymous works continuing to decline, because authors provided their names, and sometimes even the year of composition, more readily than in earlier centuries. Inwardly too, significant changes were to take place, though these were by no means limited to narrative works, and reflect, as does so much French literature of the later Middle Ages, a growing preoccupation with the realities of human existence. Generally speaking, works of fantasy, whisking the reader along with the hero through countless incredible adventures, were by this time adaptations of earlier compositions. The original works of the period were commentaries not so much on life as it might be or ought to be, but as it is, although the view expressed was frequently ironical or even embittered.

Dating apparently from the very dawn of the century, the *Quinze Joyes de Mariage* is a lively prose work of quite modest dimensions.[1] Attempts to date it more precisely, and to identify the author, have so far proved inconclusive. It is part of the substantial body of medieval anti-feminist literature. If the irony of the title, which extends throughout the work and permeates down to stylistic details, were to be discarded, it would have to be renamed *The Fifteen Miseries of Marriage*, for that is what it is all about. It is an irreverent parody of a devout theme, the fifteen joys of the Virgin Mary, treated by Christine de Pisan. Among the several misogynistic works to which it is related, special mention must be made of Deschamps's *Miroir de Mariage*,[2] to which it is so close that it seems certain that one influenced the other, although it has not been established which of the two was the earlier. It shares with certain other fifteenth-century works, in both verse and prose, a succinctness which eluded most earlier writers. Each section is carefully constructed, having an introduction, a development, and a conclusion linking it to the central theme. The characters are stock figures, unnamed – the outwitted, overburdened, cuckolded husband; the wily, pleasure-seeking wife; the bullying mother-in-law. They can be found also in the farces and *fabliaux* and in countless jokes down the ages on the ever-vulnerable subject of marriage. Each 'joy', whether it be the wife's spendthrift nature, her love of finery, parties, and the attentions of 'gallants', or her pregnancy, a fresh source of expense, or daughters who grow up to be as pleasure-loving as their mother and who already before marriage indulge in the game of 'la beste à deux dos', ends with the same mock lament, resembling some *ballade*-refrain, except that the wording varies slightly:

Ainsi use sa vie en paines, en douleurs et gemissemens, ou il est et sera toujours, et finera miserablement ses jours' (Fifteenth 'Joy') (And so he spends his life in pain, toil, and tribulation, now and in the future, and will end his days in misery).

It is a sort of nuptial *Huis Clos* based on the premise 'l'enfer, c'est le mariage'. The author is quite ruthless and never lets slip the slightest opportunity of mocking the husband: the mere mention of the wife's finery (in the second sentence of the First 'Joy') leads to the remark that the husband may not have paid for it himself and will have been led to believe (poor fool!) that it was bought for her by her parents; a reference to the wife's pregnancy immediately attracts the inevitable comment: 'et a l'aventure ne sera pas de son mary, comme advient souvent'[3] (and peradventure it will not be by her husband, and it frequently is not). It is intriguing that this work should have appeared about the time when, in Paris, the *Cour Amoureuse* was attempting to revive the old courtly spirit, roundly condemning works disrespectful of the fair sex. It is doubtful, however, whether this provincial text, whose author may have belonged to the Poitou region,[4] was known in the capital in the early fifteenth century.[5] No information has survived concerning its dissemination at this time. The five extant manuscripts date from the later fifteenth century and only one appears to have been prepared for a wealthy patron.[6] A considerable number of early printed editions in Lyons and Paris testifies to its continuing and no doubt growing popularity among the reading public at the end of the Middle Ages, in the early Renaissance, and beyond.

II. THE 'CENT NOUVELLES NOUVELLES'

Deceived husbands and libidinous wives also figure prominently in the *Cent Nouvelles Nouvelles*, a collection of tales modelled loosely on Boccaccio's *Decameron*, fourteen of them showing the more direct influence of Poggio's *Liber Facetiarum*.[7] They were told at the Court of Philip, duke of Burgundy, fourteen by the duke himself, most of the others by various members of his household, and written down probably between 1464 and 1467. Thirty-six authors are named altogether. Philippe Pot, 'échanson' (cup-bearer) to the duke, supplied fifteen tales, more than any other author, and either he or another of the duke's retinue, Philippe de Loan, author of eleven of the tales, may have assembled and 'edited' the whole series, giving them a certain unity of style and a certain overall irony. That these bawdy tales flourished in the luxurious Court of the duke of Burgundy, which attracted artists, writers, musicians, miniaturists, and sculptors, and that they provided 'une forme de divertissement destiné à passer le temps agréable-ment',[8] testifies to the coarseness of this aristocratic milieu for at least part of its time, probably when the men were alone together. In any case, that the duke was known as 'the Good' was certainly no reference to his morals, for he had a score of mistresses and many bastards. The atmosphere of the *nouvelles* resembles that of the farces and *fabliaux* which were appreciated no doubt in the Courts as well as elsewhere, and also that of certain poems, far off in time and distance, of Guillaume IX, duke of Aquitaine, first known troubadour.[9] It may well be that this is not simply a sign of the relaxed atmosphere of Burgundian *milieux* in the mid-fifteenth century, but that courtly concepts never supplanted completely, at least among the male members of court circles, the old, freer *gaulois* attitudes. More truly characteristic of the fifteenth century is the decline of the heroic and chivalric ideals which certain tales betray,[10] but this must not be seen as an invitation to use the word 'decadence' too readily of this period when new values and attitudes were rapidly emerging. One of their modern editors finds in *Les Cent Nouvelles Nouvelles* 'la solide santé de la vieille France', and before summaries of a few of them are given below, it is as well to recall his exhortation: 'Ne soyons pas scandalisés'.[11]

Tale No. 1: told by the duke of Burgundy

During her husband's absence, his wife slips through a postern gate to the house of a rich neighbour, with whom her husband is friendly. The husband returns unexpectedly, calling first at his friend's house. He catches them in bed but sees only the woman's backside and her 'cuisses, qui blanches et grosses estoient'. He admires her beauty and swears that never has he seen such a close resemblance to his wife. He is sent back home the long way round, having been led to believe that the postern is locked. His wife returns the short way, meets him, and accuses him of trying to deceive her. She receives his humble apologies, and so arranges things that subsequently she is able to slip many a time through the postern gate without her husband's knowledge.

Of particular interest here is the highly ironical use of the traditional Ovidian-inspired love vocabulary in a bourgeois setting:

les yeulx d'elle, archiers du cueur, descocherent tant de fleches en la personne dudit bourgeois que sans prochain remede son cas n'estoit pas maindre que mortel[12] (her eyes, the heart's archers, let fly so many arrows at the said bourgeois, that without a swift remedy his case was not less than fatal).

Tale No. 3: told by Philippe Pot

A knight tells the miller's buxom wife that her front is about to drop off. Simple-minded, she asks him what can be done about it. He tells her that she will have to have it 'recoigner' (i.e., fastened on again). This he proceeds to do on numerous occasions 'd'un outil qu'il avoit' (with a tool in his possession). The miller finds out and determines to get his own back. During the knight's absence the miller gives the knight's wife a pike, and, as a friend of the family, is allowed to hand it to her while she is in her bath. He steals her diamond placed on the edge of the bath. He later suggests that it must have disappeared inside her and offers to look for it. This he proceeds to do with great vigour, using the same sort of tool that the knight had used earlier to fasten his wife's front on. He eventually returns the diamond. The knight finds out, and next time they meet, he exclaims 'Dieu gard, Dieu gard ce bon pescheur de dyamant', receiving the rejoinder 'Dieu gard, Dieu gard ce recogneur de cons'.

Tale No. 4: told by the duke of Burgundy

A Scotsman begs a lady for a rendezvous. Her husband finds out and tells her to go ahead. He will hide behind the tapestry with his sword. The Scotsman arrives, brandishing his sword, declaring that if anybody comes, 'je luy fendray la teste jusques aux dens'. The husband dares not intervene. The Scotsman returns and the husband dives under the bed. On his departure husband and wife blame each other, but the former was really responsible.

Tale No. 5: told by Philippe de Loan

A Frenchman already taken prisoner meets an Englishman who claims that the Frenchman has broken the terms of his surrender because he is wearing his 'aguilletes', the laces used to strap armour in to place. He accordingly claims the Frenchman as his prize. The English captain, Talbot, hears of this, arms the Englishman with 'aguilletes', and tells the Frenchman to attack him with his sword. The Englishman is forced to beg for mercy. In a second case, finding that one of his men has robbed a church, Talbot forbids him ever to set foot inside a church again.

This is the first non-sexual tale of the series, and it is likely that the two anecdotes were true.[13]

Tale No. 6: told by Lannoy

A drunken Dutchman meets a priest and insists that he should confess him on the spot. Being assured that, having received absolution, he will go to Paradise if he dies, he gives the priest his sword and begs him to kill him. The priest whacks him with the flat of the sword and leaves him in a drunken stupor. When his companions pick him up, he exclaims: 'Put me down, I'm dead'. When they offer him a drink, he says 'I'm dead'. To everything they say to him, he replies 'I'm dead'. They take him home, where, for the next two days, he remains dead.

Tale No. 7: told by the duke of Burgundy

A coal-merchant delivers a load to the goldsmith, and stays chatting so late that he has to stay the night. He is invited to sleep in the goldsmith's bed with his wife between them. His wife puts her hand on her husband's chest and her 'gros derrière' on the coal-merchant, whose physical reaction is beyond his control. The goldsmith is woken by his wife's movement and tells the coal-merchant that, had she been awake, she would have scratched his eyes out. But according to the coal-merchant, she was awake.

Tale No. 10: told by Philippe Pot

A young man, one of whose duties it is to supply his master with mistresses, assumes that this will end when his master marries. His master asks him for his favourite dish, and, being told that it is eel-pie, has him fed on nothing but this. When, 'plain de pastez', the young man complains, the master points out that he would like a change from his wife from time to time. Either the young man will continue his earlier duties, or be fed on nothing but eel-pie.

Tale No. 98: told by 'L'Acteur' (i.e., the anonymous compiler of the series)

A girl loves a knight of her own age, but is promised by her parents to a much older one. She elopes with her lover, but they are attacked by four ruffians ('charruyers ou bouviers'). The knight defeats and pursues them, but as they run away, one of them suddenly turns round and runs the knight through with his sword, killing him instantly. The girl, powerless to resist them, pulls out a tiny knife and cuts her throat.

This last tale, a miniature tragedy of love skilfully told, is included here to show (as does Tale No. 5) that not all the stories are bawdy and lascivious, though this is the dominating note. Lacking the finesse of their Italian counterparts, they substitute a coarse explicitness for a subtle suggestiveness.[14]

III. THE 'ARRÊTS D'AMOUR' OF MARTIAL D'AUVERGNE

A rather gentler satire of love, and a more original one, is provided by Martial d'Auvergne's *Arrêts d'Amour*.[15] Their author was born in Paris in the 1430s, about the same time as François Villon. He became an attorney, spending his whole life in the capital and dying there in 1508. He was wealthy, owning several houses in the Ile de la Cité, and successful, acting for various prominent persons such as the duc de Bourbon. He is the author of several works: the *Vigilles de la Mort de Charles VII*, a long poem in praise of that king, with whose reign that of the ruling monarch, Louis XI, is compared unfavourably; the *Dévotes louanges de Notre Dame* in praise of the Virgin Mary;[16] and the work for which he is best remembered, the *Arrêts d'Amour*, in prose apart from a short prologue and epilogue in octosyllabic verse. Written between 1460 and 1466, in the same decade, that is, as Villon's *Testament* and the *Cent Nouvelles Nouvelles*, the author draws on his legal background to imagine a court of love trying cases involving lovers' tiffs. The principal aim was to amuse, the humour, mostly light-hearted and gently ironical, depending in large measure on the use of serious legal jargon in the discussion of frivolous, sometimes highly improbable or even farcical, situations. It may be considered as part of the abundant literature engendered by Alain Chartier's *La Belle Dame sans merci*, taking up a position akin to that of Chartier himself, many of the fifty-one cases involved being concerned with 'dames sans merci' and with the by now near figure of fun, the 'amant martyr' whose garb was donned by that 'bon follastre' François Villon. One of Martial d'Auvergne's mock court-cases concerns a lover's complaint that his lady who has sworn to be loyal to him is in breach of promise when she smiles at others and accepts bouquets of flowers from them. She stoutly defends her freedom in such matters and her right to use nature's gifts in such a way that she should not be considered unsociable. The lover loses his case and is ordered to pay expenses, his appeal being dismissed. Another case involves a lady who, while being serenaded by her lover, accidentally upset a bowl of blood on to his white shirt. The watch had arrested him on suspicion of murder. The lover prefers charges against his lady, who is condemned to give him six kisses, each the length of a *De Profundis*. Here, as in numerous works of the fifteenth century, the courtly ideal receives short shrift, and the general atmosphere is brisk and matter-of-fact. The importance in literary matters of the legal *milieux* of fifteenth-century Paris is once more revealed. Villon's *Testament* is also a parody of legal procedures and jargon, as are some of Henri Baude's poems, and those of other talented writers not included here such as Guillaume Coquillard.[17] We have seen also that writers of the preceding century, such as Jehan Maillart and Gervais du Bus, belonged to the same milieu, whose importance and activity in literary matters during the later Middle Ages would clearly merit special study. The success of Martial d'Auvergne's *Arrêts d'Amour* was considerable. More than thirty-five editions appeared between 1500 and 1724, and this work gave rise to the fanciful notion that in the Middle Ages courts of love – as distinct from that favourite theme of aristocratic literature, the Court of the God of Love – actually existed and heard cases similar to those described by Martial d'Auvergne, a belief which, however erroneous, was reinforced by certain earlier works such as the *tensons* and *jeux-partis*.[18]

IV. THE 'AMANT RENDU CORDELIER'

An anonymous works sometimes attributed, wrongly, to Martial d'Auvergne, is the *Amant rendu Cordelier*.[19] In this poem of 1,872 octosyllabic lines, arranged in stanzas identical in form to those of Villon's *Testament*, the poet dreams that he encounters a despairing lover who has decided to become a Cordelier (Franciscan of the strict rule) and who, before doing so, discusses at length with the prior ('damp Prieur') the disastrous effects of love. The analysis, much of it put into the mouth of the prior, has that sly, penetrating wit characteristic of much later French writers on the subject of love. The devastating effect of the lady's 'doux yeulx tous fretillans' (line 1498) (gentle fluttering eyes) is described in a passage of 160 lines, counterbalanced, however, by a description of the ascetic existence awaiting the novice monk, so severe that one inevitably suspects an ironical intent. The poet, on waking up from his dream, does not condemn love, but the despairing lover: 'Telz gens sont mauvais amoureux' (1853) (such folk make poor lovers). In this respect the *Amant rendu Cordelier* provides a distant comment on Alain Chartier's *La Belle Dame sans merci*, condemning, not the lady, but feeble-hearted lovers such as the one Chartier portrayed, since '. . . en leur cueur espoir point n'abonde' (1854) (in their hearts hope does not abound).

V. THE WORKS OF ANTOINE DE LA SALE

Outstanding among prose writers of the fifteenth century was Antoine de La Sale, born in Provence, possibly near Arles, in 1385 or 1386. From the age of fourteen he served the house of Anjou for almost fifty years, as page, then squire, eventually becoming tutor to René d'Anjou's eldest son, Jean de Calabre, probably having special responsibility for his education as a knight. In 1448 he was appointed tutor to the three sons of Louis de Luxembourg. In the course of a busy and adventurous life he travelled extensively and spent a period of several years in Italy. He appears to have turned to writing late in life, influenced in the first instance by his peda-gogical duties. His first extant work, *La Salade* (an obvious pun on his name), is a compilation on the art of government, composed in 1444 for Jean de Calabre, incorporating accounts of his travels in

Italy; *La Sale*, a moral and didactic treatise, was written in 1451 for the three sons of Louis de Luxembourg.[20] He also wrote a treatise on tournaments and feats of arms for François II, duke of Brittany.[21] The work usually regarded as his masterpiece is *Petit Jehan de Saintré*, a prose romance which has the dimensions and something of the psychological interest of the modern novel. Not without reason has it been called 'le premier roman français digne de ce nom'.[22] It was written in 1456, when its author was over seventy, and dedicated to Jean de Calabre. Two years later it was followed by the *Réconfort de Madame de Fresne*, resembling the preceding work inasmuch as it was set at the time of the Hundred Years War, but in certain important respects it too anticipates future developments.[23]

The story of Petit Jehan de Saintré[24] begins in the reign of King John II (1350–64), son of Philippe de Valois. Jehan de Saintré, thirteen years old, 'debonnaire et gracieux', attracts the attention, at Court, of a young widow whose real name will not be given 'a cause de ce que aprés pourrez veoir' (because of what you will see later). She is referred to as the 'dame des Belles Cousines' (the queen normally addressing her as 'belle cousine'), and more frequently as 'Madame'. She teases him about his lady-love for her own amusement and that of her ladies-in-waiting, to whom she promises 'vous verrez tost la bataille du petit Saintré et de moy' (you will soon see the battle between the young Saintré and me). Totally inexperienced, he is tongue-tied in her presence, nervously twisting the pendant of his belt round and round his finger 'sans mot parler'. Madame raises many laughs at his expense, but her attitude gradually becomes ambiguous, outwardly teasing and mocking, inwardly charmed by his good looks and naïveté. She keeps up the pretence with her ladies, but in private undertakes his education, giving him a long, stern warning about the Seven Deadly Sins, ordering him to love and serve with all his heart and soul God, the blessed Virgin Mary, and the very Cross, instructing him in the Ten Commandments and the twelve articles of faith. She gives him money for new clothes and cannot stop admiring him: 'le petit Saintré les yeulz de Madame ne cessoient de regarder' (Madame could not keep her eyes off little Saintré). Her double game continues, teasing him in the presence of others 'par maniere de farsse' (as a farce), encouraging him in private, giving him ever-increasing sums of money (which he tells others are from his mother) to help him secure promotion at Court. For sixteen years they manage to keep 'ceste loyale et bonne amour secrete' (this loyal and good love secret). On her recommendation he is appointed 'varlet tranchant' with the duty of serving the king at table. Madame is now in love with him, using in their secret meetings terms of endearment such as 'mon cuer, mon bien et mon tres loyal servant'. He is virtually her creation, even his reading (Livy, Suetonius, Sallust) being decided by her. At her suggestion a big feast is held, uniting 'seigneurs, dames ... bourgois, bourgoises de Paris', at which Saintré, now a promising young knight, swears 'aux dames et au paon' that he will wear a jewel-studded bracelet for a year and will yield it only to the knight able to defeat him in the lists. She swears to him that during all the Fridays and Saturdays of his absence she will do without underwear! At their leave-taking 'la furent donnez baisiers, et baisiers renduz sans compte et sans mesure, tous acompaigniez de piteux soupirs' (there kisses were given and exchanged without number accompanied by pitiful sighs). In the ensuing years Saintré achieves great distinction in the world of tournaments, on which the author makes the significant remark 'dont l'on tenoit assez plus de compte que l'on ne fait au jour d'uy' (which were held in far higher esteem than nowadays). The procedure followed in tournaments is described in great detail, and the story becomes at times a veritable Who's Who of the world of chivalry, the names of knights being given and their coats of arms and battle cries carefully described. On his triumphant return, their secret meetings resume, there are many 'baisiers donnez et baisiers renduz', though there is no hint of sexual relations. So far all Saintré's exploits have been initiated by Madame, but after a period of idleness he decides to depart on an adventurous enterprise of his own. She is greatly shocked that he should intend to leave 'sans mon sceu et congié' (without my knowledge and leave), and the king too disapproves of a mission to be undertaken 'sans mon congié'. This brings about a change in their long relationship, 'le tres doleureux cuer de Madame' prevents her from eating, drinking, and sleeping, and she is jealous when she sees other lovers happy together. For the first time in sixteen years she asks the queen's permission to leave Court and return home. On the way she stops at an abbey founded by her ancestors, where the abbot, the handsome, athletic, twenty-five-year-old son of a rich bourgeois, treats her to a sumptuous repast, rather against her will, advancing the clock an hour and a half to persuade her that it was time for lunch. The effects on Madame of the abundant food and drink, combined with her loneliness and despair, are extraordinary: 'Les prieres de faire bonne chiere et de boire les ungs aux autres y furent bien faites et tellement que grant temps avoit que Madame n'avoit fait si bonne chiere, dont en buvant, Madame a damp Abbés et damp Abbés a elle, les yeulz, archiers des cuers, peu a peu commencerent l'un des cuers a l'autre traire, et tellement que les piez couvers de la tres large touaille jusques a terre commencerent de peu a peu l'un a l'autre touchier et puis l'un sur l'autre marchier' (The entreaties to feast well and to drink to one another were well done, so much so that Madame had not feasted so well for a long time, and so, as they drank, Madame to the abbot, the abbot to her, their eyes, the heart's archers, began to attract the other's heart, so much so that their feet, covered by the large tablecloth, began gradually to touch, and then one foot climbed on to the other). A passionate love-affair follows, and she finds a 'nouvel feu d'amours' (a new fire of love), as a result of which 'de ses amours premieres ennuyee estoit' (she was tired of her first love). After an absence of three and a half months Saintré returns and is astonished at her change of heart. The abbot, at first ironically described as a 'gracieux seigneur', but now revealed in his true colours as an 'omme dissolut et de chaitive vie' (a dissolute man of wretched habits), insults Saintré, and all such knights as he, and then challenges him to a wrestling match, easily beating him at this sport to which he is unaccustomed. Saintré obtains his revenge the next day, fighting the way he knows best, sparing the abbot's life but running his dagger through his cheeks and tongue. He tears off Madame's sash of blue, the colour symbolising loyalty, and brings about her discomfiture at Court. After this sad end of a long and important stage in his life, Saintré goes on to conquer further glory. The author quotes his Latin epitaph which gives the date of his death as 25 October 1368.

Petit Jehan de Saintré is one of those works, rare in any period, in which new meanings may constantly be discovered. It is a psychological study rich in ironical observations of human nature by an old man (over seventy at the time of writing) wise in the ways of the world. He portrays a woman whose love lasts as long as it can remain a form of possession and domination, but which quickly wilts when her erstwhile 'loyal servant' develops a mind of his own and is no longer the puppet who obeys her every tug at the strings. Her change of heart is by no means unmotivated. Well described is her shock on realising that Saintré will now go his own way without her permission if need be. Her resultant feelings of despair, of loneliness, and jealousy, form the fertile seedbed of change. The hero, for his part, changes only in the gradual unfolding of his character from the callow youngster to the knight of dauntless courage and unfailing chivalry, whose fame spread throughout Europe. Had Madame not deserted him, we assume that he would have remained loyal to her, yet basic weaknesses were present already in the early stages of their relationship: the duplicity of the lady, of which she was herself the principal victim when a mere fad became an infatuation; the inequality between them, surpassing the traditional one of haughty lady and humble lover, giving her a moral superiority which was inevitably threatened once the inexperienced page had become the most valiant knight of the age; however great his courtesy, he was bound to chafe at this bondage, once so valuable to him, but which he had now quite outgrown. The author's bias tends towards misogyny,[25] for this widow, high-minded, full apparently of concern for the moral welfare of the page, cannot herself resist the temptations that flesh is heir to, even though, in our more cynical age, it may be felt that sixteen years of undivided loyalty to a man to whom she was not bound by any marriage vows, is not such a negligible record. On the other hand, the author is ever ready to idealise the knight and the world to which he belongs, for much of the story is a re-creation of the atmosphere, the activities, and creed of a vanishing society.[26] But what an extraordinary world he creates, in which a young knight's vows to a roasted peacock should be observed more rigorously than the vows of a monk in his dedication to religion! That a monk should be so mercilessly satirised is neither unique nor surprising in this age, any more than the idealisation of that society which the author had served for so long at the Court of Louis II d'Anjou and his successors. Does he show the knight's world threatened by bourgeois pretensions, as has so often been claimed? Was his story a warning to Jean de Calabre and such as he: your world is being challenged, it is up to you to defend it and uphold its honours with all the vigour shown by Saintré a century before your time? If such was its effect on its readers, Antoine de La Sale, we may be sure, would not have been displeased.

Whatever his attitude towards Madame or the abbot, the author saves his severest shafts of censure for Love:

Hé! amours tres faulses, mauvaises et traitres, semblerez vous tousjours enfer qui de angloutir ames onques ne fut saoul? ... Dieu et nature vous ont ils donné telle puissance que de prendre et mectre en voz las cuers de papes, d'empereurs, d'empereris, de cardinaulz, de roys, de roynes, de arcevesques, de ducz, de duchesses, de patriarches, de marquis, de marquises, d'evesques, de princes, de princesses, cuers d'abbez, d'abbesses, de contes, de contesses et de gens de tous autres estas et religions espirituelles et temporelles ...[27] (Oh, love very false, evil and treacherous, will you for ever resemble hell that is never tired of swallowing souls? ... Have God and nature given you such power that you can capture and keep in your snares the hearts of popes, emperors, empresses, cardinals, kings, queens, archbishops, dukes, duchesses, patriarchs, marquesses and marchionesses, bishops, princes, princesses, abbots, abbesses, counts, countesses, and all manner of people of obedience both spiritual and temporal).

If we look for some basic message at the story's end, it is surely here: love comes to all of us so full of promise; it can indeed bring us so much; but in the end love is a deceiver ever, and a man cannot build his life on it. At heart Saintré is no romantic, he is clear-headed enough to understand the situation and to react accordingly. He is no Tristan at the mercy of an uncontrollable force. Whatever he owed to love he had outgrown, and his deeds of valour, as the author is at pains to tell us, continue even when his love is dead and forgotten. Does the author mean to challenge the age-old romantic notion that love is the source of all valour and virtue? Does he not show in effect that a man in his mature years must find his qualities, his justifications, his motives, not in his lady's eyes, but within himself, and within himself alone?

More interesting than the actual legend recounted by Antoine de La Sale in his *Paradis de la Reine Sibylle*[28] is his own attitude towards it. During his travels in Italy, he visited in 1420 the Monti Sibillini, which terminate the central Apennines, about 80 miles north-east of Rome. He gives a remarkably precise description of the mountain scenery, which he finds 'si treshideuse de roideur et de parfondeur que c'est forte chose a croire' (p. 13) (so very hideous in steepness and depth that it can scarcely be believed), and pays particular attention to its flora, describing plants which caught his eye with minute detail and drawings. With a local doctor and guides he enters a cave in which they hear

une haulte voix criant ainsi que ce feust le cry du paon, qui sembloit estre moult loings. Si dirent les gens que c'estoit une voix de paradis de la Sibille. Mais, quant a moy, je n'en croy riens; ains croy que ce feussent mes chevaulx qui au pié du mont estoient ... (p. 15) (a loud voice like the cry of the peacock, which seemed very far away. And people said that it was the Sibyl's voice from paradise. But as for me, I do not believe a word of it; I believe it was my horses at the foot of the mountain).

They did not explore its innermost depths, but he hears of the local legend concerning the German knight's visit to this mysterious and

secluded realm, ruled by Queen Sibyl, whose inhabitants lead apparently idyllic lives where none grow old and pain is unknown,
but at night they turn into serpents, for they are in the land of the
Devil. The knight, realising that he had had contact with the Devil,
journeyed to Rome to seek absolution of the pope, and when this
was refused, returned to the cave and was never seen again. The
close resemblance to the Tannhäuser legend has often been pointed
out. Throughout, Antoine de La Sale's attitude is one of strong
scepticism. It is all a matter of 'choses controuvees par l'ancien
commun parler des simples gens' (things invented by the age-old
gossip of simple folk); expressions such as '. . . se ainsi est, laquelle
chose je ne croy' (if it is so, which I do not believe) abound. His
final assertion that 'c'est toute faulceté' (it is all false) is based on
two arguments: Christ's Passion destroyed all such tricks of the
Devil; Greek and Latin literature makes no mention of the existence
of 'ceste faulse Sibille' (this false Sibyl). A fascinating mind is revealed: cool-headed, not easily swayed by superstition, curious
about natural phenomena and about the ways and beliefs of others,
erudite, showing some knowledge of Greek as well as Latin, a firm
Christian still, his faith untainted by his scepticism.

Further aspects of Antoine de La Sale's mind, and qualities of a
kind rare in medieval literature, are revealed in *Le Réconfort de
Madame de Fresne*, written in 1457.[29] The author addresses
Madame de Fresne directly, offering her consolation for the death
of her son. After a brief introduction, he describes, in two short
stories, the reactions of mothers faced with the death of their sons.

The first tells how Monseigneur du Chastel, besieged by the prince of Wales
in the castle of Brest which he holds in the king's name, is compelled to ask
for a truce, and hands over as hostage his only son, thirteen years old.
Fresh supplies of food then reach the castle, so that surrender is no longer
necessary. Du Chastel is now placed in a dilemma: either to yield the
castle and face disgrace, or to resist and so be the cause of his son's death.
His wife, despite her deep love for her son, advises her husband to sacrifice
him. The situation is Cornelian: 'Vous n'avez qu'ung honneur . . . et sy
n'avez qu'ung seul filz'. His duty is to hold on to his honour, and this is the
course taken. He hears from his herald an account of his son's last moments,
spent in terror of the death which he realised awaited him, calling out to
his prison guard: 'Ha! Thomas, mon amy, vous me menez morir, vous me
menez morir; hellas! vous me menez morir! Thomas, vous me menez morir!
hellas! monsieur mon pere, je vais morir; hellas! madame ma mere, je vais
morir, je vais morir! hellas, hellas, hellas, je vais morir, morir, morir, morir!'
His shrieks are renewed when he catches sight of his father's herald who,
unable to stand the horror of the scene, turns away and faints. The child's
limbs have to be lashed together before he can be killed. The body is
delivered to his father who later obtains his revenge, killing or maiming
over a hundred of the besieging forces, whom he compels to withdraw.

In the second example, a lady learns of the death of her only son while
he had been defending the king of Portugal's son in a battle with the

Saracens for the town of Ceuta in 1415. The king comforts her with well-chosen words: men can never be certain of their end; some die a lingering death as a result of illness, others die suddenly in bed, at table, or while out walking, some die fighting, some are murdered, some are sentenced to death. He tells her that her son died absolved of his sins, fighting in defence of his lord and religion. The mother gives thanks to God for having 'lent her a true son', and comforts the prince to whom her son had been 'a second father'.

The remarkable feature of this work is the element of compassion which it shows, not only in its portrayal of the mothers in their tragic situations, but also, and principally, in the scene in which the boy of thirteen realises that he is doomed and shrieks aloud his terror of death. No earlier work, it has been claimed, has a scene of greater pathos than this, all the more effective for its simplicity. The author refrains from intervening with comments of his own. The scene tells itself, and has far more impact as a result. Such compassion, expressed without the interspersion of long moralisings, is rare in medieval French literature. In the course of the texts analysed in this survey, we have encountered it only in certain brief passages of the works of Chrétien de Troyes, Etienne de Fougères, Rutebeuf, and Villon, always, except for the last-named, at a lower level of tragic intensity. Why did Antoine de La Sale present the story in this way? It would have been easier to make the son's heroism match that of his parents; the mother's heroic sacrifice (the crux of the matter) would not have been belittled, the tale would have been all the more edifying, a greater source of comfort, surely, for Madame de Fresne. There was no artistic necessity for such a scene. Historical accuracy was not the guide, since the story in any case was a travesty of the facts.[30] Antoine de La Sale knew, quite simply, how dreadful and pathetic is the death of a child, particularly in such barbarous circumstances. Here, as in *Petit Jehan de Saintré*, he did not gloss over what he knew to be the reality, remaining faithful to the truths of human nature as he saw them. In *Petit Jehan de Saintré* fiction demanded that the Dame des Belles Cousines should remain faithful to the gallant knight she had created; in the *Réconfort de Madame de Fresne* fiction demanded that the son, despite his youth, should share his father's steadfastness of purpose. But it was not in that light that Antoine de La Sale envisaged his characters.

NOTES

1. ed. J. Rychner, Geneva–Paris, 1963; and J. Crow, Oxford, 1969.
2. This long but incomplete work of 12,103 octosyllabic lines fills the whole of vol. IX of the edition of Deschamps's complete works, see above, p. 238, note 13.
3. Crow, ed. cit., 14.
4. Rychner, ed. cit., xlvii–lvii.

5. ibid., lvii.

6. Crow, ed. cit., x.

7. The most recent edition of the *Cent Nouvelles Nouvelles* is by F. P. Sweetser, Geneva, 1966. The older, by P. Champion, Paris, 1928, remains invaluable for its informative introduction.

8. ibid., x.

9. See above, pp. 107–12.

10. L. Sozzi, 'La Nouvelle Française au Quinzième Siècle', in *Cahiers de l'Association Internationale des Etudes Françaises*, May 1971, 67–84, esp. 82.

11. Champion, ed. cit., lxiv.

12. F. P. Sweetser, ed. cit., 23.

13. John Talbot (1384–1453), member of one of the oldest families in the English nobility, was created earl of Shrewsbury in 1442 and earl of Waterford in 1446 for his distinguished services in France.

14. Sozzi, op. cit., 72–3.

15. ed. J. Rychner, Paris, SATF, 1951.

16. No modern editions exist as yet of these two works, published in *Les Poésies de Martial de Paris dit d'Auvergne*, Paris, Coustelier, 2 vols., 1724.

17. Of whose works a much-needed new edition is being prepared (1973) by M. J. Freeman.

18. See above, pp. 119, 182.

19. ed. A. de Montaiglon, Paris, SATF, 1881; reproduced New York, 1966.

20. The former has been edited by F. Desonay, Liège–Paris, 1935, and the latter by the same scholar, Liège–Paris, 1941.

21. Published in *Traités du Duel Judiciaire* by B. Prost, Paris, 1872, 193–221.

22. F. Desonay, *Le Petit Jehan de Saintré*, Paris, 1928, 93 (a study first published in the *Revue du Seizième Siècle*, XIV, 1927). The most recent editions are by J. Misrahi and C. A. Knudson, Geneva, 1965, and Y. Otaka, Tokyo, 1967.

23. For details of the ed. of this work, see below, note 29.

24. Jehan de Saintré was a historical figure, 'que l'on tenoit pour le meilleur et plus vaillant chevalier de France' (considered to be the best and most valiant knight in France), according to Froissart. He distinguished himself against the English, but was captured at Poitiers in 1351. The story, however, is not a biography, but a synthesis of various figures and episodes. That it contains certain autobiographical elements is possible. Desonay, *Le Petit Jehan de Saintré*, 67–9.

25. For Desonay 'misogyny' is too strong a word, but he confesses that the author did regard women 'avec quelque défiance' (ibid., 98).

26. '. . . le *Petit Jehan de Saintré* est l'apologie de la chevalerie expirante, vers 1450 . . .'. ibid., 72.

27. Misrahi and Knudson, ed. cit., 300–1.

28. ed. F. Desonay, Paris, 1930.

29. J. Nève, *Antoine de la Salle, sa vie et ses ouvrages d'après des documents inédits*, Paris, 1903, 101–55.

30. It was the French who put some English hostages to death; there were several of them, and they were not children. A factual account is given by Froissart; Nève, op. cit., 61–5.

CONCLUSION

THE vastness and complexity of the period of six hundred and fifty years with which this volume is concerned, the consequent incompleteness of this survey based, as was pointed out earlier,[1] on the study of a number of focal points, the neglect of the immense intellectual output of the age, written almost entirely in Latin, all mean that any conclusions reached here can be no more than tentative. We have seen that the very term Middle Ages arouses misgivings,[2] for it is obviously inadequate save in so far as all epochs are transitional, influenced by the past, influencing the future, and all become a Middle Ages at some stage in their history. Although any single label for so long an extent of time can only be misleading, as regards the French language, which by the fifteenth century had acquired many of its modern characteristics, this was the First Age; as regards literary themes such as the importance of love in human relationships, as regards particular forms such as the romance, the novel, the short story, as regards French versification, the use of a fixed number of syllables in the line, of rhyme and refrains, as regards certain fixed forms of poetry, such as the *ballade*, the *rondeau*, the *épître*, this was the First Age.

Any neat patterns of evolution which we think we can discern are more likely to be of our own invention than a reflection of reality. One feature, however, is worthy of comment. The *chansons de geste*, the love-poetry of the troubadours, the romances of that most active and creative period extending from the early twelfth century to the middle of the thirteenth, when the kingdom of France, under the dynamic leadership of the later Capetian monarchs,[3] was rapidly becoming the foremost power in western Europe, may be said to represent, each genre in its own particular way and in its most outstanding works, an art-form at its peak. Each plunges its roots into the prevailing social and historical conditions, each has its comments to make on those conditions, but each transcends its ambiance, aspiring to a higher domain where ideals are triumphant: the *chansons de geste* the warriors' paradise to which the stern duties of the militant Christian led; the troubadours' poetry a far-off realm in which a purer love replaces the erotic

desires on which this verse is founded; the romances a world of symbolism epitomising ideal relationships between the sexes, between
the individual and his ego. All were involved in a quest for something beyond their own horizons, and all, in their very different
domains, were successful.

In the second half of the thirteenth century a change, discernible a good deal earlier in certain works, became manifest in Jean
de Meun's lengthy addition to the *Roman de la Rose*. Owed to
social and intellectual developments which had been gathering
momentum over a long period – the emergence of the commercial
and trading class, the bourgeoisie, on the one hand; the attempt on
the other hand to reach a rational, philosophical outlook on religion by thinkers such as Alanus de Insulis, Abelard, and Jean de
Meun's contemporary Thomas Aquinas – a preoccupation appeared in literature with the practicalities of existence and with
human nature as it actually is, no longer with its endeavours to
reach beyond itself. The voyage to that mysterious, distant realm
beyond the furthest horizon, like the crusades themselves, was
postponed *sine die*. Ideals of the past were not forgotten, but they
tended to appear, precisely, in works protesting that they had been
forgotten, or in works whose bias was all towards the glories of the
past. The more limited horizons of later medieval literature, the
growing preoccupation with the observed world, had important
consequences: a more uniformly ironical, disillusioned view of
human society, a closer, cooler appraisal of the individual in his
whole being, no longer just in certain crucial, but isolated, aspects
of his life. The great heroes of the past – Alexis, Roland, Tristan,
Perceval, and others – are replaced by lesser men who strive to continue the quest, but they have forgotten its ultimate purpose. It can
all be symbolised in that abortive crusade attempted in the midfifteenth century by Philip the Good, duke of Burgundy. It began,
not in an inspired series of sermons, but in a sumptuous banquet to
which many notables were invited, and at which Philip swore, to
God, to the Virgin Mary, and to a pheasant wearing a necklace of
precious stones – such was the extravagant fashion of the age[4] – that
he would proceed to the rescue of the Church. An expedition was
dispatched, ten years later, with good intentions but feeble support.
It got as far as Marseilles, and there it ended.

The medieval literature of France, despite the lowly position of
the vernacular compared to Latin, is the work of professional men
of letters, whether clerics, jongleurs, troubadours, or *trouvères*.
Although there were always exceptions, and although the degree
of training received and skill attained inevitably varied at all times,
it was in the later Middle Ages that this well-established literary

tradition began to falter. We may find a man turning to writing late in life after a career in quite a different occupation, or he may turn against concepts inherited from the past even though he may not have defined to himself or others why he was doing this; he may repudiate his education and declare that personal experience is the better teacher. These trends make their appearance, in very different ways and in different degrees, in the works of several writers of the fifteenth century: Alain Chartier, François Villon, Charles d'Orléans, Martial d'Auvergne, Philippe de Commynes, Antoine de La Sale. However much indebted to literary traditions of the past – and writers like Alain Chartier and Charles d'Orléans were steeped in them – all were carried at times outside the realm of the professional man of letters, away from the well-worn *topoi* and conventions, towards the realities of the world around them, as they saw them and conceived them. Such developments, an impoverishment in some respects, represent an enrichment in others. In periods when ideals are not strong and motivation is uncertain, literary dogma and creed lose their conviction. At such moments it is necessary for writers to forsake the Muses and to renew contact with the fundamentals of human existence. This was the achievement of several fifteenth-century writers. Paradoxically enough, literature as an art-form now had new peaks in perspective, and it is no mere coincidence that the six names mentioned above are acknowledged to rank among the foremost writers of the French Middle Ages.

The extent to which the fourteenth and fifteenth centuries can properly be represented as a period of decline is a matter of debate. The very structure traditionally imposed upon the literary history of France, the very term Renaissance in its application to the sixteenth century and in its implications for those immediately preceding, should inspire caution. It is true that the aftermath of a warfare which lasted several generations and which was fought entirely on the soil of France was long and bitter, and undeniable that, from the fourteenth century onwards, the idealisms of the past were declining, but clinging on still to existence in revised and mutilated literary forms which could only earn the contempt of sixteenth-century writers. The temptation to paint too gloomy a picture becomes very strong, and the brilliantly argued hypothesis of an influential book sanctioned the view that in these centuries all was on the wane.[5] However, literary history cannot stand still, and in recent years a less prejudiced view has begun to emerge. Attention has been drawn to the strong current of humanism in fourteenth-century France, fostered by the papacy moving to Avignon (1309–1377), and by its close links with the French Court.[6] Attention has been drawn also to Pierre Bersuire's translation of Livy, and Nicole Oresme's translation of Aristotle, in the latter half of the fourteenth century. The activities of a group of French scholars of the late fourteenth and early fifteenth centuries – Jean Muret, Nicolas de Clamanges, Jean de Montreuil, Pierre and Gontier Col – who wrote principally in Latin, are being investigated at the present time.[7] Their interest in classical literature for its own intrinsic merits justifies their being looked on as humanists. That their influence was not more widespread and profound was owed in the main to prevailing conditions in France. But no balanced judgement can justifiably ignore their activities. The fact that these activities existed at all points to an intellectual awareness and a scholarship of a type long denied by literary historians to the later Middle Ages. That the fires which smouldered for so long did not break through until long afterwards was one of the accidents, perhaps one should say ironies, of history.

NOTES

1. See above, p. 1.
2. See above, pp. 1–2.
3. See above, pp. 13–14.
4. See above, pp. 329, 345.
5. Huizinga, op. cit.
6. See in particular Simone, op. cit.
7. See E. Ornato, *Jean Muret et ses amis Nicolas de Clamanges et Jean de Montreuil*, Geneva–Paris, 1969; also *L'Originalité du XV⁰ siècle* (see above, p. 4, note 3), no. 23, 9–103.

THE KINGS OF MEDIEVAL FRANCE (9TH–15TH CENTURIES) AND SOME OUTSTANDING FEATURES OF THEIR REIGNS

I. CAROLINGIAN DYNASTY

814–40 Louis I the Pious (also known as the Debonair), king of the Franks, emperor of the West

Quarrels among Louis's sons Lothair, Louis, and Pépin greatly weakened his power, and in 833–34 he was dethroned for a time, until quarrels among them enabled him to regain his position. 838 Charles II, Louis's son by a later marriage, was crowned by his father in order to ensure the succession

840–77 Charles II the Bald, king of the Franks, but emperor of the West only from 875 to 877

843 Treaty of Verdun (p. 5)
845 Normans attacked Paris
862 The future Louis II led a revolt against his father

877–79 Louis II, the Stammerer

879–82 Louis III

881 Louis III defeated the Normans at Saucourt

882–84 Carloman

884–88 Charles the Fat (regent)

Charles deposed because of incompetence in the face of the Norman invaders

885–86 Odo defeated the Normans at Montfaucon

888–98 Odo (member of Capetian family)

888 Odo elected king because of his military prowess, though subsequently he was not always victorious against the Normans

356

APPENDIX I

898–923 Charles III, the Simple	910 Foundation of Cluny (pp. 7–8) 911 Treaty of Saint-Clair-sur-Epte gave Normandy to Rollo (p. 281), ancestor of William the Conqueror
922–23 Robert I (member of Capetian family)	923 Charles the Simple dethroned after his defeat at the battle of Soissons, in which Robert I, his rival for the throne, was killed 923 Raoul of Burgundy, son-in-law of Robert I, was elected to the throne on the death of Robert
923–36 Raoul of Burgundy	Struggles against Norman invaders continue Raoul defeated them in 930
936–54 Louis IV, d'Outremer ('from Overseas')	950 End of Norman invasions Beginnings of Romanesque architecture about this time
954–86 Lothair	Several attempts by Lothair to conquer Lorraine failed
986–87 Louis V, le Fainéant ('Do-Nothing')	Last of the Carolingian kings, died without leaving an heir

II. CAPETIANS OF THE DIRECT LINE

987–96 Hugh Capet	Not the first Capetian king (see Odo and Robert I above), but the first of the line to be succeeded by his son, so beginning a dynasty which was to rule without interruption for nearly 350 years.
996–1031 Robert II, the Pious	1023 Manichaean heretics burned in **Rouen** **Peasants' revolt in Normandy**
1031–60 Henry I	1050–1127 Cluniac reforms of Church 1054 Separation of Greek Orthodox and Western Churches
1060–1108 Philip I	1061 Beginning of Norman invasion of Sicily 1066 William of Normandy conquered Harold at Hastings and was crowned king of England 1086 Domesday Book in England 1090 Normans occupied Sicily

	1095 Council of Clermont 1096–99 First Crusade 1098 Founding of Cistercian order 1099 Crusaders took Jerusalem Late 11th–early 12th centuries: towns gained their independence and were granted charters. Rising prosperity of the bourgeoisie
1108–37 Louis VI, the Fat	Louis VI the first Capetian to make the enforcement of law and order at home a prime feature of his policy Arabic numerals appeared in Western manuscripts of the 12th century
1137–80 Louis VII, the Young	Beginnings of Gothic style 1147–49 Second Crusade. Louis VII took part 1152 Henry, count of Anjou and duke of Normandy since 1149, became duke of Aquitaine on his marriage to Aliénor d'Aquitaine. In 1154 he became king of England, thereby influencing the whole course of French and English history up to 1453 1170 Murder of Thomas Becket
1180–1223 Philip II, Augustus	1183 Beginning of Inquisition. First inquisitorial court set up in 1231 1189–92 Third Crusade Late 12th century: Beginnings of University of Paris 1202–04 Fourth Crusade 1204 Crusaders seized Constantinople 1206 Founding of Dominican order 1209–29 Albigensian crusades 1210 Founding of Franciscan order 1215 Magna Carta in England 1219–21 Fifth Crusade
1223–26 Louis VIII, the Lion	1226 Louis VIII led an army against the Albigenses
1226–70 Louis IX (Saint Louis)	1228–29 Sixth Crusade 1229 Treaty of Meaux, Languedoc annexed 1244 Christians lost Jerusalem 1248–52 Seventh Crusade, led by Louis IX 1250 Serfs granted freedom in France 1254–65 Royal ordinances greatly strengthened the administration of the kingdom: prostitution, gambling, duels,

carrying of arms, were forbidden
1258 Treaty of Paris. Henry III of
England recognised as duke of Aquitaine,
and renounced claim to Normandy,
Maine, Anjou, Touraine, and Poitou

1270–85 Philip III, the Bold

1270 Eighth Crusade. Death of Louis IX
at Tunis
1271–95 Travels of Marco Polo in China
1282 Massacre of French in the Sicilian
Vespers

1285–1314 Philip IV, the Fair

1309–77 Papal schism. Popes at Avignon
as well as in Rome

1314–16 Louis X, le Hutin
('the Stubborn')

1315 Charters setting out rights and
privileges were granted to the nobles of
most provinces

1316 John I, the Posthumous

John I was born and died (4 days old) in
1316

1316–22 Philip V, the Tall

1320 Peasants in revolt (the
'Pastoureaux', lit. 'Shepherds')
imprisoned the king in his palace,
sacked Paris, and marched south. They
were eventually defeated by the
seneschal of Carcassonne

1322–28 Charles IV, the Fair

Last of the Capetian dynasty, dying
without male issue

III. VALOIS DYNASTY

1328–50 Philip VI

1328 Edward III of England laid claim
to the throne of France
1340–1453 Hundred Years War
1346 French defeat at Crécy
1346–50 Black Death in Europe
1347 First meeting of the *états-
généraux* (p. 17)

1350–64 John II, the Good

1356 John II captured by the Black
Prince at the Battle of Poitiers, freed in
1362 after payment of a large ransom
and handing over hostages. On flight of
one of these, John returned to his
imprisonment in London, where he died
1356–58 Revolts in Paris and elsewhere.
The *Jacquerie* (revolt of peasants,
so called from the name Jacques given
by nobles to peasants) began in Beauvaisis

	and spread to several regions. It was put down with great severity
1364–80 Charles V, the Wise	Charles V freed monarchy of its dependence on the *états-généraux* by securing permanent grant of taxes 1370 Bertrand Du Guesclin, constable of France, occupied Poitou and Saintonge, and drove the English out of the country By 1380 only the ports of Calais, Bordeaux, Bayonne, Brest, and Cherbourg were still in English hands
1380–1422 Charles VI	1392 madness of Charles VI Rivalry of the houses of Burgundy and Orleans 1407 Assassination of the duc d'Orléans 1415 Henry V's victory at Agincourt 1419 Assassination of John the Fearless, duke of Burgundy 1420 Treaty of Troyes imposed on Charles VI by Anglo-Burgundian alliance. Henry V acknowledged as heir to the French throne.
1422–61 Charles VII	1429 Joan of Arc raised the siege of Orleans and had Charles VII crowned at Rheims 1431 Joan of Arc burned at the stake 1435 Treaty of Arras marked the end of the Anglo-Burgundian alliance 1436 Charles VII entered Paris 1453 English driven out of France (except Calais) for good. End of Hundred Years War 1453 Turks captured Constantinople, and Athens in 1458
1461–83 Louis XI	1470 First printing-press in France
1483–98 Charles VIII	1492 Columbus discovered America 1494 Beginning of wars with Italy

Appendix II

A NOTE ON THE READING OF MEDIEVAL FRENCH

Medieval French differed from its modern descendant in several ways.

1. There was no standard, national language. After the disintegration of the Roman Empire in the fourth and fifth centuries A.D., the Vulgar Latin established in northern France gradually developed into a number of related dialects. By the twelfth century, there are indications that the dialect of the Ile-de-France, the Francien from which present-day French has developed, was considered superior to others because it was the language of king and Court, but as late as the fourteenth century an important writer such as Froissart could still use the dialectal features of his native region. In any case, dialects did not remain separate entities, but reacted on one another; Francien was influenced to some extent by the Picard dialect.

2. A vestige of the Latin case system remained in literary use for periods of time varying according to regions. Anglo-Norman, an important dialect in which numbers of early extant works are written, began to abandon the case system in the twelfth century, whereas it remained in the Ile-de-France, in central and in some northern regions, into the fourteenth century.

3. Spelling was not fixed. One may sometimes suspect that writers took pride in varying their spelling. For example, when Charles d'Orléans copied out one of his own *rondeaux*, he spelled the same word, recurring three times in one line, in three different ways:

> Alez vous ant, allez, alés,
> Soussy, Soing et Merencolie

rather as though he wished his old enemies Care, Worry, and Melancholy to see his peremptory dismissal of them in a variety of orthographical forms or took pleasure in assigning a different form to each of them.

4. There are very few grammatical works dating from the medieval period. The frequent absence too of information concerning authors' lives, the regions to which they belonged, and the periods when they were writing means that as much information as possible has to be gleaned from the linguistic features of the text itself.

From what precedes it will be obvious that no short essay of this kind can deal adequately with the many complexities of medieval French. The reader anxious to develop his knowledge of the medieval language should refer to a work for long acknowledged as authoritative: M. K. Pope, *From Latin to Modern French*, Manchester, 1934, reprinted 1952. Also extremely informative, less complex, are A. Ewert, *The French Language*, 2nd ed. London, 1943, reprinted 1947, 1949, 1964, and, a more recent publication, G. Price, *The French Language: Present and Past*, London, 1971, the bibliography of which is comprehensive.

The following notes are for the general guidance of the reader, and deal only with a few of the most obvious differences between medieval and modern French.

That the five or six cases of Classical Latin nouns and adjectives should have shrunk to two only in medieval French is less surprising than that they were not reduced much earlier to a single case as happened in most other Romance languages. The retention of two cases, one for the former nominative and vocative, one for all other Latin cases (the accusative, preceded where necessary by a preposition such as *ad* or *de*) is usually ascribed to the conservative influence on the language of the many schools established in Gaul at the time of the Empire. The extent to which the two-case system really corresponded to oral usage, or was, or became in later centuries, an anachronistic survival limited to the written language (rather as the Past Historic tense is today), is a moot point. In several ways this case system remains the most important difference between medieval and modern French texts. The following account, necessarily over-simplified, is arranged under three headings: definite article, substantives, adjectives.

(i) *The definite article.* This developed from the Latin demonstrative adjective and pronoun 'ille' (that) and retained a demonstrative sense closer to English 'the' than to modern French 'le'. As in modern English, where no 'definition' was needed, no article was used: ... 'France en ert hunie...' (*Chanson de Roland*, line 969; France will be disgraced by this...). Both the subject masculine singular and plural are *li* (<*illi*),[1] while the object masculine singular and plural forms *le* (<*illum*) and *les* (<*illos*) are those retained by present-day French. Feminine forms show no equivalent traces of a case system, the sole form for the singular being *la* (<*illa, illam*) and the plural *les* (*illas* having supplanted *illae* and having given the same result as *illos*). For examples of these forms and their usage, see the passages quoted on pp. 190–1.

(ii) *Substantives.* Forms of substantives in Old French depended in large measure on their Latin sources. Feminine forms of the original first declension varied only according to number, as in modern French: *table* (<*tabula, tabulam*), *tables* (<*tabulas,* used for the subject as well as for the object plural). Neuter nouns used frequently in the plural were absorbed by this group: *folia, arma, vela*, etc. Feminine nouns of the original third declension were unaffected by the case system except that the nominative singular sometimes ended in an *-s* (e.g., *la flors*), which could be either etymological (<*floris*<*flos*) or added on analogy with masculine counterparts.

Masculine nouns of the second declension gave two forms for the singular if the Latin endings were *-us, -um*: subject singular *murs* (<*murus*); object singular *mur* (<*murum*). Former neuter singulars such as *vinum, castellum* were made to conform to this pattern, also infinitives used substantivally (e.g., *li avoirs, l'avoir*). Corresponding nouns ending in *-er, -um*, like those of the former third declension ending in *-er, -em,* had only one form in the singular except when an *-s* was added to the nominative on analogy with *murus, annus*, etc.: *maistre* (<*magister, magistrum*), *pere* (<*pater, patrem*). Plurals of all *-er* forms behaved in the same way irrespective of the former declension in Latin. The subject plural had no *s*: *maistre, pere* (<*magistri,* analogical *patri* replacing *patres*), whereas the object had an *-s*: *maistres, peres* (<*magistros, patres* or analogical *patros*). Other nouns, particularly those liable to be used as forms of address, sometimes differed considerably in their subject and object singular forms, according to the particularities of phonetic development: *sire–seignor, emperere–empereur* (earlier *-eour, -eeur*), *trovere–troveur* (earlier *-eour, -eeur*), *cuens–comte*, etc.

(iii) *Adjectives.* Adjectives, including the numeral *unus*, conformed to the system according to their respective endings in Latin, and were subject to the same analogical remodellings (e.g., subject plural masculine *grandes* became *grandi*, whence *grant*, the same form as that deriving from the accusative singular *grandem*). *Grant, vert, tel, fort*, etc., could be feminine as well as masculine.

Simple though this case system is, it is deceptive in that presence of *-s* is not necessarily a sign that the word is plural, whereas absence of *-s* is not necessarily a sign that the word is singular. The object, representing four cases of Latin (accusative, genitive, dative, ablative), was in more frequent use than the subject (representing former nominative and vocative) and therefore was usually the one to survive when the case system disintegrated. Exceptions are provided by nouns used frequently as forms of address (*fils, soeur, Charles, Georges*, etc.) and by (*l'*)*on*, the modern indefinite pronoun, the only word derived from a nominative substantive (*homo*), which can still be used solely as a subject form.

Two further considerations must be mentioned briefly. Where form indicated function, word order was free to vary and so to play a stylistic role: *Paul frappe Georges* (with the nuance: it is *Paul* who is being struck by Georges). That this could not apply to those feminine nouns which had only one form for the singular and one for the plural (cf. *Anne frappe Paulette*) explains why the word order subject-verb-object gradually became standardised, so rendering variation of form according to function unnecessary. From its beginnings the Old French case system was only a partial one, affecting some forms and not others, and hence unlikely to survive.

Verbs. Since endings were more fully pronounced in medieval French than they are today, verbal forms were more distinctive and less dependent in consequence on the use of personal pronouns. Among the many passages quoted in this work, many will be noted where translation into modern French would necessitate the addition of personal pronouns. Presence of personal pronouns in early texts may have served to stress the subject. In the course of their evolution, verbal endings, like those of other parts of speech, became less distinctive, so that the use of personal pronouns became more necessary, although even at the end of the Middle Ages it was still more limited than it is today.

Vocabulary. Many words in common use in medieval French have not survived into modern French. The two best dictionaries of medieval French are the following:

Fr. Godefroy, *Dictionnaire de l'ancienne langue française et de tous les dialectes*, Paris, 10 vols., 1880–1902.
A. Tobler and E. Lommatzsch, *Altfranzösisches Wörterbuch*, Berlin–Wiesbaden, first vol. 1915, still in process of publication.

Adequate for daily use are two compact dictionaries published by Larousse:

R. Grandsaignes d'Hauterive, *Dictionnaire d'Ancien Français*, Paris, 1947.
A. J. Greimas, *Dictionnaire de l'Ancien Français jusqu'au milieu de XIVe siècle*, Paris, 1969.

Particularly common words liable to puzzle or mislead the reader unfamiliar with the medieval language are:
si<*sic*, not 'if', but 'and' or 'so'.
se<*si*, 'if'.
ainz, ains <Late Latin *antius* 'sooner', 'rather', 'but'.
ainc ... ne, like 'mais ... ne' $\left.\begin{smallmatrix}\text{'onques}\\\text{onc}\end{smallmatrix}\right\}$ ... ne' or 'ja ... ne', means 'never', whereas 'jamais ... ne' (or the reverse order) means 'nevermore'.
car often reinforces the imperative, rather like 'pray' in English.

illuec 'there'.
jus 'down'.
sus 'up'.

Spellings. It is particularly difficult to attempt to generalise on questions of spelling, and the following equivalents are all liable to have their exceptions:

medieval	*modern*
ei (stressed)	= oi (lei>loi, creire>croire)
ue (stressed)	= eu, œu (puet>peut, cuer>cœur)
ou (stressed)	= eu (flour>fleur, lour>leur)

Anglo-Norman texts may use *u* for modern *eu* (*flur, lur*) or for modern *o* (*mun, sun*). *l* before a consonant is frequently retained in medieval spellings, thus *albe* = modern *aube*, *halt* = modern *haut*, etc.

Final consonants are usually voiceless: grant, quant, etc. (cf. pronunciation in modern French un grand homme, quand il . . ., etc.)

Information on how these medieval spellings came about, and on the pronunciations to which they corresponded, is given in the works of Pope, Ewert, and Price quoted above.

NOTE

1. Not to be confused with the pronoun *li*, which in front of a verb was used as is modern *lui*, and after a preposition (e.g., *avec li*) was used as is modern *elle* (*avec elle*).

BIBLIOGRAPHY

Bibliographical details concerning modern editions of medieval texts, and studies of them, are given in the notes at ends of chapters. Particular works may be traced by looking up the author's name, or the title of the work, in the Index. Fuller bibliographies are given in the following:

R. Bossuat, *Manuel bibliographique de la littérature française du Moyen Age*, Melun, 1951, and two supplements, Paris, 1955, Paris, 1961. Beyond 1961, reference should be made to:

O. Klapp, *Bibliographie der französischen Literaturwissenschaft*, Frankfurt (Main), annual publication since 1960.

R. Rancœur, *Bibliographie de la littérature française du Moyen Age à nos jours*, Paris, annual publication since 1967 (earlier volumes did not include medieval literature).

The Year's Work in Modern Language Studies, annual publication since 1931 by the Modern Humanities Research Association.

The following are also invaluable:

Dictionnaire des Lettres Françaises. Le Moyen Age, prepared by R. Bossuat, L. Pichard, G. Raynaud de Lage, Paris, 1964.

J.-C. Payen, *Le Moyen Age I: Des origines à 1300*, Paris, 1970.

D. Poirion, *Le Moyen Age II: 1300–1480*, Paris, 1971.

(Both of these volumes in the *Littérature française* series contain a *Dictionnaire des auteurs et des œuvres*, very useful indeed for quick reference and for finding the essential bibliographical information.)

Outdated but still useful is

D. C. Cabeen, *A Critical Bibliography of French Literature: I. The Medieval Period*, ed. U. T. Holmes Jr, Syracuse, 1947.

INDEX

Roi Marc et d'Yseut la blonde, Del,
149
Roland, La Chanson de, 27, 55, 60,
61–78, 81, 85, 91, 92, 95, 96, 97,
99, 101, 102, 103, 104, 135, 138,
204, 205, 243, 329, 331, 336,
362
Roland, La Chanson de, origins of,
75–8, 85
Rollo of Normandy, 357
roman à thèse, 155
Roman Empire, 1, 3, 15, 106
romance, meaning of the term, 174
Romanesque style, 8
Romania, 2
Romans, 3, 106, 240–1
romans byzantins, 153
romans courtois, 331
Rome, 2, 3, 56, 152, 159, 264, 323,
348, 361
Rome, Le Roman de Marques de,
214
rondeaux, 98, 293, 327, 352
rondelet, 295
rondels, 123, 307, 325, 326
Ronsard, 322
Ronsjö, E., 57
Roques, M., 162, 163, 175, 176, 177,
178, 222, 239, 259, 337
Rosa, Tractatus contra Romantium
de, 273–4
Rose, Roman de la, see Dole
Rose, Roman de la, 137, 189, 216–24,
232, 261, 271, 272, 273, 293, 300,
324, 353
Rose, Roman de la, moralisé, 319
Rostand, 114
Rotelande, Hue de, 173
Rou, Le Roman de, 148, 176, 279,
280, 281
Rougemont, D. de, 131
Roy, M., 277
Roy Modus et de la Royne Ratio, Le
Livre du, 334, 335
Royal Annals, 75
Roye, Journal de Jean de (La
Chronique scandaleuse), 289, 292
Rudel, Jaufré, 114–16, 120, 131
Ruelle, P., 195
Runnalls, G., 259
Russian, 140
Rutebeuf, 19, 53–4, 57, 187, 189–95,
196, 236–7, 248, 249–50, 253, 326,
350
Rychner, J., 55, 168, 178, 350, 351

saddle, 19
Saint-Amour, Guillaume de, 224
Saint-Benoît-le-Bétourné, 310
Saint-Cloud, Pierre de, 232, 233, 234,
238
Saint Louis, Histoire de, 283–5

Saint-Martial, abbey of, 109, 112,
131
Saint-Quentin, Dudon de, 280
Sainte-Maure, Benoît de, 121, 134,
137, 138, 279, 281
Saintré, Le Petit Jehan de, 345–8,
350, 351
Saintré, Jehan de, 351
Saints, Lives of, 4, 7, 17, 240
Salade, La, 344
Sale, Antoine de La, 344–50, 354
Sale, La, 345
Salic Law, 3
Salisbury, John of, 224
Sallust, 224
Saracens, 58, 88, 248
Savoie, Philibert de, 323
Scheler, A., 325
Scheludko, D., 103
Schlösser, F., 133
Schoepperle, G., 175
Schutz, A.-H., 131
Sckommodau, H., 55
Scotland, 38, 148, 175, 286, 330, 332
Scotland, Maud of, 36
Scoumanne, A., 326
Sebourc, Baudouin de, 329
Seebiger, G., 103
Semilli, Richard de, 188
Sémur, La Passion de, 253, 259
seneschal, 16
Sermon des maux que l'homme a en
mariage, Le, 260
sermon joyeux, 257
Serper, A., 196
serventoys, 325
Seven Sages of Rome, 173, 179, 214,
331
Sézanne, Aubouin de, 188
Shakespeare, 173, 177
Sibylle, Le Paradis de la Reine,
348–9
Siciliano, I., 103, 326
similiter cadens, 25
Simone, F., 4, 355
Sinbad, 34, 39, 331
Sir Tristrem, 140
sirventes, 119
Sobres Sots, Les, 260
Söderhjelm, W., 238
Solente, S., 277
Sommer, H. O., 222
Songe de Pestilence, 335
Songe en Complainte, Le, 306
Sorbon, Robert de, 15
Sorbonne, 16
Sots Ecclésiastiques, Les, 260
sottie, 257, 259, 260
Sozzi, L., 351
Spain, 6, 7, 12, 16, 58, 59, 75, 76,
105, 106, 123, 140
Spence, N. C. W., 174, 175

Printed in Great Britain
by Western Printing Services Limited
Bristol